Introducing Anthropology of Religion

"This book is the best example I know of its kind – an introductory text that combines sophisticated, cross-cultural, and historically nuanced discussion with an intuitive ordering of subjects. Eller is especially good at weaving together contemporary perspectives with classical anthropological theory. The book's accessibility and erudition make it perfect for advanced undergraduate courses and graduate seminars alike."

Liam D. Murphy, *California State University, Sacramento, USA*

"The first edition of *Introducing Anthropology of Religion* was one of the most engaging, comprehensive, and theoretically sophisticated overviews ever published. Eller's second edition includes a range of new and revised material as well as expanded web resources. Beginning students and specialists alike will learn much from this volume."

Stephen D. Glazier, *University of Nebraska-Lincoln, USA*

This clear and engaging guide introduces students to key areas of the field and shows how to apply an anthropological approach to the study of religion in the contemporary world. Written by an experienced teacher, it covers major traditional topics including definitions, theories, and beliefs as well as symbols, myth, and ritual. The book also explores important but often overlooked issues such as morality, violence, fundamentalism, secularization, and new religious movements. The chapters all contain lively case studies of religions practiced around the world.

The second edition of *Introducing Anthropology of Religion* contains updated theoretical discussion plus fresh ethnographic examples throughout. In addition to a brand new chapter on vernacular religion, Eller provides a significantly revised chapter on the emerging anthropologies of Christianity and Islam. The book features more material on contemporary societies as well as new coverage of topics such as pilgrimage and paganism. Images, a glossary and questions for discussion are now included and additional resources are provided via a companion website.

Jack David Eller is Associate Professor emeritus of Anthropology at the Community College of Denver, USA. He is author of the major introductory textbook *Cultural Anthropology: Global Forces, Local Lives* (second edition, Routledge 2013).

The accompanying website can be found at
www.routledge.com/cw/eller

Introducing Anthropology of Religion

Second edition

Jack David Eller

Routledge
Taylor & Francis Group

LONDON AND NEW YORK

First edition published 2007
This second edition published 2015
by Routledge
2 Park Square, Milton Park, Abingdon, Oxon OX14 4RN

and by Routledge
711 Third Avenue, New York, NY 10017

Routledge is an imprint of the Taylor & Francis Group, an informa business

© 2007, 2015 Jack David Eller

British Library Cataloguing in Publication Data
A catalogue record for this book is available from the British Library

Library of Congress Cataloging in Publication Data
Eller, Jack David.
Introducing anthropology of religion / Jack David Eller. -- Second edition.
pages cm
1. Anthropology of religion. I. Title.
GN470.E37 2014
306.6--dc22
2014022505

ISBN: 978-1-138-02490-8 (hbk)
ISBN: 978-1-138-02491-5 (pbk)
ISBN: 978-1-315-74015-7 (ebk)

Typeset in Sabon
by Taylor & Francis Books

Printed and bound in the United States of America by Publishers Graphics, LLC on sustainably sourced paper.

Contents

ch.10
religious
violence

List of Figures

List of Boxes

Preface

The Lenca people of Honduras are quite renowned potters. In the village of La Campa, some two hundred potters, almost all women, share the local natural resources, which include clay, sand, and colored soil, as well as wood and water. These resources are communally owned, guaranteeing access to all. The local potters cannot prohibit anyone from using the available materials, and no one can build fences or otherwise block access to streams and lakes, forests, or soil deposits. These practical, economic rules are enforced by a set of beliefs about beings who inhabit the sites and punish people who treat resources selfishly or destructively. The Lenca "believe that each place on earth has a spirit or angel responsible for its protection"; the clay beds in particular are guarded by Benigna, "a powerful earth spirit who punishes any potter who uses clay without respect" (Tucker 2010: 47). As well as acting respectfully of the world and of other people's rights to it, "it is also important for potters to perform a periodic *pago a la tierra* (payment to the earth) for Benigna"; at the same time, "they must also offer *pagos* to the spirits of the spring and forests that provide water and firewood to make pottery and an additional *pago* to the spirit of the spot where pottery is tempered" (48). Individuals who do not compensate the spirits may be prevented from finding the needed resources, or worse—their pots may break and they may fall ill.

I, like most people and most anthropologists, am intrigued by religion. I have studied the subject for over thirty years and taught it for over fifteen. The current book emerged out of my teaching and research experiences and develops a number of themes that are crucial to understanding not only religion but the anthropological approach to religion. The first theme is the diversity between religions: there are many religions in the world, and they are different from each other in multiple and profound ways. Not all religions include gods, nor do all make morality a central issue, etc. No religion is "normal" or "typical" of all religions; the truth is in the diversity. Since anthropology is the study of the diversity of human thoughts and actions, this perspective is natural for us. A second theme, less obvious, is the diversity *within* religions: ordinarily we think of a religion as a single homogeneous set of beliefs and practices. The reality is quite otherwise: within any religion there is a variety of beliefs and practices—and interpretations of those beliefs and practices—distributed throughout space and time. Within the so-called world religions this variety can be extensive and contentious, one or more variations regarded as "orthodox."

A third theme is the integration of religion with its surrounding culture. In anthropology, this is the familiar principle of holism or cultural integration—that all of the parts of a culture are interconnected and mutually influencing. Beyond simply being integrated, we will find that religion tends to be, as Mary Douglas phrased it, "consonant" with its culture and society as well. Each culture and society has a style, a feel, an ethos, which religion tends to replicate, making the experience of culture—even the "bodily" experience—consistent and symmetric.

A fourth theme is what we will call the "modularity" of religion: a religion is not even a single, monolithic "thing" but a composite of many elements or bits, virtually all of which have their non-religious cognates. That is, there is religious ritual and there is non-religious ritual; there is religious violence and there is non-religious violence. Further, not all of the modules in a religion are necessarily "religious"; rather, religion may integrate non-religious components like politics, economics, gender, technology, and popular culture.

A fifth theme is the relativity of language, which is a particularly subtle yet crucial problem in the anthropological study of religion. We describe and analyze religions in words, as we must, but our words are seldom if ever neutral or universal. In the Western study of religion, our terminology generally comes from the Christian perspective, where "god" and "heaven" and "sin" and "soul" and "worship" and even "belief" and "religion" itself are appropriate and intelligible. However, in discussing other religions, these terms may not be appropriate or intelligible. We must, then, be alert to the danger of imposing alien concepts and ideas to foreign religions that do not possess them.

A sixth and final theme is the *local* and *practiced* nature of culture and of religion. Since religions are internally diverse, the same religion in different times and places will vary. Of course, "traditional" or "tribal" religions—the ones with which anthropology is most associated—are local; that is often taken to be one of their defining qualities. However, even translocal or "world" religions like Christianity or Islam ultimately consist of a congeries of local variations, shaped by the individuals and institutions that introduced them, the other religion(s) in the society, the specific actors and their interpretations, and the surrounding culture. Then, anthropologists do not focus on the "official" or "high" or "canonical" version of religions, particularly as we find them in texts and scriptures or in the understandings of officials and specialists. Anthropology instead emphasizes how real human individuals conceive and use their religious resources—beliefs, objects, texts, rituals, and specialists—in specific social contexts for specific social and personal reasons. That is, we are less interested in the doctrine of a religion than in the lived practice of the religion.

In the book that follows, religions from around the world—familiar and very unfamiliar—are examined with these six themes in mind. In addition, the topical coverage goes beyond the conventional treatment in the anthropology of religion. Like all texts on the subject, I discuss beliefs and ritual and myth and so on. However, I place these standard topics in wider contexts—myth in "religious language," ritual in "religious behavior," and the like; each of these is further relativized as a cultural concept that we may not find at all in another culture or may find to be quite different than our own. Even more, I introduce topics that usually receive little or no attention in standard texts, such as morality, world religions, violence, secularism, and fundamentalism. One might be surprised to learn—to an extent, I myself was surprised to learn—that anthropology has approached or can approach these subjects with its presumed emphasis on the small and the traditional. But if, as we have asserted, all religion is local, and if it is always evolving and adapting to its social circumstances, then anthropology is perfectly, maybe even uniquely, equipped to investigate all of these matters. And as not only scholars but citizens of the twenty-first-century global society, it is absolutely essential to investigate all of these matters. An anthropology of religion without a commitment to contemporary developments like violence or fundamentalism renders itself quaint, tangential, perhaps even inconsequential for the modern world. I hope that this book not only conveys some insight into the religions of the world but into how anthropology is relevant, even essential, for understanding and inhabiting this world.

New to the Second Edition

The second edition represents a substantial revision of the first. Every chapter includes more and new material, combining classic anthropological research with work done as recently as 2013. Some of the changes and enhancements include:

- an ethnographic vignette to open each chapter;
- three boxes per chapter, all ethnographic, with many new topics such as ayahuasca religions, beliefs in *jinn* and *mana*, Himalayan god-masks, Petalangan verbal magic, South American funeral games, Amazonian moral substances, the Indian Sai Baba movement, Islam in France and Aboriginal Australia, Bolivian Pentecostalism, African Pentecostal television, corporate Islam in Indonesia, Jain female ascetics, Jewish secularism, an atheist center in India, and a Hindu fundamentalist children's camp in the United States;
- more material on contemporary societies, especially in Europe, Asia, and the Middle East;
- coverage of new topics including pilgrimage and paganism;
- up-to-date theoretical discussions of "modes of religiosity," materiality and embodiment, "little rituals," anti-syncretism, "occult economies," and "formations of the secular";
- discussion questions at the end of each chapter;
- a significantly modified chapter on the emerging anthropologies of Christianity and Islam;
- an entirely new chapter on vernacular religion;
- a glossary;
- a companion website, featuring three original supplemental readings per chapter (identified at the end of each printed chapter), study materials, useful links and resources, and a bonus chapter on sex, gender, and religion. Available at: www.routledge.com/cw/eller

Students and instructors will find the new edition more current, more global, more ethnographic, and hopefully more exciting and eye-opening than the first, illustrating the major advances in anthropological thinking on religion in recent years.

1 Studying Religion Anthropologically
Definitions and Theories

The Egyptian event called *mulid* is usually a small local celebration of a Muslim (and sometimes Christian) saint or "friend of God" (see Figure 1.1). Literally meaning "birth" or "birthday/place" and based on the celebration of Muhammad's birthday, the *mulid* is most associated with Sufi Islam and is focused on the shrine or saint's tomb. A key feature of a *mulid* is *dhikr* or "collective rituals of ecstatic meditation held in tents" in public squares (Schielke 2012: 29), and as such they are occasions of great *baraka* or blessing. However, Schielke finds that the *mulid* combines this serious spiritual business with joyful activity like "dancing, magic shows, puppet theater, shopping, sitting in cafes, and generally 'partying'" (36). Sometimes "female dancers, alcohol, and prostitution" were part of the fun (30). Not surprisingly, many Egyptians are critical of the *mulid*, branding it as backward or even un-Islamic, and there have been efforts to stop it. Is this behavior "religion"? Or is it "superstition"? Sacrilege? Folklore? Carnival?

All around the world, humans do and say things that are strange, even incomprehensible, to people outside their group. Some of these things we call "religion." Sometimes members of the society engaged in such practices call them religion, sometimes they do not. More importantly, some societies have a term for "religion" while others lack it altogether, and when we label an idea, behavior, object, or institution "religion" we are distinguishing it from other categories such as "magic," "superstition," "spirituality," or, of course, "science" or "politics."

Like every other aspect of human existence, both physical and cultural, religions are remarkably diverse. It is the business of anthropology to study human diversity. And as with the study of other aspects of cultural diversity such as language or kinship, it is not the business of anthropology to judge religion, let alone to falsify it or to verify it. Anthropology is not the seminary, attempting to indoctrinate the novice into any one particular religion. It is not apologetics, attempting to prove or justify some religion; neither is it an exercise in debunking any or all religion. Anthropology starts out with a different interest and a different agenda, and therefore with different tools and concepts. What does it mean to study religion anthropologically? The most profitable approach might be to answer this question backwards, beginning with anthropology, then turning to religion, and ending with study.

Studying Religion "Anthropologically"

Many disciplines explore religion—psychology, sociology, theology, even biology in some instances. Each has its own focus and interest. The anthropological study of religion must be distinguished and distinguishable from these other approaches in some

Figure 1.1 Mulid: an Egyptian man beats on a traditional drum as others chant during a procession to commemorate the birth of Prophet Muhammad in Cairo. © epa european pressphoto agency b.v. / Alamy

meaningful ways; it must do or offer something that the others do not. It must raise its own specific questions, come from its own specific perspective, and practice its own specific method.

Anthropology can best be thought of as the science of the diversity of humans, in their bodies and their behavior. Thus, the anthropology of religion will be the scientific investigation of the diversity of human religions. The questions it might ask include:

- What is the range of diversity of religion—how many different kinds of religions and religious beliefs, practices, institutions, etc. exist?
- What commonalities or even universals are there between religions—are there any things that all religions do or believe?
- What relationships exist between various parts of any single religion, or between a religion and its social and even natural environment—are there any regular patterns that we can discern across religions?

Anthropology, like every discipline, starts to address its questions from a unique disciplinary perspective. Studying religion biologically implies a biological perspective (emphasizing physical traits, perhaps most importantly the brain), while studying religion psychologically implies a psychological perspective (focusing on internal "mental" phenomena and processes). Anthropology has been open to and has profited from these and many other approaches. Still, it has developed some distinctive concepts, tools, and emphases. Central to anthropology is the concept of culture, the learned and shared ideas, feelings, behaviors, and products of those behaviors characteristic of any particular society. To study anything anthropologically—language, politics, gender roles, or eating habits—is therefore to look at it as learned and shared human behavior. Since it must be observable, anthropology also treats it as *public* behavior, not primarily something that is "private" or "in people's heads"; it is certainly not *initially* in people's heads but rather, since it is learned and acquired instead of innate, initially "outside" the individual in his or her social environment. In a word, culture is a *set of practices* in which humans engage and, among other things, about which they talk and in terms of which they act. Therefore, anthropology does not limit itself to texts or history (although it certainly considers these) but rather to culture lived by the actual members of the society.

This basic orientation leads to three aspects of the "anthropological perspective." First, anthropology proceeds through *comparative or cross-cultural description*. Anthropology does not consider only one's own society and culture or others similar to it. It begins from a premise of diversity and attempts to embrace the full range of diversity of whatever is under investigation. It aims to explore and describe each culture or aspect of culture in rich detail. This tends to manifest in a process and a product. The process is *fieldwork*, traveling to and living among the subjects of our study for long periods of time, observing and participating in their lives. Hence, the principal method of anthropology is generally considered to be *participant observation*. The product is the "case study" or *ethnography*, an in-depth and up-close account of the ways of thinking and feeling and behaving of the people we study. Therefore, anthropological writings tend to be "particularistic," to describe the "small" or the "local" intensively. However and fortunately, anthropology does not emphasize the local for its own sake; as Stanley Tambiah wrote, the point of ethnography is "to use the particular to say something about the general" (1970: 1). This is a crucial approach because no particular group or culture is typical or representative of humanity—in fact, there is no such thing as "typical" or "representative" language or politics or religion—yet each sheds some light on the general processes by which culture works. Such an insight will be particularly valuable when we turn below to discussions of large-scale and even "world" phenomena, which we often take as typical or consistent across vast expanses of area and numbers of people. Rather, we will find that these phenomena vary widely from place to place—that all religion, like all politics, is local. Not only that, but we find that ideas, practices, and values differ *within* a society, that not all members of even the smallest societies act or think exactly alike. In other words, cultures are internally diverse, and culture (including religion) is more "distributed" than shared.

Second, anthropology adopts a position of *holism*. We start from the presumption that any culture is a (more or less) integrated "whole," with "parts" that operate in specific ways in relation to each other and that contribute to the operation of the whole. From our examinations of cultures, anthropology has identified four such areas of function in all cultures (although not always equally elaborated or formalized in all cultures). These four "domains" of culture are economics, kinship, politics, and religion. Each makes its distinct contribution to society, but each is also "integrated" (although sometimes loosely) with all of the others, such that if we want to understand the religion of a society, we must also inevitably understand its political arrangements, its kinship system, and even its economic practices. These major cultural domains are also connected to, reflected in, and affected by more pervasive matters of language and gender. And finally, all of these elements are located within some environmental context.

Third, anthropology upholds the principle of *cultural relativism*. Cultural relativism grasps that each culture has its own "standards" of understanding and judging. Each occupies its own universe of meaning and value—of what is true, important, good, moral, normal, legal, and so on. It is patently obvious that the same behavior may be normal in one society, abnormal or criminal or non-existent in another. We know that the same sound, gesture, symbol, or action may have an entirely different meaning (or no meaning) in another society; applying one society's standard of meaning or judgment to another is simply not very informative and may actually be misleading. This does not mean, of course, that we must accept or endorse or even like what other societies do; however, we must understand them in their terms, or else we do not understand them at all. Maintaining a culturally relative perspective is profoundly important and profoundly difficult. Most of the time we do not think of our language or our political system or our gender roles or religion as "cultural" at all but rather as "what we do" or "what is done." We assume that all people wear clothes and marry monogamously, while in reality other peoples may not. And we tend to assume that all religions entail a belief in God (or "belief" at all) as well as prayers and rituals and ideas about heaven and hell, while in reality many religions do not. If we were to act on our taken-for-granted cultural assumptions, we would conclude that all people think and behave as we do and inter- rogate them for *their* versions of *our* concepts, practices, and values. We would be pro- foundly and dangerously wrong. A quick example will suffice. Imagine that a Warlpiri (Australian Aboriginal) person were to do non-relativistic ("ethnocentric" or "culture- bound") research on your society. He or she would come to the task with a battery of culturally specific concepts, like *jukurrpa* (usually translated as Dreaming or Dreamtime). If that researcher were to ask about your notions of *jukurrpa*, you would say none, since you have never heard that word before. If he or she were to interpret your actions or ideas through the concept of *jukurrpa*, he or she would surely get you wrong. And if he or she were to condemn you for lacking this key concept of theirs, it would surely be an inappropriate conclusion.

Cultural relativism is a consequence of cross-cultural and holistic study. If we are to consider extremely diverse cultures and to understand them in relation to their web of ideas and practices, then we must be—indeed we *are* being—relativistic. This is critically important for two reasons. First, it re-orients our notion of what anthropology is or does. As Talal Asad has suggested, anthropology is not just its method (fieldwork and participant observation) or its end-product (ethnography); if it were, there are many things we could not accomplish, such as studying past cultures. Instead, he posits, the mission of anthropology is "the comparison of embedded concepts (representations) between societies differently located in time and space [and] the forms of life that articulate them, the power they release or disable" (2003: 17). Our job is precisely, then, to expose and comprehend a society's embedded concepts, a people's view of reality.

This raises a second and major question about the use of the concepts of one culture (your own) to describe and understand the concepts of another culture. The problem is particularly thorny in the realm of religion. We necessarily approach religions with a vocabulary, a terminology; we must have some words to discuss things. However, the vocabulary we bring to the study is not a neutral, technical language but *the language of a particular religion*—from the Western perspective, usually Christianity. Like the ima- ginary Warlpiri researcher, we may find ourselves imposing concepts on a culture or religion when they do not relate or even exist. We may ask the wrong questions, make the wrong assumptions, and arrive at the wrong conclusions. While we cannot eradicate the problem completely, we must be constantly on guard against it.

Box 1.1 Buddhist Language in China: From Non-self to Self

A religion is a language, with its own vocabulary, literature, and "scripts" or common and appropriate things to say. A religion also operates within the wider context of a normal spoken language, that is, Americans "speak Christian" in English, while Poles "speak Christian" in Polish and Russians "speak Christian" in Russian. The introduction of a religion into a new social and linguistic context therefore often poses fascinating challenges. Over its history, Buddhism has developed a highly sophisticated, and diverse, vocabulary and doctrine; familiar terms like *nirvana*, *samsara*, and *Buddha* are only the beginning of an extensive linguistic-belief system. Central to most understandings of Buddhism is the term *anatta* or *anatman*, the doctrine of "non-self," which is an explicit critique of the earlier Hindu notion of *atman* or self. Standard Buddhism lacks an idea of an eternal, enduring self that survives death—or even survives from moment to moment. This does not mean, of course, that all schools of Buddhism think alike. According to Jungnok Park, early forms of Buddhism taught that the self was impermanent and composite, "a compound, all of whose components are impermanent" and "dependent on certain conditions" (2012: 66). Over time, Buddhist philosophy struggled with the problem of self and salvation, with some schools concluding that the original Buddha and subsequent enlightened ones continue to exist, to help free others from suffering. Eventually they argued that humans or even all sentient beings have a Buddha-nature or *tathagatagarbha* (embryo of a Tathagata or "thus-gone"), or an eternal soul/self. When Buddhism entered China, these Indian and Hindu-derived concepts and debates underwent dramatic changes. Many Buddhist words had no Chinese equivalent and no clear meaning in Chinese, so "Buddhist translators in China sometimes had to insert words or sentences that do not appear in the original texts, or remove words or sentences from the originals" (5). Further, to make the translations sensible and attractive to Chinese readers, translators had to be "familiar with Chinese literature, ethics, philosophy, and history" (10) and to conform to Chinese style in regard to word order, connotations, and aesthetics, even as they lost qualities of stress and meter in the originals. The result was that Chinese Buddhists developed "a Buddhism that was peculiar to China" (36), including gradually introducing and building a concept of Buddhist self. Chinese words like *hun* (spirit), *jing* (mind), and *shen* (essence of mind) entered Chinese Buddhist language and thought, leading Buddhists speaking Chinese to deviate from the early Buddhist concept of non-self to a Chinese Buddhist concept of "an imperishable soul" (177), in the process ironically arriving at "an idea of self that is closer to the Brahmanic [Hindu] *atman*, though they had no accurate knowledge of Brahmanic doctrines" (183).

It is difficult to remain relativistic in any area of human culture; for instance, people often judge other societies for their marriage or sexual practices. When it comes to religion, that relativistic objectivity has been even harder to maintain. For example, James Frazer, the great twentieth-century scholar of comparative mythology, distanced himself from the myths he recounted in *The Golden Bough* by testifying that "I look upon [them] not merely as false but as preposterous and absurd" (1958: vii). Of magic he concluded that "every single profession and claim put forward by the magician as such is false" (53). The more recent and highly respected anthropologist E. E. Evans-Pritchard, writing on witchcraft among the Azande of Africa, asserted: "Witches, as the Azande conceive them, cannot exist" (1937: 63). These men follow a long tradition, going back to the Greek historian Herodotus, who wrote: "My duty is to report all that is said, but I am not obliged to believe it all" (1942: 556). Perhaps it is at least good when they are honest enough to admit their struggles with foreign ideas, although declarative statements like "Witches cannot exist" are not part of our anthropological trade. Ultimately, we might be chastened by the fact that an Azande anthropologist could preface his or her ethnography of Western religion with the disclaimer: "God, as the Christians conceive him, cannot exist."

Studying "Religion" Anthropologically

When we are studying religion, what exactly are we talking about? What is "religion" after all? This raises the issue of definition. Let us begin by recognizing that definitions are not "real" things; they are human and therefore cultural creations, not facts that we find in nature. A definition is not "true"; it is only more or less inclusive and productive. A narrow definition excludes phenomena that would be included within a wider definition. For instance, if we were to define religion as "belief in one god" we would be disqualifying as religions all of the belief systems that lack a single god, so very few belief systems would qualify as religions. If we define it as "belief in god(s)," we would still be disqualifying the religions that say nothing at all about god(s). By imposing one view of religion on others, we would be defining them into non-religion (i.e., "if you don't believe in a god, then you don't have a religion"). This attitude echoes the character of Parson Thwackum in the Henry Fielding novel *The History of Tom Jones*, who said, "When I mention religion I mean the Christian religion; and not only the Christian religion, but the Protestant religion; and not only the Protestant religion, but the Church of England." That is not an attitude that an anthropologist—or anyone else—should take.

The act of defining is an attempt to get at what is unique and distinct about the subject, the *sine qua non* or "without that, not" that makes it what it is. Probably no single definition of something as diverse as religion could ever quite capture it. Rather, what we find is that various definitions emphasize certain aspects of the phenomenon or betray the theoretical orientations of their authors. For instance, one of the earliest anthropologists, E. B. Tylor, offered in his 1871 *Primitive Culture* what he considered to be the "minimal" or simplest possible definition of religion: "the belief in spiritual beings." A more compact definition can hardly be imagined, but it faces at least one complication: it introduces other terms—"belief" and "spiritual beings"—that beg for definitions. Others have subsequently offered more elaborate definitions:

James Frazer: "a propitiation or conciliation of powers superior to man which are believed to direct and control the course of nature and human life" (1958: 58–59)

William James (psychologist): "the feelings, acts, and experiences of individual men in their solitude, so far as they apprehend themselves to stand in relation to whatever they may consider the divine" (1958: 34)

Émile Durkheim (sociologist): "a unified system of beliefs and practices relative to sacred things, that is to say, things set aside and forbidden—beliefs and practices which unite into one single moral community called a Church, all those who adhere to them" (1965: 62)

Paul Radin: "it consists of two parts: the first an easily definable, if not precisely specific feeling; and the second certain acts, customs, beliefs, and conceptions associated with this feeling. The belief most inextricably connected with the specific feeling is a belief in spirits outside of man, conceived as more powerful than man and as controlling all those elements in life upon which he lays most stress" (1957: 3)

Anthony Wallace: "a set of rituals, rationalized by myth, which mobilizes supernatural powers for the purpose of achieving or preventing transformations of state in man and nature" (1966: 107)

Sherry Ortner: "a metasystem that solves problems of meaning (or Problems of Meaning) generated in large part (though not entirely) by the social order, by grounding that order within a theoretically ultimate reality within which those problems will 'make sense'" (1978: 152)

And perhaps Clifford Geertz provided the most commonly quoted definition: "(1) a system of symbols which act to (2) establish powerful, pervasive, and long-lasting moods and motivations in men by (3) formulating conceptions of a general order of existence and (4) clothing these conceptions with such an aura of factuality that (5) the moods and motivations seem uniquely realistic" (1973: 90). Meanwhile, Rudolf Otto thought it was the mysterious experience of the "holy"; Karl Marx thought it was false consciousness intended to complete the exploitation of the laborers, "the opiate of the masses"; Sigmund Freud thought it was a projection of unconscious psychological processes; Lucien Levy-Bruhl thought (at least for a time) that it was a product of a "primitive mentality"; and so on.

Clearly, scholars do not agree precisely how to begin to talk about this thing called religion. They emphasize different aspects of it: is religion fundamentally belief and ideas, or ritual, or feeling, or morality, or community? Further, they introduce other terms in the definition that plunge us into a definitional spiral: what is "spirit," "divine," "belief," "sacred," or "holy"? Finally, does it refer to something real "out there" or merely something "inside us"?

The truth is that religion probably involves all of these issues simultaneously, but disparately for different religions. Ritual, for instance, is certainly a key element of religion, although not all religions valorize or elaborate it equally. Ideas and concepts are universal aspects of religion, although not all religions have the same concepts or necessarily very conscious and consistent ones. Language or verbal action, including "myth," is important, as is "morality" or notions of good and bad behavior, and of course community. But then rituals and ideas and verbal actions and morals and communities exist apart from religion too; they are not essentially religious phenomena. What makes religion "religious"?

It would be foolish to attempt to adjudicate between the definitions of religion. Each highlights a piece of the puzzle. Even more, since there is no "true" definition, it would be a waste of time. Instead, we want to mark out an approach to religion that distinguishes it from other human endeavors and thought systems and yet connects it to them. What unifies religion with other social actions and institutions is physical (embodied) ritualistic and verbal behavior, a concern with good or correct action, the desire to achieve certain goals or effects, and the establishment and perpetuation of communities. What distinguishes religion is the object or focus of these actions, namely, nonhuman and typically "superhuman" being(s) and/or force(s) with which humans are understood to be in relation—a recognizably "social" relation—that is mutually effective. As Robin Horton has expressed it:

> in every situation commonly labeled religious we are dealing with action directed towards objects which are believed to respond in terms of certain categories—in our own culture those of purpose, intelligence, and emotion—which are also the distinctive categories for the description of human action. The application of these categories leads us to say that such objects are "personified." The relationship between human beings and religious objects can be further defined as governed by certain ideas of patterning and obligation such as characterize relationships among human beings. In short, Religion can be looked upon as an extension of the field of people's social relationships beyond the confines of purely human society. And for completeness' sake, we should perhaps add the rider that this extension must be one in which human beings involved see themselves in a dependent position vis-à-vis their nonhuman alters.
>
> (1960: 211)

That is to say, religion is an extrapolation of culture, to include in society and as cultural those beings and/or forces that would otherwise be described as natural or supernatural.

The key for anthropology is that religious beings and/or forces are almost universally "social," with the qualities of "persons" or at least "agents" of some sort. If they were not, how would we make sense of them, and what would we do with/about them? In other words, humans see themselves, in a religious context, as occupying a certain kind of relationship with some being(s) and/or force(s), which we can rightly and only call a *social relationship*. It is a relationship of communication, intention, reciprocity, respect, avoidance, control, etc. The being(s) and/or force(s) *are like us* in some ways, despite the fact that they are greatly unlike us in others. They may have a language (usually ours), personality or intentionality, desires and interests and likes and dislikes; they may "live" in their own social arrangements; and they can be approached and influenced. This takes us to the real significance of religion as a cultural factor and its real distinction from the other domains of culture. Economics, kinship, politics—these are all about humans. The characters in religion are different, but they are not so different. They are the nonhuman: the dead ancestors, or "spirits" of plants or animals or natural objects (the sun and the moon) or natural forces (the wind and the rain), or "gods," or impersonal supernatural forces like *mana* or *chi*. Yet they interact with us. *They are social, because they are part of society.*

In other words, religion is the discourse, the language and practice, or the means by which human society and culture is extended to include the nonhuman. This is not making any truth-claims about what being(s) and/or force(s) actually exist or what traits they possess. It simply clarifies that, for members of a religious community, the being(s) and/or force(s) that they "believe in" are part of their real and social world. A. Irving Hallowell reported asking an Ojibwa elder if all stones are alive and animate, and the man replied, "No! But *some* are" (1960: 24). A colleague of mine and Osage professor of theology, George Tinker, told a story of going with a Native spiritual leader to gather stones for a ceremony; asked how he would know which stones to gather, the spiritual leader responded, "The stones will tell me."

The evidence of the "socialization," the "culturization," of the nonhuman is clear when you consider how humans talk about religious beings and forces. In Christianity, God is the father—a kinship term. Australian Aboriginals speak of the kangaroo-grandfather or the moon-mother, in terms very similar to most societies. In fact, for them and many others, their religious beings are ancestors, sometimes even literally part-human and part-animal or part-plant. The kangaroo-grandfather may have been an actual kangaroo-man. Furthermore, religious being(s) and/or force(s) often have temperaments and tastes like people: again, the Judeo-Christian god as depicted in the Torah/Old Testament enjoyed the smell of cooking meat, and he was jealous and angry. The same god in the New Testament feels love but also justice and vengeance—all human traits. In whatever religious tradition, the beings or forces almost always have personalities: they are friendly, hostile, deceptive, indifferent, or what have you. Animals are believed to talk, plants to think, rocks and stars to feel. But they are human-like. Indeed, religion makes part or all (depending on the tradition) of the nonhuman world social—participants in the norms and values and relations of culture.

Assuming that we have some general and workable idea of what religion is and what we will be studying, perhaps it is more profitable to talk about what religion *does*. So we can ask, what is the function of religion? Why do humans have such a thing, and what does it do for them? Of course, a member might answer that we have religion because it is "true" and because we are the kinds of beings who can perceive or receive the truth. This is not very helpful from an anthropological point of view, especially since different societies have perceived or received such different truths across time and space. No doubt there is something unique about humans that makes it possible (and necessary?) for us to have religious notions, but let us set aside questions of "truth" and concentrate on social and cultural nature and functions of religion, which include:

1 Filling individual needs, especially psychological or emotional needs. Religion can provide comfort, hope, perhaps love, definitely a sense of control, and relief from fear and despair.
2 Explanation, especially of origins or causes. Humans wonder why things are as they are. How did the world start? How did humans start? How did society start? Most religions not only explain cosmogony (the creation of the world) but the origin of specific cultural institutions, like marriage, language, technology, politics, and the like. Religions also explain why things happen in the present: why do we get sick? Why do bad things happen to us? Why do we die? In some societies, much if not all of sickness and misfortune is attributed to "spiritual" rather than natural causes.
3 Source of rules and norms. Religion can also provide the answer to where the traditions and institutions of the society came from. All religions contain some element of "order-establishment" or "culture-founding." This is the *charter* function of religion: it acts as the "charter" or guideline or authority by which we organize ourselves in particular ways and follow particular standards. Why monogamy? Because a superhuman being ordered it, or because the first humans set the precedent, etc. Why kings? Because a superhuman being ordained the office of king, or because the kings are chosen by superhuman beings or possess superhuman force, etc.
4 Source of "ultimate sanctions." Religion is among other things a means of social control. Even in the Judeo-Christian tradition, a large part of the religion is about what we should do, how we should live. Politics and even kinship provide a measure of this control. However, the limitation of political social control is its scope: human agents of social control cannot be everywhere and cannot see everything, and the rewards and punishments they can mete out are finite. For instance, they cannot continue to reward or punish you after you die. But religious "sanctions" can be much more extensive, exquisite, and enduring. In other words, religious being(s) and/or force(s) not only make the rules but enforce them too.

5   Solution of immediate problems. If religion is the "cause" of a variety of human ills, then religion can be the solution as well. If we are sick or distressed, are the beings or forces angry with us? What should we do about it? If there is an important social or political decision to make (say, going to war), is there a way to discover the preferences and plans of the beings and forces—to "read their mind"? Can we ask them for favors, give them gifts, or do anything at all to influence their actions and intentions?

6   Filling collective needs. Beyond the individuals who compose society and their individual needs, it is also possible to view society as an entity in its own right, with its own higher-level needs. Certainly, not everything that a religion teaches or practices is beneficial for every individual: human sacrifice is not about fulfilling the needs of sacrificial victims. Nor does religion always soothe individual fears and anxieties; for instance, the belief in a punitive afterlife may cause people to be more fearful, and concerns about proper conduct of rituals or about witches can cause anxiety. However, belief in a punitive afterlife can cause people to obey norms, which is "good for society." The primary need of society, apart from and often at odds with the needs of individuals, is integration, cohesion, and perpetuation, and religion can provide an important "glue" toward that end.

"Studying" Religion Anthropologically

Anthropology as a science has carved out for itself a territory to investigate, and that territory includes all of human behavior in its dazzling and bedeviling diversity. Religion falls within that territory. But what precisely does anthropology hope to accomplish? What does it mean to "study" religion, or anything else, from an anthropological or any scientific point of view? The one thing it does not mean is to *acquire* a religion, to *convert* to one, to become a member or functionary of one. Candidates for the priesthood "study religion," as do theologians, but their interests are to adopt and defend a religion, to believe more deeply and convince others to believe in it, which cannot be the interest of anthropology. Anthropology is not apologetics. What anthropology, like any other science, ultimately wants to do with its chosen subject matter is to *explain* it.

To "explain" religion or any other social or physical phenomenon is to construct a model of it, to identify processes or mechanisms at work in it, and/or to give reasons for it. As an example, some people might study dogs: they learn about all the different kinds of dogs and their bodily and behavioral characteristics. That is a worthwhile pursuit but ends up with a mere catalog of dog details; in essence, it allows them to answer the question, "What is a dog?" What are the qualities that make a dog a dog, and how many different kinds of dogs are there? That is the descriptive agenda. However, if they want to *explain* dogs, this would be a matter of asking a very different kind of question—not "What is a dog?" but "Why is a dog?"

The anthropological study of religion, which is a scientific study, is similar. We can describe and catalog religions, but at some point we want to advance to explanation; no longer content with definitions ("what is religion?") or cross-cultural descriptions ("how many kinds of religion are there?"), we move on to the question "Why is religion?" One obvious answer is "Because it is true" or "Because God/the gods put it in us." These are answers that anthropology or science in general cannot be content with. Rather, anthropological, or any scientific, explanations of religion (or anything else) explain it *in terms of something else*. What that "something else" might be varies, but fundamentally the process of explaining anything is giving a reason for it in terms of something other than itself—finding its foundation or its function outside of itself.

The ultimate goal or form of scientific explanation is a theory. A theory orients us to the data in a particular way: what are the most important or irreducible or universal elements to look for, what relationship are they in with each other, and how do they interact to produce the facts under investigation? A theory ought to offer us a model with some specific mechanisms or processes that give rise to and shape the phenomenon; it also ought to make some predictions which are testable in some way, allowing us potentially to verify or falsify the theory. It should, therefore, offer the possibility of using it to acquire further knowledge or understanding, as well as to eliminate error. Anthropologists and other scholars of religion have offered a variety of theoretical perspectives, each productive and each limited in its own way. No single theoretical perspective, like no single definition, can probably ever capture the entire essence or nature of religion. Above all we should avoid reductionism, the attitude that a phenomenon like religion can be explained in terms of ("reduced to") a single non-religious cause or basis, whether that cause or basis is psychological, biological, or social. At the same time, we cannot help but notice that scientific/anthropological theories of religion find the "reason" or explanation for religion in non-religion.

Pre-scientific Approaches/Apologetics

With the exception of a few ancient Greek philosophers, the pre-modern approach to religion tended to involve not explaining religion but *offering justifications for the truth of a religion*. This is the realm of apologetics, the systematic argumentative defense of a particular religion. While apologetics is an interesting subject in its own right, it is not "anthropological" in any sense and will not be pursued here; besides, the very point of the apologetic exercise is *not to explain* one's religion but rather to *prove* it. Any religion can, and many religions do, engage in this mutually exclusive effort.

Since inquiry begins when certainty ends, so it was with the first ancient "doubters" or skeptics that theorizing about religion commenced. Xenophanes in the fifth century BCE was among the first to comment on religious diversity and the relation between a religion and its society. He wrote:

> Ethiopians have gods with snub noses and black hair, Thracians have gods with gray eyes and red hair. ... If oxen or lions had hands which enabled them to draw and paint pictures as men do, they would portray their gods as having bodies like their own; horses would portray them as horses, and oxen as oxen.
>
> (quoted in Wheelwright 1966: 33)

The historian Herodotus extended this "comparative method," suggesting that the various tribal and national gods he encountered were all local names for the same universal deities—his so-called "equivalence of gods" principle. Thus, he concluded, the Egyptian god Horus was the same god as the Greek Apollo, and the Egyptian Osiris was the same as Dionysus. This led him naturally to the notion of cultural borrowing and diffusion to explain the recurrence of the same beliefs in disparate locations. Euhemerus developed this questioning into a nearly explicit humanistic theory of religion, in which he posited that the gods were merely deified human ancestors or leaders, a position known as euhemerism. There is no doubt that this accurately describes at least some pre-modern (and sometimes even modern) cases, as when pharaohs were deified in their own lifetimes or when deceased Mayan kings were left sitting on their thrones, allegedly still issuing orders. Even today, the "cult of personality" of some living leaders and the reverence they receive after death (e.g. placing Lenin's corpse in a clear glass sarcophagus in the former Soviet Union for display) suggest a "sacred" attitude toward very powerful humans.

Another pre-modern, in particular medieval, approach to religion—one that carried over strongly into the modern era—was the comparative or classificatory approach. For instance, the Muslim writer Shahrastani organized religions (not including traditional tribal ones) into four classes: Islam, the literary religions or "religions of the book" (Judaism and Christianity), the quasi-literary religions (e.g. Zoroastrianism and Manichaeism), and the philosophical religions (Buddhism and Hinduism—failing to note, apparently, the expansive literature of these faiths, including the Vedas, Upanishads, and Sutras). Roger Bacon in thirteenth-century Europe also developed a typology, including pagans, idol-worshipers (such as Buddhists and polytheists), Mongols, Muslims, Jews, and of course Christians. These systems of classification do not have much if any explanatory value, and they tend to be very judgmental and ethnocentric, but at least they were taking other religions seriously after a fashion.

Historical/Evolutionist Theories

Even some of the ancient "theories" of religion had a historical or evolutionist flavor; diffusion is a historical process, and Herodotus reiterated the even older Homeric notion of a series of historical "ages" in culture and religion, from the "golden" age of gods to the "silver" age of heroes to the "iron" age of normal humans, each inferior to its predecessor. The works of Charles Darwin and Karl Marx reinforced the pattern of historical, "progressive" analysis. Early in the nineteenth century, the philosopher Georg Hegel (1770–1831) proposed a comprehensive historical system progressing from the age of religion to the age of philosophy to the final age of science, in which each phase is a clearer step in self-knowledge of the Universal Spirit. The early sociologist Auguste Comte (1798–1857) described a similar three-stage history, with the eras of theology, metaphysics, and science or positivism. Herbert Spencer (1820–1903), a proponent of social Darwinism, echoed this idea in a more down-to-earth version but still with science eventually replacing religion and superstition. Early anthropologists like E. B. Tylor (1832–1917) also had a determined evolutionist streak in their work. Finding animism or "nature worship" to be the first phase of religion, Tylor then traced the development of religion to polytheism and finally monotheism (finding, predictably, that the local form of faith is the "highest").

Another historical approach in anthropology was diffusionism. Fritz Grabner (1877–1934), Father Wilhelm Schmidt (1868–1954), and G. Elliot Smith (1871–1937) represented this tradition in various versions. All diffusionists traced the diversity of the world's religions back to a few—or in Smith's case, one (ancient Egypt)—sources; the common origin explained the similarities, and the subsequent historical development of each independent spin-off explained the differences.

Psychological Theories

Some of the earliest modern theories of religion were psychological in nature, that is, appealing or referring in some way to the thoughts or experience of the individual. However, this appeal could differ profoundly. Psychological theories of religion include emotionalist, psychoanalytic, intellectualist, "primitive mentality," structuralist, and neurological theories, among others.

Emotionalist Theories

Many scholars emphasized the emotional quality of religion as its most distinguishing and driving feature. Which particular emotion they emphasized varied. For the seventeenth-century political philosopher Thomas Hobbes, it was fear; bad things happened to people beyond their understanding or control, so religion was invented to assuage unavoidable fears. Although writing long before anthropology emerged, he made the relativistic observation that out of this universal emotion grew such religious diversity that peoples could hardly recognize let alone accept the religions of others.

Another famous focus for emotionalist theory is the experience of "awe" or "wonder," advanced by Max Mueller (1823–1900) and Rudolf Otto (1869–1937). Mueller addressed himself to the awareness of "the divine" or "the infinite," expressed through conventional media like the sun or the moon or the seasons and so on. In his 1856 *Comparative Mythology* he argued that pre-modern and tribal societies felt the vastness and power of the cosmos but could only express their feelings in poetic symbolism incorporating natural objects; later, they forgot or confused their poetry with literal fact, resulting in religious belief. In other words, religion starts with overwhelming emotion and ends with linguistic error. This led him to characterize religion as "a disease of language." For Otto, author of *The Idea of the Holy* (1917), the religious emotions—both fear and fascination, love and dread—were a response to the "transcendent," the overwhelming power of that which is outside humans, the Holy that is "wholly other." The experience is primary, and religious ideas and practices follow to make sense of it and to harness it in some way.

In another vein, the "functionalist" theory of Bronislaw Malinowski (1884–1942) held that religious beliefs and institutions exist and function to fill the needs of individual humans, primarily psychological needs. Religion, as in his famous account of ritual in the Trobriand Islands, came into play when individuals needed a feeling of reassurance, control, and of course relief from fear; in other situations, where there was little threat or a fair chance of practical success, people did not resort to religion but focused their efforts on "practical" concerns.

Psychoanalytic Theory

A special type of theory was proposed by Sigmund Freud (1856–1939), who related or even reduced religion to mental processes, explaining it quite literally as a "symptom" or manifestation of our mind. For Freud, all humans shared a common set of unconscious drives and instincts. These drives and instincts, many of them antisocial and most of them asocial in a way, must and will be expressed. However, both physical and social reality force us to curb, control, direct, sublimate, and in some cases completely deny or "repress" our nature—to push or hold things down into the unconscious. In particular, Freud suggested in his 1913 *Totem and Taboo* that a scene had been played out in real history in which men acted on their desire to kill their father and take possession of his women (recapitulated in the infamous Oedipus complex, which he thought was part of the deep psychology of all males); subsequently, out of guilt, they reified or deified the dead father, making him an object of veneration and authority—perhaps more powerful dead than alive. The dead but divine father was both the first god and the first conscience or "superego." From that experience (literal or mythical) flowed a complex of "religious" beliefs and practices like the incest taboo, totemism, sacrifice, propitiation of spirits, and so on.

Even more basically, religion, like all behavior (including the behavior of "high culture" like art and of course dreams) was a symptom and neurosis in the Freudian view. Our unconscious, instinctive nature must and will come out, but the ways that it can come out are circumscribed by society. So, our unconscious mind often substitutes an (unacceptable) expression with another (more acceptable) one. Very human kinds of psychological and social dramas, like family dynamics, are played out in the "spiritual" realm, being essentially symbols for the "real" processes in our minds and lives. The living flesh-and-blood father is the prototype of the god, with his power to judge and punish. The child, unable to resist or even respond, becomes the model for the believer, putting his or her faith in the all-powerful adult. Religion, in this interpretation, is "an infantile obsessional neurosis" and one that Freud hoped we would grow out of as we understood and gained control over our own lives and drives (as evinced by his 1927 book *The Future of an Illusion*).

Intellectualist Theories

Other students of comparative religion have downplayed the emotional or "feeling" part and highlighted the explanatory or "thinking" function. In the intellectualist tradition, religion arises from question-asking or problem-solving. For instance, while Tylor's framework was evolutionist, his attitude was intellectualist. Primitive humans, he reasoned, had certain experiences that puzzled them, such as dreams, visions, and hallucinations, and the difference between living and dead beings. To explain these uncanny phenomena, they invented an invisible, non-mortal, detachable part of the self called the soul or spirit. From there, other concepts and behaviors would suggest themselves, such as cults of the dead and propitiation of spirits, etc.

James Frazer (1854–1941) also took an intellectualist if not quite "rationalist" stand in regard to religion. In fact, his contribution was that religion is an answer to a question or problem, just not a rational answer. He too held a "developmental" or "historical" opinion about religion, except that religion was not in his view the first step in the process. Before there was religion, he said, there was magic, which is a kind of faulty reasoning, a brand of pseudoscience. People want to know what causes what, or what they can do to cause or prevent what. Primitive humans had the right general idea—cause and effect—but they got the causes all wrong, indulging in magic instead of effective causal behavior. But still, magic was *technique*, a kind of "technology." When magic failed, humans then attributed events to intelligent, willful sources, namely spiritual beings. Thus the age of genuine religion began.

Malinowski also noted the "pre-scientific" but rational nature of magic, making the distinction between magic and religion. Both magic and religion he linked to emotional needs, as we saw. However, magic was more purely goal-oriented or "instrumental," whereas religion had no specific "goal" but was more social or moral in nature. Furthermore, no human, even a "primitive" human, was so backward as to rely exclusively on magic (or religion) to get a job done; while they may pray or perform rituals over their crops, they also plant seeds. So magic was like one tool in the individual's practical toolkit rather than a comprehensive way of life.

Primitive Mentality versus Psychic Unity

These contrary notions fall within the intellectualist school, but they are unique enough to deserve a separate comment. One of the very first, foundational notions in modern anthropology was Adolf Bastian's (1826–1905) concept of *elementargedanken* or "elementary ideas." All humans, he suggested, share a certain set of basic, fundamental ideas or experiences (what Carl Jung would later call "archetypes"). All humans are thus mentally the same; there is no profound and unbridgeable difference between "primitive" and "modern" or "religious" and "scientific" humans. There is, in other words, a common "psychic unity" of humanity. What does differ is the local expression or formulation of these elementary ideas, which he called *volkergedanken* or folk ideas or ethnic ideas. Thus, while all humans may have some idea of a transcendent power or a survival after death, the particular forms that these ideas take may and will vary from place to place and from time to time. Religious diversity, then, was to be examined not for the "surface variation" but for the deeper and more universal patterns and truths that were expressed in them.

The exact opposite position was formulated by Lucien Lévy-Bruhl (1857–1939), who stated that the thoughts and beliefs of "primitive" people came from a completely different way of thinking than that of modern people. We moderns, he argued, are logical, especially when it comes to the "law of exclusion": something cannot be itself and something else at the same time. Primitives, however, knew nothing of this. Instead, they were "pre-logical," operating on the "law of participation," which allows different or even contradictory things to co-exist or co-reside simultaneously. For instance, a statue could be a statue and a god all at once, or a being could be a human and an animal at the same time. If this analysis is true, then there is a deep gulf between them and us; however, even Lévy-Bruhl himself disavowed it in his lifetime, and it is easy to see that "primitives" are not always pre-logical (they may perform hunting rituals but they sharpen their spears too) and that "moderns" are not always logical (they may use jet planes and cell phones but still believe that a wafer is simultaneously a human body—the well-known doctrine of the transubstantiation, that the Catholic communion wafer literally "becomes" flesh). We will return to the discussion of mental dualism in Chapter 3.

Structuralism

Structuralism generally refers to the view that the meaning or the functioning of a phenomenon depends less on the nature of its individual "bits" than the relationships between those bits and the rules for combining them. Language is perhaps the paradigm of a structural system, in which the meaning of a word is determined by its place in an array of words, and the meaning of a sentence is determined by its place in an array of sentences. Ferdinand de Saussure (1857–1913) revolutionized linguists with this structuralist approach, emphasizing the "grammar" or transformational practices that allowed people who have mastered the general rules of language (*langue* in his terminology) to produce specific acts of speech (*parole*).

Claude Lévi-Strauss (1908–2009) was hugely influential in applying this grammatical approach to religion, especially mythology. Providing anthropology with a "method" to analyze and interpret myths, he suggested that the symbols and events in myth can only be understood as utterances within a grammar or pattern of transformations; as he wrote in *The Savage Mind*, religious facts such as myths or totems "are codes suitable for conveying messages which can be transposed into other codes, and for expressing messages received by means of different codes in terms of their own system" (1966: 75–76). Thus, the analysis of myths and other religious facts involves the discovery of the underlying relationships between the units or details of the whole.

While all versions of structuralism claim something similar, Lévi-Strauss' version goes further, which is why it is placed under the heading of psychological theories. He asserted that at the foundation of mythical transformations was the nature of the human mind itself, which operates in binary fashion. The human mind classifies things into pairs, such as nature/culture, male/female, alive/dead, raw/cooked, and so forth. The mind also seeks to resolve and unify these binary contradictions, but since such resolution is not permanent if even possible, humans generate repeated, different, yet recognizably similar attempts to do so. Thus, any myth, for instance, will appear to be struggling with the same issues over and over. Add to this Lévi-Strauss' suggestion that the mind is a *bricoleur* (1966: 20–21) or playful creator of meanings and manifestations, and we see the religious results: an ongoing attempt to examine basic existential themes in multiple ways through "analogies and comparisons," metaphors and poetry. We will return to this theory in our discussion of myth in Chapter 4.

Neurological theories

Where psychology meets neuroscience, there is an assortment of approaches to religion that emphasize the physical substrate that makes belief possible if not necessary. This has sometimes taken the form of talk about a "god spot" in the brain, an area or structure that is "tuned" or "designed" for religious functioning. Whether the brain makes the religion or the religion makes the brain (that is, supernatural beings or forces arranged our brain as a "receiver" for spiritual "transmissions") is open to dispute.

A popular study by Newberg, d'Aquili, and Rause (2002) examined mystics during their meditative practices and identified measurable differences in their brains in and out of mystical states, with differing levels of activity in the left temporal lobe during meditation. Their conclusion was that, since ostensibly brains react to the external world, the brain activity of adepts was evidence of their experience of some real external phenomenon or power. Others, such as Michael Persinger (1987), have used medical technology to assert quite the opposite: by stimulating certain areas of the brain with an electrical device, Persinger was able to generate "religious experience" in subjects, leading him to conclude that religion is a result of the brain's own activity rather than of some reality outside of the brain. It has also been clinically observed that patients who suffer from left hemisphere epileptic seizures often develop obsessive interest in religious matters, which lasts long after the actual brain events.

Finally, Lewis-Williams and Dowson (1988) have proposed another neurological basis of religious notions and motifs in what they refer to as "entoptic" images. These are the kinds of patterns that are produced spontaneously by the nature of the human eye and nervous system, consisting of geometric forms like dots, lines, zigzags, and so on. These patterns and shapes are commonly reported by people in trance and other altered mental states and represented in the art of traditional societies, such as rock paintings. These physiological experiences, then, would have been interpreted as "supernatural" in origin and meaning and attributed with significance and power beyond their organic sources.

Box 1.2 Bringing Gods to Mind: Entheogens and Ayahuasca Religions

Humans use many techniques to induce religious experiences, including chanting, sleep and food deprivation, pain, and of course psychoactive substances. Such substances, from peyote to LSD, are referred to by scientists as "entheogens" (from the Greek for "within-god-making"), since they generate sensations that are frequently interpreted and employed as encounters with the divine. One entheogen that has

Figure 1.2 Ayahuasca: a shaman in the Coafan region of Ecuador boils leaves for their psychoactive properties. Photo by Wade Davis/Getty Images

been widely used, and around which entire sects and religions have formed, is ayahuasca, a brew made out of the Amazonian vine *Banisteriopsis caapi* (see Figure 1.2). Also known as *yagé*, the concoction has powerful hallucinatory effects, as well as unpleasant physical effects like vomiting and diarrhea, which are considered by users as "a manner of purifying spiritual and corporal ills" (da Silva Sá and Gialluisi 2010: 170). Already known to the indigenous peoples of the Brazilian Amazon, the arrival of European settlers and African slaves developed ayahuasca in new directions. The outcome was religions "that build their systems of ritual, myth, and principles" around brewing, ingesting, and experiencing the feelings of ayahuasca (Labate, MacRae, and Goulart 2010: 1), which have become known aptly as "Brazilian ayahuasca religions." Three such religions are Santo Daime, Barquinha, and União do Vegetal. These religions are "a manifest combination of the Amazonian ayahuasca folk healer (*curandeirismo*) heritage with popular Catholicism, and with the African-Brazilian tradition, Kardecist spiritism, and European esotericism" (2). Santo Daime was the first to emerge, in the 1920s and 1930s, believing that the beverage endowed drinkers with "health, healing, knowledge, revelation, peace, love, etc." from "a divinity or spiritual entity" (3). In 1945 another sect appeared, eventually called Barquinha or Little Boat, which also uses *yagé* in healing ritual services. Finally, União do Vegetal (UDV), officially known as Union of the Vegetal Beneficent Spiritist Center, formed in 1961. Among adherents of UDV, ayahuasca and several other plants are used to acquire "light" and "knowledge," and the altered state of consciousness that it induces, called *burracheira* (drunk), includes feelings of gratitude, power, and goodness. Practitioners may also experience *miraçöes* (miracles), visions that convey a sense of well-being and oneness with the universe—the very thing that Rudolf Otto described.

Social Theories

Not all scholars did or do turn to the individual or the workings of the mind to explain religion. They note that, while religion certainly has some root or origin in the brain/mind, it is a public or social phenomenon, which cannot be explained in psychological and subjective terms alone; further, many individuals never have a "religious experience" or even believe in religion. Such scholars, anthropologists among them, turn to an "external" and more social style of explanation. As a school of thought, social theories emphasize the role of groups and institutions, community, and/or morality, which were often conspicuously lacking in the previous theories.

Functionalism

Much of the pioneering work on the sociology of religion was done not by anthropologists but by classicists studying ancient Greek, Roman, and Hebrew sources. (This was problematic work, as it was not popular to treat the Christian scriptures as just another document to be analyzed scientifically.) One brave soul was William Robertson Smith (1846–94), who lost a teaching job for searching for the origins of Old Testament/Torah rituals and beliefs. His discovery was that ancient peoples had gods and religions *as peoples*, that is, that religious beliefs and practices had "national" or "tribal" or "ethnic" roots. Each group had its own god(s), which, as Xenophanes noticed twenty-five hundred years earlier, resembled the people of the group and legitimated the ways of the group. In fact, the essence of religion, Smith decided, was the communal ritual, a social act by definition. Explicit "doctrine" or creed came later as an explanation for the rituals, but the bedrock of religion was social behavior and, even more so, the social group that engages in the behavior.

The most influential early sociologist, Émile Durkheim (1858–1917), took this idea and developed it extensively, particularly in his groundbreaking 1915 book, *The Elementary Forms of the Religious Life*. He asked the question, what is most basic in religion? If we take away every other layer and accoutrement, what is left? His answer, as we saw in the definitions above (p. 6–7), was an irreducible dichotomy between the "sacred" and the "profane." The sacred is the special, powerful, set-apart realm—the one that we dare not touch or approach carelessly, if at all. The profane is the ordinary, the mundane, the everyday realm—the one that we dwell in most of the time but that would disrespect or corrupt the sacred by contact. But where could such a notion as "the sacred" come from? Other analysts would point to the psychology of awe and wonder, but Durkheim pointed to the sociology of the group—literally. What is it that is more powerful than the individual, that exists before the individual, that survives after the individual, and upon which the individual depends? It is the social group: "this power exists, it is society" (1965: 257). The group is a "social fact" and an important one. There is the society as a whole, and within it the family and the clan and the village and other concrete social aggregates. These social realities are symbolized, with a name or a banner or a "totem." They have their stories, their songs, their designs, their dances. They have their god(s). As he reasoned: "The god of the clan, the totemic principle, can therefore be nothing else than the clan itself, personified and represented to the imagination under the visible form of the animal or vegetable which serves as totem" (236). In other words, when the group celebrates or worships its spirits or gods, it is really celebrating or worshiping itself.

But tribal, social religion does more than celebrate; it creates. The main issue is social integration and cohesion, the creation and perpetuation of the group as a group. This is accomplished in two ways. The first is the establishment of a moral community, a group of people who share common norms, values, and morals. Religion not only tells them what to worship and how to make it rain but what kind of person to be and what the correct behaviors are in their group. By recognizing common rules and authorities, individuals become a community, with shared identity and shared interests. The second means of achieving group cohesion is through the effectiveness of ritual. This communal activity not only gives members ideas and beliefs in common, but it operates at a lower and more instinctive level as well through a psychological power he called "effervescence."

> When they are together, a sort of electricity is formed by their collecting which quickly transports them to an extraordinary degree of exaltation. Every sentiment expressed finds a place without resistance in all the minds, which are very open to outside impressions; each re-echoes the others, and is re-echoed by the others. The initial impulse thus proceeds, growing as it goes, as an avalanche grows in its advance. And as such active passions so free from all control could not fail to burst out, on every side one sees nothing but violent gestures, cries, veritable howls, and deafening noises of every sort, which aid in intensifying still more the state of mind which they manifest. ... So it is in the midst of these effervescent social environments and out of this effervescence itself that the religious idea seems to be born.
>
> (1965: 247)

Whether or not this is an accurate portrayal of traditional ritual (and in many ways it is not), it does show a keen appreciation for the power of collective action. It is well established that human beings are more excitable and suggestible in groups than individually, and the more active the group the greater the effect.

Historical Materialism

One of the dominant perspectives on religion over the past century and a half has been that of Karl Marx (1818–83). His theory, identified most closely with political economy and the ideology of communism, is actually a theory of social structure and social change. Basically, his argument was that the driving force, the motor, of society and culture is not ideas but action or practice. He was talking about the way that humans relate to the world through their work or labor—the ways that we express and "objectify" ourselves in our productions—and through the social relationships into which they organize themselves to perform that work.

The central concepts in historical materialism are "mode of production" and "relations of production." However, Marx also recognized that a society is not a simple, homogeneous thing but is composed of various subgroups with different positions in the relations of production—different roles to play, different perspectives on the system, different interests, and different power. He called these subgroups "classes." In class-differentiated societies, ordinarily one class has more control over the mode and relations of production than the other(s). The "upper class" is not only richer and more powerful but is also dominant in ideas and values. As he concluded, the dominant ideas of a society are the ideas of the dominant group of the society, not least because that group controls not only the "economy" but the educational system, whatever forms of "media" exist, and the institutions of society, including the religion.

Thus, religion, he opined, reflects the on-the-ground realities of social life. If the economy and the politics are very centralized, then religion will be centralized too, with one or at most a few gods that rule everything. However, religion is more than reflection; it is also legitimation. That is, people in the society—especially those who are not in the upper class—may ask why they should participate in it. What is the benefit to them? Religion provides the answer, by setting up and enforcing a view of the world that explains and authorizes the current social arrangement. Perhaps the purest version of this idea is the "divine right of kings" conception from European history, which "proved" that the contemporary political system was correct; the traditional Chinese "mandate of heaven" and the Hindu caste system accomplished the same end. In all societies, in the "charter" function mentioned above, religion helps to account for why things are the way they are and why we should go along with it. However, religion does not always *accurately* represent society; it can misrepresent and even mystify social relations. Leaders may intentionally foster religious views that prop up their power and prevent challenges. This is why Marx (1843) called religion an "opiate of the masses" and the "heart of a heartless world." This is also why Marx, like Freud, hoped and expected that religion would disappear.

A variation on the materialist perspective can be found in the work of Marvin Harris. In such books as *Cows, Pigs, Wars, and Witches* (1974) he argued that religious practices like cow-worship in India or pig-aversion in Judaism can be attributed to immediate material (namely, economic and environmental) causes. In India, cows are worth more alive than dead, so religion created an aura of supernatural significance around them to encourage people to preserve them. In the deserts of Israel, pigs were economically unviable, so the same supernatural aura castigated them. In whatever case, a practical, non-spiritual reason for the belief or behavior can be found, which is then wrapped in a shroud of religious meaning as a form of legitimation and compulsion.

Structural Functionalism

Within professional anthropology, functionalism as propounded by Malinowski was the first significant theory of culture and of religion. However, Malinowski's version of functionalism as usually understood is not a very social theory; each individual could theoretically invent his or her own unique language, religion, or eating utensils to get the practical job done (we will see in Chapter 4 that this is hardly the whole of Malinowski's approach to religion). But individuals do not (mostly) invent their own solutions to life's problems; they learn and inherit the solutions of their ancestors and peers.

A. R. Radcliffe-Brown (1881–1955) was the main rival for anthropological theory in the first part of the twentieth century. He agreed that function was a central issue but not the function that Malinowski and the "individualists" identified. Rather, Radcliffe-Brown emphasized the needs of the group or of society. But what needs could society have other than the cumulative needs of its constituent members? The answer is, as Durkheim pointed out, integration and cohesion. It is entirely possible for every individual to be well fed and relieved from fear but for society to fragment or collapse. Radcliffe-Brown, on the other hand, saw society and its groups and institutions as having their own needs and therefore emphasized the function of all items of culture or society as "the contribution that they make to the formation and maintenance of a social order" (1965: 154).

Structural functionalism insists that religion plays its most important role in the creation and maintenance of the group and society, not the comfort of the individual. One argument for this perspective is that without social maintenance society may come to an end, endangering the lives of all the individual members. So, as Durkheim stated, religion gives members of society a common identity, activity, interest, and destiny. It makes one out of many. Even more so, there are moments in the "life" of a society when its very existence is threatened—say, times of death, war, or other crisis. Ordinary ritual and belief may get society through the ordinary times, but extraordinary rituals and beliefs may be necessary for these extraordinary times. Thus, funeral rituals might be viewed as giving comfort to the grieving survivors, or they might be viewed as holding them together as a society at a time when fights or other conflicts could rip it apart. Some rituals have purely social functions; Fourth of July festivities are fun for American individuals, but more importantly they remind and refresh the solidarity that binds them together as Americans.

A second argument for social functions of religion follows from the first. Individual functionalism depends on religion relieving fear and stress and other negative emotions. Radcliffe-Brown astutely realized that religious beliefs and actions sometimes actually increase fear and stress; after all, if one does not believe in hell, one has no fear of hell. There is the additional fear of the powerful and often capricious or malicious spirits, as well as the fear of performing a ritual wrong and suffering the effects. There is the fear of the shaman or witch or sorcerer who can use spiritual power for good or ill. So, a simple "religion makes life better" view is naïve and inaccurate. Sometimes, the individual may have to be worse off for the group to be better off. Even "scapegoating" and sacrifice mean pain and loss for the victim but (hopefully) gain for the group.

Symbolic/Interpretive Anthropology

Most of the above theorists (with the exception of Malinowski, as we will see in Chapter 4) have relied heavily on the concept of "symbol." It seems self-evident that humans use symbols and that religion in particular is a system of symbols, although we will have the opportunity to critique this assumption in Chapter 3 and beyond. Nevertheless, a school of anthropology developed in the 1960s, at least partly influenced by the "revolution in philosophy" occasioned by the emphasis on symbols as conveyors and enablers of thought. Suzanne Langer in 1942 had announced that all human thought was symbolic in the sense of condensing meaning into some sound, gesture, image, etc.; symbols were thus "vehicles for conceptions," and conceptual thought would be impossible without them.

Anthropologists like Mary Douglas (1921–2007), Victor Turner (1920–83), and Clifford Geertz (1926–2006) pioneered a symbolic or interpretive approach to religion or, in the case of Geertz, of culture in general. As noted above (p. 7), religion in Geertz's definition is a system of symbols, and culture itself is a yet more extensive and complete system of symbols, a "web of significance" of our own making upon which we are consequently suspended (1973: 5). So symbols play a decisive role in Geertz's understanding: they "are tangible formulations of notions, abstractions from experience fixed in perceptible forms, concrete embodiments of ideas, attitudes, judgments, longings, or beliefs" (91). Even more, they are *effective*; Geertz regarded them as extrasomatic control mechanisms for organizing experience and governing behavior. Thus, symbols are not mental but social, observable in the "flow of behavior" and the "pattern of life" (17)—and shaping both.

Victor Turner developed the symbolic approach even more explicitly in the direction of "performance," eventually (e.g. 1974) offering a theatrical model in which religion, especially ritual, is a drama unfolding over time, through various acts and stages. Elsewhere and earlier, he regarded ritual as a "process" (1969). For both Turner and Geertz, religion and its rituals and symbols were not static but alive, embedded in and constitutive of social order and individual experience. The "effectiveness" of symbols, therefore, resides not only or mainly in human minds, but in political systems (Geertz 1980) and the very human body (Douglas 1970).

Modular Theories

Recently, but not only recently, scholars within and outside of anthropology appear to be converging on an approach to religion that emphasizes the modular or composite quality of religion. The idea of modularity is not new or unique to religion. We know that the brain is not a single homogeneous organ but a modular one, composed of various specialized functional areas, which combine to give us our human mental experience. Similarly, the modular view of religion is grounded on the notion that religion is not a single homogeneous thing and perhaps not a "thing" at all. Rather, it is a composite and therefore a particular cumulative expression of elements—elements that may not be specifically "religious." As William James (1842–1910) noted over a century ago, for instance, in regard to "religious emotions":

> There is religious fear, religious love, religious awe, religious joy, and so forth. But religious love is only man's natural emotion of love directed to a religious object; religious fear is only the ordinary fear of commerce, so to speak, the common quaking of the human breast, in so far as the notion of divine retribution may arouse it; religious awe is the same organic thrill which we feel in a forest at twilight, or in a mountain gorge; only this time it comes over us at the thought of our supernatural relations; and similarly of all the various sentiments which may be called into play in the lives of religious persons. ...
>
> As there thus seems to be no one elementary religious emotion, but only a common storehouse of emotions upon which religious objects may draw, so there might conceivably also prove to be no one specific and essential kind of religious object, and no one specific and essential kind of religious act.
>
> (1958: 40)

In light of these observations, our quest for "religion" may be a misguided one and more of a product of the Western historical and cultural perspective than of religion as such.

The "Building Block" Approach: Wallace

Anthony Wallace (b. 1923), in his influential discussion of religion, suggested that religion may ultimately be "a summative notion and cannot be taken uncritically to imply ... one single unifying, internally coherent, carefully programmed set of rituals and beliefs" (1966: 78). His view was that religion starts from a single premise, the "supernatural premise" that "souls, supernatural beings, and supernatural forces exist" (1966: 52). This premise must be elaborated, and he suggested that there are thirteen "elementary particles" or categories of religious action that serve as building blocks for religion, including (1) prayer, (2) music and dancing and singing, (3) physiological exercises, including substance use and physical hardships and trials, (4) exhortation or orders, encouragements, and threats, (5) myth, (6) simulation/imitation such as magic, witchcraft, and ritual, (7) *mana* or the power one gets from contact with powerful objects, (8) taboo or the prohibition from contact with certain things, (9) feasts, (10) sacrifice, (11) congregation or group activity, (12) inspiration, such as hallucination and mysticism, and (13) symbols. Notice that most if not all of these, as James indicated, have their secular alternative as well.

These elementary particles can be aggregated into bundles or sequences of behavior, resulting in "ritual complexes," which are accompanied by "rationalization" in the form of beliefs (for him, beliefs were quite secondary). A particular ritual complex may incorporate any set and order of elements and exclude others; in fact, any religion may prioritize one or more elements over others, for instance stressing myth or sacrifice while minimizing prayer or mysticism. Next, ritual complexes and their associated beliefs and social roles are combined into higher-level "cult institutions," which he defined as "a set of rituals all having the same general goal, all explicitly rationalized by a set of similar or related beliefs, and all supported by the same social group" (1966: 75). Finally, when "a loosely related group of cult institutions and other, even less well-organized special practices and beliefs" (78) is agglomerated, the result is "a religion." Thus, any specific religion may differ from any other specific religion in the selection and organization of its constituent pieces. The pieces may not even be essentially "religious"—and non-religious modules can be added on—but each specific combination and arrangement is one specific "religion."

The Cognitive Evolutionary Approach: Guthrie, Boyer, and Atran

Observers have noted since the time of Xenophanes that religious entities tend to have human-like traits, a phenomenon called anthropomorphism. In 1993 Stewart Guthrie offered his "new theory" of religion based on a serious application of the anthropomorphic idea. However, from his perspective, anthropomorphism in regard to the supernatural (and the natural) world was not a mistake but rather a "good bet": "It is a bet because the world is uncertain, ambiguous, and in need of interpretation. It is a good bet because the most valuable interpretations usually are those that disclose the presence of whatever is most important to us. That usually is other humans" (1993: 3). Of course, supernatural entities are not *exactly* like humans: they are often larger or more powerful or invisible or immortal, but still these are extensions or negations of human qualities (humans mortal, supernatural beings immortal). The key to humanness is not, ultimately, in our bodies or our mortality but in our *intentionality*, our minds and wills.

Pascal Boyer's project to "explain religion" begins with the now-familiar premise that human thought is not a unitary and homogeneous thing but the result of inter-operating thought modules, a "confederacy" of explanatory devices, which he calls "inference systems." Among these systems are three with particular significance—concept formation, attention to exception, and agency. Thought proceeds via the creation of concepts and even more abstract "templates"; templates are like blank forms with certain fields to be filled, and concepts are the specific way that the form is filled. For example, the template "tool" has certain options, and the concept "hammer" fills those options in a particular way. Likewise, the template "animal" or "person" has certain qualities with a set of possible variables. One of these qualities of persons is agency—the ability to engage in intelligent, deliberate, and more or less "free" action.

As interested as humans are in our concepts, we are drawn to exceptions and violations of them. Humans are mortal animals with two arms; a three-armed human would be interesting, but an immortal human would be even more so. Some ideas, he claims, have the potential to "stick" in our minds better because they are just exceptional enough: as he offers, a being that is immortal has sticking power, but a being that exists only on

Tuesdays does not. Not surprisingly, "religious concepts *violate* certain expectations from ontological categories [but] they *preserve* other expectations" (2001: 62). Among the most critical expectations that religion preserves are agency and reciprocity/exchange. Supernatural entities "are not represented as having *human* features in general but as having *minds* which is much more specific" (144), which is not such a stretch for human thinking, since even animals manifest some agency, having their own desires and intentions. Furthermore, it is advantageous, as Guthrie opined, to attribute mind to nature and supernature, since (to paraphrase Pascal's famous wager), if we are correct it could be critically important but if we are wrong no harm is done.

As Boyer concludes, religion is constructed out of "mental systems and capacities that are there anyway … [therefore] the notion of religion as a special domain is not just unfounded but in fact rather ethnocentric" (311). In this view, religion does not require a separate explanation at all but is rather a product or by-product of how mind in society functions in all, including non-religious, contexts. In particular, he points to the evolved mental predispositions of humans, the nature of social living, processes of information exchange, and the processes of deriving inferences. If nonhuman agents exist, and they can be engaged as social beings—as "social exchange partners"—this is clearly worth thinking about and acting on.

Scott Atran expands this view further and in his own direction. He too asserts that religion involves "the very same cognitive and affective structures as nonreligious beliefs and practices—and no others—but in (more or less) systematically distinct ways" (2002: ix). Since "there is no such entity as 'religion,'" there is no need to "explain" it in a unique way. Religion is once again a by-product and epiphenomenon of other, generally human processes or modules, of which he identifies several: perceptual modules, primary emotional modules (for "unmediated" physiological responses like fear, surprise, anger, and disgust), secondary affective modules (for reactions like anxiety, guilt, and love), and conceptual modules. Agency is also high on his list of human priorities, and we have elaborate and essential processes for detecting and interpreting it, especially because we can be fooled and faked by others. Supernatural agents are a mere and fairly reasonable extrapolation of human and natural agency, "by-products of a naturally selected cognitive mechanism for detecting agents—such as predators, protectors, and prey—and for dealing rapidly and economically with stimulus situations involving people and animals" (15). No wonder, he concludes, that "supernatural agency is the most culturally recurrent, cognitively relevant, and evolutionarily compelling concept in religion" (57). Justin Barrett, in his 2004 *Why Would Anyone Believe in God?*, posited a "hyperactive agency detection device" (HADD) and has conducted many experiments to test the intuitive "natural" assumption that agents are at work around us.

Box 1.3 Modes of Religiosity

The focus on the evolutionary origins and cognitive foundations of religion leads to an interest in psychological processes like attention, motivation, and memory. The question is, what kinds of religious ideas get created in the first place, and which ideas attract our attention, stick in our memory, and motivate us to action? In 1995 Harvey Whitehouse published his research on religious movements among the Mali Baining, a people of Papua New Guinea, which eventually sparked his thoughts on "modes" of religion. By the 1970s the Pomio Kivung movement, a kind of "cargo cult" (see Chapter 7), was widespread among the Mali Baining; however, later yet another movement, Dadul-Maranagi, arose in the community and largely displaced the first sect.

The competition between these two religious formations led Whitehouse to develop his model of two distinct "modes of religiosity." Related to processes of memory and motivation, Whitehouse designates one mode as the "doctrinal mode," while the other is the "imagist mode." The doctrinal mode depends on frequent repetition of religious behaviors, on explicit religious teachings and formal leadership, and on religious centralization, all of which satisfy the more "semantic" or language-based memory processes. The imagistic mode, by contrast, functions through religious behaviors that are "invariably low frequency" but "also, without exception, highly arousing" (2004: 70). These behaviors activate a different kind of memory, "flashbulb memory," and stick in the mind because of their drama and sensory power. Exciting the senses and the emotions, they tend to downplay leadership, centralization, and orthodoxy; they also tend to appeal to small/local and exclusive communities. Whitehouse finally claims that particular religions tend to "gravitate toward" (76) one end of this spectrum or the other, although the two modes are not mutually exclusive.

Social Integration and Cooperation: Costly Signaling Theory

One last fact about religion that needs to be acknowledged is that is often *hard*. Religions require behaviors that are expensive, time-consuming, and sometimes difficult or painful; religions often ask people to believe claims that are frankly difficult to accept. Recently, a number of scholars have contended that the difficulty of religion may be the source of its integrative accomplishments.

In a society, individuals need to know that they can trust each other—that everyone is committed to the group and that everyone is contributing to the group, not "free riding" on the efforts of others. In 1996 William Irons proposed "honest-signalling [sic] theory" as a solution to the problem of religious behavior, suggesting that the demands of religion signal or demonstrate social commitment, which thus enhances cooperation and the good of the group. Since then, Richard Sosis, Candace Alcorta, and Joseph Bulbulia have collaborated on a series of essays promoting "costly signaling theory" (e.g. Sosis and Alcorta 2003; Bulbulia and Sosis 2011). The claim is that religion is socially integrative *precisely because* it is expensive and uncomfortable: social living depends on cooperation and mutual trust, but there is always the potential of deception in the group. Thus, lazy deceivers find themselves in an evolutionary arms race with their comrades who, as deceiver-detectors, erect ever more demanding tests of honesty and commitment, including and especially apparently impractical and arbitrary ones like religion. "The result of such escalation would be increasingly complex ritual behaviors, as senders attempt to deceive receivers and receivers seek to determine the truthfulness of the sender's signal" (Sosis and Alcorta 2003: 266). In a word, if religion was easy, it would not prove one's social commitment and willingness to cooperate and to conform; anyone could do it—or fake it. The costly signaling idea might help explain some of the extreme ordeals that believers put themselves and others through, including sacrifice, self-injury, and war (see Chapter 10).

Conclusion

Religion has been notoriously difficult to define, and every proposed definition has some value, emphasizing some important dimension of religion. No single definition is entirely adequate, and no definition is ever "true," only more or less inclusive and more or less productive. How we define religion determines what we accept *as religion*, and however we define religion, the definition presents new definitional problems. What is "spirit"? What is "belief"? Anthropologists have found that "religion" itself is a culture-specific concept in the first place, since not all cultures even have a word or concept for religion.

Like definitions, theories are attempts to formulate what is important and unique about religion, and different disciplines naturally see religion in different ways. Religion undoubtedly is emotion and idea and ritual and institution. Like definitions, theories set boundaries and suggest lines of research. Recently, some of the most productive suggestions for research have come from modular and evolutionary theories of religion, offering a convergence of many disciplines but dominated by a psychological/cognitive perspective.

Yet, as promising as these theories are, anthropology is not fundamentally a psychological discipline. In fact, it could be argued that anthropology is not fundamentally a theoretical discipline. Whatever takes place inside people's heads, religion lives outside the mind, in social actions and institutions, and anthropology itself has always lived—and been most alive—in the field and in the ethnographic description of experiences in the field. The power of anthropology has always been in the dynamic interplay between theory and ethnography, encountering cultures and religions that are always more complicated and exciting than any definition or theory can ever be, as we will see in upcoming chapters.

DISCUSSION QUESTIONS

- What does it mean to study religion anthropologically? How is the anthropological perspective on religion different from the perspective of other disciplines?
- What are the major schools of thought or theoretical approaches to religion in anthropology and related sciences?
- What is the contemporary cognitive evolutionary approach to religion?

SUPPLEMENTARY READING (see website)

- *Religion by Any Other Name: Do All Cultures Have "Religion"?*
- *What is Sacred? Sacredness as Specialness*
- *The Epidemiology of Religious Representations: Dan Sperber and Cognitive Theories of Religion and Culture*

2 Religious Belief
Entities and Concepts

The Akha of highland Burma have a word (*tjhŷa*) that we can translate "belief," and they have a word (*zán*) that we can translate as "religion." However, according to Deborah Tooker, *zán* is not a matter of belief: "For the Akha, you cannot *believe* or *not believe* in *zán*" (1992: 804). Rather, *zán* is something to do, not religion in the Western sense but "something like a 'way of life,' 'way of doing things,' 'customs,' or 'traditions,'" including elements we would call religion but others we would not, such as the correct way to plant rice, build a house, or boil an egg. Thus, the Akha say that they "carry" *zán* rather than "believe in" it. Behaviors may be "correct" (*zán-tsha-e*) or "incorrect" (*zán ma tsha-e*) according to *zán*, but "truth and falseness are not an issue" (804). The Akha worldview even includes spirits, but they "do not say anything like *neq djan-e* ('to believe in spirits')" (802). If one is Akha, one carries *zán*; if one is not Akha, one does not carry *zán*; and if one stops carrying *zán*, one ceases to be Akha.

Whatever the ultimate definition and cause of religion, any religion contains certain ideas and conceptions about what kinds of things exist in the world, what they are like, and what they have done. We might refer to this as the ontology that each religion embodies, in the sense of the "existents" that it posits—the beings, the forces, and the facts of religious reality. These are commonly referred to as the "beliefs" of religion.

Not all anthropologists and other scholars of religion have stressed the belief dimension equally. Anthony Wallace regarded behavior and ritual to be paramount and "myth" and "belief" to be an adjunct to them. However, Western people, including scholars, typically concentrate on if not privilege the "idea" or "intellectual" side of religion. This is partly because Western culture accentuates thought or ideas, especially over "ritual," which often seems to be only empty form. Even more so, academics prize thought, ideas, and concepts as our primary interest and medium. Partly it is an artifact of Christian religious habits, in which belief or "doctrine" is held in high esteem. Beliefs are "discursive," something to talk about and to "know," both flowing from and to a view of religion and culture as a language or a "text" to be spoken or read.

Accordingly, many definitions of religion feature if not highlight the concept of belief. Recall that E. B. Tylor's minimal definition of religion was "belief in spiritual beings." Durkheim insisted that religion is "a unified system of beliefs and practices." In other, although not all, anthropological definitions, its beliefs represent the essence of a religion, and belief represents the essence of religion. Scholars and laypeople alike have regularly assumed, often uncritically, that belief is the most important aspect of religion, that to understand a religion is to describe its "beliefs," and that we can study and know the "beliefs" of a religion in a straightforward way.

In this chapter we will investigate the range of topics that religions tend to include and the range of claims that religions tend to make. In the best anthropological tradition, we want to interrogate concepts and relativize understandings, making sure not to impute to other cultures what they do not avow of themselves. This may and does include familiar notions like "god" or "soul" or "heaven." This may include the very notion of "belief" itself, which may not be central—or even present—in any particular religion. Finally, it is important to realize that "belief" is not unique to religion; having ideas and making claims about reality is a human universal, and religious ideas/claims/beliefs are a subset, unique in some ways and quite familiar in others.

The Anthropology of Belief

Belief is so self-evident to most of us, so pervasive in our vocabulary, that we cannot help but speak and think in terms of it. Often enough, the term is not even defined, since it seems so patently obvious; we think that we could not speak of religion at all unless we spoke the language of belief. Melford Spiro, in his study of Burmese religion, did take the time to define the term, by which he meant

> any cognition concerning human beings, society, or the world that is held to be true. By "religious belief" I mean any belief that directly or indirectly relates to beings who are held to possess greater power than humans and animals, with whom human beings sustain relationship (interactions and transactions), and who can affect human lives for good or for evil. In short, "religious" beliefs are beliefs related to supernatural beings.
>
> (1978: xii)

Thus Spiro ended by affirming the conventional view that religious beliefs are allegedly true convictions about supernatural beings. But more interestingly for our purposes, he affirmed that belief is not unique to religion; religious beliefs are a subset of beliefs in general. What is distinctive about beliefs in general is that they are "cognitions" and that they are "held to be true" by those people who have these mental contents.

Such a definition and attitude does not depart much from the conventional sense of belief and believing. However, others have asked whether belief is (1) as simple as we think and (2) as universal as we think. Rodney Needham offered an extended analysis of belief across cultures. He started with the observation that the notion that humans "can be said to believe, without qualification and irrespective of their cultural formation, is an implicit premise in anthropological writings" (1972: 3). However, anthropologists cannot and dare not leave premises implicit, including or especially their own premises. He went on to find that belief is a much fuzzier concept than we realize and that it is a much more culturally specific, rather than culturally universal, concept than we think.

Needham discussed, for instance, a wide variety of cultures and languages in which the word for and the experience of belief is very complex and not necessarily like our everyday notion of it. Nuer, Navajo, Hindi, Kikchi (Guatemala), Uduk (Ethiopia), Penan (Borneo), and Chinese are some of the languages he surveyed, and he found three important consequences:

> The first consists in a clearer and more evidential recognition of the bewildering variety of senses attaching to words in foreign languages which are indifferently

translated by the English "believe." The second is that, whereas it may often seem possible, in comparing other languages, to isolate this as the equivalent in each of the English word "believe," there are languages in which senses that to an English interpretation are quite disparate are nevertheless so conjoined, and so equally expressed, as to make it unjustifiable to abstract any one of them as definitive. Thirdly, there are apparently languages in which ... there is no verbal concept at all which can convey exactly what may be understood by the English word "believe."

(37)

In fact, Evans-Pritchard did warn us in his classic study of Nuer religion that "belief" is not an indigenous concept for this society: "There is, in any case, I think, no word in the Nuer language which can stand for 'I believe'" (1956: 9). Instead, the Nuer say that they *ngath* their god/spirit (*kwoth*), which Evans-Pritchard argued we should translate as "trust," not "believe in."

Other societies have given us equal reason to pause. Feinberg, for example, claimed that the Anutans of the Solomon Islands do have a local belief concept. "The word *pakatonu*, literally 'make straight,' is used in almost precisely the manner of the English 'to believe.' Anutans are very much concerned with truth and falsity. After relating a story or an incident, they ask each other whether they 'believe' (*pakatonu*) the narrative's assertions" (1996: 107). On the opposite side, Howard (1996: 135) concluded that inhabitants of Rotuma had no word for belief prior to missionization, when the missionaries had to coin a new word, *pilifi*, to represent the Christian idea. Thus, anthropologists do not say that no religions—or no religions other than Christianity—have a concept of belief. Rather, they say that we cannot attribute such a concept to them unless they actually do have one. If they have a local belief concept, and understand their religious experience accordingly, so be it. However, "we are not sharing their apprehension and are not understanding their thought if we foist this typically Western distinction on to them" (Needham 1972: 175) when they do not recognize it themselves. My surmise is that we would find more exceptions to the "belief assumption" if we thought to question it.

A further problem with the belief concept in cross-cultural studies is that it has both "objective" and "subjective" aspects. In other words, "belief" has a propositional and a psychological nature. As an objective, propositional issue, a belief is a publicly available "truth claim," an assertion about something "real" in the world. If a person or society is said to "believe" something—or to "believe in" something—that means that the individual or group is making a claim about reality. Of course, as Needham reminded us, such a belief "is not a guarantee of reality, and it does not necessarily depend on the reality of what is believed" (66). In fact, a belief can quite easily be false, and in some ways the typical English usage of the term implies uncertainty or the possibility of falseness (i.e. one does not say that they "believe" that two plus two equals four or that they "believe in" their foot).

As a subjective or psychological issue, beliefs are additionally and necessarily construed as mental states of individuals. That is, if we say that a person believes X, we are making a statement about that person's mental representations. A person who believes X should *know* that he/she believes X and be able and willing to affirm X. Is there such a thing as "belief" if a person does not and cannot avow the belief? Can we attribute perhaps "tacit" or "implied" belief to individuals and societies? This is one of the key questions in anthropology. Further, can we attribute it *equally strongly* and *equally clearly* to all members? Spiro's response was that the psychological element of belief is not one-dimensional but multi-dimensional, yielding at least five levels of personal belief: acquaintance or familiarity with the belief, understanding of the belief in the conventional way, advancing the belief as "true," holding the belief as important or central to the believer's life, and following the belief as a motivational or guiding force (1978: xiii–xiv). For any given belief in any given society, individuals will fall anywhere along this spectrum.

This is particularly significant because anthropologists often seek out the "specialists" on religion in a society to discover its beliefs. However, as Spiro urged, "there is no a priori reason to assume that the meanings attributed to beliefs by religious virtuosi are shared by the other members of the group" (1978: xv). Even worse, Needham found no consistent or "essential" component to the psychological aspect of belief—no specific mental or physical state that goes with it or distinguishes it—making the entire approach problematic. Even in vernacular English, "belief" is a word with three quite distinct senses. First, it can be used in the propositional sense, to claim that a proposition is true, such as "God exists"; other religions are thus assumed to have beliefs like "*jukurrpa* exists" or "*hekura* spirits exist." Second, it can be used in the sense of confidence or trust, as in "I believe my wife will pick me up from the airport"; here, the existence of my wife and the airport are not in question but rather her trustworthiness. (Jean Pouillon makes the same distinction in French, between *croire à*, "to state that something exists," and *croire en*, "to have confidence" (1992: 2).) Third, it can be used in the sense of commitment or value, as in "I believe in democracy," in which one is not disputing the existence of democracy but the goodness of it.

These senses can be conjoined or disjoined in any particular language or religion, and their interrelation can change over time. For example, Malcolm Ruel (1997) demonstrated that the conception of belief in Western (including ancient Greek) civilization and Christianity has evolved, from a kind of "trust" in god(s), to specific propositions *about* God and Christ (the *kerygma* or "creed"), to the notion of "grace" based on the personal experience of and commitment to God and Christ, to a conception of belief as an "adventure of faith" which does not have any particular destination or make any specific claims. The evolutionary trajectory of belief in Christianity is, then, distinctively "local" and historical—that is, culturally and religiously relative—and not to be found in every religion. Many religions do not have any "creed" of explicit propositions about their supernatural worlds, and many do not mix fact, trust, and value in the English/Christian way (many do not "trust" their spirits at all, or even like them). Ruel arrived where Needham arrived, concluding that the English and Western concept of belief is "complex, highly ambiguous, and unstable" (Needham 1972: 43) and "is demonstrably an historical amalgam, composed of elements traceable to Judaic mystical doctrine and Greek styles of discourse" (49).

Box 2.1 The Changing Nature of "Belief" among Danish Jews

In contrast to Christianity, Judaism is often portrayed as a religion more interested in behavior—in performing rituals and following laws—than in belief. This view is not entirely accurate or fair, as Jews have engaged in lively debates about their scriptures and the correct meaning and interpretation of those writings, but Andrew Buckser does endorse the notion that, compared to the Lutherans of Denmark, "theological beliefs had a secondary place in the meaning of religious activity" for Danish Jews (2008: 41). But while belief is not absent from Danish Judaism, it also "is not something fixed; rather, it emerges out of a fluid interaction of religious ideas, cultural understandings, and political agendas" (41). Buckser identifies two stages in modern Danish Jewish thinking about belief. In the early 1800s, reformers began to encourage "active, intellectual engagement with religion rather than the rote traditionalism of the established community" (43). Belief was seen as a rational and modern form of religion. In the late twentieth century, attitudes shifted, such that belief came to be seen as "traditional," non-modern, and even anti-modern. Traditionalists "turned increasingly to belief as the cornerstone of Jewish identity" (50), although among the followers of Chabad House, their version of Jewish belief "includes a kabbalistic mysticism that is foreign to traditional Danish Judaism, as well as a flamboyant style of proselytizing that clashes with the subdued ethos of Danish culture" (52). What is clear, though, is that belief "as an idea has changed, along with the people who endorse it" (52).

Fortunately, in a way, the problem is not insurmountable. Members of a society might not advance and analyze propositions about the supernatural the way we do, but they communicate and inform us about their worldview in various ways. Not only in their (potentially rare) explicit avowals but in their behaviors, their stories, their rituals, and their everyday lives they give us clues about their religious ideas. "Belief" might be the wrong word for it, but they probably have their own way of speaking about it. Following Clifford Geertz, religious ideas may be, for the member, more along the line of "common sense" than proposition. Just as it would be inaccurate or unfamiliar to say that we "believe" that rain makes you wet or that microbes make you sick, so it might be inaccurate or unfamiliar (to them) to call their ideas "beliefs." What both of us share is a "taken for granted," "doesn't everybody know this?" attitude toward our ideas, even if on different subjects and with different views on those subjects. For many people (remote and nearby), religion is like common sense in that both seem self-evident, immediate, even obvious, no questions asked or needed. In fact, that is the very appeal of common sense and often of religion: "the unspoken premise from which common sense draws its authority [is] that it presents reality neat" (Geertz 1983: 76), just the way it is to anyone who has eyes and brains.

To be more explicit, Geertz proposed that common sense "as a cultural system" has five properties, which we recognize in many religious systems as well. They are (1) "naturalness," that it presents matters as being simple and as simply what they are, (2) "practicalness," that it tells us what we need to do to get by, (3) "thinness," that what seems true on the surface really is true, (4) "immethodicalness," that ideas are not "theoretical," elaborated, or particularly thought out, and (5) "accessibleness," that anyone can, and everyone should, "get it" (85–91). Ultimately, common sense, and religion with it, "represents the world as a familiar world, one everyone can, and should, recognize, and within which everyone stands, or should, on his own feet" (91).

Religious Ideas: Beings and Forces

Anthropologists have become chaste about the use of belief as a descriptive and analytical category. Yet we can, with some trepidation, talk about the ideas or cognitions that constitute a religious ontology or worldview. Every religion does of course contain ideas of and about nonhuman and superhuman agencies in the universe; however, not all of these agencies are equally "agentive," that is, not all equally have "personalities" or "minds" or "wills." This is another reason why Tylor's venerable definition is insufficient: not all religions have supernatural *beings*. At the same time, all religions contain much more than just "beliefs" about the supernatural; they also have more or less elaborated and explicit stories about them, more or less formal activities to perform with and in regard to them, and more or less specific behavioral or "moral" principles or codes that are demanded of people because of them. All of these will be subjects for discussion in later chapters.

In any particular society there may be many religious entities or a few, although no religion actually includes only one. Some religions do not include beings at all but rather one or more forces—*impersonal* energies or principles that underlie the world. And some include a combination of beings and forces, which is why we cannot speak of these as "types." Furthermore, "supernatural" is another one of those problematic terms; not all cultures have exactly this concept in the Western/Christian way. Often, what we would call supernatural beings are quite "natural," or on the borderline between natural and not, from other religions' perspectives. And supernatural or spiritual beings are not necessarily immaterial or disembodied; some have bodies or may occasionally or temporarily acquire bodies.

Religious Beings

Most but not quite all religions have notions about more or less well-known religious beings. But what precisely is a religious being? All of the beings that we ordinarily encounter are "physical" or "material"—that is, they have corporeal bodies, they take up space, they are constrained by laws of motion, they age and die, etc. Religious beings are different in some (but not every) way. In some instances they do not have physical bodies or might be able to coexist in the same space as physical bodies (i.e. "possession"), or they may move and act in ways that defy natural law, or they do not age or do not die. That leaves a great deal of room for diversity, but the one thing that religious beings have in common is that they are *beings*, even *persons*, that is, that they are individuals with wills and "minds" and "personalities" of their own. Beyond that, the variation is almost limitless.

Some observers have attempted to distinguish "spirits" from "gods." According to the definition given by Levy, Mageo, and Howard, spirits and gods stand at opposite ends of "a continuum of culturally defined spiritual entities ranging from well-defined, socially encompassing beings at one pole, to socially marginal, fleeting presences at the other" (1996: 11). Apparently, gods are intended to be the former, spirits the latter. They offered four variables by which gods and spirits differ—structure, personhood, experience, and morality. By structure they meant that gods are the focus of more detailed social institutions, including priesthoods, shrines, and festivals, as well as specific territories; spirits are not the subject of such elaboration, being more "fluid," "emergent, contingent, and unexpected" (14). By personhood they meant that gods are more physically and socially human, while spirits are "vague … only minimally persons" (15). By experience they meant that gods are actually less directly experienced whereas spirits are more commonly encountered and often more immediately the objects of human concern. Finally, by morality they meant that gods are more likely agents and paragons of moral order than are spirits, who tend to be "extramoral" or evil. Gods, they argued, "are clear models for social order" (21) who establish and sanction human morality, but spirits "are threats to order and frequently must be purged so that order may be re-established" (16).

As hopeful as this dichotomy is, it does not conform to the empirical evidence. First, as we will see, gods are not always particularly good or moral, nor do they always take an interest in human affairs. Spirits may be the objects of extremely elaborate ritual behavior, while gods (especially distant "high gods") may be so abstract and remote as to invoke little human interest and activity. Also, spirits, since they are more immediate, are often better known and actually *more* like social persons than gods. Finally, as the authors admitted, this continuum leaves all kinds of other beings—"giants, gnomes, fairies, phoenixes, and the like" (12)—as well as plant and animal spirits, zombies, vampires, and an unlimited number of others unaccounted for.

It is probably more apt to consider "spirit" the most general category, with "god" as a subset of this category. In other words, gods are a particular kind of spirit, a kind that may not appear in all religious systems. In some situations, it may not be clear and unequivocal whether a spirit is a god or not, and the distinction may be trivial in the end. Even more, there may be no sharp line between spirits and "natural" (including human) beings. Indeed, most religions depend on the notion that humans are or have a "spiritual" component too (a "soul"). Thus, any attempted typology of spirits is bound to founder on the rocks of religious diversity.

Human Spirits

One of the most persistent and "natural" ideas across cultures is that humans have a spiritual part or parts, which co-habit(s) the world with the body to some extent and which survive(s) the body (for a time at least) after death. In the Christian tradition, this is called the "soul." In Hinduism, it is known as the *atman*. The concept has not only different names but different descriptions and destinies in different societies. The crucial thing is that humans, even now, *are* spiritual beings in a manner of speaking. Again in the Christian tradition, it is asserted that this spiritual-human part is implanted in us from outside (it was originally "breathed into" the first created human), dwells in our body in some obscure way, and detaches from the body at death to continue its existence in some other form.

The precise characteristics of the human spirit—alive or dead—vary widely from culture to culture. The notion with which we are most familiar is a single, permanent, integral soul, not situated in any particular part of the body, which preserves our "personality" or individuality in its single, permanent, integral destination (namely, heaven or hell). That is not a universal idea. Some cultures tell of multiple souls or a soul with multiple parts. The Tausug of the Philippines believed that humans are composed of four parts: the body, the mind, the "liver" or emotion, and the soul. The soul itself is composed of four parts: the transcendent soul, which is all good and always in the spiritual realm, even while you are alive; the life-soul, which is related to the blood and attached to the body but which wanders from the body in dreams; the breath, which is the essence of life and always attached to the body; and the spirit-soul, the person's "shadow" (Kiefer 1972).

The Nupe of Africa identified three "soul-like entities" in addition to the body: the *rayi* was the life-force, the *fifingi* was the "shadow," which remained visible after death and occasionally haunted people physically or in their dreams, and the *kuci* was the "personal soul" that entered the body at birth and gradually integrated with it. However, this *kuci* was not completely "personal," since it was reincarnated in another person and could incarnate simultaneously in more than one person, ideally in the same family or clan. S. F. Nadel accordingly called it "an impersonal principle of descent and heredity" (1954: 24), linking the individual with the kin group. The Mandinko, also of Africa, had a four-part human person, including the body, breath, intelligence (located in the heart), and the soul; both the intelligence and the soul continue on in the afterlife (Schaffer and Cooper 1980). The Huron of North America talked of two souls or *atisken*, both the same size and shape as the body, one of which remained with the body after death while the other departed (Trigger 1969). The Konyak Nagas of India were reported to believe in several different soul parts that separate at death: the *yaha* contained the individual's personality and goes off to the land of the dead, while the *mia* stayed attached to the skull (which explains their practice of headhunting), and the *hiba* became a ghost if the person died a violent death (Von Fuerer-Haimendorf 1969). Finally, the Dusun of Borneo mentioned seven soul parts, one inside the other. They were not "born" full-sized but grew as the body grew, the smallest the width of the little finger and the largest the thickness of the thumb. The six "outside" souls or *magalugulu* were visible in human form, but the innermost soul or *gadagada* was formless and invisible (Williams 1965).

The mention of the Nagas' ideas about souls and ghosts reminds us that humans are not spirits only or mostly while alive but even more so after death. Of course, the ultimate spiritual fate of former humans also varies from society to society. Even in modern Western/Christian societies, many people believe that souls can become ghosts, at least temporarily. Ghosts are spiritual parts of dead humans that continue to exist and participate in the human world, usually to the detriment of the living. The Burmese villagers that Spiro studied, while being nominally Buddhist, recognized the spirits of the dead or *leikpya* as potential mischief-makers that remained around the house or village and haunted its living inhabitants; former government officials were particularly likely to end up this way, since they did not like relinquishing their power. More worrisome yet than the ordinary dead were the spirits of those who lived wicked lives, for they were transformed into *tasei* or *thaye*, evil ghosts. Members recounted that these beings were usually invisible but could become visible, with a "flimsy and resilient materiality." They were enormous (over seven feet tall), dark or black with huge ears, tongues, tusk-like teeth—"repulsive in every way" (1978: 34). These bad ghosts camped on the edge of the village, especially near burial grounds, where they ate corpses or attacked and consumed the living.

Other if not most societies also fear or worry about their dead. The Navajos told Downs (1972) that the ghost was the evil part of the deceased person, so ghosts were all evil by definition. The Dani of New Guinea too claimed that most ghosts were malevolent and tended to attack living adults, usually from the front (Heider 1979). The dead do not always become troublesome, though. One Christian belief is that dead souls become angels, either disembodied or embodied spirits in a "heavenly" dimension or reality (see Figure 2.1). Sometimes these angels interact with humans, as in "guardian angels"

Figure 2.1 Guardian angel. Courtesy of the Library of Congress Prints and Photographs Division

(the word "angel" derives from the Greek *angelon* for messenger). There are other angels who were reportedly created before humans and never were humans at all.

Finally, in some religions or sects of religions, especially pious and virtuous former humans can become saints, who also may continue to act on behalf of humans, protecting travelers and the like. In Islam, the veneration of saints is common, particularly in certain "popular" sects and interpretations, and prayers, rituals, and vigils may be held at their tombs or shrines (see Chapter 1). In many traditions a body part (a relic) or artifact of a deceased holy person may be revered and incorporated into worship and ritual. This can take any form from the bones of a saint to the Buddha's tooth to a piece of the "true cross" or the burial shroud of Jesus (the "shroud of Turin").

Many societies assert that the individual soul eventually "puts on another body," in other words, is reincarnated. The person cannot always remember the life of the previous body; the spirit of the person may not even be completely "personal," as in the case of the Warlpiri, where it is essentially nonhuman or pre-human first and incarnates in human form but does not change its essential nonhuman character. Other twists on the dead-spirit theme exist too, like the idea of a zombie who is a dead individual who has somehow been reanimated but without his or her soul; this is not completely dissimilar to the European concept of a vampire, a dead person without a soul who is now "undead."

In some instances beliefs about the dead can coalesce into systems and institutions concerning ancestor spirits. An ancestor spirit is the non-physical aspect of a dead kin-group member that continues to inhabit the area around the family and to interact with them, for better or for worse. The !Kung or Ju/hoansi viewed the //*gangwasi* or recently deceased as the main element of their religious reality (see Box 2.2). Meyer Fortes (1959) described the importance of ancestor spirits for the Tallensi of Africa, to whom the living not only owed allegiance but who supernaturally affected the lives of the living through the control of "destiny." Chinese homes, as in many other societies, traditionally had altars to the spirits of the kin group, where prayers and other offerings were made, again suggesting that the fundamental bonds of kinship do not expire with death.

Nonhuman Spirits

Many other kinds of spiritual beings never were and never will be humans, although they may be like humans and interact with humans. Perhaps the most common of these are the "nature spirits," the spirits that "are" or "are in" plants and/or animals and/or natural objects and/or natural forces. This was the observation that led Tylor to formulate what he termed *animism*. Animism, derived from the Latin *anima* for soul or more literally "alive" or "moving," is the general conception that nonhuman beings can and do have spiritual parts too. Not necessarily every nonhuman thing is thus "animated." For the Warlpiri, some trees and rocks have spirit or *pirlirrpa* and some do not; they can point at one tree and say that it is "just a tree," while another of the same species is a spirit. Some entire animal and plant species are spiritually important, and others are just natural beings. This relationship between humans and nonhuman material objects is sometimes called totemism, a term not much in current usage. The idea behind totemism is that an individual or a group (family, clan, village, etc.) has a unique spiritual relationship with a particular species or object; this species or object is the person's or group's "totem." The relationship commonly results in some special behavior toward the totem, such as not eating it; however, some societies do eat their totem species. So totemism is not a consistent phenomenon and is probably just one form of a greater spiritual relationship between humans and the nonhuman.

The spirits of plants and animals, etc., may be "individual" or "mass." That is, each particular kangaroo may have its own "personal" spirit, or there may be a "kangaroo spirit" that animates all kangaroos. Either way, "spiritualized" plants or animals or natural forces cannot be ignored; if there is a seal spirit or a spirit of the lake, those spirits have an intelligence and a will not unlike our own. They communicate with us and interact with us. The Ainu of northern Japan, for example, claimed that plants, animals, and even man-made objects were "spirit-owning" or "spirit-bearing" beings who had to be treated accordingly. In "life" there were restrictions on how humans could interact with them, and even (and perhaps mainly) in death these restrictions held; for instance, people had to maintain a separate location for the disposal of each type of spirit-owning being, called *keyohniusi*, and negligence of their duties toward these beings could bring sickness or worse (Ohnuki-Tierney 1974). The Huron spoke of plant, animal, and even inanimate objects having spirits, which were the same size and shape as their physical bodies. The Dani of New Guinea, like many peoples of the world, experienced the spirits of or in natural objects or places like hills, rocks, ponds, and whirlpools. The Anutans described by Feinberg made claims about a type of spirits called *tupua penua* or land/totemic spirits, associated either with species like the shark, octopus, or sea turtle or with natural features and sites. These spirits were god-like in some ways—with names, individual personalities, and power, who are bound to locations, prayed to, and invoked in song and story—yet also amoral, egotistical, and dangerous.

In addition to spirits of specific plants, animals, and objects, many societies recognize spirits that are not attached to any specific material forms but have their own independent "reality." These beings may be good, bad, or indifferent to humans; they may be helpful, harmful, mischievous, or unaware of their effect on humans. Such beings include demons, devils, and any of a wide array of culturally local characters such as fairies, elves, sprites, muses, furies, *kinkis* (in Warlpiri culture), *hekura* (in Yanomamo culture), and many others. A good example of a type of spirit that escapes easy categorization is the *jinn* of classical Islam. Not an angel or a demon but also not a human, *jinns* were often thought to have bodies made of fire or light. Made by Allah, most were Muslims themselves and lived in tribes and nations of their own. With the power to shift their form, they often took the shape of animals, sometimes "to hide from humans, or trick them, or deliver a message to them" (el-Zein 2009: 92). They even took human form on occasion, entering bonds of love with humans.

More than a few spirits had the ability to assume human form and the tendency to seduce humans. Among the Mapuche of Chile, a "person" (*che*) is considered to be productive, both economically and sexually, but they also recognize a class of "nonperson humans" who have bodies but lack the capacity to enter productive relationships. One such nonperson human is the *pun domo* or "night woman," a being like a woman who appears at night to bachelors; a human male may join the being in an emotional or sexual relationship for years before realizing that she is not a *che*. Another nonhuman person is the *witranalwe* or "cowboy demon" who blocks the path of travelers at night; created by witches, the *witranalwe* looks like a white person, wears black clothing, and rides a horse. He will eventually kill and eat animal herds and their human owners (Course 2011).

One of the most elaborate spirit systems on record comes from Spiro's work in Burma. In addition to the ghosts and the witches, there were various demons such as the *bilus* or ogre that eats humans. However, the really extensive part of the religion was the set of *nats*, which included the nature spirits, the *devas* or Buddhist and therefore benevolent beings, and the "thirty-seven *nats*." Nature spirits were associated with and guarded their particular locations, personified in such beings as *taw-saun nat* and *taung-saun nat*, the guardians of the forest and hill, respectively. Collectively they made the world a treacherous place. But worse were the thirty-seven *nats* or powerful beings, called *thounze khunna min nat* or "thirty-seven chief *nats*." They were distinctly malevolent, each with a name and its own mythical story, and they had to be propitiated with gifts of food. Interestingly, Spiro reports that most villagers could not name or describe more than one or two of them, and when it came to the notion of "personal *nats*" that supposedly associate with and protect individual humans, two out of the twenty households he questioned had never heard of them, four had only general ideas about them, and four denied that they existed at all (1978: 55).

Of the nonhuman spiritual beings, the greatest are the gods. There is no perfect, universal definition for gods, but we tend to think of them as extremely powerful, mostly moral or beneficent, usually creative, and utterly "other" spiritual beings. By "utterly other" we mean that they are not part of nature or in nature nor do they always interact directly with humans. Richard Swinburne, a prominent Christian philosopher, has defined god as "a person without a body (i.e., a spirit) present everywhere, the creator and sustainer of the universe, able to do everything (i.e., omnipotent), knowing all things, perfectly good, a source of moral obligation, immutable, eternal, a necessary being, holy and worthy of worship" (1977: 2). However, this is not so much a *definition* of god as a *description* of a particular god, namely the Christian god. It does not fit all cases. Among the ancient Greek gods, for instance, some were good, some bad or both or neither. Some were more or less eternal, but many were born of other gods (or humans), and many died. Some played no part in creation, as creation was all in place by the time they came along. Often, each had his or her "domain" in a supernatural "division of labor"—i.e. a god of the sea, a god of war, a god of love, a god of wine, etc. Many societies that recognize gods do not attempt to communicate or relate directly with them but rather through lower-level spiritual intermediaries, like saints or ancestors or other lower spirits.

A religion that not only includes but focuses on god(s) is called a theism (from the Greek *theos*, god, from which derive the Latin *deus* and our word "deity"). There may be in any particular theism one or more (sometimes many more) than one god, and there may be—and always are—other religious beings as well. A theistic religion that contains many gods is known as a polytheism, while a theistic religion that contains one god is known as a monotheism. Ancient Greek religion is a familiar example of polytheism, with its "pantheon" (from *pan* for all and *theos* for god) residing on Mount Olympus. Judaism, Christianity, and Islam constitute the dominant monotheisms in the world. Some versions of Christianity posit a "trinity" of three "persons" in God, while Islam insists that God is one (the doctrine of *tawhid*)—no son, no trinity, and nothing else like God.

Theism can take a few other less familiar forms. For instance, deism is the position that there is or was a god who created the world and put it in motion but then withdrew from it; this god is more or less "impersonal" and may take no active part in the daily affairs of humans at all. Monolatry refers to the worship of one particular god without necessarily denying the existence of others; some scholars regard the earliest sections of the Judeo-Christian scriptures as representing monolatry, in which Hebrew leaders like Abraham and Moses were given "their god" to worship, while other peoples (presumably) had their own. Finally, some thinkers have come to the conclusion that god is everything and everything is god, a belief known as pantheism. Baruch Spinoza was an articulate pantheist, and Albert Einstein seemed to hold this position. Some "mystical" traditions within larger religious systems, and to an extent the entire system of Hinduism, maintain that the whole universe is really god or the "mind of god" or one great cosmic soul (the *Brahman* in Hinduism), of which the human soul (*atman*) is one small alienated piece.

Within these major classes there is incredible diversity in ideas about gods. Some gods are creators, others are not. Some are moral guarantors and arbiters, others are not. Some are near and well known, others are not. The Konyak Nagas, for instance, referred to a sky god called *Gawang* or *Zangbau* who was a highly personal being and the creator of the universe. He had the form of a gargantuan human and was called upon in daily life and the main social occasions in culture; he was the protector of morality and punished wrongdoing. On the other hand, the Azande of Africa talked about a god named *Mbori* or *Mboli*, who Evans-Pritchard (1962) tells us was morally neutral and not terribly interested in human affairs. Locals did not even have clear and consistent "beliefs" about him: some said he moved about on the earth, but others disagreed.

Between these extremes are all sorts of complex variations on the god theme. The Kaguru of East Africa knew of a god named *mulungu* who was a universe creator, but the people did not know the story of this creation nor care very much; the god itself was imagined as human-like but with only one foot or arm or eye or ear (Beidelman 1971). The islanders of Ulithi in Micronesia made claims about several gods, none of whom was a creator, and their religion contained no creation story, according to Lessa (1966). There was a high god, *Ialulep*, who was described as very large, old, and weak, with white hair, and who held the "thread of life" of each person and decided when a person would die by breaking the thread. Under him were numerous sky gods and earth gods, including his son *Lugeilang*, who liked the company of human women and fathered the trickster god *Iolofath*. The earth gods included ones with more or less specific natural and social jurisdictions, like *Palulap* the Great Navigator, *Ialulwe* the patron god of sailors, *Solang* the patron god of canoe builders, and so on.

It is entirely possible and indeed common for gods to coexist with other kinds of spirits, most obviously human spirits but also animistic and ancestral spirits. The Ainu, who believed that all animate and most inanimate things have spirit, also had notions about gods or *kamuy*. There were several categories of gods, including gods of the shore, of the mountain, of the sea, and of the sky. Among the shore *kamuy* were God of the House, Grandmother Hearth, and God of Ground; among mountain *kamuy* were *iso kamuy* or bear god, *horokew kamuy* or wolf god, and *sumari kamuy* or fox god.

Finally, the line between gods and other kinds of spirits is not always clear or firm—if it exists at all. The Tewa, a southwestern US indigenous society, had a six-tiered theory of "personhood," of which the lower three were humans and the upper three spirits. When a person in the lowest tier of humans died, he or she became the lowest tier of spirits; likewise, when members of the highest tier of humans (what they call "Made People" or *Patowa*) died, they became and joined spirits of the highest tier, the "Dry Food Who Never Did Become" or the spirits who never took human form. These spirits or gods were the remote, detached types of deities who were not discussed much or known in much detail. They were talked about as *opa pene in* or *opa nuneh in*, meaning "those from beyond the world" or "those from with and around the earth, respectively. Eight named gods, in the class of *oxua*, were associated with each moiety or half of society, in a ranked order (Ortiz 1969).

Perhaps the single most famous discussion of the god problem in anthropology comes from Evans-Pritchard's *Nuer Religion* (1956), which is an extended struggle with that society's concept of *kwoth*, which he translates as "god" or "spirit." *Kwoth* seems to be a particular being, a "god." It is construed as in the sky and is associated with the sky and celestial objects and events (like rain and lightning), but it is not the same thing as these physical phenomena. It is the creator, *cak ghaua* or creator of the universe; it is also a person or *ran*, with *yiegh* or breath or life. At the same time, *kwoth* manifests itself as various types of named spirits, including *kwoth nhial* (spirits of the sky) and *kwoth piny* (spirits of the earth). *Kwoth*, then, as spirit is one and many at the same time.

Religious Forces

Not all religions include beings at all, and not all of those that do have beings have exclusively beings. There is also a regular occurrence of claims about impersonal forces— ones that are not associated necessarily with any particular living thing nor have an individual mind or will. Often these forces are more like spiritual water or electricity—a (super)naturally occurring power that exists in and flows through nature, giving it the qualities that we find there. The usual name given to religions that highlight these forces over beings is animatism.

Box 2.2 What Is "the Religion" of the !Kung or Ju/hoansi?

When we examine a specific society, even one as reputedly "simple" as the !Kung or Ju/hoansi, the identification of its "religion" can become highly problematic. The !Kung are a much-studied foraging society in the Kalahari desert of southwest Africa. Conventional wisdom says that foragers are usually animists, "worshiping" nature and lacking a conception of "gods." The reality is not so simple. In actuality, the !Kung cannot be fitted into any one "type" of religion. A prime concern of theirs was the dead ancestors, known collectively as the //gauwasi or //gangwasi, who were not "worshiped" at all and were regarded with ambivalence. They constituted a prime source of danger to humans, not out of malice but out of their loneliness; still aware of and sad for their living loved ones, they would try to bring the living to the land of the dead to be with them, with undesirable consequences for the living. In addition to the //gangwasi or //gauwasi, the !Kung also knew of gods, including the great god *Gao Na* and the lesser god *Kauha*. Each god has a wife and children and lives in the sky. *Gao Na* has human form and gives both good and bad to humans, via the dead ancestors and other intermediary spirits. He was known for having human emotions—including "passion, stupidity, and frustration"—and enjoyed food and sex. He was not a moral paragon but performed immoral acts like incest and cannibalism, and the people did not defer to him in awe and reverence. Their "prayers" typically took a somewhat accusatory tone, implying the god's injustice in doing bad things to those who do not deserve it (Katz 1982: 31). Finally, along with ancestors and gods, they held a concept of an energy called *n/um*. Richard Lee defined *n/um* as a "substance that lies in the pit of the stomach of men and women … and becomes active during a healing dance. The !Kung believe that the movements of the dancers heat the *n/um* up and when it boils it rises up the spinal cord and explodes in the brain" (1984: 109). This force was crucial to their conception of shamanism and healing (see Chapter 3).

The classic example of a spiritual force is *mana* as understood in numerous Melanesian cultures. On the island of Tikopia, *mana* was a word that could be a noun, an adjective, and/or a verb. According to Raymond Firth, it was accurate to say either that a person "has *mana*" or "is *mana*," and the key sign of having/being *mana* was potency, efficacy, power, that is, the capacity to make things happen. A chief had/was *mana*, as did/was a great warrior or hunter. *Mana* should not be understood as a possession or property of a chief, though; rather, the "only real source of *mana* is in the spirit world. *Mana* does not mean the exercise of human powers but the use of something derived from gods or ancestors" (1940: 501). The message, then, was that "nature does not work independently of man; fertility is not merely a concatenation of physical factors but depends on the maintenance of a relationship between man and spiritual beings" (505). Humans, nature, and the supernatural were one great system of power.

The Chinese notion of *chi* is another familiar animatistic principle. It is probably a very old idea but is most clearly and poetically discussed in the ancient work *Tao Te Ching*, historically attributed to a sage named Lao Tze. In this book, the *tao* is described as the "way" or "path" of nature and the *chi* that animates and flows through it. In Chinese and Chinese-derived thought systems, *chi* operates in two modes—a fast, bright, dry, male mode (*yang*) and a slow, dark, moist, female mode (*yin*). Both modes are present in all things in various proportions, the sun being the most *yang* thing and the moon the most *yin*. *Chi* flows through the world and through humans, affecting every aspect of human life. An imbalance or blockage of *chi* can cause illness, which can be corrected by diet, movement, or treatment like acupuncture or acupressure. The way of *chi* even informs such mundane matters as architecture and home furnishing: the practice of *feng shui* takes advantage of the flow of *chi* to construct healthy, efficacious spaces.

Variations on this idea of force abound. The Dusun of Borneo worried about a notion of "luck" which was a finite spiritual resource, such that a person could expend his or her luck in one area of life and so endanger other areas (e.g. acquisition of property, success in disputes, etc.). Also, luck was finite in society, making one person's gain in it another person's loss; this naturally led to arguments about surreptitious efforts to steal or damage each other's luck. The Apache functioned in terms of a power known as *diyi*, which for them was in infinite supply. Individuals who possessed or controlled *diyi* were markedly different from those who did not. Many forms of this power were recognized, related to different animals or natural phenomena. In a twist on the animatistic theme, *diyi* did have some "personal" attributes, including the ability to seek out people to attach to (individuals could also seek *diyi*) and to experience anger, which could of course be harmful to humans (Basso 1970). The Menomini of North America also knew of a power which they called *tatahkesewen* ("that which has energy"), *meskowesan* ("that which has strength"), or *ahpehtesewesen* ("that which is valuable"). They described it as nonmaterial and invisible but like a bright light. This form of power could also be sought and mastered, through dreams, vision quests, and the guidance of guardian spirits (Spindler and Spindler 1971).

Meyer Fortes (1959) recounted the Tallensi conception of "fate" or "destiny," not unlike the ancient Roman concept that gives us the English term. In the Tallensi version, humans were born with a good or evil destiny, which determined the course of their lives; in a sense, their ultimate lot was "pre-destined." An evil destiny was indicated by the person's refusal or inability to execute his or her social roles and obligations; a person's successful fulfillment of social expectations was proof of a good destiny. Thus, human social failings were traceable to supernatural sources and "no fault of our own." In a view that ties animatistic and ancestral "beliefs" together, it was the dead ancestors who provided a person with his or her fate. But fortunately not all was lost for the person born with evil destiny: rituals could be performed to help, on the premise that ancestors were potentially amenable to reversing their original assignment of destiny.

Religious Conceptions: The Universe and Human Existence

While ideas about beings and forces underlie all religions, there are many other subjects that those traditions teach about. These include origins and ends, reasons and relations, health and sickness, morality and meaning, and virtually any topic that might come to the mind of humans. In the next section we consider a few of these areas and some of the diversity in claims and doctrines about them.

Cosmology and Cosmogony

Nearly all religions offer a view of what the universe is "really like"—what it is made of, what parts or layers it has, and how all of this relates to humanity. Cosmology deals with the order or structure of ultimate reality, whereas cosmogony deals with the origin of that structure or order. Both words derive from the Greek root *kosmos* for "universe" or "order" (as opposed to "chaos"), and the former has been picked up by science to name astronomical and physical theories about the universe, while the latter has not found any scientific application.

The cosmologies and cosmogonies of different religions vary extensively. The Christian version tells of a fundamentally three-layered reality, with a heaven (above) and a hell (below) sandwiching an intermediate world inhabited by humans and other material beings (interestingly but not surprisingly, contemporary fictional cosmologies, like that of *The Lord of the Rings*, echo this same design, with a Middle Earth where humans and hobbits reside). Other religions envision ultimate reality in very different terms. The Yanomamo worldview as presented by Napoleon Chagnon included a four-layered reality, "like inverted dinner plates: gently curved, round, thin, rigid, and having a top and bottom surface" (1992: 99–100). These four layers included the highest one, called *duku ka misi*, which was of least concern to them, being "empty" or "void." The second highest level, *hedu ka misi*, had the sky as its lower surface; on it, animals and plants and dead ancestors lived very much as we do. Humans resided on the third level, *hei ka misi*, which formed when a bit of the upper layer broke off and fell. The bottom layer, *hei ta bebi*, was described as "almost barren" except for an odd race of Yanomamo-like people called the Amahiri-teri. Since their netherworld was so lifeless, they sent their spirits on cannibalistic expeditions to the "real world" above to capture Yanomamo, especially children.

The Navajo conceived the universe as a "stack" of fourteen "world structures" or platter-shaped worlds laid out on top of each other. Sam Gill does not tell us how these world structures came to be, but within this system a process of "emergence" began at the center of the lowest level, moving upward through a series of events told in myth. Living in the lower levels were insect-, animal-, and bird-people with their own languages and societies, and the "upward journey was a forced movement due to the misconduct of these peoples. Each world offered the promise of happiness and a good life to its inhabitants, but they were unable to maintain proper relationships with one another" (Gill 1981: 51). For each layer along the way, detailed descriptions of the geography as well as of the social events were known. Emerging finally at the top world, which is the contemporary earth, First Man and First Woman "begin to whisper to each other, planning what will be created on the earth surface" (52). Out of these deliberations and their actions came the first sweat lodge, the first hogan, the sacred medicine bundle as a reservoir of spiritual power, and the birth of Changing Woman. A ceremony created the original two groups of "human forms" and a man and woman "who represent the means of life for all things as they proceed through time" (52). Finally, the Holy People who had achieved the emergence departed, ushering in the era of culture heroes and of the origins of contemporary rituals.

As we can see, many religions and cosmologies view the universe as round or circular, with the territory of the particular society as the center of the world. Often, there is a connection—sometimes a literal line—that connects the center point of the world with the spiritual realm.

One common motif to depict this relation is the "axis mundi" or "tree of life," which stands at the center of creation and reaches up to "heaven." The Hindu texts *Bhagavad Gita* and *Mahabharata* speak of such a cosmic tree (see Figure 2.2). The Norse also spoke

Figure 2.2 Detail of Tree of Life relief on a restored ninth-century Hindu temple at Prambanan, Java
© Suzanne Long / Alamy

of a cosmic tree, called Yggdrasil, the Tree of Wisdom and the Tree of Life (reminiscent of the tree in the Garden of Eden). The gods met at the ash tree, as perhaps the ancient druids did and some modern-day wiccans do, which connected and shaped all of creation. In other cases the central point is a mountain; for Hindu and Hinduized cultures like traditional Java, Mount Meru was such a focal point, while for ancient Greece the home of the gods was Mount Olympus. Even Moses met the god Yahweh on a mountain. All such images not only provide a cosmology but a "sacred geography" tying together earth, heaven, society, and spirits.

Box 2.3 The Cosmology of a Pacific Island Society

Among the Chuuk-speaking peoples of Micronesia, a region of the north Pacific with many small islands and island chains, the universe was shaped "like an inverted bowl above the surface of the sea" (Dobbin 2011: 39). The floor of the sea formed the lowest level of the cosmos, and the islands projected upward from the sea bottom, "almost pylons that are sunk into the sea until they reach the bottom." Including the sea floor, there were eleven levels rising up, starting with the deep sea itself, then the island pylons, and the surface of the earth and ocean. Above the earth was the horizon, then the floating sky, then the "moving or cloud sky." Higher than the clouds were the "sun or star sky" and the "long sky," which were enclosed by the "vault of heaven." These platters hovering over the earth and ocean were connected to the earth's surface by the *axis mundi* of Enuunap's "tree to heaven." Enuunap was a sky god and the "chief of the gods" whose name meant "great spirit" (27). Despite being the high god, he was "for the most part, unconcerned with the daily needs of humankind," although he was thought to possess "very human characteristics in the little he does from his lofty place in the sky." Human-like, he was not thought to be "almighty or eternal" (28), but he did have numerous children who "performed valuable functions for humans, especially in canoe and house building, sailing and navigation, fishing, growing breadfruit, and controlling the Pacific Ocean weather" (30). On the highest level of the universe (the long sky), "there are houses for Enuunap's parents, in-laws, and his main children," where his kinfolk, "filled with foibles, fights, and feuding," resided (42). At the other end of the cosmos, the sea god Sowunoon ruled the space below the sea floor and occasionally emerged from his abode into the sea through a trapdoor on the bottom of the ocean.

Theodicy: Explaining Evil

It is eminently clear in all places and times that bad things happen to people, even good people. Humans look for explanations for these misfortunes, as well as ways to control or prevent them. No matter what the precise form of explanation, it tends to involve an "intentional" or even "personal" source. Theodicy is the Christian term for explaining evil or suffering, especially in a world made and ruled by an omnibenevolent God.

The concepts of beings and forces and of cosmology will obviously affect the concepts of evil; in fact, they will even determine what is considered evil in the first place—or whether "evil" as a concept exists. For instance, in a tradition that believes in the existence of an all-good spirit, evil is a particularly vexing problem. One solution is to blame humans for it, through a subordinate concept like "free will." Another, often in tandem with the former, is to attribute it to one or more beings of evil (a devil or satan or demons). A third and less appealing possibility is that the good spirit creates evil too, or at least allows it. "I form the light and create darkness: I make peace and create evil: I, the Lord, do all these things," prophesied Isaiah (45:7), speaking in the name of his god Yahweh. The Book of Job is centrally concerned with the problem of evil, demonstrating that there is no relationship between the goodness of the person and the evil that befalls him.

Christian theodicy represents the general solution of "dualism" for the problem of evil, that is, that there are two distinct and opposing forces or beings, the clash between which results in visible evil. This is a recurring theme, as seen in the even older religion of the Persian prophet Zoroaster or Zarathustra, who believed in a universe with two equal forces—light (Ahura Mazda) and darkness (Ahriman or Angra Mainyu)—at odds with each other. Angra Mainyu was a kind of "counter-creator" or "anti-creator," who was responsible for bringing the serpent, plagues, "plunder and sin," unbelief, "tears and wailing," and 99,999 diseases into the otherwise perfect creation of Ahura Mazda. Accordingly, the two gods or forces were perpetually at war, making the universe a battleground. Thus all of religion and all of human existence was or should be directed toward combating Angra Mainyu and his forces of evil, and all humans were in fact warriors in the struggle between light and darkness.

Other belief systems locate the cause of misfortune in other agents, human and not-so-human. This might consist of ancestral spirits, as we described above. It might also consist of human operators—witches, sorcerers, and the like—as we will discuss in the next chapter. Another way to approach the problem of evil is to accept it as inevitable, as part of the nature of existence. Buddhism finds suffering or brokenness (*dukkha*) to be an inherent quality of physical reality. The ancient Greek poets never pretended that their gods were all good. The gods, like humans, were good and bad, grand and petty, full of all the emotional and intellectual foibles that a being can exhibit. They were arbitrary and capricious, doing what they will. Sometimes evil was just the result of dumb luck or bad choices, as when Pandora opened her box.

In some religious views, the world is simply dangerous. For the Piaroa of Venezuela danger flowed from the actions of the two creator beings, Kuemoi and Wahari (Overing 1986). Kuemoi, the Master of Water, was a violent—even insanely violent—ugly cannibal, and Wahari, the Master of Land, was the creator of the Piaroa people. Invading Wahari's land domain, Kuemoi created fire, plants and animals, and "culture," the knowledge and skills of farming and hunting. Wahari, in addition to creating humans in his own domain, created fish and fishing in Kuemoi's. More consequentially, he transformed the nonhuman species into their present edible forms, depriving them of their original spiritual and anthropomorphic nature. They thus became proper food for humans. The extreme and almost unbearably contradictory message in this tale is that poison is everywhere in their world. Culture is poisonous because it was created by a mad god. Food is also poisonous; animals and large fish are dangerous to eat, but so are small fish, birds, and even plants. Consuming any of these things is dangerous, not because they cause physical harm but because they cause spiritual, invisible harm. After all, animals and fish are jealous and angry for losing their human forms and their ability to have culture. Therefore, while we humans eat them, they try to avenge themselves by "eating" us. The world, thus, is an inescapably violent and dangerous place. If we do not eat, we die, but if we eat, we may also die. Every choice, every step, is fraught with peril.

A final way to "solve" the problem of evil is to deny, in a sense, that there is any problem. In other words, a tradition may assert that evil is only apparent and that from another, more enlightened, point of view it does not exist at all. The *Bhagavad Gita*, the most famous and popular of the Hindu scriptures, makes this point clearly. In this tale, the warrior Arjuna finds himself on the eve of battle looking across the battlefield at his enemies, who include some of his own kinsmen. He is about to throw down his bow and arrow in desperation, when his chariot-driver, the god Krishna in disguise, begins a discourse on the proper actions of a righteous man. Arjuna is a member of the *kshatriya* or noble/warrior caste, whose duty is war. He would be at fault to refuse his duty, which would condemn him yet again to a demotion in the great cycle of *samsara* or rebirth, which is the greatest evil. But even more than this, Krishna instructs the reluctant warrior why neither he nor any man should worry about taking a human life: since the true essence of a person cannot be killed, and since the body is a mere temporary receptacle for that essence, then the fate of that body is of little import. In fact, killing a *kshatriya* is helping him achieve a higher existence.

Human Conception, Birth, and Death

Human birth and death are widely regarded as spiritual or religious phenomena, hedged about with beliefs, rituals, and moral value. Death in many religions is the transition from a mundane to a spiritual condition; birth may be such a transition as well (especially if the religion entails that humans pre-exist in some supernatural way). Among the Azande, for instance, conception was understood to follow from sexual intercourse, semen or *nziro* containing the soul of the unborn child. In the womb male and female "soul-stuff" mixed, and whichever parent's part was stronger determined the sex of the child. A fetus was regarded as "a soul with an undeveloped body, and even when the child is born the soul has not become completely and permanently attached to its abode," making it susceptible to "flying away" and death (Evans-Pritchard 1962: 246). The fetus was strengthened and built out of the blood of the woman and the repeated insemination of the man, as well as the mother's food.

The Dinka said that men and women give birth jointly, with divine intercession to "create" the child and the ancestors' assistance to protect it from malevolent forces. In other words, two supernatural media (a god and ancestor spirits) joined with humans to make life and guard it against a third supernatural medium (evil powers) (Deng 1972). The Ainu asserted that conception and birth were not caused by sex at all but by the god *Aynu Sikohte*, since humans do not have the power to make life. Similarly, Australian Aboriginals allegedly did not see a link between sex and child-making; in many of their societies, babies came from the Dreaming spirits and were "spirit children" born into human form. These spirits dwelt in the landscape and entered a woman's womb when she sat, lay, or camped at sacred sites. Human women were sometimes considered to be passive "hosts" of the spirits that desired to be born, while men played no part at all except perhaps to "open the way."

The Kaguru of East Africa (Beidelman 1971) had one of the most interesting takes on human birth. According to their religion, when a human died he or she went to the land of the dead or the ghosts. However, when a human child was born, that person was born *out of* the land of the ghosts, such that a human *birth* was a ghost *death*. Just as the living mourned the loss of one of their own from death, the ghosts mourned the loss of their own from "birth." Hence, there was a reciprocal life-and-death relationship between ghosts and humans in which each was born and died into the other.

Once birth has occurred, not all societies consider this a completion of the making of a human, certainly not "socially" and sometimes not even physically. Newborns are widely held to be particularly vulnerable to supernatural threats, whether from demons, witches, or spirits; accordingly, they are often subjected to periods of ritual seclusion. The Konyak Nagas closed the house of a newborn to strangers for six days out of concern for evil effects. But beyond this, infants must not only physically but socially mature into real humans. The Tewa, for example, conducted a series of initiations from the fourth day after birth until about age twenty in which the child was transformed into a full human (a "Dry Food person" or *seh t'a*, literally meaning "dry food"). An *ochu* or moist/unripe ("green") person was not quite a person at all, because they were ignorant and innocent: "To be innocent is to be not yet Tewa; to be not yet Tewa is to be not yet human, and to be not yet human is to be, in this use of the term, not entirely out of the realm of spiritual existence" (Ortiz 1969: 16). At the end of the initiation cycle, not only was the child a real Tewa, but he or she was situated firmly in the kinship (moiety) system; he or she had taken his or her place in society.

Eventually every life ends (see Figure 2.3), and in many if not most societies, something is believed to follow it. The Kaguru, like many peoples, envisioned their domain of the dead to be very similar to the domain of the living, where dead spirits "lived," farmed, hunted, fought and quarreled, and in numerous ways conducted familiar lives, including "dying" and being mourned by their survivors. They were not particularly clear on where this ghost world was (some said above, some said below). For the Huron too, the "village of the dead" resembled the habitations of the living. Even more, different dead had different courses to follow: the very old or very young might linger around their families, while those who died in combat gathered to make their own unique community. And of course, the departed were often threats to the living, especially if they died badly (Trigger 1969).

Figure 2.3 Graves in an urban Japanese cemetery. Courtesy of the author

Many religions understood death as a kind of journey between worlds that can, literally, take time and involve challenges and obstacles. The Ainu said that the dead spirit remained around the body through the funeral and then sojourned to the land of the dead to be rejoined with the body; in fact, the dead were called *yayasirika* or "reborn." They traveled to a dead world called *auru n kotan* that was similar to the living world except reversed in seasons. The living could visit the dead, although the dead could not see them (while, interestingly, dogs could smell them). The Konyak Nagas declared that the dead needed to carry weapons on their trip to their future home, since each would meet and fight again all of the warriors they had killed in battle during life. In the afterlife, conditions were similar to life, and men were always reunited with their first wife. Among the Tewa a dead body (from which the spirit escaped via the mouth) was buried with an amount of food, depending on how long the voyage to the next life would take; good people took a "straight" and short path, but bad people would travel a long and winding road, sometimes encountering beasts along the way. The dead spirit wandered with its ancestors for four days, during which time the living were nervous about its effects on them, since the dead get lonely and may return to take relatives with them, especially children. On the evening of the fourth day, a "releasing" ritual was performed to send the spirit on its way, with a repeat performance on the first anniversary.

Clearly not all societies considered death to be an immediate and total phenomenon and transformation. The Mandinko believed that a person was not entirely dead at death but was a "transitional corpse," who would be interviewed by the angel Malika in the grave before moving on. The Dusun said that the dead soul waited near the village for seven nights before going on to its final destination of *Nabalu* on the summit of Mt. Kinabalu. But some souls would never make it, since they could be captured and imprisoned by other dead spirits or by "disease-givers" or such evil-workers. A related idea is the practice of zombification of the dead or the creation of "undead."

Among the Trobriand Islanders, there were two different and incompatible beliefs (Malinowski 1948). One was that the dead had a "short and precarious existence" on the outskirts of their village in the form of *kasi*, where they pestered the living. The second and much more elaborated view was that the soul or *baloma* traveled to a physical location, the island of Tuma, where it waited on the shore crying until other spirits of the dead heard the grief and came out to join it. Then the deceased encountered Topileta, the chief of the village of the dead, who had to be compensated; for this purpose, the dead body was buried with valuables like jewels and artifacts. Those who could not afford to pay never reached the land of the dead and were condemned to become denizens of the ocean, mythical sea-creatures called *vaiaba*. For those who were able to continue, three different paths led to Tuma, based on the style of one's death (magic, poison, or combat). At their destination, they discovered their dead ancestors and made a home for themselves. Women outnumbered men in the land of the dead, and these dead women tried to lure the men with irresistible love magic, making them forget their previous existence.

End of Time: Eschatology

Many but not all religions have some conception of the "death of the world," of an end at least of the present age if not of all of creation. This is the area of eschatology, from *eschaton* for end or last or farthest. Christianity is a highly eschatological religion, warning of a final confrontation between good and evil in which evil will be defeated and consumed, the earth as we know it destroyed, and the final victory of God enshrined in a new earth where Jesus rules supreme. Linear traditions like Judaism and Christianity believe in a single creation, existence, and destruction, but other cyclical traditions believe in multiple recurring creations. Hinduism describes a reality which is repeatedly made and unmade, as god Brahma sleeps and wakes, bringing the universe into existence in his dreams. Each cycle of creation undergoes a decline from its perfect initial stage to its eventual destruction and replacement with a new, pristine godly dream. The present age, the *Kali yuga* or age of Kali (the goddess of death), is the end-stage of the most recent creation. It is distinguished as a time of troubles, of power and injustice, and of the breakdown of social institutions and the loss of piety. According to one version, as the end of the cycle approaches, the earth becomes an uninhabitable wasteland, killing off most of the beings who once lived on it. Then the god Vishnu himself completes the devastation, drinking up the last waters and allowing seven suns to scorch the desiccated surface. After that, torrential rains extinguish the fires but inundate the land with floods, which is finally ripped by high winds. Only after all life is crushed and all energy expended does Vishnu again take the form of Brahma and bring about a new cycle of creation, which in turn will pass through thousands of ages until it too ends harshly.

Another well-known version of the end is told in Norse tales of Ragnarok. According to the *Edda*, winter will engulf the land, during which time social order will break down. Brothers will fight, taboos will be broken, wars will flare, all ending in the world's ruin. A wolf will swallow the sun, and another wolf will swallow the moon. Earthquakes will tear down great trees and mountains, followed by floods and tidal waves. Out of the shattered sky will ride the sons of Muspell, and the gods will awaken and meet in counsel. Odin and his court will battle Muspell's sons and their evil hordes until all the gods and men and even the tree Yggdrasil have been laid waste. However, out of the sea a new earth will rise, with new good lands and new good gods and new people and a new sun.

Eschatological views are not particularly common among the small-scale, "traditional" religions of the world. Most appear to have a more continuous notion of existence, in which things persist much as they are. However, as we will see, eschatological ideas have diffused around the modern world and penetrated many religions, generating new beliefs and new movements of great historical and cultural importance.

Conclusion

Every religion makes a (more or less integrated) system of claims about the "super-natural" world and its relationship with the natural, human, and social worlds. Whether or not we can call these "beliefs" is an interesting relativistic problem. Nevertheless, ideas or concepts or categories of religious entities are a universal and necessary component of religions. We cannot always, however, divide these ideas and resulting religions into neat "types," and perhaps we are better served if we do not attempt it. Rather, it might be more meaningful and accurate to think of components—building blocks or modules—of religious conceptions, which can be assembled in various combinations to yield particular religions. Then, we might be better off to speak of a "religious field" than a "type of religion," recognizing that any religious field may contain some and not other elements, may elaborate some elements more than others, and may mix elements in ways that at first would seem to us unlikely or incompatible. Precisely because religions are often *not* explicit cognitive systems, such (apparent) incompatibility is less of a problem than we usually think.

DISCUSSION QUESTIONS

- What is the anthropological critique of "belief"? Is "belief" part of all religions or critical to religions?
- How are religious or supernatural beings "agents" like, but different from, human beings?
- What are the main areas or topics on which religions offer ideas or explanations?

SUPPLEMENTARY READING (see website)

- *Belief or Relational Action? Papua New Guineans in a Christian Hospital*
- *Reviving Animism: Contemporary Anthropological Thoughts on the Concept of Animism*
- *Miracles and Religious Experiences among the Samburu*

3 Religious Symbols and Specialists

The Apiao people of southern Chile carry their saint in their arms. San Antonio de Padua is a fifteen-inch tall statue made of painted chalk; further, he is privately owned, not church property. He is "not particularly old or aesthetically pleasing" but "is believed to be extremely powerful and miraculous" (Bacchiddu 2011: 26). When someone wants to benefit from his power, the seeker fetches him from his owner and takes him home for a few days. The presence of the saint in the user's home "transforms an everyday family space into a sacred space" (28). Further, although he is a saint, and a chalk saint at that, an Apiao person treats him "as if he were a person of flesh and bone," like a human being "who listens, delivers, warns, punishes, [and] guides people's actions" (31). The Apiao engage in a dialog with him, "formulating a question and waiting for an answer, making an offer and thereby agreeing on an exchange, or otherwise offering an apology and expecting the apology to be accepted" (31–32).

Although concerned ultimately with the "spiritual" or "supernatural" realm, religion must and does find its expressions and effects here in the mundane material and especially social world. Even more, humans cannot relate to entirely disembodied or abstract beings or forces, and even if we could, as long as we live in the physical world those beings or forces will be expressed or made manifest in and through specific objects and specific persons. However "transcendental" it may be, religious reality must be made immanent for humans to know it and to interact with it—to communicate *with* it and *about* it. It must take concrete forms, both nonhuman and human.

This chapter deals with two manifestations of spiritual meaning and power in the physical and social world—"symbols" and "specialists." We usually take symbols to be things that "stand for" other things. However, symbols are things themselves, and powerful things at that; their power may be more important than their "meaning"—or *may be* their meaning. The same is true for religious specialists: although they do not stand for religious beings and forces, they may *stand in for* these entities, serving as their representatives or intermediaries in the human world. As Victor Turner, one of the most influential symbolic anthropologists, phrased it in discussing the symbolic work of the Ndembu of Zambia, symbols and the specialists who use them (and in a certain sense *are* them) "make visible, audible, and tangible beliefs, ideas, values, sentiments, and psychological dispositions that cannot directly be perceived" (1967: 50). This will take us on a journey through the diversity of religious symbols and specialists across religions. We will find that the conventional concept of symbol may be inadequate to understand what members are doing in their religion. A concept like "symbol" seems perhaps too anemic to convey all of this significance—and we must be wary, as before, that it may be *our* concept but not theirs.

The Anthropology of Symbolism

Symbols, in the very simplest construction, are things—objects, images, sounds, actions, gestures, utterances, and almost any other medium—that "mean" something, that "have a meaning." The meaning is that which the symbol "stands for," the phenomenon of which it is a representation or a place-holder. Moreover, the relationship between the symbol and its meaning is arguably *arbitrary and conventional*—that is, there is no necessary connection between the particular meaning and the particular symbol. It is only cultural habit that unites the two. In other words, humans could and do use any linguistic symbol (i.e. word) for "dog" and still mean "dog." Humans could use any symbol to represent the USA or Christianity, and the meaning would be the same (in fact, the USA and Christianity have been represented by different symbols at other times). Also, any symbol could have different meanings, like the swastika for Nazi Germany or Hinduism.

Symbols are clearly not the only kind of "meaningful" things. For example, in *Symbols: Public and Private*, Raymond Firth (1973) distinguished symbols from "indexes," "signals," and "icons." An index for him is a signifier that is directly or objectively related to what it signifies, perhaps as part-to-whole or particular-to-general, like the tail of a dog signifying a dog. A signal is something that is "made" by or co-occurring with the signified, like the bark of a dog or the crash of thunder. An icon is a "sign" that bears some similarity or resemblance to the thing it signifies, like a picture or statue of a dog. Finally, a symbol is not directly or objectively related to its meaning and is "meaningful" through a chain of associations, for instance, the dog being a symbol of companionship or loyalty.

Making and using symbols entails the cognitive ability to find and place meaning where it otherwise "is not." Leslie White referred to the process of "bestowing meaning upon a thing or an act, or grasping and appreciating meanings thus bestowed," as *symboling* (1959: 231), and he offered holy water as a prime example. Holy water is water, a physical material thing, but humans add a dimension of holiness to it. People who have learned to "grasp and appreciate" the notion of holy water comprehend it as holy; for everyone else, it is just water.

While symbolism has come to be an important element in anthropological thought, it hardly originated with anthropology. Freudian psychoanalysis took the notion of symbol particularly seriously and particularly far. In fact, Weston La Barre, one of numerous twentieth-century anthropologists to apply psychoanalytic thinking, gave it credit for being "the first psychology to preoccupy itself with the symbolic *content* and *purpose*, as opposed to the mere modalities and processes, of thinking" (1972: xii). According to Freud, the mind operates on two principles, a "primary process" and a "secondary process." The latter involves effective action on "reality" or the external world whereas the former is not in touch with or even particularly interested in reality. The primary process is the spontaneous working of the isolated unconscious mind, before the "reality principle" sets in. The unconscious mind, he proposed, is full of inexpressible and even unacceptable drives and wishes and memories—most of them sexual in nature—which nevertheless must find their outlet. This outlet is creative and imaginative via meaningful indirectness or substitution, of which dreams are the most conspicuous instance. Dreams, then, are a symbolic "language" for a specific set of mental phenomena. And not dreams alone: neuroses and other mental illnesses are symbolic (e.g. hysterical blindness might be a symbol of seeing something terrible and painful), as well as "slips of the tongue" (so-called Freudian slips), making both significant for diagnosis. As Freud's thinking expanded, he also attributed "higher" cultural achievements—like art, ritual, and myth—to this same symbolic process, as well as "primitive" culture in general. Carl Jung, while more sensitive to religion, echoed Freud's approach. In his famous essay "Concerning the Two Kinds of Thinking," he argued that while dreams are "apparently contradictory and nonsensical," they arise from a distinct and important mental process, which is a symbolic one (1949: 9). He too saw symbolism arising from a different thought process than the mundane, discursive, language-based mode, namely an undirected or "dream" or "fantasy" mode of thinking, which "turns away from reality, sets free subjective wishes, and is, in regard to adaptation, wholly unproductive" (22). Jung located this same mentality in two other realms: ancient history and "primitive society," in particular religion.

An advance (some would say a revolution) in symbolism came in 1942 with the publication of Suzanne Langer's *Philosophy in a New Key*. She contended that symbolism was a much more pervasive thought process than previously suspected. In fact, she opined that the problem of "meaning" was not a strictly symbolic problem but the fundamental human problem. All experience, including the experience of supposed "sense-data," is "primarily symbolic" (1942: 16). Symbolization, the process of making and using symbols, then is "the starting point of all intellection in the human sense, and is more general than thinking, fancying, or taking action" (33). All thinking starts with concepts, not isolated perceptions, and all concepts are symbolic in that they refer to "types" or "classes" of things, not individual things: "Rover" may mean a specific dog, but "dog" means a general kind of being.

Rather than looking for "the meaning" of a symbol—that is, its translation into another "language" (for instance, the Freudian language of sex or unconscious drives)—she proposed that symbolism was not linguistic in the strict sense or at least that it constituted a kind of "non-discursive language." She distinguished language and symbolism as shown in Table 3.1.

The key to Langer's new philosophy is *metaphor*, the use of one thing to suggest another through the similarities between the two (for example, "time is money" in that both can be saved, spent, wasted, and so on). Another name for this is *analogy*, that is, one thing is like another in certain ways, although not in all ways. Metaphor or analogy is still thinking, she insists, but it is not "rational" or fact-related thinking; even though the "grammar" of such statements looks literal, they are not to be taken literally. It is not essentially "denotative" talk, and it is often not talk at all. In fact, she proposed that much of symbolism is image-based and image-driven, and images quickly crowd in on images, forging additional analogical or associative links. The result is a flight along metaphoric chains that go where nobody knows or predicts: "Metaphor is the law of growth of every semantic" (119), as people make more and more analogies and

Table 3.1 Langer's comparison of language and symbolism

Language	*Non-Linguistic Symbols (Music, Art, etc.)*
Has vocabulary and syntax	Has no vocabulary—cannot be broken into "words" or "morphemes"
Dictionary possible (one word can be "defined" by or "translated" into others)	No dictionary possible (one symbol cannot be "defined" by or "translated" into another)
Translatability (words in one language can be rendered by equivalents in another language)	No translatability (symbols in one medium or genre cannot be rendered into equivalents in another medium or genre, i.e., you cannot re-state a symphony as a poem, etc.)

associations and play with the ones they have. The end-product is a tangled and virtually impenetrable forest of meaning and metaphor, which she called "vegetative thought," in which "the very use of language exhibits a rampant confusion of metaphorical meanings clinging to every symbol, sometimes to the complete obscurance of any reasonable literal meaning" (120–21). One name that she gave to this process, as opposed to the denotative or "factual" type of thinking and speaking, is *poetic significance*.

Ernst Cassirer expanded the scope and import of the symbolic function. In his *An Essay on Man* he noted that as history or as explanation, symbolism fails, being full of "errors and heresies" (1954: 97), "a logic of absurdity" (29), but only if we mistake it for logic. However, what we should see, he urged, is the thorough and inescapable symbolic nature of all of our experience—that symbols mediate our perceptions utterly:

> man lives in a symbolic universe. Language, myth, art, and religion are parts of this universe. ... No longer can man confront reality immediately; he cannot see it, as it were, face to face. Physical reality seems to recede in proportion as man's symbolic activity advances. Instead of dealing with the things themselves man is in a sense constantly conversing with himself. ... His situation is the same in the theoretical as in the practical sphere. Even here man does not live in a world of hard facts, or according to his immediate needs and desires.
>
> (43)

This excursion into psychology and philosophy has been necessary because anthropology owes so much to those disciplines. Clifford Geertz's definition of symbol, for example— "any object, act, event, quality, or relation which serves as a vehicle for a conception—the conception is the symbol's 'meaning'" (1973: 91)—reflects and is explicitly credited to Langer. He also picked up philosopher Gilbert Ryle's suggestion that mind and meaning are fundamentally "public" and to an extent "objective" and echoed it in his subsequent statement that symbols "are *tangible formulations* of notions, abstractions from experience fixed in perceptible forms, concrete embodiments of ideas, attitudes, judgments, longings, or beliefs" (91, emphasis added).

With symbols playing such a powerful role, it is no wonder that Geertz viewed religion as exactly a system of symbols, as his definition (see Chapter 1) shows. Even more, culture itself is a system of symbols, of which religion is one component or cluster, though a particularly important one.

> The concept of culture I espouse ... is essentially a semiotic one. Believing, with Max Weber [and Ernst Cassirer], that man is an animal suspended in webs of significance he himself has spun, I take culture to be those webs, and the analysis of it to be therefore not an experimental science in search of law but an interpretative one in search of meaning.
>
> (5)

Victor Turner was another influential promoter of the symbolic perspective in anthropology. In his aptly named *The Forest of Symbols*, he explored the ritual symbolism of the Ndembu. For him, ritual and symbolism were intimately linked; in fact, he posited that the symbol "is the smallest unit of ritual which still retains the specific properties of ritual behavior; it is the ultimate unit of specific structure in a ritual context" (1967: 19). Symbols were construed incredibly widely, to include "objects, activities, relationships, events, gestures, and spatial units" (19). Surveying the types and uses, he arrived at three properties of symbols—condensation, unification of disparate significata, and polarization of meaning. By condensation he meant that one symbol can and frequently does carry multiple meanings or representations simultaneously. These multiple or disparate meanings or significata "are interconnected by virtue of their common possession of analogous qualities or by association in fact or thought" (28). A central example for the Ndembu was the milk tree, which he asserted stands at once for "women's breasts, motherhood, a novice at *Nkang'a* [an initiation ritual], the principle of matriliny, a specific matrilineage, learning, and the unity and persistence of Ndembu society" (28). Finally, symbols bring together two "poles" of experience, the natural/physiological and the moral/social. Thus, a symbol integrates the physical qualities and associations of the symbolic object (e.g. the red and therefore "bloody" quality of the *mukula* tree) and the emotional and even visceral reactions it inspires with the ideas, norms, and values of the group that uses it.

In conclusion, then, both Geertz and Turner describe and implement what we might call "the symbolic project." If culture generally and religion specifically is a system or pattern of symbols, then the task of anthropology is to "interpret" or "translate" or "decode" these symbols. As Geertz put it, anthropology becomes an essentially "semiotic" exercise, looking for the "meanings" within which people act. Real-life social action is never lost or ignored; we cannot study symbols in abstract isolation from social life.

> Behavior must be attended to, and with some exactness, because it is through the flow of behavior—or, more precisely, social action—that cultural forms find articulation. They find it as well, of course, in various sorts of artifacts, and various states of consciousness, but these draw their meaning from the role they play ... in an ongoing pattern of life, not from any intrinsic relationships they bear to one another. ... Whatever, or wherever, symbol systems 'in their own terms' may be, we gain empirical access to them by inspecting events, not by arranging abstracted entities into unified patterns.
>
> (Geertz 1973: 17)

But still, social life and culture as such could be treated as a "text" to be read or a "language" to be spoken.

Is Religion Symbolic?

While no one could deny that symbols exist and that much of religion and culture is symbolic, the treatment of culture and religion as essentially or universally symbolic is not shared by all. For instance, Bronislaw Malinowski rejected the symbolic approach to myth, if not all religion: in his essay "Myth in Primitive Psychology" (to which we will return in Chapter 4) he asserted that myth "is not symbolic. ... We can certainly discard all ... symbolic interpretations of these myths of origin" (1948: 101).

Dan Sperber asked the surprising question of *why* we seek symbolic explanations in the first place. He suggested that when anthropologists hear certain accounts from informants, we conclude, "'That's symbolic.' Why? Because it is false" (1975: 3). In other words, most of the time, we dub symbolic "all activity whose rationale escapes me" (4). For Sperber, Radcliffe-Brown would probably represent the standard social science position when the latter pronounced:

> [W]e have to say that from our point of view the natives are mistaken, that the rites do not actually do what they are believed to do. ... In so far as the rites are performed for a

purpose they are futile, based on erroneous belief. ... The rites are easily perceived to be symbolic, and we may therefore investigate their meaning.

(1965: 144)

False or impractical behavior, that is, requires a "symbolic interpretation," whereas true or practical behavior does not: we do not ask the *meaning* of planting seeds in the ground, but we do ask the meaning of performing a ritual over the field.

Further, Sperber insisted that interpreting a symbol or an entire symbol system would require a "key" or "decoder," the sort of which does not exist in most societies. We might query the members as to the meaning of their behavior, but the explanation they offer (its "exegesis") is not, in most if any cases, the "meaning" of the symbol but merely a further extension of it (1975: 34)—just more symbol. And if we told the members that their behaviors or beliefs were symbolic, often enough they would disagree. For example, Joseph Campbell, a friend to religion, wrote throughout his career that "God is a symbol," one that can and must be interpreted "in psychological terms ... [such that] what is referred ... as 'other world' is to be understood psychologically as inner world" (2001: 25). "God is not a fact" (17). However, presumably few believers would accept such an "interpretation"; they would respond that their god is a very real being. Ultimately, Sperber decided that the entire discussion of symbols and meaning may be our imposition on the ethnographic data: "The attribution of sense is an essential aspect of symbolic development in *our* culture. Semiologism is one of the bases of *our* ideology" (1975: 83–84).

John Skorupski, a philosopher examining the anthropological treatment of religion, carried the critique further. He noted that anthropologists have largely absorbed the symbolic approach of Durkheim and others. The reason for this is twofold: one, as "explanation" religion has so often proven to be patently and obviously false and therefore members could *not* use it in that way, and two, it seemed disrespectful to point out number one. So instead, description and analysis moved to the symbolic arena, where, as Durkheim said, all religions are true "in their own fashion." Skorupski argued that religion could be symbolic in different senses: it:

(a) may be unconsciously symbolic, (b) may turn out to be symbolic when its logic is properly surveyed and construed, (c) may have been originally symbolic and then become literalised, or (d) may be symbolic in the interpretation of the observer, but not in that of the actor.

(1976: 36)

How the first might be true is difficult to ascertain. The evidence for the third would be in the lost past, making it also difficult to determine. That leaves two choices—either it "really is" symbolic, or its symbolic character is an attribution of the outsider, not a part of the insider's understanding. But if the latter is true, then the notion that symbols can and must be interpreted is itself an interpretation, and a foreign one at that.

Skorupski came down against a symbolic approach and in favor of a more "literalist" one—that is, for taking the natives at their word. If they think they are making it rain or curing illness, then that is important ethnographic data, not something to be translated (away) into the anthropologist's preferred code. Of course, he was not saying that it actually is true but that the participants think it is, and that is what is interesting. As with "belief," it is a mistake to attribute "symbolism" where it does not apply: sometimes even the members know or think they are being symbolic, but sometimes they think they are being deadly serious. We should take the religious worldview more seriously our-selves, a worldview that rests "on an agency-based cosmology which will extend the social order, so to speak, up the hierarchy" from merely humans to the superhuman (169). To do otherwise leads us down tricky paths: "If Trobriand canoe magic is a ritual which 'stresses the importance of canoe-building for Trobrianders,' then presumably running away from a lion is a ritual which expresses the importance of not being eaten for the runner" (172). In other words, if we report "symbolism" in one situation and not another, we must look at whether it is the situations or ourselves that make the difference: *we* can see the pragmatic value of escaping lions, but we cannot see it in magic, ritual, myth, etc.

From the ethnographic side, Ladislav Holy concurred. He found that "meaning" or "interpretation" or "speculation" is not an indigenous aspect of Berti religion. From their point of view, religion was more instrumental and "practical" than symbolic and expressive; they were "more concerned with means than with meanings, with results than with reasons, with controlling than with explaining" (1991: 76), borrowing language from Keesing's study of the Kwaio. The Berti did not know or care *how* religion worked; they were simply sure it worked. This led him to a critique of the anthropological tradition of treating culture as "first of all a cognitive device. ... If it is seen as an instrumental device at all, it is seen as such, not for achieving practical goals, but for imposing meaning on experience and for expressing that meaning" (202).

What Are Symbols For?

It is doubtful that Sperber, Skorupski, and Holy would argue that there is no such thing as a symbol or that some cultures and religions do not use them some of the time. Nevertheless, they raised several provocative points that make us more circumspect about symbol-talk. First, we may be attributing "symbolism" where the locals do not. Second, we may be imputing meanings to symbols that they do not. And third, "meaning" may not be the only or key consideration in analyzing symbols when we do find them.

The conventional approach to symbols, as we have seen, stresses their cognitive aspect: symbols are "vehicles for a conception," depositories of cultural ideas, which are their "meaning." Precisely what meaning(s) to ascribe to a symbol has been a contentious issue. Some observers, like Holy, insisted that certain symbols do not "mean" at all for the users, and S. F. Nadel among others has urged that we should not ascribe meanings other than the ones members themselves avow. In other words, the only possible meaning of a symbol is the symbol-user's meaning; there cannot be, Nadel insisted, "uncompre-hended meanings," let alone "uncomprehended symbols." As he explained, the entire point of a symbol is to mean something, and if symbols mean "nothing to the actors, they are, from our point of view, irrelevant, and indeed no longer symbols" (1954: 108).

Turner fundamentally disagreed. According to him, symbols may mean and therefore be interpreted in three different ways—by the members' explanations, by the overt qua-lities of the symbols themselves, and by the contexts and ways in which the symbols are employed. In fact, there are two reasons why members *might not be able* to express all the meanings of a symbol. First, each individual sees only one social "angle" on a symbol, while the anthropologist has a more "inclusive" view, not being committed to just one position in society. Second, the society may have an "official" interpretation that more or less intentionally rules out certain understandings. "On these grounds, therefore, I consider it legitimate to include within the total meaning of a dominant ritual symbol, aspects of behavior associated with it which the actors themselves are unable to interpret, and indeed of which they may be unaware" (1967: 27). In fact, since a symbol can have multiple meanings, and since it can and tends to embrace all of the ambiguities and contradictions in social life, many meanings escape or are unacceptable to the members themselves.

Gananath Obeyesekere elaborated this latter point with his notion of "personal symbols." Using the case of hair, an important Hindu symbol, he showed that the life experiences of specific individuals shaped the meaning and valence of public "cultural symbols." Public symbols and their conventional meanings certainly exist; these symbols precede the individual and make certain experiences possible and typical. Thus, "the Hindu's consciousness is already influenced by his culture, facilitating the expression of intrapsychic conflict in a cultural idiom" (1981: 21). However, through selection and application to the individual's life and unique biography and personality, the public symbol is appropriated, recreated, "reloaded" with meaning. In other words, a personal symbol is one of society's public symbols "whose primary significance and meaning lie in the personal life and experience of individuals" (44). Importantly, once an individual personalizes a symbol, that symbol and its meaning are available to others once more as a public symbol.

But even Geertz and Turner did not limit their analyses to the "intellectual" dimension of symbols. As Turner expressed it directly, "Symbols instigate social action. In a field context, they may even be described as 'forces,' in that they are determinable influences inclining persons and groups to action. ... The symbol [is] a unit of action" (1967: 36). For Geertz, the function of symbols was "controlling behavior" (1973: 52); symbols, the constituents of religion and culture, "are 'programs'; they provide a template or blueprint for the organization of social and psychological processes" (216). That is, symbols may not be so much about thinking as doing.

In her influential essay "On Key Symbols" Sherry Ortner (1973) explored the multiple powers of symbols. She discovered two major classes of symbols, which she named "summarizing" and "elaborating." Summarizing symbols capture or condense a major and powerful concept or experience or feeling for the society; they do so, however, in a fairly "undifferentiated" way, that is, they do not ask members to think or feel any one thing in particular nor to reflect on or analyze those feelings nor their source. Elaborating symbols are exactly the opposite: they are "analytical" and provide opportunities and tools for "sorting out" the complexities of concepts and emotions and, of course, translating them into specific experiences and actions. These are "modes" of symbolism, naturally, and may therefore occur in the same symbol.

The precise differences between the two types are broken down into content versus form, quality versus quantity, and vertical versus lateral. Summarizing symbols are more about "content" or meaning, while elaborating symbols are more about form, especially their ability to enter into structured relations with other formal symbols. Summarizing symbols also emphasize quality, the "ultimacy" and "priority" on which other experiences and meanings depend, whereas elaborating symbols are more important as elements or bits in symbolic "clusters" or chains. Finally, summarizing symbols are vertical in the sense that they "ground" meanings to deeper or "higher-level" concepts and feelings, while elaborating symbols are lateral or horizontal in the sense that they can and do interrelate with other like symbols to form chains or "scripts" or "narratives."

Elaborating symbols received more attention from Ortner, partly because they are more "active" than summarizing ones; being more "fundamental," the latter are more static in a way. Elaborating symbols are broken down further into what she called *root metaphors* and *key scenarios*. Root metaphors are those big analogies that help us organize our thinking on a particular subject; a minor example would be the metaphor of an atom as a miniature solar system, while a major example would be the metaphors of the human body as a machine (or the brain/mind as a computer) or of society or the universe as an organism or body. They are about modeling and thinking. Key scenarios, on the other hand, are about acting; they are the "scenes" or "plots" or bits of "story" that we tell ourselves to organize our expectations and our goals. It is not hard to see—in fact, it is probably the whole point—that these root metaphors and especially these key scenarios can be added together, associated with each, and strung end to end to create more complex models and narratives, including "myths" and "rituals." That is exactly their power and their function. They help us think about who we are and what we are supposed to do.

Box 3.1 The Sherpa Temple as a Model of Buddhist Experience

Western/Christian philosophy and religion often pronounce a radical break between humans and nature, spirit and matter, and the "inner" mental world and the external world. Robert Paul argued that these dualisms are not part of Sherpa religion, where "the whole cosmos is essentially mind and our individual minds at their inner core merge with the greater mind of the universe" (1976: 131). It follows that Sherpa Buddhists would externalize their ideas and "give material reality to as many symbolic objects as possible arising out of the inexpressible inner experience" (132). Indeed, the temple itself "may be seen as an objectification of the subjective internal experience of the Sherpa experiencing his religion" (133)—and should also be seen as a means, a technique, for instilling that subjective experience. Merely by entering the temple, a person is turning her "consciousness away from an absorption in the everyday world" and making "a commitment to a process of contact with the divine" (134). Thus, entering the temple is *going into* a Buddhist symbol and embarking on a Buddhist experience. The first stage, in the first space that the voyager encounters, is filled with more symbols—icons, artifacts, and murals—which provide a sensuous embodiment of Buddhist ideas, which in fact "represent the senses, the passions, represented by the sexual and aggressive *takbu* gods" (139). But that is the lowest level of Buddhist knowledge and reality; on the second floor, the mood shifts to contemplation. The primary objects there are books, which are "holier than images or idols" (140), although a huge statue of Ongpame, eyes half-closed in meditation, indicates that deities and humans alike are on a "mind-trip." The chapel, open only to celibate monks, features Srungma, a pre-Buddhist god who demands absolutely purity of his followers. But Paul claimed that the high point of "this initiatory process" that is the journey through the temple is a painting of Kuntu-Zangbu, the Perfectly Good One. Affixed to the ceiling, he is in meditation, but his female consort sits on his lap "in a sexual embrace" (144). "Here, finally, life, sex, and generativity have been separated from fear and death, which have been overthrown" (144). The power of life has been purified, and with it the pilgrim who has completed his journey.

Religious Symbols and Objects

Symbols, religious and otherwise, mean something, but they also *are* something. They are objects or words or actions. But they are often more; they *are* the things, powers, or persons that they "stand for." Those things, powers, or persons are *present* in the symbol. For instance, Victor Turner found that the Ndembu spoke of their symbols as *ku-solola*, not "representing" but "revealing" or "making visible" a truth or a power (1967: 48). In other words, for members of the religion, the "symbols" may be *manifestations* or *results* or *remnants* of spiritual activities or events, or else conduits through which the beings or forces act—what Mircea Eliade, the great student of comparative religion, calls a "hierophany," from *hieros* for "holy" and *phany* for "appearance" or "manifestation" (1970: 447).

In order to substantiate our claim, another brief excursion is necessary. In 1977, addressing a tradition of literature about religion and personhood in India, McKim Marriott and Ronald Inden offered the term "dividual" to describe a person who, unlike the Western "individual," is not an indivisible whole but is divisible, "partible," a composite of elements that may "come in" from the outside or "go out" from the inside. Much more recently, Karl Smith (2012) has deemed such personhood "porous" and "permeable" and insisted that we find it in Western thinking as well: we often think of having a loved one "in us" and of "putting ourselves into" our creations. Marilyn Strathern (1988) picked up this concept in her work on personhood in Melanesia.

A decade later, Alfred Gell adopted the notion of partible or "distributed" personhood in his anthropological study of art. A person, he maintained, "may be 'distributed,' i.e. all their 'parts' are not physically attached, but are distributed around the ambience" (1998: 106), including and especially in objects. That is, it is easy to experience that "a person and a person's mind are not confined to particular spatio-temporal coordinates" (namely, the organic body) but are dispersed in and among "material objects, traces, and leavings" (222). For instance, as we have already seen, a chalk statue can be an inanimate object *and at the same time* (part of) the person of San Antonio de Padua. And if religious beings (and sometimes forces) are persons, then they too can be, sometimes must be, present in material objects in the here-and-now—objects that we are inclined to call "symbols."

Sacred Spaces

One of the most persistent forms of material religious objectification is the sacred site or place. In most if not all religious traditions, "place" is deeply important for belief and worship, and such a location is not a random space but a space where *something happened* or where *something is* (the Ndembu called it *isoli* or *chisoli*, a "place of revelation"). For Judaism and Christianity, the city of Jerusalem is a "holy" place, for concrete historical reasons. Within the city, some sites are more sacred than others; for Christians, these include the locations where Jesus reportedly walked and suffered and was buried. Modern-day Christian pilgrims still perambulate along the Via Dolorosa, the path their savior trod on his way to crucifixion. Modern-day Jews still perform prayers and leave prayer-messages at the Western or "wailing" wall on which the Temple once stood (see Figure 3.1). Islam too has its holy places, in particular Mecca, the home city of the prophet Muhammad. Within the borders of Mecca, some sites are yet more sacred or holy, climaxing in the structure called the Ka'aba, regarded as the center of the Muslim world.

Other societies and religions have their sacred spaces. Mount Fuji is a center of power for Japanese, as is Mount Meru for Hindus. Rivers are often sacred sites, like the Ganges in India. Of course, wherever a spirit is believed to reside—potentially any body of water, any mountain or hill, any tree, any cave—is a candidate for sacredness or at least spiritual concentration (see Figure 3.2). It is also possible for humans to create a sacred space, either by focusing attention on an event that transpired there or by importing spiritual power or significance to the site. Christians have repeatedly built churches on sites where important events occurred, most notably the cathedral of St. Peter, the site of the

Figure 3.1 The Wailing/Western Wall in Jerusalem (early twentieth century). Courtesy of the G. Eric and Edith Matson Photograph Collection, Library of Congress Prints and Photographs Division

Figure 3.2 Offering to the mountain spirits (Japanese drawing). Courtesy of the Library of Congress Prints and Photographs Division

Catholic Vatican; this was the spot where Christians believe that the disciple Peter was killed. Cathedrals constructed where no historical precedent consecrated the ground were often provided with a sacred object—in particular a "relic" or body part of a saint—to "plant" sacredness there. In many Islamic societies the tombs of saints are sacred sites.

Spaces are religiously significant for additional reasons. The souls of the recently or remotely dead may also inhabit places, and one or more places may be the official abode of the dead (like Mt. Kinabalu or the island of Tuma; see Chapter 2). It is a widely held opinion in Native American cultures that the four (or six, if you include "up" and "down") cardinal directions are sacred. The Tewa of the American Southwest have the added benefit of four prominent mountains that stand at the cardinal directions for them. Each of these sites is regarded as an "earth navel" and as an entry way into the underworld, and even more as a place where the three levels of the world (above, middle, and below) most closely intersect. At the center of these points is the center of existence, which they refer to as "Earth mother earth navel middle place."

The Manggarai of West Flores Island in Indonesia go further than recognizing sacred sites on their land. According to Catherine Allerton, "spirit-beings merge with spirit-places" (2013: 107), and these spirits or *poti* "animate and merge with a material landscape of energies, effects, and practical consequences" (108). Still more, the spirits may be understood as a code or "shorthand" for "an energy that belongs to the land itself" (108). For the Manggarai, "the land has agency" including "appetite" and an "ability to talk"; ultimately, what appears to be spirits, the people say, is "really the land" (122). And the agency of places extends to more specific, local sites, such as the house and even the particular room; houses and rooms too are persons, and they are permeable persons that absorb the sounds, smells, and energies of their human inhabitants.

Icons/Idols

"Idol" has a negative connotation in English and in Judeo-Christian parlance, but many if not all religions—including Christianity—have had ways to represent (*re-present*, as in to make present again) the gods or spirits amidst humans. Ancient Mesopotamian and Egyptian religions included life-size or larger than life-size statues of gods, often with fantastic traits like the heads of birds or other animals. Ancient Greeks also erected likenesses of their gods, including Athena in the Parthenon at Athens. Hinduism pictures its gods in paintings and sculptures and various visual media (see Figure 3.3).

Arjun Appadurai's discussion of Hindu temple practices indicated that the objects are not "symbolic" to the worshipers: the deity located at the center of the temple

> is not a mere image. It is conceived to be, in several thoroughly concrete senses, a person. ...
>
> The ceremony of vivifying the idol (*prana pratistai*), in Puranic and Agamic texts having to do with the temples, does not seem to imply allegory or metaphor. The daily cycle of worship in the temples, involving waking up the deity, dressing and periodically feeding it, and putting it to sleep at night, implies the literal personality of the deity.
>
> (1981: 20–21)

Judaism and Islam in particular explicitly forbid visual representations of divinity, on the belief that divinity cannot possibly be visualized and that such attempts lead to "idol worship." Although an officially "aniconic" religion, Islam nevertheless has its tradition of iconic images, like the paintings and tapestries depicting key persons and events (such

Figure 3.3 Hindu god resting on a bed of snakes. Courtesy of the author

as the Battle of Karbala) used by Iranian Shi'ites in their rituals and worship (Flaskerud 2010). At a Japanese Shinto shrine (referred to as a *jinja* or "god-home") the innermost sanctuary contains a *shintai* or "god-body" in the form of a stone, a text, a weapon (e.g. sword), paper, hair, jewels, pictures, or recently a mirror (Holtom 1965: 10). Sherry Ortner (1978) reported that during Sherpa rituals the gods were invited to "take a seat" on a *torma* or molded dough figure, which became a temporary body for the gods—a body in which they could not only accept human gifts but also share human emotions.

Charms, Amulets, and Relics

All religions make or find, keep, and use objects—natural or artificial—as foci of meaning and power. Such objects of power have been called "fetishes," although that word is not frequently used anymore. Evans-Pritchard referred to Nuer fetishes or *kulangni*, pieces of wood which the Nuer testified could speak, move, and especially harm. *Kulangni*, which could be bought or inherited, were "amoral" in the sense that anyone could use their power for any purpose, and they and the people who owned them (*gwan kulangni*) were feared as dangerous (1956: 101). The Bagandu of central Africa used their power-objects as "counter-magical" protections; these items, purchased from specialists in spirituality and medicine, included natural objects like a mole's tooth, which was supposed to keep away witches (Lehmann 2001: 159). Hoebel (1960) mentioned the Medicine Arrows of the Cheyenne as a sacred object, given to them by a mythical ancestor called Sweet Medicine; the sacred Arrows had to be cared for and ceremonially renewed, or else their neglect would cause the decline of the people as well. The Arrows were also used in hunting and war, where they conferred power and success on their users.

Various religions employed a wide array of other objects. In fact, Burch and Forman maintained that for the Yupik or Inupik people of arctic North America all objects were in a sense sacred, that they "did not distinguish between the sacred and the profane, for every object had a spirit of its own, and every act, no matter what its purpose, was observed and reacted to by some spirit or other" (1988: 114). For example, they used amulets for protection and luck, usually made of natural objects or the occasionally carved piece. Such amulets, called *iinrug* or *inogo*, were normally small things, a few inches long at most, sometimes as simple as a stone or feather or animal part. Individuals would often collect up to dozens of *iinrug*, some original, some inherited, and some acquired from spiritual leaders. Owners would carry their amulets with them at all times, hung on belts, sewn on clothing, dangling around the neck, or tucked away in pouches. Charms were more often used to communicate with and control spirits and were therefore most likely the property of shamans. Sometimes small and sometimes larger (and more often human-like than amulets), persons of power would fashion them and display them on houses or boats or wield them in curing rituals.

The Islamicized Berti of Sudan provide an example of the combination of objects and texts. Their religious specialists or *faki* made amulets (*hijbat*) consisting of a piece of paper inscribed with words from the Qur'an and/or divine names and astrological symbols. The recipients sewed the paper into a leather bag or strip of cloth and used them to counteract sorcery or the evil eye, to ward off diseases or weapons, to attract wealth or customers or lovers, and to prevail in court; they could also be used for malicious purposes (Holy 1991). The Bosnian Muslim villagers of Dolina (Bringa 1995) also used amulets (*zapis*) of writing, wrapped into red cloth triangles and pinned onto clothing close to the body, like an undershirt. These charms were thought to combat evil spells and to bring happiness and good luck.

Masks

Many societies make and use masks during ritual cures or re-enactments of myth. The Yupik exercised great creative freedom in the styles they produced, from the realistic to the surreal. Formally, they were made of wood, some as long as four feet, and painted brightly in white, black, red, and blue-green. They were often decorated with feathers, quills, down, hair, fur, grass, and other materials and had amulets and charms suspended on them (see Figure 3.4).

Figure 3.4 Nunivak ceremonial mask. Courtesy of the Edward S. Curtis Collection, Library of Congress Prints and Photographs Division

They represented human, animal, and other less realistic and more or less grotesque figures. Functionally, the most visually stunning and spiritually powerful masks were made and used by specialists in ceremonial activities. Each mask existed, then, not as an "art" object or even a stand-alone power object "but as part of an integrated complex of story, song, and dance in religious and secular activity" (Ray 1967: 6).

Masks are remarkably common in both religious and secular contexts across cultures. They enable human participants to portray and impersonate, to *become* the figures, including spiritual figures, represented in ritual. The Hopi wore masks of their *kachina* spirits in their ceremonies. Balinese use masks extensively in their narrative and ritual traditions, portraying both historical and divine characters, among them the all-good Barong and the all-evil Rangda. African masks are rightly famous, used by societies all over the continent, including the Dogon.

In perhaps more familiar settings, masks were incorporated into "dramatic" activities like ancient Greek and traditional Japanese theater. Behind masks, the "actors" were not encouraged—or in fact able—to display individual expressions but were rather presenting highly stylized forms of stock characters. In fact, in a real sense, the whole point of a mask is to "hide" the individuality of the actor and to replace it completely with the person of the character he or she played.

Box 3.2 Fashioning God's Face: Masks of the Divine in a Himalayan Village

For the ritual of Dashera, Himalayan villagers carry a float (*palkhi*) through the mountains between temples and villages. Aboard each float is a *mohra*, "the material manifestation of divinity" (Hingorani 2013: 15), the face of a god. A *mohra* is usually between eight and twelve inches tall, made of cast metal and covered with a

Figure 3.5 Himalayan procession with god-masks. © Fernando Garaizabal / Alamy

thin foil of gold and silver. Actually, the *palkhi* bears more than one face of the god but up to twenty-four copies of the face, all depicting the same deity; occasionally "multiple gods travel on a single *palkhi*" but "each is nevertheless represented by more than one *mohra*" (18). Some of the *mohras* are quite old, even centuries old, but others are newer, and *mohras* are continuously remade, as artisans melt down the faces of the gods and recast them. Thus, villagers and believers know that the faces are the handicraft of humans, but the faces are the presence of the god all the same. The *mohra* is the god-in-metal, distributed across multiple objects yet one person. In fact, the very "body of the carrier becomes the instrument of the deity but is not read as contiguous with the body of the deity" (18). And the voyages that the gods make on their various chariots reflect and embody the relationships between villages: like any local citizen, the gods "leave their temples to visit gods in neighboring villages and receive them in their turn," and "the sustenance of exogamous village alliances relies on the visits of village deities" across great distances and between related sites (7).

The Human Body

Among the many ways that a community embodies its ideas and values—and its identity *as* a community—is through its treatment and manipulation of the human body itself. Indeed, Mary Douglas (1970) called the human body the ultimate "natural symbol." This can include standards of dress and comportment, including grooming. In at least some Muslim societies or subcultures, men are expected to wear beards, and of course women are expected to wear some version of the veil, from a light scarf over the head to a thorough draping of every inch of the body. Traditionalist Jewish men can still be seen wearing the long curls of hair hanging from their temples (earlocks), and many Jewish men wear the skullcap or yarmulke. At least on ritual occasions, including prayer, they may also don the prayer shawl and phylactery, a small box on a leather strap worn on the arm and the forehead which holds a verse from scripture (not unlike the Muslim amulets described above).

Other cultures ordain other forms of dress or personal presentation, especially on ceremonial occasions. The Sikhs, at least in their most "orthodox" or Khalsa community, are distinguished by five traditional markers—unshorn hair (*Kesh*); the sword (*Kirpan*), which should be worn at all times; a special type of undergarment (*Katcha*); a comb (*Kanga*); and a bracelet or bangle (*Kara*). Clothing can and often does have symbolic significance. The Muslim women of Dolina wore a type of baggy trouser (*dimije*) and headscarf to state their identity vis-à-vis the Catholic women in the village, and the men wore dark blue berets. Certain colors can have religious meaning, such as green in much of Islam. Of course, religious specialists and people participating in religious activities tend to dress and comport themselves in distinguishable and typically more "formal" ways.

From Amish farmers to Hindu yogis, people indicate their religious beliefs and their spiritual state by the manner in which they appropriate their bodies. Australian Aboriginal men scarified their chests, knocked out a front tooth, pierced their nasal septum, and circumcised and subincised their penises. Nuer pastoralists in East Africa cut scars or *gar* into the foreheads. Women across a swath of Africa and the Middle East undergo female circumcision of more or less extreme kinds. Hindu women wear a dot between their eyes to indicate their marital status, whereas mainstream Americans wear a golden ring on their left hands. Many cultures, like the Iban of Borneo, tattooed themselves grandly.

Texts

All literate religions include a set of writings in their kit of religious objects. Some of these texts are to be read by all members of the society. In other cases, the texts are secret or esoteric and only intended for the initiated or the full-time practitioners of the tradition. One function, therefore, of religious specialists may be to read, memorize, and recite these texts on religious occasions.

The fundamental text in Christianity is the Bible, and in Islam it is the Qur'an along with the Hadith, record of deeds and sayings of Muhammad. The earliest writings of Hinduism are the Vedas, books of hymns and ritual rules and practices. Epic tales like the *Ramayana* and the *Mahabharata* came later, as well as the teachings known as the Upanishads, which are more philosophical in nature. Buddhism has a huge scriptural component, including the oldest *sutras* in the Pali language but continuing into current times with books and commentaries by Tibetan, Zen, and other masters. Still more ancient religions possessed writings, from the Egyptian Book of the Dead to the Sumerian *Enuma Elish* and *Epic of Gilgamesh* to the Zoroastrian *Avestas*. Chinese religions have their *Tao Te Ching*, *Chuang Tzu*, and the works of Confucius and others, while Sikhism has its *Sri Guru Granth Sahib*, which is believed to be literally a textual "person." And new scriptures continue to appear or be written. For instance, the *Book of Mormon* was revealed in the 1800s. The *Kitab-i-Aqdas* forms the basis of the Baha'i faith, while L. Ron Hubbard's Scientology and Mary Baker Eddy's Christian Science stem from these individuals' writings. Even more non-mainstream works, from *The Urantia Book* to Gerald Gardner's works on Wicca, have provided foundations for new religions.

Texts are sometimes regarded as conveyers of ideas, but they can also be regarded as objects of power in their own right; even the very skill of writing itself may be powerful. Ladislav Holy noted that literate religious leaders (*faki*) hesitated to use literacy for any purpose other than religion. Verses from the Qur'an were respected for their inherent power to cure diseases or achieve other effects, and part of the training of a *faki* was learning which verses "worked" for which problems. Each *faki* would also assemble his own book or *umbatri* ("that which mentions everything") in which he would collect knowledge from orthodox and unorthodox sources such as astrology, dreams, and any other "secrets" he discovered (1991: 25). In some traditions, including the Islamic one, the scriptures were and are treated as sacred physical objects, which must not be mishandled or profaned.

Religious Specialists

As in all other walks of life, there are some individuals who have more knowledge or ability in religion than others. This skill may come from training, personal experience, inherent talent or spiritual power, or other such factors. These individuals may be leaders and functionaries, but they may be much more—the "conduit" through which the spirits interact with the human world or vice versa. They may "represent" and "embody" the spirits on earth as emissaries or spokespeople, or they may be those who, for one reason or another, have "broken through" the barrier between the two dimensions and can thereby interact with both.

There is great variety among religious specialists, in terms of their abilities, their practices, and the beliefs or concepts underlying them. Scholars often try to organize this diversity into types with discrete abilities and functions; however, as in other instances we have seen, actual specialists often slip through such typologies, merging aspects of different "types" and/or lacking one or more of the "typical" features. Rather, it might be better to think of religious specialization from the modular perspective—as roles that combine various powers and functions. There are certain religious "jobs to do" in a society (curing different ailments, leading specific rituals, bringing luck or preventing bad luck, enhancing fertility, producing rain, and a host of others), and those jobs can be apportioned in any number of ways. One specialist may perform a bundle of tasks, or the tasks may be assigned to an assortment of specialists. And the very tasks that exist in a society will depend on what kinds of concepts and "beliefs" and interests and goals the society has.

Shaman

One of the most celebrated of all religious characters is the shaman, sometimes called (much less politely and accurately) a witch doctor or medicine man (see Figure 3.6). The term "shaman" derives from the Siberian (specifically Tungusic) word *saman*. The unique and important thing about the shaman is that he or she is a spiritually "able" person with unique talent to achieve certain spiritual states and purposes. In fact, Mircea Eliade referred to shamanism as the "technique of ecstasy" (1964: 4).

The shaman is typically a person who shows a propensity or tendency toward certain abilities early in life, such as talent in singing, facility in entering trance, susceptibility to visions, or such other qualities. One very common element in the biography of a shaman is a serious illness in youth, from which the patient dramatically or miraculously recovers. This is evidence that he or she "has the power," and it is also often the first significant contact with the spirit world. The aspiring shaman often then becomes a student or apprentice to a senior shaman, who "teaches" the novice in ways that would not quite qualify for education in our society. The master will seldom "lecture" or "instruct" him or her about how to be a shaman. Instead, the teacher may subject the student to

Figure 3.6 Yebichai, giving the medicine: Navajo shaman with participant. Courtesy of the Edward S. Curtis Collection, Library of Congress Prints and Photographs Division

trials, like sleep deprivation, long hours of chanting, drug ingestion, seclusion, quests of various kinds, and other difficult and even painful ordeals.

A key factor in becoming a full-fledged shaman is often acquiring a helper-spirit, sometimes called a "spirit familiar." This spirit will show the apprentice things that cannot be known any other way. It will teach him or her about the spirits and give him or her a personalized set of songs, dances, symbols, and other spiritual tools. That is why a shaman cannot simply learn the knowledge of past shamans; each must have his or her own "kit," which he or she may acquire in dreams, trances, or bouts of illness. Paramount in many of these kits is the ability to enter into a dissociated state, during which the most "spiritual" of shamanic work—the shaman's "technique"—is done.

!Kung or Ju/hoansi shamans, for example, were called upon when a member of the band was sick or troubled. According to Katz (1982), nearly all men and most women attempted to become shamans, or *n/um kausi* ("master/owner of *n/um*"). Spiritual power was mostly acquired by doing the trance dance; those who demonstrated a talent for the trance state (*kia*) were said to receive *n/um* from the gods, who put the power in songs and visions; another source for the apprentice was senior shamans, who were said to give their juniors *n/um* "to drink" by shooting them with invisible arrows of power by snapping their fingers. Fortunately, there was an infinite supply of *n/um* in the world, so about half of men and one-third of women succeed in their spiritual quest.

The !Kung shaman began his or her work by singing and chanting until the *n/um* located at the base of the spine heated and boiled, rising up the spine in a painful manner. They fell, literally, into a trance; the body collapsed on the ground, because the "soul" had left it and was sojourning in the spiritual dimension. Having become a spirit, they might struggle with the ancestors (*//gauwasi*) or, in the case of especially serious illness, the great god *Gao Na*. The shaman, still in trance, regained his senses and conducted "operations" that include rubbing their own sweat on the patient, with the belief that the sweat of the shaman is spiritually potent. They also practiced a technique called *twe*, which entailed pulling the sickness out of the victim. The shaman eventually literally "swam" back to consciousness.

In Australian Aboriginal societies, shamans would often accomplish their cures by pulling objects—like stones or feathers—out of the body of the victim. Shamans also might incorporate more "mundane" elements into their cures, including potions, charms, sacrifices, and suchlike. According to Trigger (1969), Huron shamans in southeastern Canada recognized four different kinds of shamans or *arendiwane* (meaning "his supernatural power is great"): those who could make wind and rain, those who could predict the future, those who could locate lost objects, and those who could cure the sick. The last, called *ocata* or *saokata*, were considered the most important. Among the Tausug of the Philippines, the curer or *magubat* tended to be an older man, often with a reputation for odd behavior, who conducted healing ceremonies in private using a combination of spells, potions, ritual bathings, palm reading, and social advice on restitution or redress for past wrongs the sufferer may have committed (Kiefer 1972).

Priest

In conventional thinking, the priest is all of the things that a shaman is not. He or she is often a full-time specialist occupying the formal "office" of priest achieved by study, testing, and ordination by a religious institution or structure with the power and authority to invest priests. Priests may or may not be powerful individuals—some are quite ordinary people—but they hold a powerful office. Many, probably most, societies, have nothing as formal as a priest. Certainly small-scale, foraging societies do not; the !Kung and the Aboriginals did not. Even some larger-scale societies like the Swazi in Africa did not; despite the fact that they achieved a level of political integration including a king, the leader of spiritual activities was merely the family head (Kuper 1963: 60).

One becomes a priest by very different means than one becomes a shaman. Commonly, acquiring a priesthood means mastering a body of knowledge and dogma, becoming an expert in some orthodoxy (*ortho* for "correct/straight" and *doxa* for "opinion"). Individuals with deviant or heretical ideas do not tend to receive priestly offices; thus, priests tend to be agents of conservatism. In fact, they represent the institution in which they belong, rather than being the "free agents" that shamans are.

The activities of priests tend to be different as well. The occasional priest may engage in curing practices. However, more often priests are ritual leaders, functionaries who organize, conduct, and preside over more formulaic ritual situations. Priests are not as encouraged to improvise or receive their own private spiritual instructions or resources; they do not, for instance, have spirit familiars. In many societies, every time a priest performs or leads a ritual, it should be exactly the same, down to the finest detail. The efficacy of the ritual may depend on each bit of it being correctly done.

The priesthood, while not always hereditary, may have a hereditary component. In the Jewish Torah and the Christian Old Testament, one particular lineage or clan, the Levites, was presented with the honor of being the priestly group. This suggests and requires a certain amount of social stratification: presumably, it is better and more prestigious to be in the priestly clan than a non-priestly one. Hindu *brahmans* also constitute a closed succession (caste) of priests, and in traditional Hawaiian society priesthood was an inherited rank.

So, priesthood tends to be associated with social stratification, institutionalization of religion, and even the equation of religious with political power. In South India in particular, as described by Beals, the system of priests followed the system of gods; there were various kinds of gods, from the benevolent "high" gods served by a class of vegetarian priests, to lower goddesses that protected or punished humans and were approached through non-vegetarian priests of lower caste (1962: 47–48). Priests, especially in larger, richer, and more centralized societies, tended to be full-time employees of the religious establishment, depending on a considerable surplus to support them, and they often exercised "secular" or political power as well as religious. In fact, as we have noted, high political office may mix politics and religion, as with the king or emperor controlling the priests or being the chief priest or even a god himself.

Even more so, in societies with blended traditions—especially one in which a "world religion" like Christianity or Islam has mingled with and superimposed itself on an indigenous tradition, we may find priests coexisting with shamans or other specialists in a kind of spiritual "division of labor." Among the Tausug, shamans and curers handled the indigenous spirits and ghosts through shamanic skills and practices. However, the "official" religion was managed by Islamic priests who formed a hierarchy from novice (*bilal*) to master (*imam*) and even high master (*imam muwallum*). The priests acquired their position through knowledge of the Islamic literature and ordination. Likewise, among the Aymara of Bolivia, curers or magicians (*yatiri*) shared the spiritual field with Catholic-based priests, who presided over masses, funerals, Christian holidays, and the ceremony having to do with twins (Buechler and Buechler 1971). We will return to this issue in Chapter 8.

Diviner/Oracle

Especially in societies with gods or powerful and well-known spirits, it can be extremely valuable to know what those beings want or intend. The diviner/oracle has the ability to read or interpret the will of spirits, sometimes by asking direction questions and examining some material manifestation of an answer. Astrology has traditionally been a divining activity, looking for traces of divine communication in the stars. Any number of other kinds of signs are read for spiritual meaning, from tea leaves and coins to the bones or entrails of animals; a diviner may put a question or request to the spirits, then kill and study the body of an animal for indications of an answer. The Azande chicken-oracle administered poison to a chicken for a quick answer. Probably the most famous oracle in Western history was the Greek oracle at Delphi, where citizens—including kings and generals—would ask advice from young priestesses who would give cryptic responses while in a trance. Decisions to go to war and other epoch-making decisions were settled this way.

The Bunyoro of Uganda practiced divination for illness, childlessness, theft, and other offenses and misfortunes. Beattie (1960) characterized most diviners as "doctors" too, diagnosing and curing physical problems in shamanic style. The most common method of divination among Bunyoro was throwing cowry shells and reading the resultant pattern; however, other techniques included throwing small leather squares, sprinkling water, rubbing blood on a stick to see where the hand sticks to it, and reading the entrails of animals. The Swazi of South Africa also practiced divination, and diviners or *tangoma* were regarded as more important and powerful than curers or medicine men, although their role was diagnosis, not cure. Their abilities came from spirit possession, which explains why women were more often diviners than men, since they were more easily "possessed" than men. Swazi diviners conducted seances to communicate with the dead, tossed bones to read the pattern, and performed a poison oracle similar to the Azande.

Among the Kaguru, the diviner or *muganga* was almost always a senior male, and his power was used regularly to combat the effects of witchcraft and sorcery. For their divination (*maselu*) work they incorporated various techniques such as "gazing into bowls of water, casting stones, seeds, or sandals, or poisoning chickens and watching how they flutter" (Beidelman 1971: 36). The Barabaig diviner or *sitetehid* manipulated a pile of stones and studied the patterns for messages, usually involving witches or angry ancestor spirits, although he did not actually perform the cure, which was turned over to another specialist. Outside of Africa, the Menomini Indians had a role called *ceseko*, sometimes translated as "juggler," who combined the functions of diviner and shaman: they would diagnose spiritual illness, listening for voices in the wind that blew against their special-purpose lodge and responding via the medium of a turtle. To cure witchcraft they would call the victim's soul to enter a small wooden cylinder, which they would return to the family, or they would suck out the witches' infection (an "arrow"), which they spat out in the form of "a maggot, a fly, a quill, or some other small object" that had entered the body (Spindler and Spindler 1971: 45).

Prophet/Medium

Prophets offer another solution to the problem of divine silence. A prophet is an individual who receives direct communication from the spirits, often quite involuntarily (recall how Moses and other Hebrew patriarchs were often reluctant to take on the role), and is then charged with the obligation to pass that communication along to other humans.

Prophecy, which is often confused with telling the future, is a bulwark in the Christian tradition, and Muhammad is revered among Muslims for being not only a prophet but "the seal of prophets"—the final and authoritative one. His prophecy, received as a recitation or Qur'an from God and his angels themselves, was to complete and correct all prophecies. Obviously, though, there have been many since who believed they were prophets, both within and outside the Judeo-Christian-Muslim tradition.

In a way, both shamans and diviners are mediums in that they provide the "mediation" between the mundane and spiritual worlds. Dozier (1967) referred to the medium as the only religious specialist among the Kalinga of the Philippines and went on to attribute to them many of the skills or powers of the shaman or diviner, including curing illness (by guiding the soul of the ill person back after its capture by a malicious spirit or ancestor). Kalinga mediums underwent a "calling" similar to a shaman, and most of them were women.

Ascetic/Monk/Mendicant

In a variety of religious traditions, there are those who voluntarily remove themselves from society and cloister or even scourge themselves, either for their own benefit or for the benefit of their family, village, society, or species. Ascetics are specifically people who choose a difficult, even painful, existence for themselves out of some religious motivation. There is certainly an ascetic tradition in Christianity, flowing from a combination of the general sinfulness of human nature and the need to avoid physical (especially carnal) pleasure together with a condemnation of wealth as an obstacle to spiritual pursuit. Hence, some Christians, at least since the time of St. Anthony (*c.* 300 CE), who withdrew into solitary existence in Egypt, have valued a rejection of "worldliness"; in fact, Anthony's example set the standard for monasticism, in which groups of men (or women, in the case of nunneries) would seclude themselves from the world and focus on their spiritual business.

From the monastery comes the monk, who chooses (usually) this set-apart life for himself. Again, he may do this for his own personal spiritual advancement. The Buddhist tradition, especially in its Theravada form, emphasizes this course: the spiritual seeker should abandon worldly goods, or at least worldly attachments, and become a full-time spiritual practitioner. However, one person's quest cannot possibly aid another person's, any more than one person's antibiotic treatment can cure another person's infection. Eventually, various local Buddhist traditions developed the notion of having monks perform their spiritual exercises for the good of the whole family or community or even the dead. At the same time, this is often the path to an education, since the monastery may be the center of literacy in the community.

The life of the mendicant (who lives off of alms and donations) or ascetic is a difficult one. In its most complete form, it entails the rejection of family and other social obligations, often a wandering lifestyle, and usually a deprived condition in terms of food and comfort. The ascetic, monk, or mendicant may own little or nothing and beg for his/her meal; a classic Buddhist mendicant owns only a robe, sandals, and a begging bowl, and they can be seen today looking for offerings of food, which "make merit" for the giver. In Hindu theory, asceticism or mendicancy is not so much a choice as a life stage. Although not all follow the prescription, the life of a man should culminate in the phase of *sannyasin* in which he renounces his home and family and embarks on the itinerant spiritual life; this stage only comes in later life, after he has completed the stages of student and householder. At this final stage of life, his main concern is and must be his own spiritual progress. In more than a few cases, asceticism crosses the line to self-mortification (see Chapter 10).

Sorcerer

Sorcerers are generally people who are believed to exercise spiritual power, typically for the worse, through specific technical means. That is, sorcery might be classed as a subset of *magic*, which is normally thought of as an instrumental action in which certain gestures or behaviors "automatically" lead to certain results. The sorcerer, then, can be conceived of as a person who performs "black magic" or such activities as ordinarily cause evil or harm.

Among the Bunyoro, sorcery was not only a great but actually a growing concern. Like many societies, they believed that little if any misfortune befalls people accidentally; there were few if any "natural" causes. The Bunyoro sorcerer used a mixture of natural and supernatural means to inflict intentional harm, usually on those fairly close to him in proximity and kinship. As one of Beattie's informants told him:

> A sorcerer is a person who wants to kill people. He may do it by blowing medicine toward them, or by putting it in the victim's food or water, or by hiding it in the path where he must pass. People practice sorcery against those whom they hate. They practice it against those who steal from them, and also against people who are richer than they are. Sorcery is brought about by envy, hatred, and quarreling.
>
> (1960: 73)

Similarly, the Kapauku of New Guinea feared and disliked the sorcerer or *kego epi me*. The Kapauku sorcerer had his own supernatural powers, not emanating from any spirit-familiar like that of a shaman. Rather, he secretly performed spells and magical processes (including imitative magic) to injure or kill his victim. Anyone suspected of sorcery was avoided or even ostracized, and in extreme circumstances might be killed by the family of his alleged victim (Pospisil 1963).

On the Pacific atoll of Ulithi, people hired sorcerers clandestinely to do evil to those "whom they feel are guilty of ill will or overt action against them" (Lessa 1966: 71). The materials utilized in this setting included "magical starfish, live lizards, and coconut oil" that had been sung over and planted in or near the victim's house; also potions might be poured on the victim's comb or clothing (72). Apache sorcerers had an array of techniques to draw from, including poisons, spells, and "injection" of a foreign substance into the person's body. Males were more often sorcerers because they were held to be more prone to *kedn* or "anger" than women. Spell sorcery, the most varied type, tended to involve ritual actions in fours, such as walking around the victim's person or home four times or situating four pieces of wood in the cardinal directions around his or her residence. Sorcery could be aimed not only at the person but at other things, including their animals and even personal property.

Witch

The traditional image of the witch in the Western world is female, old and ugly, wearing a wide-brimmed pointy hat. This is a cultural picture at best. As a cultural concept, witchcraft is very diverse, but the common thread across cultures is that witches are responsible for bad things that happen to people—often all bad things. In one of the classic studies of witchcraft, Evans-Pritchard, who is largely responsible for the anthropological conception of witchcraft and sorcery, argued that the Azande of the Sudan saw witches at work everywhere:

> If blight seizes the ground-nut crop it is witchcraft; if the bush is vaingloriously scoured for game it is witchcraft; if women laboriously bale water out of a pool and are rewarded by but a few small fish it is witchcraft; if termites do not rise when their swarming is due and a cold useless night is spent in waiting for their flight it is witchcraft; if a wife is sulky and unresponsive to her husband it is witchcraft; if a prince is cold and distant with his subjects it is witchcraft; if a magical rite fails to achieve its purpose it is witchcraft; if, in fact, any failure or misfortune falls upon anyone at any time and in relation to any of the manifold activities of his life it may be due to witchcraft.
>
> (1937: 18–19)

Some societies believed that a witch was a person with an innate, even anatomical, power to do harm; the witch may have an extra organ in his or her chest that holds negative spiritual power. Witch-power may actually be involuntary, at least initially; they may simply exude negativity in ways that even they do not understand or control. Or they may practice, sharpen, and intentionally employ their power for their benefit, especially against rivals, including rival witches.

The Swazi recognized witches as well as sorcerers, which they categorized together as *batsakatsi* or "evil-doers." As noted, they believed that witches had an innate physiological and psychological potential for evil, whereas sorcerers depended on "technique." The talent for witchcraft belonged to men and women, but only women transmitted it to children. Further, the inborn ability must be developed into real witchcraft skill by training and by infusions of evil power. To this end, witches formed congregations or covens, in which they practiced their craft and ranked themselves according to their malevolent achievements. The Kaguru also said that witches (*wahai*) were congenitally evil people, the ontological opposite of normal human beings. Like the Bunyoro, they also believed that witchcraft was actually more, not less, common than in the past—no doubt reflecting the increased stresses associated with the modern age. The Dani of New Guinea held a mutated view on witchcraft: they themselves did not do it—they didn't even know how. However, their neighbors practiced it, by physical (e.g. poison) or supernatural (e.g. pointing a stick at a victim) means. There are even tales of Dani hunting down and killing suspected witches among their neighbors, although witchcraft did not seem to be as relentless a preoccupation for them as for some societies (Heider 1979). Finally, the Menonimi took it to be the case that all powerful elders were potential witches.

According to the Burmese studied by Spiro, witches filled out a spiritual world that also included souls of the dead, ogres, Buddhist deities, and the multifarious *nats*. Some informants claimed that witches were not even human but evil spirits in a human guise; also, they did not make a sharp distinction between sorcery and witchcraft. A witch might have innate evil powers or the learned and acquired power more usually associated with a sorcerer. They distinguished two main types, the witch (*soun*) and the master witch (*aulan hsaya*). The *soun* was almost always female, recognizable by her dimly colored eyes; her power could be inherent or learned, with the learned witches being less powerful but more deliberately evil (since they sought out the ability actively). They were believed to cause various illnesses and to eat feces by detaching their heads and rolling along the ground. They might also work in conjunction with bad spirits. The master witch was much more powerful and always male. He did his dirty work by controlling evil spirits, feeding them raw meat until they became dependent on him. Interestingly, though, there were also good master witches (*ahtelan hsaya*) who could counteract the malice of *aulan hsaya*.

Box 3.3 The Field of Religious Specialists in Thai Buddhism

According to Stanley Tambiah, whom we met in the previous chapter when discussing cosmology, village Buddhism in Thailand consisted of a range of mutually dependent specialists (see Figure 3.7). The most orthodox of the Buddhist specialists was the *bhikkhu* or monk, who lived separated from society in the temple or *wat*. Most young males entered monkhood and during their time in the temple seldom visited the village or interacted with other people. The only service they performed, other than providing laypeople with an opportunity to earn merit by offering alms, was funeral rituals. Most monks eventually left the *wat* and resumed their ordinary lives. In addition to the *bhikkhus*, there was another category of specialists called *paahm*, from the Hindu term "brahman." These men were elders and former monks who performed *sukhwan* rites to bind or strengthen the soul or *khwan* to the body during occasions when that bond was likely to weaken. Such occasions included travel, marriage, illness, and starting new ventures—the kinds of activities that young people tend to engage in. Thus, a cycle of specialists and specialist performances characterized the village, in which young males became Buddhist *bhikkhu* to earn merit for their elders and to perform funeral rites for them, while older males became *paahms* to perform ceremonies for the young.

Figure 3.7 Buddhist monks in Thailand. Courtesy of the author

But even these two categories did not exhaust the specialist diversity in the village. Beyond the *tapassi* or hermit/ascetic, there was an entire spectrum of functionaries in a spiritual division of labor. The *mau song* was a diviner and diagnostician, while the *mau du* was an astrologer and fortune teller, the *mau mau* was a finder of lost objects, and the *mau ya* was a herbal healer. Then there were the individuals who specialized in dealing with particular kinds of spirits. The *mau ram* was a medium for the *phii* spirits, and the *cham* and *tiam* were exorcists of major spirits such as Tapubaan or Chao Phau Phraa Khao. The *tiam* would be possessed by the latter spirit, whereas the *cham* would not be possessed, but both attempted to placate the spirits with offerings, including meat and alcohol, both forbidden by orthodox Buddhism.

Conclusion

Religion is about ideas and beliefs but even more about power and effectiveness. And while transcendent and abstract, it must be made immanent and concrete in order for it to have that power and effectiveness. Objects, actions, places, and people can all be manifestations of and conduits to religious beings and forces. Sometimes these manifestations may be "symbolic" in the familiar sense, as standing for or reminding of other, non-natural and nonhuman phenomena. Sometimes, though, they are not mere stand-ins or reminders but, to the believers and practitioners, real containers, products, or presences of supernatural power. Geertz called symbols vehicles for meanings, but at least in some cases they are vehicles for actions, vitalities, and effects. We should not impose intellectualist interpretations where the members view themselves as *doing* something. And of course doing requires a doer, a human actor or intermediary. Since religion is fundamentally a "social" relationship between the human and the nonhuman, some persons must take their place as the partner or contact-point with the supernatural—a role of power and danger, precisely *because of* the power involved.

DISCUSSION QUESTIONS

- What is materiality, and why do (and must) all religions take some material forms?
- What is Alfred Gell's notion of "distributed personhood," and how is it relevant to religious objects and practices?
- What are the main kinds of religious specialists, and what tasks do they characteristically perform?

SUPPLEMENTARY READING (see website)

- *Spirits' Matter: Spirit and Body among the Iu-Mien of Laos*
- *Sharing Sacred Space: Co-existence in Religious Places*
- *The Problem with Shamans: Shamanism in Contemporary Nepal and Mongolia*

4 Religious Language

In the Taiwanese Taoist rite of *che ngo-kui* ("controlling/propitiating the Five Ghosts"), the specialist who called himself *ang-thau hoat-su* or "Red-Head Master of Magic" engaged in a negotiation with demons. The divination process involved a number of physical objects, including a writing brush, a plate of uncooked rice, a basket, and paper dolls representing specific demons. However, the most important part of the negotiation, like any negotiation, was talk. First the master addressed the demons, respectfully identifying the patient and demanding "that the demons take his patient's offering and leave her alone" (McCreery 1995: 149). Next, in even more respectful verse, he invoked the god, asking for help while claiming authority for himself and issuing a threat to destroy the demons. Third, he consecrated a "substitute" or effigy of the patient (a doll made of rice straw and dressed in the patient's shirt), uttering an incantation in a "peremptory" tone, "like an adult addressing a child," commanding that the substitute carry away the sufferer's afflictions (152). Fourth, in an informal and "jocular" verging on rude style, he attempted to bribe the demons with "extra offerings of spirit money" (152); in this manner the master "displays contempt for them" (153). Finally, the demons were exorcised; his voice rose to a shout, "both fierce and controlled, the embodiment of authority" (156).

As (distributed) persons, religious beings, forces, and objects interact socially with humans, and one universal form of human social interaction is language. Religious beings/forces/objects talk to us, and we talk to them. And just as humans adopt different linguistic styles (words, grammar, titles, tones of voice) depending upon whom they are talking to and what they are talking about, so religious language relies on a variety of styles appropriate to the occasion. Indeed, Webb Keane has argued that "no single set of formal or pragmatic features is diagnostic of religious as opposed to other marked uses of language, such as poetic or ceremonial speech. Rather, different religious practices seem to select from among the entire spectrum of linguistic possibilities" (1997: 48). So, just as religious emotions are simply human emotions directed toward religious figures, and religious action is simply human action directed toward religious figures, so religious language is simply human language directed toward religious figures.

The present chapter explores religious language. Often, including in anthropological analyses, this has been taken to mean *myth*. Myth is in fact an extremely common and important form of religious speech but by no means the only form. There are other major genres, such as prayer, incantations or "magical speech," songs, proverbs or wisdom literature, and liturgies, which also deserve our attention. Accordingly, we will begin with myth in this discussion but also refer to these other verbal forms.

Central to the anthropological perspective on religious language is the notion that it, like all language, is *action*. Even telling a myth (or more commonly, acting out a myth) is social behavior, and as for the Taiwanese master of demons above, speaking to spirits is social interaction. This means that we must pay attention not only to the "ideas" and the "meanings" in speech but to the actual *performance* of language. And attention to performance also directs attention to results. What is interesting and important is the "effectiveness" of speech: people often speak not so much to describe something as to *achieve* something. Words have—words are—power.

Myth as Religious Language

Humans can do many things with language—state facts, ask questions, issue commands, express emotions, etc. One thing all humans do with language is to tell stories, to present happenings in a "narrative" format such that they are connected in a processual way (i.e. occurring or unfolding in time). Events, in a narrative form, do not occur randomly but have coherence and significance, that is, they signify something; there is a theme (often a "moral") to the story, even (or especially) if it is a life story or biography.

A myth is a particular kind of story, specifically one involving the doings of the spirits or human ancestors. Myths, in a word, are narratives about the activities and adventures of these beings. As Mircea Eliade expressed it:

> Myth narrates a sacred history; it relates an event that took place in primordial Time, the fable time of the beginnings. In other words, myth tells how, through the deeds of Supernatural Beings, a reality came into existence, be it the whole of reality, the Cosmos, or only a fragment of reality—an island, a species of plant, a particular kind of human behavior, an institution. Myth, then, is always an account of a "creation"; it relates how something was produced, began to *be*. Myth tells only of that which *really* happened, which manifested itself completely. The actors in myths are Supernatural Beings. ... Hence myths disclose their creative activity and reveal the sacredness (or simply the supernaturalness) of their works.
>
> (1998: 5–6)

Thus, myths are frequently creation or origin stories, in which superhuman beings are the characters and protagonists. The myths tell us what transpired "in the beginning"—not always or necessarily in the beginning of time, but in the beginning of some particular fact or phenomenon, natural or social. As such, they are treated as *true* stories, an accurate account of events, by those who tell them (i.e. no one calls their own myths "myths").

Myths, thus, not only represent an explanation for things but also, like many religious symbols, a *hierophany*, an appearance of the sacred amidst the profane or mundane. Eliade added that "myths describe the various and sometimes dramatic breakthroughs of the sacred (or the 'supernatural') into the world. ... It is this sudden breakthrough of the sacred that really *establishes* the World and makes it what it is today" (6). The interventions or manifestations of the superhuman give the natural and social world its shape and character; the natural and social come from and depend on the supernatural and superhuman in some essential way.

While myth is characteristically taken to "explain" something, to answer some factual question about the origin or disposition of reality, as explanations myths confront one serious objection—that they are fanciful, contradictory, usually unprovable, and often enough patently false. One religion's myth might explain the origin of humans in one supernatural way and another religion's myth in another and completely incompatible way. Especially when it comes to *other people's religions*, it has been common, as Radcliffe-Brown said, to treat them as "systems of erroneous and illusory beliefs" (1965: 153). In fact, people typically regard their own religious stories as true, retaining "myth" to designate other people's (false) stories.

To avoid this attitude, and to emphasize the social value (regardless of the "truth") of myth, Bronislaw Malinowski proposed a very different approach. Myth for him was not explanatory or "etiological" (concerned with causes) at all. He strenuously suggested that myth is not speculative storytelling or question-answering or even holy history but something else. "Myth is not a savage speculation about origins of things born out of philosophic interest. Neither is it the result of the contemplation of nature—a sort of symbolic representation of its laws," he wrote (1948: 83–84). If myth is not speculative and explanatory, then what is it? He answered this question in what is probably the most oft-quoted passage in all his writings:

> Studied alive, myth … is not symbolic, but a direct expression of its subject matter; it is not an explanation in satisfaction of a scientific interest, but a narrative resurrection of a primeval reality, told in satisfaction of deep religious wants, moral cravings, social submissions, assertions, even practical requirements. Myth fulfills in primitive culture an indispensable function: it expresses, enhances, and codifies belief; it safeguards and enforces practical rules for the guidance of man. Myth is thus a vital ingredient of human civilization; it is not an idle tale, but a hard-worked active force; it is not an intellectual explanation or an artistic imagery, but a pragmatic charter of primitive faith and moral wisdom.
>
> (101)

In other words, myth "is not merely a story told but a reality lived. It is not of the nature of fiction, such as we read today in a novel, but it is a living reality, believed to have once happened in primeval times, and continuing ever since to influence the world and human destinies" (100). Therefore, he concluded, myth should not be treated as explanation or as symbol but rather in terms of how it motivates people and shapes their lives and realities. Rather than a factual description, it is a plan, a model (a "model *for*," as Geertz put it), or—in Malinowski's own word—a "charter" or guideline for life.

Others continued to stress the symbolic approach to myth and religion but also to apply it to the problem of living in social reality. Cassirer, we noted, saw that as history or as explanation, myth fails, being full of "errors and heresies." The only option was to view myth as "nontheoretical in its very meaning and essence" (1954: 99). Myth does not attempt to make factual and true statements or explanations about the natural world, because such a world "does not exist for myths. The world of myth is a dramatic world—a world of actions, of forces, of conflicting powers. In every phenomenon of nature it sees the collision of these powers. Mythical perception is always impregnated with these emotional qualities" (102). For Suzanne Langer too, while myths are told in language, they should not be treated like ordinary discursive or propositional speech. Myth is more like a dream (also a narrative) than a fact, "the primitive phase of metaphysical thought, the first embodiment of general ideas" (1942: 163). But we cannot look to myth for "explanations" and certainly not for "solutions," as that is not its function or intent. It is a different kind of talk than empirical and descriptive (let alone scientific) talk.

This approach has been given its most recent treatment in the work of Karen Armstrong. Following the tradition of Freud and Jung, she distinguishes between *mythos* and *logos* as two modes of thought and speech. *Mythos* refers to a perspective that is not directed toward or concerned with "practical" matters and is not meant to be taken "literally." It is an ancient form of psychology, bringing into the light obscure and otherwise inaccessible regions of the unconscious. It is not and does not attempt to be "factual" or rational, and so it cannot be demonstrated or verified. It tends to speak the language of history, or cast itself in historical terms, but the historical events of which it speaks are not specific and unique occurrences in the past but rather "external manifestations of constant, timeless realities" (2000: xv). *Logos*, on the other hand, is the logical, the rational, the pragmatic, the literal and, in our time, the "scientific." It is propositional, that is, it makes claims that are either true or false and can be verified or falsified as such. It is functional rather than expressive, goal-oriented rather than contemplative or playful. The relationships that it suggests between phenomena are causal rather than metaphorical or analogical, and the events that it describes are particular and unique rather than "typical" or "eternal."

What myth, then, purports to do is to express or clothe the timeless or eternal or at least "non-temporal" in a specific and temporal guise. For instance, when a myth tells of the Creation, what it is really expressing is something about creativity. Or when it speaks about a Birth and Resurrection, it is really talking about the general cycle of birth and death and rebirth. The "events" in myth, from this perspective, are not events at all but rather ideal or typical situations—situations that did not happen just once long ago but that happen (or should happen) continuously. To say it another way, myths are less about the "then" than the "now." They set the stage—and the standard—for our present lives.

Types and Themes of Myth

Myths are highly diverse. Still, perhaps because humans have a limited set of typical or even archetypical experiences, there are certain recurring motifs and elements across cultures. Creation is one obvious and compelling theme, understandably since religion attributes most of the creativity to non- and superhuman beings and forces. Myths often describe how the universe as a whole, the earth in its present form, human beings, and social institutions began (see Chapter 2). There is a tremendous amount of latitude in such matters, yet some motifs appear again and again. For instance, Rooth (1957) investigated 300 North American Indian creation myths and determined that 250 of them fell within eight general types:

1 Earth-diver, in which some being retrieves mud or sand from the bottom of a primordial body of water, from which the earth grows;
2 World-parents, in which creation ensues from the joining of a Sky Father and an Earth Mother;
3 Emergence, in which the human world begins when ancestral beings emerge from a lower world;
4 Spider as Creator, in which a spider-like being weaves the world like a web;
5 Creation of the World through Struggle and Robbery, in which a supernatural being (like Prometheus) steals something and gives it to humans, or else fights other supernatural beings (giants, dragons, etc.) out of which the world is made;
6 Ymir Type, in which the world is created out of the dead body of a slain giant or a primordial man or woman;

7 Two Creators, in which two beings—sometimes brothers, sometimes father and son or uncle and nephew—create the world jointly, often as part of a competition or a display for each other;

8 Blind Brother, in which one brother blinds the other in some sort of trick, such as getting him to open his eyes before reaching the surface during an emergence moment (note in the supplemental reading the significance of keeping one's eyes closed until the right moment in the Huichol pilgrimage).

Many of these themes can also be found in other cultural areas, and other themes can also be found in those areas. In fact, Clyde Kluckhohn (1965) conducted a more extensive survey of recurrent themes in world mythology and derived a list of six common motifs across the fifty societies he studied: a flood element in thirty-four of the fifty societies, a monster-slaying element in thirty-seven, an incest element in thirty-nine, a sibling rivalry element in thirty-two, a castration element, including four cases of actual castration and five of threats, and an androgynous deity element in seven.

Myths are repositories for cultural ideas about issues like cosmology and cosmogony, which are usually if not always portrayed in mythic terms. Evans-Pritchard retold an Azande story, which he maintained was the only creation myth in their religion. In it:

> Bapaizegino, or Bapai, who is the same person as Mbori [the high god], put mankind with the rest of creation into a kind of round canoe which he completely closed except for a small hidden entrance by which it could be opened. The entrance he closed with wax. Bapaizegino sent a messenger ... to his sons, the Sun, the Moon, the Night, the Cold, and the Stars, to say that he was dying and that they were to come immediately. All the sons of Bapaizegino received well their father's messenger at their homes and each showed him the path to the home of the next son, but it was the Sun alone who treated him with the consideration a messenger from their father deserved. Here we find Zande notions of princely obligations colouring the story. The sons of Bapaizegino should have behaved as a son of King Gdubwe would have done had a messenger from his father arrived at this court. This is just the way a Zande king might have tested the character of his son. For the messenger, in one version, acting on his master's orders, chose the Sun on account of his munificence to the greatest of the sons of Bapaizegino and explained to him the secret of opening the round canoe which contained mankind. He told him to look for a stain, made with fruit of the *mbiango* ... tree, on its surface, and when he saw that he would know that there was the hidden opening.
>
> When the sons of Bapaizegino arrived he told them that he had sent for them to open the round canoe of the universe and had it placed in the centre of them. Each in turn made an attempt to open it without success. When the Sun was called upon he saw this stain but pretended he had seen nothing and so appeared to meet with failure like the other sons. Their father upbraided them for their inability to open the canoe and the Sun then stepped forward a second time and scraped away with his nail the wax beneath the stain and with a great noise poured out men and beasts and trees and grasses and rivers and hills. The first clan of men to emerge were the Ambata, the Men, so-called because Bapaizegino has used up all the names he could think of on the other clans.

(1962: 315–16)

Myths can also recount the origins of human institutions or social relations, making those institutions or relations good and right. A Bunyoro myth narrated the origins of servitude and kingship, based on the primordial actions of a set of siblings. The first human father, Kintu or "the created thing," had three sons. The boys were given two tests. First, six objects were placed where the boys would find them—an ox's head, a cowhide thong, a bundle of cooked millet and potatoes, a grass head-ring (for carrying loads on the head), an axe, and a knife.

> When the boys come upon these things, the eldest picks up the bundle of food and starts to eat. What he cannot eat he carries away, using the head-ring for this purpose. He also takes the axe and the knife. The second son takes the leather thong, and the youngest takes the ox's head, which is all that is left. In the next test the boys have to sit on the ground in the evening, with their legs stretched out, each holding on his lap a wooden milk-pot full of milk. They are told that they must hold their pots safely until morning. At midnight the youngest boy begins to nod, and he spills a little of his milk. He wakes up with a start, and begs his brothers for some of theirs. Each gives him a little, so that his pot is full again. Just before dawn the eldest brother suddenly spills all his milk. He, too, asks his brothers to help fill his pot from theirs, but they refuse, saying that it would take too much of their milk to fill his empty pot. In the morning their father finds the youngest son's pot full, the second son's nearly full, and the eldest son's quite empty.
>
> (Beattie 1960: 11–12)

These decisions settled the identity and fate of the sons and their descendants forever. The first son and his line would always be servants and farmers, laboring for his younger brothers and their descendants; he was named "Kairu" or peasant. The second son and his descendants would have the elevated status of cattle herders; he was called "Kahmua," little cowherd. The youngest son would be political heir and leader, so he was named "Kakama," little Mukama or ruler. His descendants became the kings of Bunyoro.

Some societies, like the Kaguru, apparently lacked a cosmogonic myth altogether, although they did have social-origin myths, especially to account for the kinship (clan) distinctions within their society. Beidelman recounted:

> Kaguru sometimes compare this birth of Kaguru society to the birth of a person; as humans are born from out of the land of the ancestral ghosts, so too the Kaguru nation emerged from the north and west, two directions associated with the dead and birth. Some even say that the people marched in a column with the women to the left and the men to the right, directions associated ... with femininity and masculinity, and with subordinate and superordinate status. While there is a general legend common to all Kaguru, this varies in detail from clan to clan. Kaguru may cite this legend to prove their common origin and thus explain their common culture, but they also use it as a means to account for the differences in Kaguru society, differences which provide the most basic feature of Kaguru social organization. That feature is clanship: Kaguru are divided into about one-hundred exogamous, matrilineal clans (*ikolo* or *kolo* or *ikungugo*). Clan size varies from a few hundred to several thousand members. ... Kaguru say that although they may have left their original homeland without such social distinctions (no one stresses this point, however), somewhere en route clans came into being. Most clans derive their names from a series of events

said to have occurred during the migration to present-day Kaguruland. Some clans are also said to be related to one another, and this too is explained through such legends.

(1971: 32–33)

Myths often account for specific roles in society, including religious roles themselves. Hence, a specialist position like shaman or priest is often given mythical origins and sanction. Goldman reported the myth of the first Cubeo shaman or *paye*.

> Once there were no *payes*. A youth named Djuri wishing to become a *paye* went to the forest … and sat in a small clearing and thought about how he should go about making thunder. While he was deep in thought, Onponbu [Thunder Man], the owner of *dupa* appeared. He knew the thoughts of the youth and he could see that he had a clean body. He decided to make him *yavi* [literally "jaguar," another term for shaman] and set down beside the boy three objects—a fragment of *dupa* [a resin believed to have supernatural origin], a small container of beeswax, and a tray of eagle down. The youth prepared the *dupa* and beeswax for inhaling and he also inserted the eagle down up his nostrils from where it moved to lodge in his head.
>
> That night he had visions, and he then understood how to make thunder. In his visions, he saw the houses where the *payes* gathered and saw that there were very many in them. He slept and when he awoke before dawn, he heard the first thundering in the East where the rivers fall off the earth. He fell asleep again and dreamt that Onponbu was asking him if he was satisfied with what he had been given and if he believed he had learned how to make thunder. Onponbu advised him how to live. He cautioned him not to sleep with a woman. "You must guard the conduct of your life," he told him. "You must not eat what others eat. You are to eat only farinha of starch. … You should not eat anything hot or take food directly from the hand of a woman. Set hot food aside until it turns cold, and it will cause you no harm."

(2004: 303–10)

Onponbu proceeded to give the boy many gifts, including thunder and lightning. He also taught him to seek out specific powerful plants. And he transformed the boy into a shaman by literally changing his body, inserting spines into his forearms and putting a stick in his mouth. Finally, he received ritual objects, like a rattle with small stones inside, a feather crown, and stone and bark ornaments.

Humans cannot help but note, and therefore myth cannot help but deal with the fact, that all is not well in the natural or social world. Thus, one recurring motif across cultures is the "trickster" or ambiguous spirit character, who causes misfortune through its ignorance, innocence, or mischief. Especially well known in Native American cultures, the Pacific Islanders of Ulithi also had a version of the trickster myth, involving the god Iolofath, son of Lugeilang and a human woman and grandson of Ialulep the Great Spirit. He was responsible for some of the noisome qualities of life. According to the story, as he ascended to his father's domain in the Sky World he stopped at each of the four levels to make his unfortunate mark. First he was rebuked by some boys who were fishing, and he gave the fish spines to pierce the boys. On the second level other boys rejected him, so he gave the shark they were playing with teeth to bite them. Rebuffed on the third level, he made the stinger of the sting ray to harm those boys.

Reaching the fourth level he finds men fetching timber to build the great house of the Sky World known as Farmal. They are all fish but have human attributes, gliding back and forth, imperceptible in their appearance between the piscatory and the anthropomorphic.

The people of the fourth level are digging a hole into which to plant the great housepost of the Farmal. On seeing Iolofath they decide to kill him because he is a stranger. They induce him to go into the posthole and then they ram the post down on him. Red and green fluids squirt upwards and the people think this is his blood and bile, but he has tricked them by taking refuge in a pocket he has dug to the side of the hole. The fluids are merely red earth and green mountain apple leaves that he has put in his mouth. Our ingenious hero escapes from his subterranean prison by having termites eat a hole upward through the great housepost. He has ants bring him small morsels of coconut meat and an arum, and magically causes these to attain full size. He increases the size of a grain of sand until it becomes a rock. Dashing the coconut against the rock he cries out "Soro!" to the workmen below. They are astounded and immediately realize that he is the son of Lugeilang. Thenceforth they treat him with deference.

(Lessa 1966: 31–32)

If there is any general lesson from such trickster stories, it is that the undeniably unpleasant features of nature and existence have a source (originally did not exist and might not have existed) and that socially appropriate behavior is not always followed (with negative consequences for self and others).

The Structural Study of Myth

The verdant plenitude of myth has made it very problematic to study. What exactly do we do with all of these fantastic, ambiguous, and almost certainly fanciful stories? Even worse, what do we do when we collect different and even contradictory versions of the same story? Is it possible to treat myth, which is evidently non-scientific, scientifically? Around the middle of the twentieth century, Claude Lévi-Strauss introduced an immensely influential approach—literally a *method*—for the scientific study of myth, based not on the "contents" of myth so much as on its "structure."

Lévi-Strauss began developing his method in the area of kinship. Taking the notion of a kinship system as a language seriously, he suggested that the meaning of utterances is not so much in the individual items (e.g. words) of which they are composed as in the "grammar" or relationships between the words, that is, the *structure*. Language in this view (derived from the linguist Ferdinand de Saussure) is a set of combinatory and transformational rules or syntax or grammar for arranging its "bits" or words. The structural model thus suggests that the meaning is not *in* the words or symbols but *between* them, in how they are related to each other. Thus, actual speech can convey the same meaning in many different ways as well as using the same bits or words to convey very different meanings.

Lévi-Strauss applied this notion to religion in the analysis of "totemism" or the spiritual link between natural species or phenomena and human individuals and groups (see Chapter 2). Before structuralism, the interpretation was often that the totem was chosen because of some characteristic that it and the individual/group possessed that established a commonality (e.g. people of the bear totem might be strong, etc.). This realist or literalist perspective on religion generally and on myth specifically is precisely what the structuralist approach avoided. As Lévi-Strauss wrote in *Structural Anthropology*, "If a given mythology confers prominence on a certain figure, let us say an evil grandmother, it will be claimed that in such a society grandmothers are actually evil and that mythology reflects the social structure and the social relations" (1963: 202). However, that would be a case of looking for the meaning of the myth in the individual item rather than in the structure or context in which the item is deployed.

Despite linguistic and cultural difference, Lévi-Strauss argued, myths across cultures are remarkably similar and mutually intelligible. His explanation for this similarity and intelligibility was the one thing that all humans have in common—the human mind. All myths being products of the same human mental processes (see Chapter 1), they have a common and analyzable nature. The fundamental quality of this mind is its *binary* nature: humans think in pairs of opposites. Some key oppositions in his view were male/female, living/dead, nature/culture, matter/spirit, and us/them. The mind then operates on these oppositions or contradictions with a battery of transformational rules, generating the assortment of myths we find cross-culturally to "resolve the contradiction" or synthesize the opposites. Myth achieves this goal, finally, by mixing or manipulating two different variations of time, the eternal or timeless (universal) and the temporal (particular). Myth, then, is both historical and ahistorical, the manifestation in time of timeless truths.

If myth "works" to resolve or synthesize oppositions and contradictions, then in the end it does not and cannot succeed; life and death, matter and spirit, male and female, and so on cannot be resolved or synthesized, at least not permanently. But this helps explain the productivity, the duplication, the "vegetative quality" of myth: we cannot stop at one resolution or synthesis, one story uniting the timeless and the temporal. Rather, we must make and tell the stories over and over again, in endless variation, in a kind of playful seriousness that Lévi-Strauss called *bricolage*. Myths in this sense are more like dreams than we realize; no single dream can definitively capture or exhaust an unconscious thought or desire. We can and must express it again and again. The contradictions that myth manipulates are not changed or eliminated by the manipulation, and so another myth, like another dream or another work of art, will follow in an unending stream of temporal manifestations of timeless themes.

Lévi-Strauss went on to demonstrate how to put this theory into practice, to provide a "method" for the structural analysis of myth. First, he said, we must break the myth down into its smallest possible narrative pieces, which he called "mythemes." Literally we might write each scene or event in the myth on an index card and lay them on a table. We would then begin to arrange the mythemes into a scheme of rows and columns, rows representing time (flowing from left to right) and columns representing similar types of events or themes that occur at different places in the myth. In his famous dissection of the Oedipus myth he had one column for scenes that invoke problematic or incestuous family relations, another column for murders, and yet another column for slaying of monsters. The result, he claimed, is a kind of "musical score" of the myth, with the melody and harmony, rhythm and counterpoint, laid out graphically. The product will be the "structure" of the myth, the particular kinds of oppositions or contradictions dealt with by it, and the means by which they are resolved or synthesized.

Naturally, different myths will deal with different contradictions, but there will be in the end a finite list of such topics, and some—like life/death or male/female—will appear repeatedly. The structural method, then, should identify these recurring patterns as well as doing one other important thing, namely, removing any "observer bias" in the analysis. Structural analysis should be completely "objective" such that all analysts achieve the same results. Another benefit of such an objective study should be the elimination of the "translation" and "version" problems of myth. In other words, if the meaning of myth is in specific words or in the culturally relative value of actions or ideas, then translating a myth would distort or destroy exactly what we seek. However, if myth is a manifestation of a "deep grammar" that all myths share, then we can confidently translate without fear of loss. Also, we know that different informants will sometimes give different versions of the same myth, or that different regions will have a variant of the myth. That is a huge problem for realists, who must study each version separately or else continue looking for the "true" or "original" myth. For structuralists, each version is little more than a new twist on the same deeper structure; there is no true version of the myth, and every permutation of the myth is just as good as another.

Myth as Oral Literature

Myth is before all else narrative of a specific kind, concerning the exploits of supernatural or extraordinary actors (like the first humans, etc.). But myth is not the only kind of narrative (religious or non-religious), and narrative is not the only form of "literature." Anthropologists and scholars of myth and oral literature often characterize myth as a subgenre of the much more inclusive genre of *folklore*. First used as a technical term by William Thoms (1846: 862) to refer to "the lore of the people" the concept of folklore has expanded to embrace a vast array of verbal cultural behavior. William Bascom, one of the influential early folklorists, held it to include "myths, legends, tales, proverbs, riddles, the texts of ballads and other songs, and other forms of lesser importance" (1953: 287) but not behavioral genres like dance or art or costume and such. A much more recent compilation on folklore edited by Richard Bauman (1992) contains entries on folktales, oral poetry, proverbs, riddles, insults, gossip, oratory, song, mime, dance, clothing, and masks, among others. Perhaps Alan Dundes, the noted anthropologist of folklore, offered the most comprehensive list:

> Folklore includes myths, legends, folktales, jokes, proverbs, riddles, chants, charms, blessings, curses, oaths, insults, retorts, taunts, teases, toasts, tongue-twisters, and greeting and leave-taking formulas. ... It also includes folk costume, folk dance, folk drama, folk instrumental music ... , folksongs ... , folk speech ... , folk similes ... , folk metaphors ... , and names. Folk poetry ranges from oral epics to autograph-book verse, epitaphs, latrinalia (writings on the walls of public bathrooms), limericks, ball-bouncing rhymes, jump-rope rhymes, finger and toe rhymes, dandling rhymes (to bounce children on the knee), counting-out rhymes ... , and nursery rhymes. The list of folklore forms also contains games; gestures; symbols; prayers (e.g., graces); practical jokes; folk etymologies; food recipes; quilt and embroidery designs; house, barn, and fence types; street vendor's cries; and even the traditional conventional sounds used to summon animals or to give them commands.
>
> (1965: 3)

While we might quibble about the details of the list (for instance, Bascom and others would exclude art, dance, music, costume, and such non-verbal media), it does alert us to the fact that there are many things humans do with language other than tell myths.

According to most students of folklore, the items on these more or less extensive lists share certain key features, particularly being *oral*, *traditional*, and *face-to-face*. Dundes and others disagree with or at least problematize this definition, since obviously not all folklore is oral (some has long been committed to writing) or therefore face-to-face, nor is all oral behavior folklore; in addition, "traditional" is relative (some folklore is very old, but some is much more recent). And even precisely who the "folk" are is debatable. In other words, Dundes concluded that if we accept this conventional view, then "the folk of today produce no new folklore" (1965: 1)—in fact, "new folklore" would be an oxymoron.

These concerns and objections notwithstanding, within the category of folklore we can identify at least two main genera, namely narratives and non-narratives, with myth falling in the genus "narrative folklore." Other species of this genus include *legends* and *folktales*, *fairy tales*, *epics*, and more. Elliott Oring distinguished the three major species of narrative folklore—myth, legend, and folktale—less by "form" than by the "attitudes of the community toward them." More explicitly, myth, he claimed, is a story "generally regarded by the community in which it is told as both sacred and true," and myths "tend to be core narratives in larger ideological systems." Typically the narrative setting of the story is "outside of historical time." Also, the delivery of myths differs:

> Myths are frequently performed in a ritual or ceremonial context. There may be special personnel designated to recite the myth; the time and manner in which it is performed may also distinguish it from the other forms of narration in the society. Indeed, the language of the myth may be as sacred as its message.
>
> (1986: 124)

Legend, on the other hand, refers to narratives "which focus on a single episode, an episode which is presented as miraculous, uncanny, bizarre, or sometimes embarrassing"; it is usually if not always set in familiar historical time, and it might be "regarded as false, or true, or false by some and true by others" (125). Finally, a folktale is "related and received as a fiction or fantasy" (126). Its characters are normally stereotypes (the beautiful princess, the evil witch, the innocent child, etc.), often in contrasted pairs, and the plot "proceeds as a logical sequence of events" although this logic is "not always the logic of the everyday world" (130).

Significantly, Bascom recognized that myths, legends, and folktales are not "universally recognized categories," but he still argued that they are "analytical concepts which can be meaningfully applied cross culturally even when other 'native categories' are locally recognized" (1965: 5). While that may be true, anthropologically there is great value in understanding and using local categories, concepts, and terms. For instance, Douglas Parks (1996) in a detailed examination of narratives of the Arikara people of South Dakota found that they had their own terminology for their narrative talk. At the most general level, they distinguished "true stories" (which did not have a genus name but were spoken of as *tiraanaaNIs* meaning "it is true") from "tales" or *naa'iikaWIs*. Under the heading of true stories were the sacred stories and the non-sacred stories, both taken to be true. Sacred stories included what he called "genesis traditions" in which the origin of each village was recounted as coming from a religious being in a dream. "Myths" were a second type of true stories, consisting of

> traditions of incidents that occurred during a period before the earth had fully taken its present form, before or at a time when human institutions were developing. Arikaras refer to this as a holy period, the time when mysterious events occurred. Stories set in this era are said to be holy (*tiraa'iitUxwaaRUxti'*, "it is a holy story"). It was a time when animals were the actors in dramas and deities came down to earth

from the heavens above, when animals killed humans and buffalo ate people rather than the reverse.

(49)

Finally, legendary events were regarded as true stories and fell into three subtypes— (1) "etiological narratives," which told of the beginning of a particular social institution or tradition; (2) "dream stories," in which human characters interacted with animals or supernatural agents who help the humans by giving them special powers in hunting, war, or medicine; and (3) stories of supernatural occurrences, in which uncanny events took place, like "a girl is shamed and turns into stone" (50).

Alongside the sacred stories under the top-level category of "true stories" were the non-sacred stories, which "in general describe events that are more recent in time and, more importantly, do not have a predominant supernatural component—although nearly every story has some supernatural reference" (50). These included accounts of historical events, personal/biographical stories, and war reports. All of these "true stories" contrasted with the second major category of "tales" or essentially non-true stories. These included trickster tales and other animal stories as well as stories about humans, with a limited and well-known cast of characters such as Bounding Head, Lucky Man, Bloody Hands, Scalped Man, and Stays in the Lodge Dressed in Finery. It is worth noting that the Arikara were not totally unanimous about this narrative typology:

> What are true myths for some Arikaras today are tales for others. For many stories, in fact, it is doubtful that consensus in regard to their historical validity could be achieved now—or even, perhaps, could ever have been achieved in the past—since in no culture does everyone hold identical beliefs.

(51)

The other genus of folklore is the non-narrative, composed of other speech-acts than stories. This category may actually contain more of a society's oral literature, since there are so many things humans can do with language besides tell stories. A very few types are proverbs and sayings, jokes, and riddles, all which can be and are used in various religious contexts; take, for example, the Buddhist *koan* or riddle, which is understood to help facilitate enlightenment.

More germane to religion are categories of spells, chants, curses, incantations, poetry, and song. According to Enongene Mirabeau Sone, poetry is an essential part of the religion of the Bakossi, a society in Cameroon. Such poetry "is concerned mainly with the Bakossi people's relationship with God, with their fellow men, and with nature" (2011: 308). Poems are chanted by men near shrines in times of collective crisis such as "drought, warfare, or an epidemic" as well as on the occasion of individual illness. Incantations, which Sone characterizes as "the use of magical formulae," are the most important kind of religious poetry among the Bakossi. People employ incantations to aid in hunting, calling on the ancestors "to release the forest animals to the hunters" (310), and to combat witchcraft; incantations can also be used to place curses. The following is an incantation that was used to cure a woman of witchcraft:

> If you have been asked to assemble here today,
> It is because one of our daughters
> Has been bewitched,
> And we ourselves are the wizards.

Shall we become the wild cat
That eats itself when caught in a trap?
Shall we kill our daughter?
Our fathers always said,
That a man who always has people
Is greater than a man who has wealth.
Plums near the house
Are never harvested using a fork stick.
We should give our daughter her health.

(322)

An important verbal form in many religions is the divine epithet, a word or phrase expressing a conventional name or trait of a superhuman being. Islam is renowned for the ninety-nine names of God, including *al-Rahman* (the compassionate), *al-Rahim* (the merciful), *an-Nur* (the light), and *al-Barr* (the good). Writing about ancient Assyrian and Babylonian religion, Peter Westh shares a number of divine epithets, as in this invocation attributed to the king Assurbanipal:

O great lord who occupies an awe-inspiring dais in the pure heavens,
Golden tiara of the heavens, symbol of royalty,
O Samas, shepherd of the people, noble god,
Seer of the land, leader of the people,
Who guides the fugitive on his path,
O Samas, judge of heaven and earth,
Who directs the heavenly gods,
Who grants incense offerings to the great gods,
I, Assurbanipal, son of my god,
Call upon you in the pure heavens.

(2011: 48)

Notice how the piling-on of honors and titles resembles how a commoner would speak to human royalty.

Box 4.1 Multiple Speech Genres in Petalangan Religion

The linguistic forms of religion among the Petalangan, a society on the island of Sumatra in Indonesia, are two quite different genres, the *belian* and the *monto privadi*. *Belian* is the style used in public healing rituals, while *monto privadi* is appropriate for personal (often private) spells including beauty and love spells. Although officially Muslims, the Petalangans "believe in the existence of spiritual beings other than Allah, and they still practice magic spells in almost every daily pursuit," from health and hunting to sex and childbirth (Kang 2006: 4). Further, they divide their spells into "social magic" (*lomu masyarakat*) and "personal magic" (*lomu privadi*), the former addressing communal needs and activities and the latter focusing on personal matters. Social magic tends to involve a religious specialist, while any individual can recite a spell (*monto*) for his/her own benefit. Petalangans claim that utterances work through the invocation of spiritual beings, in which case the spells engage the spirits in a "conversation" (*bercakap*), or through the immediate power of the words themselves. Although both kinds of speech are regarded as "ancestor's words" (*kato o'ang tuo-tuo dulu*), they differ in that *belian* speech incorporates songs called *anak iyang* sung by shamans to spirits as part of a ritual. Because they are performed in public, Kang finds that *belian* utterances are becoming more "modern" and literal, even "staged" as if for a non-Petalangan audience. *Monto privadi*, being more private, have preserved more of their pre-Islamic elements, although even those spells have begun to absorb more Muslim words and phrases.

Perhaps one of the most overlooked verbal genres across religions is prayer. Not all religions contain prayer, at least in the familiar Western/Christian sense, but many do, and for many it is an essential form of religious language. Sam Gill conducted an analysis of Navajo prayer, which, he argued, cannot be understood apart from the beliefs and myths of the society; "prayers are considered to be complex ritual acts whose performances engage and are informed by elements of mythology and the cultural contexts in which they are performed" (1981: xxii). In fact, this context is critical, since any particular prayer can be used in different ways with different meanings, e.g. "in one context to request and effect a smooth and healthy birth and in another to request and effect rainfall in a period of drought" (xxiii).

Reviewing three hundred different instances of prayers, Gill identified eight general types: (1) blessings, (2) prayers of restoration/recovery by reidentification/reassociation with the means of health, (3) prayers of restoration by expulsion of foreign malevolence, (4) prayers of restoration by expulsion of the malevolent influence of native ghosts or witches, (5) prayers of restoration by the removal of the malevolent influence of Holy People, (6) prayers of restoration by the recovery, return, and reassociation with the means of health, (7) prayers of procurement of protection against potential attack, and (8) prayers of restoration by remaking/redressing the Holy Person's means of health and life (39–42). He determined these eight types by a form of structural analysis different from and less theory driven than that of Lévi-Strauss. Gill's structuralism considered the elements or segments of which prayer utterances are composed and the arrangements of those segments, and then the relation between the resulting structure and the function or use of the prayer.

For instance, Gill found that there are twenty identifiable constituents of Navajo prayers, such as "place designation," "name mention," "offering," "plea for assistance," "assertion to affect," "procurement of protection," "journey of a Holy Person from his home to the home of an Earth Surface Person," and so on (14) (see Figure 4.1). He assigned each of these segments a letter value, from A to V. Any particular type of prayer, then, is a particular combination of these building blocks. Thus, he could name and describe each prayer type (in terms of its ceremonial classification) and its unique structure of components, as follows:

Prayer Classification	Structure
1. Blessingway	(A) ... (F) G (U) (V) or
	(A) ... (F) V or
	(A) ... (F) $G^n V^n$ (U) (V)
2. Lifeway	(A) ... (F) P G (U) (V)
3. Enemyway	(A) ... (G) K (V)
4. Uglyway	(A) ... (F) M (N)
5. Holyway	(A) ... (G) H M (U) (V)

Figure 4.1 Yebichai prayer—Navajo dancing. Courtesy of the Edward S. Curtis Collection, Library of Congress Prints and Photographs Division

And so on. To take one example, an Enemyway ceremony seeks the expulsion of foreign malevolence, and that is what the prayers ask. The structure in this case is an opening reference to a place or places ([A] in the list of constituents), which is common to all prayers, followed by the naming or association with one or more Holy People ([G]), a section asking for the removal of the foreign malevolence ([K]), and one or more references to a state of blessing ([V]). The result might be such a prayer:

He of "Waters flow together"!?   (A)
His feet have become my feet, thereby I shall go about,?   (G)
By which he is long life, by that I am long life,
By which he is happiness, by that I am happiness,
By which it is pleasant at his front, thereby it is pleasant at my front,
By which it is pleasant in his rear, thereby it is pleasant at my rear,
When the pollen which encircles sun's mouth also encircles my mouth, and that
    enables me to speak and continue speaking,
[replace "feet" with "legs" and "body" and "mind" and "voice" and repeat]
You shall take the death of the upright, of the extended bowstring?   (K)
out of me! You have taken it out of me, it was returned upon him,
it has settled far away!
Therefore the dart of the Ute enemy's ghost, its filth, by which it
bothered my interior, which had traveled in my interior, which had absorbed
    my interior, shall this day return out of me! This day it has returned out of me! ...
Long life, happiness I shall be, pleasant again it has become,?   (V)
pleasant again it has become, pleasant again it has become,
pleasant again it has become, pleasant again it has become.

(based on Gill 1981: 106–7)

Religious Language as Performance

A serious approach to myth as folklore and particularly as oral literature leads to other crucial considerations. At the heart of these is the fact that oral genres, whether they are myths, legends, riddles, proverbs, prayers, or whatever, are *performed* and, to a greater or lesser extent, only exist *in the performance*. What this means is that we do not have the luxury of examining only the "content" or the "symbols" or even the "structural relations" within the myths and other oral "texts" but that we should and must include much more in our analyses.

Scholars have tended to focus on the content—the characters, the events, the "beliefs"—of myth and religious language to the exclusion of what we might call "style." Even worse, when we commit oral literature to writing, all other qualities of speech are usually washed out and lost. And what we as ethnographers often report of myths and oral literature are after-the-fact or outside-the-fact summaries or commentaries of them rather than actual "live" versions—that is, we sit down with knowledgeable members of society and have them talk *about* myth rather than *do* the myth. Often enough our ethnographic accounts summarize the summary (convert it into a Western discursive description) or excise the non-content elements, the non-plot-advancing parts, of the story. Notice, for instance, that the prayer given by Gill ends with a repetitive section of "pleasant-becomings" which could easily be, and often would be, dropped.

According to Dennis Tedlock, this summarizing and rendering of myth and oral literature was deemed good enough by early anthropologists: "Franz Boas advocated a 'faithful rendering of the native tales,' which for him and most of his followers meant what professional translators would call a 'crib' or a 'trot'—not a true translation into literate English, but rather a running guide to the original text, written in an English that was decidedly awkward and foreign" (1983: 31). For an analysis like that of Lévi-Strauss, this was sufficient, since the form and style of myth were irrelevant; any translation and any version would suffice, since each was a variation on a deeper "grammar" of myth. But in Lévi-Straussian analysis as well as in less theoretical cribs and collections of myth, something—maybe the main thing—is lost.

Dell Hymes was an advocate for a more performance-based approach to myth and oral literature. Hymes attributed the obsession with content and structure to a linguistic theory and tradition that privileges *rules* or *knowledge* over *action*, that is, the underlying regularities of language over the actual practices of speech. Instead, he proposed that a speech performance, whether it is reciting a myth or greeting someone in the morning or telling a joke, "as an event, may have properties (patterns and dynamics) not reducible to terms of individual or standardized competence [that is, rules]. Sometimes, indeed, these properties are the point" (2001: 65). In the main, there are two sets of these properties: stylistic components and social context. Gill too wrote in his study of Navajo prayer that descriptions of oral literature that emphasize performance "have begun to show us that the elements of context and style in specific performances of any oral act are essential to our fuller understanding of it" (1981: xxii–xxiii). Myths, for instance, are not normally if ever told like other kinds of stories; they may not be "told" at all but may be recited or enacted or "sung" alone or as part of ritual performances. And different cultures will have different traditions for doing so. Just as English has certain stylistic conventions and options for storytelling, so do other cultures and languages.

Douglas Parks, for example, offered a rich description of the stylistic qualities or devices of Arikara storytelling. "Narrative perspective" was one device: the teller usually removed himself or herself from the account, speaking in the third person. Also, Arikara language included grammatical forms like "evidentials," verb variations that indicated the action was being reported second hand and that its truth could not be verified. Two examples were the "quotative," indicating that the speaker was repeating something previously heard rather than witnessed, and the "evidential proper," signifying the action was "apparently the case" but was not personally observed (1996: 65). Besides narrative perspective, Arikara myth-telling counted on indirect discourse or the use of quoted speech, in which the speaker quoted other speakers, often who themselves were quoting other speakers. The sequencing of events and episodes marked a story, by stating the result of an event first and then telling the event itself; also, actions might be described before the actor was named, and generalities would be described before the details were given. "Discourse bracketing" involved formulaic introductory and closing forms, such as "This is what he did" or "Then he said" or "This is what he said." A final remark like "That is what I want to say" ended the story. Finally, other devices such as repetition, indeterminacy (marking when details are missing or left out), abbreviation, and numerical patterning were used to build a good Arikara performance.

The very words and phrases uttered may distinguish a myth or other story from everyday speech. Parks noted that the Arikara used various unique words or grammatical forms to make stories. These included sentence introducers and connectors, like *nawah* ("now" or "well") and verb prefixes. Also, "existential constructions" provided emphasis as well as expressions of surprise. Demonstratives like "this one" or exclamatives like "oh my" added narrative color. (English-speaking fairy-tale tellers use similar devices, like "Once upon a time" and "They lived happily ever after.")

Because of the awareness of these performative qualities, a specialized field within anthropology has developed to attend to the linguistic devices or options that exist in a culture for making different kinds of religious speech and how they relate to other non-religious kinds of speech. This subfield is known as the *ethnography of speaking*. Joel Sherzer applied the concepts of the ethnography of speaking to the Kuna people of Panama. In his *Kuna Ways of Speaking* (1983), he described several different linguistic variants depending upon what kind of talk is occurring. To fully appreciate the specialized styles, we must contrast them with everyday speech or *tule kaya*. Unlike ordinary English speaking style, Kuna everyday talk typically took the form of a dialog between a speaker and a responder, with the speaker engaging in reports or retellings of things that he or she has heard or even previously said. Thus, quotations and quotes within quotes were a major part of their speech. Within the major genre of *tule kaya* fell minor subgenres such as lullabies, play languages (akin to "pig Latin"), and humorous stories called *kwento*.

The first specialized way of speaking was political or chiefly speech (*sakla kaya*). This type of speaking was done only at the meeting house and was characterized by what the Kuna called "chanting" (*namakke*), which could last for an hour or two, starting softly and building in volume over time. Like everyday speech, it too took the form of dialog, with a "chanting chief" and a "responding chief" as well as a spokesman or interpreter for the crowd. Words were spoken more slowly and formally, with vowels fully enunciated. There was more repetition, parallelism, and length in the language and many occasion-specific alternative words. There were also special words and phrases to indicate the beginning and end of "verses" in the chant, as well as elaborate and creative use of metaphor (as a really good English speechmaker might do).

Further along the spectrum of specialized and formalized speech was the curing song (*suar miimi kaya*), performed in "stick doll language." In this case, the "partner" in the dialog was not another person, not even the patient, but a doll, to which the words were spoken or sung (to Sherzer's ear the speech sounded like song, but the Kuna claimed that it was spoken or *sunmakke*). The formalization of this style included even more retention of phonemes and words and phrases, more specialized vocabulary, and a unique set of pre-fixes and suffixes. It was also highly standardized and "routinized," with fixed metaphors and figurative language.

At the extreme end of formality was the ritual language associated with girl's puberty rites (*kantule kaya*). The Kuna described this speech as neither spoken nor chanted but "shouted" (*kromakke*). The dialog here was conducted with the spirit of the ceremonial flute. The speech style was more conservative than any other, with the most retention and elaboration of sounds, words, and phrases and the most specialized lexicon. Finally, the lines were recited identically in each performance, and the recitation had to be letter perfect—no creativity or clever improvisation was allowed.

In order to capture and convey such performance qualities, a new and different kind of anthropological writing is required. Tedlock demonstrated the possibilities of creative notation in his study of Zuni narrative poetry, entitled *Finding the Center* (1972). He literally used upper-case and bold letters to express louder speaking, even placing the letters at rising or falling angles to indicate tone of voice, as in the following:

> SON'AHCHI. [a conventional story-opening]
>   SONTI ^{LO} ––––––––– ^{NG A}GO
>   [pause]
> AT STANDING ARROWS
> OLD LADY JUNCO HAD HER HOME
> And COYOTE
> Coyote was there at Sitting Rock with his children.
> He was with his children
> And Old Lady Junco
> was winnowing.
> Pigweed
> and tumbleweed, she was winnowing these.
>
>   (based on Tedlock 1972: 77)

Box 4.2 Word, Voice, and Gesture in Amazonian "Somatic Poetry"

Few anthropologists have followed Tedlock's lead in representing the performance qualities of religious language on paper. One remarkable exception is Michael Uzendoski and Edith Felicia Calapucha-Tapuy's study of Napo Runa myth and poetry. Among the Napo Runa, "communicative action is not limited to humans but also includes spirits and beings from the nonhuman phenomenological world," including plants and animals (2012: 23). One way that humans interact with these beings is "somatic poetry," a kind of speech that engages the entire body "by lis-tening, feeling, smelling, seeing, and tasting." Obviously this interaction depends on "the creative use of words and music and also plants, animals, and the landscape," since all such entities are "recognized as having subjectivity and creative powers" (23). Not surprisingly, then, when a shaman conducts a healing ritual or when a storyteller recites a myth, he or she uses not only voice but gesture to make the experience as vivid and multisensory, as *bodily*, as possible. So, in presenting these performances, Uzendoski and Calapucha-Tapuy not only adopt Tedlock's method of using bold letters and rising/falling print but also enhance the written account with simple line-drawings of the gestures that the speaker makes, such as raising the arms, clasping the hands, pointing, adjusting clothing, and moving the head. All of these movements are part of the performance/experience, and all would be lost if we treated myth and poetry as mere text or grammar.

The following is an extract from a story explaining the origins of the anaconda told by Grandfather Alberto Grefa of Pumayaku (text and illustrations courtesy of Michael Uzendoski). The story is about the culture heroes, the twins, named "Kyullur." In this story the younger brother Kyullur sexually desires a very attractive woman who appears as a yutu bird. She realizes Kyullur's intensions, however, and attacks Kyullur by stabbing his penis with her sharp beak. She then flies away, stretching it very far. The older, wiser brother then cuts the penis to normal length and throws the leftover pieces into the various rivers around Napo. The cuttings transform into anacondas. The story not only explains the origins of the anaconda but also is metaphorical of the process of life and the poetics of human–animal somatic flow.

The Kyllur brothers
    were walking through the forest
when they came up on a yutu bird
    yutu (*tinamus major*)

so while they were going
      just like this from above (yutu cried out)

Figure 4.2 a, b, c Gesture drawings for a Napo Runa story explaining the origins of the anaconda

UW UW UW UW UW UW Uw uw uw uw
    (she) got scared and flew off
      getting scared

AYYY AYYYY [she cried] while flying away
    "They scared me so much …
    and in a bad way"

"If they would have caught me …
    they would have had their way [sexually] with me."
    she said they say

  and so going far away to land
    landing far away saying [thinking]

   and then
     to that Kyullur brother with bad intentions
      right there
       all of a sudden

Figure 4.2b

> she flew right back over
> >   attacking him [Kyullur] right in his "thing"
> >   >   [laughter]
>
> **TSAK** [ideophone = stabbing]
> >   sticking it
> >   >   [she] she took off flying
> >   >   >   way over there
> >   >   >   >   she went very far
>
> And so going so far
> >   his penis was stretched long
> >   >   very long
>
> And so Kyullur could no longer walk
> >   he could not even move
> >   >   with such a heavy penis

Figure 4.2c

At the most general level, Bauman (2001) offered a list of common or potential performative qualities or "keys" to performance, including the following:

1 "special codes, e.g. archaic or esoteric language, reserved for and diagnostic of performance";
2 "special formulae that signal performance, such as conventional openings and closings, or explicit statements announcing or asserting performance";
3 "figurative language, such as metaphor, metonymy, etc.";
4 "formal stylistic devices, such as rhyme, vowel harmony, other forms of parallelism";
5 "special prosodic patterns of tempo, stress, pitch";
6 "special paralinguistic patterns of voice quality and vocalization";
7 "appeal to tradition";
8 "disclaimer of performance." (171)

As we can see from Sherzer's material above, each culture and each oral genre may have its own distinct set of these keys.

Finally, in addition to the linguistic styles employed in the production of the myth or other genre, there are extra-linguistic contextual elements. These may include who can perform the speech-act and when they can perform it. Oring asserted that oral narratives

> are performed in specific social contexts. These contexts are constituted by a specific group of people, by a specific set of principles governing their interrelationship, by a specific set of behaviors and conversations in which the narrative is embedded, and by a specific physical and symbolic environment present at the time of narration. The understanding of a narrative is governed to some extent by an understanding of the specific situation or situations in which it is told.
>
> (1986: 136–37)

Parks noted that Arikara storytelling was mostly a male prerogative. Some myths or parts of myths should be told only during certain seasons or at certain times of day;

Arikara myths and tales were to be told only during the winter. Some myths or parts of myths might be recited only in the midst of rituals. They might also be told only before certain audiences—or, as in the case of many Australian Aboriginal societies, different (less "esoteric") versions might be told in front of general audiences, the "inside" or esoteric versions reserved for initiated men. There might be specialists with the prerogative to tell myths—priests, shamans, or designated story-keepers. And other performative features might accompany the story, such as singing, dancing, noise-making of various kinds, and so on. Irving Goldman describes how he was reviewing his field notes on mourning rituals with an informant

> when the traditional dance leader rose from his chair to dance a few steps while illustrating a mourning song. He turned to me and said, "It cannot be done this way. I cannot sing without dancing." Then after a long pause he said, "I cannot dance without wearing the mask."
>
> (2004: 5)

A special symbolic or sacred space may be reserved for the telling or created by the telling. Finally, speakers and/or participants may have to be in special ritual conditions (e.g. purified) in order for the telling to occur. The narrative cannot be told—or least it may not work—otherwise.

In conclusion, neither myth nor any other oral folklore genre can be regarded as a mere rote enactment of a grammar or set of rules nor of an "ideal" and unchanging "original" narrative. The performance is relative to a range of variables and in the end is a particular "event" in the linguistic and ritual world of the society. Whether myth or chant or prayer, the performance can and must be

> creative and responsive to heartfelt needs while the words ... are utterly formulaic. The relevance and immediacy and the creativity and freedom ... are not fully apparent at the level of simple reference, but they become so when [oral performance] is considered also as a highly symbolic religious act which incorporates much more than the words.
>
> (Gill 1981: 187)

There is, therefore, no "real" or "true" or "perfect" version of an oral literature; there are only different versions. Myths and other narratives "exist in multiple versions. No single text can claim to be the authoritative or 'correct' one. Rather, different narrators perform narratives differently in different circumstances. A folk narrative, in other words, must be re-created with each telling" (Oring 1986: 123). And this is not a fact to be lamented or elided but to be studied and celebrated.

The Power of Words

The preceding discussions converge to make a single point: we should not and dare not approach myth or religious language in general solely in terms of its content, that is, the "facts" or "ideas" or "beliefs" it seems to transmit. Language—religious and otherwise—might ultimately be less about describing something or believing something than about *doing* something. That is, language is, like all behavior, a form of action, often intended to achieve effects or inspire further action. In a way, the content of religious speech may be its least important aspect; it may be meant not so much to "inform" anyone of anything as to "accomplish" something. Ultimately, its *content* may be less crucial than its *consequences*.

The notion that words can make things happen is not completely unfamiliar; after all, the Judeo-Christian deity created the entire universe through speech. And many if not all cultures would insist that their speech-acts—whether prayers or songs or myths—have or at least seek demonstrable effects on the world. J. L. Austin, in his short but influential book *How to Do Things with Words* (1962), showed how this is less exotic than we think and not limited to religion. He distinguished various functions of speech, including the customary propositional quality which he designated as its "locutionary force"; this is the "meaning" of a statement in the ordinary sense, its content or claim. As such, an utterance is either true or false. If I say, "The cat is on the mat," I am making a factual claim about the world, and either the claim is true or it is not. Much of our speech is of this sort—but less than we might usually assume.

An entirely separate mode or function of language consists of its "illocutionary force," by which he meant the *effect* that the speech has or the way in which it brings about a state of affairs. In other words, if I say, "The cat is on the mat," my saying so does not make it so. However, when a priest or minister says, "I now pronounce you man and wife," the saying so does make it so. The utterance *accomplishes* the act of marriage. Other examples might include a college dean or president conferring degrees on graduates or a monarch knighting a servant. By speaking the words "I knight thee" or "I confer this degree on you," the recipient *becomes* a knight or a college graduate. Of course, in the modern Western world, where not only language but official pageantry and symbolism have lost much of their power and significance, we would probably feel equally graduated without the dean's speech-act (we might not even attend the ceremony), but the point is that for many people in many times and places speech has been much more than a *description* of events but an actual *doing* of events.

Finally, Austin also mentioned the "perlocutionary force" of speech, in which words neither describe facts nor make changes but have psychological impact on the hearers. For instance, the function of an utterance or a series of utterances (namely, an "argument") can be to convince or persuade people to believe a claim or to come to a conclusion or, more importantly, to take an action. Clearly much of political speech, not to mention advertising, is of this variety. Hopefully a politician or a commercial employs true facts, but that is not the real point of the exercise, and certainly when a politician asks "Vote for me" or a commercial pleads "Buy this product," the saying so does not make it so. The goal is to alter the listeners' thoughts and actions in particular ways, and as such the speech may succeed or fail.

A hugely important consequence of this analysis is that some kinds of talk can be subjected to true/false judgment, while some kinds cannot—or at least that is not the most important thing to do with them. We can assert that a proposition is either true or false and in principle determine which: the cat is on the mat or not, or the earth is round or not. Other kinds of speech do not fall within the true/false discourse—what Langer called "factual reference" and Armstrong called *logos*—at all. Questions ("what time is it?"), imperatives ("open the window!"), and expletives ("liver again, yuk") are among the non-propositional uses of language. Utterances that sometimes sound like propositions may not be propositional but illocutionary or perlocutionary in function (e.g. "You are under arrest" or "Be very afraid"), and non-propositional speech cannot in any meaningful way be assessed as true or false. It might, however, be more or less *successful* or *effective*. I might decide to vote for a candidate or not, to buy the product or not, to halt for the police or not, or to act scared or not.

In order to be successful or effective, the speech must meet certain culturally and situationally relevant conditions. It must be performed correctly, that is, the right words must be said in the right way. It must be performed by someone authorized to perform it. For instance, only an ordained priest can conduct a Catholic mass; it would not "work" or "count" otherwise. It must be performed in the right or "official" context and circumstances—which explains the difference between a wedding rehearsal and a wedding. And perhaps the performer must be in the correct social or spiritual or ritual condition (e.g. be purified, have observed prohibitions, or be in the right state of mind, including "sincerity," since performances can be "faked").

Bronislaw Malinowski, as we saw earlier in the chapter, called myth a "charter," and Clifford Geertz in his discussion of religion emphasized its "modeling" function (1973). Both referred not to description but to creation or production: religious language in particular, and language in general, not only portrays the world (*model of*) but *produces* the world (*model for*). Language is productive, effective, because for many societies *words have power*. Uttering the divine epithet, speaking the spell, chanting the incantation—doing these things changes reality, either directly or through the intervention of the spirits, who listen, respond, and act. However, as Webb Keane emphasized, the problem with spirits as communicative partners is that their very spiritual nature makes communication uncertain. While, as we noted above, there is fundamentally nothing different about religious language from language in general, one crucial difference is that "the presence, engagement, and identity of spiritual participants in the speech event cannot always be presupposed or guaranteed" (Keane 1997: 50). As they are often invisible, we are not even sure of their presence; if they are present, we cannot be sure if they are listening, taking an interest, understanding, or responding. Christians confront this issue in their question as to whether God answers all prayers.

Finally, because of the dangers inherent in any situation of speaking to superiors, and because of the particular dangers in saying the wrong thing, religious speech may evince special qualities (not totally unknown in mundane speech), such as repetition, formalization (especially speaking in highly respectful ways), standardization and formulaic utterances, and even the use of specialized "religious languages" (like Latin in Christianity or Arabic in Islam). And other actions may be added to get the attention and approval of the spiritual interlocutors, such as noise, pageantry, and material offerings.

Box 4.3 Power Beyond Understanding: The Efficacy of Words not Understood—or Even Heard

It seems credible to us that words that are heard and understood could have their social force. However, in many traditions, religious language need not be comprehended, or even heard, in order to "work." For instance, monks may be isolated from general society in their monasteries, offering their prayers for the good of society. Sometimes, as Tambiah noted, specialists like Thai Buddhist monks may chant in public in an obscure or esoteric language (ancient Pali, in this case) that is unintelligible to layfolk. Such chants "are meant to be heard but paradoxically they are not understood by the majority of the congregation (nor by some of the monks themselves)"; yet the villagers were "emphatic that through listening to the chants the congregation gains merit, blessings, and protection" (1970: 195). He calls this attitude "the virtue of listening without understanding" (196).

In other circumstances, words are believed to be "objects" of power whether they are spoken or read or whether they merely have physical existence. For many Muslims, the physical Qur'an is a potent force. We mentioned above how *faki* in Berti society made amulets out of Qur'anic verses. Even more remarkably, they would also write verses on a wooden slate, wash the words off with water, and have people drink the liquid (*mihai*) (see Figure 4.3). Individuals would consume the liquid words routinely as religious precautions, and the entire society would drink together to ward off disasters and misfortunes like drought, fire, locusts, or diseases. For the Berti, the Qur'an "is considered to have an immense power which guarantees the well-being of those who have internalized it" (Holy 1991: 33)—and not just internalized it "intellectually."

Figure 4.3 Drinking the Qur'an in East Niger. Courtesy of Swiatoslaw Wojtkowiak (http://swiatoslaw.com/)

Conclusion

Humans use language. They speak to and about other humans. They speak to communicate objective facts and subjective feelings. And they speak in many different and subtle styles depending on the subject, the situation, and the relation between speakers. But they speak for other purposes—and to other listeners—as well. One subject or subset of language is religious language, with most if not all the same processes and properties of nonreligious language, plus some distinct ones of its own. Religion, positing nonhuman beings or agents, encourages humans to speak to and about them as well. It encourages humans to communicate objective facts and subjective feelings to spiritual entities and to employ styles for these specific subjects, situations, and relations that may not be used in any other aspect of culture. And they speak of and to the supernatural in order to unleash and direct the power of the religious dimension.

Myths are typically the narrative repository of the knowledge of the past actions of the religious beings, and they receive most of the attention from students of religion. However, many significant language behaviors comprise religious speech, each for its "audience" and purpose. In total, religious talk provides a source and therefore model or paradigm for human thought, action, and organization as well as "practical" ways to influence and control other humans and society, the natural world, and the supernatural itself.

DISCUSSION QUESTIONS

- What are the similarities and differences between ordinary language and religious language? Why are they similar, and why are they different?
- What is myth, and why has it been such a central topic in the study of religion?
- What was Lévi-Strauss' structural approach to religious language?
- How is religious language a "performance," and what are some of its performative types and traits?

SUPPLEMENTARY READING (see website)

- *Stories of Spirit and Animal in Ainu Culture and Religion*
- *The Power of Words in Mongolian Divination*
- *Evangelical Christian Conversion as Language Learning*

5 Religious Action
Ritual

A number of tasks must be accomplished at a Chinese funeral, especially in the late Imperial era. One, of course, was disposing of the body; another was providing a good fate for the soul. Additionally, the "inauspicious effect" or pollution of death was handled, the relationships between the living were regulated and reinforced, and the guests at the ceremony were cared for (Chau 2012: 82). These many needs required the work of religious specialists—but not specialists of only one religion. Rather, "Four groups of religious specialists would be hired to chant scriptures: Tibetan Buddhist monks (lamas), Daoist priests, Buddhist monks, and Buddhist nuns" (84). Each category of specialist and his/her ritual performance was called a "shed," since sheds or platforms/stages were constructed for each troupe to occupy during their chanting. The funeral of General Wu Peifu in 1939 involved ten sheds constructed on three levels. Adam Yuet Chau has dubbed this approach to ritual "Confucian-Buddhist-Daoist polytropy" (89), since many different religions contributed to any ritual occasion. Indeed, ordinary Chinese people did not consider themselves *members of a religion* but rather were "free to employ a Confucian, Buddhist, or Daoist to conduct rituals" (89). The point was not to "belong to" a religion but instead to maximize the *efficacy*, the effectiveness, of rituals.

In the very early days of anthropology, R. R. Marett proclaimed that religion "is, fundamentally, a mode of social behavior" (1909: ix), like all social behavior in that humans do it together in groups but unlike other social behavior in that it also involves nonhuman/ superhuman agents. In fact, in contrast to the reigning intellectualist approach of E. B. Tylor and others (see Chapter 1), Marett thought that action was more important than ideas: religion, especially but not exclusively "primitive" religion, "is something not so much thought out as danced out," favoring "emotional and motor processes" (xxxi). This attitude goes against the modern preference for ideas, explanations, and "meaning" with its devaluation of behavior as mindless and rote. However, not all religions have shared the modern (some say Protestant) perspective, and all religions engage in some behavior.

In the previous chapter we discussed various types of religious speech, and speaking is acting. Further, religious speech is often if not usually part of a larger performance, including bodily motion and religious objects. We call such behavior *ritual*, which can be a protracted multimedia performance of multiple "scenes" that may take hours or days to complete. Victor Turner wrote that a ritual "is segmented into 'phases' or 'stages' and into subunits such as 'episodes,' 'actions,' and 'gestures.' To each of these units and subunits corresponds a specific arrangement of symbols, of symbolic activities and objects" (1981: 3). Accordingly, a ritual typically entails many genres of action, from language to dance to stillness and silence to material items (masks, body painting, sacred objects of various kinds) and food and any number of other elements.

In this chapter we will consider the meaning and function, the "origin," and the variety of ritual. We will notice and explore the fact that ritual as communication and social action is not unique to religion—in fact, much of human life is "ritualized"—nor even to humans. It is quite clear that social species, including humans, can and often do communicate or interact ritually. Ultimately, ritual interaction may not be "communication" in the normal sense—that is, the transmission of information—so much as social behavior intended to establish, maintain, influence, or break relationships, including relations with the nonhuman and superhuman. Humans may interact ritually with the superhuman precisely because ritual is how humans interact.

The Anthropology of Ritual and Ritualization

Ritual is not necessarily or essentially a religious phenomenon. College graduation is a ritual with little or no religious content or significance. Some hold that getting your first driver's license and going on your first date are rituals. We even speak of someone washing their hands or engaging in some other such mundane behavior "ritualistically." As Anthony Wallace commented, "although ritual is the primary phenomenon of religion, the ritual process itself requires no supernatural belief" (1966: 233).

Ritual is such a crucial part of religion and of culture in general that anthropologists have studied it intensely and defined it in many ways, including the following:

> Victor Turner: "prescribed formal behavior for occasions not given over to technological routine, having reference to belief in mystical beings or powers. The symbol is the smallest unit of ritual" (1967: 19).

> Stanley Tambiah: "a culturally constructed system of symbolic communication. It is constituted of patterned and ordered sequences of words and acts, often expressed in multiple media, whose content and arrangement are characterized in varying degree by formality (conventionality), stereotypy (rigidity), condensation (fusion), and redundancy (repetition)" (1979: 119).

> Anthony Wallace: "communication without information: that is to say, each ritual is a particular sequence of signals which, once announced, allows no uncertainty, no choice, and hence, in the statistical sense of information theory, conveys no information from sender to receiver. It is, ideally, a system of perfect order and any deviation from this order is a mistake" (1966: 233).

> Thomas Barfield: "prescribed, formal acts that take place in the context of religious worship" as well as "any activity with a high degree of formality and a nonutilitarian purpose. This usage includes not only clearly religious activities, but also such events as festivals, parades, initiations, games, and greetings. In its broadest sense, ritual may refer not to any particular kind of event but to the expressive aspect of all human activity. To the extent that it conveys messages about the social and cultural status of individuals, any human action has a ritual dimension. In this sense, even such mundane acts as planting fields and processing foods share a ritual aspect with sacrifice and the mass" (1997: 410).

> Edmund Leach: "Behavior which forms part of a signaling system and which serves to 'communicate information,' not because of any mechanical link between means

and ends, but because of a culturally defined communication code"; and "Behavior which is potent in itself in terms of the cultural conventions of the actor but *not* potent in a rational-technical sense ... or alternatively behavior which is directed towards evoking the potency of occult powers even though it is not presumed to be potent in itself" (1966: 403).

As different as these definitions are, they evince a few recurrent features. They emphasize action (although not always "practical" or "instrumental" action), patterning, and communication—even if, at least in some cases, that communication is regarded as "empty." Catherine Bell pointed out that these theories tend to stress "formality, fixity, and repetition" as central aspects (1992: 91–92). Further, she noted that anthropological treatments of ritual have often if not ordinarily separated it from the more "cognitive" or "conceptual" aspect of religion. As she asserted:

> Theoretical descriptions of ritual generally regard it as action and thus automatically distinguish it from the conceptual aspects of religion, such as beliefs, symbols, and myths. ... Ritual is then described as particularly *thoughtless* action—routinized, habitual, obsessive, or mimetic—and therefore the purely formal, secondary, and mere physical expression of logically prior ideas.
>
> (19)

She concluded that "beliefs could exist without rituals; rituals, however, could not exist without beliefs" (19).

Ritual and the "Interaction Code"

Although ritual is a fundamental component of religion, as we have already stated it is not unique to religion in any way. As Jack Goody asserted, "'routinization,' regularization, repetition, lie at the basis of social life itself" (1977: 28). Indeed, from this perspective— and there is some merit to it—all of culture is "ritualistic" in the sense that it makes patterned, fixed, communicative habits out of behavior.

The philosopher John Skorupski (1976) provided a fruitful commentary of anthropological theories of symbolism and religion, which elaborated the notion of ritual and ritualization. Beginning with a discussion of the intellectualist tradition from Tylor and Frazer, he indicated how the symbolist school of Durkheim and most subsequent social scientists disregarded the content or beliefs of the religion and emphasized its expressive and representative functions. This conveniently exempted them from having to engage the truth-claims of a religion, which are often false. However, to do so, he said, is to mischaracterize religion from the member's point of view: "If Trobriand canoe magic is a ritual which 'stresses the importance of canoe-building for Trobrianders,' then presumably running away from a lion is a ritual which expresses the importance of not being eaten for the runner" (172). This satirical example makes Skorupski's point that perhaps the people mean what they say and do—and expect it to work.

His analysis turned on his description of most if not all rituals as "interaction ceremonies" in which humans as agents interact with other agents, generally other humans. Interaction ceremonies "communicate" between the parties in a conventional "language" that he called the *interaction code*. "The point of interaction-code behavior is to establish or maintain (or destroy) an equilibrium, or mutual agreement, among the people involved in an interaction as to their relative standing or roles, and their reciprocal commitments and obligations" (77). Thus, there is an available "vocabulary" of coded actions which participants master and from which they select to construct their interactions with each other.

Interaction-code (IC) behavior is not unique to humans. In fact, Skorupski considered it "part of a more general form of social life" (77), which we would expect to see and do see in virtually all social species; indeed, he noted that a "parallel with what animal ethnologists call ritual ... is obvious" (84). Certain species-specific behaviors "mean" a challenge or a surrender or an invitation to mate, if they are performed correctly. And if all goes well, the behaviors should also invoke the appropriate response.

Interestingly, just as cats or birds or fish need not "understand" or "agree to" the interaction code, so humans need not necessarily either. Humans only have to be able to perform the code, with or without "believing" it or "meaning" it. This code is not explicitly articulated in most cultures (being more tacit or implicit) and is generally not written down. The point of IC behavior rather is "that people should use the code to establish the relationship which ought—in accordance with other norms—to hold between them, to maintain it, to re-establish it if it is thrown out of equilibrium and to terminate it properly" (83–84). And this code permeates human society, from the grand religious gestures through the high-level political ones of prostrating oneself before the king and kissing his ring to the minor and mundane ones that pervade everyday life like handshaking and exchanging greetings—what John Haviland (2009) has aptly called "little rituals."

While IC behavior is part of daily life, it is also distinguished from other kinds of behaviors by its qualities of *elaboration* and *formality*. Many of our routine actions are relatively "free" and voluntary, although still enacted within a culture that provides familiar and stock actions and responses. Even much of our non-ritual life is remarkably conventional and routine. However, IC behavior, and especially ceremonial and ritual behavior, is particularly distinct in its seriousness, precision, stereotypy, and detail. Part of this elaboration ensures that the ritual is done correctly, but another part is self-referential, that is, a way "of marking out, emphasizing, underlining the fact of code behavior" (87). In other words, it must be clear and apparent to participants that this is not normal everyday behavior but something special and something that demands a (perhaps equally elaborate, formal, and specific) response.

The IC actions that are intended to evoke a response, set a particular counteraction in progress, or even institute a new norm or relationship are called "operative acts," which reminds us of Austin's illocutionary acts (see Chapter 4). "Operative acts are performed to set up new patterns of rules. Hence one can also say that they can establish people in new statuses or roles, and can set up new institutions" (99). Operative acts "are produced, then, by being *said* to be produced (the 'saying' need not be verbal, of course)" (103). Thus, interaction code behavior, of which the most striking is religious ritual, does not in his view so much represent social realities as make and maintain them.

The essential aspect of interaction rituals is that they *are* interactions that "call out" and expect certain responses. They are symbolic in the sense that we are not directly saying or doing what we mean—for example, a Japanese person could say in words, "I am of a lower status than you," instead of bowing deeply to a superior—but not in the sense of "representing society" in some other medium and definitely not in the sense of being "nonutilitarian." And ultimately, religious ritual as a distinct species of coded behavior cannot be understood, Skorupski insisted, without considering and taking seriously the religious "beliefs" of the society.

If humans are ritually interacting persons, then we would expect humans to ritually interact with other persons too. Accordingly, Skorupski concluded that "to a large extent religious rites *are* social interactions with authoritative or powerful beings within the actor's social field, and … their special characteristics are in large part due to the special characteristics these beings are thought to have" (165). In other words, if you bow deeply to a human superior, you would likely bow (maybe more deeply) to a superhuman one. What humans do in religious ritual is extend their interaction code beyond the human realm into the nonhuman, to include those nonhuman agents that the particular society "believes in." Recall Robin Horton's definition of religion (Chapter 1), "an extension of the field of people's social relationships beyond the confines of purely human society" (1960: 211).

A Continuum of Ritual Behavior

We might think of ritualization as the process by which rigid patterning or stereotyping of behavior takes place, so as to de-emphasize the everyday mundane qualities of the behavior and to emphasize its special communicative and interactive consequences. The highly stylized and typically non-instrumental behavior of one individual not only communicates to the other(s) and also communicates that it is communicating. That is, not only the content but the *form* of ritual is critical and communicative. And part of what ritualization in general does is not only communicate *between* the participants but communicate *about* them; it is a commentary on the relationship.

The formality and fixity of ritualized behavior helps to assure communicative success; if the action is always done the same way, there should be no confusion over its intention. Finally, these same qualities help to guarantee the *practical* success of the action; if it worked this way before, it should work this way again. Communication in this sense means not so much the conveyance of information as the achievement of goals. It follows, then, that different kinds of communicative/interactive situations, between different kinds of actors, would have different kinds or levels of ritualization. In other words, ritual behavior is not all or nothing but falls along a spectrum, from *individual/compulsive* to *casual* to *etiquette/diplomacy* to *normal religious* to *liturgical*. Individual rituals would include repetitive behaviors that a single person engages in, often not "learned" at all and even "neurotic," such as superstitious gestures or obsessive hand washing, etc. These behaviors often have meaning for the individual but, more important, they (are believed to) have effect too—perhaps to insure success in sports or love or to protect one from the harmful consequences of germs or a more general loss of personal control.

Casual rituals occur continuously in human social life; they constitute the first level of interaction-code behavior. From saying hello and shaking hands to more elaborate and situational actions, humans have a set of culturally appropriate interactional patterns that would seem odd if omitted or if done improperly. When we offer a hand for shaking, we expect a hand offered back; when we say, "How are you?" we expect a simple "Fine, thanks," not a detailed litany of complaints. Etiquette typically appears at more formal social occasions, such as weddings or ceremonial dinners or political functions. There is a correct way to send thank you notes after a wedding and a correct fork to use at a dinner. There are the polite things to say to a host or friend (or an enemy). Mastery and performance of these rituals shows one's own social skill and status as well as respect (or disrespect) for one's interaction partners; it is easy to accidentally (or intentionally) send other messages—including slights and insults—by subtly modifying the expected gestures. Specialized rituals pertain to particular occasions. In courtrooms, for example, there are ritualized ways of standing and speaking and unique rituals for swearing oaths and such. Diplomacy, on the other hand, tends to emerge when persons of power interact, like heads of state. The formality and predictability of diplomatic rituals minimizes misunderstandings when respect is due and the stakes are unusually high.

Normal religious rituals tend to escalate the formality and stereotypy, since for the first time on the ritual continuum nonhuman and superhuman agents are participating. These greater beings must be approached with more respect and caution, although not all religions or religious occasions are necessarily solemn. In some instances, humor and even intentional sarcasm or disrespect are intended (not all spirits disapprove of such attitudes). Further, while a certain degree of formulaic repetition is typical of religious ritual, we have already seen that there is also a degree of freedom and creativity in how the formulas are assembled and deployed. Even religious rituals may allow for some deviation, invention, or interpretation.

Box 5.1 Four Games and a Funeral: Ritual and Play in Salasaca (Ecuador) Mortuary Rites

Funerals are among the most serious, even somber, occasions for Christians, but among the Salasaca of the Ecuadorian Andes, as for other South American societies, the "ability (and obligation) for certain people to laugh and play at a time of death is considered part of the proper way to observe the rites" (Corr 2008: 5). During the wake or vigil for the deceased person, adult men play games, while "children perform mimetic acts as they imitate adult performers, laymen parody priests, and people imitate animals" (4). Among the games indulged in by men are The Rooster, in which "men line up to jump off the roof of the house, holding a rooster, into a pile of burning branches" (8), as well as a kind of Blindman's Bluff. But the most common and significant game is called *huayru*, named after the six-sided dice made of animal bone and used during play. Interestingly, close kinsmen of the deceased do not play; instead, a son-in-law bears primary responsibility to organize the festivities. Rachel Corr describes the game as follows:

> a man will give the first toss, and all see what number it lands on. Then he gives it to each man in turn to throw, and if it is a lower number, the first thrower slaps him on the back of the hand very hard. If it is higher than the first throw, the one with the higher number slaps the first thrower's hand. ... [A]nother man, who is passing out shots of sugar cane alcohol at the wake, will come and say, "Here have some 'blood' (*yawar*) to calm you." The sugar cane alcohol is figuratively referred to as "blood" in this context.

(10)

Meanwhile, adolescent boys mock the men's game, using sticks instead of dice, and otherwise imitate and parody the adults. Even more remarkably, attendees perform actions that might seem odd or disrespectful to outsiders, such as "marrying" the deceased to a chicken if s/he was a young unmarried adult. They also conduct mock versions of official Catholic rituals, for instance imitating how Catholic priests perform the sacraments. Such behavior, Corr argues, "blurs the boundaries between sacred ritual and humorous play" (8), and games and other forms of jocularity "juxtapose death and humor, grief and laughter, danger and fun" (2).

Liturgies are the most formal, fixed, and weighty of rituals, in which the exact gestures, objects, and words must be used in the precisely correct ways in order for the ritual to "succeed." In fact, a poorly or wrongly done liturgy can be worse than no liturgy at all. The Catholic mass is an example of a highly formalized liturgy, and other Christian and non-Christian religions also have liturgical aspects or moments, like the Kuna rituals discussed in Chapter 4.

Speaking of etiquette and diplomacy reminds us of the criticism of politicians (among others) who "talk without saying anything." Clearly, language, that most informational of media, can be and often is used to avoid or distort informative communication. And while liturgy communicates after a fashion, ideally it says and does the exact same thing every time. For these reasons, Anthony Wallace, one of the key promoters of ritual among anthropologists, called it "communication without information"; the whole point of ritual, he maintained, was behavior that "allows no uncertainty, no choice. ... It is, ideally, a system of perfect order and any deviation from this order is a mistake" (1966: 233). The essence of ritual, he claimed, is orderliness, providing predictability. Therefore, the point of ritual is not transmission of information, since nothing is said or done that we do not already know; rather, the "particular function of ritual communication is quickly to prepare an individual or individuals to execute an action with maximum efficiency" (234).

Frits Staal famously took this idea a step further. He insisted that ritual is *meaningless*, in contradiction to the standard notion that "it consists in symbolic activities which refer to something else" (1979: 3). He by no means implied that ritual was pointless but instead that ritual "is primarily activity"; even more, "It is an activity governed by explicit rules. The important thing is what you do, not what you think, believe, or say" (4). Studying Brahmin priests in Hinduism, Staal said that they never offer symbolic interpretations of their ritual activity: when asked why they perform a ritual, they say "we do it because our ancestors did it; because we are eligible to do it; because it is good for society; because it is good; because it is our duty; because it is said to lead to immortality; because it leads to immortality" (3). In short, Staal argued that people engage in ritual because they feel that they must engage in ritual. Ritual is "pure activity" (9), done because that is what you do.

The Diversity of Religious Ritual

Despite the common qualities of all religious (and non-religious rituals), there is also great diversity among them, both in structure and in their function. As mentioned in Chapter 1, Anthony Wallace suggested that we regard religion as a composite of discrete bits, a cumulative phenomenon composed of identifiable and not necessarily distinctively religious building blocks. Rituals, he proposed, are built out of even more elementary particles, the thirteen different activities including prayer, music/dancing/singing, physiological exercise (e.g. self-mortification, drug ingestion, food and sleep deprivation, sensory deprivation, etc.), exhortation (messages or commands to other people, including orders, threats, and words of comfort or encouragement), myth, simulation/imitation (e.g. magic, ritual, and witchcraft), *mana* or power, taboo or restrictions, feasts, sacrifice, congregation, inspiration, and symbolism and symbolic objects.

A ritual in Wallace's view is a composite phenomenon, and any actual ritual could contain any or all of these parts in any combination, including multiple instances of each (that is, a number of different prayers or simulations or symbols). Of course, this analysis is not perfect or universally accepted. Turner and Geertz would not place the concept of symbol as just one in the list of ritual constituents, but rather they would see all of these elements as symbolic. The list could be longer or shorter, and not every entry on it is necessarily elementary: a constituent like physiological exercises or sacrifice or congregation may itself be a composite of multiple ritual objects and gestures.

Anthropologists have also attempted to arrange rituals into typologies. Catherine Bell (1997) proposed a short list of ritual types based on their functions, including:

1 rites of passage or life crisis rituals;
2 calendrical or commemorative rituals;
3 rites of exchange and communion;
4 rites of affliction;
5 rites of feasting, fast, and festival;
6 political rituals.

There is no perfect or universally accepted typology of rituals; any attempt would, as with typologies of beliefs or specialists previously discussed, almost certainly leave gaps and overlaps. Specific rituals do not always fit nicely into any one or only one category. Nevertheless, for the purpose of imposing some order on the diversity of ritual, we can consider the well-known system adopted by Wallace, who divided rituals into technical, therapeutic/anti-therapeutic, salvation, ideological, and revitalization.

Technical Rituals

Technical rituals are those intended to achieve natural or supernatural effects through "technique," the more or less mechanical manipulation of objects and words that is more or less guaranteed to bear results. We might think of it as a version of "spiritual technology" or "spiritual cause and effect": do X and Y will result.

One subtype of technical rituals is *rites of intensification*, which function to increase the fertility or number of natural species. It is widely claimed across the world's cultures that humans have a power if not a duty to preserve and reproduce the natural life of the earth. The Inuit, like most foraging societies, felt that they shared a fundamental and inescapable spiritual relationship with nature. Most acutely, they believed that the seal was or had a spirit, and there was a Seal Goddess who animates and guides the beasts. Seals, being spiritual as well as material beings, participated reciprocally with humans in the hunt; far superior to humans, they could easily elude capture if they chose, but they volunteered their lives for the benefit of humans. This was a gesture that humans cannot take lightly, for to disrespect the seal would be to abuse it and to cause it to stop offering itself for the hunt.

Therefore, the Yupik people, for instance, had a complex of three rituals in which they honored the seal and requested its continued self-sacrifice. In the first of these, the Bladder Festival, fallen seals were honored by returning their preserved bladders to their ocean home. The bladder was the chosen body part for ritualization because the Yupik believed that it was the seat of *yua*, roughly translated as "spirit." (*Yua* comes from the same root as *yupik*, their word for themselves, literally "person.") In the Bladder Festival, songs and dances were performed to entertain the animal spirits. The Messenger Festival, so named because communities sent messengers to their guests to inform them of the event, also invoked the hunted animals; masked dancers would imitate the behavior of seals as well as the actions of hunting and killing them. However, masks were most intricately involved in the Inviting-In Feast (*Agayuyaraq* or "way of requesting"), in which masked dancers entreated the animals to offer themselves up to the hunters again during the next season—in other words, the animals were "invited in" to participate in the hunt along with the hunters who were ready to receive them. As a critical part of the ritual, shamans wearing masks would travel to the moon, where the moon-man spirit who controls the movements of all animals lives.

Another subtype of ritual placed by Wallace in this category is divination. This assignment is more problematic, because divination, as we have seen, is not always "technical" although it does centrally involve the gods or spirits who are the authors of the messages received from the practice. However, in some cases it can be distinctly technical. Either way, the main point of divination is the acquisition of information, as discussed in Chapter 3.

Although Wallace does not mention it, perhaps this is the right place to put *magic* as well. Magic is frequently distinguished from religion in that the former is more technical and the latter more social; this is Frazer's classic analysis. Magic supposedly works directly on the object of the behavior, while religion tends to depend on an indirect relationship between means and ends, mediated by spirits or gods. For instance, rain magic or "voodoo" function by immediately affecting the clouds or the human victim by way of manipulation of materials (water, perhaps, or an effigy of the victim). Magical behaviors cause or compel their effects. Religion, on the other hand, requires the assistance and will of spiritual others; humans cannot cause effects but can petition for them. As Malinowski expressed it, religion is a social thing, an end in itself, whereas magic is a means to an end.

Most famously, Frazer divided magic into two types, imitative/sympathetic and contagious (1958). Imitative magic, he asserted, depends on some similarity between the technique and the end: a rain-making ceremony in which water is poured onto the ground imitates the goal of rain falling from the sky. Resemblance between the object of the ritual and its target also qualifies: a doll that represents a human victim can substitute for the victim in a magical or sorcery ritual. Turner's discussion of Ndembu symbolic use of the milk tree rests on the similarities between its sap and milk (1967). Contagious magic, on the other hand, depends on a physical contact or connection that exists or has existed between the technique and the goal. This might involve the manipulation of a lock of hair, a bit of fingernail, or a piece of clothing of a person in order to make magic on it, thus transferring the effects from the part to the whole. Touching someone with a magically powerful object could also qualify.

Therapeutic and Anti-Therapeutic Rituals

Many rites are performed as therapy, for the purpose of curing or preventing illness or other misfortune (e.g. bad luck), or alternatively for causing such misfortune. In many societies, it is believed that much if not most or all harm, sickness, and death are attributable to spiritual causes, human or otherwise. Forest Clements (1932) proposed that there are six sources of misfortune understood across cultures, one natural and five spiritual: magic, object intrusion, soul loss, spirit intrusion (possession), and breach of taboo. Therefore, the appropriate solution for (or way to cause) such circumstances is ritual.

One familiar form of therapeutic ritual is shamanism. In shamanic rituals, the specialist diagnoses and treats a specific complaint by a combination of means, both spiritual and material (e.g. medicinal plants) (see Figure 5.1). Other specialists like witches and sorcerers cause harm, sorcerers classically by manipulation and ritual whereas witches

Figure 5.1 A shaman performing a ritual to heal a sick child in Sikkim (India). Courtesy of the Alice S. Kandell Collection, Library of Congress Prints and Photographs Division

are often viewed as people with "natural," even organic, powers to cause harm when they project malice or negative emotions such as anger or jealousy. A witch or sorcerer alternatively might use his or her power to ward off the evil effects of others, either for themselves or for their clients.

In a more familiar context, Christianity has a place for therapeutic and anti-therapeutic practices. Faith healers are believed to channel divine power, often through their hands and touch, which can cure the faithful of all manner of diseases, commonly including sensory loss (e.g. blindness and deafness), pain and paralysis, and maladies like cancer. In many cases this curative function also entails combating the destructive power of demons or the very devil himself. Other specific traditions, such as Christian Science or Seventh Day Adventism, have taken the health effects of religion and spiritual forces even further.

Box 5.2 An Ndembu Ritual of Affliction

Victor Turner was particularly interested in so-called "rituals of affliction" (e.g. 1981), which are intended to identify and relieve the spiritual causes of ailment and which can involve many different beliefs, specialists, and ritual episodes. For instance, the entire process among the Ndembu of Zambia started with a visit to a diviner, who was the spiritual diagnostician but not the therapist. This type of divination was not about revealing the future but discovering the past: what particular spirit is afflicting the patient? Turner went on to describe in great detail one subsequent ritual, known as *Nkula*, which was intended "to remove a ban imposed by the shade of a deceased relative on the patient's fertility" (55), a condition usually reserved for women and indicated by such symptoms as infertility, sexual unresponsiveness, menstrual disorders, and irregular births (breach or stillbirths).

The ritual occurred in two large phases, each consisting of a number of scenes or episodes.

In phase one, called *Ku-Lembeka*, medicinal materials were collected and administered in an overnight ritual sequence. First, various substances were gathered from various sources, such as the *mukula, musoli,* and *mujiwu* plants. The symbolic-sympathetic quality of much of their action was apparent even to them, for instance using *mujiwu* for infertility since it "has many roots, therefore many children" (61). After collection, the substances were prepared and then applied, mostly by rubbing on the victim's body. As this was done, songs were sung, reminiscent of the Navajo prayers discussed above, such as: "It is good, let us just dance, it is good, it is good. It is good, *Nkula* manifestation, it is good, it is good, the position of clasping a baby in one's arms. Having to do with a child, it is good, it is good" (67).

The second phase, *Ku-Tumbuka*, was more extensive and public. It also began with the collection and preparation of medicinal substances. Then the patient was dressed in ritual garb—a waistcloth, animal skins draped over the shoulders, a quill in the hair, and clay rubbed on the face. This was followed by a nighttime ceremony in which the women danced around the sufferer. Next came a procession known as *Isoli* and a prayer at a *mukula* tree. When the prayer was complete, the tree was cut to be used for ritual carvings. The cuttings were carved into figurines described as "highly stylized representations of babies," although one informant asserted that they symbolized the shade called *mukishi*. During this procedure a red rooster was decapitated and roasted. Medicines were applied to the head of the figurines, made of a mixture of rooster entrails, feathers, hair and nails from the patient, clay, bark, and other material, which formed a thick red liquid, likened to a mass of coagulated blood. For the Ndembu, the menstrual and fertility metaphors were immanent. Finally, another dance named *Kutumbuka* was performed, and a payment was made to the ritual leaders. Throughout the *Nkula* time the patient observed various taboos, against touching or carrying water, for instance; the Ndembu said that water leaks and therefore would make the medicine leaky and weak (77).

Salvation Rituals

Wallace applied the term "salvation ritual," perhaps a little unfortunately, to those rites that seek to cause change of personality. Salvation as a Christian notion refers to something much different than personality change, so another term like "transformation ritual" or "psychological ritual" might have been more appropriate and cross-cultural.

An example of such rites might be the initiation of shamans, in which the future specialist is transformed into a new kind of person, one with spiritual powers, even one who is "dead" in a certain sense or has died and returned to the living. Master shamans prepare and instruct apprentice shamans not only (or mostly) by conveying information to them but by exposing them to experiences and perils that alter their consciousness. Typically this exposure includes sleep and food deprivation, long periods of singing or chanting, painful ordeals, and psychoactive drugs. At a point in the process, the former mind or personality of the novice breaks and is replaced by the new.

"Mystical" experiences in general have the capacity for personal transformation. Mysticism, an imprecise term, refers generally to the direct and immediate contact between the human and the supernatural, however conceived. The person may see a vision, hear a voice, feel the presence of the sacred, or sense a unity between him/herself and divinity or the universe. Commonly, the mystic describes the experience as a loss of self, as a collapse of the boundary of individuality, and an "oceanic" feeling in which he or she is one with the cosmos. Beyond that, the particulars of mystical experiences are incredibly diverse. Some mystics claim that the encounter is ineffable, that no words can communicate it. Others have written voluminously and systematically on the experience. For some, mystical union conveys no particular knowledge, while others claim to learn specific things as a result. For some, the experience is warm and comforting, while others find it alien or even frightening. Above all else, people tend to have the experiences that their culture prepares them for: Christians tend to experience God or Jesus, Muslims tend to experience Allah or Muhammad, and so on. Finally, some people claim to be changed by the experience, although others do not, and no definitive follow-up studies have been done to determine whether the transformation is permanent or significant.

Expiation is another form of personally transformative ritual. Expiation refers to the process of shedding guilt or sin, and rituals with this intent change the person by relieving the burden of spiritual negativity, lightening him or her spiritually. Confession might be an example within the Catholic tradition, in which sins are forgiven by being admitted and then paid for with various ritual acts, verbal and manual (e.g. repeating Hail Marys or counting rosary beads). Sacrifice is a way for an individual or community to expunge guilt or other negativity, by symbolically transferring the burden to the sacrificial victim and then destroying it, thereby destroying the burden (see Chapter 10).

Spirit possession is one remaining form of salvation ritual on Wallace's list (see Figure 5.2). This might strike us as strange, since possession by spirits is viewed as wholly negative from the Western perspective and is regularly the very condition to be cured rather than

Figure 5.2 A Colombian spiritual healer performs a ritual of exorcism on a woman who claims to be possessed by spirits. Using fire, dirt, candles, flowers, eggs, and other natural-based items, in conjunction with Christian religious formulas, he attempts to drive the supposed evil spirit out of the victim's mind and body. Photo by Jan Sochor/Latincontent/Getty Images

to be sought as a cure. Exorcism of spirits in Christian practice transforms the person by removing the causes of spiritual oppression and allowing the person to live his or her own life.

In other religious settings, however, the situation is not so simple. Erika Bourguignon (1976: 9), for example, found that there are at least three different ideas about and attitudes toward possession cross-culturally. One is the familiar view that possession is wholly undesirable, to be avoided, and to be cured when it happens. However, in other circumstances societies may regard the initial possession experience as bad and even sickness-producing but then respond by inducing a possession trance in an intentional and controlled way. In still other contexts possession is actually seen as a positive state and is literally sought and voluntarily induced.

The most interesting alternative for our purposes is the second, in which possession is not seen as desirable but, once it happens, is accepted and even accommodated in significant ways. Michael Lambek (1981) in his ethnography of possession on the island of Mayotte (off the African coast between Mozambique and Madagascar) related the concept to gender, ethnomedicine, and of course religious belief, both "native" and Islamic. In Mayotte society, spirit possession was indeed a form of affliction, alongside "natural disease" (which was still caused by God) and sorcery, which was the work of humans. Spirit possession or *menziky lulu* occurred when one of the many types of spirits known to the society entered a human's body, rose into the head, and took control of the victim's body. At such times, the person's own soul or essence or life-force or *rohu* was said to be displaced by the spirit, although no one could say where it went.

When a person suspected he or she was, or was suspected to be, inhabited by a spirit, a specialist induced a trance in the victim, during which the spirit was interrogated as to its intentions; typically, the spirit "makes a list of excessive, if predictable, demands, and there ensues a process of bargaining and exchange, which stabilizes the relationship between spirit and host" (46). At no time did the Mayotte consider exorcising the spirit, which they thought would be harmful to the person. Rather, they worked out a peaceful coexistence between the victim and the spiritual inhabitant, which may last for the rest of the person's life.

Lambek could not help but notice that the vast majority of the victims of possession were women: of a total of seventy spirit-possession cases, fifty-nine were women and only eleven men. He also noticed that Mayotte society had a layer of Islamic belief over the beliefs about spirits and possessions. He suggested that women found themselves burdened if not oppressed by social and religious roles and structures, especially Islamic ones, and that possession for women "is not so much an expression of opposition toward Islam as freedom from it" (64). That is, because society was so burdensome and restrictive for women, and even contradictory in its demands on her, she could not possibly find escape or respite in any "natural" or cultural medium; instead, her only recourse might be the release that spirit possession provides. Men, on the other hand, were less restricted in their options and less exposed to contradictory situations; even when they were, "they may more readily escape from the situation. They have less opportunity to learn to respond to paradox by 'blanking out' or by role playing than girls do, and they are, therefore, not as prepared to enter trance" (68–69). This analysis corresponds to the conclusion that Bourguignon reached:

> Possession trance offers alternative roles, which satisfy certain individual needs, and it does so by providing the alibi that the behavior is that of spirits and not of the human beings themselves. And furthermore, in order for human beings to play such

assertive roles, they must be totally passive, giving over their bodies to what are ego-alien forces. In a hierarchical society, demanding submission to those in authority, one acquires authority by identification with symbols of power, identification with which goes as far as the total assumption of the other's identity, total loss of its own. In this authoritarian society, it is possible to act out dominance fantasies by pretending, to self as well as others, total passivity and subjection.

(1976: 40)

Ideological Rituals

We might think of Wallace's ideological rituals as rites of social control (including perhaps Bell's "political rituals"), in which individuals, groups, or society in its entirety are moved, influenced, and manipulated. These rituals function to structure social reality and to adjust individuals to that reality, creating the rules and experiences that shape and perpetuate the members' reality. Some of these rituals are instructional or informative, while others are intended to instill "moods and motivations" upon which society depends. Or, most often, as in the case of the Christian passion play that recounts the story of Christ's suffering, both are accomplished simultaneously.

Rites of social intensification are among the most obvious and important such rituals. As Radcliffe-Brown commented, contrary to Malinowski, the function of religion is often not to satisfy the needs of the individual, especially the need for freedom from fear and anxiety (1965). Religion and ritual can actually *increase* the fear and anxiety of individuals, not least their fear and anxiety about religious matters: only people who do believe in demons or hell, or a punishing god, are afraid of them. Rather, Radcliffe-Brown suggested that much of religion and ritual functions above the personal level, for the benefit of society as a structured whole. Especially in times of crisis, but often on a day-to-day basis, society is threatened with disintegration, with the collapse of groups and order and the atomization of individuals or families. When there is a death (particularly a suspicious one, and recall that death is often if not always suspicious in some societies) or a natural disaster or merely an internal feud, society could disintegrate. Rituals, even negative ones like witch inquiries or hostile funerary rites, can prevent the disintegration of society by giving people things to do and ways to direct their feelings and concerns.

Australian Aboriginal societies, for instance, often responded to a death with an aggressive duel between kin groups (see Figure 5.3). Dancing in opposing lines, the event would turn into a confrontation in which the sides tossed spears at each other. Usually, no mortal injury was desired or achieved; one side or both would draw blood (normally by bouncing spears off the ground so that they would strike at unpredictable angles), and when the blood-vengeance was satisfied, the ritual could end and people could return to their common lives together.

Taboos and ceremonial obligations form a genus of ideological rituals. These types of beliefs and behaviors center around things that people must or must not do or touch. The very essence of these restrictions is the notion of sacred power, as Durkheim hypothesized. Some objects, actions, or persons are so powerful that they are dangerous, at least for the normal person in normal circumstances. When a person is properly prepared (purified, ritually protected, etc.) he or she might approach these same items or perform these acts safely. Perhaps the social significance of taboo is the experience of ritual *seriousness*—that all things are not equal and that our behavior must reflect this fact. And of course it is not only things that are unequal but *people*. Rituals of kingship, for

Figure 5.3 Australian Aboriginal (Warlpiri) men and boys practicing a ritual dance. Courtesy of the author

example, establish the powerful or even sacred character of the king or ruler, and ideologies such as the "divine right of kings" justify and perpetuate that power. The ritual obligations that individuals observe in relation to each other create and maintain social structures as well as spiritual ones, as we will discuss in the next chapter.

Under ideological rituals Wallace included rites of passage, which are important and pervasive enough to deserve a separate treatment (see below). Finally, he mentioned "rituals of rebellion," which we might, in some cases anyhow, regard as *anti-ideological* rituals. That is, these rituals of rebellion can comment upon, criticize, and even invert everyday social relations and structures. Carnival in the traditional sense was one such occasion, where the point of the event was to break intentionally many of the rules and norms of society; nonconformity, sexual license, and "political" inversions (making fun of or even desecrating the king, among others) were common forms, and we can still see some of this in the New Orleans Mardi Gras festival or more so in the Brazilian *carnivale*. Halloween is a faint echo of such a practice, when people deliberately conceal their identity and adopt fictional and even sacrilegious personae for the day. At the same time, these rule-ordered rule-breakings also have the effect of restating and reaffirming the structures and power relations of society; the very fact that you can belittle the king on one day a year (with his permission) establishes his power every other day of the year (see Chapter 6).

Rituals of Revitalization

Religion and ritual can be not only conservative and stabilizing but also creative, liberating, resistant, and even revolutionary. When a society, or at least some segment of a society, is in crisis, religion can provide the language for rethinking rules, roles, and realities and for responding to the critical challenges with a "program" intended to breathe new life into a failing social, natural, and supernatural order. Among the types of rituals or ritual movements in this category, all of which we will return to later, are messianic and millenarian ones, "cargo cults," nativism and fundamentalism, syncretism, separatism/schism or the founding of new religious sects within an existing tradition or church, and "new religious movements" with more or less novel spiritual views and agendas. Most often, by the time a society is deep enough in crisis for these phenomena to appear, many of these various forms are appearing simultaneously, making of a society a bubbling broth of religious innovation and competition. Such is the modern world and modern American society. We will delve into these processes in Chapters 6 and 7.

Rites of Passage: The Structure of Ritual

Students of religion like Victor Turner have suggested that there is a "ritual process" that cuts across the superficial differences between rituals to unify them at a deeper level. Turner wrote extensively on the ritual process, developing the ideas of Arnold van Gennep on so-called *rites of passage*. Many rituals around the world seem to occur at key moments in the life of individuals, groups, or society as a whole. Rituals accompany these key moments—moments when things are changing or threatening to change in some way, such as puberty, adulthood, marriage, parenthood, and death. Even more, though, the rituals help or serve to *accomplish* the change occurring at that moment; along the lines of illocutionary speech acts, the ritual facilitates the change rather than merely acknowledging or celebrating it.

The ritual process involves three stages, the middle of which drew the bulk of Turner's attention. These three stages can be conceptualized as follows:

Separation → Marginality/Liminality → Aggregation

The best way to think of this progression is in terms of the condition or status of the subjects before and after the ritual. Prior to a ritual, a person is in some state—say, unmarried or juvenile or ill. Subsequent to the ritual, the person is in a different state— say, married or adult or well. Something happens in between that transforms or delivers the individual from one status to another. However, that cannot happen without two concomitant things happening—the loss or falling away or "death" of the old status and the journey through an ambiguous transitional phase.

Thus, a rite of passage typically begins with a symbolic break from the previous status. In some societies, an initiation ritual of youths into adulthood (perhaps the classic rite of passage) or of a shaman into his or her new vocation starts with a capture of the candidate and even a mock "death." In the case of coming of age initiations, adult men may enter the community and seize the young males while their mothers wail that they will never see their children again. In a certain sense, they are correct. The adolescents may be sequestered from the rest of society for the duration of the ritual or for weeks or months at a time, where they are put through trials including physical operations like circumcision or scarification, shown sacred objects, and instructed in religious knowledge. Or there may be little such "training." The Gisu of Uganda traditionally practiced an initiation ritual in which males aged eighteen to twenty-five were circumcised in public and then given gifts signifying their entry into manhood, such as farming implements. However, what they did not receive was any specific teaching. The main function of the

Figure 5.4 Young men wearing Gisu circumcision regalia consisting of a headdress of black and white Colobus monkey, tails of cowhide, and cowrie shells. Under the direction of a song leader (left), this is part of the first phase of ceremonial dancing where the boys are expressing an interest in going through the rites later in the year. Courtesy of Pitt Rivers Museum, University of Oxford

ritual, other than to announce maturity, seemed to be to generate a particular emotional or psychological trait in the men, which the Gisu called *lirima*. *Lirima* was the manly quality of violent emotion, connected with anger, jealousy, hatred, and resentment. It was not totally wild emotion, though; it also implied or required self-control, strength of character, bravery, and will. It was the characteristic that enabled men to overcome fear (the ritual itself was a test of overcoming fear), but it was also a dangerous characteristic, one that produced aggressiveness in men that even the Gisu themselves regretted (Heald 1986).

To return to our general discussion, having been separated from their social world and their previous lives, the candidates of rites of passage enter into the second or "liminal" (from the Latin *limen* or threshold) stage. This is a condition that Turner referred to as "betwixt and between," not another status but a *non-status*. It is the absence of status, a social no-place, but a condition of potential. It is the doorway or portal between statuses, the road that links the origin and destination. This non-status takes a variety of symbolic forms, often likened to or expressed as death, wilderness, return to the womb, even bisexuality. It is without name, rank, or social identity. Occupants of this threshold may be deprived of possessions including clothes; they came into life naked, so they must come into their new life naked. They are often expected to be obedient, passive, receptive, and non-assertive. In other situations, including periodic rituals partaken by adults, the language of liminality may involve opposites, doing things "backward" or "upside down," and other forms of contradiction or violation of everyday behavior, as we will see below.

In a way, the liminal condition is a lowly one, virtually outside of society altogether. In another way, though, it is a sacred condition—special, powerful, and perhaps dangerous. One particular way in which liminality combines all these features is in the elimination of distinctions, social and otherwise. It is a manifestation of the unnamed state, the circumstance when all things are equal but therefore unstructured. Turner referred to this condition as *communitas*, a kind of undifferentiated and structureless existence. There are no children or adults, no males or females, no kings and commoners. As an example, when Muslim pilgrims undertake the *hajj* or journey to Mecca, they shed their markings of nationality and rank and don the same white robes, indicating the shared (and therefore undifferentiated) status of pilgrim (see pp. 120–3).

It should be easy to see that, while this is a creative state, it is also an unstable one. Neither individuals nor society can endure there for long. In other words, "all sustained manifestations of communitas must appear as dangerous and anarchical, and have to be hedged around with prescriptions, prohibitions, and conditions" (Turner 1969: 109). Interestingly, Turner identified this communitas experience in other social locations besides the liminality of ritual passage, including the status of "hippies," monks, prophets, and jesters/comedians, and no doubt poets and artists—all those people who are at the margins or the "interstices" or the bottom of society. Structured society tolerates them, even benefits from them, but their "anti-structure" always poses a threat to social order. They also represent the creative corner from which new social orders will emerge. Thus, ultimately, society, via religion and ritual, is a cycle or dialectic of communitas and differentiation, anarchy and order.

Ritual Fields, Ritual Performances, and "Social Theater"

In the ethnography of religious behavior, as of religious language, we find not a single monolithic practice but a diverse "field" in which different kinds of rituals are performed. It is perhaps possible—but frequently erroneous—to conceive of myths and other verbal genres without the performance, as Lévi-Strauss and others have actually done (see Chapter 4). However, in the case of ritual, performance is fundamental to their reality, let alone their effectiveness; while one could summarize or describe a ritual, in no way would the summary or the description equate to doing the ritual. In fact, Roy Rappaport wrote that ritual "is an order of *acts* and *utterances* and as such is enlivened or realized only when those acts are performed and those utterances voiced" (1992: 252). For this reason alone, ritual cannot be understood apart from its performance.

It is also true that, in any given society, a variety of rituals or entire ritual genres may coexist, and that any particular ritual is a temporal combination of elements from the ritual field (as Wallace suggested). Turner, one of the central contributors to the performative analysis of ritual, went so far as to reject the "obsessional" aspect of ritual—the compulsive repetition of formulaic acts—and to highlight its creative and multimedia aspects. He regarded ritual as "an immense orchestration of genres in all available sensory codes: speech, music, singing; the presentation of elaborately worked objects, such as masks; wall paintings, body paintings; sculptured forms; complex, multi-tiered shrines; costumes; dance forms with complex grammars and vocabularies of body movements, gestures, and facial expressions" (1984: 25), and presumably much more. Each specific such orchestration—with its attendant beliefs and specialist roles—would generate a specific kind of ritual. For instance, Seneviratne (1978) distinguished between two types of rituals in pre-colonial Kandy, a kingdom on Sri Lanka. One type concerned the maintenance of sacred objects, including daily and weekly rites for tending temple artifacts and symbols, as well as the annual New Year ceremonies consisting of bathing, boiling milk until it overflowed and flooded the site, and food offerings. The second type focused on common social ends, such as the New Rice festival (itself composed of a series of events from processions to the fields to measurement of the crop to distribution among the temples to presentation of a bowl of rice to the *Dalada* or relic of the sacred tooth of Buddha). Tambiah, also working in a Buddhist context, found an even more crowded ritual field with four types of rituals: formally "Buddhist" ones (performed by monks), *sukhwan* rites (performed by elders to "bind" individuals' personal spirits to their bodies), ceremonies for the cult of village guardian spirits, and rites of possession aimed at evil spirits (performed by a panoply of specialists depending on the complaint and the spirit involved). Tambiah concluded explicitly that "the four ritual complexes are differentiated and also linked together in a *single total* field" (1970: 2). We began this chapter with an example of such "ritual polytropy" from China.

On an even grander scale, Turner related rituals and ritual behavior to what he called "social dramas" (1974). Social dramas are public, symbolic scenes in which the conflicts or disharmonies of society are played out; they might also be, although he stressed the disharmonic side, scenes in which the harmonies or essential relationships or truths of a society are played out. Social dramas are built from basic components which he called *fields* and *arenas*. Fields in this sense are defined as "the abstract cultural domains where paradigms are formulated, established, and come into conflict. Such paradigms consist of sets of 'rules' from which many kinds of sequences of social action may be generated but which further specify what sequences must be concluded" (17). Arenas then are "the concrete settings in which paradigms become transformed into metaphors and symbols with reference to which political power is mobilized and in which there is a trial of strength between influential paradigm-bearers" (17). Social dramas, as a result, are the performed processes of this social contest, played out in public and over a (more or less protracted) period of time. They are characterized by four phases, from the initial breach in social relations, to a social crisis of some sort, to "redressive action" aimed at healing the breach, to the ultimate reintegration of actors into society and (ideally) the restoration of social relations and institutions.

Rituals as social dramas are many things, including socially appropriate interaction with the supernatural, communication, effective action, social and political power, and entertainment. All of these features combine into the notion of social theater, in which people and groups put on performances for each other, even if they are not intentionally "putting on" their performances at all. One scholar to take the notion of social theater seriously was sociologist Erving Goffman, whose highly influential *The Presentation of Self in Everyday Life* (1959) portrayed a theatrical account of social life, in which all human beings are actors taking on roles and in which all social encounters are potentially stages upon which these actors play their roles. The most minute situations may be opportunities for individuals to demonstrate their social competence or to manipulate the impressions that they make upon others, and in some cases individuals realize they are doing so and play these roles self-consciously.

If Goffman described human social action as performative and theatrical at the smallest scale, Clifford Geertz described it as such at perhaps the greatest possible scale. In his discussion of traditional Balinese culture, he referred to Bali as a "theater state" where ritual was politics and politics was ritual. In the theater state,

> the kings and princes were the impresarios, the priests the directors, and the peasants the supporting cast, stage crew, and audience. The stupendous cremations, tooth filings, temple dedications, pilgrimages, and blood sacrifices, mobilizing hundreds and even thousands of people and great quantities of wealth, were not means to particular ends: they were the ends themselves, they were what the state was for. Court

ceremonialism was the driving force of court politics; and mass ritual was not a device to shore up the state, but rather the state, even in its final gasp, was a device for the enactment of mass ritual. Power served pomp, not pomp power.

(1980: 13)

Ritual was theater indeed—a great display of the society, by the society, and for the society—in which people enacted their roles and their rules and, in enacting them, made them real. A ceremony like a royal cremation (recounted in detail by Geertz) was a performance of the deepest and most important themes of Balinese culture: "the center is exemplary, status is the ground of power, statecraft is a thespian art" (120). This is probably not much less true today, even in the Western world, and it is perhaps more visible today than at any time in its past: politics is performance, political leaders are actors, and the public is the audience, and together they create and maintain the cultural and political world they inhabit. The ceremonialism of society is never merely superficial decoration, because in the West and in pre-colonial Bali, and arguably in all societies at all times, "the pageants were not mere aesthetic embellishments, celebrations of a domination independently existing: they were the thing itself" (120). Rituals, in other words, are "great collective gestures" (116), realizations in the sense that they "make real" cultural ideas and ideals. In the final analysis, the "dramas of the theatre state"—and probably of all states and societies—"mimetic of themselves, were, in the end, neither illusions nor lies, neither sleight of hand nor make-believe. They were what there was" (136).

Pilgrimage: Religion in Motion

One of the most prolonged and potentially dramatic of rituals and social dramas is the pilgrimage. Christians have been making pilgrimages to Jerusalem and to various sites in Europe for centuries, and the *hajj* or pilgrimage to Mecca is one of the obligatory "pillars" of Islam, yet anthropology arguably overlooked pilgrimage until the 1970s (see Figure 5.5). Barbara

Figure 5.5 Pilgrims at Mecca (*c*.1910). Courtesy of the Library of Congress Prints and Photographs Division

Myerhoff's (1974) rich description of the sacred journey of the Huichol people of Mexico known as the Peyote Hunt was one of the first extended analyses. However, in her introduction to the 2011 edition of Victor Turner and Edith Turner's *Image and Pilgrimage in Christian Culture* (originally published in 1978), Deborah Ross credits the Turners as "the founders of pilgrimage studies" (Turner and Turner 2011: xxxiv).

Naturally, for the Turners pilgrimage was understood as a rite of passage, as exiting the mundane state and crossing a threshold into a different place and a different time—that is, into liminality. The place of pilgrimage is literally often far away and difficult to reach, yet for the pilgrim it is the most important place, even the true home from which s/he is separated and alienated in everyday life. It is "the center out there," as Victor Turner (1973) phrased it in another essay. Sometimes the site is a hierophany in Mircea Eliade's sense, a place where something significant once happened and/or where power and meaning reside today. According to Turner, the journey of the pilgrim "reenacts the temporal sequences made sacred and permanent by the succession of events in the lives of incarnate gods, saints, gurus, prophets, and martyrs" (1973: 221), and the pilgrim adds his/her effort to the historical accumulation of energy on that route.

As a path that others have trod—at the very least, the spirit or ancestor who established the path, and most likely a train of previous pilgrims—the space of pilgrimage is not spontaneous or idiosyncratic but typically well marked. There may be and often is a designated pilgrimage "course," as in Japan, where the standard pilgrim course "is a visit to a series of temples in a set order, resulting in a circuit" (Usui 2007: 29) (see Figure 5.6). For instance, the pilgrimage of the Thirty-Three Holy Places of Kannon involves a circuit of thirty-three temples dedicated to the deity Kannon, while eighty-eight temples constitute a pilgrimage circuit on Shikoku Island. Altogether, Sachiko Usui indicates 234 pilgrimage courses around Japan, linking 4,423 temples.

Figure 5.6 Worshipers at a Japanese temple. Courtesy of the author

Obviously, an inherent aspect of pilgrimage is *movement*, both in the sense of *moving out* of one's everyday space and of *moving through* the pilgrimage space. As such, the issue of pilgrimage fits well with anthropology's increasing interest in flow and circulation, in crossing boundaries and frontiers. Pilgrimage also raises important questions about the body, since the pilgrim's body undergoes many new and sometimes trying experiences, not the least of which is walking. A pilgrim's commitment, Turner wrote, is to "full physicality," to *being there*, and the pilgrim thus "becomes himself a total symbol" (1973: 221) who enacts and embodies the message and power of the place and its history.

Box 5.3 Walking the Spirit: Spain's *Camino de Santiago*

While the "center out there" for Christianity is Jerusalem, and many Christians do in fact make pilgrimages back to the "holy land," Europe itself is crisscrossed with pilgrimage courses. One of the most famous is the *Camino de Santiago* or path/way of St. James, which ends in Santiago de Compostela in the northwest corner of Spain. Actually, as the *camino*'s website (www.santiago-compostela.net) depicts, and as Nancy Louise Frey discussed, the *Camino de Santiago* is

> really a network of routes, many of Roman origin, extending throughout Europe that have been used regularly by pilgrims since the eleventh century … The various *caminos* are based on other historical pilgrimage roads to Santiago. The *camino inglés* (English way) led British pilgrims arriving by sea at La Coruña south of Santiago, the *camino portugués* (Portuguese way) brought pilgrims north, and the *via de la plata* (silver way) was used by pilgrims from the south and center of the peninsula to join the *camino francés* (French/ Frankish way) at Astorga.
>
> (Frey 1998: 5)

Every year, thousands of people from around Europe and around the world travel the *camino*, some because of the Catholic Church's doctrine of salvation and remission of sin, others in pursuit of "transcendent spirituality, tourism, physical adventure, nostalgia, a place to grieve, and esoteric initiation" (4). Despite their many motivations, an important commonality among pilgrims is that many "believe they will find 'something'—God, friendship, themselves, others—while on the road" (87). Accordingly, while the novice may think that the point of the *camino* is to reach the city at its end, in actuality the goal "is often the road itself, not the city" (45). That is, the point of the pilgrimage is the journey, not the destination. And the journey is often as much internal and psychological as external and geographic. Interviewing pilgrims on the road, Frey found that many of them were "making a life-cycle transition—from youth to adulthood, from midlife reflection and crisis to retirement. More serious wounds—or 'critical life gaps,' as one pilgrim put it—also draw pilgrims to the *Camino*" (45). Victor Turner would approve of this as classic rite of passage. Indeed, often the effect was a personal transformation in the pilgrim, the achievement of "the reorientation they seek in their own lives" (46).

The transformation begins long before the actual voyage, during the days or years of preparation. During the pilgrimage itself, two main experiences are anonymity and solitude, both highly typical of liminality. In solitude, pilgrims can commune with nature and introspect. With anonymity, everyone is equal: "That a diplomat walks with a field hand and a teacher with a policeman and a graduate student is very appealing among pilgrims. Feeling oneself anonymous and equal can be remarkably liberating for many" (86). And the third main experience is *walking*, since the ideal pilgrim makes the journey on foot. Frey wrote

> When pilgrims begin to walk several things usually begin to happen to their perceptions of the world which continue over the course of the journey: they develop a changing sense of time, a heightening of their senses, and a new awareness of their bodies and the landscape. Marina begins her statement with "I began to walk," immediately linking basic human movement with joy and discovery. The walking reveals a world of natural beauty existing out of ordinary time. In this moment preparation and chance meet. No matter how much one prepares physically, mentally, and spiritually one cannot prepare for the unanticipated that the Way presents. Launching oneself into the unknown is an important first step into one's role as a pilgrim.
>
> (72)

Since the founding work of the Turners, the anthropological study of pilgrimage has grown. In their examination of Muslim pilgrimage, Dale Eickelman and James Piscatori (1990) questioned whether pilgrimage is necessarily an extraordinary experience as opposed to everyday life and routine. John Eade and Michael J. Sallow (1991), as the title of their *Contesting the Sacred* implies, stressed the divergences and disagreements in the experiences and interpretations of pilgrims rather than their imputed communitas. Finally, anthropologists and other scholars could not help notice the similarities between pilgrimage and "tourism": as the Turners themselves opined, "A tourist is half a pilgrim, if a pilgrim is half a tourist" (2011: 20). Both travel in search of something, and both are perhaps transformed by their voyage. People may even visit religious sites as tourists rather than as pilgrims. At the same time, ultimately, people may visit secular sites and walk secular circuits with the attitude of a pilgrim: Elvis Presley fans may treat a stop at Graceland as a pilgrimage and sacred experience (see Davidson and Gitlitz 2002), just as Americans may treat a tour of Gettysburg or Plymouth Rock as a pilgrimage to a sacred place.

Conclusion

Rituals are a key component of religion. However, the tendency to see ritual as uniquely religious and uniquely symbolic distorts both religion and ritual. Religion is not so much a thing to believe or to "mean" as a thing to *do*. Humans have goals—practical and social—to accomplish. If language is effective, though, then action is doubly so. Social action—religious or otherwise—is *interaction*, and it makes sense that humans who ascribe supernatural agency to the world would interact with those agents in the only ways they know how. Since all human social interaction takes place within an "interaction code" which not only comments on but *performs* and achieves those interactions, then religious interactions can be understood as instances—and particularly formal and serious instances—of a behavioral code as well. And while much human behavior is symbolic (and some may be purely symbolic), religious behavior must be understood, from the actor's perspective, as at least partly "real" too. Religious rituals, whether or not they have practical effects, have social effects, but it is hard to imagine that people would perform healing rituals solely for the social effects. They must think, rightly or wrongly, that the ritual has some healing effects as well. In other words, rituals are not merely informative (and often not informative at all) but *transformative*—establishing certain states of being (like wellness), certain kinds of persons or social statuses, a certain kind of society, and ultimately a certain kind of world.

DISCUSSION QUESTIONS

- What is ritualization? How does the "interaction code" help explain the special qualities of ritual?
- What are the main types of ritual, and how do they differ?
- What is Victor Turner's "ritual process," and how is ritual a kind of performance and "social theater"?

SUPPLEMENTARY READING (see website)

- *Ritual and Experience: The Japanese Tea Ceremony*
- *Cognitive Science of Religion and Ritual Competence: McCauley and Lawson*
- *Two Turkish Pilgrimages: The Islamic Hajj and the Return Home*
- *Return to Paradise: The Peyote Hunt of the Huichol*

6 Religion, Morality, and Social Order

In the United States and Europe, most Christians expect their churches to "do good"—to engage in charity such as providing food or clothing for the poor. Islam includes an obligation on each member to offer charity (*zakat*, literally "purification"), as well as the institution of *waqf* (a religious endowment) to provide benefits to individuals or organizations. But Tobias Köllner contends that the Russian Orthodox Church "has tried to avoid taking up a role as a provider of social support" (2011: 193). In fact, one priest interviewed by Köllner, a Father Vladimir, actually

> opposes a Western understanding of charity in order to overcome misery, poverty, and illnesses. Referring to the Bible, he argues that misery and poverty will always exist and there is no way to prevent them. Rather, donations are perceived as a way of securing one's own salvation, and not as a feasible way to change the world.
>
> (194)

Such donations "are perceived and described as a form of penance (*pokaianie*) for one's sins" (199), but what are they used for, if not to assist people in need? They are spent "primarily for the erection of new churches and the adornment (*ukrashenie*) or reconstruction of existing ones" (195).

Morality is often presumed to be the essence or greatest contribution of religion. People who know or value little else about religion may esteem it for its moral qualities; parents may expose their children to religion solely for the purpose of making them "good." In fact, some argue that it is impossible to be "good without God" (which raises the doubly awkward problem that "good" is a relative term and that not all religions have gods).

While there is no doubt that all cultures feature behavioral exhortations and injunctions, the relationship between morality and religion has been a controversial one. E. B. Tylor wrote rather dismissively that the "moral element which among the higher nations forms a most vital part, is indeed little represented in the religion of the lower races" (1958: 29). Indeed, it was the moral or ethical dimension that most separated the "lower" and "higher" religions. Durkheim, on the other hand, placed morality in the very definition of religion: "beliefs and practices which unite into one single moral community called a Church, all those who adhere to them" (see Chapter 1).

In this chapter, we will explore the relation between religion, morality conceived as codes or standards for individual behavior, and the order and institutions of society. From an anthropological perspective, we are less interested in the particulars of any moral system, let alone in ranking such systems as low or high, than with how such systems contribute to society and to the construction and transformation of individuals in society. Religion is by no means the only source or sanction of rules, but in its Malinowskian function as a "charter" for society, it is potentially the firmest source. At the same time, we must acknowledge the role of *disorder* or at least of the violation, transgression, and inversion of order as part of social reality, with its inevitable tensions, complexities, and ambiguities.

The Anthropology of Morality

Millennia of philosophers have struggled to define and document morality, with little success or consensus, so we will not be able to solve the problem here. What anthropology brings to the discussion of morality is attention to diversity, to social construction, and to the relativity of language. First, then, it is immanently obvious that morality actually exists as a widely varied congeries of *moralities*, just as religion actually exists as a widely varied congeries of *religions*. Accordingly, most studies of morality have been attempts not so much to describe and explain morality as to propose a—or *the*—"true" or "best" morality. In other words, most "moral theories" have in reality been advocacy for a certain morality. The idea of moral diversity has been generally lacking.

Yet, when we look cross-culturally, we find, as the philosopher Nietzsche put it, a thousand and one different tablets of good and evil. There are many moralities, each different in ways—some small, some great—from the others. In some societies, polygamy is regarded as immoral, and in others it is held as the ideal kind of marriage. Certain behaviors are immoral in one while the same behaviors are accepted and lauded in others. Even killing is tolerated or celebrated, at least in some forms, in virtually all societies. The Judeo-Christian scriptures, while they forbid killing in one passage ("Thou shalt not kill"), make time for killing in another ("A time to kill, a time to heal"), and most Westerners regard killing in self-defense and "just war" to be morally acceptable. Certainly killing insects is of no moral consequence to most Westerners, but a Jain in India might find it a serious moral failing.

On closer inspection, then, it is not clear what morality means. It is not even clear what is or is not a moral matter in the first place. In the United States, public nudity is a moral concern, but in other societies it is not. In the United States, premarital sex is at least a subject for moral argument, but in other societies it is not. In his portrait of Nuer religion, Evans-Pritchard painted them as remarkably "Christian" in their attitudes and practices, but he also warned us that "we have to be more than usually on guard against thinking into Nuer thought what may be in our own and is alien to theirs. From this point of view the ethical content of what the Nuer regard as grave faults may appear to be highly variable, and even altogether absent" (1956: 188). Indeed, what the Nuer judged as "grave faults, or even as faults at all," may appear to a Westerner as "rather trivial actions" (189)—and no doubt the feeling would be mutual. Incest and adultery are major issues for both of us, but the Nuer injunctions against "a man milking his cow and drinking the milk, or a man eating with persons with whom his kin are at blood-feud" (189) seem oddly irrelevant to Westerners, as many traditional Judeo-Christian injunctions—such as prohibitions on eating meat on Friday or eating pork or shellfish at all—would seem oddly irrelevant to the Nuer (and, honestly, to many modern Christians).

So it seems that there are no universal moral answers, *because there are no universal moral questions*. Rather, when most English-speakers talk about morality, they mean something vague about "good behavior" (or, as in the United States, "morality" tends to be a code word for sexual and reproductive matters). But there are varying definitions and standards of "goodness" across societies and religions. One way that anthropologists and other scholars have tried to settle the dispute over "goodness" is in terms of "prosociality," which Ara Norenzayan and Azim Shariff define as "acts that benefit others at a personal cost" (2008: 58). But it is hard to see how some "moral" issues, such as public nudity or premarital sex, have anything to do with "benefit," and the fact that many religions offer rewards for good behavior mitigates the personal cost.

Further, even in Western society, not all undesirable actions are "immoral." "Moral" as an adjective is part of what philosopher Kai Nielsen called "appraisal language," the set of words that English-speakers use to appraise or judge their own and each other's behavior, including such terms as "(ab)normal" or "(un)ethical" or "(il)legal" or "(in) sane." Not every action that is immoral is illegal and vice versa (e.g. speeding is not immoral by any familiar standard). Ethics and morality are not completely synonymous, since we can speak of "business ethics" but not usually of "business morals." Even etiquette and propriety shape our behavior and our evaluations of others' behavior: it may be unetiquette, but not immoral, to refuse a handshake or to use the wrong fork.

Sin and Pollution

Just as in the case of belief, symbol, myth, and sacrifice (see Chapters 2, 3, 4, and 10), the discourse of morality in Western societies, and in much of anthropology, is the Judeo-Christian discourse. In this particular religious tradition, morality is generally perceived as explicit, formal (even written down), abstract, and legalistic. It is also typically seen as an individual (rather than collective) and "existential" matter, that is, a commentary on the individual's essential state of being. A crucial part of this language is the concept of "sin," a condition of moral and spiritual fault. However, like belief and symbol and myth, sin in particular and morality in general may be impositions of one religion's worldview on others.

Sin is a concept that does not appear in all religions; it is also a concept with varied and evolving meaning in Judeo-Christian religion. One Hebrew root for sin in the scriptures is *chet* or *khate*, meaning going astray or missing the mark—literally the term used in archery for missing the target. Three varieties of sin are recognized: *pasha* or *mered* for intentional defiance of God's laws, *avon* for lust or other strong emotions (which are intentional but not defiant), and *cheit* for unintentional violations of law. (In fact, the first occurrence of the word "sin" comes in Genesis, or *Bereishith* in the original Hebrew, chapter 4, *before* any specific laws had been instituted.) Christians eventually developed the concept of "original sin," a congenital and therefore inescapable state of flaw or guilt, for which divine salvation is the only remedy.

However, in the original usages of the sin-concept, congenital, permanent, and even "moral" connotations were not necessarily implied. Sin was often temporary, fading over time, or it could be removed and "cleansed" through specific ritual actions such as washing or sacrifice. In fact, many things that Christians interpret as "sins" were actually referred to as "abominations" or "uncleanness" and applied to areas of conduct that most modern Westerners would consider outside the scope of morality. Dietary laws, for instance, identified particular plant and animal species as fit or unfit to eat; likewise, men and women were instructed not to wear clothing of the opposite sex (Deuteronomy/ *Devarim* 22:5). A word meaning "unclean" (*niddah* or *tum'ah*) was employed to describe the effects of actions as disparate as touching a dead carcass or any prohibited animal, committing adultery, or merely giving birth. A woman was unclean for seven days (for a boy-child) or fourteen days (for a girl-child) after birth, and adultery with a brother's wife was not immoral but unclean, resulting in childlessness (Leviticus/*Vayiqra* 20:21).

According to Evans-Pritchard the Nuer too had a notion of sin (*nueer*), but he admitted "that Nuer do not express indignation at sin and that what they get most indignant about is not thought of as sin" (1956: 194)—in other words, "sinful" actions were not their greatest "moral" concern. Further, the threat of an act was not its "immoral" quality but the "state of grave spiritual danger" it engendered: for example, it was not wrong to kill a man in fair combat, but it was still spiritually dangerous. Thus, the real issue for the Nuer was not with "people's morals, whether according to Nuer ideas they are good or bad people, but with their spiritual condition, though good or bad conduct may affect this condition" (195).

Notice that, for the Nuer, actions were not punished because they were "bad" but rather were bad because they were punished; the badness lay in the consequences, not the "morality," of the behavior. *Kwoth* (spirit) punished what *kwoth* punished, even or primarily "unwitting offences," which made people feel worried but not guilty. The consequences of course could be quite severe, including physical illness. However, the response to spiritual danger and punishment was *woc*, to wipe it away, through religious as well as material means such as medicines and other cleansing actions but especially through sacrifice.

As dissimilar as they are, the Nuer and Judeo-Christian views of sin and danger share two qualities. The first is that they result from violations of supernatural strictures. The second is that they are "infectious" in the sense that they infect or contaminate the individual and, potentially, the family, society, and physical world itself. Various terms that might be and have been applied to this conception are pollution, defilement, impurity, uncleanness, and profanation. (Recall that Durkheim suggested that the core of religion is the separation of the sacred and the profane.) Immorality in this sense is like a disease— but mostly a curable one—that corrupts the person, body or soul or both.

One of the first anthropologists to take seriously the idea of purity, cleanness, and "dirt" and their relation to religion and danger was Mary Douglas. In her *Purity and Danger*, first published in 1966, she connected dirt with disorder, including social disorder. Notions of dirt or impurity, along with those of (physical and spiritual) hygiene, constituted "a set of ordered relations and a contravention of that order" (1988: 35). Pollution or profanation "offends against order. Eliminating it is not a negative movement, but a positive effort to organize the environment," both natural and supernatural (2). In her most famous analysis, she explained the Jewish dietary laws, the so-called "abominations of Leviticus," in terms of classification and violation of classification. Some animals, she reasoned, belonged to the category of species that "split the hoof and chew the cud," and such animals were "clean" and proper to eat. Animals that deviated from this type were unclean and improper to eat. Likewise, a "true fish" had fins and scales, and any exception to this type, like shellfish, was not a fish at all and therefore unfit for consumption. As she concluded, "in general the underlying principle of cleanness in animals is that they shall conform fully to their class. Those species are unclean which are imperfect members of their class, or whose class itself confounds the general scheme of the world" (55).

In the same year as Douglas, Louis Dumont published his *Homo Hierarchicus* stressing the significance of "purity" for India and the caste system. Humans themselves are classified into castes, he insisted, on the basis of their spiritual or ritual purity, and the highest and purist caste (the priestly Brahmans) literally worried about the defilement that came with the touch of a low-caste individual, especially the "outcastes" or "untouchables." Lower castes were certainly not "immoral" as such, but they were polluted and polluting. Mixing castes, then, like eating the wrong animal or performing the wrong action for Douglas, was a violation of the order of things—of the rules and categories that comprise society—and was *dangerous*. Douglas thus concluded that beliefs about impurity, pollution, and "sin" and the dangers thereof

> are a strong language of mutual exhortation. At this level the laws of nature are dragged in to sanction the moral code: this kind of disease is caused by adultery, that by incest; this meteorological disaster is the effect of political disloyalty, that the effect of impiety. The whole universe is harnessed to man's attempts to force one another into good citizenship.
>
> (3)

Box 6.1 Food, Sex, and Pollution among the Hua of Papua New Guinea

As described by Anna Meigs, Hua religion was centrally and almost solely composed of rules about pollution, mostly expressed through food regulations, related intimately with gender and to a more general ontology. The context was a firm ideology of male superiority; not only were men politically and culturally dominant, but women—especially their sexual organs and bodily fluids—were held to be "disgusting and dangerous" to men. This attitude was closely associated with their notion of *nu*, a semi-spiritual but also quite concrete substance carried by matter, including human matter such as "blood, breath, hair, sweat, fingernails, feces, urine, footprints, and shadows" (1984: 20). Food conveyed *nu* as well and was "in some sense congealed *nu*" (20). It also shared in the *nu* of those who acquired or prepared it, leading to an elaborate system of dietary and other restrictions. For instance, some foods, by their own properties, were more associated with female qualities, *korogo* or soft, juicy, fertile, fast-growing, and cool. Others were more masculine, *hakeri'a* or hard, dry, infertile, slow-growing, and hot (79). Males needed to avoid feminine foods or foods prepared by women, but more so at certain times of life than others: they were especially vulnerable in late childhood and adolescence, when their maleness was building, but in adulthood there were fewer limitations and by old age almost none. Food, however, was not the only threat to men, since sexual activity also endangered their *nu*: men were relatively deficient in the substance to begin with, and intercourse was believed to deplete it. Women, on the other hand, with their surplus of *nu* were fertile, and their special quality was to feed others. In order to maintain the separation between the substances of the genders, men would practice rituals for purging female influences from their bodies, including induced vomiting, sweating, and nose bleeding. Bodily material and the *nu* it carried, when in the wrong place, was referred to as *siro na* or dirt or pollution. However, these substances were not exactly "immoral," and even their polluting quality was affected by social relations and applications. For instance, a child's *nu* was said to be polluting but not morally objectionable to the parents. Even more, seemingly *siro na* substances like hair, feces, urine, and dead bodies were sometimes incorporated into medicines and growth-promoting concoctions, and a man would smear "sweat, oil, and vomit over the bodies of his real and classificatory sons to increase their growth" (109). As Meigs concluded for the Hua, "pollution is not inherent in bodily substances, as in our own feces model. Instead a substance that in other situations may be nourishing may be temporarily polluting through the contexts of its production and distribution," and one that in other situations may be polluting may be temporarily nourishing (113). In our own culture, someone's saliva might be disgusting, but we would permit a little of our mother's to slick down our hair or remove a spot of dirt from our face.

Morality and the Demands of Social Living

While the details of morality or proper conduct differ greatly from one society to another, some form of appropriate behavior, and some standard for appraisal of behavior, appears in all societies. Durkheim went so far as to state:

> Law and morality are the totality of ties which bind us to society, which make a unitary, coherent aggregate of the mass of individuals. Everything which is a source of solidarity is moral; everything which forces man to take account of other men is moral; everything which forces him to regulate his conduct through something other than the striving of ego is moral; and morality is as solid as these ties are numerous and strong.
>
> (1933: 398)

Morality in an important sense *is* society, or perhaps society *is* morality. That is, humans living in social arrangements will have normal, or at least "channeled" and habitual, ways of doing things because we must have them. Social normality depends on regularity and predictability in human affairs, such that I know what I am supposed to do, that I know what you are supposed to do, and that I can reasonably assume that you are going to do it—and judge you if you do not. It seems that social life without such traits would be virtually inconceivable, and that in their absence new ones would be quickly established.

This goes not only for human social life but the lives of all social species. Significantly, Charles Darwin observed in *The Descent of Man* that "any animal whatever, endowed with well marked social instincts, the parental and filial affections being here included, would inevitably acquire a moral sense or conscience" (1882: 98). In other words, some sort of behavioral order is a social necessity. We have seen that humans are not the only species with an "interaction code" that ritualizes behavior (see Chapter 5); an interaction code is one of the prerequisites of a social species. Accordingly, studies of human and nonhuman social animals alike have shown evidence of "moral" kinds of qualities, including attachment and bonding, cooperation and mutual aid (including altruism or "self-sacrifice"), sympathy and empathy, direct and indirect reciprocity, conflict resolution and "peacemaking," deception and deception detection, concern with the evaluations of other members of the group, and an awareness of and responsiveness to group rules or norms. What humanity essentially adds to this list is self-consciousness of these traits and the ability to speculate on them and to elaborate or "theorize" about them—that is, to create moral "systems" or "interpretations" where moral "behavior" already existed.

This discovery supports Durkheim's assertion that morality, "in all its forms, is never met with except in society" (1933: 399)—but also that it is *always* met with in society. Societies—of humans, apes, fish, or bees—are all "moral communities" in the sense that there are right and wrong ways to behave within them. Morality, in a fundamental way, is basically an effect of living in and being sensitive to a social group. Again, a social group without some "moral standards" (however tacit and unconscious, even instinctual) could probably not survive; its members would either kill each other or scatter.

But it is not just as a mundane order of human relations that society provides both form and substance for religious/moral concerns; "society also consecrates things, especially ideas" (Durkheim 1965: 244). That is, one of the properties or functions of society is to surround its social realities with what Geertz called an "aura of factuality" and (or perhaps by way of) an aura of sacrality. We will discuss this much further in the final section of this chapter. For now, let us think of Radcliffe-Brown's notion not only of "social function" but of "ritual value." He proposed that the central function of any social fact, including religion or morality, is the contribution it makes "to the formation and maintenance of social order" (1965: 154). This order is itself a social fact: people really *are* in various relationships, groups, and institutions with various rights and responsibilities to each other. (Many of these social realities even predate Homo sapiens and spoken language, etc.) There *are* rules and norms and "customary" arrangements between individuals. He wrote:

> For every rule that *ought* to be observed there must be some sort of sanction or reason. For acts that patently affect other persons the moral and legal sanctions provide a generally sufficient controlling force upon the individual. For ritual obligations conformity and rationalization are provided by the ritual sanctions. The simplest form of ritual sanction is an accepted belief that if rules of ritual are not observed some undefined misfortune is likely to occur.
>
> (150)

Morality in this sense is an extra layer of value and of obligation or coercion: the practices, rules, or institutions are not only valuable in themselves but "morally" valuable too. That is, they are not only real but right. Even if those practices, rules, and institutions entail war, headhunting, or human sacrifice, they are important because they are done (and perhaps *only* because they are done), and they attain the status of "moral" duties or concerns.

The Efficacy of Religion: Formation and Transformation

Morality is, ultimately, not just an idea or belief but a *practice*. Therefore, producing moral behavior means producing moral human beings, which in turn means producing individuals with particular attitudes, habits, and dispositions. Or, as Geertz's classic definition phrased it, the point of religion is to "establish powerful, pervasive, and long-lasting mood and motivations" in people (1973: 90). We might say then that the power of religion is not so much to "inform" humans (to give them knowledge or beliefs) as to *form* and *transform* them—to turn them into certain kinds of individuals who behave in certain ways. Religious information *in-forms* humans in the sense that it instills form in them; religious instruction *in-structs* in the sense of creating structure in them. And religion, among all the elements of culture, is particularly successful at this because it is presented as "the really real."

Durkheim spoke fundamentally of the *effectiveness*, the *efficacy*, of religion: it *works* by transforming humans individually and collectively. Through doing religion, "men become different" (1965: 241). Specific ideas, and still more so sentiments, are aroused and established in them. A society has—perhaps is—a set of such ideas and sentiments; that is what he meant by "moral community." The "social facts" (the families, lineages, clans, tribes, villages, etc.) are there. The members of society must not only *represent* these realities to themselves; they must also *commit* to them, be swayed by them.

Durkheim saw religion, or more precisely religious ritual, as the process by which this goal is accomplished. During ritual, a psychological force that he called "effervescence" is achieved, a state of excitement, suggestibility, and mental "contagion." "In the midst of an assembly animated by a common passion," he stated, "we become susceptible of acts and sentiments of which we are incapable when reduced to our own forces" (240). At such times, "Every sentiment expressed finds a place without resistance in all minds, which are very open to outside impressions; each re-echoes the others, and is re-echoed by the others" (247). The entire experience is "ecstatic" in the sense of the individual getting outside of himself or herself and feeling the presence and power of a greater external reality, which is society.

Durkheim greatly exaggerated the immediacy and unanimity of the mental effects of ritual experiences; not all people—whether "primitive" or "modern"—come away with exactly the same ideas and attitudes to the same degree. Nonetheless, Radcliffe-Brown agreed, almost in the same words, that

> an orderly social life amongst human beings depends upon the presence in the minds of the members of a society of certain sentiments, which control the behavior of the individual in his relation to others. Rites can be seen to be the regulated symbolic expressions of certain sentiments. Rites can therefore be shown to have a specific social function when, and to the extent that, they have for their effect to regulate, maintain, and transmit from one generation to another sentiments on which the constitution of the society depends.
>
> (1965: 157)

And Malinowski, who is better known for elevating individual needs over social ones, concurred at least this far in discussing particular ceremonies, including initiation rites:

> they are a ritual and dramatic expression of the supreme power and value of tradition in primitive societies; they also serve to impress this power and value upon the minds of each generation, and they are at the same time an extremely efficient means of transmitting tribal lore, of insuring continuity in tradition, and of maintaining tribal cohesion.
>
> (1948: 40)

So religion is a profound ingredient in the creation and perpetuation of social order by being a profound ingredient in the minds and experiences of the beings who make up (in both senses of the phrase) society. Religion is about the social realities and the social relationships in which humans find themselves, independent and regardless of their own actions or intentions. Religious reality is "just there" in the same way that social reality is.

The overall effect, as Geertz indicated, is to give these social and religious realities such an "aura of factuality" that humans take them for granted and experience them as "really real." Religion contributes to this effect by attaching social relations to, or founding them on, a *non-social* ground. One of the best and strongest expressions of this idea came from Marshall Sahlins (1976), who talked about "the culturalization of nature and the naturalization of culture." That is, the source of and thus the reason and justification for culture are displaced from culture onto non-culture; they are certainly not human inventions but are independent and real. This is not only true of religion. He discussed how Darwin's theory of natural selection represented a projection of nineteenth-century capitalist concepts and practices, particularly competition and the elimination of competitors, onto nature and thereby provided a basis for arguing that those very *cultural* concepts and practices are *natural*. Throughout history, before and since, people have appealed to nature for models of culture or to culture for models of nature, often if not usually unconsciously. Marx alleged to found his social laws and predictions on natural/historical laws, and even the Enlightenment spoke of "natural rights" as if these rights were something you could find in nature. The argumentative force of this approach is obvious: if your social and cultural principles are "natural," they are intellectually true and morally obligating.

Religion goes one step further. It appeals not only "below" human life and culture (to nature) but "above" human culture (to the supernatural) as well. So we should restate Sahlins' proposition to include the *culturalization of super-nature and the super-naturalization of culture.* The source, model, and authority of human relations, regulations, and institutions is, then, not merely nature, and certainly not humans themselves, but the superhuman agents and realities named in religion. Culture is thus extra-human and super-human, but above all it is *given* to or established for humans. Human society and culture is one dimension in a trans-human system, all of which dimensions reflect the same basic natural/supernatural truths.

If Nietzsche was correct that "everything you like you should first let yourself be commanded to do" (1976: 160), then the missing piece of morality is "command." Roy Rappaport (1999), accordingly, suggested that the key aspect of ritual and religion is not the acts and the "content," let alone the doctrine or beliefs, nor even the meanings of the acts and symbols, but the attitude toward all of these things and what they stand for, namely, the attitude of *commitment*. He proposed that the very doing of rituals, the very manipulation of symbols, generates moral states and expresses and accomplishes commitment to them. For him, religion and its performance had two "offices." The first is *acceptance*: to do or participate in a rite is to publicly accept its right if not its rightness. He was adamant that acceptance is not "belief" and can happen separately from or without belief. The point is to embrace the *obligations* that come with the ritual, the morality, the religion, and the culture. When people take part in a ritual, they communicate that such behavior is the "right thing to do" and that those who lead the ritual have the right to do so. This recognizes not only obligation but authority. The second office, then, is the establishment of convention, of those "right things to do," in the first place. Once established, the convention is endowed with importance, with "sacredness," which makes it obligatory. Hence, the obligatoriness of the conventional behavior *becomes* morality: "Breach of obligation may, then, be *the* fundamental immoral act. … failure to abide by the terms of an obligation is universally stigmatized as immoral" (132). Here, then, is perhaps a theory of the very genesis of morality.

In Meyer Fortes' description of Tallensi religion and morality, he found exactly these forces at work. The Tallensi observed an array of behavioral restrictions, some of which Fortes referred to as matters of propriety, while others were matters of "moral or ritual injunction." Moral/ritual rules distinguished between "ritual custom" (*malung*) and "taboo custom" (*kyiher*), the difference being that "Fear of embarrassment is the sanction of the former. In the case of the latter it is the likelihood of mystical retribution" (1987: 125). Despite the differences, all of their customary regulations were "accepted as absolutely binding," "moral imperatives complied with in acts of individual observances or abstention" (126).

> The observance of a taboo signifies submission to an internal command which is beyond question. ... Transgression is tantamount to repudiating one's identity, or one's identification with a locality or office of status ... [Such] taboos ordain rules of conduct that are binding on the individual, in the first place because he is the person he is in the situation he is in. Compliance with them means that he identifies himself with, appropriates to himself, the capacities, the rights and obligations, the relationships and the commitments that devolve upon a normal person of his status in his situation. He has, it must be remembered, been cast in these roles or in roles preparatory to them since childhood. Being with him all the time taboos keep him aware of his enduring identity, as a person in contraposition to other persons.
>   There is, however, a second factor of fundamental importance in these prescriptions. They are defined as obligations to the founding ancestors and to the Earth. ... They represent acknowledgement of a particular form of dependence ... to bonds that amount to inescapable bondage.
>
> (126–27)

Religion and the "Embodiment" of Morals

As Fortes indicated, humans are carefully and continuously groomed to take their place(s) in society and in religion. This means that, although religious concepts and morals supposedly emanate from the nonhuman realm, they are incarnated in real flesh-and-blood humans and real social institutions. The concepts and morals must become part of actual human minds and personalities as well as shared practices, relations, and institutions. This includes beliefs and other such intellectual components, but also emotional states. The goal is to produce persons who think and feel certain things and therefore *do* certain things, and to suspend and bind them in social relationships that support these actions and that are in turn reproduced by these actions. This may include literally "inscribing" religion in or on the bodies of members.

For Durkheim as mentioned, rituals are the occasions when religious ideas and sentiments are given overt form and emotional force. Yet this cannot be sufficient. For one, rituals are not always particularly informative: the Gisu (see Chapter 5) explicitly did not communicate much "content" in their initiation rituals. For another, rituals do not always convey the seriousness that Durkheim attributed to them; recall the playfulness of the Salasaca funeral. There is no single "ritual attitude," but rather rituals may be characterized by gravity, levity, and every emotion in between. Most importantly, it is *unnecessary* that ritual carry the entire weight of religious transformation, since ritual is not the only opportunity people have to experience their religion. Indeed, if it were, religion would be much impoverished, since people do not spend most of their time in ritual activity, and when they *are* in it the words and gestures and objects they encounter would be new and meaningless.

Geertz is well known for emphasizing the role of symbols in religion and culture, which may lead us to conclude that he saw symbols as performing the role that rituals perform for Durkheim. However, Geertz went on to state that religion and culture exist as a "traffic" of symbols (1973: 45), which occurs not only during ritual but incessantly in social life. We might say, then, that the meaning of symbols and the power of rituals are "overdetermined" in society: long before a person experiences a ritual, he or she has seen (at least parts of) that ritual before and has definitely heard about it. Very much training and preparation for ritual occurs repeatedly before and after its performance. People hear accounts of rituals, retell the myths that inform the rituals, and generally rehearse the skills and habits that are communicated by ritual. For example, while a wedding ceremony may be a rite of passage and establish a marriage, that ceremony is hardly the first occasion on which the couple has heard of marriage and its norms and expectations. They may have attended other services, observed their own parents and other adults in marriages, and overheard an endless stream of discussion about marriage. Their nuptials "bring it all together," but much of the knowledge and many of the habits that they will practice are already well known and well established.

The acquisition of "moods and motivations" means literally training the mind, the emotions, the very body, to act and respond in certain ways. Charles Hirschkind (2001) made the point when he examined the behavior of listening to religious tape-recordings among Muslims in Egypt. Rather than following the typical method of studying the "big" moments of ritual, he instead looked at the repetitive, everyday activity of playing pre-recorded lectures and sermons and the effects of this behavior. What he concluded was that acquiring and practicing a religion is more (and less) than adopting a set of beliefs or participating in formal rituals. A religion, like a culture in general, is a complex of "perceptual skills," the ways that we think, feel, concentrate, emote, even sit or stand or otherwise use our bodies. The "practices" that people undergo and perform, trivial as they seem, generate a "sensibility" that is an effect of and a further cause of the practices. This is the same point made by Pierre Bourdieu (1977): a way of thinking and feeling and acting, what he called a *habitus*, must be instilled in the person, and once instilled it will produce more of the same experiences, right down to how the senses and organs function. A "socially informed" body, in particular a "religiously informed" or "morally informed" body, will have been constructed.

Other versions of this social and moral in-formative process can be found. Simon Coleman, for instance, emphasized how the proselytizing practices of Swedish Christian Pentecostals achieve the same results. For the new convert, "telling and retelling conversion stories is a central ritual of faith, framing personal experience in canonical language and recreating that experience in the telling" (2003: 16–17). Likewise, all of the day-to-day activities like knocking on doors, training Bible school students, making trips abroad, public witnessing, and so on—including consuming their own media like tape recordings, newspapers, and television programs—are part of the ongoing structuring of the self and the group. John and Jean Comaroff (1991) and Michael Gilsenan (2000) also described the role not only of everyday religious but also more pedestrian practices in constructing religious experience and "moral" attitudes in Christianity and Islam, respectively, as we will see in Chapter 8.

Minds, emotions, and bodies cannot therefore be separated in our consideration of religious and moral behavior. Bodily comportment is a source and expression of experience and of moral concern. Standing, sitting, dressing, etc. constitute one dimension of bodily experience. Often enough, religion is more literally inscribed on or in the body. Scarification, circumcision, tattooing, jewelry, body paint, and other decorations are among the forms by which the body itself becomes a religious object and by which religious states and orientations are produced in the body. Much of what we would regard as violence against self or other (see Chapter 10), such as sacrifice, asceticism and self-denial, and self-mortification, are ways of training the body and emotions to have conventional religious attitudes and motivations. In other words, it is not only—maybe not mainly—by shaping minds (with beliefs and concepts) that religious members are made but by shaping feelings and bodies too.

Our conclusion is this: religion, in its forms grand and small, particularly as expressed as "morality," is less about doctrine than about preparing human individuals to act in certain ways, guaranteeing that they do, and appraising them when they do or don't. This may and commonly does entail making those actions so real, so obligatory, so natural, that most people never seriously consider acting otherwise—in fact, never seriously consider the actions at all. Anthony Wallace and Frits Staal seemed to suggest this when they emphasized the behavioral efficiency (Wallace) and the meaninglessness (Staal) of ritual. The very stereotypy and moral urgency of certain actions virtually (but not completely) guarantee their successful performance. All of social life is structured and organized, but religion "is orderliness raised to an extraordinary degree" (Wallace 1966: 238)—and given the sanction not only of man but of nature and super-nature. In the end, the goal and function of ritual, religion, and morality "is to prepare a human being for the efficient performance of a task by communicating an image of a highly organized world system, already described in the belief system, and by suggesting a role during a ritual learning process" (270) that the individual must play in this system.

Box 6.2 Bodies, Behaviors, and Moral Substances among the Amazonian Muinane

The Muinane, who refer to themselves as People of the Center, are very concerned with moral behavior. In fact, they assert that humans are "intrinsically moral" (Londono Sulkin 2012: 48), tending toward "loving care, a sense of purpose, coolness or calm equanimity, respect, and good humor" (30). However, Muinane morality is not fundamentally about spirit or even emotion but about *body* and more generally about *substance*. They claim that they are "alive, aware, articulate, and capable of competent, moral, and sociable action in part because of 'speeches' and 'breaths' that constituted their bodies and resonated inside them" (31). It is these multiple speeches/breaths, rather than some single unitary "soul," that makes people naturally moral, and the person or body is built of these speeches/breaths from interaction—not only social interaction but interaction with the physical world. Each plant, animal, and other substance has its own speech/breath, which is related to human society and gendered bodies. Tobacco is perhaps the most moral of substances, giving humans "proper thoughts/emotions and the capacity to learn, remember, and discern" (96). Both male and female bodies consist of tobacco juice, but only men can trade and share tobacco. Coca is only consumed by adult men and is closely associated with morality in its cultivation, preparation, and consumption. Women's bodies and morality, by contrast, are associated with and composed of manioc, chilies, and cool herbs.

The connection between bodies, substances, and morality in Muinane culture can be traced to two ideas. First, different people had different substances—even different tobaccos—that bred different behaviors in them. For instance, "other lineages and clans had intrinsically violent, antisocial, promiscuous, or authoritarian tobaccos and thus similarly undesirable speeches and thoughts/emotions" (35). More, nonhuman animals are said to be essentially immoral, not observing the social and sexual norms of humans. Animal species have their own speeches/breaths, even their own tobaccos, but if an animal speech/breath/tobacco invades a human, immoral behavior results. Thus, "it was not rare for people to claim that a man who misbehaved had a jaguar inside, or that he spoke the speech of a jaguar" (55). In short, the Muinane assert that "hot speeches or breaths ensuing from animals' tobaccos and other substances altered people's sensibilities so much that they did not perceive or act as real people" (50)—that is, as moral people.

Religion and the Social Order

If mind, body, society, culture, nature, and super-nature are all dimensions of an integrated system, then we should expect to find connections between and reflections of each in the others. We would expect the myths, rituals, beliefs, and values of a religion to relate to the kinship, political, and even economic practices and institutions of the society. According to Durkheim, this fact is not only not surprising but virtually mandatory, since religion is "a system of ideas with which the individuals represent to themselves the society of which they are members, and the obscure but intimate relations which they have with it" (1965: 257). Society provides the "inspiration" for religion by being omnipresent, external, "real," and coercive or at least inevitable; however, it also provides the particular "content" of the religion, being as it is the model upon which the group's religion is based.

Durkheim's theory is perhaps too simplistic and causal, but it was highly influential in the social-scientific study of religion and has been developed by anthropologists from Radcliffe-Brown to Mary Douglas. Most famously in Douglas' book *Natural Symbols* she laid out a view of religion in which the quality of religious experience is shaped by the quality of general social experience, which she called the "symbolic replication of a social state" (1970: 82). Humans therefore not only get the idea of religion from society but get specific religious forms from it. Society provides the experience and sentiment from which religion springs but also the particular categories or order that inform religion. In other words, "Religious forms as well as social forms are generated by experience in the same dimension" (16), which is the dimension of everyday lived existence.

She identified certain variables of qualitative experience that have detectable impact on religious expression, dubbed "group" and "grid." Grid in her theory refers to the individualistic or ego-focused experiences or categories, such as the available titles, roles, statuses, and names in a society, that is, the order within which individuals define their identity. In any particular society, "grid" qualities may be strong or weak. Group, on the other hand, stands for the macrosocial organizational patterns such as class, caste, lineage, and other institutional or political structures to which individuals belong or in which they participate. Group can also be strong or weak. Thus, human beings live within a social context in which "personal"/grid and "structural"/group experiences intersect in some way: grid and group may both be strong or both be weak, or one may be strong while the other is weak. The result is an overall "feel" or ethos to social life. Societies with a particular combination of group and grid qualities will be prone to particular religious attitudes and practices, she argued, such as spirit possession, trance, and so on.

Finally, Douglas stressed a psychological process to link the personal, social, and spiritual dimensions. She named it *consonance*, literally "sounding like/with," to suggest that social experience and spiritual experience establish a harmony that almost becomes a unison. She wrote that there is a "drive to achieve consonance between social and physical and emotional experience" (149) which explains "the power of social structures to generate symbols of their own" (151). People who inhabit a specific kind of psychological and social order are going to learn to think and feel in specific ways; their very bodies will be trained and attuned to certain habits and sentiments. To have institutions or beliefs that are "out of tune" with the quality of their lives would create a kind of "dissonance." Hence, "Just as the experience of cognitive dissonance is disturbing, the experience of consonance in layer after layer of experience and context after context is satisfying" (70). It is a very human way of bringing one's social order, emotional order, and spiritual order into one great consistent order.

Thus we should expect to find some social organizations and some mythical/ritual/ moral systems that co-occur and others that do not. Small, egalitarian societies do not tend to possess concepts of hierarchical religious arrangements—pantheons of judgmental gods, for instance. Societies tend to see their own economic and political institutions reflected in their religions: the Dogon, a horticultural society, had an elaborate cosmology concerning grains, granaries, and blacksmiths, whereas pastoralists like the Nuer or Dinka saw cattle as central to their symbolic and ritual practice. Societies that have unequal or even tense gender relations have those relations reflected back to them in myth and ritual. Meanwhile, via a cross-cultural survey of 186 societies, Frank Roes and Michel Raymond (2003) found a correlation between large societies that engage in high levels of external conflict and beliefs in "moralizing gods."

Around the world and throughout time, human societies have developed the religion and morality that suits and strengthens their social order. Chinese Confucian ideals of proper behavior or *li* (translated alternately as etiquette, propriety, morality, or ritual conduct) were expressed in and productive of the so-called Five Relationships—father and son, husband and wife, elder and younger, older brother and younger brother, and ruler and subject. Each relationship reiterated the same pattern, a rightfully dominant but benevolent superordinate and an obedient and respectful subordinate. In fact, the Chinese character for the fundamental value of *jen* or "humaneness" is a composite of two characters, one meaning human person and the other meaning "two" (Brannigan 2005: 296). Thus, humaneness, morality, and social order are overtly about humans in social relations.

There are many other ways in which religion relates to its cultural context. Lenora Greenbaum (1973) illustrated that there are strong correlations between spirit-possession and other cultural variables. Spirit-possession is a very common concept worldwide, but 86 percent of cultures that practiced slavery, for instance, also had spirit trance compared with 14 percent of cultures without slavery. Likewise, 58 percent of societies with a stratification system of two or more classes experienced such trances, while 74 percent of those without class inequalities also lacked trances. Societies that practiced patrilocal marriage were twice as likely to include spirit-possession, and larger societies (more than one hundred thousand members) were more than twice as likely. Agricultural societies (87 percent), societies that practiced bride price or bride service (89 percent), and societies with multiple levels of political power (83 percent) were all dramatically more likely to believe in possession.

Wallace (1966) identified an even wider array of religious phenomena with social correlates. Witchcraft, for instance, was more common in societies that lacked "political superiors" to administer punishments or in societies without a central social authority; this suggests that witchcraft provided the missing function. In addition, a concept of a "high god" occurred more often in societies with multiple distinct and sovereign subgroups and seldom in homogeneous societies. A pantheon of gods and a "supernatural sanction for morality" was much more associated with social stratification than with egalitarianism.

Legitimating Order

It is a well-known and well-established idea that religion legitimates human relations and institutions; members of religious communities tend to believe that their institutions and practices (their language, their knowledge and skills, their kinship arrangements, their political systems, etc.) were given by spiritual sources—perhaps the ancestors, perhaps the gods, perhaps "culture heroes" of some sort—which is *why* those institutions and practices are morally obligating. Indeed, their lives and the very shapes of their bodies may have been established in a supernatural way. The legitimation of the human order amounts in the end to the claim that the order comes from or is authorized by a nonhuman reality— the natural and/or supernatural realms themselves. As Sahlins characterized it, culture becomes naturalized (and supernaturalized), and nature (super-nature) becomes culturalized.

There are many examples of this effect. Perhaps the clearest and most complete expression is the caste system of India, studied by Louis Dumont. The Hindu caste system was and is an immensely complex social phenomenon, actually not a single unified phenomenon at all but a diverse and intricate set of beliefs and practices distributed across the South Asian subcontinent and beyond (i.e. Bali and other "Hinduized" societies). It essentially involved the stratification of society through a holistic network of kinship, economic, political, and religious concepts and institutions. It may be the most fully worked-out moral–religious system in the world. Kathleen Gough (1971: 11), for instance, gave these characteristics of castes, although we must keep in mind that the system functioned differently in different areas of southern Asia:

- Inherited by birth
- Endogamous, that is, in-marrying
- Associated with an occupation
- Ranked and hierarchical in prestige, power, and usually wealth
- Separated by "social distance" and sometimes by physical distance as well (e.g. living in different districts or neighborhoods of the same village)
- Based on a notion of ritual purity and pollution.

Thus all of the functional domains of culture are involved in this comprehensive system.

Most readers will be familiar with the four major "caste" categories, namely *brahmans* (the highest rank, of priests and scholars; see Figure 6.1), *kshatriyas* (the second rank, of warriors and political leaders), *vaishyas* (the third rank, of merchants, craftspeople, and farmers), and *shudras* (the fourth rank, of laborers and servants). At the bottom of or even outside the system was the *panchama* or *pariah* class, sometimes called "outcastes" or "untouchables" (legally designated as *harijan* or "children of god" today), who did and do the absolutely most menial and dirty work, such as cleaning streets and sewers, handling dead bodies, and so on. However, in reality the system contained hundreds, if not thousands, of distinct occupational statuses called *jati*; fisherman is one *jati*, carpenter another, potter another, barber another. A caste category, then, included a host of various *jati*, which may be ranked against each other as well as against the other major categories.

Figure 6.1 Indian *brahman* painting his forehead with the red and white marks of his sect and caste. Courtesy of the Library of Congress Prints and Photographs Division

Not surprisingly, caste status tended to affect wealth and standard of living. Gough wrote that in the southeast Indian village she studied *brahmans* were typically much richer than the next three castes, who were in turn slightly richer than the bottom-dwellers, called *Adi Dravidas* or "original Dravidians" in her setting. Not only did each category tend to be residentially segregated but it possessed its own norms and morals: *brahmans* notably practiced cremation, widow celibacy, proscription of divorce, avoidance of animal sacrifice, and other specialized behaviors. They also could interact with some lower castes but not the very lowest; the most degraded *jati*, the Pallan or landless serf rank, could not even stand within several feet of a *brahman* nor walk on the street in a *brahman* neighborhood, let alone enter one of their houses, and vice versa (53–54).

It is obvious that there is something more than occupational specialization going on here. As Gough explained, the gap between castes (especially the highest and the lowest) was a *ritual* as well as a natural one (according to Dumont, a matter of purity). *Brahmans* were not merely socially or economically superior to their underlings but spiritually better too. A *brahman* was a higher spiritual incarnation of human being, burdened by comparatively less *karma* and closer to the attainment of the goal of religion. "Naturally" they deserved the status and the advantages that they enjoyed, for truly they were better human beings. As Gough pointed out, one's wealth and power did not confer caste status but rather one's caste status conferred wealth and power:

> Ritual rank inheres in castes by virtue of birth, and has connotations of worth. A high caste is often called a "good" caste, and a low caste a "bad" one. … A rich or powerful

man is not thereby a "good" man but a "big" man; a poor or powerless person not a "bad" man but a "small" one.

(51)

The most revealing aspect of the legitimating value of religion is how it adapts to changes in social institutions and relations. Society is not written in stone, so neither can the religious sources of society be fixed and settled. Australian Aboriginal groups had mechanisms for sharing, trading, and redistributing religious knowledge as well as religious sites, as we will discuss in the next chapter. Beidelman gave another example of religion flexing to keep up with and to legitimate changing social realities. Among the Kaguru, clans owned particular parcels of land and performed annual rites (*tambiko*) to rejuvenate the land, guaranteeing rainfall and fertility largely through the agency of clan ghosts (*misimu*). However, he also reported:

> These annual rites are a useful means by which the members of an owner clan enforce their rule upon the other residents in their land. Although Kaguru always speak of this enforcement in mystical, ritual terms, however, these activities are invariably the expression of the power relations within a local area; when in the past these relations changed and a clan's power was lost, ritual was usurped by others, who quickly put forward a new legendary justification for their powers.
>
> (1971: 34)

Observers of modern religions have noticed this property again and again—how a group that enters new relations, like occupying new territory, develops mythico-ritual bases for their changed circumstances. Often the newcomers will appropriate part of the displaced group's beliefs and practices; sometimes they will superimpose their rituals or myths on the prior ones, for instance adopting the same days for ritual activities (the Christian use of Sunday for its sabbath was an appropriation of the pagan Roman sun cult, as was the adoption of December 25 as their incarnated god's birthday, a belief inherited from the worship of Mithra) or literally locating their sacred sites on top of previous sacred sites (the Dome of the Rock on the Jewish Temple Mount in Jerusalem being a prime example). Then, the transfer of divine legitimation from old to new goes along relatively unproblematically.

Box 6.3 Legitimating the State in Japan

Shinto is widely recognized as the traditional religion of Japan. However, as Daniel Holtom argued, it is particularly treacherous to attempt to define or classify Shinto; it has been described as

> the indigenous religion of the Japanese people; it is the Way of the Gods; it is "*kami*-cult," a form of definition in which *kami* signifies the deities of Japan as distinct from those brought into the country through foreign contacts; ... it is the racial spirit of the Japanese people (*Yamato Damashii*); it is the sacred ceremonies conducted before the *kami*; it is the essence of the principles of imperial rule; it is a system of correct social and political etiquette; it is the ideal national morality; it is a system of patriotism and loyalty centering on emperor worship ("Mikadoism"); it is, in its pure and original form, a nature

worship or, over against this, Shinto, correctly understood, is ancestor worship; or, again, it is an admixture of the worship of nature and of ancestors.

(1965: 5–6)

Most likely it is all of these at once. Holtom characterized Shinto as having four simultaneous fields of activity: domestic or household worship, sect observances, "state" ceremonies at public shrines (see Figure 6.2), and the rituals of the imperial residence. The earliest Shinto shrines were locations or objects in nature, and the religion evinces a clear relation to agriculture; in fact, "The ancient interests of the rice culture in which the lives of these ancient people centered have penetrated Old Shinto deeply" (101). However, as the unified Japanese state under the hereditary emperor coalesced, Shinto came to reflect and support this political reality. According to Robert Bellah,

The earliest records we have of Shinto indicate the emergence of a state cult out of what is clearly a primitive tribal religion. The Yamato people consolidated their hegemony over central Japan in the early centuries of the Christian era and apparently in connection with this political predominance, they managed to establish their own version of the mythology.

(1957: 86)

In this mythology, the sun goddess Amaterasu-Omikami plays a prominent role: she "has become the symbol of practically everything that is most precious and most characteristic in the evolution of the Japanese people" (Holtom 1965: 124).

Figure 6.2 Itsukushima Shinto shrine, Japan. Courtesy of the Library of Congress Prints and Photographs Division

This includes, significantly, the imperial family itself; the emperor is a direct descendant of the goddess. Holtom quoted a Japanese school text which taught that the goddess herself proclaimed, "This country is a land over which my offspring shall rule. Do thou, Imperial Grandson, go and rule over it. And the prosperity of the Imperial Throne shall be as everlasting as heaven and earth" (127). In terms of ritual practice, the public/state cult is designed to represent and instill key Japanese values, particularly military ideals, honor and loyalty toward superiors, and respect for the emperor. Not surprisingly, with the revised and modernized state of the Tokugawa (1603) and Meiji periods, Shinto was elevated and edited to become what Bellah termed "a sacred form of nationalism" (53).

Inverting Order

Order is a necessary and standard condition in human society, but as Turner among others has reminded us, it is not the only condition. Humans also experience and actually require some disorder too, or at least disorder is an inevitable concomitant of order. Also as Turner has hypothesized, disorder can have its own functions, positive or negative. In some cases, inversions or transgressions of social order may actually be reaffirming of that order. In others, such violations may be the explanation for the problems in society, providing a "solution" to those problems.

Turner himself explored how structured exceptions to structure can themselves be structuring, generally in the concepts of liminality and communitas and specifically in the case of sociopolitical rituals such as those involved in installing a new leader or in renewing that leader's power. The leader must be respected and obeyed most of the time, but there may be instances when a controlled overthrow of the hierarchy is allowed or even required, during which the leader is mocked, ridiculed, perhaps even attacked. However, the chief or king (almost) always emerges from the event safely—and restored to power.

Even in situations where there is no formal reversal of social relations, there is always an uncertain and liminal aspect to transitions of power. Beattie wrote that the Bunyoro kingdom of Africa conducted coronation and "refresher" ceremonies for its kings. The reigning king or *mukama* was always, according to belief, descended from the original king in an unbroken patrilineal succession (thus establishing the religious charter for kingship, flowing from the first family of humans). When a king died, there was an institutionalized period of chaos and social disturbance, during which sons of the deceased king were supposed to fight to the death for the throne. The king's demise was deliberately concealed to allow time for the succession competition to play out. When the new king was finally installed, his ascension was surrounded with ritual, including "the placing on the throne and the subsequent killing of a 'mock king,' who would, it was believed, attract to himself the magical dangers which attended the transition to kingship, protecting the real king" (1960: 28).

In the case of Shilluk kings, the violent confrontation was more protracted but also more symbolic, although the conception of a religious continuity of the institution of king was similar. All kings inherited the place and power of the first great king, Nyikang. In fact, as Evans-Pritchard described it, "it is not the individual at any time reigning who is king, but Nyikang who is the medium between man and God (*Juok*) and is believed in some way to participate in God as he does in the king" (1962: 201). Accordingly, the installation of a new king involved a symbolic war between the king-to-be and Nyikang himself, present in effigy. Priests displayed the effigy of Nyikang, which traveled through the northern part of the kingdom literally collecting up the subjects of the mythical king. Finally, the army of Nyikang confronted the army of the king-to-be.

> The army of the king-elect is defeated and he is captured by Nyikang and taken by him to the capital. The kingship captures the king. There Nyikang is placed on the royal stool. After a while he is taken off it and the king-elect sits on it in his stead and the spirit of Nyikang enters into him, causing him to tremble, and he becomes king, that is he becomes possessed by Nyikang.
>
> (205)

In an important and symbolic sense, after and thanks to the confusion and disorder, order was re-established—and it was the same order (literally the same royal spirit) as before.

Another noteworthy illustration of limited liminality and constrained communitas is the practice of "carnival," as seen in the lingering and pale instantiations of Mardi Gras (see Figure 6.3) and perhaps Halloween in the United States, where the strange, the evil, and the immoral are allowed and celebrated. In other times and places, the purpose and practice of carnival has been much more serious. Peter Stallybrass and Allon White (1986) did some informative work on the social meaning of such intentional inversions. Carnival, for instance, was an opportunity to step out of the mundane state of affairs, put on a mask, play a different role, sometimes break the everyday rules and indulge in the different, the grotesque, even the immoral. They followed Mikhail Bahktin who opined that an event

Figure 6.3 Mardi Gras parade, New Orleans. Courtesy of the Carol M. Highsmith Archive, Library of Congress Prints and Photographs Division

like carnival "celebrated temporary liberation from the prevailing truths of the established order; it marked the suspension of all hierarchical rank, privileges, norms and prohibitions. Carnival was the true feast of time, the feast of becoming, change and renewal. It was hostile to all that was immortalized and completed" (1984: 10). Even in the USA today, people put on masks of often ghoulish characters one night each year, although the ritual has been mostly consigned to children, and almost all of its transgressive meaning has been lost in favor of the quest for candy.

The point of the analysis by Stallybrass and White is that the "high" culture and the "low," the ordered and the disordered, even the moral and the immoral are not detachable but are mutually dependent. The normal social order often tries to deny or at least ignore this fact: kings are kings, rules are rules. However, at moments the "official" independence of order and disorder is truly actualized, and disorder temporarily rules; kings may be pulled down, institutions (even priests and gods) may be parodied, tricksters and pranksters may be celebrated (hence "trick or treat"), and major taboos may be broken. Rightly they refer to carnivalesque events as inversions, hybrids, transgressions, and rites of reversal.

However, two facts are certain. First, the transgressive moment will end. Ideally, it was never really a danger to order at all. It was always, as Terry Eagleton put it, "a licensed affair in every sense, a permissible rupture of hegemony" (1981: 148). The authorities usually even sanctioned and condoned it and provided security so that it could take place but not get too rambunctious. The order allowed a symbolic inversion, perhaps so that a real inversion did not occur. Second, as the recent marketing slogan goes, "What happens in Las Vegas stays in Las Vegas." People are expected not to carry their transgressions across the line that separates carnival from "real life"; that would be a *real* transgression. Instead, symbolic inversion remains a game played on a circumscribed field—a game, potentially, with real and positive effects but one that is not allowed to continue outside of the time and place set aside for it. It is, in the end, a legal illegality, an ordered disorder, a moral immorality.

Not all immorality or transgression is so playful and contained, though. There are real social and moral inversions with usually negative consequences. One of the clearest and most common forms is witchcraft and sorcery. We have seen that many if not most societies have attributed much or all of human misfortune to supernatural forces, including the gods and dead ancestors; by no means are these religious phenomena always benevolent. The malevolent spiritual beings also include especially powerful and malicious humans who in some ways violate or invert the normal order of things.

As discussed in Chapters 3 and 5, sorcerers were ordinarily people who used objects and techniques to achieve (often negative) supernatural results. By engaging in such behavior, they were acting antisocially and immorally (in most instances—some few societies considered it normal for people to attempt to injure each other). Witches, however, were a different story; they were often humans with an inherent spiritual badness to them, or even nonhumans in a human guise. The Barabaig claimed that a witch was a person whose very presence caused trouble (Klima 1970: 100). The Kaguru, more extremely, believed that witches were innately evil, or even worse, "the physical opposites of humans even though they may appear to be like ordinary humans" (Beidelman 1971: 37). They were thus some kind of perversion or corruption of human nature. Most revealingly, they were said to be "backward," literal opposites of human normality: they were cannibals, they "walked and danced upside down," went about naked, committed incest, and did their work at night.

All this is the reverse of what is normal for humans; they confound humans with animals, kin with nonkin, up with down, day with night, and shame (clothing) with shamelessness (nakedness and incest). What Kaguru seem to be saying is that witches do not recognize the rules and constraints of society, and those accused of witchcraft are those who do not seem to fulfill their basic social obligations to other humans.

(37)

If abnormality is the inverse of normality, witches represented that inversion to the ultimate. The social dimension of witchcraft has been commented on by various observers. For one thing, witchcraft talent was often thought to be inherited, so there was a kinship aspect to it. The Swazi of Africa, for instance, maintained that a female witch passed her abilities on to her children of both sexes (although a male witch did not). And not only were the practitioners of such evil socially structured but so were the victims: Kuper wrote that Swazi witchcraft was "usually aimed at persons who are already connected by social bonds" (1963: 66). For them as for many societies, the "automatic" character of witchcraft was invoked in situations of "hatred, fear, jealousy, and thwarted ambition," all social emotions. Basso said of the Apache that people who were "suspected of witchcraft are by definition guilty of hatred" (1970: 87). It should be no surprise, then, that witchcraft tended to be suspected or perpetrated more often against neighbors and family than against those who were "farther away" physically and socially.

A particularly illuminating case of witchcraft belief comes from the Apache, who thought that *itkasn* were the most dangerous kinds of witches. Male *itkasn* were more common than female for the reason that men felt more *kedn* or hatred than women. There were both structural and personal signs or indications that someone was a witch. The structural elements included being in a category of "power" (such as shaman or rich man), belonging to a clan other than that of the victim, and being older than the victim (since younger people did not usually have power over older ones). The personal and behavioral elements of witch suspects were still more telling: they included selfishness, anger, bellicosity, meanness, dishonesty, gossip, threats, adultery, and thievery—all clearly "wrong" and antisocial and immoral acts (Basso 1970: 81).

Obviously one consequence of the idea of witchcraft in a society is that it offers a reason for people to conform to the behavioral norms; those who are antisocial stand a chance of being accused as witches. However, there is one final way that this feature of social control can work. Among the Menomini, the Spindlers found that witches were not the usual antisocial deviants but the category in society with the most power and prestige, the elders. They noted that "social control is achieved ... by the threat of witchcraft by power figures rather than through accusation of the witch by the community" (1971: 73). All elders were believed to be potential witches which, in a society of relative equals, was one of the few "power relations" available. One way or another, witchcraft represented a potent ideology: conform and be good, or the witches will get you.

Mystifying Order

One of the crucial aspects of the legitimation of society is that humans must not recognize that they themselves originated the order, nor that their behavior perpetuates it. The very authority and reality of the order comes from its "givenness," the fact that humans are more or less passive recipients of it. This is especially true when the relations of society are unequal, even exploitative or oppressive. If humans made the system, they could question it and unmake and remake it. However, if the system is natural or supernatural—"just the way it is" or "ordained from on high"—it is obligatory and there is nothing humans can do about it. In fact, as the Hindu or Tallensi perspective demonstrates, struggling with and attempting to "reform" the system would be tantamount to immorality itself—rejecting one's social and spiritual duties.

The very process of naturalizing and supernaturalizing culture and of culturalizing nature and super-nature purportedly removes culture from the realm of human doing. There is a "moral" value in this move, in that it gives people a stronger reason to conform to cultural norms and makes those norms themselves more normal, those morals more moral, those values more valuable. However, from a social-constructionist perspective, the naturalizing/culturalizing dialectic also hides the social basis of culture and morality from people, leading them to believe that their culture and morality are natural or supernatural. For some scholars, this amounts to a "mystification" of social realities, making those realities more mysterious and opaque than they would otherwise be. This is a particularly significant factor when we consider two things—first, that social realities continually change and the natural and supernatural justifications change with them, and second, that some of these realities are exploitative or even oppressive and the natural and supernatural justifications make them seem necessary and unquestionable.

Marx was one of the harshest critics of the mystifying power of religion. For him, a society is founded ultimately on practical and material activity, which gives rise to particular social relations (the "relations of production"). These relations have evolved over time, as the "means of production" have evolved; however, while many philosophers and social observers saw the relations—and even the ideas and beliefs—of society driving the practical actions, he saw it precisely the other way around. The means of production were the "most real," the relations of production were the "next most real," and the ideas, beliefs, and values were the least real, mere epiphenomena to explain and legitimate the means and relations. He expected that, if people would unveil the mystery and under-stand the real foundations of their society, then they would no longer need religion, nor would they accept the unproductive sacrifices (such as supporting an idle class of priests) that it demands.

Not all students of religion follow Marx. However, almost all have noted what he noted, that religion is an effective discourse for representing and justifying society to itself. This is the essence of Durkheim's entire approach, although he ended up much less critical, even saying that all religion is "true" after a fashion. But still society is the ground and religion is the reflection of that ground. Malinowski too wrote that religion can associate itself with and legitimate "any form of social power or social claim. It is used always to account for extraordinary privileges or duties, for great social inequalities, for severe burdens of rank, whether this be very high or very low" (1948: 84).

We see this process at work across cultures and throughout time. The Hindu system illustrates it well. Similarly, the European concept of "divine right of kings" made a solid explanation of and basis for the sovereignty of a single individual in a more or less elabo-rate hierarchy of personal power and privilege: individual kings—and the very institution of kingship—were ordained by God, not made by human social practices (like war or class). Traditional Chinese politico-religious thinking had a corollary in the "mandate of heaven," which asserted that an emperor ruled with the blessing of the gods and that he could be removed only by someone else whom the gods had selected over him. The Bunyoro and Shilluk cases above illustrate the same phenomenon: the new king is the old mythical king, making his claim stronger and more unimpeachable. Finally, the concept of *mana* in Polynesian societies provided a supernatural foundation for the power and success (or the weakness and failure) of powerful persons, including chiefs and kings.

Some analysts have pushed the argument much further. Maurice Bloch (1979), for example, in discussing kingship in Madagascar, insisted that mystification, inversion, and legitimation are all intimately linked. The relationship between the king and the society (and the land itself) in the Merina and Betsileo kingdoms was based on the idea of *hasina*, an animatistic force not unlike *mana* or others found around the world. *Hasina* was a super-natural power associated with life and reproduction, both human and natural (e.g. farming). Like *mana* or the Apache concept of *diyi*, some people possessed more of it than others, and those who did were more important and more influential both on society and on nature itself.

Possessing or controlling *hasina* thus entitled a person to greater honor and greater authority, as the application of this mystical power helped society and nature itself to function better; the little people depended on the holders of *hasina* in a way that was not reciprocal. Or so the system said. Bloch reinterpreted the relationship between *hasina*-holder and *hasina*-needer as an obfuscation of real social and political relations. Super-natural power allegedly flowed "down" from the kings, but social/political power actually flowed "up" from the people, in both symbolic (obedience and other obligations) and literal (wealth and gifts) forms. The same thing can be seen in Hinduism in the transactions between *brahmans* and non-*brahmans*: the highest caste performed ritual functions for the lower castes, and the lower castes offered deference and respect—and money—to their betters.

Thus Bloch concluded that *hasina* created an illusion of rank and an illusion of the necessity and truth of rank distinctions. Specific politico-religious rituals in which the king and his subjects interacted communicated and reconstituted the unequal relations between them, making those relations appear to be natural and supernatural rather than cultural and historical. They represented social realities, as Durkheim thought, but also *misrepresented* them, as Marx thought. The result, in the Madagascar case as in many others, was that the political system and the religious system, while clearly interrelated, actually became disconnected for the people who participate in it, and the direction of social production was reversed: rather than rulers and subjects creating and maintaining the stratified system, the natural and supernatural stratification seemed to create rulers and subjects. And the ritual and mundane interactions of the various strata, conducted in terms of mystical giving and taking, reproduced the system continuously.

Conclusion

Every society gives its members a sense of the correct, valuable, or good things to do, and not only through religion. As discussed in the previous chapter, religious ritual falls on a continuum of other more general forms of socially appropriate behavior. The same is true of morality, which is itself a form of social sanction specific to certain cultures and religions. The very concept of "morality," not to mention the details of moral conduct, is relative, but the underlying force and motive perhaps are not. Different cultures and religions ordain different behavioral standards, but the key is that all cultures have such standards and that these standards are *ordained*—religion being the most profound source of ordi-nation. What precisely humans are supposed to do is less important than the fact that there is something to do and that humans are supposed to do it. Herein lies religion's "charter" function, its "model of/for" function, and its function to in-form and in-struct individuals, groups, institutions, and society as a whole. Religion communicates that the relationships and orders of the social and natural world are "given"—they have been established, and this establishment comes from outside, from the super-social and supernatural realm. Human life is thus based ultimately on *obligation*, on *commitment*, and not only are humans pressured to acknowledge and comply with these standards, but they are given continuous opportunities to experience and practice them. Society depends on it.

DISCUSSION QUESTIONS

- What is the anthropological perspective on "morality"? How are notions of pollution central to cultural and religious concepts of morality?
- What does it mean to talk about the "efficacy" of religion—individually and collectively?
- How does religion legitimate society—and sometimes contest society's legitimacy?

SUPPLEMENTARY READING (see website)

- *The Evolutionary Origins of Morality*
- *The Moral of the Story: Persons, Places, Stories, and Morality among the Apache*
- *The Moral Power of Witchcraft among the Sukuma of Tanzania*
- *What is Allowed, What is Forbidden: Halal Goods and the Global Halal Industry in Islam*

7 Religious Change and New Religious Movements

Most people know Rastafarianism through reggae music. But Rastafarianism, or simply Rastafari, is much more—a religion, a culture, and a political movement. Since it emerged in the 1930s, followers of Rastafari have believed "that they and all Africans in the diaspora are but exiles in 'Babylon,' destined to be delivered out of captivity by a return to 'Zion,' that is, Africa, the land of their ancestors" (Chevannes 1994: 1). The biblical allusions are clear. When Africans were forcibly transported to the Caribbean, they encountered Western Christianity, and many new hybrid religions, mixing African, Christian, and indigenous ideas and practices resulted, such as Santería and Voudun ("voodoo"). On the island of Jamaica, Rastafari was preceded by a movement called Revivalism, but in the 1930s two new elements were added—the "black nationalism" and back-to-Africa notion of Marcus Garvey's Universal Negro Improvement Association and reverence for Haile Selassie, the emperor of Ethiopia, who was known by the title Ras Tafari (Tafari was part of his given name and Ras was a noble title). Many Jamaicans came to see Ras Tafari as more than the hope of African liberation but as a divine figure, even as *Jah* or God. Thus these "Rastafaris" saw Africa not only as their lost homeland but as a sacred place, as the biblical Zion, from which they were exiled in the biblical Babylon. By the late 1940s some especially adamant young Rastafaris, known as the Young Black Faith, adopted the hairstyle of dreadlocks, signaling the fact that they were fearsome, "dreadful" warriors. Others who did not adopt this look were called "Comb-somes," splitting the religion into two "houses." Chevannes characterized the Dreadlocks as "zealots" (163) who not only opposed much of Jamaican society but developed their own speech codes, such as the extensive use of "I" as an object pronoun (instead of "me"), as a second-person pronoun (instead of "you"), and as a plural pronoun ("I and I" instead of "we"). They would also say "overstand" instead of "understand" and "downpression" instead of "oppression." Eventually a contingent of Dreadlocks known as Bobo splintered off, living in communes and "marked by the wearing of tightly wrapped turbans, sometimes long flowing black or white robes, and attractively handmade sandals" (171).

Religion is often perceived as a mainly or even totally conservative force. That is, religion seems—or claims—to ordain a way of life and a system of meaning and morality that is settled once and for all and that cannot change without being corrupted. But this notion of permanence and immutability is less a fact about religion than an *ideology of religion*; its alleged ancient and unchanging nature is part of its claim to authority and legitimacy. However, it is immanently clear that religions change and always have, entirely new religions commonly appearing. Indeed, every religious *tradition* was at some point in time a religious *novelty*. Christianity and Islam, as we will describe in the next chapter, were once new religions, although each tried and succeeded to offer itself as a continuation of an older religious truth. And according to one source, two or three new religions are invented every day (Lester 2002: 38).

Rather than seeing religion as a static and strictly conservative force, we should see it as a dynamic and highly adaptable one. As part of culture and as a composite phenomenon, religion can and must absorb aspects of the wider culture while diffusing out into the wider culture. Of course, religions meet and interact—sometimes clashing but almost always borrowing. Thus in this chapter we will explore the ongoing construction of religion. Even "traditional" religions were dynamic, and no particular version or moment of such religions was the "true" or "traditional" one. Further, by the time anthropologists arrived on the scene, many "traditional" religions had already encountered missionaries or members of other religions like Christianity, Islam, or Buddhism. In more recent times, the processes of religious change have accelerated, as and because the more general processes of cultural change and globalization have accelerated.

The Anthropology of Religious Change

As Malinowski noted long ago, "The figment of the 'uncontaminated' Native has to be dropped from research in field and study. The cogent reason for this is that the 'uncontaminated' Native does not exist anywhere" (1961: 2). Therefore, "the scientific anthropologist must be the anthropologist of the changing Native" (6). Of course, contemporary anthropology is also the science of the modern global citizen and society too. Nevertheless, in the realm of religion, the scientific anthropologist must be an anthropologist of changing religion. In fact, religious change is a species of cultural change in general, which Malinowski defined as "the process by which the existing order of a society, that is, its social, spiritual, and material civilization, is transformed from one type to another" (1). The significance of this appreciation is twofold: that changes in religion will be holistically related to changes in other aspects of culture, and that the same basic change processes will operate in both.

In religion specifically and culture generally, the two most basic change processes are *innovation* and *diffusion*. In the former, an individual or group within the society invents or discovers some new idea, object, or practice—in the case of religion, a new entity to believe in, a new myth to tell, a new symbol to use, a new ritual to perform, etc. In the latter, an idea, object, or practice from another society is introduced into the first society, which entails further cultural processes such as contact, migration, intermarriage, invasion, or conquest. Whichever is the ultimate source of novelty, the course of change only begins with the appearance of the new item, as we will see below.

We can be considerably more precise about the forms and outcomes of religious and cultural change. The result may be *addition* of an item to the pre-existing repertoire. Evans-Pritchard commented, for instance, that several aspects of Nuer religion appeared to come from outside Nuer society, specifically from their Dinka neighbors. The *kwoth nhial* or "spirits of the air," according to informants, "had all 'fallen' into foreign lands and had only recently entered into Nuerland and become known to them" (1956: 29). Ideas about totems, nature sprites, and fetishes were also often attributed to the Dinka. Conversely, *deletion* may occur when an item is dropped from the repertoire, as when a society stops performing a certain ritual. Often, a *reinterpretation* of previous beliefs and practices takes place, with old forms given new meaning; this can occur due to changing social circumstances and experiences or the mere passing of the generations, new members bringing new perspectives. Other outcomes, or perhaps versions of reinterpretation, include *elaboration*, in which a pre-existing notion or practice is extended and developed, sometimes in quite unprecedented directions; *simplification*, in which a pre-existing notion or practice is trimmed of detail or sophistication; and *purification*, in which members attempt to purge (from their point of view) false or foreign elements and to return to the "real" or "pure" form.

One of the most common and well-studied change processes is *syncretism* (see pp. 161–3 below), in which elements from two or more cultural/religious sources are blended, more or less intentionally, to create a new culture or religion. The result may not be a simple combination of sources but a truly original and creative hybrid, like Rastafari; in the same way that an alloy of two metals is not merely an intermediate of its constituents, so alloys of cultures or religions can also develop new and unique properties. On the other hand, for any number of reasons, the consequence of religious processes may be *schism* or *fission*, the speciation or proliferation of religions as branches from prior beliefs and traditions, leading to "sects" and "denominations" and ultimately entire religions; a classic example would be the Christian schism of Protestantism from Catholicism. In some cases, the result of all of these processes may be the *abandonment* of a religion and its replacement or substitution by a new or foreign one, leading perhaps at the extreme to the *extinction* of the former religion.

The Invention of (Religious) Tradition

Anthropologists have conventionally stressed the stability and continuity of culture generally, and of religion specifically, especially since anthropology has been largely associated with—and has associated with—"traditional" societies. Often the sense is that such societies are unchanged from time immemorial, living fossils that shed light on the early stages of humanity and society. The implication is antiquity and authenticity; however, as just noted, Malinowski quickly dispensed with the suggestion that "traditional societies" were ancient and unchanged. In fact, the word "tradition" does not necessarily imply absolute continuity: from the Latin *tradere* ("across-give"), its connotation is to deliver, transmit, or hand down, but this does not tell us how long or how perfectly the transmission process has occurred.

In religion, the issue of tradition is particularly acute, because religion obtains much of its authority from its antiquity and from its supposed unchanged purity. However, in 1983 Eric Hobsbawm and Terence Ranger published their groundbreaking study on "invented traditions," showing that many purportedly old traditions (like Scottish tartans or various rituals or texts) were actually of surprisingly recent vintage. Hobsbawm thus insisted that, while traditions usually claim to be about "the past," this past does not have to be old nor even real.

> The historic past into which the new tradition is inserted need not be of length, stretching back into the assumed mists of time ... However, insofar as there is such reference to a historic past, the peculiarity of "invented" traditions is that the continuity with it is largely factitious. In short, they are responses to novel situations which take the form of reference to old situations, or which establish their own past by quasi-obligatory repetition.
>
> (1983: 2)

Even more than anthropologists, folklorists and religion scholars were immediately sensitive to the problems of changing or even inventing traditions. Dell Hymes, both a folklorist and anthropologist, went so far as to recommend thinking of tradition as a *verb*, as "to traditionalize," saying that "every person, and group, makes some effort to 'traditionalize' aspects of its experience" (1975: 353). That is, individuals and groups try to establish their ideas, practices, and institutions *as* traditions, to have those things transmitted or handed down and to attach them to "the past" in some way. What we call tradition is, at any given moment, actually the current point in a process of traditionalization, leading him to conclude that "intact tradition is not so much a matter of preservation, as it is a matter of re-creation, by successive persons and generations, and in individual performances"; in short, there are no non-traditionalized traditions, if by non-traditionalized "is meant the absence of creative interpretation and effort" (355). Yet esteemed biblical scholar Walter Brueggemann affirms the "traditioned" character of the Judeo-Christian scriptures themselves, arguing that "there was a long process of traditioning prior to the fixing of the canon as text in normative form" (2003: 11). Ironically, one of the ideologies of the "traditioning" process (the invention of tradition) is that each moment's version or interpretation is the absolute and authoritative one:

> each version of the retelling (of which there were surely many in the long-term process) intends, perforce, that its particular retelling should be the "final" and surely the correct one. In the event, however, no account of traditioning turns out to be the "final" one, but each act of traditioning is eventually overcome and in fact displaced ("superseded") by a fresher version. The later, displacing form of the tradition no doubt is assumed to be the "final and correct" one, but is in turn sure to be overcome and, in part, displaced by subsequent versions of the memory.
>
> (9)

Ultimately, Brueggemann refers to this traditioning, this "work of tradition," as "imaginative remembering" (7).

The Invention of "Traditional" Religion

While traditioning or traditionalization is easy to observe in contemporary and literate cultures and religions (especially in literate ones, where we can compare present texts, interpretations, and practices with older ones), the invention of tradition is not unique to the modern world. The traditionalization of "traditional societies" has been harder to see and to accept. If there is a paragon of "traditional culture," it is Australian Aboriginals. In fact, Durkheim used them explicitly as his model for "elementary religion"—the simplest, oldest, most unchanging, and therefore "purist" religion (even the name "Aboriginal" derives from the roots *ab origine* for "from the beginning"). Aboriginal societies themselves often present their religions as models of immutable relations between the spiritual, human/social, and physical worlds, expressed by the Warlpiri for instance in terms of the *jukurrpa* or Dreaming. The Warlpiri told me personally that "the Law" (their English-language gloss for religious knowledge and order) cannot be changed, and Françoise Dussart stated: "If one asks the Warlpiri whether the *Jukurrpa* ... is susceptible to change, they will say, point blank, that it is not" (2000: 23). Richard Waterman and Patricia Waterman asserted that Westerners have been seduced by this indigenous attitude to think that "Aboriginal culture is set up in a way calculated to stifle inventiveness" (1970: 101), while in reality, Aboriginal religions have been remarkably flexible and have even included "traditional" methods of innovation and change. We might go so far as to insist that innovation and change are Aboriginal religious traditions.

There were three processes by which novelty could be introduced into Aboriginal religions without appearing to be novelty at all. The first was revelation. While it would appear that the *jukurrpa* is closed and that no new knowledge or practice could come from it, the Aboriginal view was that there were always more spiritual truths to learn. One obvious doorway through which new knowledge could come was dreams. *Jukurrpa* also literally meant "night-time dreams" among the Warlpiri, so a person could dream a song or dance or symbol or design or entire ritual, and that person was "seeing" a previously unrevealed piece of the Dreaming. Individuals were not regarded as the personal "authors" of these bits of religion but as recipients of the ongoing and never-completed revelation of the Dreaming. Humans could also discover previously unknown religious sites or objects. At the same time, old content could be dropped out. As Dussart wrote, "If, however, you ask them whether a specific Dreaming segment ... can be forgotten, they will readily admit that such amnesia is quite common" (23). This, like addition, does not affect the *jukurrpa* itself but only people's knowledge of it.

The second process was diffusion and exchange. Aboriginal Australia was a huge trading sphere of religious ideas, material resources, and entire complexes of spiritual (and other cultural) knowledge and practice. Franz Josef Micha (1970) found evidence of trade and diffusion of different types of stone, of techniques like tool-making, and of cult objects, myths, and rituals. It was only too clear that major religious elements like the myths of the Wawilak sisters, or the Rainbow serpent, or the Kunapipi, or the Kurangara cult, were sweeping Aboriginal Australia by the mid-twentieth century. Sylvie Poirier (1993) detailed a particular exchange of knowledge and ceremonial forms, focusing on two women's rituals called Tjarada and Walawalarra. In March 1988 thirty women from the Balgo area traveled to a Pintupi community called Kiwirrkura to transfer the Tjarada ritual to the local people there. Apparently, this was the final stage in a long, multi-stage process of ritual exchange between the two groups, one moment in "an ongoing process that involves the participation of various groups from different cultural areas, and in which the fulfillment of any exchange in its entirety might last for years, sometimes even for decades" (758). Accordingly, the Walawalarra ritual, which had been traveling at least since the 1950s, was simultaneously being passed northward to Kiwirrkura. In the final analysis, circulation of "traditional" religion was the norm; in fact, she declared that "the very possibility of long-term 'ownership' or 'accumulation' of such bodies of knowledge appears to be ruled out, and groups seem to insist upon an ongoing circulation" (771).

The third process of novelty was social distribution and interpretation of religious knowledge. Poirier noted that religious forms "are 'open,' and that new sequences and elements can be added to an already existing corpus" (758), just as older material "might pass into oblivion" (772). In other words, one society could and almost certainly would and must adjust the ceremonies and attendant mythology to their own circumstances, and if and when they transferred that corpus to another society, the new recipients would do the same. Even with a society's "own" beliefs and practices, such reworking could occur, and Australian Aboriginal notions about knowledge almost guaranteed it. In order to understand this, it is important to grasp the nature of Aboriginal knowledge, which was located in a context of "ownership" and "rights" that had a profound impact on its construction and constitution. Different individuals and social and local groups had different kinds and degrees of rights over knowledge and objects, depending on various factors and determining various outcomes.

Howard Morphy gave a sense of the complexity of rights over paintings, from "ownership" to "the right to produce certain paintings, the right to divulge the meanings of a painting, and the right to authorize or restrict the use of a painting" (1991: 57–58). The effect on religious knowledge was necessarily a kind of distribution: different individuals had access to different parts of it and/or arrived at different meanings depending on a variety of social factors. Two key factors were, of course, age and gender. Much of Aboriginal religion was strongly gender segregated; also, younger people had less knowledge and less right to knowledge than elders. Beyond that, individuals and social groups—families, "clans," Dreaming "lodges," and local/residential groups—had different access to knowledge of and interpretations about religious matters.

So Aboriginal religious knowledge was not only distributed but restricted, or what Morphy called "layered." In Warlpiri society, this layering of knowledge was captured in the indigenous classification of "cheap," "halfway," and "dear" knowledge and performance (Dussart 2000). "Cheap" was public, relatively non-powerful and therefore without spiritual risk, and available to all. "Halfway" was somewhat powerful and dangerous and as such restricted to ritually active members of both sexes. However, "dear" knowledge, objects, or practices were very powerful and dangerous, secret, and restricted only to initiated men. Interestingly, the very same object or ritual or tale could be cheap or halfway or dear depending on how much of its "inside" detail and meaning were revealed; that is, the power and significance of a religious item can be "hidden in plain sight."

From Religious Change to Religious Movement

Despite the fact that "traditional" religions like the Warlpiri were anything but static and traditional, there is a qualitative and quantitative difference between those processes and products and the processes and products we see in the present. Even for the Aboriginals today, religious (and other cultural) change comes faster and diverges more greatly from previous patterns. In other words, indigenous Aboriginal cultural processes did not create completely new religions but rather permutations of recognizably "traditional" forms. At a certain point, however, a conspicuously new *kind* of religion enters the picture, which is widely referred to as a "new religious movement."

The study of new religious movements (NRM) is even more problematic than the study of religion in general. For one thing, what does "new" mean? It is unclear how *recent* in time and how *different* in doctrine a religion must be to qualify as a "new religion" and therefore when a religion ceases to be "new" and becomes "established" or "orthodox." For another, it is not always obvious what is "religious" about NRMs. Many NRMs integrate non-religious as well as religious elements or modules, like Scientology, "Heaven's Gate," and Raelianism. Many NRMs also express non-religious as well as religious goals, including political, economic, and personal/psychological ones. In his study of "cargo cults" (see p. 169 below), Peter Lawrence went so far as to characterize them as incipient political movements, which gave members "a sense of unity they had never known before European contact and, especially, its last stage, developed into a form of 'embryonic nationalism' or 'proto-nationalism'" (1964: 7). Others like the Taiping "Rebellion" in China expressly combined spiritual and political and even military ends.

Third and finally, NRMs are not understood or offered merely as religions but as religious *movements*. As such, they represent a sub-category of social movements or even "mass movements," which tend to have certain common features. Primary among them is the social condition out of which they emerge. William McFarland, in his investigation of new religions in post-World War II Japan, called them "crisis religions," fashioned "to shelter the masses from the impact of a threatening world" (1967: 13). The same pattern is reproduced in other times and places: NRMs arise as responses, accommodations, or protests to new and unsatisfactory social circumstances. So, as he urged, to explain them is "to explore the dynamic relations between these religious movements and the emergent society" in which they occur (13). In other words, each movement is a unique product of various social factors, including the particular society where it transpires, the particular external forces that impinge on it and the particular ways in which those forces are manifested, the particular individual(s) who offer the response, and the particular intersection of all of these factors.

Despite their diversity, NRMs in the modern world tend to share some qualities. McFarland identified seven such qualities in Japanese new religions, which are more or less typical:

- Charismatic leadership, with a founder or prophet who claims or is endowed with supernatural authority and/or power;
- Concrete goals, or a program for improving individual or collective life, including health, happiness, success, and wealth, etc.;
- Community identification, which often involves seeking recruits among the "hopeless and lonely," the "disinherited" of society, and forming them into a new group;
- Highly centralized organization, frequently quite controlling and "undemocratic";
- Ambitious construction projects, such as headquarters for the movement;
- Mass activities, not the least of which are aimed at proselytization;
- Syncretism, mystery, and novelty, such as a sense of chosenness or possession of a special revelation or message or responsibility.

Finally, the ways in which the general public, and often enough the academic community, talks about such movements tend to evidence two prejudices: first, a negativity toward such groups and second, a distinctly Western/Christian bias. NRMs, which are usually small and almost by definition "unorthodox," are often branded as "cults," with accusations of "brainwashing," abuse, exploitation, extremism and antisocial tendencies, and even violence, and of course sheer falsity and delusion. People forget all too readily that the "orthodox" religions were new religions at first, held in as much contempt by their surrounding societies as "cult" groups are today. Christianity was a cult to the ancient Romans, and early Protestantism was a cult (or a collection of cults) to the Catholic Church. Every new Christian sect—from the Church of Jesus Christ of Latter Day Saints or Mormons, to Seventh Day Adventists, Jehovah's Witnesses, Branch Davidians, the various Pentecostal churches, etc.—has been condemned as a cult by someone, and less mainstream religions like Scientology, Aum Shinrikyo, and Raelianism frequently still are.

It should be obvious that "cult" is not a technical term but a judgment. In popular language, it is a pejorative term used to express disapproval of certain kinds of "strange" or "unacceptable" or "bad" religion. Nobody ever describes their own religion as a cult; it may be unorthodox, but it is not bad from the member's perspective. The academic treatment of cults has too often and too closely followed the popular one, which itself is dominated by sectarian interests. The Christian apologist Jan Karel van Baalen literally named a cult "any religion regarded as unorthodox or spurious" (1956: 363), and notwithstanding that the new religion must be regarded so *by someone*, this usage has found its way into some dictionary definitions. Not surprisingly, he equated orthodoxy with mainstream Christianity. Walter Martin made his definition even more dependent on Christianity, calling a cult "a group of people gathered about a specific person or person's interpretation of the Bible," such that cults "contain not a few major deviations from historic Christianity" (1976: 11). By this definition most cults would not be considered cults at all, since they have little or nothing to do with Christianity—and many or most contemporary Christian groups would be considered cults.

Box 7.1 Cult or New Religion: The Sathya Sai Movement in India

In 1925 or 1926 in the village of Puttaparthi in India was born a boy, Sathyanarayana Raju, who would have a remarkable religious career: beginning as a local guru, he would evolve into a "global godman" (Srinivas 2010: 51). In retrospect his followers regard his birth as miraculous, but his holy mission really began in 1940, when he was reportedly stung by a scorpion and lapsed into unconsciousness. "When he awoke, he appeared to be a different person, weeping, or catatonic, spouting Vedanta philosophy, singing songs in Sanskrit, and describing faraway places and images of deities that his family had never seen" (56). He manifested mystical powers, including the ability to materialize objects out of thin air. Taking the name Sathya Sai Baba, he claimed to be the reincarnation of Shirdi Sai Baba, a Muslim Sufi mystic who had died a couple of decades before. Tulasi Srinivas maintains that his life "follows the ideal Indic template for self-realization" (58), including leaving his home and family and adopting the physical style of a spiritual master. Because of his magical and healing powers, he attracted a following; his miracles grew to include "teleportation, telekinesis, mind reading, appearance in dreams to give guidance, speaking many languages, and resurrecting people from the dead" (61). Even more, his supernatural claims expanded: in 1963 he declared himself "the reincarnation of the Hindu god Shiva and his consort Shakti" (65), and by the early 1970s he identified himself as "the cosmic Christ," inviting devotees to address him as Krishna, Allah, Christ, or any divine name (69). Within a few years he had integrated symbols of many religions—the cross of Christianity, the crescent of Islam, the dharma wheel of Buddhism, the fire of Zoroastrianism—into his movement. Devotees meanwhile were following Sathya Sai Baba's travels, making pilgrimage to his birthplace (which has developed into a major religious destination), and attending his audiences (see Figure 7.1). Sathya Sai materialized gifts, such as candy and rings, for his followers, who rewarded him with chanting and singing, as well as obeying his commands (e.g. dietary rules) and buying his products—not only recorded music and lectures but "jewelry, pens, watches, statues, prayer beads, snow globes, with pictures of Sathya Sai Baba, ... picture postcards of the ashram, calendars ... and other paraphernalia that cater to global spiritual seekers" (300). The Sai Baba

Figure 7.1 Praying to a picture of Sai Baba at Sri Sathya Sai Super Speciality Hospital in Puttaparthi, India © Tim Gainey / Alamy

movement fell into disrepute over allegations of sexual abuse, and the Great One himself died in 2011, but not before planting temples around the world, including in Chicago, Illinois (www.saibaba.org) and the United Kingdom (www.srisathyasai. org.uk), not to mention Sri Sathya Sai University, several Sri Sathya Sai hospitals, and drinking water projects in various parts of India.

Religion and Revitalization: Using Religion to Bring Society Back to Life

Throughout history, societies and their religions have found themselves in crises of various kinds—wars, disasters, contact with hostile or merely different peoples and religions, and the like. Or sometimes they have simply discovered that their expectations did not match reality or that their predictions or their practices did not produce results. From that experience, a kind of innocence was lost, and tough new questions were thrust upon them. Even more profoundly, individuals and societies have often found themselves exposed to forces well beyond their control and their comprehension, world-historical forces like urbanization, colonialism, capitalism, industrialization, and detribalization. Their Durkheimian "moral communities" may be smashed and atomized, or at least mixed and remixed, by these forces. Without "traditional" moral communities, the solutions adapted for such communities will not suffice. New ones must and will be found.

Humans in these situations may feel a disconnection, a sense of loss, a cultural (and often enough literal) death of their way of life, their people, and their very world. They may also see themselves reduced to an impoverished group, a minority or lower class in a larger social system not of their making and not in their interest. They may experience "deprivation"—deprivation of independence, of meaning, of wealth, of control, of life itself. Many such societies have long since disappeared from human history, physically or culturally. Many individuals have been absorbed into larger, "modernizing" entities—cities, states, mass movements, world religions, etc. However, there is always the possibility and hope of new life, new community, and new meaning. This is why many religious (as well as non-religious) movements take the form of some type of "revival" or "revitalization."

Revitalization Movements

Such activities to revive a moribund culture or to modify a dissatisfying one often take the form of revitalization movements. Anthony Wallace defined revitalization movements as "deliberate, conscious, and organized efforts by members of a society to construct a more satisfying culture" (1956: 265). They are therefore a subset of culture change, specifically a type of directed change in which people more or less consciously set out to effect changes that they think will improve their lives and society in some way. They may not write a proposal for revitalization, but someone will propose a specific change or set of changes. Like all innovations or diffusions, revitalization efforts have certain characteristics.

According to Wallace, revitalization movements emerge when individuals find themselves in chronic psychosocial stress, caused by the mismatch between their existing beliefs and behaviors and the workings of their new social world. In other words, social conditions change first, and religious conceptions and practices adjust to try to establish some new consonance. The first inclination of humans is to make the new conditions conform to the old conceptions or to assume that they do, but often this simply will not work. At a certain point, perhaps (and usually) one person will arrive at a new idea, a new interpretation, a new view that is intended to lead society out of its impasse and into a better tomorrow. This is the revitalization.

Wallace described a consistent pattern among such movements, starting with the original cultural situation before any jarring social change appears. He called this the "steady state" (although we know that this "traditional" state was not always so steady or so traditional): the worldview of the society fits the world adequately enough, and any threats to that worldview or society can be accommodated within the existing beliefs and practices. However, because of contact, conquest, disaster, globalization, or other experience, a period of *increased individual stress* begins; changes in the real-life, on-the-ground conditions no longer match the traditional worldview or beliefs. People may continue doing what they always did but with diminishing or no effect. Their traditions are clearly failing them, and their world does not quite make sense.

This is followed by a phase of *cultural distortion*, where the prolonged and serious stress of cultural failure may lead to negative responses like alcoholism, depression, violence, neurosis, suicide, and the breakdown of social institutions. People perceive that things are going wrong fast, but most do not know how to respond effectively. Many give up, perhaps assimilating into another social system, often the one that brought the disjunction in the first place; for instance, after conquest by Rome, ancient Israelites sometimes chose to collaborate with Rome or even become Roman citizens. In many other cases the society simply disintegrated.

However, in more than a few instances in human history, a response has emerged; this is what Wallace called the *period of revitalization*. This phase of cultural or religious innovation has several significant sub-phases:

1   Cultural/psychological reformulation. Existing elements of society and/or new elements are put forth by a creative individual, a prophet or a leader. It is extremely note-worthy that the innovator usually is a single individual, someone who has a "moment of insight, a brief period of realization of relationships and opportunities," which seems to him or her and to others as a revelation or inspiration—a gift from outside (270). Often enough, this insight comes from a dream or vision, a purportedly supernatural or spiritual experience in which the innovator is shown or taught something. The dream or vision may be apocalyptic or utopian; Wallace suggested that "such a dream also functions almost as a funeral ritual: the 'dead' way of life is recognized as dead; interest shifts to a god, a community, and a new way" (270). What kind of person is prone to such experiences? The potential revitalizer is a person in crisis, perhaps someone given to visions and dissociative breaks. He or she is very often someone who suffers a serious, even life-threatening illness or other personal failure. But whatever the impetus for the experience, they "come back" with some specific "content"—some suggestions for what to do, what to believe, and how to live. These suggestions can be more or less articulate and thorough, but they are often remarkably so.

2   Communication. In the next step, the innovator must express and spread his or her vision of things to come: what is wrong, why is it wrong, and what must we do to remedy it? The prophet may achieve a kind of prestige from having survived the illness—having "come back from death's door." Two recurring themes in this "proselytization" phase are the establishment of a new community under the care of the spirits and a promise of success (in whatever terms) for the members of that community; they may attain material wealth, or regain control of their land, or bring back the dead ancestors, etc. The precise methods of communication can and will vary, and of course many a revitalization program has no doubt been offered but found no takers.

3   Organization. Usually a small number of converts become the core of the new movement; often this is the family of the prophet. A basic organizational structure emerges: leader, "inner circle" of disciples or apostles, and the rest. Often enough, effective lea-dership of the movement may pass into the hands of "men of action," practical "political" leaders who act for or in the name of the spiritual messenger. As the movement gains momentum—and numbers—it will have to reorganize again, since the simple "primitive" community cannot handle its own success. It must often "bureaucratize" to cope with its growing membership and its growing influence in society.

4   Adaptation. Like any instance of culture change, a revitalization movement may not and most likely will not remain the same—doctrinally, behaviorally, or organizationally— over time. It will encounter resistance, incomprehension and miscomprehension, challenges and failures, and rivals and threats, since there may be more than one revitalization effort in any society at any time. The movement, if it achieves any growth at all, will employ a variety of adaptations, including "doctrinal modification, political and diplomatic maneuver, and force" among others and in various combina-tions (274). Modifications may adjust it to the tastes, preferences, and preconceptions of the believers as well as to changes in the social context since the movement first appeared. Often enough, hostility from some or all of the society (and forces outside the society) radicalizes the movement, transforming it "from cultivation of the ideal to

combat against the unbeliever" (275). Those who resist or fight the movement, or simply fail to join it, may be branded as demonic or subhuman.

5   Cultural transformation. If the movement achieves sufficient proportions, a new cultural pattern is created by and around it. A sense of excitement, of reversal of fortunes and of ascending power and success, can arise. The previous deterioration seems to have ended. However, this new plan and culture "may be more or less realistic and more or less adaptive: some programs are literally suicidal; others represent well-conceived and successful projects for further social, political, or economic reform; some fail, not through any deficiency in conception and execution, but because circumstances made defeat inevitable" (275).

6   Routinization. If the movement survives all of the traps and pitfalls above, it will and must eventually settle into a routine pattern. The initial "revolutionary" spirit cannot be sustained forever, and probably should not be (recall Turner's warnings of the dangers of liminality). Organizational structures are put into place, lines of succession are established, and doctrines are worked out and formalized. If the movement is sufficiently successful, it can even become the "new orthodoxy." What was once innovative and radical becomes familiar and mainstream.

Having passed through all of these stages, the final destination of a revitalization movement is *the new steady state*, in which the movement has not only institutionalized itself but matured into a culture and worldview that solves the problems it set out to solve, giving people that sense of security, certainty, and satisfaction that they so palpably lacked in the pre-movement era. However, Wallace maintained that the vast majority (99 percent) of such movements fail, that the most likely moment to fail is the "cultural transformation" phase, and that most of those that survive remain small subcultures in their respective societies, not dying out completely, but stalling as minority or alternative systems— "sects," "denominations," or even "cults"—in a greater religious field. It stays on the "fringe" of society as yet one more religious and social alternative.

Types of Revitalization Movements

Anthropologists have distinguished a variety of different "types" of revitalization movements, based on their aims and methods. But, as in all of the typologies we have examined previously, these types are not pure or mutually exclusive. An actual movement can and generally does show features of two or more of these categories; it may also not show all of the features of any one category. Finally, these types or processes are not exclusive to religion. Still, the categories proposed by Wallace are analytically useful.

Syncretism

Syncretism refers to an attempt to mix or blend elements of two or more cultures or belief systems to produce a new, third, better culture or system. Some anthropologists and other scholars, like Rosalind Shaw and Charles Stewart (1996), have defended the position that syncretism refers exclusively to religion and, more, to the interactions between two or more distinct religions. Others, like André Droogers (1989), following J. H. Kamstra, hold that syncretism can occur *within* a single religion, by absorbing elements of the non-religious culture. While it may be desirable to have a term for specifically religious blending processes, such processes are in no way unique to religion: blending (by the name of syncretism or by any other name) occurs in food, clothing, music, and every domain of culture.

In a very real sense, all religion is syncretistic. Shaw and Stewart admitted that "all religions have composite origins and are continually reconstructed through ongoing processes of synthesis and erasure" (1996: 7), or, in terms of our earlier discussion, all religions are the product of traditioning. Indeed, it is fair to say that all culture (and potentially all life and physical existence) is syncretistic, mixing and blending down to the genetic level. However, for our purpose, religions not only consciously or unconsciously borrow from each other, but individuals and groups may intentionally practice such borrowing in the interest of inventing a new sect or denomination or even an entirely new religion. And since syncretism is so ubiquitous, Shaw and Stewart suggested that "rather than treating syncretism as a category—an 'ism'—we wish to focus upon *processes* of religious synthesis and upon *discourses* of syncretism" (7).

Religious syncretism can obviously draw from diverse religious sources. Cao Dai, a new religion that originated in Vietnam in the early twentieth century, overtly incorporated conceptual and organizational elements from Buddhism, Chinese religions (especially Confucianism and Taoism), and Christianity (especially Catholicism). Aum Shinrikyo, the group responsible for the subway gas attacks in Japan in 1995, also merged Hindu–Buddhist with Christian components. Smaller-scale or so-called "tribal" movements, like cargo cults, the Ghost Dance, and the Handsome Lake movement, tended to intermingle traditional beliefs and practices with those of the invading religion, frequently Christianity.

Syncretism, even in religion, can and often does draw upon other non-religious sources too, which can contribute modules to a new religious composite. Aum Shinrikyo mixed aspects of Nostradamus together with modern technology (like preparing poison gas) and "Y2K" or turn-of-the-millennium concerns. The suicidal group popularly known as Heaven's Gate (see Figure 7.2) but formally as TELAH (The Evolutionary Level Above Human) borrowed from computer technology and the internet as well as UFO beliefs. Scientology not only got inspiration from but actually started out as a psychological and health movement. Finally, the women's spirituality movement, in various forms, exhibits qualities of many different religious traditions (Christian, Eastern, tribal, pagan, etc.) joined with political, psychological, and gender issues and goals.

Figure 7.2 Heaven's Gate website © Pictorial Press Ltd / Alamy

The mention by Shaw and Stewart of the discourses of syncretism reminds us that not all observers perceive the phenomenon equally. For anthropologists, ideally, it is a neutral process; however, especially for members of an orthodox religion, as well as for scholars with an investment in an orthodox religion, syncretism is "often taken to imply 'inauthenticity' or 'contamination,' the infiltration of a supposedly 'pure' tradition by symbols and meanings seen as belonging to other, incompatible traditions" (1996: 1). While anthropologists could argue with such a viewpoint or simply exclude it from consideration, Droogers advised that "*the controversy* within a religion on the acceptability of syncretism should not be left out of the definition of the concept" (1989: 9).

Accordingly, Shaw and Stewart stressed that we should also pay attention to the opposite of syncretism, which they called "anti-syncretism," "the antagonism to religious synthesis shown by agents concerned with the defense of religious boundaries" (1996: 7). Often expressed in terms of the purity or authenticity, even the "truth," of a religion, anti-syncretism prevents mixing or purges already mixed foreign elements. Islam, for example, explicitly forbids *bid'a* or "innovation/novelty," just as Christianity worries about orthodoxy versus heresy, although the history of both religions has been schism and continual reinterpretation. Small-scale religions too sometimes oppose the encroachment of world religions. Catherine Allerton, who reported the personhood of Manggarai land (see Chapter 3), also reports that the Manggarai have so far resisted syncretism in their land-related beliefs and rituals. Although most Manggarai today identify as Catholic, many of them continue to feel that Christianity is foreign and "not applicable to practices concerned with the land, its energies and fertility" (2009: 277). They go so far as to "reject the possibility of a fully Catholic landscape" (271), at least partly because in Christianity land is inert matter, not a living person, and because to "have a fully Catholic landscape … one would need to change the name of the land from Manggarai, and change the names of all the hills, rivers, mountains and villages. In short, one would have to make it a completely different land" (278).

Millenarianism

Millenarianism (from the Latin *mille* for thousand) is a familiar concept to those versed in Christianity, which is an inherently millenarian religion. Christianity teaches that at some point in the future the world as we know it will end. Opinions about the specific order of events, and what is to follow, vary between denominations and sects, but it is generally agreed that the transformation will not be easy or painless. Naturally, not all religions contain such eschatology (see Chapter 2), and most that include a prediction do not conceive of it in thousand-year terms; this is an artifact of the base-ten system of the West (in which 1,000 is 10^3). Societies that do not operate in base ten, like the ancient Maya, or that start their calendars on different dates, do not reckon time the way Westerners do. So the point of millenarianism is not literally the thousand-year period but the notion that the world proceeds through historical or spiritual periods, the current one of which will end—and often soon. Thus millenarianism as a general cultural phenomenon is a type of movement based on the conception that the present age of the world (an inferior, unhappy, or wicked one) is about to end and that a superior age is about to begin. The followers of the movement must either prepare for the coming change (which may be opposed by the forces of evil and darkness or by the human forces of power and wealth) or act to set the change in motion.

Although not universal, millenarianism is a surprisingly common dimension of new religious movements. There are probably two reasons for this. One is the global influence of Christianity, which has transported the expectation to other cultures. The second reason is the general "protest" nature of many NRMs, which are explicitly aimed at modifying or eliminating the reigning religious and cultural circumstances. The Taiping rebellion was clearly millenarian (as well as syncretistic), expecting and determining to achieve a new divine society in China. Many if not all cargo cults have a millenarian ring, as did TELAH and Aum Shinrikyo and older movements like the Ghost Dance. In fact, if there is one thing that new religions commonly anticipate—and seek—it is the end of "life as they know it" and the establishment of a better life, at least for followers.

Messianism

Messianism is another term drawn from the Judeo-Christian tradition, which insists that a *messiah* or "anointed one" will appear (or has appeared) to lead the society to salvation and happiness. As such, it is probably either a subtype of millenarianism or a concomitant of it: when the millennium comes, a messianic figure will be the one who ushers out the old and ushers in the new. Perhaps one of the key traits of a messianic movement is the belief that some individual will appear to found and/or lead the movement. This figure may not always be a *messiah* but is generally a prophet or innovator or founder of some sort.

Various characters, ancient and modern, have claimed or been attributed to be messianic figures. In Christianity-inspired movements, the messiah figure is often believed to be an incarnation of Jesus; such was the case in the Branch Davidian sect, where David Koresh (who had even changed his name for the occasion) was accepted as more than a religious leader but as literally *the* messiah returned to carry out the promise. In Mormonism (formally, the Church of Jesus Christ of Latter Day Saints, or LDS), Joseph Smith played the role of founder and prophet, and all subsequent leaders (and even regular members) are prophets. Shoko Asahara performed the function for Aum Shinrikyo (see Figure 7.3),

Figure 7.3 An Aum Shinrikyo follower meditates before a portrait of founder Shoko Asahara. Photo courtesy of TORU YAMANAKA/AFP/Getty Images

while Sathya Sai Baba was the focal figure of his movement. In fact, since movements are almost always the inspiration of an individual, there is almost always a single identifiable founder. In Seventh Day Adventism it was Ellen Harmon White; in Scientology it was L. Ron Hubbard; and in the Unification Church it was Sun Myung Moon (significantly, a name meaning, at least in some translations, "he who has clarified the Truth").

The role of the founder, and of his/her personal qualities, has been noted since Max Weber if not before. Weber regarded "charisma" as a critical non-traditional as well as non-rational form of power and authority, based on the extraordinary and even supernatural characteristics of the leader—his or her ability to perform miraculous acts, display wisdom and answer questions, prophesy the future, and achieve results. Peter Worsley stressed charisma in his investigation of cargo cults, noting that charisma as a personality trait is never enough to sustain a movement; it must be institutionalized, crystallizing

> individual beliefs into a belief *system* and believers into a social collectivity, the perceptions [of which] must further generate a disposition to behave in socially meaningful and causally significant ways, and to do so in coordination with others in a goal-directed and normatively controlled fashion.
>
> (1968: xii)

In other words, while a charismatic movement "is non-routine behavior par excellence" (xlviii), it must settle into an organization or institution—and not only that, but produce some effects. "This is why 'signs,' 'proofs,' the behavioral acting out or demonstration of the abstract 'promise' are a *sine qua non* for the continuation of the movement" (xii–xiii).

Box 7.2 A Messianic, Millenarian Movement: The Ghost Dance

One of the earliest ethnographic accounts is James Mooney's (1896) report on the Ghost Dance. Mooney felt the Ghost Dance to be an unprecedented religious development in Native American culture, but others including Leslie Spier (1935) showed convincingly that it was related to previous revitalization activities as well as traditional Indian beliefs and rituals far from the site of the 1890 incident at Wounded Knee, South Dakota. There had been an earlier wave of Ghost Dance activity in 1870 in northwest United States, specifically the Oregon area, affecting the Modoc, Klamath, and Paviotso peoples. However, going back even further in time Spier discussed the "Prophet Dance" and the apocalyptic views of various Northwestern tribes. He described the Southern Okanagon belief in natural disasters (earthquakes, falling stars, etc.), dreams or visions of god or the land of the dead, a "doomsday" when the world will end, and dances and songs aimed at human salvation at the end time. Seers would dance for days at a time until the crisis passed, returning to their normal lives until such time as another visionary issued another warning. He also mentioned the "confession dance," which would spring up at some perceived sign of the final days, during which the people would stand swaying in a circle confessing their sins. The "circle dance" would emerge as a key element of the Ghost Dance. Whatever its roots and precedents, the beliefs and practices spread into previously unaffected regions in the late 1800s. Those were dark years for Plains Indians. The initial incursions of the whites into Indian territory had been followed by treaties and wars, leading to the final defeat of formerly independent tribes. Not only were the people crushed and consigned to reservations, but nearly the entire population of buffalo was wiped out. By the 1880s even reservation lands, small and dismal as they were, were being carved up and distributed under the policy of "allotment." On the remaining reservation land, people suffered hunger, contagious diseases, and general cultural dislocation. Obviously, enormous numbers of indigenous people had been sent off to join their dead ancestors.

The prophet of the Ghost Dance is generally known as Wovoka (the woodcutter), probably a variation of *Quoitze Ow* or *Kwohitsauq*; he was also called Jack Wilson. As a youth he showed interest in religious matters and even purportedly participated in a Baptist temperance society in his adulthood; he may have been prone to minor religious experiences. Then, as Michael Hittman (1997) recounted from primary sources, on January 1, 1889, he supposedly heard a "great noise" while out chopping wood, causing him to faint. He had a near-death experience and was unconscious for an unspecified time, regaining consciousness simultaneous to a solar eclipse. Other Indians viewed his recovery as a spiritual cure by the Sun, reasoning that he had saved the world from destruction according to beliefs like those just mentioned. He declared that he had visited heaven during his coma and talked with "God." In heaven, all the dead ancestors were alive and young again, dancing and happy. God then gave Wovoka power over nature, along with a moral code including rules against lying, stealing, and fighting. Finally, he was given a dance—the Ghost Dance—and promised life and youth in heaven for compliance (see Figure 7.4). Apparently the prophet had some successes in his prophecies and natural powers, for his fame spread; not only did he send representatives to other tribes with the good news, but as many as thirty tribes sent delegations to him to learn the news.

Among these were the Lakota or Sioux, who sent Good Thunder, Cloud Horse, Yellow Knife, and Short Bull to meet Wovoka in 1890. When the Lakota received it, their conditions, having just been settled onto reservations, were very different from other tribes, including the prophet's own. Nevertheless, much of Lakota Ghost Dance belief and practice was consistent not only with Wovoka's instructions but with the Northwestern apocalyptic tradition described above. They danced in a circle, or several concentric circles, in a shuffling step holding hands. They anticipated the restoration and rejuvenation of earth and society, as soon as spring 1891. At that time, they would be reunited with their dead ancestors; presumably the whites would be eliminated, for the Lakota had a more aggressive tradition than the Paiutes or the Northwestern tribes, not to mention a more violent recent history. One innovation that may have been original to the Lakotas was the Ghost Dance shirt, a garment not only attributed with spiritual significance but magical power. It was believed at least by some to protect the wearer from bullets. It was allegedly believed, both by the prophet and his followers, that he himself was invulnerable to arrows or bullets, but it is unclear whether this was through any special clothing or merely through his own unique spiritual person. Either way, when the Lakota commenced their Ghost Dance activities in view of reservation authorities (as secret as they tried to be), a sense of alarm was raised among the whites, since a mobilized Indian population, together with no more susceptibility to or at least fear of soldiers' bullets, presented a dangerous situation for the whites. Two days before the end of the year, following an attempt to arrest the great chief Sitting Bull in which he had been killed, tension erupted into violence as guards

Figure 7.4 Sioux Ghost Dance (nineteenth-century engraving). Courtesy of the Library of Congress Prints and Photographs Division

fired on a crowd of men, women, and children at Wounded Knee, killing three hundred in the last "battle" (or massacre) on the Plains. It was the end of Lakota resistance and of the Ghost Dance.

Irredentism

Irredentism (from the Italian *irredenta*, "unredeemed") is another recurring if less familiar feature of movements. Irredentist movements are efforts to reclaim and reoccupy a lost homeland; not all are religious in nature, but religion can serve as a mighty justification for the movement. They are at the heart of many of the ethnic conflicts in the modern world. The Sinhalese/Tamil struggle over Sri Lanka is a sort of irredentist movement: the Tamils claim to be fighting for their former homeland, Tamil Eelam, which they justify on the basis of their distinct culture, their prior occupation, and their present-day majority status. We can also appreciate the irredentist aspects of the 1990s Yugoslavian wars, in particular the Serb demands for chunks of Bosnia and even more so for Kosovo.

The Zionist movement, beginning officially in the late 1800s but with much older roots, set as its goal the recreation of a Jewish national state in the Jewish "holy land." On the basis of a variety of justifications—divine intent and "covenant" (the "promised land"), prior occupation and political control (the ancient kingdom of Israel), right of conquest (the biblical Hebrews under Moses and Joshua had fought to take the land they were promised), and in the modern context cultural rights and cultural survival (living in Europe had proven to be a risky proposition)—Zionists like Theodore Herzl, author of the *The Jewish State*, set about reclaiming their lost homeland, from which they had been dispersed (referred to as the Diaspora) for nearly two thousand years. The subsequent establishment of the modern state of Israel in Palestine in 1948 was the end result of this movement, and contemporary Zionist extremists like the organization called Gush Emunim envision a day, based on scriptural and historical grounds, when all of ancient Israel and beyond—"from the Euphrates River in Iraq to the Brook of Egypt" (Aran 1991: 268)—will be returned to the Jewish people (see Chapter 12).

Of course, a place is not just a physical geographical location; it is also an idea and (invented) memory. "Zion" is the strip of land on the eastern Mediterranean coast for Jews. Recall that "Zion" was relocated to Africa, specifically Ethiopia, for Rastafaris—an imagined lost homeland, imagined because Caribbean African slaves were largely taken from western Africa, not eastern Africa. And as early as the 1940s some Jamaican Rastafaris did "return" to Ethiopia, but what many found was not exactly "home": they have had difficulty obtaining Ethiopian citizenship or rights to own land, and their Jamaican/Rastafari identity sets them apart from native Ethiopians (Niaah 2012). Subsequently, some Rastafaris have reinterpreted "Zion" again, arguing that Zion is Jamaica. Most fascinatingly of all, Rastafarianism has flowed around the world, even to places where Afro-Jamaicans have not traveled, such as New Zealand. Some Maori, the indigenous people of New Zealand, have adopted Rastafarianism, mixing Rastafari styles with traditional Maori culture like *moko* face tattoos, and of course for them Israel, Ethiopia, and Jamaica hold no significance. For them, the lost homeland is their colonized islands of New Zealand, and their Zion is the local Mount Hikurangi (Douglas and Boxill 2012).

Modernism/Vitalism

Modernism or vitalism seeks to import and accept alien cultural ways, in part or in total. Modernism does not always take the form of religion. For instance, when Japan was finally "opened" to the West in 1854, it began to adapt itself to this new contact by appropriating much from the Western world. Technology, military organization, language, and styles of dress and music were absorbed. By 1868, a revolution known as the Meiji (Japanese for enlightenment) was underway. A modern constitution was written, establishing the emperor as the head of state. The feudal system was abolished, mass state-sponsored education was put in place, and concentrated efforts to industrialize and to modernize the army were made.

The most complete form of modernism in religion is conversion, the wholesale acceptance of a foreign set of beliefs, values, and practices, and in the realm of religion this means conversion to a foreign religion, especially a world religion and proselytizing religion like Christianity or Islam. We will have much to say about this process in the next chapter. Indigenous religions can also modernize themselves by incorporating aspects of new and foreign religion and culture, in particular beliefs in a single god or in an apocalyptic end time, or values and practices like monogamy or avoidance of alcohol. Members may go so far as to condemn and reject their traditional religion and associated practices and institutions (often under the influence of foreign agents of change like missionaries).

At the same time, probably all movements show some degree of modernism, even if only in the adoption of modern technologies to preserve and propagate old beliefs and practices; many indigenous societies, for instance, maintain websites and use cell phones, automobiles, and airplanes. Thus modernism/vitalism is not a total phenomenon; rather, ordinarily we find a combination of old and new—and new seen through the eyes of old—in unique and surprising ways.

Box 7.3 Cargo Cults: Local Religion, Translocal Politics

Among the most colorful forms of syncretistic movements in the anthropological literature are the so-called "cargo cults" that swept through the Pacific Islands, particularly Melanesia and the southwest regions, between about 1900 and 1950 as a result of large-scale invasion and colonialism. Cargo cults tended to involve the mimicking of Western religious, social, and moral behavior in order to obtain the wealth that Westerners possessed, "based on the natives' belief that European goods (cargo) … are not man-made but have to be obtained from a non-human or divine source" (Lawrence 1964: 1). However, Julia Zamorska saw such movements as much more than efforts to be rich but as "ways of adaptation, adjustment to a new situation, attempts to find a new place in the changing world and ways of searching for a new definition of Melanesian culture and a redefined cultural identity of the native people" (1998: 7).

Louise Morauta described the complex interplay between the native/local and the foreign/global in the so-called "Yali cult" which broke out in the Madang region of New Guinea in the 1960s. The area had a history of cargo cults reaching back to the 1920s. Yali Singha became the leader of a widespread movement, covering more than two hundred villages whose representatives followed his teachings, held meetings, and collected offerings for their leader. The size of Yali's movement was unusual, most previous and contemporary cargo cults (for his was not the only one in the vicinity) being smaller and more local, sometimes restricted to a single village. At the same time, Yali's movement had two contradictory characteristics. First, it was relatively centralized, with "local bosses" answering to Yali; it was more regularized and standardized than most movements, conducted in pidgin (the hybrid of local and foreign language) rather than the indigenous language, and "not limited to traditional channels of communication" (1972: 436). Yet his followers were a distinct minority in the area: in some villages he had no supporters at all, and most villages were divided between members and non-members. Significantly, the villages where Yali had little or no support were those most effectively integrated into the colonial system, linked by roads, providing employment, and served by schools and hospitals. Yali was actively opposed by the local Lutheran Church as well as those who favored the colonial administration and modern economic development. Yali's influence was strongest in the more remote and less acculturated villages, where literacy and income were lower and where, most importantly, many of the pre-colonial practices and institutions that had provided social cohesion had broken down. Yali's movement seemed to offer not only a new means of social integration and of material success but a new political vision and identity. It was both traditional and modernizing, uniting residents of disparate villages into a regional and potentially national society; his movement exploited internal divisions within villages to "forge strong links between villages" (446), to serve the needs of a partially de-traditionalized society that sought more than cargo but also a way to relate to each other and to the outside world.

Nativism/Fundamentalism

At the opposite end of the revitalization spectrum are nativist or fundamentalist movements. Nativism or fundamentalism is a form of movement that emphasizes indigenous or traditional culture and resistance to or even expulsion of alien culture. Ralph Linton defined a nativistic movement as "[a]ny conscious, organized attempt on the part of a society's members to revive or perpetuate selected aspects of its culture" (1943: 230). This is a significant definition, since it indicates that nativism or fundamentalism is not merely "tradition" but tradition *selectively and intentionally revived or perpetuated*. Thus it can never be entirely traditional, in spirit or in content: for instance, the Ghost Dance emphasized certain aspects of traditional culture but also specifically embraced "the use of cloth, guns, kettles, and other objects of European manufacture," which, they were guaranteed, would be theirs when the whites were "swept away" (231).

Linton further specified four subtypes of nativistic movements: (1) revivalistic-magical, (2) revivalist-rational, (3) perpetuative-magical, and (4) perpetuative-rational. In terms of their goals, revivalist movements strive to bring back lost cultural elements, while perpetuative movements struggle to keep alive existing ones; in both cases, there are no strong claims that the elements of interest are particularly ancient or pristine. In terms of their attitudes or practices, magical movements resemble the sort we have been discussing—often promoted by a prophet or charismatic founder with "supernatural and usually … apocalyptic and millennial aspects" (232). Items of culture are focused on

> not … for their own sake or in anticipation of practical advantages from the elements themselves. Their revival is part of a magical formula designed to modify the society's environment in ways which will be favorable to it. … The society's members feel that by behaving as the ancestors did they will, in some usually undefined way, help to recreate the total situation in which the ancestors lived. Perhaps it would be more accurate to say that they are attempting to recreate those aspects of the ancestral situation which appear desirable in retrospect.
>
> (232)

On the other hand, rational movements are primarily psychological and self-consciously "symbolic" and social: their function is to provide self-esteem to the individual members and to maintain solidarity for the collective society. Interestingly, Linton concludes that all of the subtypes are quite common except perpetuative-magical, of which he claims to know no examples. At any rate, we will return to fundamentalist movements in Chapter 12, of which there are many in the modern world; indeed, fundamentalism may be one of the, if not the, most frequent forms of religious revitalization forms in the present.

Case Study: The Blending of Religions in Cao Dai

Vietnam had come under French colonial authority by the time that Ngo Minh Chieu was born in 1878 as the only child of a poor family. Exposed early in life to Chinese religious notions, in particular Confucianism, as well as to French culture (working in the headquarters of the Governor General of Indochina in 1903), he stood at the crossroads of cultures and religions. He studied not only Asian traditions as well as Western ones but practiced spiritism and séances; at one of these events, he received a spiritual message that purportedly cured his mother of her illness. At a subsequent séance in 1920, he was visited by *Duc Cao Dai*, the Supreme Being, in a series of revelations that would lead to a new religion.

Following three years of ritual vegetarianism, Chieu began to spread his lessons around Saigon. He met with great success, especially among the lower class of peasants; Susan Werner concluded that the new religion "claimed more followers within a year of its founding than Catholicism had gained in over three hundred years of proselytization" (1981: 4). On October 7, 1926, when the "Declaration of the Founding of the Cao Dai Religion" was signed, 247 members were present, and the congregation grew rapidly. The original name of the movement, *Dai Dao Tam Ky Pho Do* or "The Third Great Universal Religious Amnesty," illustrated how the new religion saw itself as a continuation or renewal of much older traditions (see Figure 7.5).

Chieu soon withdrew from daily administration, and Le Van Truang came to act as the "Pope" of the church. Not only that, the new church took on some of the structural characteristics of the Catholic Church, with one *Giao-Tong* (Pope) presiding over a "college" of church administrators (*Cuu-Trung-Dai*), considered to be the "executive branch." Three *Chuong Phap* or "Legislative Cardinals" headed up the three "legislative branches," one for each of the old Asian religions (Confucianism, Buddhism, and Taoism). Beneath that, thirty-six *Phoi-Su* or "Archbishops" (twelve for each "branch") held authority over one thousand *Giao-huu* or "priests," each, with *Le-Sahn* ("student priests"), *Chuc Viec* ("lay workers"), and *Tin-Do* ("adepts" or followers), arrayed in an elaborate order.

Doctrinally, Cao Dai was an ecumenical, universalist syncretism. Although resembling Catholicism institutionally, its explicit agenda was to unify the great Asian religions. It was monotheistic, believing in God the Father (*Duc Cao Dai*) but also a Universal Mother. It recognized a number of divine beings including Siddhartha, Confucius, Lao-Tzu, and Jesus. According to Hum Dac Bui, its cosmogony and theology were probably closest to Taoism:

> At the beginning, there is nothing but one principle, one monad, no heaven, no earth, no universe. This monad is Dao or God. God has no name, no color, no beginning, no end; God is invariable, unfathomably powerful, everlasting, and is the origin of all. After creating the universe, God has divided His spirit and with it made all creatures, plants, and materials.
>
> (Bui 1992: 22)

The new religion then explicitly mixed the teachings of its three predecessors—the "three jewels" (matter, energy, and soul) and the "five elements" (mineral, wood/vegetable, water, fire, and earth) of Taoism, the "three duties" (king and subject, father and son, and husband and wife) and the "five virtues" (love, justice, good behavior/politeness, wisdom, and loyalty) of Confucianism, and the "three refuges" (Buddha, *dharma*, and *sangha*) and the "five prohibitions" (no killing, no stealing, no alcohol, no luxuries or temptations, and no bad speech) of Buddhism. The end goal of the religion was basically that of Buddhism: to achieve enlightenment through the careful management of one's karma, by avoiding bad action and engaging in good, including the teaching of others about the right path. Reincarnation in a higher state or ultimate escape to a better reality, heaven or nirvana, was the reward.

Cao Daist practice combined worship of the one God, spiritism, and veneration of the ancestors. Observances could take place at home or at a local temple. These daily rituals involved four ceremonies at sunrise, midday, sunset (roughly eight o'clock), and midnight. At the beginning of the (lunar) month, calendrical rituals were performed along with ones for the Father, the Mother, and the other Divine Beings. Even more propitious was carrying out one's ceremonial duties at the "mother temple" located at Tay Ninh.

The temple, called the Holy See, was constructed in 1928 and houses a mural of the Three Saints of Cao Dai, who are Trang Trinh (a fifteenth-century Vietnamese nationalist poet), Sun Yat-sen (the leader of the 1911 Chinese nationalist revolution), and Victor Hugo (the French writer). These three figures not only represent the "Third Alliance" of Vietnam, China, and France but communicated with followers during séances. Séances, in keeping with Chieu's early personal experience, made up a critical part of religious practice, using Ouija boards or having spirits tap out messages on tables or write them with ritual pens. Mediums were obviously necessary officiates at such events.

These outward demonstrations of religion comprised the "exoteric" side of Cao Dai, but there was also an "esoteric" side. The "inside" version, as in all traditions, was more demanding and more "advanced," and it followed the example set by Chieu himself when he withdrew from outward observance into deeper practice and insight. Esoteric Cao Dai required thorough vegetarianism, meditation, and asceticism. This path was not for the faint of heart and was mostly adopted by the priests.

Cao Dai met with initial official resistance, but by 1935 it was tolerated as a religion. In 1941 the French administration closed the Holy See and tried to eradicate the movement, and the coming of Communism in the 1940s only steeled the faithful more. On February 7, 1947 a Cao Dai army was introduced under the rubric of the "Great Community for Guarding Righteousness and Humanity"; followers were recognized as "Soldiers of the Heavenly Path." The Cao Dai militia grew to ten thousand men and fought both the French and the Communists. The end of the Vietnam war in 1975 with the victory of the North Vietnamese Communists meant the abolition of all observable religion and "re-education" of believers as socialists. Even so, Cao Dai claims some five million believers internationally, with at least 1.5 million in Vietnam, making it the third largest religion in the country—and a new "world religion" with temples in the United States, Australia, and Europe (see www.caodai.org).

Figure 7.5 Cao Dai temple. Courtesy of Shutterstock

Case Study: Change within Religion in the "Emerging Church" Movement

As Droogers insisted earlier, religious change and even religious movements can occur *within* a religion as well as *between* religions, and in fact such intra-religious dynamics are common when people find the received ideas, practices, or institutions of their religion unsatisfying. In the contemporary United States, one of the most interesting recent developments in Christianity has been the "emerging church" movement. Advocates Eddie Gibbs and Ryan Bolger of the Fuller Theological Seminary have defined emerging churches as "communities that practice the way of Jesus within postmodern cultures" (2005: 44). That is, the emerging church movement is a new way that Christianity adapts to the present-day culture around it. Specifically, Gibbs and Ryan suggest that such churches "live highly communal lives" in order to "transform the secular realm" (45).

James Bielo is one anthropologist who has turned the anthropological gaze on American Christianity, and he finds that what he calls Emerging Evangelicals "are religious subjects reflecting and responding to the cultural conditions of modernity and late modernity" (2011: 17), those conditions including urbanization and suburbanization, capitalism and markets, mass media, and reflexive self-awareness. Bielo describes Emerging Evangelicals as "white, male, middle-class, well-educated, urban, Gen-X pastors, church planters, church consultants, and concerned laity" (5). In search of modern and postmodern "authenticity," many of these individuals became dissatisfied with existing churches, even evangelical ones; they tend to have a common "deconversion" story and then reconversion to emerging-church Christianity with a "narrative of critique, of contrast, of rethinking, of recovery, of revelation, and ultimately of keeping the faith" (46). As such, they distinguish themselves not only from the secular materialistic American culture but from mainstream evangelicalism.

As postmodernist Christians, one of the remarkable traits of Emerging Evangelicals is irony. If contemporary American culture entails a certain self-awareness of symbolic mediation, a certain dabbling in surface forms, a certain "indirectness, inversion, circumlocution, satire, parody, pretense, and other ironic forms" (49), then postmodern Christianity can and should demonstrate these qualities. Bielo suggests that, both in regard to commodities and to language, irony is a "centerpiece" of Emerging Evangelical performance (50). Another key aspect of Emerging Evangelicalism is what members call their "ancient-future" orientation, which has them conspicuously—and surprisingly— mixing the old and the new and even "worshiping God in ways that seem patently non-Evangelical" such as

> public reading of monastic and Catholic prayers, burning incense, replacing fluorescent lighting with candles, setting early Protestant hymns to contemporary music, chanting Eastern Orthodox prayers, using icons, creating prayer labyrinths, following the church calendar for sermons and lectionary readings, using *lectio divina* to read the Bible, and increasing the role of silence.
>
> (71)

In these and other ways, Emerging Evangelicals borrow and blend, innovate and simulate, all while claiming to get back to the "basics" or "fundamentals" of their religion.

Most Emerging Evangelicals are committed to "being a missionary to one's own society" (119), which is not particularly unique among Christians. However, because they can see themselves in the wider American social context (i.e. they possess a postmodern reflexive identity), they take an approach to Christian missionizing that they call the "now, not yet kingdom." In other words, the Christian society they seek is both here and not yet here. Emerging Evangelicals have what they call "missional hearts," and part of their strategy of missionizing and of moving toward the "now, not yet kingdom" is church planting, which sometimes carries them into poor and troubled neighborhoods to start new congregations. Bielo urges that this church planting "can be read as a religious incarnation of late modernity's entrepreneurial disposition" (164), and church planting does indeed appear to be supported by an articulated rhetoric, literature, and institutional base of "neoliberal economics." Additionally, Bielo posits that church planting also makes ancient-future the reality of "place" in religion, especially what they call "thinplaces" or "physical spaces on the earth where God's presence could be most readily felt" (76).

Ultimately, the emerging church movement represents an example of what Droogers, after Kamstra, called syncretism *within* a single religion, although practitioners would almost certainly reject the term "syncretism." The result is what Scot McKnight (2007) of North Park Theological Seminary, writing for the evangelical magazine *Christianity Today*, calls "the quilt of evangelicalism," with Emerging Evangelicalism taking its place alongside "the Jesus and charismatic movements of the 1960s." As such, contemporary American Christianity evolves and multiplies, to become more contemporary and more American while expanding the meaning and diversity of Christianity—or Christiani*ties*.

Conclusion

Religion, like all of culture, is in a constant state of change, or it might be better to think of it, like all of culture, as dynamic. Social and cultural processes and practices continuously produce and reproduce religion; when they reproduce it as it was previously, we have "religious stasis" or apparent stability, but when they reproduce it with modifications, we have "religious change." Religions have a tendency, indeed a vested interest, to portray themselves as unchanging, eternal, and immutable, but this is part of religious ideology rather than a fact of religion. The apparent permanence and stasis of religion allows it to claim the "prestige of the past" that Eliade mentioned (see Chapter 4). Even new religions typically claim to perpetuate or perfect previous beliefs and practices, or else they assert that they receive their new messages and revelations from "beyond," from some extra-human source. Thus in the phenomenon of religious change we observe not only the holistic relationship between a religion and its sociocultural and historical environment, as well as the convergence of the personal/psychological and the social/institutional, but also the essential process by which culture—here, change in culture—becomes supernaturalized while the supernatural becomes culturalized. In the following two chapters, we will further explore the consequences of religious dynamism, in the form of "world religion" and "vernacular religions."

DISCUSSION QUESTIONS

- What do anthropologists mean by "the invention of tradition"? How do even "traditional" religions invent their beliefs and practices?
- What are the processes of cultural and religious change, and how is change different from "movement"?
- What is a revitalization movement, and what are the types or elements of revitalization movements?

SUPPLEMENTARY READING (see website)

- *The Making of a Modern Zoroastrianism*
- *The Classical Study of Cargo Cults*
- *Making Money the Sufi Way: The Murabutin Movement*
- *An Old Religion as a New Religion: Druidry in the United States*

8 Translocal Religion
Islam and Christianity

"One of the fruits of the nineteenth- and twentieth-century missionary enterprise in Ghana," a small country in northwest Africa, is the Presbyterian Church of Ghana or PCG (Biney 2011: 53). However, the PCG is hardly the only form of Christianity in Ghana; instead, Christianity exists as "a tapestry of different denominations and independent churches," belonging to categories such as mainline, African independent, Pentecostal, Neo-Evangelical, Neo-Pentecostal/Charismatic, not to mention Jehovah's Witnesses and Mormons. Missionary Christianity inevitably confronted and interacted with local African traditions, including ideas about ancestor spirits, witches, and spiritual qualities of human beings. Since national independence in 1957, many Ghanaians have immigrated to the United States, bringing their Ghanaian Christianity with them. In New York City, Ghanaian immigrants, predominantly of the Akan society or ethnic group, formed the Presbyterian Church of Ghana in New York (PCGNY) in 1983 as a place for religious worship and community gathering. Most interestingly, the PCGNY sees itself not only as a church specifically for Ghanaians (although 99 percent of its members are from Ghana) but as an "overseas mission," which "attempts to propagate the message and mission of the Christian church in the United States through its own brand of Ghanaian presbyterianism (sic)" (68). In other words, the West missionized Africa, but at least in a small way now Africa is missionizing the West.

Anthropology has made its living investigating small, local, "tribal" or "traditional" religions. But religions have never been as isolated and as local as we imagine: Dinka and Nuer religions interacted in East Africa, Warlpiri traded religion with their neighbors in central Australia, and Buddhism coexisted with non-Buddhist ideas and practices in Thailand, as we have seen in previous chapters. Thus some religions became translocal, even international, achieving the status of "world religions."

It might seem at first thought that anthropology is ill suited to study translocal religions, since methods of participant observation favor intimate knowledge of a local setting. However, as in Africa or Thailand, the translocal or the global is present in the local, and translocal or global religions like Christianity take specific local forms, like the Presbyterian Church of Ghana. Most importantly, anthropologists have found that their concepts and methods are by no means limited to local or "traditional" religions but are equally applicable—and critically necessary—to the study of translocal or "world" religions.

This chapter will primarily focus on two translocal religions, Islam and Christianity, not because they are the most important or the most representative religions (they are not) but because anthropologists themselves have been especially active in establishing an "anthropology of Islam" and an "anthropology of Christianity." Moreover, both of these efforts are remarkably recent: just a few years ago some anthropologists insisted that, while there were anthropological studies of Christian groups, there was no anthropology of Christianity, and much energy has gone into the debate over the anthropological treatment of these two massively translocal religions, which between them claim at least half of humanity.

Additionally, the anthropological study of translocal religions raises issues of crucial significance to anthropology. One issue is the formation and spread of new religious movements, the subject of the previous chapter. Another is the diversity within religions, which adapt to and become more or less consonant with their local social and cultural surroundings. A third issue is the interactions between religions, which often share a religious field where they compete and/or cooperate. A final issue is the question of religious identity, that is, how and why people come to affiliate with one (or more than one) translocal religion and how this affiliation shapes their identity and their relations with other religious communities and the wider society.

The Anthropology of the "Great Transformation"

Until recently, we could speak of the world's religions but not of "world religions." There were literally thousands and thousands of religious beliefs and practices and myths and rituals and specialists; in fact, virtually every identifiable social entity had one of its own. Or to say it another way, there were literally thousands and thousands of societies, each with a distinct religious or spiritual tradition. Religion was "local." A few anthropologists have proposed that, at certain times in certain places for certain reasons, a "great transformation" occurred: in addition to, or out of, some local "traditional" religions, not only new religions but *a new kind of religion* sprouted. These theories depend on a considerable amount of cross-cultural generalization, but they are interesting and important.

Robert Redfield (1953) was one of the first to attempt a comparison of local and translocal religions, or what he called "small traditions" and "great traditions." According to him, small or local religions were products or experiences of a specific kind of society, the kind that all societies arguably once were. Small and isolated, "self-contained and self-supported," they were socially homogeneous, with a strong sense of group solidarity. Kinship was the basic organizing principle, so social relationships were personal and informal. Social control was therefore informal and almost unconscious: people behaved in particular ways "because it seems to the people to flow from the very necessity of existence that they do that kind of thing" (14). Religion provided the glue or the threads that held society together and made it seem necessary and self-evident; in fact, religion was and perhaps depended on being largely unreflective and unsystematic. The result was a "moral community" of the sort described by Durkheim; as Redfield put it, "the essential order of society, the nexus which held people together, was moral" (15). "'Moral order' includes the binding sentiments of rightness that attend religion, the social solidarity that accompanies religious ritual, the sense of religious seriousness and obligation that strengthens men, and the effects of a belief in invisible beings that embody goodness" (21).

But all of this changed when social and political circumstances changed. The experience of living in a "great society," what he called a "civilization," requires a different religious ethos. Civilizations are characterized by large and/or interconnected communities, which are socially heterogeneous. Social relationships cannot remain personal but become institutional and "rational." Kinship as an organizing principle gives way to "politics," in the shape of formal government, contractual relations, and the stratification of power and wealth. Specialization and differentiation within the society come to include religion itself, which becomes an institution among other social institutions, albeit one that supports the political institutions. In the process, religion becomes more "professional"—with religious specialists—and more reflective, self-conscious, and systematic. The old moral order cannot integrate such a society, but neither can a new moral order of the old variety. Instead, "In civilization the moral orders suffer, but new states of mind are developed by which the moral order is, to some significant degree, taken in charge. The story of the moral order is the attainment of some autonomy through much adversity" (25).

Ernest Gellner also explored this hypothetical break between local and translocal religion. Local religions, he opined,

> took the overall meaningfulness of the world for granted, even though they had done so much to maintain it. They did not feel obliged to supply guarantees of the overall goodness of the world. Meaning was conferred on the world absent-mindly, without a codified revelation.
>
> (1988: 91)

They were "concrete," not particularly given to "speculation" and intense philosophical introspection. Rather, they "take for granted" the truth of their beliefs and the efficacy of their actions as "self-evident." So they were more "ad hoc," in the sense that they dealt with specific spiritual or practical problems when those arose rather than establishing a permanent self-sustaining "institution" and "orthodoxy." In particular they were non-codified, not written down or "settled" into a "canon" of official dogma. Instead they were "patently social," by which he meant that, while all the details may not be worked out in rationalized completeness, nevertheless the religion and its society were tightly interwoven. People did not so much *believe* their religion as *do* it. The "beliefs" of the religion mirrored and reinforced the "morality" or behavioral imperatives of it, which themselves were embedded in cultural practices and social institutions.

In what Gellner called one of the "big divides in human history," a few religions began to spread from their original sites to other and potentially all places, peoples, and times. These religions, sometimes also designated as "high" or "universal" religions, were not only "bigger" than the local ones but different in some fundamental regards. The main factor in the creation and diffusion of a translocal or "world" religion is, necessarily, its detachment and separation from place. This is not to say that a world religion cannot have sacred places; they can and do. However, a religion that can be practiced only in one location is hobbled in its aspiration to be a translocal religion.

Translocal/world religions are "uprooted" from their original social context to become traveling and often enough missionizing and proselytizing religions. After all, they must recruit members and create for them a new community and sometimes a new identity. Translocal religions therefore tend to be *voluntary* movements or associations, which individuals can join by intentional decision. This leads to another common trait of translocal religions: they tend to be "individualistic" in a critical sense. This is not to say that there is no religious community nor that the individual can think or do whatever he or she likes. Rather, it is to say that individuals may have to choose to join the religion and to accept its doctrines as a personal act. It follows that translocal religions will be deeply concerned with doctrine, with dogma, with belief ("orthodoxy" deriving from Greek words meaning correct or straight belief). In a very real way, what holds the religion together and makes it a religion and a community is doctrine. It is thus crucially important that those doctrines be clear and, more so, accepted without diversity or dissent (a divergent or dissenting belief being "heresy").

One of the fundamental requirements for this elaboration and dissemination of orthodoxy is writing—and specifically the writing of a standard, official body of religious literature, that is, a *canon*. In pre-literate societies, varying versions and interpretations could coexist. For example, ancient Greeks myths could and did exist in varying forms, which further varied from performance to performance. However, once they were set down in writing, the tales became "fixed" or "frozen" into an orthodox version. Likewise, differing versions or pieces of Christian and Muslim texts existed (and still exist) before they were "settled" into the canonical literature that became the Bible and the Qur'an respectively. Other variant versions or writings became unorthodox at best and schismatic or heretical at worst. Along with the settlement of an official doctrine based on an official written work, a "scripture," came a specialized class of individuals to study, represent, perform, and preserve those doctrines—that is, an *ecclesiastical institution* of priests and other officials. Religion thus became institutionalized and professionalized in unprecedented and fateful ways.

Christianity and Islam have been the most prolific of the translocal religions, carried along by missionary zeal, long-distance trade, and military force. The other religions generally regarded as world religions are Hinduism, Buddhism, and Judaism, although none of those three boast the levels of membership of Christianity and Islam. Further, many younger religions such as Sikhism, Baha'i, and Cao Dai have memberships in the millions and members spread around the globe.

Given the prominence of Christianity and Islam, which both were initially local religions, one of the livelier debates in anthropology was whether other local religions could and would have launched into translocal religions without contact with those two foreign traditions. That is, if the conditions described by Redfield and Gellner had obtained elsewhere, would they have spawned translocal religions from their own local predecessors? In 1972, Robin Horton was a champion of the notion that African local religions had the potential of going translocal on their own. His famous "thought experiment" imagined African societies undergoing their own "great transformation" without colonization or missionization, what he called "the modern situation, *minus* Islam and Christianity" (1972: 102). Would they independently breed a translocal/world religion? He answered yes, that African religions had the potential to develop into a world religion in their own right.

First, he believed, "faced with the interpretative challenge of social change, [a traditional religion's] adherents do not just abandon it in despair. Rather, they remold and develop it" (102). In particular, he identified what he regarded as a universalizing potential in African religions in the form of a two-tiered belief system, made up of lower and lesser spirits (who, he argued, represent the local or "microcosmic") and a higher or supreme being (who represents the global or "macrocosmic"). Over time, he expected that people would ignore the lower spirits and "develop a far more elaborate theory of the supreme being and his ways of working in the world, and a battery of new ritual techniques for approaching him and directing his influence." In addition, they would

> begin to evolve a moral code for the governance of this wider life. Since the supreme being is already defined as the arbiter of everything that transcends the boundaries of the microcosms, he is seen as underpinning this universalist moral code. From a position of moral neutrality, he moves to one of moral concern.

> (102)

Horton's conclusion was that religious change in Africa was inevitable; he reduced Islam and Christianity "to the role of catalysts—i.e., stimulators and accelerators of changes which were 'in the air' anyway" (104). This explains, he said, why Christianity and Islam had so little success in converting locals in the absence of wider social changes. Horton received passionate disagreement, though, from Humphrey Fisher, who in a pair of articles (1973; 1985) contested both Horton's notion of a distinct African cosmology and his assessment of the minor and recent role of Christianity and Islam in Africa. Fisher responded that Islam in particular was more than a catalyst for indigenous change but was a "juggernaut" with "its own momentum" in Africa (1985: 156), one that had been present for centuries. In other words, Islam was already an African religion by the time of Horton's thought experiment, and Islam in Africa had already wrought "a new cosmology" (166) on the continent, which he contended that Horton ignored or denied.

"Conversion" to Translocal Religions

Whether local religions have the potential to transcend their original social and spatial contexts, the truth is still that most societies have received an already existing translocal religion (and often more than one). Further, translocal religions tend to be accompanied by other social and cultural changes, part of a package that Horton called "the modern situation." Accordingly, new concepts, institutions, and relationships arrive and arise as a consequence of culture contact and culture change, and new individual attitudes and identities are proffered and accepted in what is conventionally recognized as "conversion."

The standard model of religious conversion is represented by A. D. Nock (1933), who distinguished between primitive or organic religion and prophetic or world religion. He called primitive/organic religion "the collective wisdom of the community": "Those who follow such a tradition have no reason to interest themselves in other traditions, and no impulse to commend their own tradition to others" (2). In other words, members of "traditional" religions do not convert to them or seek to convert others. Prophetic religions, as *new* religions, are different. They are not traditions but *movements*. Since they are new, they tend to stand out from, and sometimes actively oppose, the past and "tradition" (see the discussion of Pentecostalism below, pp. 194–7). And since they do not initially have a community, they must construct their own community by drawing individuals away from previous religions. From the individual's point of view, then, to participate in a new religion constitutes a *choice*, a decision to break from tradition and to try something else. To do so, it must operate on the individual at a psychological level, "to create in men the deeper needs which it claims to fulfill" (9). That is to say, "traditional" individuals would not be attracted to "new" religions; the person must be transformed before the religion can be transforming.

Most religions, Nock reckoned, have been more absorptive than substitutive: elements of foreign systems could be integrated into an existing religion without radically altering it, and (as in the case of ancient Roman religion) entire foreign cults could be added to existing religion to simply produce "more religion." In other words, there was a critical difference between the processes of "adhesion," or adding onto/absorbing into a religion, and "conversion," defined as

> the reorientation of the soul of an individual, his deliberate turning from indifference or from an earlier form of piety to another, a turning which implies a consciousness that a great change is involved, that the old was wrong and the new is right.

(7)

In short, conversion was seen as a complete replacement of religion—*sudden, total, exclusive* (that is, the individual can only affiliate with or "belong to" one religion), *irreversible, "doctrinal"* (that is, based on the acceptance of the "truth" of the new religion), and *personally profound.*

Despite the impact of Christianity and other expanding and missionizing religions, anthropology's interest in conversion is surprisingly recent, and anthropological research does not support the standard model as expressed by Nock. In a review article published in 2012, Frédéric Laugrand argued that a mere thirty years ago, "the conversion of natives and their views of Christianity did not yet comprise an area of study in anthropology" (2012: 15). Less than forty years ago, Raymond Firth judged that, apart from Robin Horton, "not many anthropologists (or missionaries) have written systematically about conversion as such" (1976: 4), so his comments were some of the earliest in the anthropological literature. Still referring to the people of Tikopia as "pagans," Firth described how missionaries from the Church of England made "almost no progress" on the island for sixty years, until one chief adopted Christianity largely for economic reasons including "special access to steel tools, calico and other goods made available through the Mission teachers" (5). The common folk under the chief's authority "converted" subsequently because "they were ordered to go to Church by the chief's eldest son" and "threatened with violence should they refuse" (5). Schooling provided by missionaries was another factor in "conversion," since "Christian affiliation offered the prime avenue of advancement" (5). Finally, Christian Tikopia pressured their families to join the religion. Naturally, in many cases "conversion was not 'complete' in the sense that intellectual conviction had been only partly modified" (5).

The discipline's interest in conversion was enhanced greatly by the 1993 volume *Conversion to Christianity: Historical and Anthropological Perspectives on a Great Transformation,* edited by Robert Hefner. In his often-quoted introduction to the anthology, Hefner stressed that the unique and powerful nature of translocal religions like Christianity or Islam is not simply doctrinal but "social-organizational" (1993: 19). In other words, while the "message" of such religions is novel, what is really effective about them is their capacity to *institutionalize,* to establish and maintain "institutions for the propagation and control of religious knowledge and identity over time and space" (19). But they must dominate more than *religious* knowledge, identity and institutions, which demands that they must establish—or at least establish interdependencies with—non-religious knowledge, identity, and institutions as well. This will implicate political, economic, educational, and many other domains of society. Failure to institutionalize in the non-religious realm can result in the failure of conversion.

Even before this publication, ethnographic studies suggested the need for a more careful analysis of "conversion." Marshall Murphree's (1969) research on the "conversion" of the Shona in southern Rhodesia made the point clearly. Not only did locals interpret and construct conversion idiosyncratically, but various Christian sects presented it differently. Methodist missionaries emphasized personal ecstatic experiences; for Catholic priests, on the other hand, "conversion involved not a subjective experience, but rather commitment to a given system of beliefs and practices, coupled with loyalty to the organization" (80). Since Methodism supposed a mature religious experience, adults were its focus, while Catholicism focused on children, who could be recruited and socialized into the religious institution.

As Catholic practices indicated, conversion did not always require prior training in or acceptance of Christian doctrine and probably seldom required or proved real understanding or orthodoxy of beliefs, let alone a personal transformation. Often, the ritual of baptism *was* conversion from the Catholic stance, so a person could be baptized first and educated later. Maia Green (2003) likewise noted that in the 1920s in southern Tanzania most of the baptisms were of infants, and as late as the 1950s the majority of "converts" were either children or the dying—or even the dead, who were past having any conversion experiences.

The inevitable result of these "conversion" practices was, to say the least, religious heterodoxy and sometimes a total lack of comprehension or serious concern for right doctrine. In Murphree's research, as elsewhere, pre-contact religious beliefs and practices survived and even provided the lens through which new religions were perceived. He explained that many Shona Christians continued to believe in traditional spirits, while some Shona non-Christians absorbed concepts such as heaven. Other people, like a sub-chief he interviewed, explicitly claimed to practice tradition along with Christianity: "'It is best,' he says, 'to believe it all'" (132)—a thoroughly unorthodox, if not heretical, position according to Christianity.

Not only was conversion less than complete among the Shona, but it was also often not irreversible. Murphree found that many people converted more than once and in multiple directions—from traditional to Christian, or from Christian to traditional, or from one Christian sect to another or to some other religious movement. In fact, he rejected the concept of conversion altogether in this case, preferring to discuss "religious mobility" (137). Worse, individuals regularly did not comprehend or share the notion of an exclusive "religious affiliation" or "religious identity" at all. Rather, "a person, *at certain times and in given circumstances,* moves out of the pattern of beliefs and practices standard for his religious group, and temporarily and for specific purposes aligns himself with that of another" (140), for instance on occasions when a Christian had to partake in a traditional ceremony or vice versa.

Finally, as in Firth's case, "conversion" or religious mobility was not always about "believing" the new religion. Maia Green stressed that conversion or at least affiliation to Christianity sometimes had less to do with truth of foreign doctrines than with the perceived power of the foreign specialists. The Tanzanians in her research thought that the Christian priests controlled energies, literally substances or "medicines," which were supernaturally present in waters and oils employed by priests. Accordingly, they sought out baptism or other sacraments not for their Christian spiritual meaning but for their (traditional) practical effects, "to incorporate Christian substances and objects into themselves" to promote growth, wealth, success, etc. (2003: 67). In still other situations, foreign religious authorities held literal control of resources like food and money, as well as of institutions like marriage, employment, education, and even government; in Tanzania, the church interjected itself into marriage arrangements and bridewealth payments in order to influence who married who and how (specifically, to guarantee that Christians married Christians within the church).

These and many other anthropological studies show that the standard Judeo-Christian model of conversion does not apply in all circumstances. As Diane Austin-Broos concluded in a more recent volume, *The Anthropology of Religious Conversion*, conversion is not a "singular experience, paranormal or otherwise, or an absolute breach with a former life. ... [Rather] conversion is a passage: constituted and reconstituted through social practice and the articulation of new forms of relatedness" (2003: 9). In fact, cases like the Pentecostal church in Kyrgyzstan described by Mathijs Pelkmans (2009) illustrate that "conversion" is often temporary; therefore, anthropologists should not consider conversion "complete" when individuals join a church, as they may later leave. In other instances, for example with Islam, "conversion" might not be the operative concept at all (see p. 185 below).

Finally, ambitious translocal religions may encounter passive indifference or active resistance. Aram Yengoyan (1993) insisted that the moods and motivations of Christianity were simply too foreign for Australian Aboriginals. He discovered that between the 1960s and 1980s only eight or ten real conversions were made among the Pitjantjatjara; most people found Christianity "incomprehensible," although many others hung around the church because they enjoyed the singing. He suggested that Christian concepts like salvation, damnation, and sin had no resonance for the locals; that the notion of a "single omnipotent force" with no "physical referent" (248) made no sense to them; and that their lack of "individualism" made religious "choice" unappealing. For these cultural and religious reasons, "it is apparent that the Pitjantjatjara and other desert-dwelling Aboriginal societies simply do not convert to Christianity" (244).

Charles Keyes (1993a) argued that Thais were resistant to Christianity for very different reasons. In this case, Christian missionaries failed to compete successfully with another world religion—namely, Buddhism—for converts among the traditional villagers. Keyes proposed that the reasons are two. First, unlike Christianity, "conversion to Buddhism does not require that people radically reject their previous beliefs" (268); resident and visiting monks emphasized that local spirits were not false but were subject to Buddhist concepts like *karma* too. Once villagers had had their traditional beliefs subsumed by Buddhism, Christian missionaries were unable to persuade them that Christianity "offers greater insight into ultimate Truth than does Buddhism" (277). Second, the local political and economic institutions were sufficiently strong and independent to prevent Christian penetration and domination; with no way to control and exploit resources and opportunities—and no way to "institutionalize"—Christianity had no way to gain a foothold in the villages.

The Anthropology of Islam

In the early twenty-first century, there is a greater need than ever to understand Islam, in all its diversity and in all its global locations, not simply the Middle East. Indeed, not all Muslims live in the Middle East (the largest population of Muslims inhabits Indonesia), and not all inhabitants of the Middle East are Muslims. There are Muslims in Europe and the United States; more than 1.3 million Muslims reside in the USA, approximately two-thirds of whom are immigrants and one-third American converts, including many African American Muslims. Most Westerners are at least familiar with the main division in Islam, between Sunnis and Shi'ites, but too many know little else and actually suffer from stereotypes and what has been called "Islamophobia" or fear and loathing of Muslims.

Orientalism and the Anthropological Study of Islam

Anthropologists, along with other scholars, have a long history of descriptions of Islamic societies. As early as 1926 Edward Westermarck published *Ritual and Belief in Morocco*, and more than two decades later E. E. Evans-Pritchard released his *The Sanusi of Cyrenaica* (1949). However, in retrospect anthropology's record with Islam has been subjected to some intense criticisms. One criticism is that anthropologists tended to focus on "nomads or pastoralists" (McLoughlin 2007: 280), perpetuating a set of dichotomies between rural and urban Islam and between "'folk'/'popular'/'local' forms of Islam and 'high'/'reform-minded'/

'book-centred'/'doctrinal' Islam" (Marsden and Retsikas 2012: 5). Ironically related to this first critique is the assumption that Islam is a monolithic whole, that there is "a single object called 'Islam'" and that "we can find that object directly in scripture" (Bowen 2012: 2). This scriptural or textual obsession in analyses of Islam tends to make the religion seem particularly static and particularly totalistic: Ernest Gellner's *Muslim Society* called Islam "the blueprint of a social order" the rules of which "exist, eternal, divinely ordained, and independent of the will of men" (1981: 1). Thus Islam has been characterized as uniquely immune to, even hostile to, modernization, democracy, human rights, and secularization. All in all, Islam is chronically portrayed as radically other, as different from the West (which, by the way, is never referred to as "Christian society") in every significant way. In a very influential book, Edward Said proposed the term "orientalism" for this tendency of Western society and scholarship to construct and use Islam and Muslims as the total opposite and other.

In a pithy summary of the subject, Samuli Schielke concluded that "there is too much Islam in the anthropology of Islam" and not enough anthropology, that is, not enough awareness of society, culture, politics, and "the existential and pragmatic sensibilities of living a life in a complex and often troubling world" (2010:1). Clifford Geertz was one of the first to try to contextualize the cultures of Islam, explicitly comparing the religion in two widely separated contexts, Morocco and Indonesia. He firmly reminded us that a translocal religion like Islam,

> even when it is fed from a common source, is as much a particularizing force as a generalizing one, and indeed whatever universality a given religious tradition manages to attain arises from its ability to engage a widening set of individual, even idiosyncratic, conceptions of life and yet somehow sustain and elaborate them all.
>
> (1968: 14)

What emerged was two local Islams, a distinctly Moroccan Islam and a distinctly Indonesian Islam, each consonant with its local culture, politics, and history. In Morocco, the basic style of life—and therefore of religion—was "strenuous, fluid, violent, visionary, devout, unsentimental, and above all, self-assertive" (8). "Activism, fervor, impetuosity, nerve, toughness, moralism, populism, and an almost obsessive self-assertion" being cultural norms (54), it is no surprise that "holy-man" piety evolved to match strong-man politics. The central figure was the saint or religious leader (*marabout*) who possessed blessing or divine favor (*baraka*). Followers organized into brotherhoods (*awiya*) around such leaders, and dead saints (*siyyid*) and their tombs were religious foci. The basic Indonesian style of life was "remarkably malleable, tentative, syncretistic, and most significantly of all, multivoiced" (12), leading to norms of "inwardness, imperturbability, patience, poise, sensibility, aestheticism, elitism, and an almost obsessive self-effacement" (54). Indonesian Islam did not seek purity of religion or a single dominant figure; instead it produced "a proliferation of abstractions so generalized, symbols so allusive, and doctrines so programmatic that they can be made to fit any form of experience at all" (17).

In the light of Geertz's work, Abdul Hamid el-Zein in 1977 initiated "a search for an anthropology of Islam," accusing all sides of approaching Islam "as an isolable and bounded domain of meaningful phenomena inherently distinct from other cultural forms such as social relations or economic systems and from other religions" (1977: 241). Ultimately he concluded that there was no such thing as "Islam," at best rather a congeries of local "islams." Talal Asad responded in 1986 with "The Idea of an Anthropology of Islam," accepting the heterogeneity of Islam but offering the productive suggestion that these diverse local forms share a *discursive tradition*, defined as

> discourses that seek to instruct practitioners regarding the correct form and purpose of a given practice that, precisely because it is established, has a history. These discourses relate conceptually to a *past* (when the practice was instituted, and from which the knowledge of its point and proper performance has been transmitted) and a *future* (how the point of that practice can best be secured in the short or long term, or why it should be modified or abandoned), through a *present* (how it is linked to other practices, institutions, and social conditions). An Islamic discursive tradition is simply a tradition of Muslim discourse that addresses itself to conception of the Islamic past and future, with reference to a particular Islamic practice in the present.
>
> (2009: 20)

Michael Gilsenan made a contribution to healing this rift between tradition and the present, and between religion and the wider society, in his *Recognizing Islam*. In that book, he explored Islam in a number of different settings, from the Middle East to North Africa and Pakistan, surveying both history and contemporary society. Intentionally "dissolving" the essentialist and orientalist approach to Islam, he asked "what the term *Islam* comes to mean in quite different economic, political, and social structures and relations," investigating such diverse issues as "the furnishing of the *salon* of the Lebanese bourgeoisie; sexuality, honor, and violation linked to God's grace; the street plan of modern Cairo; tribal markets; family feuds; genealogies" (1982: 19), as well as of course Islamic authorities and young modern Muslims.

"Conversion" to Islam

Most of the attention to conversion has been focused on Christianity; however, as the fastest-growing religion in the world, conversion to Islam is an equally important issue. Yet, as many observers and members have noted, including Anna Mansson McGinty in her study of Western female converts, "There is no word in Arabic for 'conversion,' rather there is the idea of 'becoming a Muslim'" (2006: 18). This specifically Muslim notion of conversion—or what might better be called *reversion*—is based on the notion that "all human beings are born as Muslims, and that they hopefully will find their way and revert to the only faith" (18). Thus, while Islam does have a concept of *da'wa* or "inviting," sometimes understood as proselytizing, it is sufficiently different from the Christian notion to suggest some new ways to think about affiliating with a translocal religion.

Like other translocal religions, Islam was spread by migration, trade, and conquest. By the time that European colonialists landed in places like Africa and Southeast Asia, it had become an "indigenous" religion for many societies, yet anthropologists tended to perceive it as a foreign imposition. S. F. Nadel echoed this view in his classic study of religion among the Nupe of Africa. Nadel persisted in considering Islam "an intrusion" upon the "indigenous religion," although he admitted that what he observed was not Islam replacing tradition or functioning parallel to tradition; rather "Nupe Islam" was not even "so-and-so much Nupe religion plus so-and-so much Islam but a fundamentally novel phenomenon, unprecedented, integrated, self-contained" (1954: 256). Islam had originated from above, brought with the conquering Fulani in the late eighteenth century. "Islam thus added to the unification of the conquest-state, extending the area of a common culture over a population otherwise unified only by political means" (233). Nupe joined Islam for various reasons, including exemption from slavery and closer client ties with the Muslim nobility. However, at the same time the Nupe assimilated Islam to their own culture. They accommodated the mosque to local design (an open area under a shady tree), applied obligatory prayers to traditional concerns, identified their local god Soko with Allah, and picked and chose among orthodox Islamic festivals. Nupe Muslim "scholars" (*mallam*) often held and taught "a medley of incongruous" knowledge about the religion, and average members thought that Muhammad was the first human being (247). In Nadel's time, finally, young people were converting to Islam "not for any particular benefits they were expecting of Islam" but out of personal, practical, and political considerations: their conversion "meant abandoning religious practices which, more or less openly, stood for the status quo, for parental authority and an outmoded family structure" (251).

Although people have been joining Islam for centuries, Anne Sofie Roald asserts that scholars have been examining Muslim conversion only since the 1980s and that the academic habit was "to view Muslims' conversion experiences as following the pattern of conversion to Christianity" (2012: 348). This habit included, unfortunately, only following individuals until the moment of their conversion, that is, concentrating on the events or stages *before* conversion. Roald takes the novel approach of following individuals *after* conversion, to study the process as it evolves in the life of the convert. She suggests four post-conversion stages, beginning with "zealotry," the extreme enthusiasm characteristic of the new member, which is like "falling in love" (349). Like many romances, excitement gives way to "disappointment," a brief stage in which converts become bored or disillusioned with their new religion and, interestingly, critical of "born-Muslims" whose behavior does not seem to live up to Islamic ideals. If converts survive this stage (and not all do), the third phase is "acceptance," an appreciation of the limitations of human beings and a return to the reality of their own selves, with a commitment to be the best Muslims they can realistically be. Finally, while in the first three stages there is a tendency to perceive "Islam as a way of life" (356), in the fourth stage of "secularization" Islam becomes more personal and private, with a greater awareness of "the possibility of understanding the sacred texts in various ways" and therefore "of being a Muslim without necessarily having to accept every detail in the Qur'an" (357).

Islam has begun to win converts in areas that were only recently converted to Christianity, and this second conversion often accompanies cogent criticisms of Christianity. One case is the Solomon Islands, where 98 percent of inhabitants identify as Christians (McDougall 2009). However, one attraction of Islam is the perception that Christianity has caused a social and moral decline in society, especially in regard to gender and sexuality: missionaries "destroyed male cults and lifted social and spatial restrictions on women" (481), undermining tradition and male authority. Further, many locals view Christianity as hypocritical, divisive (with too many competing sects and denominations), and racist; others disagree with doctrines like the trinity, preferring the simple monotheism of Islam. But McDougall writes that while early Muslim converts found Islam's monotheism, unity, and racial inclusiveness appealing, later converts "seem preoccupied by the problem of sin" (486). Many, she writes, "are deeply disappointed by Christianity" (486) and, fascinatingly, not only understand Islam as morally superior to Christianity but also as more convergent with traditional, pre-Christian culture and values. Some Muslim converts from Christianity think that Islam is more similar to their old religion in its moral and gender regulations; others go so far as to insist that "Islam is in fact their own lost ancestral religion" (487), that is, that they really are *reverting*, not converting.

Box 8.1 Islam in Aboriginal Australia

Long before Europeans stepped ashore on Australia, Makassan fishermen from predominantly Muslim parts of Southeast Asia were visiting the northern edge of the continent; later, Western colonialism brought a contingent of Afghani camel-drivers into the central desert. This means that Australian Aboriginal societies have been in contact with Islam as long as or longer than with Christianity. These mostly male Muslims interacted with the native peoples more than their white counterparts and more often married Aboriginal women. Not surprisingly, there have been Muslim Aboriginal individuals and families for decades, maybe centuries, observing Muslim customs, absorbing Muslim values, and adopting Muslim words, like the term *walitha 'walitha*, which allegedly derives from "Allah." Peta Stephenson, in a long-overdue study of Aboriginal Islam, describes much of this conversion as "kinversion" because it is funneled through marriage and family connections. Remarkably, like the Solomon Islanders just mentioned, many Aboriginals see Islam as similar to, if not actually, their traditional religions; simultaneously, they share with the Solomon Islanders and other missionized peoples a condemnation of "the devaluation of their cultural and religious heritage through the processes of missionization and Christianization" (2010: 183). Lately, Aboriginals (especially men) have been attracted to the apparently racially tolerant message of Islam, which has become a factor in the emerging Aboriginal identity movement. Anthony Mundine, an Aboriginal boxer and convert/revert to Islam, became a model for Aboriginal men who "emphasized the universality of Islam 'as opposed to nationalist or racialist doctrines'" (251) (see Figure 8.1). Another inspirational figure has been Malcolm X, an American leader of the Nation of Islam, and many Aboriginal men, like black men in the United States, have discovered Islam while imprisoned.

Figure 8.1 Boxer Anthony Mundine holding a book about Malcolm X and Islam. Courtesy of Wade Laube/Sydney Morning Herald/Fairfax Syndication

Islam in Majority Non-Muslim Societies

Islam is not and never has been restricted to the Middle East or "Islamic" societies. Islam was carried rapidly after its formation to North Africa, Central Asia and India, Southeast Asia, and Europe. Spain was controlled by Muslims (known as Moors) for almost a millennium, and Islam traveled to the Americas with African slaves and later African, Middle Eastern, and Asian immigrants. As just mentioned, Islam has won converts/reverts among African Americans (for example, the Nation of Islam) but also among white Americans and Europeans. Anna Mansson McGinty's study of female converts/reverts finds them in both the United States and Sweden.

Islam in societies where the majority is non-Muslim presents a fascinating subject for anthropology, as well as a vexing problem for the majority populations and governments, not to mention for Muslim minorities. Translocal religions that claim universal truth and seek new members almost inevitably find themselves suspicious of and competitive with each other; even if universal claims are not in competition, religious and social differences can cause tensions. Add the hostility toward Islam as an alleged agent of terrorism, and inter-religious relations can be understandably difficult. In the United Kingdom, the English Defence League (www.englishdefenceleague.org) was formed to resist "Muslim extremists" and the threat of "Islamization" of British society. Some Americans have also expressed dismay at the prospect of Islamization in the form of sharia courts, mosques, Islamic centers, and practices like the veil, honor killing, and female genital mutilation. McDougall reports that the small Muslim minority in the Solomon Islands (around 1 percent of the population)

> is seen as a threat by church leaders and Christian politicians. ... Solomon Islands Muslims are called "terrorists" when they wear their distinctive white robes and caps. Some Solomon Islander Christian leaders worry, moreover, that Islam threatens the national unity that results from a shared Christian faith and may undermine postconflict reconciliation work that is being carried out in Christian idioms.
>
> (2009: 483)

In nearby Papua New Guinea, some Christian organizations have literally demanded a ban on Islam in the form of a constitutional amendment "curtailing freedom of religion" (Flower 2012: 205).

Tensions between Muslims and non-Muslims have exploded into real political and physical action, not the least of which was the partition of colonial India into two states, Hindu-majority India and Muslim-majority Pakistan, as well as their ongoing rivalry. Irfan Ahmad (2009) chronicles the Jamaat-e-Islami (Party of Islam) from its founding to its contemporary transformation. Organized by Syed Abul Ala Maududi in 1941 with the goal of an Islamic state out of colonial India, the party originally practiced a "political Islam," mixing religion with twentieth-century state politics. Another innovation was a school, the Darsgah-e-Jamaat-e-Islami (Jamaate-e-Islami School), which began as a separatist and factional institution but gradually joined the mainstream, changing its name to something less political, opening its curriculum, altering its internal culture, and most dramatically affiliating with the previously hated government education system. In Ahmad's estimation, the party itself moved from rejecting secular democracy to accepting and participating in it, even establishing a Forum for Democracy and Communal Amity. Meanwhile, inside India as elsewhere, Muslims have sometimes been the victims of violence: for instance, the Babri Mosque was destroyed by Hindus in 1992 and reclaimed as the site of the temple to Ram Llala. Such violence has radicalized Muslims in some places, but it has encouraged others to strive for peace, often in the name of Islam. Raphael Susewind (2013) has identified four kinds of Muslims working for peace in India, including not only the "secular technocrats" but additionally the "doubting professionals" who appreciate the ambiguity of Islam, the "emancipating women" whose personal journey through Islam leads them to assist and liberate other women, and the "faith-based actors" who take religion and scripture as the source of their peacemaking activities.

Muslims in non-Muslim majority societies also face the problem of how to relate to the wider society and how to practice Islam when dominant laws and institutions are not Islamic. Such Muslims face dilemmas such as whether they should vote, whether they should attend the local schools, whether they should take out a bank loan, and generally how far they should integrate into the dominant society. At the same time, host states adopt varying policies toward their Muslim minorities. Ahmet Yükleyen (2012) considers Turkish Muslims in two European states—Germany and the Netherlands—and finds a range of attitudes and institutional forms, including:

1 Diyanet—an "official" form of Islam, controlled from Turkey by the Diyanet Isleri Baskanligi (Directorate of Religious Affairs);
2 Milli Gorus—a "political" form of Islam, seeking to promote the recognition of Islam in Europe;
3 Süleymanli—a "mystical" form of Islam, which focuses on learning the Qur'an and performing rituals;
4 Gülen Community—a "civil" form of Islam with schools located around the world;
5 Kaplan Community—a "revolutionary" form of Islam, which is currently banned for its insistence on the merger of religion and state.

Box 8.2 Being Muslim in France

Can Muslims also be good French citizens? Can Islam itself be French, so long as France is not Islamic? Being Muslim in France is especially challenging, given the country's official secularism (known as *laïcité*; see Chapter 11). Thus Muslims living in France must answer the question, "what forms of Islamic ideas and institutions enable those Muslims wishing to practice their religion to do so fully and freely in France?" (Bowen 2010: 5). As anthropologists would predict, multiple answers have arisen, shaped by "the active role played by the state and by certain municipalities in seeking to organize religious life for Muslims" (32) and "to build and control a French Islam" (27). Two obvious sites for constructing a French Islam are mosques and schools, which themselves have offered an array of solutions and services for Muslims, from "cathedral mosques" (see Figure 8.2) to small neighborhood institutions that provide lessons, lectures, and public forums. The attitudes of Muslims toward Islam vary too, from Islam as "a set of absolute rules" that are as binding in France as anywhere, to Islam as "one among several legal traditions," to Islam as "a set of principles based on Scripture" that can be interpreted in the local French context (63). Then there are the everyday pragmatic questions that a Muslim in a non-Muslim society confronts. For instance, can a Muslim use the French banking system, operating as it does on the forbidden principles of *riba'* or interest/usury? There are also matters of family law, such as marriage and divorce, not to mention the issue of diet and religiously permitted (*halal*) foods. The ultimate question is "whether there should be distinctive Islamic norms for France (and by extension for

Figure 8.2 The Grande Mosquée de Paris. Courtesy of Shutterstock

Europe)" or whether Islam is a single universal way that applies in all countries (136). Muslims and their non-Islamic neighbors will be dealing with these alternatives for years to come.

Finally, not all of the news is bad. In many locations, Muslims and non-Muslims not only coexist but share sacred space. One example is Macedonia, which has layers of Christian and Muslim history. Sveti Bogoroditsa Prechista is an Orthodox Christian monastery in Macedonia, visited not only by Christians but also Muslims, since the shrine is celebrated for its healing powers; Glenn Bowman explains that the imam of the nearby mosque specifically sends Muslims there if they are afflicted by "Christian demons" that "can be driven out only by beneficent Christian powers" (2010: 206). Bowman also observes that, while Muslims interact with the same spaces and icons as Christians, they interact with them differently: Muslims do not kiss the images or cross themselves, and they utter Muslim prayers while Christians offer Christian ones. Even so, although they understand that the spiritual forces in the monastery are Christian, they also say that it "is a healing place that is known to work" (208), whatever the petitioner's religion.

The Anthropology of Christianity

"Perhaps surprisingly, Christianity was the last major area of religious activity to be explored in ethnographic writing," marveled Fenella Cannell in 2006 (8). In fact, three years earlier Joel Robbins declared that he did not think that an anthropology of Christianity was yet "a going concern" (2003b: 191). He actually cited "the success of the anthropology of Islam" as proof "that it is possible to construct a viable comparative enterprise around the study of a world religion" (192).

Despite the fact, as examples throughout this book have illustrated, that anthropologists have described Christianity in many societies around the world for many years, Cannell felt that "Christianity is still an occluded object," even a repressed one. She and other anthropologists have pondered a number of reasons for the delayed development of an anthropology of Christianity. One reason, opines Chris Hann in an opinion shared by many, is that Christianity has tended to seem inauthentic to anthropologists, like "an alien intrusion that undermines a local cosmology" (2007: 384). That is, because anthropologists have specialized in societies where Christianity was not indigenous but was introduced (and quite recently), Christianity has been viewed as obscuring the "traditional culture" that we have hoped to discover. Two factors have changed this position, though. First, anthropologists have turned their attention to areas like Europe, where Christianity has been present for centuries (e.g. Jeremy Boissevain's 1965 *Saints and Fireworks: Religion and Politics in Rural Malta* or Charles Stewart's 1991 *Demons and the Devil: Moral Imagination in Modern Greek Culture*). Second, as Webb Keane wrote in his important study *Christian Moderns*, "Christianity has become 'our' religion for a large part of the non-Western world and is not seen as foreign" (2007: 45). In other words, Christianity has *become* an indigenous religion, just as it *became* indigenous to Europe after being introduced from elsewhere.

But Cannell, Robbins, and others point to greater problems. Cannell claims that anthropologists (like other scholars) have tended to exaggerate the "ascetic" and other-worldly quality of Christianity, neglecting the lived experiences of Christians and the links between the religion and the wider society and culture. Or perhaps Christianity's "meanings are 'obvious' because they are part of the culture from which anthropologists themselves are largely drawn" (2005: 340). But Joel Robbins suggests a deeper obstacle, latent in the culture of anthropology itself: Christianity emphasizes the radical, even total, break with the past that we noted above in the discussion of conversion—what Robbins calls "discontinuity thinking"—whereas anthropology is characterized by "continuity thinking," "the kind of thinking that sees change as slow and conservative" (2007: 16). If he is correct, anthropology and Christianity are foreign cultures to each other.

Christianity, Colonialism, and Modernization

As previously stated, anthropologists and other scholars of non-Western Christianity have frequently if not adamantly emphasized that the religion arrived in many locations as part of the colonial experience, both of which were part of the grander project of modernization. For colonizers from Europe, Christianity was seen and offered as *the* modern religion and as key to having a modern society and to being a modern individual in that society. In his aptly named *Christian Moderns*, Webb Keane relates the proselytization of Dutch Calvinism in Southeast Asia to "colonialism and its postcolonial wake," which speaks to "the idea of becoming modern, with all the promises, threats, and paradoxes this involves" (2007: 38).

Accordingly, the spread of Christianity cannot help but be connected to more all-encompassing processes of culture change (which is why, many argue, anthropologists eschewed the study of the religion). Michael Gilsenan (1982) was one of the first to emphasize the role of non-religious, even ordinary and mundane, practices in the perpetuation or change of religion; he saw religion as not only dependent upon everyday forms and practices—down to furniture, ways of sitting, modes of dress, and such—but as even secondary to them. So when foreign and novel models of these cultural practices burst onto the scene, religion could not help but be affected. Sometimes, of course, agents of change more or less intentionally manipulated these non-religious factors for religious ends.

John and Jean Comaroff have paid special attention to these processes. Colonialism, wherever and whenever conducted, involved changes to and domination of the political and economic aspects of subject societies, together with religion and other cultural habits like dress, speech, marriage, gender roles, and so on. All of these forms and practices, and not merely religious doctrines and rituals, carried messages about what is true, good, important, and possible. In fact, as anthropologists have increasingly realized, much of cultural and even religious "knowledge" is not explicit and formal but implicit and informal, embedded in the big and little things we do all day everyday—what Jean Comaroff called "the signs and structures of everyday life" (1985: 80). Therefore, the missionization process was designed to effect a change in these signs and structures, a "revolution in habits," "a quest to refurnish the mundane: to focus human endeavor on the humble scapes of the everyday, of the 'here-and-now' in which the narrative of Protestant redemption took on its contemporary form" (Comaroff and Comaroff 1991: 9). They have also labeled this struggle as "an epic of the ordinary" and "the everyday as epiphany":

> [I]t was precisely by means of the residual, naturalized quality of habit that power takes up residence in culture, insinuating itself, apparently without agency, in the texture of a life-world. This, we believe, is why recasting mundane, routine practices has been so vital to all manner of social reformers, colonial missionaries among them.
>
> (31)

They examined in great detail a number of cultural realms in which European/Christian habits of mind and body took residence. An important one was economics, specifically farming techniques. Missionaries offered a model for "civilized cultivation" in the form of the "mission garden"; a major aspect of this new model was a reversal of traditional gender roles, in which women had done the bulk of horticultural work. The plow became a potent symbol of Western-style farming; fences introduced conceptions of "enclosure" and property; and inequality of output, related to intensity of labor, generated Western-style differences in wealth and status as their reward. But economic change went beyond horticulture to new institutions like markets and money. Modern labor and cash were part of a new "moral economy," stigmatizing idleness and "primitive production" and promoting "the kind of upright industry and lifestyle that would dissolve [tradition's] dirt" (189).

Yet more mundane areas like clothing and household practices were valued for their civilizing and Christianizing effects. Clothes not only meant covering heathen nakedness but teaching locals the proper wear and care of these articles; native clothing, it seemed to colonists, was dirty, too "natural," and lacking the necessary markers of social—especially gender—distinctions. For this purpose, old used clothes were shipped from England to clothe, and thereby transform, the pagan body, teaching them shame and pride at the same time. And as already suggested, proper (that is, Western/Christian) gender behavior was essential: women needed to be covered modestly and reassigned to the home. Home became a "domestic" sphere, which became woman's sphere, where she would literally sit, sew, and serve. But the traditional native house would not do; the house and the community had to be transformed from what the Europeans perceived as "a wild array of small, featureless huts scattered across the countryside" (282). Missionary houses and buildings again acted as the model: with right angles, specialized spaces (e.g. a room for eating, a room for sleeping, etc.), doors and locks for privacy, and modern furniture, the mission structures "became a diorama" for how people should live (292). The collection of residences that became the "town" differentiated public from private spaces, all set in a universe of square blocks and broad streets. In these and many ways, the foreigners were doing much more than bringing a new religion; they were "teaching [them] to build a world" (296), one in which civilization itself was expressed "in squares and straight lines" (127).

Despite all of these energetic efforts, Western Christians could not guarantee the acceptance of the religion nor its specific local formations. In a classic analysis, Michael Taussig found that rural folks in Colombia, introduced to the modern concept of money as interest-bearing capital, were baptizing their money by intercepting baptisms intended for children and redirecting that spiritual force to their cash. The baptized bill even received the Christian name "that the baptismal ritual was meant to bestow on the child" (1977: 137), which allegedly made the money lively and potent (with what damage to the child we cannot know).

Elsewhere people have reinterpreted, invented, or resisted Christianity. Donald Pollock researched early Catholic activities in Brazil, where Tupi and Guarani peoples were contacted by Jesuits in 1549. Jesuit missionaries were not the first Europeans met by the natives, so in this case the priests were welcomed by the locals, "who sought refuge from brutal Portuguese and Spanish soldiers and merchants" (1993: 167) (see Figure 8.3). As a consequence, "Indians were happy to perform meaningless rituals in return for protection from the colonists, gifts from the missionaries, and the supernatural benefits of the

Figure 8.3 An indigenous slave of the Tupinamba tribe is baptized by a Jesuit priest near Bahia in 1550 (engraving, Spanish School, nineteenth century). Courtesy of the Bridgeman Art Library/Getty Images

powerful European shamans" (167). Much more recently, the Siriono accepted Protestantism for similar reasons—not out of commitment to Christian doctrines or love of Christian missionaries, but "as a means of strengthening social and cultural boundaries between themselves and non-Indians" (173). Conversely, the Kraho of central Brazil firmly resisted Protestantism for its hostility to traditional religious and cultural practices but accepted a few elements of Catholicism, such as baptism and "ritual sponsorship" (the "godparent" relation), which resembled their own practices (174).

In the case of the Uiaku, a Papuan community, Anglican contact beginning in 1891 resulted in a segregated system and the "continuing coexistence of two social environments, the mission station and the village" (Barker 1993: 199). The missionaries typically sought to incorporate the people into the religious and colonial project of the West, through education and schools, employment, and political authority. Despite these more or less successful efforts, the physical fact that the mission was located outside the village meant that village life could persist along more indigenous lines. The outcome was a dual cultural and religious universe, in which locals inhabited a tradition-oriented village but "also grew up attending school and church and modeled their roles (if not always their moral attitudes) on the teachers and on their ideas of Europeans" (209). Only a few actually converted or had "more than the vaguest notion of church doctrine; most villagers are firmly convinced of the reality of local bush spirits and sorcerers; and individuals frequently disregard church strictures on marriage and divorce" (209). When they did think about Christianity, they inevitably thought about it through traditional lenses. For instance, Christian spiritual beliefs did not displace local ones; traditional village beliefs became the "microcosm," which people could know and experience directly; while Christian beliefs represented a "macrocosm," which was revealed by missionaries. The entire relationship between villagers and missionaries was understood through traditional social concepts like the *kawo/sabu* relation, in which *kawo* or higher-ranking groups had rights but also obligations to look after *sabu* or lower-ranking groups, who owed their superiors respect but could expect care in exchange. So the locals exchanged church attendance, labor, and support in the form of food and money for the rituals, baptisms, and knowledge that the church provided (212).

One of the most noteworthy and enduring ways in which Christianity interjected a vision of modernity was in its impact on other religions. Presented as the epitome of modern religion, authorities of other religions often sought to modernize and reform their religions, especially in the image of Protestant Christianity, emphasizing monotheism, scripture, individual piety over purportedly "empty" ritual, and of course "belief." In places like colonial Ceylon (present-day Sri Lanka), Buddhist intellectuals perfected their debating skills with Christians, in the process reforming their Buddhism to meet Christianity. Anthropologists like Talal Asad (1993) have gone so far as to contend that the very concept of "religion" is a Western/Christian distinction—which was adopted by many non-Western/non-Christian cultures.

Pentecostalism

One of the most startling developments in the realm of global Christianity has been the rise of Pentecostal churches, especially in societies and countries where Catholicism formerly held a virtual monopoly. Pentecostalism sheds some interesting light on the questions of modernity and tradition, of the local and the global, and of class and gender. Yet Robert Hefner, in a new collection of essays, reveals that a program to study Pentecostal Christianity in 1985 was met "with a mixture of skepticism and bewilderment" because, once again, "most anthropologists found global Christianity inauthentic and uninteresting" (2013a: vii). However, he notes that anthropologists began to change their attitude within a decade.

Pentecostalism is not a sect or a religion so much as a style of Christianity, stressing the "gifts of grace" (sometimes also referred to as "charisma") and the presence of the "Holy Spirit" in such forms as speaking in tongues, prophecy, faith-healing, and exorcism of evil spirits. As an organized movement, it is usually associated with the Azusa Street Revival in Los Angeles, California in the early years of the twentieth century. According to Hefner, it quickly became an international missionary movement, with churches in Chile, China, England, India, and Norway by 1907, in Brazil by 1908, in Russia by 1911, and in Mexico by 1914 (2013b: 3). However, he also indicates that there is not one but many sources of Pentecostalism (there were even signs of such a revival movement in India in 1860) and ultimately not "one but many Pentecostalisms" (2).

David Martin was one of the first and remains one of the leading scholars on global Pentecostalism, focusing on Latin America, where Catholicism was the earliest and has long been the dominant and most fully institutionalized variety of Christianity. However, he found an "explosion of Protestantism" in Latin America in the 1980s, documented in his 1990 book *Tongues of Fire*. This Protestantism was mostly a "religion of the poor" in societies where the Catholic Church was often closely linked to political and economic elites and largely a force of social conservatism. (Within the Catholic Church, "liberation theology" fought for social justice and the rights of the poor but was substantially opposed by the church hierarchy, which tended to associate it with communism.)

As what Martin recently described as religion "preached in homely language with homely examples by homely people to homely people" (2013: 38), Pentecostalism in particular at first blush appears to contradict the view of Protestantism presented in Max Weber's classic *The Protestant Ethic and the Spirit of Capitalism*, where Protestantism supposedly followed and led the emerging middle class of early modern Europe. Yet Martin and others see Pentecostalism as a decidedly modern and modernizing phenomenon, one that has the potential to lift the poor to the middle class while it morphs itself into a religiosity for the middle class.

Two significant characteristics of Pentecostalism are its organizational structure and its gender dimensions. First, as a product of "deregulated religious markets" (Martin 2013: 42) in a brand of Christianity (Protestantism) that is already essentially decentralized, Pentecostalism frequently takes the shape of small independent "local house groups and store-front churches" run by "religious entrepreneurs" (43). Anyone seized by the Holy Spirit can start a Pentecostal congregation. Second, although the leadership of Pentecostal churches is almost invariably male, and Pentecostalism promotes a distinctively conservative attitude toward gender roles, women comprise the majority of members, up to 75 percent. Whether in China (Cao 2013), India (Shah and Shah 2013), Africa, or Latin America, women seem to flock to Pentecostalism, where they are widely believed to have greater spiritual gifts than men and where they can benefit in numerous ways from participation in such churches.

Box 8.3 Women and Pentecostalism in Bolivia

The realities of the lives of poor women in Bolivia did not conform to the model of Pentecostal womanhood: instead of being enclosed in the home, they, like most lower-class women, were obliged "to spend a considerable amount of time working away from their homes and families" (Gill 1990: 709). Yet the Iglesia Pentecostal

Unida (United Pentecostal Church) appealed to and served them in a number of ways, as a means to establish new supportive bonds between women and to form "new relationships between men and women" (709). It is important to note that most of the female members were first- and second-generation Aymara migrants to the city of La Paz; as such, they were typically less well educated than urbanites or male migrants, earning lower wages in a more restricted set of jobs. Also like poor women globally, they generally could not "count on men—fathers, husbands, lovers—to provide income to the domestic unit" (710); indeed, most of the women in the church were unmarried or otherwise not in a stable relationship with a man. One advantage that the church offered them was "an institutional base for developing important and enduring social relationships" with other women, and the five weekly religious services provided "the rituals to validate these emerging bonds, which help to create a shared sense of community" (712). The typically emotional quality of Pentecostal worship further allowed them to express "the desperation and despair that once plagued their lives and the peace and happiness that they encountered after a surprise meeting with God changed them forever" (714). At least as important for them, though, was the message to Pentecostal men, who were admonished to abstain from sins like "alcohol, cigarettes, gambling, and extramarital liaisons" (717). It could be said, then, that while males enjoyed authority in the church, they were also encouraged "to cultivate some traditionally 'feminine' qualities" that made them better family men. Consequently, Pentecostal women were likely to "encounter more potentially 'domesticated' mates among the male faithful than among the male population at large" (717).

To return to the previous discussion of conversion and modernization, another key characteristic of Pentecostalism is its relation to traditional culture and to "the past." Many commentators note that, while Christianity generally promotes discontinuity and a radical break with the past, Pentecostalism takes this position especially seriously. Joel Robbins has applied his continuity/discontinuity model (see p. 191 above) to Pentecostalism, arguing that it is "rich in disjunctive discourses and practices aimed at making ruptures with the past" (2003a: 224). More than most sects of Christianity, Pentecostalism "set[s] up ritual practices designed continuously to create or defend the disjunctions those discourses construct" (224), including condemnations of their old lives and cultures as well as exorcisms of the evil demons of those lives and cultures.

Perhaps no one has documented this rupture better than Birgit Meyer (1998, 1999). She found Pentecostals in Ghana literally commanding followers to "make a complete break with the past" (1998: 316). For them, tradition and local culture were satanic, so while their religion was *in* Africa it was not *of* Africa: "Pentecostalization was opposed to Africanization" (319). A crucial aspect of the church was "deliverance" from the evils of past and local religions, including the individual biographical past, the ancestors, the "occult" (which encompassed animism as well as Islam, Buddhism, Mormonism, Jehovah's Witnesses, and various African Christian churches), and of course evil spirits. Central to this achievement in the Ghanaian Pentecostal movement she studied was the "deliverance ritual," in which

> people are held to realize that they are in the grip of "the past," which is represented
> as a fearful thing out of control, and that they can only gain control over their

individual lives—and, indeed, become modern individuals—by remembering, and only subsequently untying all the links connecting them with, their "past."

(339)

Significantly, as Pentecostals break the ties to their past lives and local cultures, they forge ties with new modern lives and translocal cultures, joining an imagined non-local and universal Christian community.

Ironically perhaps, then, Pentecostalism tends to take local cultural and religious beliefs unusually seriously, and part of its appeal is its power to battle local evil. In Trinidad, for instance, Stephen Glazier suggested that "the appeal and subsequent 'growth' of Pentecostalism may be attributed partially to its handling of traditional, and decidedly unmodern, beliefs concerning Obeah and demon possession" (1980: 67). Obeah is a religion on the island concerned with (mostly bad) luck, in which practitioners cast evil spirits into people, usually at the request of a client. The only remedy for an Obeah spell was exorcism by an even stronger practitioner, and Pentecostals claimed to be more spiritually powerful and able to combat demons and pagan spells. Interestingly, not only did Pentecostals perform exorcisms but so did Methodists, Presbyterians, Seventh Day Adventists, and Catholics—each religion adapting to local situations—and locals turned to all of them, although Pentecostal rites had become the preferred solution (70).

Finally, Pentecostalism is not a static and unchanging version of Christianity but has already shown signs of evolution. Some Pentecostal congregations have achieved tremendous success and growth, morphing into "megachurches" and sometimes shedding their most extreme Pentecostal beliefs and practices in favor of "charismatic" or "evangelical" trappings. Observers have already begun to apply the term neo-Pentecostal to such developments. Hefner states that neo-Pentecostal churches tend to make peace with aspects of modernity, for instance skillfully using "modern electronic media, both to accompany religious services and to disseminate worship events through live or recorded broadcasts" (2013b: 24). Donald Miller (2009) uses the term "progressive Pentecostalism" for the (still minority of) Pentecostal churches that engage in social activism such as food and clothing programs, divorce and addiction counseling, and community development. And, of course, one of the most amazing transformations, in the United States and around the globe, has been the appearance of "the prosperity gospel" as a form of Christianity, including Pentecostalism, which promises material wealth to believers, often through a distinctly modernist and capitalist form of "investment" and "exchange" with God through "seed offerings" that virtually obligate God to reward them.

Other Christianities: Eastern Orthodox and Coptic

This section has dealt almost exclusively with Catholicism and Protestantism, because anthropology and other disciplines have been preoccupied with those familiar Western formations of Christianity. But as Chris Hann and Hermann Goltz remind us in their comparatively rare discussion of other Christianities, "The Eastern traditions of Christianity nowadays have large congregations (number well over 200 million), but they have attracted little scholarly attention to date from Anglophone anthropologists" (2010: 2).

Before there was Western Christianity, there was Eastern Christianity; indeed, Americans and Western Europeans too easily forget that Christianity began as an Eastern religion and that Western versions like Catholicism and Protestantism were much later developments. While the Roman church claimed primacy, Eastern Christianity based in

Greece and Byzantium never accepted this claim, and the official split or schism between the two Christianities, over doctrinal and political differences, is dated to 1054. Since then, Eastern or Orthodox Christianity has taken a more "national" approach, consisting of more or less autonomous national churches, such as Russian Orthodox, Greek Orthodox, and so on.

One reason for the neglect of Orthodox Christianity, unfortunately, is the Western, Catholic or Protestant, origin of anthropology as a discipline and of most anthropologists. Another reason, equally unfortunate, is that Orthodox Christianity mostly resides in societies where anthropology had little interest, or where Western anthropologists were largely excluded, until recently (Russia and its satellites being off limits during the Cold War). Today, however, an anthropology of Christianity cannot afford to ignore its Eastern bloodline, and Hann and Goltz go so far as to insist that "the Orthodox churches can stake a strong claim to be *more* global in the original Christian sense of church unity: they form a *global* structure of *local* churches, as distinct from the 'globalization' of a local church, be it the West Roman, the Wittenbergian [i.e. Lutheran], or the Genevan [i.e. Calvinist]" (3). Even more, many assumptions about Christianity are sorely tested in the case of Orthodox Christianity.

Two such assumptions go to the heart of the anthropological analysis of Christianity and to the heart of some cutting-edge anthropological theorizing on religion. The first, as Cannell notes, is an overemphasis on asceticism and otherworldliness, and the second, according to Robbins, is a perceived discontinuity or radical temporal break. Orthodox Christianity challenges both assumptions. Eastern Christianity, various observers claim, has never stressed asceticism like Catholicism or Protestantism. Further, contra Robbins, "Eastern Christians tend to emphasize continuity in their self-representations. Their basic notions of time seem (at any rate among certain intellectuals in certain periods) to be quite different from Western temporalities" (Hann and Goltz 2010: 7).

On the issue of asceticism, Alice Forbess contends that Western Christianity's other-worldliness relates to a theology that "God's 'withdrawal' has left man 'in a state of incompleteness that can be resolved only at death'" (2010: 132). In contrast, even in the Eastern monastic tradition, monks and nuns are "more concerned with *indumnezeirea* (divinization)—the feat of becoming God-like while still in the flesh, as the saints are thought to have done" (132–33); thus Eastern Christianity is arguably not as alienated from and at war with the world and the flesh as Western Christianity. This difference might be reflected in the Eastern attraction to relics and other physical manifestations of divinity (although Western Christianity is no stranger to relics: in November 2013 the Catholic Church displayed some bone fragments attributed to Peter, and Western Christians continue to be fascinated by the Shroud of Turin, the Holy Grail, and Noah's Ark).

Bridging these points and the second assumption are the Eastern reverence for icons or visual representations of saints, Jesus, or God. This second assumption is captured by Harvey Whitehouse's influential dichotomy between "imagistic" and "doctrinal" modes of religiosity (see Chapter 1). Whitehouse considers imagistic religiosity to be lower in frequency and generally less appropriate to stable, established, and modern religions than the doctrinal alternative. However, Eastern Orthodox churches use images frequently and intensely and have attained great stability (see Figure 8.4). Hann and Goltz conclude that "it might be argued that Eastern Christians confound Whitehouse's dichotomy, which is left with at most a limited heuristic value" (2010: 16). In a more damning assessment, they continue: "What is clear is that neither he nor any of the other protagonists in the current cognitive debates have looked at Eastern Christianity in any depth" (16).

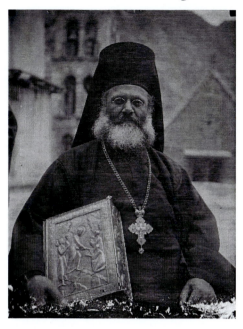

Figure 8.4 Orthodox priest at St. Catherine's Monastery in the Sinai. Courtesy of the Library of Congress Prints and Photographs Division

While not all Orthodox Christians believe in icons equally (if it is accurate to say that they "believe in" icons at all), these painted or gilded objects are central to Orthodox religious practice. The existence and use of icons evokes the ideas of Alfred Gell concerning material objects and distributed personhood (see Chapter 3). Icons are not idols that Orthodox Christians worship; instead, they are residues, presences, of holy persons and holy power. As Gabriel Hanganu explains in the case of a Romanian icon of Saint Anna, physical matter is also potentially holy and human handiwork is part of the "work of transforming nature" to realize its spirituality:

> People are asked to add their contribution to the *logoi* God originally implanted in the constitutive materials of the objects and to the flow of divine energies keeping the whole world in existence. By virtue of their free will they can make and use objects either toward or against the fulfillment of nature's sacred potentiality. ... Religious objects comprise a particular category of objects that are meant to be employed for prompting and facilitating people's relationship with God. Their "proper" use can open up invisible channels by means of which spiritual energies are directed to the various realms to the benefit of animated and unanimated elements of the cosmos. ... In addition to being material objects produced and employed in the visible world, they are also images providing representations of the invisible spiritual realm.
>
> (2010: 45)

Yet one more reason why Orthodox Christianity is overlooked by anthropology is that Orthodox Christian societies were not as actively involved in colonialism and therefore did not transplant their religion as widely in the non-Western world. This is not to say, by any means, that Orthodoxy did not travel with Eastern Christians. A fascinating site of colonial Orthodox Christianity is Alaska, where Russian explorers and colonists carried their religion. The leading chronicler of Orthodox Christianity in the American Northwest is Sergei Kan (1999), who studied Russian Orthodoxy among the Tlingit. More recently, Medeia Csoba DeHass reported on the Sugpiaq of Alaska, who were not only missionized by Russian Orthodoxy but who "interpreted and integrated the once foreign Russian Orthodox religion into their stock notions of what 'Sugpiaqness' ought to be" (2007: 208). In a challenge to standard anthropological categories, DeHass calls the Sugqpiaq "the most 'traditional' people in the area" (208) while also being thoroughly Orthodox. It is, DeHass acknowledges, "impossible to find concrete information on pre-Christian beliefs and practices, as everybody in the community is Russian Orthodox, and they proudly declare it to be their original religion" (209). Even so, one can "recognize aspects of current Sugpiaq Russian Orthodoxy that correspond with pre-Christian ideas, and which are incorporated through the process of indigenization of Russian Orthodoxy" (210).

Space allows only a brief mention of one other neglected species of Christianity—Coptic Christianity, based in Egypt. As a Christian minority in a predominantly Muslim country, not surprisingly much of the literature on Coptic Christians has focused on their political and security situation. For instance, Angie Heo recounts the fascinating story of a Coptic woman named Samia Youssef Basilious who was miraculously cured of cancer and then began to exude sacred oil from her hand. Sadly, both the Coptic hierarchy and the Egyptian government "were ambivalent and wary about the public visibility" of such an unauthorized miracle, which presented "a significant challenge to the ordering of religious truths and their governability" (2013: 151). Consequently, she was locked away in a convent for five years, during which time a printed poster (not even an official painting) of the Virgin Mary in her cell started to produce oil as well. Heo characterizes the apotheosis of Samia as a transformation "from image veneration to becoming-an-image oneself" (153) and explains the phenomenon of icons as "'pores,' portals and openings accessible at their surfaces" and therefore points "where saints travel between heavenly and earthly realms" (158), the latter including images and human bodies.

To end this discussion and this chapter and to bring it full circle, Lise Paulsen Galal describes how Coptic and Muslim co-residence in Egypt inevitably implicates the Christians in a politics of sameness and difference. In a religiously plural state, the Copts naturally emphasize their Egyptianness, thus rejecting any status as a foreign or minority group in Egypt; obviously too, "by insisting on being the same, the Church at the same time rejects any identification of Copts as inferior, second-class citizens" (2012: 47). Yet simultaneously the Copts want to endorse their difference as a religious group, since it is as Coptic Christians that they demand their place and their equality in Egyptian society. Thus they are put in the awkward and even contradictory position of promoting their "Christianity as a primary identity without compromising Egyptianness, positing the former as an integral part of the latter" (52). Not unexpectedly, over history but particularly since the collapse of the Mubarak regime, tensions and violence have flared between Muslim and Coptic Egyptians.

Conclusion

Translocal or "world" religions are among the most conspicuous and the most influential forces on the international stage today. They often claim, aim, or attempt to impose consistency and orthodoxy across their zones of influence. However, as we have learned, it would be misleading to take their claims—or aspirations—of homogeneity too literally. Homogeneity is less a fact of translocal religions than *part of the doctrine or self-identity* of these religions. The reality is that there are no sharp and absolute lines that divide religions from each other or unite all of the local versions of a particular religion with each other. A translocal/world religion in the end is not a single global "thing" but an assortment of disparate local things, linked by a discursive tradition. As such, each translocal/world religion meets, confronts, struggles with, and eventually adapts to not only "traditional" religions and other world religions but also diversity within its own religion, not to mention non-religious (including modernizing and secularizing) forces. The final outcome is a dynamic, churning, and ever-varying religious and social landscape in which religious practices and identities are contested, made, unmade, and remade continuously. In fact, some of today's translocal/world religions may not be tomorrow's translocal/world religions, and some of today's local—or even not-yet-existing—religions may be translocal/world religions tomorrow.

DISCUSSION QUESTIONS

- What are the differences between "traditional"/local religions and "translocal" or world religions? What are the social conditions that promote these differences?
- Why has the study of Islam been plagued by "orientalism," and how is the emerging anthropology of Islam different from previous analyses of the religion?
- Why has an anthropology of Christianity been so late in forming? What new directions is anthropology taking—and should it take—in the study of Christianity?
- Why is studying Eastern Orthodox Christianity essential for understanding Christianity, and perhaps other religions as well?

SUPPLEMENTARY READING (see website)

- *The Politics of Muslim Conversion in Pakistan and Papua New Guinea*
- *Why Have the Akha Resisted Christian Conversion?*
- *Hinduism and Buddhism as Translocal Religions*

9　Vernacular Religion

In November 2013, Marvel Comics announced the creation of a new superhero, Ms. Marvel, who is not only female (which is a relative rarity in the masculine realm of superheroes) but Muslim as well. Kamala Khan, a Pakistani-American teenage girl living in Jersey City, from a conservative Muslim family that worries about her purity, discovers superpowers such as the ability to alter her form and calls herself Ms. Marvel. As unusual as this character is among American superheroes, she is not the first comic book Muslim hero. Marvel previously introduced Dust, an Afghani Sunni woman with the power to turn herself into a storm of sand; she joined the New X-Men in 2002. A decade before her, Monet St. Croix, a North African Muslim known by the alias M, appeared in an issue of "Uncanny X-Men" in 1994. Meanwhile, DC Comics (the home of Superman and Batman) created Nightrunner in 2011, an Algerian-French superhero whose real name was Bilal Asselah, and the next year a Muslim-American named Simon Baz became the latest incarnation of the Green Lantern. Nor are American comic book companies the only originators of Muslim heroes. In 2006 Teshkeel Comics, based in Kuwait, released the first issue of *The 99*, about ninety-nine young Muslims who develop superpowers thanks to magical Noor stones (www.the99.org). Based on the Muslim notion of the ninety-nine names of Allah, the ninety-nine Muslim heroes with names like Aleem ("all-knowing"), Bari ("healer"), and Raheema ("merciful") even enjoyed a short cooperation with the Justice League of America in 2010–11. The producer of *The 99*, Naif Al-Mutawa, recounts the struggle to introduce his creations to the Muslim world in a film, *Wham! Bam! Islam!*, in which he states that "Muslim children need new heroes."

Nor is Islam the only religion to get treated in comic book or graphic novel fashion. Campfire Graphic Novels has published a "mythology" series featuring Hindu characters and gods like Krishna "defender of dharma," Draupadi "fire-born princess," and Sita "daughter of the earth." And of course Christian comic book companies like Christian Knight Comics (www.christianknightcomics.com) have created superheroes like Mr. Christian, Desertwind, and The Christian Knight to battle evil and spread Christianity; there are also posters, trading cards, and coloring books for the characters. Based in Orlando, Florida, the Christian Super-Hero Association (TCSHA, www.tcsha.com and Facebook) proclaims its mission "to provide 'The Official Christian Super-Hero Universe—Enter Thy Kingdom' database, local HeroCons, and community for all ministry leaders, creators, illustrators, publishers, and fans. Our vision is to glory God by 'Harvesting Souls … Through God's Super-Heroes!'"

Comic books and graphic novels may seem like an odd, even inappropriate, place to do religion. Yet religion has been "outside the box" of formal or official religion for decades, if not centuries, if not from the very beginnings of religion. Whether in the form of

"Chick tracts" (the "cartoon gospel tracts" first drawn by Jack Chick more than fifty years ago; see www.chick.com), animated cartoons like "Davey and Goliath," popular movies and music, or hats and T-shirts, religion escapes the church, mosque, synagogue, or temple and appears in any and all corners of culture.

Anthropology, with its deep commitment to practice and embodiment, is well prepared to recognize religion that operates beyond the realm of official writings, occasions, and locations. Other disciplines may identify religion with scriptures, doctrines, rituals, and sacred spaces, but anthropology identifies religion wherever it may be found, in whatever form it might be done. This religion beyond official religion, religion as practiced by regular people, has been called "popular religion" or "everyday religion" or "vernacular religion," and as sociologist Nancy Ammerman notes, this religion of non-experts "may happen in unpredictable places. It may combine elements from multiple religious sources" (2007: 9)—and it may combine elements from non-religious sources, like comic books.

The consequences of taking vernacular religion seriously are quite profound. Vernacular religion tends to rupture boundaries, first and foremost between what is "religion" and what is not. It also erodes familiar concepts and dualisms like sacred and profane. Jean Comaroff, to whom we will return below, sees that the sacred "is becoming more prominent in profane places" (2010: 17) and adds: "Commerce, government, education, the media, and popular arts—nothing seems too trivial or debased to offer grist to the spiritual mill" (20). Martin Stringer, based on his work in The Worship in Birmingham Project, studying everyday religion in Britain, goes so far as to contend that because of the academic preoccupation with written texts, church rituals, and "beliefs" we "have fundamentally misunderstood the nature of 'religion'" (2008: ix).

The Anthropology of Vernacular Religion

Particularly in pre-modern and "tribal" societies, anthropologists have found religion distributed through and integrated with the wider culture; as we have observed before, many societies lack a concept of "religion" as distinct from the rest of culture and do not institutionalize religion separately. We have even argued that the very idea of a thing called "religion" may be unique to Western/Christian society. In the last chapter, though, we discussed newer forms of religion—translocal or "world" religions—that have undergone a transformation to centralized structures, professionalized officiates, and standardized scriptures and doctrines. As we will explore in the next chapter, these more institutionalized varieties of religion are prone to novel forms of intolerance and violence. In the present chapter, we will examine how this phenomenon of a centralized, professionalized, and standardization religion leads to variations between what "the religion" says and what people actually do—which ultimately forces us to reconsider what "the religion" is.

The Language of Vernacular Religion

Observers have long noticed the deviation between the explicit doctrines of religions and the actual religious ideas and practices of people. There has been little agreement, though, on how to name this distinction. One suggestion has been to label the people's religion "folk religion," but scholars have objected to this term for a number of reasons. For instance, folk religion implies a religion *prior to* and independent of the dominant (usually translocal or world) religion, whatever survives of a religion from the past, like pre-Christian religions in contrast to Christianity. Another contender is "popular religion," which merely suggests the religion "of the people." But the official religion can also be the people's religion, and we make no claims about how popular a particular unofficial belief or practice is. Other alternatives have included "everyday religion," "lived religion," "implicit religion," and worst of all "residual religion," the religion that is left over after you subtract the official religion.

As folklorist Leonard Primiano justifiably complained, such terms (especially the last one) tend to "residualize the religious lives of believers" (1995: 38), rendering their actual ideas and practices into leftovers after the "real" religion is identified. At the same time, they imply a real religion that "somewhere exists as a pure element which is in some way transformed, even contaminated, by its exposure to human communities" (39). To avoid such a conceptual and methodological outcome, Primiano offered the term "vernacular religion," by which he meant "religion as it is lived: as humans encounter, understand, interpret, and practice it" (44). The word "vernacular" is borrowed from linguistics, where it simply means "in the native/local language" or "in plain, everyday, ordinary language." Sometimes this means literally translating the religion into a new local language; in other instances it means communicating technical terms in laymen's terms.

Religions too often have complicated and technical languages, as well as esoteric doctrines and arcane rituals, which are not necessarily known, understood, or accepted by the ordinary members. Religion may get translated (vernacularized) to the ordinary people, or they may translate/vernacularize it themselves. Regular people may even invent their own religious ideas and practices (see pp. 224–6 below). Therefore, as Primiano insisted and as Schielke and Debevec echo, vernacular religion is "characterized by ambiguity, uncertainty, anxiety, creative play and contestation" (Schielke and Debevec 2012: 7). In a much more recent statement, Primiano stresses that the lens of vernacular religion "understands religion as the continuous art of individual interpretation and negotiation of any number of influential sources. All religion is subtly and vibrantly marked by continuous interpretation even after it has been reified in expressive or structured forms" (2012: 384).

Since humans invariably create and re-create, interpret and speak, and use and adapt their religions, Primiano went so far as to claim that "it is impossible for the religion of an individual not to be vernacular" (1995: 44). Whether or not we go that far, the notion of vernacular religion debunks the "assumption that religion is synonymous with institutional or hierarchical authority" (45). Further, by encouraging us toward "understanding religion as it has been lived in the past and is lived today" (51), the lines between vernacular religion and official religion become blurred, as do the lines between different religions and between religion and non-religion. This will be especially the case when, as we considered in the previous two chapters, multiple religious traditions interact in a shared religious field, or when religious traditions encounter modern media and popular culture. Then we will find, as Bowman and Valk warn, that religion "cannot be neatly compartmentalized into the theoretical containers of academic discourse" (2012: 2).

Religion and Vernacular Religion: Two Traditions or One?

Some scholars have applied Redfield's distinction of great and small traditions, or Gellner's distinction of local and translocal religion, to the question of vernacular religion. However, as in Stringer's study of British religion, most of the time there are not two different religions at play, certainly not a pre-modern or tribal one alongside a modern one. Gananath Obeyesekere offered another way to think about the variations of religion within a society. In the context of Sinhalese Buddhism, he modified Redfield's notion of great and little traditions, holding that while the villagers practiced Buddhism differently from the official version (and different villages practiced it differently from each other), they definitely did not see themselves as practicing a different "tradition": "The average person's identifications occur within a single tradition, and his roles are meaningful mostly in relation to this tradition" (1963: 140).

Rather than conceptualizing Sinhalese Buddhism as two religions—"little" village religion and "great" translocal religion—Obeyesekere recommended that we think of various levels or styles of religion within the same society. Village religion is, he insisted, "the religion of the masses," whereas official translocal religion is the religion of "monks, intellectuals, and scholars" (142). Because of their training and their location in the institutions of Buddhism, the monks, intellectuals, and scholars have different knowledge, interpretations, and perspectives on Buddhism than the laity and villagers do. The villagers may indeed mix some non-Buddhist and pre-Buddhist elements with their Buddhism, but that is not the main or only issue; instead, ordinary people have ordinary knowledge of the religion and *apply the religion to their ordinary lives.* Thus "the religion of the masses" may diverge from "the religion of the elites," but it is not a different religion. As Obeyesekere concluded, "Sinhalese Buddhism is a single religious tradition, having important structural links and in constant interaction with the great tradition" (142). That is, the villagers learn their religion from the elites, and the elites try to make village belief and practice more orthodox. What Obeyesekere called the "common idiom" that unites villagers and elites "is derived historically from a great tradition [a tradition of the elites], though refashioned to fit the peasant world view"; this common idiom, the shared sets of beliefs and practices, "not only links the little tradition with the great, but also links the little traditions with one another" (153).

The usefulness of Obeyesekere's approach resides not only in the restoration of two alleged "traditions" into a single cultural-religious system but in the recognition of the contestation between them. Writing from the context of Orthodox Russian Christianity, Alexander Panchenko endorses Gregory Freeze's judgment that the main goal of that church or of any formal religious institution is "to 'confine the sacred'—temporally and spatially—within the ecclesiastical domain" (quoted 2012: 45). In other words, the religious leaders and elites want to monopolize belief and practice, want their particular knowledge and interpretations to be the only ones, and want to bring all religious activity under their authority and control. The so-called great tradition, or what is really the viewpoint of the scholars and officials, thus appoints itself as the *orthodoxy* of the religion. "The question of orthodoxy, in consequence, becomes a political one: orthodoxy is nothing else than the capability to credibly claim to represent the true, correct, reading and practice of a tradition— a position that is subject to change and contestation" (Schielke and Debevec 2012: 6). This is why Samuli Schielke and Liza Debevec contrast not great traditions against little ones but "grand schemes" (of conformity and orthodoxy) against "ordinary lives."

In the case of Russian religion, Panchenko describes the three types of shrines that one encounters in the countryside—individual or spontaneous ones, communal ones, and official ones. Any "separate point of the landscape" can become "an object of worship by an individual or a family" (2012: 46). Some of these are forgotten when the worshipers die. "More often, however, such holy places become objects of worship for whole rural communities or groups of communities" (47)—that is, individual shrines are adopted as communal shrines. When this happens, contestation often arises, ranging from "concurrence of various plots or motifs of narratives" to "contradiction of belief and disbelief narratives, worship, and sacrilege" (49). Meanwhile, the church maintains a set of official shrines, where the authorities dictate meaning and behavior. But to make matters maximally complicated, sometimes an individual or communal shrine "is recognized, approved, and accommodated by Church officials," while simultaneously "each official shrine is worshipped in different vernacular ways, in spite of all attempts by church and secular authorities to unify and standardize either rituals or narratives relating to the holy place or object" (49).

Box 9.1 Making Greek Saints: Where Popular Becomes Official

The case of Russian shrines just discussed illustrates the porous boundaries between vernacular religion and orthodox religion. Séverine Rey reports a similar phenomenon in modern Greece, where the canonization of new saints illustrates "an intertwining of spheres and competing discourses" (2012: 82). In the 1950s a family of villagers built a small chapel in their fields, akin to the Russian individual shrines mentioned above. After a burial and an engraved cross from the Byzantine era (thirteenth to fourteenth centuries) were discovered at the site, "extraordinary and mysterious events began to occur," including purported miracles and mystical dreams (84). The locals sought verification and approval by church officials of the religious wonders they experienced, but at first "authorities did not seem to be interested in this phenomenon and criticized it as a sign of imagination and credulity" typical of "simple people and above all women" (84). Yet in Orthodox Christianity the canonization of a new saint "is a process which endorses popular veneration in a particular way. Such veneration is actually considered evidence of divine grace affecting an individual" (86). Still, as in the case of Samia Youssef Basilious (see Chapter 8), whose miraculous production of oil was ambiguous and threatening to authorities, the Greek bishop in charge of the investigation "recognized the vitality of the new devotion, the unbreakable links between the faithful and the ecclesiastical institutions, and the necessity for the latter to control the development of the situation" (87). Ultimately the church created some new saints out of the experience, absorbing them into the official category of "neo-martyrs" and linking them to church doctrine and history. In the end, then, "Even if the Church was not the origin of those dreams and stories, it nevertheless has the means to control their development by giving (or denying) them official support" and to translate them from vernacular to orthodox (91).

Vernacularization from Above: Inculturation and the Catholic Church

When religious institutions, elites, and experts are not the source of vernacularization, their responses to vernacular religion vary. Sometimes, as in the case above, they may coopt it and institutionalize it; on other occasions they may suppress it as heresy (a Christian concept indicating choice) or *bida'* (a Muslim concept meaning innovation or religious deviation). In some instances, though, institutions may actively participate in the vernacularization of their religion.

As evinced by examples in the last two chapters, Christianity has been undergoing vernacularization as long as it has been undergoing translocalization. This was of course true even in the early centuries, as Christianity gradually adopted the trappings of the

Roman Empire, translated its scriptures into Greek and Latin, absorbed Western philosophy, and picked up Western and Northern European elements such as Christmas trees, yule logs, and Easter bunnies. Through European expansion and colonialism in particular, many more local societies were exposed to Christianity and vernacularized the religion, whether missionaries approved or not. Indeed, Christian authorities tried to stamp out much of this innovation and replace it with orthodoxy; on the other hand, Christian proselytizers also saw the value of using the local language, mixing local beliefs and traditions, and in some cases superimposing the new god on the old ones.

That is to say, Christian authorities often allowed or even initiated vernacularization. One of the oldest and most adored examples is Our Lady of Guadalupe, the dark-skinned Nahuatl-speaking version of the Virgin Mary, who reportedly revealed herself to Juan Diego in 1531, not long after Mexico had been conquered. As in the Greek case, the church eventually condoned the vision, Our Lady of Guadalupe became a Mexican national symbol, and centuries later, in 2002, Diego himself was honored as a saint.

It is obvious, then, that vernacularization is not new to, and need not be destructive to and can be positively beneficial to, the advancement of Christianity. Even so, much of this vernacularization has occurred without real theoretical comprehension. However, in recent decades the Catholic Church has become quite aware and articulate about the process, which it recognizes and promotes as *inculturation*. One of the leading documenters of Catholic inculturation is Aylward Shorter, whose *Toward a Theology of Inculturation* provides a history, analysis, and justification. Importantly, the church's policy of inculturation is highly anthropologically informed, relating to "the twentieth-century 'discovery' of culture as a plural phenomenon" (1988: xi); Shorter actually discussed Tylor, Geertz, and Durkheim in his book. Inculturation theology thus means "the recognition that faith must become culture, if it is to be fully received and lived" (xi).

As early as the second century, but not yet in the modern language of culture, the *Epistle to Diogenes* explained that Christianity entails no specific culture, that "Christians are distinguished from other men neither by country, nor language, nor the customs they observe … nor lead a life which is marked out by any singularity" (www.newadvent.org/fathers/0101.htm). The implication is the separation of Christianity from culture and the consequent cultural neutrality of the religion; in other words, Christianity could be practiced in any vernacular without losing its religious core, and the conventional Christianity established in Europe is no more than European vernacular Christianity, not "real" Christianity.

Shorter accordingly defined inculturation, following Father Pedro Arrup, as

> the incarnation of Christian life and of the Christian message in a particular cultural context, in such a way that this experience not only finds expression through elements proper to the culture in question (this alone would be no more than a superficial adaptation) but becomes a principle that animates, directs, and unifies the culture, transforming it and remaking it so as to bring about a "new creation."
>
> (1988: 11)

This sophisticated notion entails that "the Christian faith cannot exist except in a cultural form" (12)—and not necessarily in the familiar Western cultural form. But even more consequentially, Catholic scholars, both in the West and in non-Western societies, insist that the spread of Christianity is not a one-way process; rather, inculturation "implies that the Christian message transforms a culture. It is also the case that

Christianity is transformed by culture, not in a way that falsifies the message, but in the way in which the message is formulated and interpreted anew" (14).

Despite the fact that Shorter concluded that inculturation "is nothing other than the profound evangelization of a people in their culture" (63), it is actually much more than that, since it has multiple effects not only on the local culture but on the global church. For one, it moves the church out of solely Western hands, increasing the number and power of native clergy. It opens the way to multiple Catholicisms: the reforms of the Second Vatican Council in the 1960s explicitly state, in Liturgical Constitution 38, that "provision shall be made, when revising the liturgical books, for legitimate variations and adaptations to different groups, regions, and peoples." And some of these revisions can make their way back to the West (as in the case of the Ghanaian missionary church in New York mentioned in Chapter 8), altering Western Christianity.

Anthropologists have not been in the forefront of the study of inculturation, but one anthropological analysis shows the wider cultural impact of such policies. Andrew Orta reported on inculturation among the Aymara of Bolivia, which he found "strives to recuperate and revalorize indigenous culture"; instead of condemning and eradicating traditional practices, Catholicism embraces them "as profoundly Christian, or at least as expression of an indigenous religiosity that do not resist translation into a Christian frame of reference" (1998: 168). The surprising and generous-sounding quality of this approach is "to present the Aymara a way of being Aymara the way that Jesus would have been Aymara" (171)—which refracts back on Christianity by implying that Jesus' life and mission were culturally specific by him being born a Hebrew rather than an Aymara. Orta claimed that missionaries even challenged their Aymara catechists "to live and write their own Aymara New Testament" (172). Yet Orta also recognized that the surface cultural relativism of inculturation "is predicated upon a Christian universalism" (171), insisting that Christianity is true and will be the future of Aymara culture and identity. And most profoundly, he argued that, while "from the perspective of the global church inculturation is certainly localizing, in grounded practice it is deceptively homogenizing" (169), ignoring and erasing differences *within* Aymara (and other) society and assuming—and constructing—a homogeneous culture. In a word, while respecting certain aspects of the "local," it effaces others.

Vernacular Religion in Television and Cinema

In 1987–88, television in India aired serialized versions of two classic religious-historical epics, the *Ramayana* and the *Mahabharata*. Each Sunday morning, according to Cybelle Shattuck, viewers congregated to watch these televisual renderings of their sacred stories. More still,

> They treated the show as a religious event, a chance to have darshan, a "vision" of the divine, through the medium of *dur-darshan*, "distant-vision," i.e. television. In many places, before each broadcast began the viewers performed rituals traditionally used to honor images of deities. The TV sets were garlanded and offerings made to them. According to newspaper reports, work ceased all across India as the populace gathered to view the divine stories.
>
> (1999: 11)

All religions have found ways to visualize what is often (but by no means always) invisible, including Christianity, which privileges the mental and textual over the visual (especially the Protestant form of Christianity), and Islam, which is commonly held to be "aniconic" or opposed to any visual representation of Allah or his prophet Muhammad. Yet the last chapter showed how Orthodox Christians view and revere images, and Chapter 3 mentioned Iranian Muslim use of images in Shi'ite ritual. Indeed, "visual piety" (see Morgan 1998) is an important part of virtually every religion, and people in all times and places have manufactured material and visible manifestations of their religion, whether statues, paintings, carvings, masks, sand drawings, or, as discussed at the outset, cartoons.

In contemporary society, with its visual technologies of television and cinema, it is inevitable that religion will be translated into and transmitted via those media too. Religion has been the subject of movies for as long as there have been movies, from *The Ten Commandments* to *The Passion of the Christ* and *Left Behind*. It has also found its way onto the small screen, reverentially in television series like *Touched by an Angel* and satirically in *South Park* and *The Simpsons*. Other television programs, while not promoting an explicitly religious message, inhabit the world of a religion: *Supernatural* takes as real the Christian world of heaven, hell, angels, and God (although an absent God), and familiar Christian notions, including a savior-like figure, pervade non-religious plots, from *The Lord of the Rings* to *The Matrix*.

In the context of West Africa, Birgit Meyer (whose contributions to the study of Pentecostalism were acknowledged in Chapter 8) describes a "public space in Southern Ghana" that "brims with the tremendous popularity of Christianity, especially the Pentecostal-Charismatic brand" (2008: 87). She finds that "Christian popular culture has successfully colonized public space ... where Christian signs—spread via posters, songs, and radio, TV and film programs, and victorious mottos on shops ... create an all pervasive Christian environment" (84). In fact, in an earlier article she insists that religion

> cannot be analyzed apart from the forms and practices of mediation that define it. It is a resource generating distinct forms of expression that are not limited to the institutional sphere but that are articulated in, and partly (re)shape, the public sphere in the information age.
>
> (2004: 94)

In that earlier writing, she focuses on popular movies, which exhibit not only "the blurring of boundaries between religion and entertainment" but more particularly what she calls the "pentecostalite cultural style" (92). As indicated in Chapter 8, Pentecostalism in Africa (and elsewhere) tends to call for a radical break with the past, in tandem with a worldview in which satanic forces (in the form of pre-Christian religion, other non-Christian religions, modern consumer culture, and the devil himself) are invisibly at work. This perspective, she suggests, is especially compatible with the style of the melodrama, a genre that explores "the ordinary and banal" aspects of life but "sets out to reveal the underlying forces that govern what happens on the surface of everyday life" (98). For Christians and especially Pentecostals, these underlying forces are supernatural good and evil.

Accordingly, Meyer identifies some of the features of the pentecostalite visual cultural style, beginning with "Christian modernity." Christian modernity is the real and inescapable world of nice homes, fine clothes, and comfortable city life; it is desirable but also seductive and dangerous, promoting "immoral, selfish ways of achieving wealth" and other satisfactions, including sexual ones (102). "The wife and the pastor are featured as heroes" in this vision of modernity, "but husbands usually appear as weak" and easily given to temptation (102). Naturally, a second feature of the pentecostalite style is the dualism of God against Satan.

> Thus, films usually evolve around a struggle between "the powers of darkness," on the one hand, with their firm grip on irresponsible husbands, loose girls, selfish businessmen, greedy mothers-in-law, bad friends, or ritual murderers, killers, and members of secret cults and, on the other hand, divine power, which always supports the pious housewife, the innocent child, and, of course, the Pentecostal pastor. In the end, in such films good must overcome evil just as in Pentecostal sermons God is asserted to be stronger than the devil.
>
> (103)

Finally, in an effort to convey the Christian/Pentecostal experience, films incorporate visual devices and special effects intended to make the viewer feel that the films "reveal that which remains invisible to the eye yet determines the course of life" (104).

> Moviegoers are positioned in such a way that they share the eye of God, technologically simulated by the camera. Indeed, audiences are made mimetically to share the super vision that enables God to penetrate the dark; they are addressed as viewer-believers and even as voyeurs peeping into the otherwise forbidden. Far from exposing the nonexistence of invisible forces, in popular film the eye of the camera zooms in on the operations of such forces and projects them onto the screen, thereby creating the illusion of offering firsthand views deep into hell. In this way, the work of representation that constitutes film, as well as the visual technology on which such representation depends, is mystified—*mise-en-scène* appears as a revelation of the invisibly real.
>
> (104)

Box 9.2 The Pentecostal Melodrama in the Democratic Republic of Congo

Christian pastors and congregations in Kinshasa, the capital city of the Democratic Republic of Congo (DRC, formerly Zaire), take the notion of melodrama quite seriously, according to Katrien Pype. She discovers that congregations-cum-acting-companies make their own television programs or soap operas with an "explicit Christian proselytizing mission," and their members "imagine themselves as correctors of Kinshasa's society" (2012: 3). In Congolese society, "nearly everybody claims to be a Christian" (32), although Christianity sits uncomfortably alongside other religions, especially traditional religions. Worse, it sits uncomfortably alongside the "heat" of the city, with its materialism and its sexuality, confusion, and uncertainty. Kinshasa Pentecostalism adopts the conventional dualistic division of modern urban society into the good godly part and the bad ungodly part, with "a strong belief in the demonization of quotidian life and an invisible battle ... between God ... and the Devil" (38). Christianity and "witchcraft" or "the occult" constantly confront each other, although, as Pype stresses, they look less dissimilar than either might care to admit. As for the production of Pentecostal melodramas, the acting corps has a leader or patron, who in this case is a Pentecostal man with a "calling" from God. He is the "big man" and patriarch, literally, since "women rarely lead theater companies" (70). Thus the leader combines two roles, an "artistic father" and a "spiritual father" (73), and the performing group is essentially a church or ministry and therefore worries considerably about who is or is not a "real Christian" as opposed to merely a "carnal Christian" or "Christian of the flesh." The melodramas themselves are almost invariably morality plays of some sort, depicting the threats of modern city life and deploying characters like the "bad girl," "an adolescent girl with occult powers who does not belong to the earthly realm of reality but inhabits a demonic world" (211). In fact, Pype characterizes these serials as witchcraft accusations and wider condemnations of traditional religion, the power of the elders, and the immorality of the city. Not surprisingly, "Pentecostal melodramas frequently end with confessions" (163) and the victory of Christians over the forces of darkness. In order to convey this struggle televisually, Congolese Pentecostal melodramas utilize the types of special effects that Meyer mentioned, but their very effectiveness makes the shows spiritually powerful. For the actors, the experiences are not entirely fictional but quite real, so individuals are sometimes hesitant to play evil characters, and before filming begins the troupe attends "special prayer sessions at which participating members not only seek inspiration but also solicit spiritual guidance and protection" (131). Nor is it only the actors who need protection against the very forces that they portray and potentially unleash; audiences of the programs have also "expressed a fear of becoming bewitched while watching the actors perform dances originating in the dark world" (145) or otherwise bringing these evil beings and forces to life.

Christianity is quite accomplished at integrating religion into television and movies, but it is by no means unique. Mattias Krings describes Islamic films in northern Nigeria, which function as conversion tools and only emerged in 2002. Multiple genres are used, to the same general effect:

> Within the epic, set in precolonial times, Muslim *mujahids* fight against pagan tribes and convert them to Islam, thus only vaguely relating to the nineteenth century's jihads. Within the framework of the romantic melodrama, pious Muslim boys have to choose between a pagan and a Muslim girl, and in a genre crossover of Western vampire, science-fiction, and police films, a poor pagan has to be cured from vampirism before he can convert to Islam and return to his tribesmen on a proselytizing mission.
>
> (2008: 46)

As elsewhere, some Muslim traditionalists opposed the production of Islamic films and sought a total ban, but others argued that movies "can be considered a legitimate educative tool from an Islamic point of view" (49). Although the latter party has won the contest, they still must strive to legitimate the religious use of popular films and to make those films as acceptably Muslim as possible:

> To justify the moral legitimacy of their video films, several filmmakers have recast their work as religious admonition (*fa'dakarwa*) or religious preaching (*wa'azi*), and liken themselves in press interviews to religious teachers (*malamai*). According to the new terminology, the credits of a number of video films no longer list actors under

the rubric of "players" (*'yan wasa*) but as "admonition deliverers" (*masu fa'dakarwa / masu wa'azi*). Opening credits usually start with a line that reads, "In the name of Allah," thus legitimizing a video film as sanctioned by divinity. In a similar manner, many video films end with a text line reading, "Thanks be to Allah the Merciful and Almighty."

(49)

Krings contends that these "conversion films" have two goals. First, they function as "a call for individual Islamic reorientation," aimed largely at the Hausa people who are already Muslims; second, they offer "a manual for the conversion of so-called pagans" who are not yet Muslims (53). As in Pentecostal movies, witchcraft looms as a threat to true believers. "Some plots have an Islamic scholar who fights against the occult," Krings adds, "a Muslim double of the Pentecostal pastor who fights witches and magicians in many southern Nigerian videos" (54). More creative and unorthodox storylines occur too, as in the film *Qarni*, set in "a Muslim city plagued by a mysterious vampire, who kills virgins by sucking their blood during nights of the full moon"; ultimately, the vampire is surgically restored to human form, converts to Islam, and returns to his non-Muslim village as a missionary of Islam (57). In short, and identically to Christian media, such films "portray Muslims as salvationists" (58) who combat the forces of falsehood and immorality.

Finally, of course, television and movies can be used to record and broadcast activity understood as conventionally religious, such as sermons, masses, and rituals. Michael Wilmore reports on a local cable channel that televised religious festivals in the town of Tansen in Nepal. Nepal is a country where Hinduism and Buddhism coexist, and both Hindu and Buddhist rituals were shown; interestingly, though, Wilmore states that one Hindu ceremony, Krishna Jayanti, was not televised. This leads him to two conclusions. First, media broadcasts of religious activity shape and to a certain extent create a "public sphere" or "public arena" in which citizens can become aware of and part of the happenings of the entire society; this public sphere/arena can have clearly integrating effects. Yet, someone must decide which events get televised, and Wilmore argues that Tansen's broadcast religion can be seen as

> a demonstration of how media representations of religious culture may be used to repro-
> duce the power of local elites. They reproduce hegemonic political order because
> many of the festivals that they televised are obviously focused upon elite circuits of
> exchange (i.e. between upper caste members of the Parbatiya and Newar communities,
> with agents of the state, and with INGOs that supported the organization).

(2006: 331)

It is worth reminding ourselves that not all individuals appreciate the representation of their religion on screen or specifically how it is represented. A 2013 episode of the American television series *Marvel's Agents of S.H.I.E.L.D.* caused an uproar when it insinuated that Vishnu, a Hindu god, might be an extraterrestrial. Rajan Zed, president of the Universal Society of Hinduism, expressed outrage at the insult to the sacred faith of millions of Hindus.

Vernacular Religion in Business and the Economy

For many Westerners and Christians, nothing could be more remote from, even incompatible with, religion than money and business. Elements of Christianity have long condemned wealth and economic activity, from Jesus' attacks on tax collectors and money lenders to the familiar threat that the rich have as much chance of reaching heaven as a camel does of passing through the eye of the needle. Yet not all religions share the disdain for "filthy lucre," and Christianity has certainly not been consistent in its censure of wealth: there have always been rich Christians and Christian institutions (like the Catholic Church), Max Weber believed that Protestantism was central to the consolidation of capitalism in Europe, and many contemporary Christians including evangelicals and Pentecostals subscribe to the "prosperity gospel" doctrine that God wants his people to be prosperous (see Chapter 8).

Further, many corporations or corporate owners do not keep their business and their religion separate. Some high-profile companies in the United States, such as arts and crafts store Hobby Lobby and fast-food restaurant Chik-Fil-A, conspicuously promote Christian beliefs and practices (for example, Hobby Lobby often places religious advertising in newspapers and closes its stores on Sunday) and Christian values (Chik-Fil-A has been active in resisting gay marriage). In-N-Out Burger has been known to print Bible verses on their packaging (see Figure 9.1), and clothing store Forever 21, which is not above selling sexy clothes to young girls, puts the verse of John 3:16 on the bottom of its shopping bags. Other less overt businesses often object to policies that violate their religious sensibilities, such as providing healthcare that includes reproductive services or offering benefits to gay partners of employees. And, of course, all of those Christian artifacts, from Bibles and crosses to priests' robes, are manufactured by some company.

Anthropologists have discovered even more intimate connections between religion and contemporary economic practices. John and Jean Comaroff, who analyzed the practical everyday experience of colonization (see Chapter 7), also remarked on the "dramatic rise" in the late twentieth and early twenty-first centuries of what they called "occult economies" or "the deployment, real or imagined, of magical means for material ends" (1999: 279).

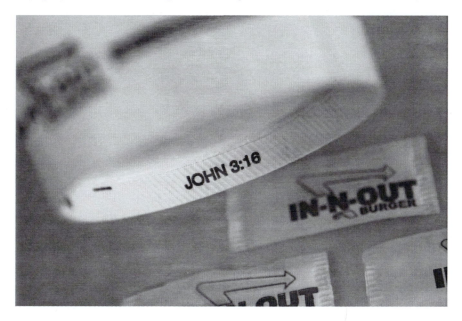

Figure 9.1 Bible verse printed on the bottom of a soda cup at an In-N-Out Burger restaurant. Photo by Patrick T. Fallon/Bloomberg via Getty Images

Among the expressions of occult economy they highlighted were "'ritual murder,' the sale of body parts, and the putative production of zombies," which led them to ask, "Why is all this occurring with such intensity, right now?" (279), especially when the world is supposedly modernizing and secularizing (see Chapter 11).

The Comaroffs argued that "the contradictory effects of millennial capitalism and the culture of neoliberalism" (279) were being experienced in spiritual terms, leading to bizarre spiritual responses. People literally felt assaulted by economic forces, as if their very bodies were being invaded; "hence the fascination with cyborgs, the fear of invasion by aliens clothed in humdrum bodily form, the dangerous promise of cloning and genetic mutation" (281). Equally if not more important, forms of work and production seemed to be perverted by global capitalism, as if evil spirits or humans harnessing evil powers were "diverting the flow" of work or wealth "for selfish purposes." The perception of bad spiritual intent in the economy led to two reactions.

> The first is the constant pursuit of new, magical means for otherwise unattainable ends. The second is the effort to eradicate people held to enrich themselves by those very means; through the illegitimate appropriation, that is, not just of the bodies and things of others, but also of the forces of production and reproduction themselves.
>
> (284)

Thus, for example, people around the world turn to witchcraft to attain success and wealth, or they accuse others of turning to witchcraft, resulting in witchcraft trials and/or the murder of alleged witches. As evidence, they reported that in the Northern Province of South Africa, there were 300 witch-related murders between 1985 and 1995, with another 676 in the first half of 1996 alone (285). All of this was taken seriously enough for the government to set up a Commission of Inquiry into Witchcraft Violence and Ritual Murders.

Witchcraft was not the only tactic to illegitimately steal other people's economic productivity. There was also widespread fear that malicious parties, "usually old people, were turning others into zombies; into a vast virtual army of ghost workers, whose life-blood fueled a vibrant, immoral economy pulsing beneath the sluggish rhythm of country life" (285). And these terrors manifested in other domains of popular culture, including in "comic strips, on the radio, on television, and the internet; almost every day newspapers and magazines advertise 'dial-in-diviners'" who could help determine who was bewitching or zombifying a victim (286–87). And the signs or provocations of witchcraft were mundane but valued commodities like "houses, televisions, cell phones" (288).

In short, the Comaroffs reasoned that occult economies were comprehensible religious responses to global capitalism, with its "ever more brutal forms of extraction" (290), its inherent unfairness, and its mysterious rules and operations. Some people got rich by inexplicable and probably illegitimate means, and occult economies were "about the desire to plumb the secret of those invisible means" and then "to stem the spread of a macabre, visceral economy founded on the violence of extraction and abstraction"

> (1) in which the majority are kept poor by the mystical machinations of the few; (2) in which employment has dwindled because of the creation of a virtual labor force from the living dead; (3) in which profit depends on compressing space and time, on cannibalizing bodies, and on making production into the spectral province of people of the night; (4) in which the old are accused of aborting the natural

process of social reproduction by preventing the next generation from securing the bases of its material and social existence—and youth, reciprocally, are demonized.

(293)

A startling example of spiritual infestation of the modern corporate world was described by Aihwa Ong in the late 1980s (Ong 1987; 1988). Women working in factories in Malaysia were, it was believed, suddenly and viciously attacked by "vengeful spirits," which caused the women to "explode into demonic screaming and rage on the shop floor" (1988: 28). Interestingly, Ong explained that prior to industrialization, spirits mainly afflicted older married women. "With urbanization and industrialization, spirit possession became overnight the affliction of young, unmarried women placed in modern organizations" (29). Accordingly, Ong judged that spirit assaults in both circumstances were related to the social pressures on women. In the village, spirit possession on women was "associated with their containment in prescribed domestic roles" as wife, mother, divorcée, or widow (32). As for young unmarried women, they were expected to be "shy, obedient, and deferential, to be observed and not heard" (33). However, in modern industrial jobs women were performing activities previously associated with males, in which they were active and exposed.

Not surprisingly, the symptoms of spirit attack mirrored their condition of being socially other-than-themselves: possessed young women would "speak in other voices that refuse to be silenced" and had no memory of the outburst afterwards (33). Even more, Ong found other cases too where it was believed that spirits afflicted females in factories "who had violated moral codes, thereby becoming 'unclean'" (33). Although, of course, not everyone interpreted the incidents as spirit possession at all—managers tended to blame it on "mass hysteria" without seriously questioning what would make young working women hysterical—Ong concluded that either way the episodes were "expressions of fear and of resistance against the multiple violations of moral boundaries in the modern factory. They are acts of rebellion, symbolizing what cannot be spoken directly, calling for a renegotiation of obligations between the management and workers" (38).

Morten Pedersen critiques the concept of occult economies in his analysis of spirit trouble in contemporary Mongolia. Emerging out of a socialist system in which, if nothing else, the economy was stable, people are subjected to the same global market forces that the Comaroffs described in South Africa. But Pedersen sees occult-economy explanations as symbolic or metaphorical projections of religious ideas onto economic experiences, whereas he opines that the Mongolian spirit world (and its associated shamanism) and economic world are "isomorphic," that they take the same basic form—that they are "both variations on one immanent state of transition" (2011: 35). To be sure, global capitalism introduces uncertainty into modern life (uncertainty of processes and uncertainty of outcomes), but Pedersen holds that this is precisely the message of spirits and shamans as well: shamans and the "restless spirits" with which they dealt "*were* uncertainty as such; they were materializations, actualizations, instantiations, and condensations of the all-pervasive state of cosmological turmoil variously called 'democracy,' 'transition,' or 'the age of the market'" (39). In short, shamanism and postsocialism share the same underlying logic, so amok spirits are not so much a new occult economy as the familiar reality of permanent and inescapable transition. Ironically, then, the problem for modern Mongolians in Pedersen's assessment is not *too many* religious actors trying to take advantage of economic opportunities (to coopt or hijack others' wealth and productivity) but precisely *too few* religious actors (that is, qualified shamans) who can manage the protean spirits.

Box 9.3 The Modern Islamic Corporation in Indonesia

Corporations can be places of spiritual havoc, as Aihwa Ong demonstrated, but they can also be sites of piety. In fact, contemporary business practices and religious ideas and values can be integrated more smoothly than many people imagine. One remarkable example is the industrial city of Cilegon in Indonesia, the most populous Muslim-majority country in the world. As Islam has become more prominent in Indonesian society, it has moved into more corners of that society. Daromir Rudnyckyj mentions the Salman mosque, located on the campus of Institut Teknologi Bandung (Bandung Technological Institute), where a professor of electrical engineering, Imaduddin Abdulrahmin, became a leader in the effort "to reconcile Islam with modernity," associating Islam with modern labor in his book *The Spirit of Tawhid* [oneness or monotheism] *and Work Motivation* (2010: 58). For Imaduddin,

> [T]he unity of God meant that all of one's activity is conducted in the name of God, not just activities that were recognizable as religious, such as going to mosque or performing requisite prayers. Thus, Imaduddin laid out the argument that there was an economic ethic inherent in Islam that could facilitate Indonesian development.
>
> (59)

Another key figure in what Rudnyckyj calls "developing faith" (that is, injecting faith into economic development, while at the same time developing the faith of modern workers) is Ary Ginanjar, a kind of Indonesian Muslim corporate guru and motivational speaker, who promotes a form of neoliberal Islam in programs like Emotional and Spiritual Quotient (ESQ) and Management of the Heart, which offer training sessions for corporate workers and managers. ESQ and similar programs operate from the simple but surprising premise that Muslim virtues are corporate virtues. "A central theme of ESQ training was that the origins of the twin pillars of Western modernity—science and capitalism—can be found in the Qur'an and the *hadiths*" (82–83). Having established that science and capitalism were authentically Muslim, the multi-day training seminars would go on to "claim that enhanced spiritual practice yields business success" (85). But much more than that, ESQ as well as Manajem Qolbu or Management of the Heart Corporation sought to construct a new kind of modern Muslim person, one who was rational and efficient, hard-working, self-disciplined, and personally responsible, attentive to time, clean, and moral. In this view, "faith itself became an object of development" (126)—and of the very same kind of neoliberal development found elsewhere, in which governmentality shifts from the formal institutions of government to other institutions like the corporation and the religion and ultimately to the self. Rudnyckyj calls this a "spiritual economy," in contrast to an "occult economy," because there is nothing occult or magical about this neoliberal Islam; rather, the whole point is that spiritual economies "focus on the process of rationalization inherent in capitalism" (133). They simply do so in the vernacular and with the legitimation of mainstream religion. Thus the three key components of spiritual economies are "(1) reconfiguring work as a form of worship and religious duty;

(2) objectifying spirituality as a site of management and intervention; and (3) inculcating ethics of individual accountability that are deemed commensurable with norms of transparency, productivity, and rationalization for purposes of profit" (131–32).

The Varieties of Pagan Experience

Paganism is often used as a synonym for vernacular religion or even more for folk religion. Many people understand paganism as folk religion or pre-Christian religion in the purest sense, which is how early Roman Christians intended the term: from the Latin *paganus* literally meaning "country folk," the word implied those people who still clung to the old, usually polytheistic religion of their ancestors rather than to the new and true religion. As paganism (sometimes written as Paganism) is found today, it does not necessarily involve pre-Christian or polytheistic religion, but it does indeed tend to convey a sense of past, even lost, religion.

Paganism does not refer to any one specific religion; in fact, some self-styled contemporary pagans do not consider themselves "religious" at all. Hence, "while there may be common threads linking current expressions of Paganism, it is important to remember that there is really no single thing that can be accurately termed Paganism" (Sage 2009: 36). Further, since virtually (some would say absolutely) no modern-day pagans actually follow ancient religions, many observers regard them as "Neopagans," which, according to Sarah Pike,

> covers a wide variety of beliefs and traditions that include re-creations of ancient Celtic Druidism (a British organization of sun worshippers who gathered in sacred groves), Wicca or Witchcraft, ceremonial magic, and neoshamanism (revivals of ecstatic journeys into the spirit world in indigenous and pre-Christian cultures).
>
> (2004: 19)

Vanessa Sage characterizes paganism as partaking in the spirit of Romanticism, an early modern European cultural movement that revered nature and sought to re-instill the "enchantment" that modernity seemed to have driven out of life and society (see Chapter 11 on secularization). Both paganism and Romanticism, she continues,

> are products of modernity; both emphasize imagination and emotion; both question the place of rationality in how we know what we know; both put stress on the individual and ask what his or her place is within a larger community; both look to the past for a model of the future; both are political, idealistic, and utopian at times; and both take nature to be the main vehicle for the realization of their goals.
>
> (2009: 36–37)

This purported attachment to the past is complicated and varied, though, since, as Pike maintains, in Europe

> contemporary Pagan organizations usually claim a lineage that is ancient and unbroken, often tied to nationalism and ethnic pride. American, British, and Australian

"Neopagan" communities differ in that they are self-conscious revivals created to be egalitarian, individualistic, and, in the American case, influenced by currents of apocalypticism and social change movements.

(2004: 19)

Thus it is necessary to treat continental European and American paganisms separately.

Continental European (Neo)Paganism

(Neo)pagan groups and movements are plentiful throughout Central and Eastern Europe, and although we might be tempted to categorize them as new religious movements, Piotr Wiench argues convincingly that they "in many respects do not fit the typical characteristics of a *religious* movement"; in fact, commonly "the groups inspired by Neopagan ideas might display a near-total lack of truly religious characteristics," being "more focused on the discourse of identity, and in some cases, even on an overtly political message" (2013: 13). Significantly, insofar as they are "religions" at all, Wiench recommends that we think of them less as pagan or ancient religions than as *ethnic* religions. Writing in the context of Hungary, Réka Szilárdi insists that the effect and intent of such religions is to "sacralize the nation," to make the society and its culture "stand out from other nations in origin and mission," and further to assert that "its fate influences the whole of human civilization" (2013: 233). The point, as Kaarina Aitamurto and Alexey Gaidukov find in the case of Russia, is to have *rodnaya vera*, "a faith of one's own" (2013: 150), that is, a faith that is specific to one's own people, history, and culture.

(Neo)pagans, both in Europe and the United States, are often avid readers of history, folklore, and ethnography, in their search for the (supposedly) authentic and often lost or suppressed origins and former greatness of their kind. In Hungary, for example, (neo) pagan movements "participate in this tradition of a radical reinterpretation of national culture and the historical origin of the nation, emphasizing 'national character,' the heroic past, and the continuity of ancient traditions," precisely because members object to what they perceive as "a 'falsified' mainstream history" that denies them their true and unique character (Szilárdi 2013: 231). As early as the mid-1800s Hungarian scholars like Arnold Ipolyi went in search of Hungarian folk culture, publishing *Magyar Mythológia* in 1854, a text that is still part of pagan discourse today. In the twentieth century, astounding claims of Hungarian historical connections to ancient Egypt or even Sumer were made. Pagan (and other) nationalism is of course also tied to land, and for some Hungarian (neo)pagans the Pilis Mountains are the site of ruins "from an ancient sacred center which was founded by Hunnish-Hungarian progenitors" (Szilárdi 2013: 233), to whom modern Hungarians are related in unbroken continuity. Key to this ancient spirituality was the shaman or *Táltos*, a religious visionary and healer. But the spirit of the Hungarian people need not be limited to this earth: Szilárdi finds that an "esoteric" version of Hungarian neopaganism, advanced by György Kisfaludy of the Church of the Universe, holds "rather astonishing views about the Huns' ancestors coming from Sirius [a distant star], and populating the ancient island of Atais in the Pacific Ocean which was destroyed in a worldwide disaster" (236). Among the more terrestrial organizations in the Hungarian (neo)pagan movement are the Community of Hungarian Religion, the Ancient Hungarian Church, Yotengrit Church, Solar Cross Movement, Firebird Táltos Drum Circle, People of Arpád Drum Circle, Church of Esoteric Doctrines (Church of the Holy Crown), and Ancient Hungarian Táltos Church (237). Running across these diverse institutions Szilárdi identifies some common themes, including the idea of the sacred nation, national/ethnic exclusivity and even intolerance, and therefore sometimes political activity that takes the shape of "xenophobia" as well as "anti-pluralist" (that is, anti-minority and anti-immigrant) and "anti-globalist" activism (244–45).

This association between paganism and intolerance, even violence, is even more pronounced in Russia (see Figure 9.2). Victor Shnirelman, following Vladimir Pribylovsky, notes two varying forms of neopaganism in Russia, one with a "less politicized folklorist" nature and the other with a "highly politicized national-patriotic" quality (2013: 63). For the nationalists, "Russian nationalism is the actual creed and ... Pagan beliefs and symbols legitimate the implementation of ethnic Russian rule and discrimination against non-Russians" (65). This has led, unhappily, to an alliance between neopagans and right-wing, including neo-Nazi/skinhead, organizations; Shnirelman mentions the Union of Slavic Communities of the Slavic Native Faith as one neopagan group with skinhead ties. Both wings of the nationalist movement can turn to actual violence against ethnic minorities as well as against Christian churches, which they view as false and foreign. Thus Shnirelman invites us to perceive Russian neopaganism "as both an ideology ... and as a fighting practice" (73). Interestingly, one other location for the vernacularization of (neo)pagan religion is hard rock, specifically heavy metal, music: Deena Weinstein (2013) calculates that pagan metal bands are most prominent in Eastern Europe, particularly in the former communist countries of Russia, Belarus, Ukraine, Lithuania, Poland, and Bulgaria. On the dark end of the hard rock spectrum, Benjamin Hedge Olson finds the origins of National Socialist Black Metal (NSBM) in Scandinavian countries; with its message that "the present is sick and degraded; the past was glorious and vital; the present must be destroyed and/or escaped in order to attain a meaningful existence" (2013: 137), Eastern Europe has developed "one of the most vibrant, fanatic and racist black metal scenes in the world" (146), although the United States "has become one of the most prolific producers of NSBM in the last ten years" (140).

Figure 9.2 Local people celebrate Ivan Kupala Day in Tervenichi, Russia. The celebration relates to the summer solstice and includes a number of pagan rituals. Courtesy of De Visu/Shutterstock

American (Neo)Paganism

Apparently the United States has its measure of nationalist/political paganism, but by and large the American version is a comparatively benign creature. Sarah Pike writes that (neo)paganism in the USA highlights "a desire to revive ancient pre-Christian nature religions" (2004: 19), and such faiths cannot generally contribute to a prickly politics of authentic ethnic American identity. Nevertheless, Americans share the (neo)pagan tendency to research the past and liberally lift elements from it:

> In the process of creating new religions in the cast of old ones, Neopagans borrow from American Indian and other available religious cultures. Neodruids often learn ancient Celtic languages and focus on their roles as caretakers of the woods. Neopagans who are intrigued by specific ancient cultures look to Tibetan, Greek, Roman, and Egyptian pantheons. They find ritual texts, usually in translation, and fashion their practice after mythological stories, such as the descent of the goddess Persephone into the underworld. Neopagans dressed as Aphrodite and Dionysus may put in appearances in Neopagan festivals, where rituals encourage participants to explore divine archetypes from ancient pantheons of deities.
>
> (19)

But the overall effect of American (neo)paganism tends to be a tolerant and inclusive religious attitude, much more in tune with environmentalist than nationalist issues.

In its earth-loving and individually empowering orientation, American (neo)paganism has much in common with nineteenth-century Spiritualism and the "mind cure" movement (see p. 222 below), which, also like Romanticism as discussed above, saw nature pervaded by and ultimately dependent upon spirit and promised people the power to live better and healthier lives. For (neo)pagans, then, the world is enchanted again, suffused with magic, which reunites what modern materialistic society has rent apart. As Pike puts it in another of her books, "Neopagans are committed to pursuing religious options that they think will bring about harmony between humans and nature, sacralize the body and sexuality, heal wounds caused by intolerance, and create healthy and peaceful communities" (2001: xiii).

In this earlier work of Pike's, as in much of the research on American (neo)paganism, the focus has tended to fall on ritual activities, including but not limited to large-scale festivals. In these collective gatherings,

> participants work to make an experience set apart from their lives "back home." They create place myths: composites of rumors, images, and experiences that make particular places fascinating. These myths may extol a place's vices as well as its virtues. Neopagans tell stories designed to locate the festival in an imaginary geography vis-à-vis the place-myths of other towns and regions which form the contrast which established its reputation as a liminal destination.
>
> (2001: 19)

What Pike calls "festival worlds" add a dimension that everyday life lacks, a dimension of the "fantastic and enchanting," and at such sites and events "the land itself, the trees, and the earth are invested with the desires and dreams of festival goers and become 'sacred' destinations for festival participants" (27). And contrary to the European experience, at such events the national and the spiritual are not merged but, if anything, the national is brushed aside in a spiritual universalism that binds spirit and earth but disregards nation, as in this song sung at Spiral Path's *Liturgy for Lady Liberty*, to the tune of "America" or "My Country 'Tis of Thee" (which by the way is also the tune of the British national anthem, "God Save the Queen"):

> Blessed and bounteous land,
> Safe in the Lady's hand,
> Of Thee I sing.
> Terrors are turned away
> Routed by freedom's ray;
> Chastened by light of day,
> All fears take wing.

(quoted in Chase 2006: 152)

Zohreh Kermani takes a different angle on American (neo)paganism, considering it as culture, since while adults may "convert" to (neo)paganism, their children are "second-generation (neo)pagans." This perspective allows us to see some of the processes, and contradictions, in the religion. As Kermani explains, (neo)pagans tend to revere children, attributing to them a singular kind of spiritual awareness and wisdom; adults also seek to cultivate childlike qualities in themselves. At the same time, (neo)pagan values of freedom and tolerance discourage adults from indoctrinating their children with their own religion, thus exposing children to (neo)pagan beliefs and practices while not imposing those beliefs and practices. Kermani cannot help but comment on the inherent threat to (neo)paganism, which unlike most religions actively eschews formal and mandatory religious indoctrination.

Another contradiction or tension is the fact that (neo)pagan adults frequently inhabit their own world of perpetual childhood, a kind of Neverland in which they "remember and imagine their own religious childhoods" (2013: 72) in ways that cannot help but affect, and even oppress, actual children. Too often, she claims, (neo)pagan adults appear to be on a mission "to reconstruct the religious worlds they wish they had inhabited" and thereby "to redeem their lost magical childhoods by shaping their own children's religious worlds" (73). A further problem of intergenerational interaction in (neo)paganism is those aspects of the religion that are too "adult" (including too sexual) for children, which makes child participation in ritual a thorny problem. Yet parents want to share their religion with their own children, but not impose it on them, so adults creatively innovate child-friendly and child-inclusive versions of ritual practices (a vernacularization of a vernacularization), which is not much of a problem given (neo)pagans' freedom to invent. Two specific inventions verging on institutions described by Kermani are the Spiral Scouts, a sort of Boy/Girl Scouts for (neo)pagan kids, and child-specific ceremonies like Wiccaning, a coming-of-age ceremony and (neo)pagan answer to christening. Whether all of these are enough to overcome the disadvantages of a generally non-institutionalized and non-imposed religion, only time will tell.

Vernacular Christianity in the United States

As the above discussion illustrates, the United States is and always has been a hotbed of vernacular religion. In fact, its most renowned early settlers were heretical groups of Christians, the "pilgrims" and Puritans, who practiced their own version of Christianity and could not find a home in England for it. From that time until today, Americans have been extraordinarily creative in their religion and extraordinarily willing and eager to express it in the vernacular. One reason is the Protestant character of America's core culture, which recognizes no central authority like the Catholic Church to check invention and deviation. American culture contains an even deeper anti-authoritarian streak, related to its egalitarian ideals, which would prevent Americans from conforming to any single vision or interpretation of religion. Additionally, the frontier nature of the United States for much of its history meant that people were remote, geographically and culturally, from centers of official religion, and there were always religious entrepreneurs who were ready to bring Christianity "to the people," in both senses of the phrase.

The First American Centuries

By the time that North America was settled, Christianity had already differentiated irrevocably into many churches, denominations, and sects. Within a century of the Plymouth colony (which, by the way, was a business venture of the Plymouth Company, which was chartered to found colonies on the eastern coast and which recruited enthusiastic Christians pilgrims to be among its settlers), the American colonies were experiencing their first "great awakening" of religious fervor. The years between 1720 and 1750 saw an explosion of Christian activity, most of it of a "grass roots" quality. New or expanding denominations like Baptism and Methodism emerged, even in the cities, but the urban and university elites were often regarded as men who studied and preached religion but did not *live* it and could not communicate it to the common folk. Their erudite sermons did not have the "fire" of a person enflamed by the Holy Spirit, and so they could not transmit that fire. This task fell to men of passion, if not learning, like Jonathan Edwards, George Whitefield, James Davenport, Charles Woodmason, Devereux Jarratt, and Samuel Morris. Such men were the first "circuit-riders" of American religion, itinerant preachers who traveled from village to farm to hamlet, stopping to spread the gospel in open-air or tent "revivals" wherever they could gather an audience. They spoke with the well-known enthusiasm of the evangelist—in fact, they were the first American evangelists, bearers of the "message" (*evangel* comes from the Greek word for messenger or bringing good news). Not only did they circulate among the masses, but they delivered the message in a style and language that the masses could digest.

About a century later (1820–50), a second great awakening and popularization occurred. One of its key features was the discourse of "primitive Christianity." Elias Smith, for instance, called for a simpler, more egalitarian kind of Christianity, one in which the masses could interpret the Bible for themselves; his followers eschewed even a name and merely referred to themselves as "Christian" or "Disciples of Christ." In this period, other more famous and enduring religious movements appeared, such as the Church of Jesus Christ of Latter Day Saints (Mormons), a truly American Christianity that asserted that Jesus had visited North America after his mission in Israel and that tribes of Hebrews had built a civilization on the continent. Followers of William Miller meanwhile predicted the end of the world in the 1830s (one of the more durable tropes in American Christianity), but when that prediction failed, some "Millerites" broke off to become Seven Day Adventists. Two wider social movements—utopianism and spiritualism/"mind cure"—spawned variations of Christianity, including, respectively, the United Society of Believers (the "Shakers") and the Church of Christ, Scientist (Christian Science).

An underappreciated current in American religion is transcendentalism, which can be traced back to Emanuel Swedenborg (1688–1771), whose writing such as *The Worship and the Love of God* and his eight-volume *Arcana Coelestia* maintained that the Christian Bible was not to be taken as a literal, historical document but as a spiritual code or allegory. He viewed existence as having three "levels" or "planes"—the physical (animal, vegetable, and mineral), the spiritual, and the celestial. Each of these planes reiterated the others, such that every entity on the physical plane (he called them "ultimates") had a corollary on the spiritual and celestial planes. Therefore there was no need for slavish obedience to or tortured interpretations of the scriptures; the point was to know one's relation to the higher realms of reality and to put one's affections and actions in order. These ideas were influential on American thinkers like Ralph Waldo Emerson and Henry David Thoreau, whose reverence for nature largely detached them from conventional Christianity; Emerson actually rejected old, literalist "religion" in favor of spiritual intuition. Religion as usually performed was little more than "the dead forms of our forefathers" (quoted in Marty 1984: 210), and Emerson and his peers literally asked Americans to "forget historical Christianity."

It might be argued that at least a contingent of Americans heeded their advice. American Christianity continued to morph into new and unprecedented vernacular forms, mixing popular notions of spiritualism and spirit-based health, esoteric doctrine, and Eastern religions and philosophies. Ever confident in the powers of the individual, even literally to think him/herself well, American adepts like Phineas Parkhurst Quimby (1802–66) conducted healing sessions after 1840, first using a hypnotized subject as his medium of diagnosis and cure. By the late 1860s Quimby dropped the partner and did his own curing, using a combination of touch, hypnotic gestures, visual imagery, and talk. For Quimby and his followers, the cause of illness was unhealthy thoughts and beliefs. Henry Wood represented another but familiar side of the mentalist movement, that is, the use of "visualization" or mental imagery. In his 1893 *Ideal Suggestion Through Mental Photography* he essentially appropriated Swedenborg's tripartite distinction (here, material, psychological, and spiritual), suggesting that humans exist on all three levels simultaneously but that disease results from fixating solely on the material. In reality, he suggested, neither illness nor healing is a purely physical process but a psychological/spiritual one too.

One other unfortunate American vernacular form of Christianity in the nineteenth century was the Ku Klux Klan, which appeared immediately after the fall of the South in America's Civil War. Offering a toxic mixture of Christianity, racism, and nationalism, it was suppressed by President Ulysses Grant in the 1870s but rose again in the 1920s, this time practicing the burning of Christian crosses along with the adoption of ancient esoteric titles like Hydra, Giant, Great Titan, and Exalted Cyclops. Yet a third incarnation of the KKK grew after the Second World War, in opposition to the civil rights movement, and its philosophy paralleled the Christian Identity movement and Anglo-Israelism, which identified true Christianity (even true humanity) with the white race or, still more narrowly, Anglo (English and American) whites.

The Twentieth Century and Beyond

The twentieth century brought deep changes to American society, facilitated by communication and transportation technologies. All of these innovations had their impact on American Christianity, beginning with the automobile and radio and followed soon by television and the internet. Jeffrey Hadden (1993) reported that the first remote radio broadcast in America was a Sunday evening service at the Calvary Episcopal Church in Pittsburgh in 1921. Meanwhile, by 1916 evangelist Aimee Semple McPherson began a preaching tour of southern states in her "Gospel Car," using a megaphone, although she soon discovered the power of radio to deliver her message. According to Hadden, a Catholic priest, Charles E. Coughlin, was the first radio preacher to reach a mass audience, going national in 1930, but none achieved the prominence of Bishop Fulton Sheen, whose Sunday night radio show "The Catholic Hour" launched in 1930 as well. The famous Billy Graham got a radio ministry of his own in 1944. Thus was born the era of televangelism, of remote and mass religious sermonizing, although the term is often reserved for television preaching.

Bishop Sheen moved into the television market in 1951 with a show called "Life is Worth Living," and many of Graham's "crusades" were televised as well. Rex Humbard held a weekly television service starting in 1952, and many national and local Christian figures joined the ranks of televangelists thereafter, including Oral Roberts, Jimmy Swaggart, Jim and Tammy Faye Bakker, Robert Schuller, and of course Jerry Falwell and Pat Robertson. It was not long before Christians were forming their own broadcasting systems, beginning with Pat Robertson's Christian Broadcasting Network in 1977, featuring "The 700 Club." Paul Crouch shortly thereafter founded the Trinity Broadcasting Network (TBN), and Jim Bakker responded with Praise the Lord (PTL) Network. In 1997, Marcus and Joni Lamb established Daystar, but by then many famous televangelists had suffered embarrassing falls from grace, including Roberts, Bakker, and Swaggart.

At the same time, following McPherson's humble Gospel Car, the automobile was reshaping the geographical and religious landscape of America. As Americans became more mobile and urban (and later suburban), American Christianity moved with them and learned to speak that vernacular. Just as Americans invented and embraced drive-in movies and drive-in restaurants, 1949 saw America's first drive-in church, when Reverend Norman Hammer of Emmanuel Lutheran Church of North Hollywood gave a sermon in a vacant lot. By 1955 Robert Schuller began holding services in a drive-in movie lot, where people could listen to preaching inside their cars through the same sound system used for movies.

As middle-class, office-working Americans moved to the suburbs mid-century, Christianity moved with them, evolving to be more suburban, middle class, and office-like. One of the most spectacular results was the "megachurch," which exploited abundant land and large dense populations to reach memberships in the thousands. Willow Creek Community Church in suburban Chicago, founded in 1975, is often credited as the first megachurch (see Figure 9.3). It was a project based on literal market surveys, investigating what kind of church experience locals wanted. According to Susan Harding, Jerry Falwell had already given the answer in 1971, insisting that "the church would be wise to look at business for a prediction of future innovation," and since business had given us "giant shopping centers," religion would do the same, "placing at least two or more services at one location to attract the customers" (2000: 16). In corporate vernacular, Willow Creek identified its "target demographic" and crafted a church service and a physical church space that middle-class suburbanites would enjoy. Revealingly, Stewart Hoover reported that a guide at the church explained that "you will see no Christian symbolism here at all. The metaphor or image we are trying to project here is corporate or business, not traditional Church" (2000: 145).

Figure 9.3 Sunday service at Willow Creek Community Church, Chicago © John Gress/Reuters/ Corbis

To some eyes, there is little religion at megachurches like Willow Creek—no crosses, no fire-and-brimstone preaching. The Sunday service is more like a show, with songs and skits and lectures. And, as Hoover added, megachurches "make certain that their parking lots are large and convenient. They provide childcare and other things which make attendance more accessible. Many have shops and coffee bars. Some provide recreational facilities, aerobics, and the like" (152). Indeed, like the megamall or shopping center of Falwell's imagination, the megachurch is characterized by a range of facilities, not all of which fall within the traditional realm of religion. Moreover, megachurches are often actually comprised of "a panoply of 'ministries'—typically support groups, fellowship opportunities, or combinations of these—pegged to the particular stresses and strains of contemporary life," including "parenting workshops; twelve-step recovery groups 'by category' (i.e., alcohol, drugs, gambling, etc.); premarital couples classes; classes for 'homebuilders'; a 'women in the workplace' brunch" (153), and so on. Justin Wilford notes the same approach in Rick Warren's Saddleback Church, the genius of which is "an infinitely specialized experience" (2012: 168), a loose congeries of micro-ministries that reflects and accommodates the fragmented quality of contemporary suburban life. As a geographer Wilford appreciates how Warren vernacularized Christianity to the spatial experience of the suburbs, promoting small groups that meet in members' homes; in Warren's strategy, not the church campus but the family home "is the center of most Saddleback members' spiritual lives" (111).

Finally, outside of the church system in the United States, Christianity has been vernacularized repeatedly in every new genre and subculture of American society. The 1960s saw the emergence of hippie "Jesus freaks," and the Gospels got a rock opera treatment in 1971 in "Jesus Christ Superstar" (made into a motion picture in 1973), not to mention the hippie Jesus in the Superman T-shirt of 1971's "Godspell." And ordinary believers have taken it upon themselves to render Christianity into every conceivable vernacular, such as

- The Church for Men (www.churchformen.com), offering ways to "man up your church";
- Christian Mingle (www.christianmingle.com), for Christian dating;
- Guitar Praise, a Christian version of the video game "Guitar Hero";
- "Veggie Tales," Christian cartoons for children;
- Christian Wrestling Federation (www.christianwrestling.com), using wrestling for "effective evangelistic outreach";
- Lord's Gym (www.lordsgym.org), for physical and moral strength;
- Gospel Light's Sonrise National Park Vacation Bible School (www.gospellightvbs. com/sonrise), for Christian camping;
- Cross the Sky Ministries (www.crossthesky.com), which teaches clown skills for Christianity.

Every imaginable genre of popular music also has its Christian version, from rock to country to rap. One of my favorites, for the gang-banger who is also a Christian, is "Banging for Christ" (www.youtube.com/watch?v=o5WLdvVEkpw). Meanwhile, even the scriptures themselves are not immune to vernacularization: the King James Version of the Bible is written in seventeenth-century vernacular, which the American Standard Version, the International Standard Version, the New Revised Standard Edition, and many more were created to update. And for those who feel that the existing Bible is full of "liberal translation distortions," there is the Conservative Bible Project (http://conservapedia.com/Conservative_Bible_Project). One unsuccessful attempt at vernacularization is the toaster that burns an image of Jesus onto bread, which Amazon removed from its site during the Christmas season of 2013.

Conclusion

Religion is found not only in the frozen words of scriptures and the orthodox teachings and rituals of experts and officials. Religion is lived and practiced by people inside religious institutions and outside of them as well. Further, as religion flows through a society it is refracted by language, class, gender, region, and other social variables, and as a composite phenomenon it absorbs the local culture as it is absorbed by that culture. The inevitable result is multiple vernacular expressions of the religion.

Religious authorities are often leery of vernacular religion, since it adds innovations and threatens the monopoly of religious institutions. But religious authorities also may endorse and adopt these vernacularizations, de-vernacularizing them and making them official and institutional. Yet, in the end, the official or institutional version of the religion is simply the vernacular that won the struggle between vernaculars and that imposes itself at any given time as *the* religion. However, if anthropologists focus only on the official religion, they will miss the dynamic diversity and ongoing evolution of religion.

DISCUSSION QUESTIONS

- What is vernacular religion, and what is its relation to official or orthodox religion?
- How and why is religion represented in popular modern media like television and movies?
- What is an "occult economy"?
- What is (neo)paganism, and how does it differ between continental Europe and the United States?

SUPPLEMENTARY READING (see website)

- *Representing Religion in Contemporary Japanese Manga*
- *Witchcraft and the Search for Fame in New York City*
- *Vernacular Muslim Education: The Gülen Movement*

10 Religious Violence

Some people would walk through fire for their religion. Christians in the Greek village of Agia Eleni do walk through fire during their ritual of the Anastenaria (see Figure 10.1). Brought to Greece a century ago by northern refugees, fire-walking is obviously not part of Orthodox Christianity, and the Anastenaria "have no sacred texts or written traditions" but acquire their special religious knowledge from experience as well as myths and legends (Xygalatas 2012: 91). Because the ritual was seen as unorthodox and even pagan, for years the church "persecuted the Anastenaria, often violently, beating the fire-walkers and burning their icons" (16). However, church leaders eventually accepted this vernacular expression of faith and even assumed some control over it, holding the ritual's icons of saints Constantine and Helen between performances. Walking on fire is the culminating act in a festival that lasts for three days and includes "various processions, music and dancing, an animal sacrifice, and ecstatic ritual dance" (90). Finally, the adepts walk barefoot over red-hot coals carrying the icons of their saints. Some walkers cross the coals more than once, some in pairs. Xygalatas noticed afterwards that "their feet showed no signs of burns whatsoever" (84).

In the early twentieth century, it is impossible to ignore the relationship between religion and violence. For example, according to Magnus Ranstorp (2003), the number of extremist religious movements of all types around the world tripled from the mid-1960s to the mid-1990s. At the same time, the number of religiously inspired terrorist groups grew from zero to about one-quarter of all known terrorist organizations. In the period from 1970 to 1995, religious groups accounted for over half of the total acts of world terrorism—all this before 9/11.

Not surprisingly, a virtual industry of literature on religious violence has appeared. However, all of these treatments, valuable as they are, suffer from three limitations. First, they tend to examine a limited variety of religions, usually only Christianity and Islam, with some mention of Judaism. Second, they tend to consider a limited variety of violence, mostly "terrorism" and "holy war." Third, they tend to defend one of two positions in regard to the relationship between religion and violence, either blaming religion for violence or excusing religion from violence.

Anthropology regards the issue of religious violence as more diverse and more complicated. A thorough comprehension of the violence that flows from religion requires a more comprehensive examination of religions. Furthermore, although understanding terrorism and holy war is vital, they hardly exhaust the variety of religion-based violence; rather, they are comparatively rare forms of violence. Finally, it is crucial to see that violence is neither inherent in nor inimical to religion. Rather, violence is a culturally constructed behavior, which arises out of specific social conditions that are not unique to religion but that are unfortunately common to religion.

Figure 10.1 Walking over hot coals in Agia Eleni © Pixelstock / Alamy

The Anthropology of Violence

Understanding religious violence demands that we understand religion and that we understand violence. The problem is that many people think that violence requires no understanding, that is a simple and obvious phenomenon, or that to understand it is somehow to condone it. The latter is particularly significant since a dominant attitude is that violence is always unacceptable. However, the near-universality of violence, the plethora of forms it takes cross-culturally, and the diversity of reactions to and evaluations of it make the anthropological approach to violence more problematic.

There are two main problems confronting those who would explain violence. The first is the notion that violence is by definition disordering, disruptive, indeed antisocial. Max Gluckman was one of the first anthropologists to redirect attention away from the presumed homogeneity and homeostasis of culture to internal division and conflict. Many if not all societies, he noted, are "elaborately divided and cross-divided by customary allegiances" that pit members of the society against each other in different ways (1956: 1). He actually considered this internal division and low-grade conflict to be integrative rather than disintegrative, since

> these conflicting loyalties and divisions of allegiance tend to inhibit the development of open quarrelling, and … the greater the division in one area of society, the greater is likely to be the cohesion in a wider range of relationships—provided that there is a general need for peace, and the recognition of a moral order in which this peace can flourish.
>
> (25)

Whether or not it is good for society, violence is certainly a part of society. The second problem, then, is the notion that violence is an objective, absolute, and unitary thing.

Such thinking should lead to a neat definition of violence, but such a definition—especially cross-culturally—has been notoriously difficult to devise. Instead, violence "is a slippery concept—nonlinear, productive, destructive, *and* reproductive. ... [It] defies easy categorization. It can be everything and nothing; legitimate or illegitimate; visible or invisible; necessary or useless; senseless and gratuitous or utterly rational and strategic" (Scheper-Hughes and Bourgois 2004: 1–2). There is little that all acts of violence share and that distinguishes them from acts of nonviolence; in fact, the exact same act can be judged as violence in one context and not as violence in another.

This raises the salient point that violence is not so much an objective quality of an act or actor as a concept and a *judgment*. As Nancy Scheper-Hughes and Philippe Bourgois go on to say,

> violence is in the eye of the beholder. What constitutes violence is always mediated by an expressed or implicit dichotomy between legitimate/illegitimate, permissible or sanctioned acts, as when the 'legitimate' violence of the militarized state is differentiated from the unruly, illicit violence of the mob or of revolutionaries. ... [M]ost violent acts consist of conduct that is socially permitted, encouraged, or enjoined as a right or a duty. Most violence is not deviant behavior, not disapproved of, but to the contrary is defined as virtuous action in the service of generally applauded conventional social, economic, and political norms.
>
> (5)

From this vantage, violence is not only a cultural judgment but a *political* one, that is, who gets to label—and therefore condemn—an act or actor is a matter of social position and power. As David Riches put it,

> violence is very much a word of those who witness, or who are victims of, certain acts, rather than of those who perform them. ... [W]hen a witness or victim invokes the notion of violence, they make a judgment not just that the action concerned causes physical harm but also that it is illegitimate.
>
> (1986: 3–4)

And the judgment of violence is a cultural and therefore a contestable one: a person, group, or society may label an act as violence, while another person, group, or society—or the same person, group, or society at another time—may label it otherwise. For instance, when I was young, whipping a child was not considered violence, but for many Americans today it is.

"Violence" as a label, then, is relative and constructed. In addition, it is one among a variety of social labels available to judge and condemn or condone behavior. The English language has a field of terms with differing but overlapping meanings, such as "conflict," "competition," "aggression," "hostility," "abuse," and so on. All such words/concepts carry some negative connotation but different definitions. At the same time, there is a parallel discourse—often enough applied to the same actions—that conveys a positive message, such as "self-defense," "justice," "right," "duty," and so on. Killing in self-defense is better than, more legitimate than, killing in aggression, even though the victim is equally dead.

Finally, various observers have commented that science, along with popular opinion, has tended to focus on the sudden, extreme, and exceptional "outbreaks" of violence—the ones that are least representative and least informative. Exceptional violence draws us away from the "violence of the everyday," what has been called "structural violence" or "symbolic violence," or merely from the routine, taken-for-granted practices and values that contribute to those outbreaks. Carolyn Nordstrom and JoAnn Martin (1992) insisted that it is not only naïve but dangerous to believe that violence only occurs when people are killing each other and ends when the killing stops; peace is not simply the absence of violence. Violence, like all other cultural phenomena, is "practiced," and it emerges from concrete circumstances, shaped by norms, beliefs, and values that are embodied by real-life individuals in particular situations.

The Constituents of Cultural Violence

The anthropological perspective suggests that violence is not (usually) something that "bad people" do but something that ordinary people do in certain social situations. To test this hypothesis, Stanley Milgram (1963) performed a classic experiment, asking average people to administer painful and potentially lethal electric shocks to other normal people as part of an alleged "teaching study." He reported that two-thirds of the subjects were willing to give the highest level of shock, even though the "victim" screamed in pain and then went silent. Of course, there was no actual victim or even actual shocking, but the subjects thought there was. His finding was that regular people will knowingly hurt others in certain circumstances, specifically ones where some authority urges them to do so and absolves them from responsibility for it.

Based on this and other research, the social psychologist Philip Zimbardo (2000) suggested that social factors are much more important than psychological ones in performing violence. In particular, he identified six factors that are effective in making good people do bad things:

1 indoctrination into a thought-system that rationalizes or legitimizes violence;
2 obedience to authority, with no opportunity for dissent;
3 anonymity and deindividuation (e.g. getting lost in a crowd or having your individual decision-making powers taken or suppressed);
4 diffusion of responsibility (e.g. "just following orders" or dividing the violent behavior among a group of people);
5 gradual escalation of violence;
6 dehumanization of the enemy or the victim.

Of these six, he felt that blind obedience to authority was the most dangerous.

One significant conclusion of these studies is that an essential ingredient for committing injurious actions is a lack of empathy for potential victims. In empathy, we feel the suffering of the others around us; when I am empathetic, it really does "hurt me as much as it hurts you." If one can inflict pain without experiencing pain, it is much easier. And if one thinks that the other *deserves* pain, or does not even feel pain, or is beneath the concern of the perpetrator (nothing more than "dirt," "a worm," "garbage," or otherwise subhuman) one can actually feel good while harming the other—or feel nothing at all.

We can thus identify a series of factors or conditions that contribute to the frequency, intensity, and "normality" of violence. The more of these dimensions or conditions that are met, the more likely and stronger the violence may be.

1. Incorporation into Groups. If humans have violent potential as individuals, that potential is increased dramatically in groups. And it is not a simple additive increase. Groups seem to have their own dynamics—not the least of which is creating an "out-group," an "other," a "not-us" against whom we can commit violence more extravagantly. Many commentators have noted the violent tendencies of groups. The philosopher Friedrich Nietzsche wrote in *Beyond Good and Evil* (section 156) that "Madness is something rare in individuals—but in groups, parties, peoples, ages, it is the rule." Sigmund Freud also argued that groups have their own distinct psychology, characterized by heightened emotionality and irrationality, increased excitability and agitation, and a kind of "suggestibility" found in hypnotic states. It is almost like, he opined, a sort of "group mind" emerges. Gustave Le Bon, writing over a century ago, gave an equally bleak assessment of the effect of groups. He maintained that groups

> do not reason, that they accept or reject ideas as a whole, that they tolerate neither discussion nor contradiction, and that the suggestions brought to bear on them invade the entire field of their understanding and tend at once to transform themselves into acts. We have shown that crowds suitably influenced are ready to sacrifice themselves for the ideal with which they have been inspired. We have also seen that they only entertain violent and extreme sentiments, that in their case sympathy quickly becomes adoration, and antipathy almost as soon as it is aroused is transformed into hatred. These general indications furnish us already with a presentiment of the nature of the convictions of crowds.
>
> (1896: 62–63)

2. Identity. Identity, one's sense of "who he/she is," is a complex cultural construction, consisting typically of four elements, all of which relate more or less directly to group integration. The first is a name. The basis for the name can be anything—language, territory, history, religion, race, or what have you—but it usually is derived from and shared by a group. The second is values or beliefs, which are also learned and shared with a group or a society and internalized as we grow. The third, which is the ground for the first two, is a certain amount of direct and personal interaction. The more continuous and intense the personal interaction, the stronger the identity, although other indirect sources—newspapers, television, etc.—can have major impact on identity formation too. Fourth, identity involves a sense of future or "destiny," of not only who we are or were but who we will be and what we will accomplish—individually or, significantly, as and with a group. Identity therefore necessarily separates individuals and groups from each other, intensifying the us-versus-them thinking that enhances violence.

3. Institutions. Groups are not merely collections of individuals but have their own structure and processes. The institutions of a group or society can promote or reduce conflict and violence, depending on their details. Social institutions include such factors as hierarchy and leadership, as well as stratification based on characteristics of class, race, ethnicity, religion, gender, etc. Gender institutions themselves often have direct effects on violence, especially on women, from generalized patriarchy and female disempowerment to specific practices like dowry or bridewealth, polygyny, or female genital operations. Government as an institution increases the violent capabilities of a society, especially its organizations of legitimate violence such as the military and police force. Some institutions like slavery are violent in their core. In short, institutions stabilize and perpetuate the group/society and, if it is violent, stabilize and perpetuate its violence.

4. Interests. Individuals and groups inhabit a world where resources are often in short supply and almost always unevenly distributed. They therefore have interests, by which we mean the practical demands or goals of the group, such as wealth, power, land, jobs, or education, as well as the "symbolic" goals like prestige, self-respect, rights, and recognition—or in the religious realm, purity or spiritual favor or heaven. Humans individually and groups collectively almost necessarily compete for their interests. Furthermore, often individuals cannot help but notice that their opportunity to achieve their interests is affected or determined by their group membership: one group may dominate or control valued resources and deny them to the other(s). The unequal and unfair distribution of resources, and the association of access or exclusion with group membership, can turn into competition, which can turn into conflict, which can turn into (deadly and prolonged, even genocidal) violence. That is ordinarily not the first step in the process; rather, competitions and disagreements escalate over time. Nevertheless, in this sense, violence can be "instrumental" or goal oriented, and it can be effective.

5. Ideology. An ideology is a model or view of how the world works, based on fundamental beliefs and values. As such, it is often immune to evidence and argument. Certain ideologies, like those of Mohandas (Mahatma) Gandhi or Martin Luther King, Jr., can contribute to nonviolence. However, other ideologies can make violence likely or even necessary. Violent ideologies tend to be *idealistic*, that is, to imagine an ideal, perfect world—often a future world—in which they have triumphed and instituted themselves. They are often *absolutist*, demanding that their way is the only way and dividing people into good and evil. Since those who share the ideology are the good ones, they are frequently *exclusivist*; outsiders or holders of other ideologies may be "enemies"—the ultimate "them" standing in the way of our ideal reality. This attitude may excuse or compel the suppression, defeat, or total eradication of the other. Thus such ideologies commonly operate on the premise of *good war*, even *cosmic war*, that the world is an arena of inevitable conflict. Finally, such ideologies are often empowered by a sense of *certainty*, that the ideas and the group are infallible and invincible and therefore that everyone else is doomed to defeat or destruction.

Notice that religion is not a unique or inherent aspect of any of these five criteria of violence. The claim we are making is not that religion is alone in fulfilling these conditions. Quite the opposite: political, racial, linguistic, gender, even "special interest" (e.g. radical ecological) groups, institutions, and ideologies can meet all of the conditions and have been observed driving people to violence. Our claim is precisely that religion is *not* unique as a source for violence. Humans are violent in many ways for many reasons. However, religion is not exempt from fomenting violence, because, in some forms, it meets these five conditions exquisitely. Religion is always a social and a group phenomenon. It frequently contributes greatly to individual and collective identity. It seeks and depends on institutionalization. It almost invariably establishes interests (spiritual as well as practical) and thereby creates not only a "moral community" but an "interest community." And its ideology *can* incorporate absolutist, idealistic, exclusivist, and unquestioning beliefs and goals. Not all religions meet these criteria equally well, but when they do, violence—seen from the members' perspective as *legitimate violence or not as violence at all*—should be no surprise.

Religion as Explanation and Justification for Violence

Religion is part of culture, and violence is part of culture. It is almost inevitable, then, that religion and violence would become entangled. Two particular ways in which religion meets violence are as explanation and as legitimation. That is to say, religion must help people make sense of the empirical and undeniable violence in the natural and social world, and it can itself also serve as a reason for and justification for violence in certain situations against certain targets.

As discussed in Chapter 1, one common theory of or approach to religion is as an "intellectual," problem-solving, question-answering phenomenon. And one of the recurring questions that humans ask is, Why do bad things happen? Why is there evil or violence or misfortune, etc. in the world? And more specifically, why did it happen to me and mine? Since the existence of pain and struggle is irrefutable, no religion would be taken seriously that did not offer some insight into—and some remedy for—these undesirable happenings. Also, as a model of and for the world, religion *can* offer explanations and answers in ways that no other human thought system can.

The religious explanations of violence are as myriad as religion itself. In large part, the explanation that a religion offers will depend on the beings, forces, concepts, and specialist roles that it posits. One familiar reason for violence in the human world is humans themselves. In the Christian tradition, human "free will" is the cause of much suffering: humans are free to help or harm and frequently choose to harm. In Christianity, human failings can even be used to explain "natural evil" like predation, aging, and death: according to Christian beliefs, there was no death at all in the world until humans disobeyed and subsequently brought death and pain down upon themselves and upon the natural world as well. In other words, all of reality suffers for the foibles of humanity.

There are also other kinds of especially powerful and pernicious humans, such as witches and sorcerers. Some religions attribute almost all hardship and misfortune to such human operators. As we saw in Chapter 3, the Azande explained everything from crop blights to hunting failures to bad moods to infertility in terms of witchcraft; "any failure or misfortune ... upon anyone at any time and in relation to any of the manifold activities of his life ... may be due to witchcraft" (Evans-Pritchard 1937: 19). Sorcerers and witches used an array of natural and supernatural substances and forces to do their dirty work and often aimed it at those who had offended or violated *them* in some way.

A common, probably universal aspect of religion is the assertion that harmful or at least capricious nonhuman beings or "spirits" exist (see Chapter 2). Some of these beings plague humans because it is their nature and pleasure to do so, like Spiro's thirty-seven *nats* in Thailand. An infinity of demons, ogres, devils, and the like inhabit the religions of the world. In addition to malevolent spiritual beings, there are the spirits of plants, animals, and other natural phenomena that simply demand the attention and respect that they deserve as "persons"—like the "spirit-owning beings" of Ainu religion—and may inflict harm on humans for failure to treat them properly. Deceased humans too, the ancestors, can cause all sorts of troubles for the living. !Kung or Ju/hoansi ancestors (//gauwasi or //gangwasi) were the direct bearers of much misfortune, and Tallensi ancestors determined a person's "evil destiny."

In other religions, impersonal supernatural forces could often account for the misery of humans. From the ancient Greek notion of fate to *mana* and *chi*, such forces were seen as influencing or setting the course of one's life, for good or ill. The Hindu–Buddhist concept of *karma* meant that the bad that one did came back to him or her, in the next life if not sooner; there was a supernatural cause and effect that explained a person's fortunes or misfortunes. Buddhism perhaps most elaborated this view and made it central to the religion, in the idea of *dukkha* or suffering. In fact, among the Four Noble Truths, the first is simply and inevitably that existence itself is *dukkha*; the subsequent truths explain the cause (attachment or desire), the cure (detachment or extinguishing desire), and the method to implement the cure. However, the religion does not promise an alleviation, much less a defeat, of suffering, but merely an acceptance and overcoming of it.

Finally, in religions with gods, the gods themselves may be the architect of human ill. For instance, one or more gods may specialize in tribulation, such as a god of war or a god of disease. Suffering may be divine punishment or "justice" for wrongdoing, if the god(s) take(s) a moral interest in humans. On other occasions, adversity could be a warning. And some gods simply have a malevolent nature. Christianity tends to emphasize the positive qualities of its god, overlooking the fact that he stated, "I make peace, and create evil: I the Lord do all these things" (Isaiah 45:7). In other traditions, the trouble that befalls humans comes from the struggle between a good god and an evil god or being, with humans caught in between. It may have been an evil god/being who unleashed suffering on the world in the first place, as in the Zoroastrian claim that Angra Mainyu—a kind of "anti-creator" god—introduced the serpents, plagues, "plunder and sin," unbelief, "tears and wailing," and the 99,999 diseases into the otherwise perfect creation of Ahura Mazda, the good god.

Not only does religion explain why violence and other burdens exist in the world, but it also frequently explains why such things are *necessary, good, even noble*. Many religions see certain kinds of violence on certain occasions against certain entities as tolerable, moral, or even commanded.

From the smallest and most "traditional," religions make room for some forms of sanctioned violence, as we will explore in more depth below. For instance, religions that accept the reality of witches often consider it acceptable and desirable to punish or execute them. Individuals who violate religious taboos, break sacred moral injunctions, blaspheme, or deny religious beliefs may be subject to sanction including death. However, there can be no doubt that the translocal religions have offered more extensive and elaborate justifications for violence and have practiced it on an unprecedented scale. A concept like "holy war" would make little sense to most local religions. "World religions" created a dualism of believers and non-believers that rendered violence possible if not inescapable: groups that feel themselves in possession of the "one true religion" have little sympathy or tolerance for divergent groups. Clearly, the god of the Torah/Old Testament ordered violence against other societies as well as disobedient or disbelieving members of his own society:

> And they warred against the Midianites, as the Lord commanded Moses; and they slew all the males. ...
>
> And the children of Israel took all the women of Midian captives, and their little ones, and took the spoil of all their cattle, and all their goodly castles, and all their goods. ...
>
> [Moses said] Now therefore kill every male among the little ones, and kill woman that hath known man by lying with him.
>
> But all the women children, that have not known a man by lying with him, keep alive for yourselves.
>
> (Numbers 31:7–18)

Islam too, inheriting the monotheistic absolutism of Judaism and Christianity, ordains violence in the name of religion.

> So when the sacred months have passed away, then slay the idolaters wherever you find them, and take them captive and besiege them and lie in wait for them in every

ambush, then if they repent and keep up prayer and pay the poor-rate, leave their way free to them; surely Allah is Forgiving, Merciful.

(Qur'an, sura 9:5)

O you who believe! fight those of the unbelievers who are near to you and let them find in you hardness; and know that Allah is with those who guard (against evil).

(sura 9:123)

Like many ideologies that tolerate violence, the perpetrators of religious violence can see *themselves* as victims of abuse or persecution and their acts therefore as self-defense; they also demonize the enemy, who deserves no better treatment.

[P]ersecution is graver than slaughter; and they will not cease fighting with you until they turn you back from your religion, if they can; and whoever of you turns back from his religion, then he dies while an unbeliever—these it is whose works shall go for nothing in this world and the hereafter, and they are the inmates of the fire; therein they shall abide.

(sura 2:217)

While monotheisms are particularly prone to such attitudes, they are not alone. Hinduism, for instance, justifies violence and war through its concepts of *dharma*, *karma*, caste, and reincarnation. The classic statement comes in the *Bhagavad Gita*, in which the warrior Arjuna contemplates the upcoming battle where he will face friends and kinsmen in the opposing army. Prepared to throw down his weapons in despair, his chariot-driver, the god Krishna, explains why war and killing are not only necessary but moral: Arjuna is a *kshatriya*, born into the caste of warriors, as are his opponents. To kill is his duty, his *dharma*, as it is theirs. It cannot be immoral to do one's spiritual duty; rather, it would be immoral *not* to fight and kill. Even more, since humans are really spiritual beings and not material bodies, no harm can come to any combatant; a warrior can only kill the body, not the spirit, and such a death actually *benefits* the spirit, which has died well and dutifully. How will you grieve for what cannot be destroyed, Krishna admonishes him, since the spirit is "unharmed, untouched, immortal"? Birth, death, and duty are all ordained, so what is there to be sad or guilty about?

The Diversity of Religious Violence

Religion and violence are clearly compatible, but they are not identical. Religion is complex and modular, and violence is one of its modules—not universal but recurring. As a conceptual and behavioral module, violence is by no means whatsoever exclusive to religion. Violence is neither essential to nor exclusive to religion. Nor is religious violence all alike. There are numerous manifestations and motivations for violence in the name or the service of religion. Any religion may condone some and condemn others. And virtually every form of religious violence has its non-religious counterpart.

A few scholars have tried to make theoretical sense of religious violence, most of them non-anthropologists. Probably the two most influential thinkers on the subject are René Girard and Walter Burkert, both of whom have argued for a vital connection between violence and religion. Girard's influential analysis, *Violence and the Sacred* (1977), posited that religion is fundamentally linked to violence but in a surprising way: religion does not produce violence, but *violence produces religion*. Humans as social creatures, he insisted, unavoidably experience tensions and conflicts with each other. The cause of this problem, Girard theorized, is "mimetic desire," that is, that members of society learn to value and desire the same things and thus to compete over them. Humans are invariably rivals and obstacles to each other, breeding hostility and violence. Allowed to proceed unchecked, this internal violence would tear society apart through fights, feuds, vendettas, civil wars, and so on. Religion provides a solution through the projection of violence away from the real rival and onto a substitute victim, a "scapegoat." This is not a "symbolic" act, he insisted, since it must be real to the actors. Girard ended up equating violence to sacrifice and equating religion to a control system to prevent the spread of violence. Religion is, in the final analysis, "another term for that obscurity that surrounds man's efforts to defend himself by curative or preventative means against his own violence" (23). Thus Girard expected to find violence (sacrifice) in societies without other more formal, "judicial" means of handling competition and conflict.

For Burkert, religious violence was related to the human practice of hunting. In his book *Homo Necans*, he theorized that humans became human through the act of the kill (hence the title, meaning "killer man"). Yet, as crucial as hunting was, the experience was horrifying: prehistoric hunters, he believed, felt shock and anxiety at the death they caused. These intense experiences—"the shock of the deadly blow and flowing blood, the bodily and spiritual rapture of festive eating, the strict order surrounding the whole process"—are the very fount of the religious sentiment, the "*sacra* par excellence" (1983: 40). "Thus," he concluded, "blood and violence lurk fascinatingly at the very heart of religion," with sacrifice again playing the paradigmatic role of religious violence (2).

Sacrifice

Since it has occupied such a central place in discussion of religious violence, it is tempting to start with the topic of sacrifice. The very word means "to make sacred" (from the Latin *sacer* for "holy" or "sacred" and *facere* for "to make or do"). Sacrifice entails the damage or destruction of some object, often a living being, for a supernatural purpose. In one of its first sociological treatments, published originally in 1898, Henri Hubert and Marcel Mauss defined it as "a religious act which, through the consecration of a victim, modifies the condition of the moral person who accomplishes it or that of certain objects with which he is concerned" (1964: 13). In Durkheimian style, they saw sacrifice as a mediation between the poles of sacred and profane, represented by the sacrificer and the supernatural entity to which he/she sacrifices. In the process, the object is removed, literally, from the profane world and "sacralized" so that it can be transferred to the sacred world in a sort of supernatural communication and exchange.

Other analysts have offered various views. Tylor saw sacrifice as a gift to the divine, while Frazer interpreted it as a ritual control of death, and Robertson Smith as predominantly a communal meal. More recently, Meyer Fortes stressed that sacrifice "is more commonly a response to a demand or command from supernatural agencies or else a rendering of a standard obligation, than a spontaneous offering"; it entails "an element of demand, certainly of persuasion, on the donor's side" (1980: xiii–xiv).

From the anthropological perspective, sacrifice is not only a destructive act and a mandated and therefore appropriate act but also a social act. The nature and meaning of the social exchange and mutual obligation implied has often been viewed through Judeo-Christian eyes, as a matter of "cleansing sin" or currying God's favor or, as Girard emphasized, scapegoating (i.e. substitutive killing). And if scapegoating is the paradigm of sacrifice, the offering of Abraham's son Isaac to God is the paradigm of scapegoating. However, Judeo-Christianity is not the only religious tradition of sacrifice, nor is scapegoating the only type of sacrifice in Judeo-Christianity. The scriptures mention "peace offerings" (Exodus 20), "trespass offerings" (Leviticus 5:19), "sacrifice of thanksgiving" (Leviticus 22:29), and "jealousy offerings" (Numbers 5:15), among others.

Evans-Pritchard studied sacrifice among the Nuer cattle-herders of East Africa, where it was a regular practice (see Figure 10.2). There it had nothing to do with scapegoating but rather seemed to occur in two circumstances. The first related to "changes of social status and the interaction of social groups" such as male initiation into adulthood. The second involved "situations of danger arising from the interventions of Spirit in human affairs," which threatened "the moral and physical welfare of the individual" (1954: 21). The key quality of sacrifice for the Nuer appeared therefore to be "the efficacy of the rite," its actual effects on people, property, and spirits, which were "regarded as physical and immediate" (25).

Blood sacrifice is a remarkably widespread practice. Hinduism began as a fundamentally sacrificial religion. Early Hindu texts like the Vedas consist primarily of hymns and instructions of sacrifice, and the god Agni, literally the deity of fire, was the "ruler" of sacrifice, and sacrifice was a critical if not *the* critical ritual act. Ancient Greeks and

Figure 10.2 Nuer sheep sacrifice. Photo by E. Evans-Pritchard, *c.*1935. Courtesy of Pitt Rivers Museum, University of Oxford

Romans practiced animal sacrifice, such as the *buphonia* or ox sacrifice to the god Zeus and sacrifices for the Roman gods. Historian Fred Naiden's recent re-examination of Greek sacrifice argues that social theories of sacrifice like those of Girard and Burkert "wrote the gods out of sacrifice" (2013: 4), countering that those rituals acts should be understood as "a performance for an invisible audience of one" (19), a performance that ordinarily included a request and expected a response.

The Aztec and Mayan sacrificial practices are particularly famous and particularly "political." At least three major themes combined to produce these prodigious religious killings, including of humans. One was a belief that the sun was a tired and hungry god who needed a constant flow of blood to rejuvenate him and keep him returning every day. The second was the model of the gods themselves. According to one Aztec myth, the god Huitzilipochtli had been born fully grown and fully armed for battle from the womb of the goddess Coatlicue. Born a war god, Huitzilipochtli fought with his sister Coyolxauahqui and other gods and defeated them. His sister's broken body, beheaded and dismembered, landed at the bottom of the stairs of his temple (Matos Moctezuma 1984: 136). Subsequent human sacrifices at the main temple at Tenochtitlan in present-day Mexico City re-enacted this victory: human victims were killed at the top of the temple, ideally by having their beating heart ripped out, then they were bled, and finally their bodies were tossed down the stairs to land where and as the vanquished goddess had fallen. In some particularly macabre rituals, priests would flay the skin off of the victims and wear it themselves, transforming themselves temporarily into gods. The third theme was an overtly political one: the Mayan and Aztec emperors proclaimed their political and military prowess by leading vast sacrifices, often of defeated enemies, in a theater of absolute power over life and death.

In the kingdom of Dahomey the living king and the spirits of dead kings demanded sacrifice on such occasions as a royal death, the construction of a new palace, the initiation or conclusion of a war, the opening of a new market, and the ceremonies to feed his ancestors (Herskovits 1938). The existence of sacrifice practices in societies like those presented above contradicts a prediction by Girard, that sacrifice should disappear where complex political and judicial systems replace substitutive-symbolic justice. Further, there is no ethnographic evidence of sacrifice traditions in foraging societies, where both Girard and Burkert most expected to find them. Instead, sacrifice is closely associated with animal domestication (it is almost always domesticated animals that are offered) and with centralized governments, in which victims are killed for and by the ruler.

Box 10.1 Sacrifice in the Hawaiian Kingdom

Pre-conquest Hawaii had a highly developed political system, verging on state status. Sacrifices were common in and critical to this system. They were performed for a wide variety of purposes, including life-cycle occasions like birth, marriage, and death; work- or production-related activities such as building a house, setting fishing nets, and cultivating crops; to combat sickness and ritual and moral failures; natural increase and protection, such as to bring rain or fertility or to protect against sharks or volcanoes; and as part of sorcery and divination. Each of the many deities on the islands required their specific sacrifices, of species or objects that were associated with it. Many of the victims were also associated with humans, such as domesticated animals, or had metaphorical connections with humans, like bananas and coconuts. In some cases, humans themselves were offered. Among other things, the sacrifices were food for the gods, who ate the "essence" of the offering and left the rest to share among the human participants, who were "supposed to absorb divine mana" (Valeri 1985: 56). The king was not only the political leader but the paramount sacrificer. In this role, he was seen to partake of "the nature of the god on whom his actions are efficacious" and even to be "a human manifestation of this god" (131). The king, by conducting or at least authorizing sacrifice—especially the ultimate sacrifice, human—proclaimed and established, literally *performed*, his role as highest of men. In a word, "The king is king, therefore, because he is the head of the cult, the supreme sacrificer, the man closest to divinity" (140). Therefore, being the supreme sacrificer was not only part of his political power but *the source of his political power*: "It is precisely this that gives him authority over men, since it makes his actions more perfect and efficacious than theirs" (142). "He is, in sum, the point of connection between the social whole and the concept that justifies it" (142)—namely, the supernatural and its demand for victims.

Long before the speculations of Girard and Burkert, a lesser-known scholar named E. O. James in 1933 suggested that sacrifice is not about death at all but about life:

> In the ritual of shedding blood it is not the taking of life but the giving of life that really is fundamental, for blood is not death but life. The outpouring of the vital fluid in actuality, or by substitute, is the sacred act whereby life is given to promote and preserve life, and to establish thereby a bond of union with the supernatural order.
>
> (1971: 33)

In other words,

> [the] fundamental principle throughout [instances of sacrifice] is the same; the giving of life to promote or preserve life, death being merely a means of liberating vitality. ... Consequently, the destruction of the victim, to which many writers have given a central position in the rite, assumes a position of secondary importance in comparison with the "transmission" of the soul-substance [to whatever being or purpose it is intended].
>
> (256)

This explains why sacrifice is so common and so crucial to maintaining the *power* of supernatural beings, of social roles (like king), and of physical *but cultural* items like buildings, farms, and *domesticated* animals. Sacrifice illustrates a natural/social/supernatural complex that is caught in an *economy of life* in which vitality must be spent here to invest there.

Self-mortification

If there is a universal expression of violence across religions, it is probably not sacrifice but rather self-mortification—any of the thousands of ways in which humans deprive, injure, or even kill themselves for spiritual reasons. Its very universality makes it an incredibly diverse phenomenon, with many variations and many justifications. Shamans in training often underwent painful ordeals, such as insect bites, food and sleep deprivation, drug ingestion, and physical operations. Ritual participants frequently had to observe behavioral strictures on food or sleep or sex. Initiations typically included direct or indirect infliction of pain, in the forms of circumcision, scarification, "female circumcision" or female genital mutilation, nasal septum piercing, tooth removal, and so on. While religion is ostensibly about the spirit, it often seeks and even needs to be inscribed on the body.

The ultimate act of religious self-destruction is martyrdom, killing oneself or allowing oneself to die for a religious cause. In a way, it can be construed as self-sacrifice. Judaism to a certain extent and Christianity to a much greater extent have elevated martyrdom to a righteous act. Arthur Droge and James Tabor titled their book on martyrdom *A Noble Death* (1992), as dying is viewed by the actor and often the audience as superior to living in a desecrated state. For instance, in the text known as *Testament of Moses*, a father urged his sons to "let us die rather than transgress the commandments of the lord of lords" (quoted in Droge and Tabor 1992: 72). The Books of Maccabees give more models: Eleazar, for instance, was ordered to eat unclean food but instead, "welcoming death with honor rather than life with pollution, went up to the rack of his own accord ... as men ought to go who have the courage to refuse things that it is not right to taste" (2 Maccabees 6:18–20). The end of the siege of Masada, where the entire population killed themselves rather than be taken prisoner by the Romans, shows the extent to which they embraced death over surrender of religion.

Martyrdom became a fixture of early Christianity, partly because it emulated the paradigmatic act of Jesus. Some, like the early church father Tertullian, came to positively revel in the notion, seeing it as not just the only way to salvation but as a great and glorious choice: "condemnation gives us more pleasure than acquittal" (quoted in Droge and Tabor 1992: 136). "I strongly maintain that martyrdom is good," he preached (146), and many others concurred. Origen regarded martyrdom as a kind of baptism that removed sins, while Cyprian opined that "death makes life more complete, death rather leads to glory" (quoted in Smith 1997: 91). Ordered to worship the Romans gods, Carpus and Palylus eagerly ran to their deaths (Droge and Tabor 1992: 138). Vivia Perpetua actually assisted in her own death by steadying the executioner's sword against her neck, according to *The Passions of Saints Perpetua and Felicity*. Indeed a great number of "acts of martyrs" or "lives of martyrs" are collected in Christian literature.

Non-fatal mortification like self-flagellation has appeared recently as a practice in parts of the Philippines (where a hardy few have even been known to crucify themselves), and "penitential" self-flagellation has also been performed in European Christianity and its offshoots, such as the Penitente Brotherhood in New Mexico, which practiced it in the nineteenth and early twentieth centuries and in some areas may still do so. Michael Carroll (2002) claims that self-flagellation was introduced to Spanish colonies as a technique of Christian conversion, as a sort of "social disciplining"—a "theatricality of blood" that evoked a strong emotional reaction and commitment to Catholicism. The behavior eventually institutionalized into the "Brothers of Blood" with roles and ranks of discipline and self-mortification.

Islam has its own tradition of martyrdom, as evidenced by the verse in the Qur'an, "And whoever obeys Allah and the Apostle, these are with those upon whom Allah has bestowed favors from among the prophets and the truthful and the martyrs and the good, and a goodly company are they!" (sura 4:69). Martyrdom in Islam is called *shahadat* and a martyr a *shahid*, from the Arabic word that means "witness" (which is also the root meaning of the English word "martyr"). While traditionally Muslims have not sought martyrdom as eagerly as Christians have, it is still a noble destiny. For at least some

Figure 10.3 Self-flagellation with chains and blades during Ashura. Courtesy of Majid Saeedi/
Thinkstock via Getty Images

Muslims, martyrdom follows from the historical model of Hussein or Husayn, who was killed in the early days of the religion. Shi'ite Muslims sometimes perform self-mortification during their rituals. In the festival of Ashura, the devout flagellate themselves across the back with blades attached to whips to taste martyrdom (see Figure 10.3). Mary Elaine Hegland painted such a scene:

> different circles and rows of men, bared to the waist, were energetically beating themselves on the chest in rhythm with their chanting. They stayed in place for some time and then moved up a short way before stopping again. Whenever the sound of clanging metal arose, people ran in the direction of the noise to see men striking their backs with chain flails ending in knives, for the few moments before others forced them to quit their bloody self-mortification. As men cut away at their backs, blood ran down, soaking their shalwar [loose pants] sometimes even to the ankles and showing up in striking red contrast against their pure, white cotton pants.
>
> (1998: 245)

Although women were not free to participate with the men, Hegland explains that women found their own way to inflict pain by beating their chests and heads. During a re-enactment of the death of Hussein,

> the women started rapidly hitting their heads with the hands in agitation. They cried out their grief to Zuljinnah [Hussein's riderless horse] in verse with louder voices. The reverberation of their fists knocking their heads rang out sharply, replacing the hollow sound made by the thump, thump, thump of hundreds of palms whacking chests.
>
> (246)

Asceticism is another very common form of self-mortification across religions, in which people intentionally damage or deprive themselves. Ascetic behaviors can include extreme isolation, self-starvation, sleep deprivation, lack of sanitation, poverty, silence, and of course sexual chastity, or any other action that makes life difficult or uncomfortable (like wearing scratchy clothing, sleeping on hard surfaces, or exposing oneself to heat or cold). It can also include deliberate infliction or acceptance of pain. The monastic tradition (secluding oneself in a monastery) derived from such individual feats of ascetic rigor.

Talal Asad studied medieval Christian monasticism as a set of "disciplinary practices" intended to "regulate, inform, and construct religious subjects" (1987: 159). The first lesson, according to Asad, was obedience, which is, ironically, an act of will: the monk "who learns to *will* obedience ... is a person for whom obedience is *his* virtue" (159). Asceticism, with its confinement and continuous monitoring of the ascetic, also "aimed to construct and reorganize distinctive emotions—desire (*cupiditas/caritas*), humility (*humilitas*), remorse (*contrition*)—on which the central Christian virtue of obedience to God depended" (166–67). Because sin, most immediately experienced through the emotions and cravings of the body, was a constant problem, asceticism functioned as "techniques of self-correction" (192).

Hinduism shares some of the anti-body ideology characteristic of Christianity, as the following passage from the *Maitreya Upanishad* (1.3) illustrates:

> Lord, this body is produced just by sexual intercourse and is devoid of consciousness; it is a veritable hell. Born through the urinary canal, it is built with bones, plastered with flesh, and covered with skin. It is filled with feces, urine, wind, bile, phlegm, marrow, fat, serum, and many other kinds of filth. In such a body do I live.

Thus asceticism, especially in its more extreme forms, is founded on a religiously inspired conception of sinful or vile self and offers a method and discipline "to become a different person, a new self, to become a different person in new relationships; and to become a different person in a new society that forms a new culture" (Valantasis 1995: 547).

Most religions suggest asceticism as a path for the elite few. Buddhism, on the other hand, essentially teaches that every human is or should be an ascetic; although some practitioners commit themselves more completely to the goal than others, the ideal Buddhist life is a self-denying one. Hinduism, in addition to full-time ascetics, offers renunciation as a life stage for any man who, in his old age, wants to dedicate himself solely to spiritual advancement. After his social duties of family and household had been satisfied, a man ideally was to become a *sannyasin*, abandoning the world and its pleasures and wandering as a poor spiritual athlete. The path was not as open or proper for women, although Lynn Denton (2004) found a group of female ascetics or *sannyasini* in contemporary India who engaged in ritual fasting and sexual abstinence; they literally organized themselves into formal ascetic communities or subcultures with sects and leaders and ranks and rituals. However, for the vast majority of Hindu women, self-denial and self-destruction awaited their husbands' death, when rather than live as a widow they were ideally to kill themselves by joining their husbands on the funeral pyre to become a *sati* or "pure one." Numerous mythical and historical models established this paradigm of womanly and wifely devotion.

Box 10.2 Female Ascetics in Jainism

Jainism is an Indian religion that appeared around the same time as Buddhism, renowned for its extreme nonviolence. Named for the ideal status of a member as a *jina* or conqueror (one who has conquered the passions and frailties of the body), Jains avoid killing even animals or insects, and the "religious virtuosos" of the faith can choose to become Digambars or "sky-clad monks," who "go naked, travel widely on foot, eat only once a day, and practice difficult forms of self-mortification" (Carrithers 1989: 219). The Digambar monk may not bathe or sit while eating, and he takes a vow of *Sallekhana*, to end his life by starvation rather than continue to destroy other beings. Such asceticism is fundamentally for males, since women are typically considered unfit for such discipline and since it is considered inappropriate for women to appear nude in public or to abandon their wifely and maternal duties. Yet Manisha Sethi found a sect of female *sadhvis* (the female version of *sadhu* or ascetic) among the Jains (see Figure 10.4). Like their male counterparts, they had renounced mundane life and taken vows of poverty and chastity. Yet, in ways beyond their very existence in a patriarchal religious system, these pious women challenge stereotypes about asceticism. While accepting deprivations and a monastic-style life, they do not entirely detach themselves from the world nor do they all come from poor or tragic backgrounds such as widowhood, as is widely assumed. Sethi determines that many women voluntarily choose the way of a *sadhvi* before they marry or even while they are married. Primary among their motivations is a positive view of asceticism, that it represents "a loftier, spiritual plane" (2012: 99). Some joined after being inspired by a *sadhvi*, often a kinswoman. But most selected the hardships of an ascetic over the hardships of the normal life for women. Indeed, Sethi asserts that the life of a wife and mother can be more unpleasant and more burdensome than the life of a renouncer; within their culture, "a woman can be individuated only through renunciation" (130). Nor is the choice entirely selfless or self-destructive: "Jain *sadhvis* are firmly embedded in a web of social relations" (186), involving them in the lives of laywomen through receiving gifts of food and offering in exchange sermons, instruction, ritual leadership, and social services "that undertake welfare activities in the field of health and education" (186)—what Sethi calls "an ethic of care" (188).

Figure 10.4 Nuns (*sadhvis*) attend a religious ceremony at a Jain temple in India. Courtesy of Daniel J. Rao/Shutterstock

Persecution

Persecution ranges from mild discrimination and intolerance to active hostility to genocidal violence; the unifying aspect of these practices is the disapproval of one religious community by another. Every religion, of course, creates a community of believers, which in turn creates a community of non-believers, essentially everyone else in the world. Religion, then, establishes a fundamental us-versus-them dynamic. However, not all religions promote this dichotomy equally—or at all—and not all act on it as strenuously. "Local" religions never expected that all humans would share the same beliefs and practices; geographically and socially limited beings, forces, rituals, and symbols constituted their religious reality. But other kinds of religions—especially those that make universal, totalistic, absolute claims to truth and morality—are more prone to religion-based intolerance and conflict. These include the translocal religions.

Persecution requires not only belief but power. However, it is a tragic lesson of history that the persecuted tend to become the persecutors once they attain power. In Christianity's early years, it was persecuted. Most of this hostility resulted from their refusal to conform to Roman imperial religious conventions, like sacrificing to the emperor. Once Christianity came to power in the empire, it practiced persecution too. For example, when religious orthodoxy was established by the Council of Nicaea in 325, all dissenting views became heresy. Such heresies included the claim that God was not a trinity or that Jesus was not divine or that the sacraments of the church were wrong or unnecessary. In 380 Theodosius set penalties for deviation from official doctrine, ranging from fines and loss of property to banishment, torture, and death; in 385 Spanish bishop Priscillian and six of his followers received the honor of being the first to be put to death under the new edicts, by decapitation.

Tertullian was only the most extreme advocate of persecution when he wrote,

> How shall I admire, how laugh, how rejoice, how exult, when I behold so many proud monarchs, and fancied gods, groaning in the lowest abyss of darkness; so many magistrates who persecuted the name of the Lord, liquefying in fiercer fires than they ever kindled against the Christians.
>
> (quoted in Freke and Gandy 1999: 243)

Augustine and Aquinas agreed. In fact, Augustine asserted that persecution and execution were not only justice but kindness: the church killed "out of love ... to reclaim from error to save souls" (quoted in Levy 1993: 48). Accordingly, there was unjust persecution and just persecution, namely "an unjust persecution which the wicked inflict on the Church of Christ, and ... a just persecution which the Church of Christ inflicts on the wicked." Aquinas argued that some crimes deserved capital punishment and that blasphemy and "unbelief" were the worst of crimes. Therefore, heretics

> by right ... can be put to death and despoiled of their possessions by the secular authorities, even if they do not corrupt others, for they are blasphemers against God, because they observe a false faith. Thus they can be justly punished more than those accused of high treason.
>
> (52)

The Inquisition, established in the 1200s, was the most institutionalized form of European religious persecution, aimed first at "protesting" Christian sects and eventually at

Jews and Muslims. Non-Christians who did not convert to Christianity, or who converted but were suspected of "backsliding" or secretly following their old religion, were often tortured and killed. Martin Luther, who barely escaped the Inquisition himself, was unfortunately no champion of tolerance: in 1530 he called for imprisonment, torture, and death for *other* heretics like Anabaptists and accepted the persecution of Jews.

Many religions have conducted or suffered their own forms of persecution. Hindus and Muslims have persecuted each other, and continue to do so, along the India–Pakistan border. The religion of Sikhism in Kashmir was born, and became militarized, from religious clashes on the Muslim–Hindu frontier. Local tribal religions were widely suppressed and persecuted under European colonialism, and religions of all kinds were persecuted by communist governments in the Soviet Union, China, Cambodia, and elsewhere. In the attempt to purge society of religion, functionaries of every faith were defrocked, sometimes forced to marry, publicly ridiculed and "re-educated," and more than occasionally killed; religious properties were seized for secular uses or simply destroyed.

Jews have been particular targets of persecution in the Western world, for a variety of reasons. They have been the most populous and prominent group of non-Christians in generally Christian societies. They sometimes held positions of wealth and power. And, of course, they were often accused of being the "murderers of Christ." Throughout European history they were segregated into ghettoes, made to wear identifying clothing, barred from certain occupations or social positions, and periodically uprooted or terrorized. In imperial Russia, recurring pogroms forced them from their homes. The very model of modern religious persecution, the Nazi Holocaust, was only and overtly the "final solution" to what had been perceived as a problem by many Westerners for many centuries.

Holy War

The notion of holy war presupposes the notion of war. While virtually all societies have had their more or less violent episodes, not all have practiced war, by which we mean a prolonged, coordinated effort by a more or less formal "military institution" to conquer, often to occupy the land of, and sometimes to vanquish or even exterminate another society. Most anthropological analyses of war suggest that it is a characteristic of state-level political systems—perhaps a *defining* characteristic of such systems—and that this form of politics typically occurs, again, with the world-religion form of religion.

Holy war, then, is probably unique to exclusivist, universalistic religions. Not only does each see itself as sole possessor of the truth and therefore as in mortal competition with all other religions (local and world), but each may find itself at some time in alliance with or possession of the apparatus of state, including the military. Islam is the religion most closely associated in most people's minds with the doctrine of holy war or *jihad*, but the Christian concept of *crusade* means precisely the same thing. Both can trace their roots to the ancient Hebrew doctrine of *milhemet mitzvah* or commanded/obligatory war. As Jewish scriptures and history prove, their god regularly ordered them to war against certain neighbors, making such war not only holy but mandatory. At least according to some commentators and traditions, *milhemet mitzvah* also included or allowed for self-defense, including preemptive wars to prevent an expected attack; some commentaries even suggest that wars to expand God's territory are obligatory. Like later Islamic practice, ancient Hebrew war first required an offer of peace to the enemy, which of course meant surrender and servitude to the conqueror; if they refused the "peace offer," the godly army could destroy them or enslave them righteously. Compared to some later versions of holy war, the ancient Hebrew variety was not meant for conversion but for eliminating "abomination" and keeping the religion integrated and "pure" against foreign influence.

Islam is most often held up as the model of holy war. As in Christianity, the religion perceives the world as basically dualistic, with a domain of peace where true religion reigns (*dar al-islam*) and a domain of conflict and struggle where religion is absent (*dar al-harb*). The domain of peace is naturally where Islam is observed. The domain of strife is where it is not—but where it should and will be.

Jihad, the generally known word for holy war, actually does not mean "war" in Arabic (which is *qital*). *Jihad* means "struggle," including the so-called "greater *jihad*" of struggle against one's own immoral self and the "lesser *jihad*"—the *jihad* of the sword—of struggle against the enemies of religion. Despite this distinction, the lesser *jihad* can and does employ real weapons and cause real death. As the Qur'an instructs: "Permission (to fight) is given to those upon whom war is made because they are oppressed, and most surely Allah is well able to assist them" (sura 22:39), so "slay the idolaters wherever you find them" (sura 9:5; see pp. 235–6 above). As in ancient Hebraic war, unbelievers are given the option to give up their irreligion and accept the truth, but if they fail to, war is authorized. Islam also sees this violence as defense, namely defense against persecution.

The Sikhs of Kashmir and Punjab valued war in the name of the faith. Sikhism (from the Hindi word for "disciple") was born in struggle, specifically the struggle between Hindus and Muslims in the sixteenth century. A guru named Nanak proffered a new religious vision and movement that accepted aspects of both. However, first the Muslim rulers and later the Hindu ones opposed and suppressed the religion, martyring the guru Arjan in 1606. Thus in 1699, the last human guru, Gobind Singh, instituted a military wing of religious purists, the Khalsa or "company of the pure." As a contemporary Sikh website expresses it:

> Readiness for the supreme sacrifice or of offering one's head on the palm of one's hand to the Guru is an essential condition laid down by the Gurus for becoming a Khalsa Sikh. Seeking death, not for personal glory, winning reward or going to heaven, but for the purpose of protecting the weak and the oppressed is what made the Khalsa brave and invincible. This has become a traditional reputation of the Khalsa. Right from the times of the Gurus till the last India–Pakistan conflict (1971), the Sikhs have demonstrated that death in the service of truth, justice and country, is part of their character and their glorious tradition. They do not seek martyrdom, they attain it. Dying is the privilege of heroes. It should, however, be for an approved or noble cause.
>
> (Gateway to Sikhism: 2005)

Many religions in addition to Sikhism have not only justified war but actually established their own warrior organizations, like the various orders of knights in Christendom. Many of these orders were formed for or during the Crusades by the church, such as the Order of St. John of Jerusalem, the Knights of Malta, the Teutonic Knights, and the famous Knights Templar. Article 3 in the constitution of the Teutonic Knights is direct in saying:

> This order, signifying both the heavenly and the earthly knighthood, is the foremost for it has promised to avenge the dishonoring of God and His Cross and to fight so

that the Holy Land, which the infidels subjected to their rule, shall belong to the Christians. St. John also saw a new knighthood coming down out of heaven. This vision signifies to us that the Church now shall have knights sworn to drive out the enemies of the Church by force.

("The Rules and Statutes of the Teutonic Knights" 1969)

The same philosophy has appeared in other places and times, such as medieval Japan, where groups of fighting Buddhist monks (*sohei* or "priest warriors") were created. Wars between monks and monasteries broke out in the tenth century, at which time the temple of Enryakuji established the first standing army of monks in the country. Perhaps the greatest of these Buddhist armies was the Ikko-Ikki (Ikko meaning "single-minded" or "devoted" and Ikki meaning "league" or "mob"), which conquered an area around Kyoto in the 1500s. As T. Dugdale Pointon (2005) describes it,

> With their belief in a paradise waiting for them the warrior monks of the Ikko-Ikki were fearless and eager warriors proving very useful to whichever side they were aiding at the time. In battle they would often use mass chanting (*nembutsu*) to strike fear into their enemies and improve their own morale.

Of course, each religion constructs its notion of religious war along its own religious principles. According to Surya Subedi, "there is no justification in Hinduism for any war against foreigners or people of other faiths" (2003: 339). However, in keeping with the Hindu concept of *dharma*, there was a distinction between *dharma yuddha* or righteous war (war that follows *dharma*) and *adharma yuddha* or unrighteous war. Righteous war conformed to a number of rules, including a formal declaration; prohibitions against certain weapons; bans on harming women, children, the elderly, or soldiers in retreat; and norms of humane treatment of prisoners. Most distinctively, Hinduism provided a warrior caste, the *kshatriya* (like Arjuna in the *Bhagavad Gita* tale told above), and ruled that only the military class should make war, thus limiting war's size and scope. In other words, what made war "righteous" in classical Hinduism was not that its cause was holy but that it conformed to expectations of righteous behavior, in particular "to prohibit inequality in fighting and to protect those who exhibit helplessness" (357). War was not to be waged "to spread the Hindu religion or to contain the spread of another religion" (346).

Ethno-religious Conflict

As a modular social phenomenon, religion can easily become intertwined with other identities and interests. When a pure or hybrid religious group and/or its interests are threatened, or merely blocked from achieving its interests by another group, conflict and violence may ensue. In such cases, although religion is part of the issue and religious groups form the competitors or combatants, it would be simplistic or wrong to assume that religion is the *cause* of the trouble or that the parties are "fighting about religion." Religion in these circumstances may be more a marker of the antagonists than an actual point of contention between them.

Nevertheless, religion is an element in a number of the main "ethnic conflicts" of the twentieth and early twenty-first centuries. Catholic versus Protestant in Northern Ireland,

Christian versus Muslim in Bosnia, Hindu and Muslim versus Sikh in Kashmir, Hindu versus Buddhist in Sri Lanka, Sunni versus Shi'ite in Iraq—in all these cases, the belligerents are distinguished by religion. Still, it would be more accurate and useful to view these conflicts as clashes of *communities* and identity—of interest groups—rather than of religious doctrines. A clear example is the sectarian violence since 1969 in Northern Ireland. Protestants and Catholics were locked in violence occasionally verging on civil war for almost three decades but *not* over matters of religion. In fact, they were not different religions but denominations of the same religion. In the USA and elsewhere, Protestants and Catholics coexist without collapsing into sectarian strife. Since the same doctrinal differences hold in Northern Ireland as in the USA, those differences are not the major or real source of friction. Rather, being a Protestant or being a Catholic *in the Northern Irish cultural context* makes a critical difference, in terms of economic and political interests. For one, the Protestants—a two-thirds majority in the region—tend to be "unionists," that is, desire to maintain the union of Northern Ireland and the United Kingdom; Catholics tend to favor disassociation from the UK and integration with the Republic of Ireland. One obvious reason for the disagreement is that Catholics compose a majority of the Republic but a minority in Northern Ireland; conversely, Protestants, a two-thirds majority in Northern Ireland, would become a minority in a unified Irish state. In addition, Protestants occupy most of the positions of power and control most of the wealth in the north. Catholics perceive themselves as an underclass, with segregated neighborhoods, schools, etc., based on their religion. What originated as a "civil rights" struggle, after a failed attempt at secession from the UK, eventually escalated and transformed into an "ethnic" conflict.

Escalation and hardening of "ethnic" claims and identities is the usual process in such scenarios. In Kashmir, a contested region north of India, Sikh nationalists hope for a Sikh homeland; however, both Indian/Hindu and Pakistani/Muslim authorities claim the area as their own. Hostilities there led eventually to an Indian attack on the Golden Temple of the Sikhs at Amritsar in 1984. In the Middle East, tensions between Jews and Muslims have seethed since the nineteenth century, as Jews began immigrating to reoccupy their historical homeland. When the state of Israel was established, local Arabs/Muslims launched a campaign to crush the state, leading to a series of wars and the formation of various violent extremist groups like the Palestine Liberation Organization, Hamas, and Hezbollah dedicated to the destruction of Israel. In this case, issues of sovereignty, land, wealth, and political power blend with historical religious differences and hatreds.

Despite Buddhism's reputation as a religion of peace, Buddhist Sinhalese in Sri Lanka engaged in a struggle with Hindu Tamils for the better part of fifty years. Tamils, around 15 percent of the island's population with their own language and history, sought inclusion in the post-colonial government, but increasingly nationalist Sinhalese not only excluded them but enacted discriminatory laws against them, including an official language act (Sinhalese), an official religion act (Buddhism), and voting, citizenship, and education acts. Still worse, the Sinhalese felt like an "oppressed majority" since they existed nowhere in the world except on this island, whereas the Tamils had a "homeland" on the Indian subcontinent. Worst of all, they saw themselves as the original and therefore rightful occupants of the island—a claim even sanctioned by the Buddha himself—and Tamils as invaders or interlopers. A struggle for equality transformed into a struggle for separation and a Tamil state, a bitter war that only ended in 2009 with the defeat of the militant Liberation Tigers of Tamil Eelam (also known as Tamil Tigers).

Box 10.3 Religious Conflict and "Ethnic Cleansing" in Bosnia

The coexistence of religious groups often results from conquest followed by conversion. In the case of Bosnia, Muslim Turks invaded the area in the fourteenth century, maintaining control until late in the nineteenth. Many locals converted to Islam, for reasons discussed in Chapter 8—relief from religious restrictions, access to wealth and power, assimilation, and no doubt sometimes genuine belief. Serbs, who migrated northeast to escape Turkish influence, held tightly to their Eastern Orthodox faith, while Croats to the northwest kept their Catholicism. When the state of Yugoslavia was created after World War I, attempts were made to minimize "national" and "ethnic" differences, but by the 1990s Yugoslavia began to disintegrate along national lines. Five "nations" (*nacija* or *narod*) had been recognized—Serbs, Croats, Slovenes, Montenegrins, and Macedonians—each with a national home republic; Muslims had not been regarded as a nation but instead were considered apostate Serbs or Croats. During the 1940s and 1950s, most Bosnian Muslims identified themselves as "Yugoslavs" first and Bosnians or Muslims second, although they had been allowed to establish some religious institutions, like the office of *Reis-ul-Ulema* (the national head of Muslims) and *vaqf* (charitable) organizations. However, in 1961 a new category was added to the census—"Ethnic Muslim"—and by 1964 Muslims were recognized as a "nation."

Then, with the rise of Islamic fundamentalism in Iran and elsewhere (see Chapter 12), other Yugoslavs began to suspect Bosnian Muslim sympathies and motives. Anti-Muslim writings appeared, such as Vuk Draskovic's 1982 novel *Noz* (*The Knife*), portraying ugly stereotypes of Muslims. The Serb thinker Dragos Kalajic insisted that Muslims did not belong to "the European family of nations" but were culturally and genetically the product of foreign invasion and race mixing: "in satisfying their sexual impulses ... the Ottoman armies and administrators—drawn from the Near Eastern and North African bazaars—created a distinct semi-Arab ethnic group" (quoted in Cigar 1995: 26). Fears increased such that in 1983 Alija Izetbegovic (who eventually became the president of Bosnia) and twelve other Muslims were put on trial for "conspiring to transform Bosnia into an Islamistan," and all were found guilty. While there was undoubtedly some pure religious hatred involved, there were also political and economic motives: Serb nationalists wanted to expand Serb power and territory in the region, and other Serbs could not help but notice the relative economic deprivation of their homeland compared to more "developed" areas like Croatia and Slovenia. When these relatively wealthier republics withdrew from Yugoslavia in the early 1990s with fairly little resistance, Bosnia decided to follow, so in early 1992 it declared independence. However, the ethnic composition of Bosnia—roughly 45 percent Muslim, 34 percent Serb, and 17 percent Croat—made it largely ungovernable. Some Serbs and Croats alike regarded Bosnia, with Izetbegovic as president, as a Muslim polity with a captive Serb or Croat minority, so Bosnian Serb and Bosnian Croat militias were formed and autonomous regions declared. Between the ethnic militias and the Yugoslav army (which was basically an instrument of Serbia by this time), a policy of clearing Muslims (and sometimes Croats and other minorities) out of once or future Serb land was adopted—a policy known as "ethnic cleansing." As Cigar described it, ethnic cleansing

> was neither a spontaneous expression of communal hatreds, extending back over
> a millennium, nor was it a primeval popular emotion, which the ... leadership
> could not control. On the contrary, in seeking to develop a vehicle for its own
> acquisition and consolidation of power, the ... elite (both governmental and
> non-governmental) found it necessary to engage in a systematic and intensive cam-
> paign in order to create a nationalist movement and to exacerbate intercommunal
> relations to the extent that genocide could be made plausible.(6)

The outcome was not only a near genocide but the near destruction of a country
and a culture.

Abuse, Crime, and Murder

Not every crime perpetrated by a religious person is a "religious" crime; otherwise,
almost all crimes would be religious crimes. Also, many religious people commit abuses
and crimes not because they are religious but because they are abusers and criminals, as
the child sex abuse scandal facing the Catholic Church (but not *only* the Catholic
Church—there are Protestant and other offenders too) amply proves. However, just as
religion is not immune to violence, it is not immune to crime. Even so, in this discussion
we want to restrict ourselves to abuses and crimes that are committed for explicitly religious reasons. As such, they are often not interpreted as "abuses" or "crimes" at all by
the perpetrators but as necessary and even good actions.

Among the most lurid crimes is the murder of children by their mothers. Andrea Yates,
the Texas woman who killed her five children (named, significantly, Noah, John, Paul,
Luke, and Mary) in 2001, stated that her motivation was religious. She told doctors
afterwards that

> My children weren't righteous. They stumbled because I was evil. The way I was raising
> them they could never be saved ... Better for someone else to tie a millstone around their
> neck and cast them into a river than to stumble. They were going to perish [in Hell].
> (quoted in Baker 2002)

Two other women, Deanna Laney and Dena Schlosser (of Tyler and Dallas, Texas
respectively), also killed their children for religious reasons. Laney, a Pentecostal, beat
two of her children to death with stones because, she claimed, God told her to. Schlosser,
a member of the Way of Life Church, killed her ten-month-old because she wanted to
offer her to God. And studies indicate that they are not alone. Lisa Falkenberg cites two
studies that link religiosity with child-directed violence. One found that of thirty-nine
women who killed their children, fifteen had religion-related motivations; the other concluded
that one-fourth of its fifty-six child-killing mothers had religious "delusions" (Falkenberg
2004)—although at the time at least they did not consider them delusions at all.

In fact, in some instances the violent deaths of children or adults have been part of a more
systematic belief. The case of the Lafferty brothers became infamous in Jon Krakauer's
bestselling book *Under the Banner of Heaven* (2003). On July 24, 1984, Ron and Dan
Lafferty murdered the wife and daughter of their brother Allen because God had told
them to do it. Members of a fundamentalist sect of Mormonism, they are unrepentant to

this day, reasoning that if God orders an action, there is no way to disobey. Similarly, when Jacques Robidoux starved his infant son to death in 1999, it was on God's orders. Robidoux was a member of an offshoot of the World Wide Church of God known only as The Body. Members believed that they received "leadings" or direct messages from God, one of which told Jacques to deprive his baby of solid food. Over fifty-two days, baby Samuel wasted and died.

Christianity is certainly not the only religion that has driven people to murder. A Hindu group known as Thuggee practiced ritual murders into the nineteenth century. Members would infiltrate bands of travelers and assault them with ceremonial weapons like a magical pickaxe (*kussee*), a special scarf or cloth (*rumal*) for strangling victims, or a sacred dagger. Victims were dismembered and buried in collective graves, on top of which the successful killers would hold rituals. All of this was done at the behest of the goddess Kali, who demanded the dead as sacrifices to her. Religious models and values play at least partly into the too common modern practice of bride-burning or "dowry death," in which husbands or their mothers injure or kill wives in staged "kitchen accidents." An abusive but not generally fatal biannual ceremony known as Kuzhimattru Thiru Vizha involves burying a child alive "briefly" as a thanksgiving gesture; the child is supposedly drugged into unconsciousness and then laid in a shallow grave and covered with dirt for up to a minute while priests pray over them.

In Muslim societies, as we have mentioned, girls are most often the objects of harm and abuse, as in "honor killings" for behaving inappropriately, including having sex before marriage, dating outside of the religion or ethnic group, or just "acting too Western." In more than a few cases, especially when living in Western countries, families have sent younger brothers to do the deed, since Western law deals more leniently with minors. Females in these and many other societies are often married young and physically abused in their marriages, on the grounds that men have spiritual authority over women. And in a number of societies—at least eighteen, as surveyed by Dickeman (1975)—families killed one or both of twins, on the belief that twins are evil or unnatural or a bad omen of some sort.

Not all religion-inspired deaths are intentional murders; some, like the Robidoux case, are more like religion-inspired criminal neglect. Most modern people would consider depriving a sick person of medical care to be a form of neglect, but it is a controversial subject that a variety of religious groups claim the right to decline medical care for themselves or their children in favor of spiritual cures. Not only do many religious groups reject scientific medicine, but American law often grants a "religious exemption" from safe and effective medical treatments. The result, as Seth Asser and others have noted, is a high rate of preventable death. In the study that he and Rita Swan conducted of religiously motivated rejection of treatment, 172 child deaths occurred (from causes like diabetes, dehydration, trauma, infections, heart conditions, and tumors), of which 104 would have had a 90 percent survival rate with modern medical care (Asser and Swan 1998). The belief that parents were doing something effective, something ordained by their faith, led directly to the preventable deaths of their children. It is yet another case of people, thanks to religion, thinking they are doing good when they are really doing harm.

Conclusion

Much good has come from religion. Much harm has also come from it. And much harm has also come from sources other than religion. However, we find that the characteristics of religion—its group nature, its authority principles, its identity aspects, its practical interests, and its specific ideologies—can be and have been particularly productive of violence. And not only producing but justifying, valorizing, and virtually demanding violence. As the philosopher Blaise Pascal—who was certainly no enemy of religion—said in his *Pensées*, "Men never do evil so completely and cheerfully as when they do it from religious conviction."

Violence, aggression, and destructiveness are not only part of the human condition but part of the natural condition. It is no surprise that religion would have to take notice of it—and would more than occasionally take advantage of it. Religion is diverse, ambiguous, and cultural, and violence is equally diverse, ambiguous, and cultural. Alloyed as they can be, they produce a stunning and alarming array of religion-inspired and often enough religion-sanctioned violence. Violence, therefore, is neither native to nor foreign to religion. Rather it should be said that both violence and religion are native to humans, and they will find their way together.

DISCUSSION QUESTIONS

- What are the five variables that shape violence? How do religions provide these variables particularly effectively?
- Why are some dominant theories of sacrifice not supported by anthropological evidence? How is sacrifice related to religious beliefs and political power across cultures?
- What is self-mortification? What diverse forms does it take, and what individual and collective functions does it serve?

SUPPLEMENTARY READING (see website)

- *Predicting Human Sacrifice: A Cross-Cultural Survey*
- *Self-Mortification and Self-Discipline in the Indian Wrestler*
- *Toward an Anthropology of Terrorism*

11 Secularism and Irreligion

After the communist revolution of 1949, the People's Republic of China adopted a policy of official state atheism. Based on Marxist thinking that religion is class exploitation and false consciousness, the communist regime suppressed religion, "re-educated" believers and religious leaders, and destroyed religious buildings or converted them to non-religious uses. Since the death of Communist Party Chairman Mao, the Chinese government has relaxed some restrictions on religion, permitting "normal" religious practice and officially recognizing five major religions—Islam, Buddhism, Catholicism, "Christianity" (that is, Protestantism), and Taoism (Barnett 2012: 29). However, the regime asserts control of Catholicism in China independent of Rome and continues to suppress new religions like Falun Gong. By some measures, over 40 percent of Chinese call themselves atheists or agnostics. When China invaded (or reclaimed, from the Chinese perspective) Tibet, a deeply Buddhist society headed by the spiritual and political authority, the Dalai Lama, Tibet was at first allowed to keep its religious system; an uprising in 1959 led to the exile of the Dalai Lama and a crackdown on Buddhism including "land reform and class struggle" (34). By the mid-1990s, Tibetans who worked for the Chinese administration, as well as all students, were prohibited from practicing religion at temples or monasteries or at home. Yet through most of its rule of Tibet, China has employed the strategy "to promote Tibetan religious dignitaries to be local rulers" (32), not destroying Tibetan religion but "micro-managing the mystical rituals at the heart of the Tibetan religio-political system" (31). For instance, the government has taken control of the identification of reincarnations of traditional lamas: in 1992 a seven-year-old boy was declared the seventeenth incarnation of the Karmapa, and he was soon taken on a tour through China to be celebrated and coopted. Even more remarkably, in 1995 a ceremony known as the Golden Urn ritual was televised across China, intended to identify the next Panchen Lama. Not only did the communist government control the ceremony but apparently also invented it: Barnett claims that for the Tibetan people, "the details of the ritual indicated that it was a fabrication carried out at gunpoint" (43). But, of course, the performance was not for the Tibetans; rather, this "imitation of religion is directed to the secularized, modern audience in inland China" (44), which entertained non-believers and "appears to demonstrate official respect for Tibetan ritual but at the same time forcibly reminds Tibetan viewers that it controls that ritual, including its outcome" (45).

According to Adherents.com, there are some 1.1 billion "nonreligious" or "secular" or "agnostic" or "atheist" people in the world; if so, they would constitute the third largest category after Christianity (2.1 billion) and Islam (1.3 billion). And not all of these non-religious people are found in China; according to various surveys, as many as 15 or 16 percent of Americans do not identify with a religion, up to 12 percent of whom identify as atheists or agnostics. Much of Europe is often referred to as "post-Christian," with very low levels of religious belief and participation—in 2005 only 16 percent of Estonians avowed a belief in God (Heelas 2013: 72), and a majority of Japanese call themselves non-religious (see p. 267 below). Thus irreligion or secularism would seem to be an urgent subject for anthropology.

Yet, as Talal Asad admonished us, "anthropologists have paid scarcely any attention to the idea of the secular" (2003: 17). He even cited a recent survey of syllabi for anthropology of religion courses conducted by Andrew Buckser for the American Anthropological Association, which revealed that the topic of secularism "makes no appearance in the collection. Nor is it treated in any of the well-known introductory texts" (22). But, as Asad insisted, "Any discipline that seeks to understand 'religion' must also try to understand its other" (22).

Things are not as bleak as they were at the time of Asad's pronouncement, nor even at the time of the first edition of our textbook. Along with the anthropology of Christianity and of Islam discussed in Chapter 8, calls have arisen for an anthropology of secularism (e.g. Cannell 2010), and in 2011 *The Australian Journal of Anthropology* published an entire issue dedicated to the topic of secularism.

An anthropological perspective on secularism or irreligion or atheism (which are not, as we will see shortly, synonymous) is important not only because there is a lot of it in the world. Just as anthropology has insisted that "religion" is not a single simple thing, so an anthropological angle on non-religion suggests that it is complex and diverse. Indeed, if the concept or category of "religion" is socially constructed, then not only would the concept or category of "non-religion" or "anti-religion" be equally constructed, but *the two concepts or categories would be mutually constructed.* That is to say, by identifying or creating a phenomenon or space called "religion," an accompanying phenomenon or space of "non-religion" would appear, and, as the case of China illustrates, secularism or irreligion may exercise a sort of commanding power over what—and where—"religion" is.

The Anthropology of Secularism

The non-religious component of society has been relatively ignored for a variety of reasons. One is that it has not tended to form a distinct localized community, so there has been "nowhere to go" to investigate it—nowhere to do fieldwork. Additionally, it has regularly been presumed that the component is so small that it does not merit much attention (despite the fact that anthropology focuses on the micro-social level of analysis), but this is conspicuously untrue. Even more, it has regularly been presumed that religion is the default position of any society and of humanity as such, so that irreligion is nothing more than a *lack* of religion and therefore has no social qualities of its own. At the worst, secularism or irreligion has been construed as unnatural, antisocial, or simply non-existent. For instance, the eminent historian Arnold Toynbee opined,

> To have religion is one of those distinctively human characteristics of mankind that differentiate us from our non-human fellows on the face of this planet. This assumption implies that every human being has religion: in fact, that one cannot be human without having it in some form.
>
> (quoted in Campbell 1971: 130)

Not surprisingly, theologians and Christian scholars concur, like Martin Marty, who prejudicially dubbed secularism as "unbelief," defined as "any kind of serious or permanent departure from belief in God (as symbolized by the term 'Trinity') and from the belief that God not only is but acts (as symbolized by the historic reference 'Incarnation')" (1966: 30). But by this definition, not only are *most humans unbelievers*, since they do not have any such concepts as trinity or incarnation or even god, but many Christians would be unbelievers, since not all Christians are Trinitarians. By his own admission, such a wide net would catch "unbelievers, disbelievers, nonbelievers, the unserious, the inattentive" (27), and necessarily the two-thirds or more of humanity who are not Christians. In fact, the venerable scholar David Martin, in his *A General Theory of Secularization*, confessed that "by the term 'religion' in this context I mean Christianity" (1978: 2). But such an approach cannot possibly produce a "general" theory of anything.

Secularization Theory

Despite the disagreement and disdain around the subject of secularism or irreligion, secularization has been a hallmark of sociological and anthropological theory for more than a century. Prior to the emergence of modern social sciences, the French *philosophes* of the eighteenth century, for instance, were intensely critical of religion and expected and desired, indeed plotted, its decline and disappearance (see p. 269 below). The early sociologist Auguste Comte divided human history into three epochs, with the "theological" stage being the earliest and most primitive, followed by the "metaphysical" stage of philosophy and rational inquiry. Comte felt that within his lifetime (1798–1859) a new "positive" stage had arrived, characterized by science and the pursuit of facts, which would dispense with any lingering theological or metaphysical speculation.

Karl Marx is perhaps most closely associated with modern secularization theory. In his dialectical materialist view of history, each society is a formation founded upon its material/economic conditions. Religion is an effect of more basic material/economic forces, shaped by those forces but also legitimating those forces. As we saw in Chapter 1, Marx held that religion was a distorted or inverted reflection of society, a false consciousness that obfuscated rather than clarified the real workings of the social formation. It was the sigh of the oppressed masses and, while it indicated the true suffering of the people, it did not do anything real to address that suffering. Thus Marx predicted that when the economic inequality and exploitation of society ended (in his perfect communist order), religion would not even need to be eradicated; instead, like the state itself, religion would simply wither away due to lack of interest.

The late nineteenth century was a time of great secular expectation. The philosopher Friedrich Nietzsche in 1888 announced that "God is dead." In what may be his most famous passage, "The Madman," contained in his book *The Gay Science*, he proclaimed that God is dead and "we have killed him. Yet his shadow still looms" (1976: 95). But he also recognized that the news, the realization, of the end of God might not have reached people yet—and that they might not be able to hear or bear the news. In a series of writings, particularly his 1927 *The Future of an Illusion*, Sigmund Freud also diagnosed religion's demise, calling it an illusion without a future, akin to a neurosis; when humans solved their psychological problems directly, they would not need the indirect salve of religion.

Probably the leading statement on secularization came from Max Weber, who saw it as part—and a virtually inevitable part—of the more general process of *modernization*. In the past, in social settings like those described by Redfield and Gellner before the "great transformation" (see Chapter 8), any society's religion was ubiquitous and taken for granted, a kind of moral glue that held the society together. However, as social relations and the ethos or "feel" of society changed, the nature and function of religion changed as well. In other words, secularization, seen as the decline of religion, was an effect of other social forces.

Weber regarded the central features of modernization to include *rationalization, industrialization, bureaucratization, urbanization,* and finally *secularization.* Industrialization and urbanization are obvious enough. Rationalization meant that social goals, and the methods to achieve them, became more and more "practical" and "economic" as opposed to "moral" and "religious." Efficiency of action and cost, division of labor, market exchange relations, and technological imperatives replaced more personal and spiritual interests and relations. Bureaucratization meant that social organization became more formal, differentiated, hierarchical, and "integrated," with "managers" far removed—physically or socially—from the site of production. Also, institutions like "the factory" or "the market" or "the government" or "the family" became functionally detached from each other, separate social spaces. Altogether, the experience of society would be more complicated, more diverse, more fragmented (i.e. the people you interact with in the factory are not the same ones you interact with in the market or the family, etc.), and more "private." Modern society, Weber expected and grieved, would undergo "disenchantment," losing its spiritual and magical qualities.

The basic assertion of secularization theory, as Steve Bruce explained it, is "that modernization creates problems for religion" (2002: 2). Along Marxist lines, we might think of religion as growing in the soil of the society; different soils produce different religions—and some soil is inhospitable to religion altogether. Thus, as society evolves more rational, industrial, bureaucratic, and urban features, religion is changed or vanquished. Religion develops at best into just one more "institution" in the society, unplugged from its multiple social and moral functions; it transforms into something you "do" on Sundays in a specialized building, one part of a complicated modern life. Or religion may be transformed—or restricted—into a private matter, a personal choice and practice, not a public matter at all. In fact, it may become impolite or divisive to do religion too publicly. For some, ultimately, it simply diminishes in importance or is ignored completely, either as insignificant or impractical or *false* or in favor of other activities that compete with it in a busy secular schedule, like the football season.

Thus sociologists Peter Berger and Thomas Luckmann, like so many others, claimed to see the declining power and influence of religion in "the progressive autonomization of societal sectors from the domination of religious meaning and institutions" (1966: 74). What they meant is that, as various actions, roles, and institutions "free" themselves (become "autonomous") from religion, religion's impact on society cannot help but wane. A critical aspect of this retreat of religion from society is social diversity, in two ways. First, as societies for various historical reasons began to encompass multiple racial, ethnic, linguistic, and of course religious communities, no religion unified them all, and therefore they did not comprise a "moral community." In other words, the *pluralism* of modernity threatened religion as much as any other force: Bruce argued that the "separation of church and state was one consequence of diversity" (17). Second, even within a religion like Christianity and increasingly in all religions including the "traditional" ones, schism and syncretism led to a proliferation of alternative and competing "religions" or religious movements; the Catholic monopoly in ancient and medieval Europe had largely prevented this development, but the triumph of the Protestant Reformation generated a new kind of or new attitude toward religion, which "was extremely vulnerable to fragmentation because it removed the institution of the church as a source of authority between God and man" (Bruce 2002: 10), leaving the individual to voluntarily choose between or "convert to" any of the religious offerings. The result is a "consumer approach" toward religions in which the individual as a free and private agent "may choose from the assortment of 'ultimate' meanings as he sees fit" (Luckmann 1970: 99).

As powerful and pervasive as this modernization process is, its religious outcomes are diverse. Even within a paradigm of secularization, Bryan Wilson suggested a variety of possible consequences for religion, such as

> the sequestration of political powers of the property and facilities of religious agencies; the shift from religious to secular control of various of the erstwhile activities and functions of religion; the decline in the proportion of their time, energy and resources which men devote to supra-empirical concerns; the decay of religious institutions; the supplanting, in matters of behavior, of religious precepts by demands that accord with strictly technical criteria; and the gradual replacement of a specifically religious consciousness (which might range from dependence on charms, rites, spells, or prayers, to a broadly spiritually-inspired ethical concern) by an empirical, rational, instrumental orientation; the abandonment of mythical, poetic, and artistic inter-pretations of nature and society in favor of matter-of-fact descriptions, and with it, the rigorous separation of evaluative and emotive dispositions from cognitive and positivistic orientations.
>
> (1982: 149)

In a highly respected analysis, José Casanova (1994) boiled secularization theory down to three primary claims. First, secularization might entail structural differentiation, that is, the separation of religion from other domains of society and its isolation in a "religious institution" (like "the church") detached from other institutions (like "the state"). Second, secularization might mean privatization, something that individuals do inside their homes, heads, and hearts without wider public impact. Third, secularization might involve the decline in religious belief and participation (e.g. less church attendance, less prayer, more avowals of disbelief) and thus the diminishing influence of religious institutions.

Talal Asad and Formations of the Secular

Without doubt the most influential anthropological contribution to the study of secularism has been Talal Asad's 2003 *Formations of the Secular*. As he did for religion in his 1993 *Genealogies of Religion* and for Islam in his 2009 "The Idea of an Anthropology of Islam," Asad called for "an anthropology of secularism" that would examine secularism as a social and political doctrine and "the secular" as a cultural concept or category (2003: 1). He insisted, as we noted at the opening of this chapter, that the neglect of secularism was serious, since any "discipline that seeks to understand 'religion' must also try to understand its 'other'" (21). But so far the "category of the secular itself remains unexamined" (23).

Like the concept of "religion" and other conventional terms and categories, Asad contended that "the secular is neither singular in origin nor stable in its historical identity"; in other words, both "the 'religious' and the 'secular' are not essentially fixed categories" (25). Indeed, as the study of translocal religions and vernacular religions has shown, what is or is not "religion" is not evident or consistent; different societies construct the category of religion differently—or do not construct it at all—and those constructions vary over time. But as the understanding and range of "religion" varies, so too does "secular," if we think of "secular" as that which is not religion.

Asad contends that secularism and "the secular" as understood today is essentially a Western Christian mode of thought, and admittedly almost all of his discussion deals with Western European experience, where Christianity drew a line between "religion" and "the world," between "spirit" and "matter," between "sacred" and "profane." Western social sciences largely absorbed these culturally specific categories; note Durkheim's assertion that religion is fundamentally about "sacred things." The conclusion from this line of analysis is that other societies would define "the secular" differently—or not at all. And "the secular," rather than diametrically opposed to "religion," is intimately related to religion.

Box 11.1 Traditions of Jewish Secular Thought

Each religion provides the conditions for its own brand of secularism. Or we might better say *brands* of secularism, since, as Jewish history scholar David Biale reports, Judaism has generated a number of different secularisms, which do not necessarily reject religion so much as develop certain internal possibilities of religion. It is not insignificant that Marx and Freud, arch secularists, descended from Jewish backgrounds; for them as for many other secularists, "Jewish secularism was a revolt grounded in the tradition it rejected" (Biale 2011: 1). Further, as Asad would expect, "different local conditions created different types of secularization" (4): for some Jews, secularism "was the flight from traditional communities, rabbinic authority, and the daily routine prescribed by Jewish law," while for others it was a denunciation of "obscurantist, medieval religion" in favor of a more modern culture and identity (x). For still others, secularism was the logical outcome of certain ideas in the religion itself. One such variation is pantheism as represented by Benedict/Baruch Spinoza (1632–77). Biale explains that classical Jewish scholars like Moses Maimonides (1138–1204) reasoned that God "was utterly transcendent, so removed from the world as to have nothing in common with it" (19). Maimonides' radical separation of "nature" and "God" offered Spinoza a way to reunify them in an unorthodox and secular fashion: for Spinoza, God was not a person, had no feelings, no love for humans. This God "vanished from sight, leaving only the universe"; as Biale summarized Spinoza, "God *is* the universe—and nothing else" (26). A second species of Jewish secularism was the mystical tradition of Kabbalah, which taught that "when God begins to create the world, he contracts himself away from a central point, leaving an empty space" (47). The natural world, then, is precisely where God is *not*, leading to "a radical secular identification of God with nothingness or even death" (47). Third, Biale mentions "the resurrection of the ancient pagan gods, both Greek and Canaanite," which amounted to "an assault on the God of Israel by recourse to his ancient enemies" (57). Notice that none of these alternatives is anti-religious in the strict sense. Nor is the present-day movement of Humanistic Judaism (http://www.shj.org/), which bills itself as "a nontheistic alternative in contemporary Jewish life" that "combines the celebration of Jewish culture and identity with an adherence to humanistic values and ideas."

But Asad's case goes much further. Recall that, beyond a concept (the secular), Asad characterized secularism as a political doctrine, even an ideology. We might say that secularism is a *project*, and he tied the secular project tightly to the projects of modernity and of the modern state. The modern state project, he posited, "aims at institutionalizing a number of (sometimes conflicting, often evolving) principles: constitutionalism, moral autonomy, democracy, human rights, civil equality, industry, consumerism, freedom of the market—and secularism" (2003: 13). Specifically, the state claims for itself the authority to dictate how society is organized: it creates the disparate institutional realms of "the economy," "the household," and of course "the religion." The individual, moreover, owes his/her allegiance first and foremost to the state, although the state may adopt religion for its own legitimation. But even when the state "is said to be 'under God,' it has its being only in 'this world'—a special kind of world. The men and women of each national society make and *own* their history" (193).

The modern not only "requires clearly demarcated spaces that it can classify and regulate: religion, education, health, leisure, work, income, justice, and war" (201). Within each of those spaces, the state determines what each of these phenomena is and how it may behave. "From the point of view of secularism," Asad opined, "religion has the option either of confining itself to private belief and worship or of engaging in public talk that makes no demands on life. In either case such religion is seen by secularism to take the form it should properly have" (199). In a word, as modern society and politics circumscribed religion (as in the Chinese case described at the outset of the chapter), they both created and depended on a notion of "the secular"—and *secularized religion*.

Varieties of Secular Experience

Inspired by Asad, anthropologists have increasingly recognized that secularism is "a concept with particular geographical and historical locations and patterns of export, first from Europe and then from America" (Cannell 2010: 90). However, a few years before Asad's seminal work, Jack Goody stressed that it would be incorrect to assume that secularism, including "explicit forms of skepticism and agnosticism (even atheism)" (1996: 667), are unique to the modern West. Certainly, he argued, we can find secularist/skeptical ideas in ancient Greece, which "already had a concept of *agnostos*" (that about which knowledge is unavailable or impossible, from *a-* for no/without and *gnosis* for knowledge), and "God himself belonged in this category" (668).

One of the first to express such thoughts was the sixth-century BCE poet Theognis, who was troubled about the apparent injustice in the world: "Dear Zeus, you baffle me," he wrote, because "you make no distinction between the sinner and the good man, between the man who devotes himself to temperate and responsible acts and the man who commits deeds of hubris [pride]. Tell me, son of Cronus, how can you deal such unfairness?" (quoted in Wheelwright 1966: 29–30).

Xenophanes struggled with a similar problem: how could the gods, authors of all good and right, act so decidedly badly in the traditional stories? "Homer and Hesiod attributed to the gods all sorts of actions which when done by men are disreputable and deserving of blame—such lawless deeds as theft, adultery, and mutual deception" (quoted in Wheelwright: 33). One possible though disturbing answer was that the myths and the poets were wrong. This conclusion was bolstered by the patently obvious fact that different societies believed in different gods that were noticeably similar to the believers themselves:

Ethiopians have gods with snub noses and black hair, Thracians have gods with gray eyes and red hair. ... If oxen or lions had hands which enabled them to draw and paint pictures as men do, they would portray their gods as having bodies like their own; horses would portray them as horses, and oxen as oxen.

(33)

So all of these local portrayals of gods could be nothing more than anthropomorphisms (or horse-omorphisms) for gods that really have none of these traits—or perhaps do not exist at all.

The consequences of this line of reasoning were not long in arriving. The pre-Socratic "natural philosophers" began to ponder how the universe might work—even how it might have come into existence—without reliance on religion. Their aim, stated Wheelwright, was "systematically to explain nature in terms of nature, instead of referring to the supposed will or caprice of supernatural beings" (41). What, for instance, is the primary substance of nature, out of which all other things are made? How does the diversity of nature (the "many") come from the single source (the "one"), and how does change between forms occur? These are essentially a-theistic questions, seeking a-theistic answers.

The precise answers were various and not our concern. The point is that the explanatory function previously reserved for religion was usurped by nature, as when Heraclitus reasoned that, "This universe, which is the same for all, has not been made by any god or man, but it always has been, is, and will be—an ever-living fire, kindling itself by regular measures and going out by regular measures" (71). The new explanation was natural sufficiency and natural law: nature did not need anything other than nature to create or sustain it, and nature operated by laws which were in principle knowable by man. Parmenides wrote:

For strong Necessity holds [Being] in its bonds of limit, which constrain it on all sides; Natural Law forbids that Being should be other than perfectly complete. It stands in need of nothing; for if it needed anything at all it would need everything.

(98)

The key notion was *cause*. Natural things have a cause, and those causes are other natural things. Thucydides' history of the Peloponnesian War (432–404 BCE) described human action without reference to gods. Hippocrates argued that disease, even the "divine disease" of epilepsy, had solely natural causes. And Protagoras made the strongest statement yet, earning himself a charge of blasphemy:

As for the gods, I have no way of knowing either that they exist or that they do not exist; nor, if they exist, of what form they are. For the obstacles to that sort of knowledge are many, including the obscurity of the matter and the brevity of human life.

(240)

Anaxogoras was the first man in recorded history to be indicted for atheism; a law was even drafted around 438 BCE to "denounce those who do not believe in the divine beings or who teach doctrines about things in the sky" such as planets or meteors (quoted in Hecht 2003: 10). But it was the fate of Socrates to be the only Athenian victim of the death penalty for "impiety" and "corrupting the youth" by asking too many impertinent questions.

After the conquest of the Greek cities by Alexander and then the rise of Rome, a new cosmopolitan society emerged, which had important consequences for religion. Some people held on to the old ways; others embraced new religions and "mystery cults" like Mithraism and eventually Christianity. But others practiced what Jennifer Hecht in her study of the history of doubt "a clear-eyed resignation to chaos and uncertainty, and a conviction that reality, even painful reality, is preferable to living under false ideas," including false religious ideas (2003: 27). Two of these philosophies and lifestyles were cynicism, the distrust of all authority and often the flouting of all convention, and stoicism, a philosophy that combined rationality with tough uncomplaining resignation to the tribulations of life. Epicureanism, commonly associated with mindless pleasure-seeking, actually taught that people could be happy in the present world if they were freed from error, mistaken beliefs, and fears. The founder, Epicurus, asked one of the most enduring questions in the history of religion:

> God either wishes to take away evil, and is unable, or He is able, and unwilling; or He is neither willing nor able, or He is both willing and able. If He is willing and is unable, He is feeble, which is not in accordance with the character of God; if He is able and unwilling, He is envious, which is equally at variance with God; if He is neither willing nor able, He is both envious and feeble, and therefore not God; if He is both willing and able, which alone is suitable to God, from what source then are evils? Or why does He not remove them?
>
> (Lactantius 1871)

Finally, skepticism as advocated by Pyrrho and his successor Carneades argued that individuals could, even should, live without firm and sure beliefs and values. Certainty was impossible, since the opposite case was always possible, nothing could really be known. Since nothing could be known, then one should suspend or avoid all decisions or judgments. Carneades went still further, effectively debunking most of the classic arguments for god(s), including personal experience, design, tradition or common belief, and the "goodness" of god(s).

But Goody did not stop with the Greeks. He noted that the possibility of unbelief was acknowledged, although condemned, in the Hebrew scriptures (the Christian Old Testament): the book of Ecclesiastes reads something like an epicurean or stoic text. Goody also claimed to find skepticism in Babylonian and Egyptian writings, in non-Western traditions, and in tribal societies. He cited a medieval Indian author, Madhavacarya, who speculated that there "was no God, no soul, and no survival after death" (673), commented that Confucius was agnostic about the supernatural realm, and claimed that anthropologist Evans-Pritchard found "faith tempered by skepticism" among the Azande (677).

The Language of Secularism

Our hesitancy about terms like "secular" or "secularism" or "irreligion" or "atheism" illustrates the terminological complexities and confusions in the subject. Before proceeding further, it is essential to state that in its origin the word "secular" does not refer to "the material world" as opposed to the "spiritual realm" that purportedly concerns religion. The word "secular," from the Latin *saeculum*, is commonly and crucially misunderstood. It denotes not a place like the physical world versus heaven but *a time*, a particular era or epoch, an age or generation. Therefore, "secular" properly speaking names that which is distinctive of a specific time period, as opposed to that which is allegedly "eternal." In this new but more accurate sense, "secular" means roughly what "vernacular" meant in Chapter 9: when Hebrew or Aramaic or Greek scriptures are translated into contemporary English, those are *secular* scriptures, and when religious beliefs or stories are portrayed in movies, songs, websites, and comic books, those are examples of *secular* religion.

That is to say, "secular" does not imply the absence of religion or a hostility to religion. "Secularization" can mean the detachment of religion from culture, but it can also mean the attachment of religion *to* culture. Catholic inculturation is a form of secularization: an Aymara New Testament would be very much of a particular time. And when churches organize basketball leagues or bingo games, that is secularization too.

Even in the history of Christianity, secular did not originally mean non-religious or anti-religious. Medieval Christianity recognized "secular clergy" or priests who ministered in parishes, dealing with the common people, in distinction to the priests who took monastic vows and cloistered themselves away from "the world." "Secular" was first used with its current meaning in the mid-1800s by George Jacob Holyoake, a British non-believer in Christianity, who characterized secularism as

> A series of principles intended for the guidance of those who find Theology indefinite, or inadequate, or deem it unreliable. It replaces theology, which mainly regards life as a sinful necessity, as a scene of tribulation through which we pass to a better world. Secularism rejoices in this life, and regards it as the sphere of those duties which educate men to fitness for any future and better life, should such transpire.
>
> (1871: 11)

Another term available for centuries in the West is "freethought," which like secularism did not initially imply irreligion. Rather, a freethinker was a person who came to his/her own conclusions about religion, for instance how to interpret the Bible. By extension, of course, one might come to the conclusion that the Bible or all religion is "indefinite, inadequate, or unreliable," and freethought today tends to be a synonym for religious disbelief. Yet a third term is "humanism," which came into use during the Renaissance (fourteenth and fifteenth centuries). By no means inherently anti-religious, Renaissance humanists like Erasmus (an ordained Catholic priest) and Petrarch read and promoted classical Greek and Roman literature, devoted themselves to practical matters and the study of nature, and tended to support religious tolerance. Humanism in the twenty-first century, as defined by the American Humanist Association and as repeated in every issue of its magazine *The Humanist*, is

> a rational philosophy informed by science, inspired by art, and motivated by compassion. Affirming the dignity of each human being, it supports the maximization of individual liberty and opportunity consonant with social and planetary responsibility. It advocates the extension of participatory democracy and the expansion of the open society, standing for human rights and social justice. Free of supernaturalism, it recognizes human beings as a part of nature and holds that values—be they religious, ethical, social, or political—have their source in human nature, experience, and culture. Humanism thus derives the goals of life from human need and interest rather than from theological or ideological abstractions and asserts that humanity must take responsibility for its own destiny.

As seen above, "skepticism" is an ancient term for a questioning attitude, a desire to verify claims for oneself; it does not necessarily mean the rejection of all claims, and one can be skeptical about any subject, not only religion. Much more recently, Thomas Huxley, a contemporary and defender of Darwin, coined the term "agnosticism" in 1869 out of the Greek *gnosis* for "knowledge" and literally meaning "without knowledge," which many people still think means indecision or an intermediate position between belief and non-belief. Huxley explained his intention thus:

> Agnosticism is not a creed but a method, the essence of which lies in the vigorous application of a single principle. Positively the principle may be expressed as, in matters of the intellect, follow your reason as far as it can carry you without other considerations. And negatively, in matters of the intellect, do not pretend the conclusions are certain that are not demonstrated or demonstrable. It is wrong for a man to say he is certain of the objective truth of a proposition unless he can produce evidence which logically justifies that certainty.
>
> (1902: 245–46)

In other words, he did not see himself offering a new belief but expressing an old and trusty approach to knowledge: do not claim to know what you cannot prove you know. In this sense, agnosticism is virtually identical to skepticism and freethought and to reason itself—the process by which we gather our facts and arrive at our conclusions.

Finally, "atheism" (from *a-* for no and *theos* for god) in modern parlance means a disbelief in god(s). Some atheists and other commentators distinguish between "negative" and "positive" atheism, with negative atheism merely refuting arguments for the existence of god(s) and positive atheism advancing its own counter-arguments to justify the non-existence of god(s). There are aggressive atheists today who vociferously deny the existence of god(s) and even denigrate believers, while others simply want to be free to live a life without god(s). There are two important facts to note about atheism, however. First, in the strictest sense, it only disputes god(s); it would be logically consistent, although not common, to disbelieve in god(s) but still believe in spirits, dead ancestors, or other religious beings or forces. (Of course, atheists who are firm materialists or naturalists also reject those notions.) Second, contemporary Western atheism, operating in a theistic environment, tends to *oppose* god(s), while many religions themselves merely *lack* god(s); in other words, it is entirely possible, and fairly common, to have an atheistic religion.

This survey of terminology demonstrates that there are many overlapping but not synonymous ways to talk about religious belief or non-belief. Not all of these terms imply strenuous denial of religion, and not all of them are applicable to non-Christian or non-theistic religions.

Societies without Religion?

It is frequently asserted that religion is a universal human phenomenon, even, as Toynbee and others believed (see p. 255 above), that humanity without religion is inconceivable. This claim naturally depends on how one defines religion, and it is often intended as an argument in favor of religion. Whether there are societies without religion is a controversial but important question.

The Hua of Papua New Guinea as described by Anna Meigs (see Chapter 6) seemed only concerned with pollution, and their concept of *nu* that carried purity or pollution was part-spiritual but also immanently material, as it was found in bodily substances, even in footprints and shadows, but especially in food. Beyond this pollution system, Meigs did not report anything for the Hua that resembles "religion" in the familiar Western/Christian sense. Colin Turnbull's account of the Mbuti people of the Congo rainforest revealed little that feels like religion to us. For the Mbuti, their forest was roughly a sentient being and a benevolent one at that; Turnbull marveled at the "complete faith of the Pygmies in the goodness of their forest world" (1961: 93), but to call it sacred might be going too far. To be sure, misfortune sometimes befell the Mbuti, but their understanding was that "the forest is sleeping and not looking after its children"; the proper course of action, they taught Turnbull, was "We wake it up. We wake it up by singing to it, and we do this because we want it to awaken happy. Then everything will be well and good again" (92). For this purpose, the Mbuti sang songs and played a horn or trumpet, both dubbed *molimo*. We might be tempted to call this a "ritual," but Turnbull insisted that the molimo music "is not concerned with ritual or magic. In fact, it is so devoid of ritual, expressed either in action or words, that it is difficult to see what it *is* concerned with" (80). Turnbull confessed his dismay at the lack of seriousness or reverence, of religious attitude, with which the Mbuti performed their songs and lived their lives.

In Fredrik Barth's classic ethnography of the Basseri pastoralists of mountain Iran, religion did not even merit its own chapter. Indeed, the absence of religion among these putatively Muslim people vexed Barth sufficiently to drive him to discuss it in an appendix at the end of the book, where he wrote:

> Only few references have been made to ritual in this account of the Basseri—hardly any ceremonies have been described, and the behavior patterns have been discussed in terms of the pragmatic systems of economics, or politics, and hardly ever in terms of their meanings within a ritual system. This has followed from the nature of the material itself, and is not merely a reflection of the present field worker's interests or the analytic orientation of this particular study. The Basseri show a poverty of ritual activities which is quite striking in the field situation; what they have of ceremonies, avoidance customs, and beliefs seem to influence, or be expressed in, very few of their actions. What is more, the different elements of ritual do not seem closely connected or interrelated in a wider system of meanings; they give the impression of occurring without reference to each other, or to important features of the social structure.
>
> (1961: 135)

While the Basseri avowed Shi'ite Islam, Barth claimed that they took little interest in it. They were self-consciously "lax" in their religion and "indifferent to metaphysical problems." They lacked ritual specialists of any sort, although they might invite a village holy man to perform marriages or certain other ceremonies. For the most part their ceremonial life was quite simple and pragmatic. They observed some rituals surrounding key life events like birth, marriage, and death, but these were more social and political than religious; the supernatural seemed to play little or no role. Even funerals were "relatively little elaborated" (142), and no ritual specialists took part. They observed a few other customs, such as calendrical rites (often associated with migration patterns), but they did not pray regularly and there was "no communal gathering of worshippers within a camp or even within a tent" (136). Their religious concerns amounted to not much more than concepts of luck and the "evil eye." Perplexed at how to "explain" the Basseri's relative "lack of religion," Barth suggested that the society "invested its values" in their economic activities, especially their herds and their cyclical migrations. Presumably, then, if Basseri "secular" life were less satisfying they would have more religion.

Box 11.2 Ironic Muslims in Kyrgyzstan

As noted in Chapter 8, the stereotype of Muslims is a deeply religious people, seemingly spellbound by their religion and immune to forces of modernization, democratization, and secularization. This is part of what Edward Said called "orientalism." Imagine Maria Louw's surprise, then, to hear the Kyrgyz of central Asia assert that "the Kyrgyz people, by the way, had never been *real* Muslims" (2012: 144). Louw finds that many Kyrgyz in the city of Bishkek "display a profound discomfort with 'religion' and with people who have begun to embrace, and publicly display, a 'religious' identity" (151). Granted, Kyrgyzstan was subjected to state atheism for decades under Soviet control. But when the Soviet Union dissolved in the late 1980s, anthropologists and visitors commented that "there were hardly any signs of a religious 'revival' in the country" (148), remarking on "the lack of interest most Kyrgyz displayed in religion" (149). This does not mean that they engaged in no "religious" behavior. Louw explains that the *közü achïk* or clairvoyant is important in Kyrgyz society and that locals take omens seriously, usually encountering them in dreams. But people are "a bit embarrassed to talk about these things," and when they do talk, they refer ironically to their own religious belief and behavior. By irony Louw means that "people play with the categories that have been used to describe their ways of being Muslims and with which they circumscribe practices during 'religious' rituals" (155). In other words, "the practice of Islam is often accompanied by ironic attitudes and gestures. … I have often been met with surprised reactions and ironic comments, like, 'You know, if a *real* Muslim observed us, he/she would not think we were Muslims [laughter]'" (156). Louw classifies such behavior as

> an everyday form of secularism, a way of relating to "religion" in a context where the meaning of religion has become the object of scrutiny and great controversy and where a perceived increasing "religiousness" in society is associated with all sorts of post-Soviet—and indeed global—excesses.
>
> (144)

Finally, as far back as 1936, J. H. Driberg warned us about applying Western Christian religious concepts to traditional African religions. "'Worship,' 'sacrifice,' 'offerings,' 'prayer,' 'shrine,' and even, though to a slightly different degree, 'soul' are all words with a specialized significance in English and their application to the ancestral system of the Africans is both a linguistic and a cultural offence," he wrote, urging instead that so-called "ancestor worship" "is in fact a purely secular attitude" (1936: 6). For example, "no African 'prays' to his dead grandfather any more than he 'prays' to his living father" (6), and what we are wont to call the ancestor's "shrine" is simply a miniature house in which the dead person dwells. Likewise, "the so-called 'sacrifices' that the dead receiver … are identical with and part of the tribute received and transmitted by the living elders, and they are offered to the dead in recognition of their advice to the living" (11). What we fail to grasp, Driberg insisted, is that *age* is "the most important criterion of classification to be found in African societies" (9), and since living elders deserve respect and special treatment, the even older dead elders deserve the same or better respect and treatment. Therefore, the supposed religious attitude toward ancestors "is nothing sacred, but a social recognition of the fact that the dead man has acquired a new status and that ... he is still one with" the society of the living (7).

Thirty-five years later Igor Kopytoff seconded Driberg's conclusion in perhaps even clearer language. Researching the Suku of southwestern Congo, he found that this society actually lacked a word for "ancestor"; rather, dead ancestors and living elders together were called *bambuta*, which meant "big ones" or "old ones." As Driberg stated, age and seniority are the key issue, and indeed "eldership confers upon a person mystical powers over the junior" (1971: 131). "If there be a 'cult' here," Kopytoff wryly argued, "it is a cult of *bambuta*, of elders living and dead"; juniors owe seniors honor and respect, and "the line dividing the living from the dead does not affect the structure of the relationship" (133). In strong words, Kopytoff warned that the "Western ethnocentric conviction that 'ancestors' must be separated from living 'elders' conditions the cognitive set with which we approach African data and theorize about them" (136). Wisely he warned us that when we use such Western Christian terms "as 'cult,' 'worship,' and 'sacrifice,' we introduce semantic paradoxes which we then feel compelled to explain" (138). But when "we recognize that African 'ancestors' are above all elders and to be understood in terms of the same category as living elders, we shall stop pursuing a multitude of problems of our own creation" (138).

Shinto: A Worldly Religion of Japan

Japan is often regarded as a highly secular, indeed non-religious, society. The 2005 World Values Survey reported that 62 percent of Japanese people identified as non-religious and 13.7 percent as atheists, and 88 percent were not members of a religious organization while only 4.4% were active members of such an organization. Yet Emily Aoife Somers notes that the *Dictionary of Sacred Places in Japan* lists "thousands of shrines, temples and natural features that have supernatural connections, festival importance or other manifestations of legend" (2013: 219)—including the sacred Mount Fuji—and Japan has been a place of hectic new religious movement since the nineteenth century.

Likewise, Ian Reader claimed that contemporary Japanese people tend to assert "that they are not religious, even whilst performing acts of an overtly religious nature such as praying at a shrine or walking a pilgrimage" (1991: 1). In fact, he mentioned that two-thirds of Japanese in a 1981 survey responded that they had no religious beliefs. They can avow non-religion and simultaneously engage in what outsiders might call religion because of their particular conception of "religion" and because of the nature of their "traditional" religion, Shinto. The Japanese word for religion, *shukyo*, he argued, is a modern introduction,

> a derived word that came into prominence in the nineteenth century as a result of Japanese encounters with the West and particularly with Christian missionaries, to denote a concept and view of religion commonplace in the realms of nineteenth-century

Christian theology but at that time not found in Japan, of religion as a specific belief-framed entity.

(13)

This foreign (but familiar to Westerners) view of religion as "organized religion" or "doctrine" or "creed" has never really caught on in Japan, especially among the young: another study of college students showed that 92 percent of them maintained that they would never join any organized religious movement (14).

All of this is not to say that Japan is irreligious or secular in the Western sense of the terms. Instead, their particular religious sensibility has tended to run along naturalistic (versus supernaturalistic), social (versus spiritual), and behavioral (versus doctrinal) lines. First and most essentially, "the Japanese religious world is not separate from the general flow of life, but an intrinsic part thereof, upholding, strengthening, and giving sustenance to it" (54). The dualistic approach of Western religions, dividing the "religious" from the "secular," is not an indigenous understanding. For instance, the conception of Shinto spirits or gods (*kami*) was not transcendent and otherworldly: "Traditionally, anything that inspired a sense of awe (that is, which expressed through its nature some special quality or sense of vitality) could be seen as a *kami* or as the abode of a *kami*, including rocks and trees" (25). The world of the spirits and the world of nature and human society were not infinitely separated from each other but were continuous, such that humans could become *kami* and *kami* could act like humans; the spirits suffered pain, loss, decay, and death like any other person.

Reader further suggested that religion for traditional and contemporary Japanese has been more about fulfilling social obligations than possessing deep faith. Visiting a shrine, attending a festival, participating in a ritual were matters of "social belonging": individuals belonged to corporate groups like families, neighborhoods, villages, companies (especially in the present), and of course the nation, and these corporate groups had corporate religious duties. Significantly, this made Japanese religion particularly "flexible" and "syncretistic," even to the point of leading many people to make little distinction between Shinto and Buddhism. *Kami* and Buddhas existed side by side or were even equated with each other, and people attended whatever religious activities were available and incumbent on them. They could, as we have seen in other cases, "move into (and out of) religious modes according to requirements and circumstances" (21–22). At the extreme, as Reader put it, Japanese are born Shinto but die Buddhist, integrating both into their lives on different occasions or at different stages.

Japanese religion allowed for this inclusiveness because "belief," let alone "exclusive belief," was not a central feature. Religion was something to do, more than something to believe. It had very practical and worldly interests and goals, including creating and maintaining social relationships with the gods and ancestors and ensuring purity, health, prosperity, and tranquility for living humans. Orthodoxy was less important than orthopraxy, doing the right things to achieve the right results. People might behave religiously without any significant religious belief or understanding.

Most recently, Reader noted, Japanese religion had become increasingly "secular" in the conventional sense. For instance, civic festivals had become common: the Kobe Festival, "sponsored by the civil authorities, is intended to create a sense of civic pride and community feeling in the city and consists of pageantry, parades, and spectacular street events which have little or no religious content" (73). At the same time, businesses had absorbed and "co-opted" religion by embracing religious institutions or forms, sponsoring festivals, supporting shrines and temples, organizing visits to sacred places, and the like—all for the purpose of reinforcing the loyalty of workers and of advancing the image of the company.

France: State Secularism

France is rare if not unique in the world for being officially secular; its current constitution, adopted in 1958, declares unequivocally (Part 1, Article 2) that France is "an indivisible, secular, democratic, and social Republic." The term used for "secular" in the constitution is *laïque*, and the French term for secularism is *laïcité*.

French society has a long history of struggle with religion. In the eighteenth century, the *philosophes* of France like Rousseau, Voltaire, and Diderot were openly critical of religion, or it might be more accurate to say that they were critical of the clergy and of religious fanaticism and intolerance. Many condemned priests as useless and hypocritical, and they also distrusted the conventional notion of God, preferring instead a deistic belief of an impersonal creator god. Few went as far as Paul-Henri Thiry, the Baron d'Holbach, in openly defending atheism in such works as his 1761 *Christianity Unveiled* and 1770 *The System of Nature*.

Hostility to religion came to a head during the French Revolution, starting in 1789. As the famous historian Alexis de Tocqueville observed, "One of the earliest enterprises of the revolutionary movement was a concerted attack on the Church, and among the many passions inflamed by it the first to be kindled and last to be extinguished was of an anti-religious nature" (1955: 5). Initially, the revolutionary government attempted to bring the Catholic priesthood under secular control through the Civil Constitution of the Clergy in 1790. By 1793, more radical elements were driving the revolution, so a new calendar was promulgated, detaching time-keeping from Christianity and setting Year 1 to 1792; the seven-day week was eliminated, and of course Sunday disappeared. In what historian J. M. Thompson called a "de-christianizing campaign," churches were vandalized, church bells were melted into coins or guns, and priests were jailed, deported, and occasionally executed; the Christian god was ridiculed as "jealous, capricious, greedy, cruel, implacable" (1962: 115). In 1794 Maximilien Robespierre introduced a non-theistic Cult of the Supreme Being and of Nature, complete with national secular holidays, but the new secular religion died with him.

By the nineteenth century, *laïcité* was part of French political discourse, and referred to the freedom of social institutions, primarily schools, from Catholic authority. Official state secularism in relation to education was most recently reaffirmed in the 2013 Charter of Secularism at School, which begins with a restatement of the country's constitutional position on religion and adds articles promoting separation of religion and the state and freedom of conscience (i.e. freedom "to believe or not believe"). Further, though, the charter insists that secularism "assures to students the access to a common and shared culture" (Article 7) as well as offering "the condition to forge their personalities" free from "all proselytizing and from any pressure that would prevent them from making their own choices" (Article 6). The curriculum is also explicitly secularized: "no subject is a priori excluded from scientific and pedagogic questioning," and students cannot use religion to "dispute a teacher's right to address a question on the syllabus" (Article 12). Finally and most controversially, the school is firmly established as a secular space, where students cannot promote "religious membership by refusing to conform" (Article 13) and where "wearing signs by which students ostentatiously demonstrate a religious membership is forbidden" (Article 14).

France is thus a perfect example of Asad's notion of the state using secularism to define and constrain religion and to create a common public culture. Yet, although the target of *laïcité* was originally Catholicism, more recently it has fallen hardest on Islam. While France has accommodated Islam in various ways, with prayer spaces set aside for Muslim observance and working conditions adjusted to allow time for prayer, France has engaged in the kind of micro-management of religion noted above. For instance, in 2002 Nicolas Sarkozy (at the time the interior minister, later the president) created the French Council for the Muslim Religion, bringing together Muslim organizations under government watch; Sarkozy also saw to it that the president of the council was the head of the Paris mosque, which "had long been a favored partner of the state" (Bowen 2010: 26).

The most contentious manifestation of *laïcité* has been the 2004 law prohibiting "conspicuous religious signs" in schools, which many have seen as targeting the Muslim practice of wearing the veil (see Figure 11.1). In an enlightening analysis drawing on Asad, Mayanthi Fernando illustrates how the specific French formation of the secular made life difficult for Muslims. Fernando notes the French distinction between "the right of conscience" (to believe or not) and "the right to expressions or manifestations of conscience, which can be subject to restriction" (2010: 19). On the familiar Western premise that religion is "private" and "internal," supporters of the ban justified it because it did not interfere with belief, only with behavior. Fernando rightly points out that such an interpretation depends on "a specific, secular understanding of the relationship between belief and practice": "if religious practices are neither as integral to religion as are beliefs nor constitutive of belief, then a restriction on practice would not, by this logic, constitute a violation of religious liberty" (26). However, this approach is not consistent with Muslim women's understanding of the veil (or headscarf), which they regard as a personal decision but one that is crucial to their religious identity. French *laïcité* has no such conception: the veil, like all religious behavior, is categorized as "either a choice or an

Figure 11.1 A woman in a niqab walks down the street in Strasbourg despite the law that prohibits face covering. Courtesy of Walencienne/Shutterstock

obligation" (27); worse still, "any external pressure ... diminishes the right of individuals to choose freely, violating their freedom of conscience" (29). To secular ears, "framing the headscarf as both a personal decision and a religious obligation constituted, and continues to constitute, a kind of 'double talk' ... representative of either an incoherent subjectivity or an insidious plot to mask a 'fundamentalist' agenda with liberal-republican language" (30). In short, Muslim women were forced to speak the secular language of *laïcité*, defending the scarf as a choice—which is thereby subject to prohibition.

Turkey: Secularization, Modernization, Westernization

The modern state of Turkey was born from the ashes of the Ottoman Empire, long the political epicenter of Islam. The classic Ottoman political system had consisted of three main institutions: the sultanate or office of the head of state (the sultan), the caliphate or office of the head of Islam (the caliph, a successor to Muhammad)—both of which offices were combined in the emperor—and the *Seriat* or Islamic law (the Turkish version of *shari'a*). In the 1700s, as some Ottomans began to sense a decline in imperial power, they pushed for reforms; as early as 1720 French influences in architecture, tastes (including coffee houses and taverns), and thought had diffused to the empire. In 1731 Ibrahim Muteferrika wrote a book about "rational politics" involving democracy, parliamentary government, and popular representation, not to mention Western military science. In the most lasting early modern reform, Mahmud II inaugurated a system known as *Tanzimat* or "re-ordering" in the 1830s, which envisioned the Ottoman state as "composed of peoples of diverse nationalities and religions, based on secular principles of sovereignty as contrasted with the medieval concept of an Islamic empire" (Berkes 1998: 90). A secular council was appointed to decide judicial questions outside the *Seriat*, and the jurisdiction of *Seriat* courts was diminished; Western science was promoted, education (at the primary level) was made compulsory, and modernizations of language and literature were undertaken. A new secular vocabulary including "freedom of expression," "public opinion," "liberal ideas," and "natural rights" was advanced.

As a system to empower the empire against its European rivals, the *Tanzimat* failed, but it represented nevertheless a step in the secularization of society. It was also only one element in a changing society marked by a growing urban working class, entailing "the breakdown in several traditions, habits, tastes, and attitudes" (273) and the emergence of an educated professional class, with their newspapers and other Western-style literature, introducing new "modes of psychological states, feelings of conflict, doubt, anxiety, and, above all, the practice of philosophizing and moralizing, both of which were the signs of secularization in mind and morality" (280).

According to Jenny White, the "Young Turk" movement that emerged in the early nineteenth century advocated a French-style secularism; the Turkish term for state secularism, *laiklik*, was even based on the French and represented "state control over religion and a strong state role in keeping religion out of the public sphere" (2013: 28). For the modernizers, including Mustafa Kemal, who became the leader of Turkey after World War I, "religion was a dangerous, divisive force in society that could not be eliminated and so had to be kept under the thumb of the state" (28). In addition to dangerous and divisive, religion was backward and non-modern.

When Kemal (known as Ataturk or "father of the Turks") assumed office, the sultanate was abolished; since the caliphate now had no place in Turkish politics, it was abolished too. *Seriat* courts were closed; *medreses* (religious schools), *tariqas* (Muslim brotherhoods), and *turbe* (tombs and shrines of saints) were all shut down. The Ministry of *Seriat* was closed, and some religious roles and titles were eliminated. A new code of civil/family law was promulgated, which "signified the unmitigated secularization of civil life. The men of religion lost their function, not only in civil procedure, but also in the administration of the law" (Berkes 1998: 472), including the area of marriage, which was entirely secularized. Even dress was secularized: the traditional headgear for men (the fez) was circumscribed, and women were heavily discouraged from wearing the traditional veil or headscarf. Even religion was brought under the authority of the state, which opened its own schools for the education of *imams* (religious specialists) under the jurisdiction of the Ministry of Education. In 1924 a Department of the Affairs of Piety was created "to manage the administrative affairs of religion" (484).

Obviously, whether it is public displays of religion, education, or the bodies of Turkish men and women, secularism "has been closely connected with the staging and representation of modernity in Turkey" (Zencirci 2012: 96). Yet Zencirci among others has made the salient point, which could be applied to other efforts at secularization, that *laiklik* was largely an "authoritarian" (107), top-down, elite-driven initiative. Kabir Tambar adds that "secularism continues to lack a popular base" in Turkey and that "secularist organizers failed to 'popularize their message'" (2009: 522). Both Zencirci and Tambar see this changing, though, as secularists have literally taken to the streets in recent years to protest the rise of Islam in culture and politics (see Figure 11.2). In a 2007

Figure 11.2 A protester holds up a poster of Atatürk during anti-government protests in Istanbul (2013).
Courtesy of fulya atalay/Shutterstock

demonstration against the ruling Justice and Development Party, secularists defending Kemal's vision for the society were known to repeat, "Turkey is secular, and it will remain secular" (Tambar 2009: 519). Zencirci contends that "the public experience of secularism has shifted from an authoritarian, solemn, and orderly outlook to a site where enjoyment and pluralistic, voluntary participation have become central in its emotional appeal" (2012: 107)—what we might rightly call *vernacular secularism*.

The Contemporary Secular (Anti-Religion) Movement

In 2009, many people were surprised to learn that Harvard University had a Humanist Chaplaincy, when the chaplain, Greg Epstein, released his book *Good Without God*. In fact, Harvard's Humanist Chaplaincy is nearly forty years old, founded by a former Catholic priest, and describes its mission as "to create and connect a nationwide network of Humanist communities focused on individual, group, and societal betterment, by providing them with the tools and expertise needed to make Humanism recognized, accessible, and influential across the United States" (http://harvardhumanist.org/explore-2/mission-statement/). Among its stated values are "reason, compassion, creativity, justice, integrity, awareness, environmentalism, feminism, equality, science, progress, and pluralism"—all of which are possible without religion.

If secularism is a continuum or field, then at the far end of the spectrum or at the edge of the field are those who are not merely indifferent or worldly but more or less self-consciously and intentionally unreligious or anti-religious. There are no humanist or atheist states or towns or even neighborhoods, which has so far made them difficult to study anthropologically. This does not mean, though, that there is no such thing as a humanist/atheist/secularist culture or community or organization. The secular movement has long had formal organizations and is moving now in the direction of forming communities.

We might conceive of the anti-religion movement as a network more than a society, a network of individuals, groups, and organizations. Central to the movement have been inspirational speakers like Robert Ingersoll (1833–99) and more recently Richard Dawkins and Christopher Hitchens. But no worldview can survive and spread without some form of institutionalization, and essential to the modern irreligion, like virtually all social movements, has been print media and membership organizations. Among the most prominent publications in contemporary secularism are the journals *American Atheist*, *Freethought Today*, *Free Inquiry*, *Skeptical Inquirer*, *Secular Nation*, *Skeptic*, *The Humanist*, and *Open Society*, not to mention countless newspapers and newsletters.

Many of these publications are mouthpieces for formal organizations. One of the oldest existing anti-religion organizations in the United States is American Atheists (see Figure 11.3), founded by Madalyn Murray (later O'Hair) in Baltimore on July 1, 1963, two weeks after the successful Supreme Court case on Bible reading and prayer in public schools. O'Hair quickly became known as "the most hated person in America" for her public atheism, even though the co-plaintiff in the case was a Unitarian. Because of the rampant hostility toward atheism, the organization's original name was Other Americans (that is, those who are *not* Christian), which was changed to Society of Separationists and finally American Atheists in 1976. It owns a press (American Atheists Press) and publishes occasional books as well as two journals. It also produces a television program, "The Atheist Viewpoint," and in 2004 established a political action committee to lobby for the rights of atheists. It holds an annual conference each year over Easter weekend.

Figure 11.3 Atheist billboard in New York City © Richard Levine / Alamy

Freedom from Religion Foundation (FFRF) was formed after a schism within American Atheists. The founder of the organization is Anne Gaylor, and the other central figures in the group are her daughter Annie Laurie and Annie Laurie's husband, Dan Barker. Barker is the public face of FFRF, a former believer who speaks as well as sings songs for the cause of irreligion. Based in Madison, Wisconsin, it publishes a monthly newspaper, *Freethought Today*. The main cause of FFRF is church/state separation, including fighting religious displays on public property and use of facilities like schools for proselytizing. It does a small amount of publishing, including Barker's memoir *Losing Faith in Faith* and Annie Laurie Gaylor's *Women Without Superstition*, a collection of writings from eighteenth- and nineteenth-century female freethinkers. It holds an annual conference in Madison in the fall, with smaller occasional meetings around the country.

Atheist Alliance International (AAI) is a loosely affiliated group of atheist and freethought grassroots organizations with a "democratic" approach to their activities. It has a website and an annual conference (most recently in August 2013) but is much more informal than the other groups just discussed. It also publishes a journal called *Secular Nation*. The Council for Secular Humanism was headed by Dr. Paul Kurtz, a philosopher in Buffalo, New York, who is regarded by many as the intellectual leader of humanism. In 1980 he formed the council, which maintains a variety of activities focusing on research, education, and publishing. The organization runs a major press, Prometheus Books, which publishes on freethought, science, politics, philosophy, and other subjects. It also publishes journals including *Free Inquiry*, *Skeptical Inquirer* (an instrument of the Committee for the Scientific Investigation of Claims of the Paranormal, or CSICOP), and *Philo*. It has an outreach arm to students in schools and colleges, the Campus Freethought Alliance. Finally, it operates a series of "Centers for Inquiry" where research and education are conducted. The current locations are Amherst, New York (the home office), Hollywood, New York City, and Tampa Bay; there are even international sites in Russia, Mexico, Peru, Nigeria, Germany, France, and Nepal. Major scholars like Ibn Warraq (who recently published *Why I am not a Muslim*) and Karen Armstrong work for or with the centers. At these locations, and occasionally around the country, CSH offers training seminars on critical thinking, science, history, and other issues of interest to humanists.

Americans United for Separation of Church and State is an organization with a single agenda—the First Amendment separation of church and state. It is not directly associated with atheist issues and in fact is headed by a religious man, the Reverend Barry Lynn. AU starts or joins legal action in cases of violation of the First Amendment, and Lynn is a regular figure on national news and discussion programs.

The American Humanist Association, established in 1941, is probably the most socially oriented of the major freethought organizations. Typical issues that it tackles include environmental, political, educational, ethical/moral, social justice, and of course religious ones. It operates local chapters around the country as well as a student outreach group, the Secular Student Alliance. It publishes a magazine entitled *The Humanist* and a newsletter called *Free Mind*. It even keeps a registry of secular officiates for humanists who want a non-religious wedding or funeral.

The Skeptics Society is primarily the work of Michael Shermer, author of such titles as *Why People Believe Weird Things* and *The Science of Good and Evil*. Based in Pasadena, it publishes *Skeptic* magazine, the main target of which is pseudoscience, with typical topics ranging from UFOs and alternative medical treatments to creationism and Holocaust-denial. While not explicitly anti-religious, it does take religion to task for its false or unsupported "scientific" claims. It has published *The Skeptic Encyclopedia of Pseudoscience* and sponsors monthly lectures at the California Institute of Technology. It also promotes various educational activities, including research, speakers and local events, and training and informational guides, not the least of which is the "Baloney Detection Kit" to help people identify errors, fallacies, and pseudoscience whenever they meet it.

Crucial to late twentieth- and early twentieth-first-century irreligion has been the internet and media like Facebook. The Secular Web/Internet Infidels is one of the many initiatives that exist only on the internet (www.infidels.org). It maintains an extensive online library of articles and information on topics from religion to politics to science. It also supports local and national organizations by listing activities on its site. At present, one of the most useful resources for planning secular/atheist activities has been Meetup.com; in 2009 there were 388 local atheist meetup groups with more than 46,000 members. There are also many smaller or private internet projects, as well as a number of internet radio outlets, such as "Freethought Radio," "The Infidel Guy," "Hellbound Allee," and the like, which feature guests and discussions on secularist issues, such as *Secular Nation*'s podcast.

As mentioned above, the atheist movement has recently discovered some celebrities and heroes, including Richard Dawkins, Christopher Hitchens, Daniel Dennett, and Sam Harris, whose writings since 2004 have earned them the title "The Four Horsemen of Atheism." Figures such as these have been instrumental in inspiring local organization, and atheist/freethought communities have begun to form around the USA and around the world. A few examples of more active communities are the Atheist Community of Austin, Texas;

New York City Atheists; the Atheist Community of Topeka, Kansas; Dalhousie Atheist Community in Canada; and the Mid-West Humanists: An Irish-Atheist Community.

What is really new and fascinating is the appearance of atheism in popular culture and a popular or vernacular secular/atheist culture. Mainstream television programs or movies such as *Dogma, Blasphemy: The Movie*, Bill Maher's *Religulous*, Penn and Teller's *Bullshit*, and Jonathan Miller's *Brief History of Disbelief* would have been almost inconceivable only a few years ago. Further, secularists/atheists have begun to invent everything that has formerly been associated with religion, not only chaplaincies and officiates for weddings and funerals, but also holidays. They have put Darwin Day (Charles Darwin's birthday, February 14), National Day of Reason (in early May), National Secular Service Day (October 18), Humanlight (December 23), and seasonal celebrations for solstices and equinoxes on their calendar. They offer secular alternatives to religion-based programs like Alcoholics Anonymous, such as Rational Recovery, and they run a children's camp called Camp Quest, with multiple locations around the United States. They have proposed new terminology to substitute for more inflammatory or biased labels, some preferring to call themselves "the brights" or "the universists." They use a variety of symbols to identify themselves on Facebook and elsewhere, and they put advertisements on billboards and the sides of buses. In other words, the secularist movement is evolving from lone non-believers and angry argument to the construction of a culture and a society.

Box 11.3 An Atheist Movement in Contemporary India

The anti-religion movement in the United States and much of the West has two primary agendas—to disprove the existence of God and to combat the incursion of religion into politics and public culture. However, anti-religion movements are also found in other countries, where we can witness, to paraphrase Asad, diverse formations of atheism. In a rare ethnographic study of an atheistic organization, Johannes Quack (2012a; 2012b) describes the history, philosophy, and activity of Andhashraddha Nirmoolan Samiti (ANiS or Organization for the Eradication of Superstition) in Maharashtra, India. Quack quotes Goparaju Vijayam, the executive director of the Atheist Center in Vijayawada, who stresses that India "is not only a land of religion, superstition, and blind beliefs, but also of atheism, rationalism, humanism, skepticism, and agnosticism" (2012a: 3). Representing the latter end of the spectrum, Quack finds that the Indian atheist movement "is based on the explicit intent to challenge belief in magical powers of irrational efficacy, as well as the influence of charismatic gurus, so as to tackle the harm and injustices the rationalists see as resulting from such belief"; put another way, Indian atheists want "to show their fellow Indians a way out of their enchanted world toward a rational, this-worldly way of life" (3).

Modern Indian atheism was influenced by British colonialism and freethought, leading to two organizations in the mid-1800s, the Gujarat Vernacular Society and the Deve Samaj or Society of Excellence, the second of which published a journal titled *Science-Grounded Religion*. But the key figure for contemporary Indian atheism is Goparaju Ramachandra Rao, better known as Gora, who established the Atheist Center in 1940. According to Quack, the Atheist Center "is not only an organization, it also owns and runs a campus which includes guest houses, lecture halls, and a hospital as well as an impressive (albeit disorganized) library with collection of atheist literature and magazines from all over the world" (2012b: 71). In addition to the standard conferences and seminars,

> it is also active, for example, in the realm of promoting environmental consciousness and ecological awareness; it collaborates with socio-psychological rehabilitation centers for former criminals, promotes sex education, health education, birth control, and family planning, and supports other areas of social work. Finally, the Atheist Center also launched what it calls "comprehensive rural development programs."
>
> (71)

ANiS brings its message to the people via "science vans," which drive activists to various communities where they can engage local people on issues including "sex education, environmental concerns, gender equality, and problems of alcohol addiction and make statements about 'consumerism'" (77). What is especially interesting about these efforts is that the Indian atheist movement does not limit itself to strictly "religious" questions; it "cannot be reduced to debates about the role of religion(s) in the public sphere" (77) and does not fret much about existence of gods or the compatibility or incompatibility of religion and science. As Vijayam himself has said, "Unlike in the West, in India there was no apparent conflict between science and religion. In India, we find that the conflict is between religion and social reform. In India, we find philosophical freedom on the one side and social ostracism on the other" (79). A most revealing illustration of the difference between Western and Indian atheism is an international conference organized at the Atheist Center titled "Atheism and Social Progress": Quack notes that the papers presented by Western atheist groups "hardly address the conference topic" (78). Thus Quack usefully suggests that we think of diverse local "modes of unbelief" instead of a simple opposition between religion (which itself comprises many "modes of religiosity") and non-religion.

Conclusion

Religions, while they may refer to or even dwell on "other worlds," inhabit the here and now. As we have seen repeatedly, the radical distinction between the "spiritual realm" and the "material realm" is a Christian preoccupation not shared by all cultures and religions. And, just as Christian societies construct "religion" in a particular way, so they construct "the secular" in a particular way. These different cultural constructions are what Talal Asad meant by "formations of the secular." Anthropologists, accordingly, have become attentive to the role of culture in producing certain visions of the secular and to the role of the secular as a project of modern states in producing certain types of societies and subjectivities.

Further, while the secular has a prominent place in modern Western societies, the secular is not unique to modernity or to the West. There have been secular alternatives in earlier history, and other societies, from Japan to Turkey to India, have developed their own formations of the secular. Even more, many cultures and religions have not divided the world between religion and non-religion, and, as in African "ancestor worship," the imposition of Western Christian thinking on other societies may lead us to see "religion" where the local people do not.

Clearly, then, "the secular" is not necessarily the absence or the opposite of "the religious." Scholars have suggested the notion of "secular religion," and much of vernacular religion represents an intersection of "the religious" and "the secular." There are of course individuals, organizations, and governments that are openly hostile to religion. But more often, secularism is one (quite mixed and ambiguous) effect of modernization on religion. Another effect has been the proliferation of new religious movements, some making universalistic claims and others being quite "local." Another effect can be clinging to traditions, even when they do not entirely fit modernizing conditions. When this clinging becomes sufficiently intense and aggressive, we might even encounter a kind of "fundamentalism," which is the topic of the final chapter.

DISCUSSION QUESTIONS

- What did Talal Asad mean by "formations of the secular"? How is "the secular" shaped by social notions of "religion" as well as by modern state governments? Why does "the secular" not simply mean "no religion" or "anti-religion"?
- What is "secularization theory," and how has contemporary religion challenged the theory?
- What are some specific "formations of the secular," and how do terms like "secular" or indeed "religion" not fit all cultures equally well?

SUPPLEMENTARY READING (see website)

- *State Atheism in the Early Soviet Union*
- *Formations of the Conflict between Science and Religion: Unification Church, ISKCON, and Heaven's Gate*
- *A Secular Bible Movement in the United Kingdom*

12 Religious Fundamentalism

For too many Western people, Islam equals fundamentalism, and for those who know a bit more about Islam, Salafism equals Islamic fundamentalism. In fact, no less credible a source than Princeton University defines Salafism as "a militant group of extremist Sunnis who believe themselves the only correct interpreters of the Koran and consider moderate Muslims to be infidels; seek to convert all Muslims and to insure that its own fundamentalist version of Islam will dominate the world" (http://wordnetweb.princeton.edu/perl/webwn?s=salafism). However, as Laurent Bonnefoy explains, *salafiyyah* in Arabic denotes "the ancestors" or "the early years," in particular the founding generation of Islam and their original (and thereby authoritative) form of the religion. With roots in the Middle Ages, Salafism is a kind of Islamic traditionalism, which

> gained momentum in the course of the twentieth century. This movement is characterized in theological terms as a return to religious foundations ... [and] the devotees intend to return to the practices of the "pious ancestors" (*al-salaf al-salih*) ... that is, the earliest generation of Muslims who are treated as models of piety.
>
> (2011: 42)

Surprisingly to many Westerners, this allegedly fundamentalist Islam does not necessarily advocate violence or even extremism. Rather, Bonnefoy identifies three variations, including missionary Salafism, activist Salafism, and jihadi Salafism. Focusing on missionary Salafism, because it so exquisitely defies our assumptions, he describes it as a quietist type of religion, one that lacks interest in politics and rejects violence. Of course missionary Salafists, like all religious missionaries, aspire to spread their version of truth, but they are hardly hostile to all aspects of modernity: they depend on resources like books and audio and video recordings, as well as on an international circulation of experts, ideas, and money. And in other ways they are the very opposite of the stereotype of fundamentalists: they do not uphold the obligation of women to veil their faces nor the prohibition on driving for women, nor do they endorse violence against non-Muslims, and at least one scholar demanded that Palestinians give up their campaign against Israel. Their purism mostly concentrates on "minor behaviors and distinctive practices" like clothing and grooming, and Bonnefoy even reports on a Salafi school where differences of opinion and divergences from official Salafism are tolerated. He concludes that this "capacity to live and let live at the local level and to work around mere doctrine once again shows that the study of Salafism should not be limited to an analysis of the ideological output of its leaders" (198), let alone the assumptions of non-Muslim partisans.

The twentieth and twenty-first centuries have shown that, to paraphrase Mark Twain, the rumors of the death of religion were greatly exaggerated. Religion survived the onslaught of modernization and secularization, evincing its characteristic and almost infinite capacity to adapt to and absorb extra-religious influences. Not only did religion not quietly fade away, but it thrived and multiplied, producing more religions and new religious movements, especially in the decades after World War II, than scholars could keep track of. And at least some of these religions and NRMs offered resistance—even virulent resistance—to modernization, or to other cultures and religions, or to "the world" as we commonly know it.

Religion, some might say, has re-emerged with a vengeance as a global social force—with fundamentalism as the most vengeful. Others might say, as noted in Chapter 11, that secularization was always an elite project that overestimated its impact on religion; more than a few scholars have declared that modern society was never as secular as we thought. Most accurately, modernity (which is itself multiple and diverse) no doubt has multiple and diverse effects on religion—in some instances breeding secularism, in other instances new religions, and in still other instances religious traditionalism or fundamentalism.

Fundamentalism is not a religion per se, nor is it a sect or denomination of religion. Following Thomas Meyer (2000) we should consider it as a "style" of religion. It is not the only style of religion, of course: there are many styles, from liberal and syncretistic to conservative and purist. It is also not exclusive to any particular religion: there is fundamentalist Christianity, fundamentalist Islam, fundamentalist Hinduism, and so on. In fact, fundamentalism is not exclusive to religion at all: Meyer called it a "style of civilization" (29), which can occur in any area of culture. One can be fundamentalist about politics or economics or race or gender or baseball. Finally, while fundamentalism seems to be a distinctly modern phenomenon, or at least a type of response to certain challenges posed by modernity, it is possible without stretching the term to identify it in pre-modern contexts as well.

The Anthropology of Fundamentalism

Religious fundamentalism derives its name (and much of its energy) from the notion of "fundamentals," those elements—beliefs, behaviors, organizational structures, and/or moral injunctions—that are felt to be most essential and central, the oldest, deepest, and truest aspects of the religion. The popular and often scholarly view is dominated by Christian and Muslim fundamentalisms: George Marsden, for instance defined a fundamentalist as "an evangelical Protestant who is militantly opposed to liberal theologies and to some aspects of secularism in modern culture" (1990: 22). This definition is unsatisfactory, though, since it not only excludes all non-Christians but also most Christians (e.g. Catholics and Orthodox).

Instead of associating fundamentalism with any specific religion, or with religion at all, Richard Antoun, while still focusing overtly on Christian, Muslim, and Jewish versions, saw it as "an orientation to the world, both cognitive and affective. The affective, or emotional, orientation indicates outrage and protest against (and also fear of) change and against a certain ideological orientation, the orientation of modernism" (2001: 3). Meyer too understood fundamentalism as "a political ideology of the 20th century," which combines "elements of the late modern age in an ambiguously pragmatic manner with aspects drawn from the dogmatized stock of pre-modern traditions" (2000: 17).

Social-scientific approaches to religious fundamentalism highlight a number of common points. First, religious fundamentalism is *for* something, promoting what it

perceives to be the fundamental and crucial elements of its
worldview *and the truth* for practitioners. In the case of Ch
typically include the Bible as a literal and inerrant docum
the exclusion and sometimes condemnation of others (ev
and lost; a sharp distinction between religion and "the
inferior or actually evil; an eschatology in which the er
survive into the new kingdom; an uncompromising mora...
to participate in politics to institutionalize all of the above, incl...
scious desire to dismantle the separation of church and state. Other religi...
their own programs based on their own "fundamentals": a scriptural religion ...
finds its fundamentals in the Qur'an, while other types of religions find it elsewhere.

Second, religious fundamentalism is *against* something. Virtually all of the commentators stress the exclusivist, agitated, and even militant attitude of fundamentalism. As Marsden emphasized, fundamentalists "must not only believe their evangelical teachings, but they must be willing to fight for them against modernist theologies, secular humanism, and the like" (23). Martin Marty and Scott Appleby, in the introduction to their massive comparative study, stated that fundamentalists see themselves as fighting, specifically *fighting back*:

> It is no insult to fundamentalisms to see them as militant, whether in the use of words and ideas or ballots or, in extreme cases, bullets. Fundamentalists see themselves as militants. This means the first word to employ in respect to them is that they are reactive.
>
> (1991a: ix)

They are, in their words and often enough in their works, at war with the world.

Anthropologists apply their unique perspective to fundamentalism, asking, in the words of Susan Harding, "how 'fundamentalism' was invented, who speaks it, what are the categories, assumptions, and trajectories implicit in its narrative representations" (1991: 374). Harding insisted that fundamentalists "do not simply exist 'out there' but are also produced by modern discursive practices" (374). Central to the invention of fundamentalism, she argued, is secularism: exactly as Asad stipulated (see Chapter 11), secularism strives to define "proper religion" and to constrain religion within its proper sphere (ideally, the church and private life). Religious actors who refuse these secularist limitations become, from the secular perspective, "a category of persons whose behavior defies reasonable expectations and therefore needs to be—and can be—explained" (374). In other words, "fundamentalism" becomes a cultural category—and what she called a *repugnant* category—because "modern voices represent fundamentalists and their beliefs as an historical object, a cultural 'other,' apart from, even antithetical to, 'modernity,' which emerges as the positive term" in the struggle between secular modernity and religion (374).

Almost a decade later, but two years before Asad's *Formations of the Secular*, Judith Nagata endorsed and extended Harding's argument. Nagata noted that "fundamentalism" originally referred to religion but, as a "metaphor of choice" was being applied "to an everwidening range of ideas and behaviors" (2001: 481), including nationalism, ethnicity, language, politics, and even the market and the environment. To be sure, Nagata posited that fundamentalism or traditionalism was a reaction to uncertainty, to the "excess of openness and choice" that accompanies modern life; it is "a way of setting boundaries, an 'anti-hermeneutic'" that claims to end uncertainty by ending interpretation ("hermeneutics" is the study and practice of interpretation), identifying the putatively original or true belief. But precisely because fundamentalists take this decidedly non-modern stance, talist" becomes "an epithet for the Other, invariably negative, the archenemy, se position is to be dismissed or vilified, and the goal is demonization, regardless ogical, political, religious or moral substance" (489). Nagata called the label "funda-alist" a kind of "verbal ammunition" (489), a tactic to discredit and marginalize the ple and their position. Such a strategy is interesting and often effective politically, but s Harding stressed, it is very destructive anthropologically, serving to "blot out funda-mentalist realities" and paint all traditionalists into "aberrant, usually backward or hoodwinked, versions of modern subjects," confirming the rational modern person "as the neutral norm of history" (1991: 374).

Varieties of Fundamentalist Experience

Given the anthropological analysis just presented, it is appropriate if not essential to apply concepts previously applied to religion and secularism to fundamentalism as well. In a word, just as there are diverse "formations" of religion and of the secular, so we might conceive of diverse "formations of the fundamental." Likewise, just as there are multiple "modes of religiosity," so we can think of "modes of fundamentalism," not all political and not all violent.

In fact, among "fundamentalists," *moral and ideological purists* are probably the most common and least extreme type; they merely take their religion especially seriously and let it pervade and define more or less every aspect of their lives. Some groups and sects take this notion of community further, becoming *peaceful separatists* like the Mennonites or the Amish (see Figure 12.1), whom Larsen (1971) called "quiet fanatics." These groups reject the modern and outside world to greater or lesser degrees and hold to their convictions by not only ideologically but physically detaching themselves from the wider society. Typically, there are certain practices that can only be followed in a separatist setting, such as polygamy among the fundamentalist Mormons of the southwestern United States.

Figure 12.1 Amish life in Lancaster, Pennsylvania. Courtesy of the Carol M. Highsmith Archive, Library of Congress Prints and Photographs Division

Groups or sects that seek to engage the wider society, for purposes of bringing that society into line with their own beliefs and values, can be regarded as *activists*. The Moral Majority and the Christian Coalition, among other religiously and culturally conservative agencies, represent such an effort: they want not only to live their own moral and ideological principles but to urge them on the rest of society and are willing to use political (including electoral and governmental) methods to achieve their goals. Legislating and institutionalizing religious principles are among their techniques. More uncompromising are the *reconstructionists* who seek a total transformation or reinvention of society in line with their religious convictions (see pp. 290–2 below). However, they do not use, or at least so far have not used, coercion to reach their ends. At the extreme, then, are the *militants*, who are willing to employ force against their perceived enemies—which may include the government and the general population—in pursuit of religious agendas. These are the groups that fly airliners into towers or drive truckloads of explosives to federal buildings.

Box 12.1 Jewish Fundamentalists and Liberals Getting Along in Denmark

Fundamentalists may be the Other to modern liberal citizens, but they need not always be a "repugnant other." In contemporary Denmark, a small and well-acculturated community of Jews lives, interacting peacefully with the wider non-Jewish society, intermarrying with Christians, and maintaining "no special neighborhoods, accents, occupations, or clothing styles" (Buckser 2005: 128). We might expect the arrival of an ultraorthodox or fundamentalist group in Copenhagen to agitate modern Danish Jews, and when Yitzchock and Rochel Loewenthal established Chabad House in the 1990s, there was at first consternation over their "stringent religiosity" and "cultural otherness" (125). However, since that early suspicion and hostility, not only have emotions mellowed, but Andrew Buckser witnessed "an appreciation" and "a grudging admiration" for the local fundamentalists. The acculturated Danish Jews were certainly not impressed with the Loewenthal's beliefs: the Chabad group has had no "missionary success" nor "acquired any converts among the Danish Jews" (132). But for a number of local reasons, the liberal Jews enjoy having the orthodox Jews around. One reason is that Chabad maintains a healthy distance from the wider society: because its founders are immigrants from England and the United States, Chabad has a "decidedly non-Danish" atmosphere, including religious services predominantly in English (132). This distance insulates Chabad from the factionalism of the small Danish Jewish community. More importantly, since Chabad operates above the din of local Jewish factions, "it can engineer the kind of innovative activities that indigenous Jews cannot" (135), sponsoring, for example, community-wide events and festivals. Ultimately, in these events and in the persons of the Loewenthals, the Danish Jews can experience and celebrate an "unapologetic Jewishness" (131) that is satisfying and liberating to the acculturated Danes. "The appeal," Buckser concludes, "of Chabad lay almost entirely in its positive attitude toward Jewish identity" (132). For many secularized Jews, "the Loewenthals' willingness to flaunt their anomalous identity makes them almost heroic figures" (136), and Buckser judges that, while secular Jews do not want to join Chabad, they treat it like "a valuable resource for the Jewish community" (140).

So fundamentalism is not a single monolithic phenomenon or movement, nor does the relationship between fundamentalists and the surrounding society take only one (conflictual) form. Nevertheless, summing up their research on religious fundamentalisms, Marty and Appleby found the following characteristics recurring through history and across culture:

- Religious idealism;
- Religious claims as an irreducible basis for communal and personal identity;
- Extremism, rhetorical or actual, which "serves a number of purposes, among them the posing of a litmus test separating true believers from outsiders" (1991b: 818);
- Dramatic eschatologies;
- A dramatization, demonization, and even "mythologization" of their enemies;
- A counter-acculturation orientation, that is, a refusal to compromise with or integrate "outside" influences;
- Missionary zeal;
- A crisis mentality: "Fundamentalisms arise or come to prominence in times of crisis, actual or perceived" (822);
- Charismatic and authoritarian (usually male) leadership;
- Mass appeal;
- A stated rejection of modernity mixed with "a shrewd exploitation of its processes and instrumentalities" (827).

Fundamentalism as a Cultural System

Fundamentalisms are not, any more than new religious movements or secularization or modernity itself, purely negative programs; they are not only against something but for something. Each sees itself, as the cases below will amply illustrate, as an effort to create a good and true religion as part of a larger project to create a good and true society. As Marty and Appleby clearly stated:

> fundamentalism intends neither an artificial imposition of archaic practices and life-styles nor a simple return to a golden era, a sacred past, a bygone time of origins—although nostalgia for such an era is a hallmark of fundamentalist rhetoric. Instead, religious identity thus renewed becomes the exclusive and absolute basis for a re-created political and social order that is oriented to the future rather than the past. Selecting elements of tradition and modernity, fundamentalists seek to re-make the world in the service of a dual commitment to the unfolding eschatological drama (by returning all things in submission to the divine) and to self-preservation (by neutralizing the threatening "Other").
>
> (1993: 3)

Fundamentalisms, then, are engaged in the noble practice—indeed, the essentially and only human practice—of world-making, or what Antoun called "traditioning." By traditioning he meant an active process in which "traditions" are chosen and modified (though often not admittedly so), interpreted, and sometimes outright invented to give form to the religion. These "traditioned" traditions are then "given" as *the* fundamentals of their faith, *through which members are supposed to view and understand their past, their present, and most critically their future.* In other words, fundamentalism is a special case of the more general process of "the invention of tradition." This explains Antoun's other characteristic of fundamentalism, "selective modernization," through which such movements contend with but also adapt to modern/foreign influences.

Fundamentalisms are thus not only cultural but *cultures or potential cultures*. And, based on everything we understand about culture, fundamentalisms are doing what must be done: they are offering not only a model *of* the world but a model *for* the world, one in which "ethos" and "worldview" match. They are generating the "consonance" between religion and other domains of society and, in a certain and sometimes intentional sense, eliminating the modern "separation" of religion and the rest of society.

Part—in fact an essential part—of the fundamentalist program is the construction of institutions, religious and otherwise but necessarily authorized and legitimized by religion. The details of the institution-construction will vary from religion to religion, from society to society, and from historical period to historical period. Nevertheless, a few elements of this process are fairly standard. Fundamentalists, as Marty and Appleby put it, "are boundary-setters: they excel in marking themselves off from others by distinctive dress, customs, and conduct" (1993: 4). These distinctions are, of course, one dimension of their culture, whether it is earlocks for orthodox Jews, beards for orthodox Muslims, or "WWJD" bracelets for orthodox Christians. As for the boundaries, the group that is enclosed by them can be a single congregation, a movement or entire religion, an ethnic group, a society, or a state. One of the more interesting things we observe is the easy concatenation of religion and nationality or nationalism, as with *Hindutva* in India or Buddhism in Sri Lanka (see pp. 300–1 and 302–3 respectively below).

The relation between fundamentalisms and the state is a problematic one, as our examples will show. Depending on their theology and politics, a fundamentalist movement may be opposed to any state at all (God or religion being the sole source of authority and law) or adamantly pro-state (seeing the government as the mechanism for achieving religious rectitude on earth). In more than a few cases, fundamentalist groups have attempted, occasionally successfully (e.g. Ayatollah Khomeini in Iran or the Taliban in Afghanistan), to seize the government and use political power to implement their religious plans. Some scholars have asked whether one can reasonably speak of a fundamentalism-in-power, since fundamentalism is by definition oppositional, but the question is wrongly asked: a fundamentalist movement is not in opposition to power (in a direct way, each seeks power) but to modern or foreign influences on society. Therefore, a fundamentalism-in-power still has much to oppose, including resistance from modernized members of society, not to mention all non-members of the movement. A more serious question is whether a fundamentalism-in-power must necessarily make some concessions to secularism, that is to say, when a religious movement attains political power and runs the state, it must first participate in areas of society that it never did before—thus redefining religious institutions and practices (like Muslim *shari'a* law) in original ways—and second at least partly submit religious principle and authority to pragmatic and worldly concerns. In other words, when a religion becomes the government, it must deliver the mail, pick up the trash, and command the army.

The culture of fundamentalism brings with it other troublesome ingredients. Experience has shown that fundamentalism tends to be "essentially antidemocratic, anti-accommodationist, and antipluralist and that it violates, *as a matter of principle*, the standards of human rights defended, if not always perfectly upheld, by Western democracies" (Marty and Appleby 1993: 5). This attitude, not unique to fundamentalism (we find it in both right-wing and left-wing absolutist and idealist movements), flows from the superhuman authority of the system: power and sovereignty do not lie with the *demos* but with the divine. Also, naturally, all other positions, even loyal oppositions, are necessarily and completely wrong. Thus the legitimation of the movement and its resulting institutions and (if successful) regime almost inevitably entail the delegitimation of all possible alternatives and rivals, which are castigated as evil, corrupt, and so on. This attitude can, obviously, lead to violence.

Besides pluralism and popular sovereignty, other aspects of modern social life are questioned or rejected by fundamentalisms. One is the self-critical and uncertain nature of modernity, or even postmodernity, the collapse or failure of all "grand narratives" of human life and social meaning. As mentioned by Nagata, Peter Berger contended that modernity "undermines all the old certainties; uncertainty is a condition that many people find very hard to bear; therefore, any movement (not only a religious one) that promises to provide or to renew certainty has a ready market" (1999: 7). Nancy Ammerman (1987), in her ethnography of a fundamentalist congregation, repeatedly cited their impulse to certainty; inerrancy of their authorities (scriptural, human, and institutional) is typically the first principle of the movement.

A second aspect of modernity that is disparaged is the separation of the religious and the secular or, as it is often formulated in modern religion, the assignment of religion to "the private" apart from public social and political life. Religion is not merely private, not merely a matter of choice or feeling; therefore, it can and must be institutionalized. Religion, from this point of view, is the very ground and source of society and its institutions. This leads, as one might expect, to a perspective on religion itself which is diametrically opposed to the one that secularism (or anthropology) takes. While secularists call religion essentially "symbolic" and "social" and "functional," fundamentalists insist that it is literal and true, public and effective. In other words, the fundamentalist perspective "rejects the widespread modern idea that religion ... really doesn't mean what it actually says" (Gellner 1992: 2). A clear example is the televangelist James Kennedy, who rejected the symbolist approach when he argued that aside from obviously metaphorical parts of the Bible (like "faith of a mustard seed") the rest is to be taken literally. For him, Jonah was literally swallowed by a whale, Adam was a real person, and Jesus really walked on water; there is no interpretation, no symbolic analysis: "In living, explaining, or defending our faith, we are most likely to say, 'The Word of God says. ... ' As believers, that settles the matter, no matter what the matter may be" (1997: 20).

Finally, fundamentalists, like all culture-makers, must put their plans into action; this may mean pervading and "colonizing" the existing institutions of a society. Very often the primary institutions in contention between fundamentalists and the rest of society are the government, the education system, and the media. Fundamentalists, in the USA and elsewhere, have been active and direct in attempting to penetrate and dominate these segments of society (see also pp. 291–2 below). They have often, due to their minority status or their perceived extremism, been defeated in these initiatives. However, given their certainty and their energy, defeat is seldom the end of their culture-making efforts: as Ammerman pointed out, "Whenever fundamentalists have lost a battle, they have responded by withdrawing to establish their own alternative institutions" (1987: 211). At the extreme, like the Amish, they literally withdraw and live in a world-within-a-world of their own design. More commonly, if they cannot control the public schools, for instance, they establish private schools or home schools where they can teach their own curriculum. The Catholic Church has long operated an extensive system of schools parallel to the public ones; Muslim societies often depended on religious schools or *madrasas*, and Protestant sects have increasingly exploited the notion. Recently, fundamentalist movements have opened their own colleges (e.g. Liberty University or Bob Jones University) and law schools, as well as creating their own radio and television stations, printing their own curricula and textbooks, publishing their own journals and newspapers, organizing their own political action groups, and so on.

This is why Anthony Giddens, the brilliant social theorist, was wrong when he declared that fundamentalism is "tradition defended in the traditional way" (1994: 6). As he himself subsequently admitted, "The point about traditions is that you don't really have to justify them: they contain their own truth, a ritual truth, asserted as correct by the believer" (6). There is a vast difference between tradition and "traditionalism," between the fundamentals of a religion and "fundamentalism." But since fundamentalisms are not only movements but *arguments and ideologies*—and arguments and ideologies that share the social space with others, fundamentalist and non-fundamentalist—they act highly non-traditionally. In other words, fundamentalisms may be *about* tradition, but they are not "traditional," and they may complain against innovation, but they are essentially innovative.

Christian Fundamentalisms

While fundamentalism in Christianity is especially noteworthy in the present moment, it is not entirely unprecedented in this moment. The Protestant Reformation can well be seen as a fundamentalist movement. Martin Luther's purpose, quite explicitly, was to dispense with the accretions of time and tradition and to return to a simpler, purer, and therefore truer Christianity (a sort of Salafi Christianity), one without priests and sacraments but with only the believer and the Bible. Even before that, we could regard such dissent movements as the Free Spirits of the twelfth century as a kind of fundamentalism, which took their inspiration from a literalist reading of (some parts of) scripture for their beliefs and lifestyles. And even further back, unitarian and other such challenges to Catholic orthodoxy can be seen as attempts to dip directly from the source and to restore a lost original orthodoxy, a "primitive church" as it was in the early years of the religion. Finally, many if not all ascetic and monastic traditions are attempts to create an oasis of right belief and conduct in a desert of chaos and corruption.

The Rise of Modern Fundamentalism

Although reform and revivalism are old Christian traditions, the terms "fundamentalism" and "fundamentalist" did not enter the English vocabulary until shortly after the turn of the twentieth century. Between 1910 and 1915 a series of twelve publications named *The Fundamentals: A Testimony to the Truth* appeared. Out of this effort emerged an organization, the World's Christian Fundamentals Association, founded by William B. Riley in 1919, and the new terminology. In 1920 the editor of the Northern Baptist newspaper *Watchman Examiner*, Curtis Lee Laws, actually described a fundamentalist as a person who is willing to "do battle royal" for Christian fundamentals.

There were five basic points to the early fundamentalist position: the absolute truth and inerrancy of the Christian scriptures, the virgin birth of Jesus, the atonement of sin through the substitutive sacrifice of Jesus on the cross, the bodily resurrection and future second coming of Jesus, and the divinity of Jesus and/or the reality of the miracles he performed. Of these, the anchor is clearly the inerrancy of the Bible, which is the source (and alleged proof) of the other four claims. A more interesting question is why fundamentalism appeared at this particular moment in social history. There have been various revivals or "awakenings" in American history (see Chapter 9), and some of the most successful and respected denominations in the country, like the Methodists and the Baptists, started as energetic revivalist efforts with "circuit riders" traveling the countryside giving ordinary people a version of the religion they could understand and digest.

So "old time religion" is nothing new. But while the specifics of these and other similar movements differ, on some general points they are in substantial agreement. All invoked the purity and perfection of scripture. Each looked out upon not just a physical world but even a spiritual world that had "gone wrong" somehow; as nineteenth-century evangelist Alexander Campbell wrote, "The stream of Christianity has become polluted" (quoted in Hatch 1989: 168). And each saw itself as representing authentic Christianity. Each imagined itself—and *only* itself—as the *restoration* of religion. Accordingly, Campbell wrote a column called "A Restoration of the Ancient Order of Things," in which he set the agenda to "'bring the christianity [sic] and the church of the present day' up to the standards of 'the state of christianity [sic] and of the church of the New Testament'" (quoted in Hatch: 168). Other churches were corrupted at best, false or even satanic at worst.

However, there were other menaces afoot. A crucial one was science and its attendant secularization; Darwin's *On the Origin of Species*, after all, appeared in 1859. Humanistic philosophies and social sciences were also advancing. The Bible itself was increasingly being treated as literature rather than literal truth, to the point of questioning the authenticity of some of its passages or even the very historicity of Jesus. Finally, the American society was changing, under the forces of urbanization, industrialization, and immigration; as early as the 1840s, Roman Catholics comprised the largest single Christian denomination in the USA, which they continue to do today, displacing any single Protestant sect as the most numerous in the country (although Protestants collectively still outnumber Catholics by nearly three to one). Within Christianity itself, there were "modernizing" processes at work, attempting to accommodate scientific and social realities with religion.

By the late nineteenth century, while liberal Christians were making their peace with cultural change and modernity, conservatives were organizing their opposition. Charles Hodge, in his 1873 book *Systematic Theology*, argued that every word of the scriptures was literally true, not allegorical or symbolic; he followed with *What is Darwinism?*, where he wrote that religion "has to fight for its life against a large class of scientific men." By 1875 conservative Christians in the USA were organizing Bible conferences and other such gatherings for preachers and teachers. For instance, 1875 saw the founding of the Believers' Meeting for Bible Study (which became in 1883 the Niagara Bible Conference). In 1886 what would become the Moody Bible Institute opened, followed in 1909 by the Bible Institute of Los Angeles, and any number of books, newspapers, newsletters, and magazines.

The Resurgence of Fundamentalism in the Late Twentieth Century

American fundamentalism hit its high point in the 1925 Scopes "monkey" trial in Tennessee, in which a man named John Thomas Scopes was charged with the crime of teaching evolution. For several decades fundamentalism fell into disrepute and was replaced by the more benign and less political "evangelicalism" best represented by Billy Graham: the goal was to save souls, not change society. Even Jerry Falwell subsequently maintained that fundamentalists "are not interested in controlling America; they are interested in seeing souls saved and lives changed for the glory of God. They believe that the degree to which this is accomplished will naturally influence the trend of society in America" (quoted in Pinnock 1990: 50). However, cultural developments in the second half of the twentieth century drove fundamentalists to become impatient with this natural trend and therefore to become more politically active. First, the civil rights movement of the 1950s aggravated some cultural conservatives, as can be seen from the anti-integration activities of the Ku Klux Klan and certain Southern politicians. The 1960s saw minorities of all sorts—feminists, "hippies" and anti-war activists, and even gays and atheists—supposedly trampling on "traditional values" and conventional definitions of family and society. The school prayer cases of the early 1960s and the struggle over the Equal Rights Amendment (ERA) were two rallying causes. But the last straw was the 1973 Supreme Court decision *Roe v. Wade*, legalizing abortion rights. To some, this was tantamount to legalized murder and state Satanism. From that date, it only took a few years for organized fundamentalism to crystallize. That these are precisely the issues that preoccupy fundamentalists is evidenced by the litany of complaints featured in Tim LaHaye's influential 1980 book *The Battle for the Mind*, including the ERA, prayer in school, abortion, gay rights, and the general philosophy of "secular humanism," as well as such other matters as the limitation of corporal punishment for children, certification requirements for Christian schools, and investigations into church finances.

A newly motivated and politically active American Christian fundamentalism coalesced in the late 1970s, embodied in organizations like the Moral Majority. Figures like Falwell, Ralph Reed, and Pat Robertson rose to prominence on a new kind of philosophy and platform. Susan Harding conducted anthropological fieldwork inside Falwell's ministry in the 1990s, finding a movement that "broke old taboos constraining [fundamentalists'] interactions with outsiders, claimed new cultural territory, and refashioned themselves in church services" (2000: ix). Most clearly, a youth minister told her, "We don't practice stay-at-home Christianity. We're militant and aggressive in getting out Christ's message" (4). Unexpectedly to some critics of fundamentalism, Harding encountered "no big political meetings, no direct actions, no public political debates, no heated political conversations, and no partisan politics worth shaking a stick at" (9). Yet Falwell told his flock that "God wanted fundamentalists to reenter, to reoccupy, the world" and to use modern social and political tactics to achieve their goal (see Chapter 9). What was especially intriguing about Falwell's brand of fundamentalism (soon to be adopted by others) was the role of the preacher and the organizational structure of the church. Preachers like Falwell "'stand in the gap' between the language of the Christian Bible and the language of everyday life," translating—dare we say, vernacularizing—biblical talk "into local theological and cultural idioms and placing present events inside the sequences of the Biblical stories. Church people, in their turn, borrow, customize, and reproduce the Bible-based speech of their preachers and other leaders in their daily lives" (12). Precisely because preachers and congregants spoke the same fundamentalist language, the church did not have to institute a rigid centralized structure; instead, as in Wilford's account of Rick Warren's church, Falwell's organization "was managed by loose, fragmentary pastoral networks or weak denominational structures," leaning heavily on "parachurch organizations" (274). The result was contrary to the stereotype of fundamentalism: "heterogeneity not homogeneity, hybridity not purity, fluidity not fixity, characterized the movement at every level" (274)—producing what Harding called a kind of "flexible absolutism" (275).

Outside the "mainstream" of American fundamentalism, other more adamant groups and movements dwell. We referred earlier to separatist types like the Amish and the Mennonites who have successfully created their own society-within-a-society where they can practice their religion and traditions untroubled by the outside, modern world. Jerry Falwell actually announced a plan to establish a Christian community in Virginia where, theoretically, a person could be born, go to school, work, retire, and die without ever stepping foot outside. And a movement known as Christian Exodus has gone further; as they state clearly on their website (www.christianexodus.org):

> ChristianExodus.org is an association of Christians who no longer wish to live under the unjust usurpation of powers by the federal government, and therefore resolves to formally disassociate itself from this tyrannical authority, and return to the model of governance of a constitutional republic. We seek a republican government constrained by constitutionally delegated powers. If this cannot be achieved within the United States, then we believe a peaceful withdrawal from the union to be the last available remedy.

Their express mission, then, is to migrate en masse to a relatively small state (South Carolina is their current selection), vote themselves into office, and inaugurate a society based on their religious principles. These principles include prohibition of abortion and gay marriage, institutionalization of prayer and the Christian Bible in schools, the elimination of evolution from the curriculum, the public display of the Ten Commandments, and the right to own weapons, among others. As they intimate in their statement, if the federal government interferes with their effort to build a Christian society (no mention is made of the non-Christians or non-Christian-Exodus Christians in South Carolina), they are prepared to secede from the Union.

Further along the fundamentalist scale is the Christian Reconstruction movement. It aims to do for the entire country what Christian Exodus aims to do for one state: institute a religious society and a religious government. Also known as Dominionism and Theonomy, Christian Reconstructionism advances the following agenda:

- The reformulation of civil law in accordance with biblical, specifically Torah/Old Testament standards, including the death penalty for adultery, blasphemy, heresy, homosexuality, idolatry, and witchcraft;
- The banning of any congregation or religion that does not accept Mosaic law, including of course all non-Christian religions;
- The return of women to their ancient subordinate status;
- The elimination of income taxes and the prison system (the death penalty presumably rendering jail mostly unnecessary);
- The criminalization of abortion, also punishable by death.

The rationale behind this agenda was expressed clearly by R. J. Rushdoony, one of the founders of Christian Reconstructionism: "The law is therefore the law for Christian man and Christian society. Nothing is more deadly or more derelict than the notion that the Christian is at liberty with respect to the kind of law he can have" (1973: 8–9). And by law, they mean ancient Hebrew law; as another prominent figure in the movement, Gary North, wrote:

The *New* Testament teaches us that—unless exceptions are revealed elsewhere—*every* Old Testament commandment is binding, even as the standard of justice for all magistrates (Rom. 13:1–4), including every recompense stipulated for civil offenses in the law of Moses (Heb 2:2). From the New Testament alone we learn that we must take as our operating *presumption* that any Old Testament penal requirement is binding today on all civil magistrates. The presumption can surely be modified by definite, revealed teaching in the Scripture, but in the absence of such qualifications or changes, any Old Testament penal sanction we have in mind would be morally obligatory for civil rulers.

(1986: 242)

In other words, and unusually overtly, Christian Reconstructionism seeks to reshape the future in the image of the (ancient) past. Equally overtly, North elsewhere reformulated the fundamentalist struggle, which we tend to imagine pits religion against modernization. The battle for the mind, which other fundamentalists like LaHaye also acknowledge,

some fundamentalists believe, is between fundamentalism and the institutions of the Left. This conception of the battle is fundamentally incorrect. The battle for the mind is between the Christian reconstruction movement, which alone among Protestant groups takes seriously the law of God, and everyone else.

(1984: 65–66)

Not only is modernity wrong, but all other religions are wrong as well.

Near the far end of the scale, the Christian Identity movement is a loose affiliation of various groups and agendas, from Anglo-Israelists to white supremacists to some "militia movements." Anglo-Israelism is a doctrine inspired by the Englishman John Wilson's 1840 "Lectures on our Israelitish Origin," which asserted that white people, specifically Anglo-Saxons, are the direct and true descendants of Israel. It was first promoted in the USA by Howard Rand, who founded the Anglo-Saxon Federation of America in 1930. However, the movement received a major boost when Wesley Swift joined in the 1940s; coming from a Christian and politically right-wing position, he introduced "demonic anti-Semitism and political extremism" to the religious mix (Barkun 1997: 61). Swift started the Anglo-Saxon Christian Congregation in California, which eventually became the Church of Jesus Christ Christian. He was succeeded in 1970 by Richard Butler, who also established the Aryan Nations in Idaho (see Figure 12.2).

According to the watchdog organization ReligiousTolerance.org, the beliefs of Christian Identity groups, while various, share some common factors, including "a very conservative interpretation of the Bible," leading to condemnation of homosexuality and members of other religions; the superiority of the whites as the "Adamic race," that is, the real descendants of Adam, who was a white man; derogation of non-whites as "Satanic spawn," subhumans and "mud people" who corrupt and threaten God's true people; racial separation or, in the extreme, racial extermination; an absolute ban on interracial marriage or "racial adultery"; and more or less complex conspiracy theories, often with Jews at the center. At least some Christian Identity groups have syncretized fundamentalist religious views and racial ideologies with American

Figure 12.2 Richard Butler, founder of Aryan Nations, with his followers (*c*.1995) © Evan Hurd/
Sygma/Corbis

patriotism, producing a volatile blend of religious conviction and political extremism. As
Richard Abanes reported:

> Long before today's militias, these white supremacists/Christian Identity Movement
> followers were calling themselves "patriots." One Aryan Nations newsletter (*c*. 1982),
> for instance, lists Aryan Nations founder Richard Butler and racist leader Dan Gayman
> as "Christian patriots." … Several racist fundraising letters from the 1980s, such as
> those produced by KKK Grand Wizard Don Black, were addressed to fellow "White
> Patriots." … By the 1980s, white "patriots" were also forming paramilitary groups
> similar to militias. For example, in the mid 1980s a militia-like group of racists called
> the Arizona Patriots were arrested and convicted of plotting to bomb several targets,
> including federal buildings in Phoenix and Los Angeles.
>
> (1997: 31–33)

The potential for violence shows not only in the company that the Christian Identity
movement keeps, including the Ku Klux Klan, the Aryan Nations, the National Alliance,
and the Posse Comitatus, but also the actions of its adherents, including the Olympic and
abortion-clinic bombings of Eric Rudolph and the Oklahoma City bombing by Timothy
McVeigh.

Fundamentalisms in Cross-Cultural Perspective

Other religions have their own formations of the fundamental; in addition, the modes of fundamentalism within a religion differ depending on the society or country and, even further, on the specific group or movement within the society or country. And while "modern" fundamentalisms resist modernity, past fundamentalisms have strived against their contemporary social, moral, or ideological threats. Each clings to and elevates its own "fundamentals" and seeks to restore its own version of the past. Within this diversity, fundamentalism is a recurrent theme in human life. In fact, it is more than interesting to ponder how the decade of the 1970s was an especially fertile time for fundamentalist movements—and for the success of those movements.

Jewish Fundamentalisms

Even in ancient times, Hebrew prophets and other devotees were constantly trying to bring the people back to the right worship of their god; one of the most persistent and pernicious issues among the ancient Jews was the influence of "baals" or gods of foreign neighbors, and they were repeatedly admonished to abandon these false gods and return to their own god. When Israel came under the influence first of the Greeks and then of the Romans, this created a new fundamentalist dynamic; now they were faced with cultural as well as religious assimilation and syncretism. As in every case of culture contact, some Israelites adopted the culture of the outsider, as prestige or as defiance of traditional Jewish authority; some mixed old and new cultures and molded something locally unique from the mixture. But some held firmly to the "old religion" and even became militant champions of orthodoxy against outside and inside challenges alike. As we saw in Chapter 10, many followers were willing to die for their religious truths.

The Essenes and the Maccabees are two examples of "restorationist" groups in ancient Judaism. After centuries of foreign rule, Judas Maccabeus led a Jewish revolt and temporarily established a Jewish state in the late 60s CE which was the restoration of not just the state but the religion. And the Essenes, a monastically separatist faction, seem surprisingly modern in their attitudes, including their denunciation of the priests of Jerusalem "as being hopelessly corrupted by their accommodation to Gentile ways, and by collaboration with the Roman occupiers," as well as their doctrines "of repentance and God's coming judgment [which meant that] Jews must separate themselves from such polluting influences and return to strict observance of God's law" (Pagels 1995: 18).

The so-called *sicarii* or knife-bearers, active during the Roman occupation, backed up their convictions with violence. They were a sect of nationalist religionists who attacked enemies in broad daylight, preferably on holidays when the temple was crowded, and killed with a short sword that gives them their name. Their victims, predictably, were not exclusively or even normally the occupying foreigners but the moderates and collaborationists among their own people, again highlighting the fact that fundamentalists often target their "liberal" coreligionists as their main enemy. And their religious motivation is undeniable; the historian Josephus describes them as having "a passion for liberty that is almost unconquerable since they are convinced that God alone is their leader and master" (quoted in Rapoport 1989: 29).

Modern Jewish fundamentalism can be traced to the early 1700s as a response to the modernist or "enlightenment" shifts in Jewish culture. This is one major distinction between Christian fundamentalisms and the non-Christian ones to be discussed below: in the non-Christian cases, modernity seems not only secular but *foreign*, a force or culture of the alien West, often implicated with colonialism. Among early modern Jews, the modernist/Westernist members—the *maskilim* or enlightened men—were opposed by traditional religious teachers or rabbis as well as a new breed of more orthodox leaders who called themselves *zaddikim* ("righteous men") or *rebbes*. These men founded the movement known as Hasidism, an ultra-orthodox form of Judaism which identified itself with the Maccabees and medieval Judaism and "provided the spiritual model for what has emerged as Jewish fundamentalism" (Lawrence 1989: 124). For these *rebbes* the greatest threat of modernism was "the separation of Jews from their collective observance of the *mitzvoth*, or commandments of the Torah" (126).

In the late nineteenth century, Jewish culture and politics took a new direction with the Zionist movement, represented by Theodor Herzl and his efforts to establish a Jewish state. The movement grew until it succeeded, after World War II, in creating the state of Israel. While it might seem that all Jews would welcome this development, some of the more traditionalist elements in fact did not. One reaction came in the form of the *haredim* (literally, "those who tremble"), which is not a single unified group but a collection of like-minded organizations and communities. All such groups, including *Neturei Karta* and *Toldot Aharon*, share some ideas and values, like a strict observance of all scriptural laws and a theological opposition to Zionism and the secular state of Israel. They have attempted to purge foreign, secular learning from their religious schools (*yeshiva*) and to purify their culture, as much as possible withdrawing from the wider society. Ehud Sprinzak described them as "a totalitarian system which does not recognize privacy" (1993: 465); they contain, for example, an institution known as *Miahmarot Hatzniut* or "The Chastity Guards," who police the sexual behavior of the community. Politically, they interpret the formation of Israel as a betrayal of eschatology, an indication that divine history is not progressing but is veering in the wrong direction. They are a small segment (less than 3 percent) of a generally much more secular society (under 20 percent of Israeli Jews identify themselves as "religious," although 35–40 percent call themselves "traditional" rather than secular [Liebman 1993]), but they have been very vocal and influential.

Other groups and movements share the social space of contemporary Israel, with varying agendas and strategies. A small but effective group (with perhaps 20,000 active members) is *Gush Emunim* (The Bloc of the Faithful), which emerged in the early 1970s following the Israeli success of the Six-Day War in 1967. Adherents of *Gush Emunim* saw this event as apocalyptic, a sign of God's involvement and approval. Originating as a student movement out of the *yeshiva* of Rabbi Abraham Itzhak Hacohen Kook and his son Zvi Yehuda Kook, they have tended to be younger, better educated, and higher in social class than *haredim* members—products of the modern age. Another difference is their attitude toward the state of Israel: they are not hostile to it but rather seek to expand it, ideally "from the Euphrates River in Iraq to the Brook of Egypt" (Aran 1991: 268). They have therefore been particularly active in the settlement movement in the occupied territories of Gaza and the West Bank. They have opposed any plans to withdraw from conquered territories like Sinai and have committed vandalism and harassment against local Palestinians. Sprinzak depicted their aggression as "settler vigilantism" but also noted that they have been implicated in "messianic violence," including a plot to destroy the Muslim mosque, the Dome of the Rock, which sits atop the ancient Jerusalem Temple Mount.

Our third and final Jewish fundamentalist example is the movement associated with extremist rabbi Meir Kahane (see Figure 12.3), whom Lawrence considered "a Jewish

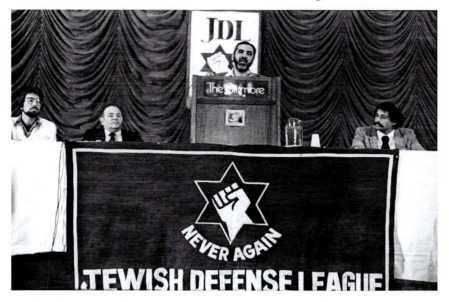

Figure 12.3 Meir Kahane, founder of the Jewish Defense League, at a press conference in New York
(1981). Photo by Fred W. McDarrah/Getty Images

activist but not a fundamentalist" (1989: 130). Kahane rose to prominence in 1968 with
his New York-based Jewish Defense League and his angry rhetoric against Israel and
non-Jews alike. The state of Israel, he taught, was sinful and its leadership secular and
corrupt. Judaism, he further instructed, was not an individualistic religion but a collective
one, such that all Jews must collectively obey Torah commandments. He also expressed
deep animosity for all gentiles and even regarded the state of Israel not as a gift to the
Jews but as revenge against non-Jews. Eventually his thinking crystallized into a violent
ideology embodied in the group *Kach* (Thus!), which saw all oppressions and humilia-
tions of the Jewish people as sacrilege against God. His group advocated and conducted
violence and terrorism against Arabs and even against other Jews.

Islamic Fundamentalisms

For most people, the very epitome of fundamentalism in the modern world is the Islamic
kind; certainly the most dramatic instances of recent violence have been carried out in its
name by its followers. This had led some observers to conclude that Islam is uniquely
prone to fundamentalist tendencies and to criticize the religion accordingly; others have
separated the fundamentalist current in Islam from the wider religion, branding it with the
derogatory term "Islamist" (although one never hears the words "Jewishist" or "Christia-
nist") or "Islamic fascist." Beyond the judgmental and orientalist tendencies, to talk about
Islamic fundamentalism is especially complex because Islam exists in so many different
countries and societies, with so many different internal variables (historical, political, and
ethnic), and with such a problematic relation to "the West." In addition to the "foreign"
nature of secularism and modernization, we must understand the connection for many
Muslim people and groups of these forces not only with Europe and the United States but
also with Christianity and with colonialism and finally with their own nationalist

struggles. Islam is also one of the few cases where fundamentalists have actually achieved political power and begun their implementation of a religious social system.

One might consider the very origins of Islam as a kind of fundamentalist movement, the recovery and re-establishment of an original and basic monotheism that perpetuated but perfected earlier revelations in Judaism and Christianity. One of the essential things to realize is that, from the beginning, Islam was ideally both a religion and a social system; in fact, the religious/secular schism did not really exist. Islam is a set of beliefs and rituals, to be sure, but it is and always has been also a set of laws and a system of jurisprudence, established first and foremost in the Qur'an and then in the "traditions" of Muhammad's rulings, the history of social and legal rulings and interpretations, and the *shari'a* law that gradually coalesced. Islam never experienced a "reformation" or an "enlightenment" like Christian Europe and never recognized a "separation of church and state."

Islam has its unique history of movements and struggles for belief and power, dating back to the earliest years and the controversy over the successor (caliph) to Muhammad. This led immediately to the split between the Sunnis and the Shi'ites (the *Shi'a Ali* or the "partisans of Ali," a kinsman of Muhammad). Thus Shi'ites in particular have tended to see themselves as the purifiers and reformers of a literally "misguided" Islam. However, the movements that have arisen since sustained contact with and colonization by the West interest us the most. Wahhabism is one of the more familiar and important developments. Muhammad Ibn 'Abd al-Wahhab (1703–92), living in what would become Saudi Arabia, led a purist movement distinguished by "opposition to popular superstitions and innovations, his insistence on informed independent judgments over against the role reliance on medieval authorities, and his call for the Islamization of society and the creation of a political order which gives appropriate recognition to Islam" (Voll 1991: 351). Specifically, this entailed a return to the textual fundamentals of the Qur'an and the other main Islamic scripture, the *Hadith* or "traditions." Wahhabism is still an influential school of thought in Saudi Arabia.

Islam was a medium of discourse, response, and resistance in all Muslim societies penetrated by Western colonialism and culture, from Africa to Asia. As in the Ottoman Empire, some local rulers attempted to embrace modernization, if only for their own interests (see Chapter 11); among them were Muhammad 'Ali and Isma'il in nineteenth-century Egypt. Traditionalist and "counter-reformation" movements arose in reaction, although Abdel Azim Ramadan (1993) noted that no Arabic equivalent for "fundamentalists" existed until recently; prior to the invention of the term *usuliyyun*, such groups were simply called "radicals." One of the most influential examples was the Muslim Brotherhood founded by Hasan al-Banna (1906–49) in the late 1920s to defend Islam against foreign contaminants, such as "their half-naked women … , their liquors, their theaters, their dance halls, their amusements, their stories, their newspapers, their novels, their whims, their silly games, and their vices" as well as

> schools and scientific and cultural institutes in the very heart of the Islamic domain, which cast doubt and heresy into the souls of its sons and taught them how to demean themselves, disparage their religion and their fatherland, divest themselves of their traditions and beliefs, and to regard as sacred anything Western.
>
> (quoted in Voll 1991: 360–61)

The Brotherhood rejected the separation of the religious and temporal worlds and called for an Islamic society and government, arguing that political neutrality was a crime against Islam. Eventually a secret military wing was established to defend the group and hopefully to someday seize power; they even attempted an assassination of the Egyptian leader, Nasser. The Muslim Brotherhood spawned other movements in Egypt, like Sayyid Qutb's *takfir*, which accused all existing Muslim societies of atheism (*takfir* literally means "branding with unbelief" or "excommunication") and therefore rejected their legitimacy. Some *takfir* groups advocated overthrow of regimes, while others proposed withdrawal from them (e.g. Shukri Mustafa's *al-Takfir w'al-Hijra* or "charging with atheism and emigrating" view). By 1975 the Jihad Organization had formed to extend the vision, calling for obligatory holy war against any society or administration not ruled by God's laws.

Undoubtedly the most inspiring model for Islamic fundamentalism in the twentieth century was the Iranian revolution, which must be understood in the context of internal and international politics. A revolution in 1906 had led to a constitution that was not anti-Islamic but not based on *shari'a* law either. In 1941 Muhammad Reza Pahlavi became ruler or shah and, after being reinstalled by the West following an insurrection in the early 1950s, became a major ally and champion of modernization, if not of political freedoms. His modernizing policies and close ties to the West, together with the repression practiced through his secret police force, made the regime increasingly unpopular. From exile in France, Ayatollah Khomeini applied continuous pressure, calling for an Islamic administration which would rule but not "legislate," since all of the laws were already provided by Islam. In 1979 the revolution was successful, and Khomeini declared Iran an Islamic Republic—the first time in modern history that a Muslim fundamentalist movement had actually achieved power.

According to Said Amir Arjomand, Khomeini's theory of Islamic government was the "Mandate of the Jurist," a thoroughly non-traditional interpretation of the role of the jurist or interpreter of the law. Shi'ite jurists had previously asserted their rights to religious authority but never to political power; not only that, but Khomeini claimed that if any single jurist ever succeeded in founding a government, all others were bound to submit to him (violating the traditional principle of the equality of *ayatollahs*). He set about building an Islamic (specifically Shi'ite Islamic) system, expressed in a new constitution that described the effort "as an attempt by the nation to cleanse itself of the dust of godless government and foreign ideas, as a way to return to God and to the 'authentic intellectual positions and worldview of Islam'" (Arjomand 1993: 92). Article 2 of the constitution explicitly inaugurated a theocracy, with all sovereignty and legislative power placed on God, and a Council of Guardians (composed of *ayatollahs*) to lead the way. Ironically, as Ann Elizabeth Mayer (1993) pointed out, the necessities of politics required a kind of de facto secularization of the religious revolution: in 1988, Khomeini ruled that the state had the authority to govern even in opposition to Islamic law or ritual duty.

Mayer went on to argue that Islamic fundamentalism, while claiming doctrinal unity and absolutism, has actually produced diverse interpretations and been used for diverse purposes: "A variety of ideological formulations of the *shari'a* that range from the radical left to the reactionary right have been proposed in recent decades" (111), employed to support democratic and even socialist worldviews as well as anti-modernist and authoritarian ones. The outcome is a complex and inconsistent movement shaped by local forces. For instance, whereas the Shi'ite majority largely supported Iranian fundamentalism, Zia ul-Haq's religious program in Pakistan in the 1980s came largely from the Sunni side and was opposed by the Shi'ite minority, which in this circumstance was liberal and anti-fundamentalist. In fact, Zia's fundamentalism may have been more self-interested than devout. In the Sudan in 1983, military dictator Jafar al-Numayri initiated an Islamization program in the midst of numerous national crises, including economic woes, famine, ethnic tensions, and threat of civil war in the south. His supposed Islamic revival oddly did not include any actual religious leaders, so that it was opposed not only by the secular part of the government but by much of the religious part of the society. Many of the rebels in southern Sudan still blame the policy for contributing to the local war.

Box 12.2 Fundamentalists in Control: The Taliban of Afghanistan

On April 27, 1978 a communist coup seized power in Afghanistan, a multi-ethnic state created by British colonialism in the 1800s. As early as the 1870s various resistance movements had arisen, generally spearheaded by religious clerics who enlisted support among the region's myriad local tribal leaders and groups; such movements had never attempted political revolution, only cultural and legal (*shari'a*) reforms, usually by appealing to the rural population. Following the same pattern, rural resisters inspired by Islam had liberated two-thirds of Afghanistan before the Soviet Union intervened in December 1979 to save the regime. Now the resistance had to contend with the Soviet army, but with US aid and leadership and financing provided by outsiders like Osama bin Laden, the *Mujahadin* fighters drove the Soviets out by 1989. In the power vacuum and factional fighting that ensued, a group of religious students (*talib* is singular for student, *taliban* plural) emerged in 1994 and captured the capital city of Kabul in 1996. The reign of the Taliban had begun. The Taliban grew out of the system of religious schools

Figure 12.4 Afghan men in front of the huge cavity where one of the ancient Buddhas of Bamiyan used to stand until they were destroyed by the Taliban. Courtesy of Majid Saeedi/Thinkstock by Getty Images

(*madrasas*) in Afghanistan and Pakistan, often in refugee camps, where they also provided other social and religious services to the communities and defended them when necessary; they were also predominantly drawn from the Pashtun ethnic group, comprising roughly 48 percent of Afghanistan's population. As sources of education, they espoused a particularly orthodox and puritanical version of Islam, associated with Wahhabism (see p. 296 above). Under their leader Mullah Muhammad Omar, the Taliban administration set about instituting its strict brand of Islam as social and political policy. Very many modern or unorthodox practices were banned, including movies and television, music of all kinds, the internet, pornography, non-Islamic books, kite-flying (seen as a Hindu behavior), smoking, drinking alcohol, and proselytizing other religions. Other "traditional" practices were mandated, such as public executions for murder and adultery, hand-amputation for theft, obligatory beards for men, and a panoply of restrictions for women—no employment outside the home, no education, complete covering of the body in public, and no printed or electronic images of women, among many others. Even wearing fingernail polish could get their fingers cut off. As already mentioned, all non-Muslim and pre-Islamic religions were wicked; hence in 2001, two immense Buddha statues were destroyed to rid the country of idolatry (see Figure 12.4). Also in 2001, eight Western aid workers were put on trial for preaching Christianity, which was punishable by death. The Taliban were removed from power by the United States after September 11, 2001 for providing haven for al-Qaeda. As of 2014, Taliban fighters continued to skirmish with American forces and had actually re-established control of some parts of the country.

Hindu Fundamentalisms

While monotheisms are particularly prone to religious fundamentalisms, they are by no means unique in that regard. Any religion—in fact, any position or ideology—can develop fundamentalist tendencies, especially when syncretized with other volatile social ideas and forces. In the context of India, tradition and modernization met through European colonialism. As Robert Frykenberg explained, there had never been a unified Indian society or state prior to the English Raj that created colonial and modern India. Instead, society had always been diverse, decentralized, and weakly integrated, "a carefully arranged hierarchy of ranked social, political, and religious contracts" (1993: 235). Not only was there no pre-colonial "national" integration of the modern, Western "state" sort, but there was no "national" *identity*. In particular, there was no such thing as "Hinduism"; what we think of as Hinduism was (and largely is) a "mosaic of distinct cults, deities, sects, and ideas" (237). Not surprisingly, the formalization and advancement of "Hinduism" paralleled the formalization of the bounded, inclusive "society" and "state" of India, essentially an achievement of modernization and colonialism. "The 'Hinduism' promulgated by mass mobilizations—the rising ideal of an all-embracing monolithic 'Hindu community'—is, accordingly, a recent development" (237).

Part of this accomplishment, as in Sri Lankan Buddhism (see pp. 302–3 below), came from activities of the Raj, both political and scholarly. The need to name the local culture and society, in distinction from Muslim or Christian, etc., led to the adoption of the term "Hindu." At the same time, Western scholars like Max Mueller were actively studying and codifying Asian cultures and traditions, providing order, attention, and legitimacy to those traditions; with efforts like the fifty-volume *Sacred Books of the East* edited by Mueller, there was now an "official Hindu literature." The Parliament of World Religions in 1893 made Hinduism a household word and a world religion.

The other part of the coalescence of Hindu culture and identity came from indigenous sociocultural initiatives. In 1871 the All-India Congress introduced a classification of religious and communal categories, including "Hindu." Shortly thereafter, in 1875, the *Arya Samaj* or Society of Aryas appeared as a Vedic fundamentalist organization, observing a strict adherence to the very oldest of Hindu texts (the Vedas) and dismissing "much of later Hindu tradition as degenerate practice that is best forgotten" (Gold 1991: 534). In 1915 the All-India Hindu Mahasabha was created in association with the Indian National Congress and as a cultural reaction to the Muslim League.

Out of such activity rose an ideology known as *Hindutva*, discussed in the 1923/4 publication of Vinayak Damadar Savarkar by the same name. Meaning essentially "Hindu-ness" or "Hindu nationalism," its principles included the idea that Hindus were not only a single nation (*rashtra*) but the authentic indigenous nation of the subcontinent. All true natives of the land, regardless of their caste or sect or language, were Hindu; the "fundamentals" of Hindu identity and belief were literally in the blood. Therefore, all of India was not only a home but a *sacred* home to Hindus (see Chapter 9 for other examples of the "sacred nation"). This ideology was institutionalized in the 1925 movement *Rashtriya Swayamsevak Sangh* (National Union of Volunteers/Servants) led by Kesnar Baliram Hedgewar. This new understanding called for a radical personal transformation, basically a conversion or re-conversion to one's true Hindu-ness. The RSS recruited "volunteers" or "self-servants" (*swayamsevaks*) to defend and advance the cause—the elite cadre, trained in *kshatriya* values and organized into military regiments.

By 1939, there were 60,000 active RSS members, and by 1989 1.8 million trained *swayamsevaks* in 25,000 national branches (Frykenberg 1993). The movement had become quite influential on Indian politics in the late twentieth century and was best summarized by Madhav Sadashir Golwalkar, who wrote in his 1938 *We, or Our Nationhood Defined*:

> The non-Hindu peoples in Hindustan must adopt the Hindu culture and language, must learn to respect and hold in reverence Hindu religion, must entertain no idea but glorification of the Hindu race and culture: i.e., they must not only give up their attitude of intolerance and ungratefulness towards this land and its age-old traditions, but must also cultivate a positive attitude of love and devotion instead ... in a word, they must cease to be foreigners, or must stay in this country wholly subordinated to the Hindu nation, claiming nothing, deserving no privileges, far less any preferential treatment, not even citizens' rights.
>
> (quoted in Frykenberg: 243)

As Kalyani Devaki Menon portrays it, the national re-conversion demanded by *Hindutva* often entails reversing Christian conversion and retrieving people who "have been tricked by missionaries or ... seduced by offers of material remuneration" (2003: 43). From the Hindu nationalist perspective, the proselytization of other religions "is part of a conspiracy to destroy 'Indian' culture and to destabilize the 'Indian' polity" (43). As such, the conversion of Indians to foreign religions, and their successful re-conversion to their true and native religion and identity, "is not seen as simply an individual expression of faith but rather as a political choice that necessarily implicates questions of national allegiance, patriotism, and cultural determination" (51).

Box 12.3 Hindutva Camp: Teaching Fundamentalism among American Hindus

Readers may be familiar with the movie *Jesus Camp* and the phenomenon of Christian (including but not limited to) evangelical and fundamentalist children's camps. Jessica Marie Falcone discovered something very similar at Shantiniketan, "a summer camp with a Hindu nationalist (*Hindutva*) political bent based in the suburbs of Washington, D.C." (2012: 164). The Shantiniketan Summer Camp was a program organized by local members of the Hindu Swayamsevak Sangh and the Vishwa Hindu Parishad, two institutions "that have vehemently, and sometimes violently, worked against the secular Indian state in favor of an exclusionary Hindu state" (170). At the four-day sleep-over camp, children and their parents were treated to *Hindutva* ideology

> through various activities, including games, lectures, and events. The children learned a set of drills and formation, as well as what I can only describe as militant yoga, that reflected the mission of the leaders to militarize Hinduism. The atmosphere of discipline was punctuated with loud nationalist chants for Hindu solidarity.
>
> (170–71)

The camp also, of course, included activities "of a more specifically religious nature, bent on celebrating and teaching aspects of Hindu ritual … to create linkages suggesting that Hindu religious practice is inseparable from Hindutva political theology and discourse" (171). And, like other fundamentalisms, Shantiniketan's *Hindutva* was not only for something but against something. Campers were taught that they must fight hard "against the so-called Muslim and Christian onslaught: 'the battle is on. The Christian missionaries are trying to destroy us. … Stand up!'" (172). In particular, they were told that Hindus should only date and marry Hindus. Interestingly, Falcone concludes that this unique brand of "Yankee Hindutva" represents an exceptional blend of Hindu nationalism and American immigrant experience. She reports that few of the parents held *Hindutva* views prior to arrival in the United States, although many did feel that Muslims had unfair advantages in India. Once in the USA, though, they associated with *Hindutva* partly "to feel they were contributing meaningfully to their native land" (170), partly because of peer pressure from their community, and partly because of perceived discrimination against Indians in their new country. She notes that American *Hindutva* groups do in fact collect significant funds for *Hindutva* parties back in India, which means that "'Yankee Hindutva' is complicit in current Indian politics" (167). But apart from the religious and political situation in the homeland, and like the Danish Jews discussed above (p. 285), living in a foreign land has made many Indian immigrants more conscious of their culture and ethnicity. Ultimately, "in the 'white supremacist' climate of the United States, many Indians have embraced Hindutva as an antidote to their humbled pride," as well as in reaction to the "guilt that some Hindu Americans feel about leaving behind 'Mother India'" (169). As a diaspora community, "Alienation in the United States awakens hunger for the romanticized narrative of belonging, acceptance, and Hindu unity that Hindutva stories have constructed" (169).

Buddhist Fundamentalisms

The popular impression of Buddhism is that it is a religion of moderation and peace and therefore not one susceptible to extremism, fundamentalism, and violence. However, in practice, although perhaps not as regularly, it too has demonstrated fundamentalist tendencies. In the mildest cases, like the one reported by Sherry Ortner in Nepal, such phenomena can take the form of movements to improve or enforce or purify religious belief and practice. Sherpa Buddhism has been characterized by monasteries staffed by married monks, a habit set in the late 1600s. However, the early twentieth century saw efforts to establish a more orthodox institution, "the first celibate Buddhist monasteries among the Sherpas of Nepal" (1989: 3). And the founding of the monasteries was only the first stage in a process of re-orthodoxification: "Once the Sherpa monasteries were built, a whole new process was set in motion: the monks launched a campaign to upgrade popular religion and to bring it into line with monastic views and values" (3).

In other instances, Buddhist restorationism has been more muscular but also more "modern" and syncretistic, particularly in contemporary Burma (sometimes called Myanmar). As in so many parts of the world, the impetus originally came from the colonial experience: by the 1800s, some religious authorities were demanding a return to and purification of Buddhism against the Christian threat, which involved a "new exegesis of the Tripitaka, the Buddhist scriptures, and a stricter adherence by monks to the 'discipline'" (Keyes 1993b: 368). Modernization and integration into the global economy brought further shocks: when the Great Depression of the 1930s impoverished many Burmese, millenarian movements like *Saya San* emerged, aimed at the expulsion of the British and the return of the Buddhist monarchy. More modernized Burmese developed a heightened self-identity as Buddhists along with a more activist and "political" agenda. One of the key figures was U Ottama, who advocated a militant and "fundamentalist" style, with a political role for monks. Even more significant was U Ba Swe, who consciously blended Buddhism with Marxism, seeing Marxism as the temporal, practical counterpart to Buddhism. The political coup of Ne Win in 1962 brought to power a regime committed to just such a "Buddhist socialism," at the same time aggrandizing religion and achieving state control over religion; for example, leadership of the *sangha* or religious community was shifted to the Burma Socialist Program Party.

Sri Lanka provides the best case of a Buddhism that rose to political power and to religious violence. Sri Lanka is an island containing two main ethnic or religious/identity groups, the majority Sinhalese (Buddhists) and the minority Tamils (Hindus). The Sinhalese also claimed to be the original and rightful inhabitants, and at various times in the past strong Buddhist kingdoms had existed, especially under the Sinhalese Buddhist culture hero Dutthagamani, who purportedly drove out a non-Buddhist king in the name of Buddhism. From that time at least, if not before, Buddhist monks (*bhikkhus*) were politically important, seeing it as their right and duty to preserve and promote the religion and the kingdom.

Immediately after becoming a British colony in 1802, Christian missionaries began to flood the island. Within decades Buddhist *samagamas* (associations) were formed, such as *Sarvagna Sasanabhivruddhi Dayaka Dharma Samagama* in 1862, to "protect and develop Buddhism," and Buddhist spokesmen like Gunananda contested with Christianity, even conducting public debates. Interestingly, the American-based Theosophical Society played a part in encouraging Buddhist self-identity, and Sinhalese journals and newspapers like *Lankapakaraya* and *Lak Mini Kirula* were established (both in 1881) to advance Buddhist identity and interests. Probably the single most important figure in nineteenth-century

Buddhist fundamentalism, though, was Anagarika Dharmapala, exclusive Sinhalese/Buddhist identity and hegemony for the island:

> The island of Lanka belongs to the Buddhist Sinhalese. For 2⁴
> land of birth for the Sinhalese. Other races have come here to .
> cial activities. For the Europeans, apart from this land, there is Canaua,
> South Africa, England and America to go to; for the Tamils there is South India; tor
> the Moors ... Egypt; the Dutch can go to Holland. But for the Sinhalese there only
> this island.
>
> (quoted in Dharmadasa 1992: 138)

As independence approached in the 1940s Buddhist elements became more active, like the political *bhikkhus* who formed the *Lanka Eksath Bhikkhu Mandalaya* (Ceylon Union of *Bhikkhus*) to advance Buddhism, by means of the overthrow of the colonial government if necessary. In 1956, the All Ceylon Buddhist Congress issued a report titled "The Betrayal of Buddhism," which complained about the condition of Buddhism, government, and society; it demanded discontinuation of aid to Christian schools and the re-establishment of unity between state and *sangha*. Not surprisingly, the same year the dominant political party, the Sri Lanka Freedom Party, turned more pro-Buddhist and pro-Sinhalese, promulgating laws to advantage the Buddhist religion and the Sinhalese language, which eventually so outraged Tamils that an ethno-religious civil war broke out between them.

Conclusion

No religion is immune to fundamentalist tendencies, especially in a modern world of religious and cultural pluralism, rapid social change, and strong religious beliefs and sentiments. All fundamentalisms share a certain reactionary or defensive nature—even a certain militancy—although they also vary significantly not only between religions and between societies/states but also within religions. They are also, it is quite clear, not utterly unique to modern times but can be found in all times of change and threat— which are almost all times. They are ultimately one of the recurring forms of "revitalization movements" that arise in all societies (and not only in religious institutions) during moments of turmoil and (real or perceived) social decline.

Fundamentalism is thus not "bad religion" nor is it "true religion" but rather one of the many variations that religion can and likely will take in particular historical and social circumstances. The fact that these very circumstances are certain to continue and even intensify in the future suggests that fundamentalisms are likely to persist, and it also proves conclusively that "modernity" is not the death of religion but may rather give it new and energetic life. Finally, fundamentalisms are a perfect illustration of the multiple formations or modes of religion (and irreligion), of the vernacularization of religions, and of the value of an anthropological perspective on religions.

DISCUSSION QUESTIONS

- What does it mean to speak of "formations of the fundamental"? How is fundamentalism constructed in and by secular society, and why does Harding call it the "repugnant other"?

- What are the varieties of fundamentalism? Do all of them advocate violence—or even political action?
- How and why did fundamentalism emerge in the United States? How do fundamentalisms in other religions and countries resemble and differ from American Christian fundamentalism?

SUPPLEMENTARY READING (see website)

- *Fieldwork among Fundamentalists: The Southside Gospel Church*
- *The Hyper-Christian, Hyper-Modern Children of God*
- *Jesus.com: Internet Fundamentalism*

Glossary

Below are handy definitions for some important terms in the anthropology of religion. Other terms are too complex or controversial for simple definitions, such as "ritual" or "secularism" or "belief," and it would defeat the point of anthropology to attempt to settle the professional debate in a glossary. Other key terms have sections or entire chapters devoted to them, and readers are urged to consult those pages for discussions and assessments of terminology.

Agency   The capacity to act on the basis of one's own subjectivity, desires, or intentions, rather than as an object of someone else's intentions.

Agent   A being that has its own subjectivity and can act upon its own desires or intentions; something that is more than a mere passive object.

Agnosticism   Formulated by Thomas Huxley (and derived from the Greek *a-* for no/ without and *gnosis* for knowledge). The position that we should not claim to have knowledge unless we can demonstrate the reasons for our knowledge—not, as commonly understood, that knowledge is impossible or an intermediate position between believing and not-believing.

Anglo-Israelism   A Christian movement that claims the English-speaking peoples (particularly the British and Americans) to be the true Christians and inheritors of God's covenant with Israel.

Animatism   The religious conception that impersonal spiritual forces exist in the world and affect human life and behavior.

Animism   The religious conception that natural objects (animals, plants, hills, lakes, moon, etc.) and forces (wind, rain, etc.) have spiritual components that interact socially with humans.

Anti-syncretism   Resistance to mixing new or foreign elements in religion.

Asceticism   A form of religious discipline that involves self-deprivation, the rejection of comforts, and sometimes the deliberate infliction of pain.

Atheism   From the Greek *a-* for no/without and *theos* for god. The absence of a concept of god(s) or belief in god(s); in conventional terms, the rejection of the existence of god(s).

Bid'a   The Arabic term for illicit innovation or novelty in religion.

Canon   The set of standardized, official writings or doctrines and practices of a religion.

Christian Exodus   An American Christian movement working to relocate a large number of Christians to a state (for instance, South Carolina), where they can institute a Christian culture.

Christian Identity   A Christian movement that attributes true Christianity to the white race, going so far as to brand other races "the spawn of Satan" or sub-human "mud people." *See also* **Anglo-Israelism**.

Cognitive evolutionary theory   The approach to religion (and other complex behaviors) that suggests that specific cognitive and social characteristics developed during human evolution that make such complex behaviors possible and likely.

Communitas   In Victor Turner's ritual model, the condition of undifferentiated and structureless existence; the unity that characterizes the state of liminality, when the ritual actor is between social statuses.

Contagious magic   The belief and practice that objects that come in contact with each other have some supernatural connection with each other.

Conversion   Used most commonly in Christian parlance; the allegedly sudden and complete break with the past and the adoption of a new religious belief and identity.

Cosmogony   Notions about the origin of the universe.

Cosmology   Notions about the order or structure of ultimate reality.

Costly signaling theory   The idea that religions feature difficult and difficult-to-fake actions because those actions demonstrate social commitment and cooperation.

Cultural relativism   The part of the anthropological perspective that insists that we understand and judge the behavior of another culture in terms of its standards of good, normal, moral, legal, etc. rather than our own.

Da'wa   Arabic for "inviting," often understood as a synonym in Islam for conversion.

Deism   The religious idea of a god that created the universe but takes little interest in humans and does not intervene in human affairs.

Diaspora   The dispersion of a social group from its historical homeland (often applied specifically to the Jewish community).

Diffusion   The spread of items of culture from one society to another.

Diffusionism   The nineteenth-century ethnological or anthropological position or theory that culture—or specific cultural practices, objects, or institutions—had appeared once or at most a few times and spread out from their original center.

Discursive tradition   For Talal Asad, discourses or ways of talking and interpreting that seek to instruct religious practitioners regarding the correct form and purpose of a given practice that, precisely because it is established, has a history.

Distributed personhood   The idea, associated with Alfred Gell, that a person can be "distributed," that is all of his or her "parts" need not be physically attached but can be located in other persons, places, and objects.

Divination The use of religious techniques to "read" information from the supernatural world.

Diviner A religious specialist who uses one of many techniques to "read" information from the supernatural world.

Entheogen A chemical substance that induces a religious-type experience.

Eschatology Notions about the end of the world.

Ethnography A written account or description of a particular culture, usually including its environment, economic system, kinship arrangements, political systems, and religious beliefs, and often including some discussion of culture change.

Ethno-religious conflict Violence between ethnic or identity groups, which has religion as one of its elements of identity or of conflicting interest.

Euhemerism The notion that the idea of gods or spirits derives from modified or exaggerated accounts of actual people and events.

Folklore The "traditional," usually oral, literature of a society, consisting of various genres such as myth, legend, folktale, song, proverb, and many others.

Functionalism The method, and eventually the theory, that a cultural trait can be investigated for the contribution it makes to the survival of individual humans, the operation of other cultural items, or the culture as a whole.

Fundamentalism A type of cultural/revitalization movement in which members attempt to address perceived social problems or disadvantages by restoring the perceived "fundamentals" or oldest, most important, and most "genuine" elements of culture.

Ghost A religious or spiritual being, generally regarded to be the disembodied spiritual part of a deceased human.

Gush Emunim The Bloc of the Faithful, an extremist Jewish group that emerged in the early 1970s following the Israeli success of the Six Day War in 1967, supporting the state of Israel and eager to expand its territory to include all of ancient Israel's land.

Haredim Literally "those who tremble." A collection of like-minded Jewish organizations and communities, including *Neturei Karta* and *Toldot Aharon*, that share some ideas and values, like a strict observance of all scriptural laws and a theological opposition to Zionism and the secular state of Israel.

Hierophany An appearance of the sacred amidst the profane or mundane.

Hindutva A form of Hindu nationalism in India, which asserts Hinduism as the true religion of all Indians and the Indian subcontinent as the sacred homeland of Hindus.

Historical materialism The theory, associated with Karl Marx, that material or economic conditions shape society, so that each particular society is a formation based on the material conditions and relations of the particular moment in history.

Holism The part of the anthropological perspective that entails consideration of every part of a culture in relation to every other part and to the whole.

Honor killing   The killing, usually of women, when their behavior has brought shame or dishonor on a family through behavior such as premarital sex or "dating" outside the preferred categories.

Humanism   A rational philosophy informed by science, inspired by art, and motivated by compassion; a philosophy that places humanity as the highest principle.

Ideological ritual   According to Anthony Wallace, a type of ritual that aims at social control, in which individuals, groups, or society in its entirety are moved, influenced, and manipulated.

Inculturation   An official policy of the Catholic Church, intended to inject religion into the wider society as well as to inject the local culture into religion, resulting in multiple local Christianities.

Innovation   The invention or discovery of new cultural items.

Interaction code   According to John Skorupski, a specialized set of behaviors that establish or maintain (or destroy) an equilibrium, or mutual agreement, among the people involved in an interaction as to their relative standing or roles, and their reciprocal commitments and obligations.

Irredentism   From the Italian *irredenta* for "unredeemed," a type of revitalization movement to reclaim and re-occupy a lost homeland.

Jihad   The Arabic term for "struggle," including both struggle with oneself and violent struggle against others.

Laïcité   The official French policy of state secularism.

Laiklik   The Turkish term for state secularism.

Liminality   Most associated with the work of Victor Turner. The condition of being "in between" or "on the margins" of social roles, in particular of being in transition (as during ritual) between one social role and another.

Liturgy   The most formal, fixed, and weighty of rituals, in which the exact gestures, objects, and words must be used in the precisely correct ways in order for the ritual to "succeed."

Mana   A supernatural force or energy recognized by some Pacific Island societies, which gives its human bearers power or efficacy.

Martyrdom   Giving one's life for a cause, including but not limited to a religious cause.

Megachurch   A modern (sub)urban form of Christianity, featuring large church facilities, multiple religious and social activities aimed at specific niches, and often very mild forms of worship.

Messianism   Based on the Judeo-Christian tradition, a type of revitalization movement that insists that a *messiah* or "anointed one" will appear (or has appeared) to lead the society to salvation and happiness.

Millenarianism   A type of revitalization movement aimed at preparing for and perhaps bringing about the end of the "present era," however that era is understood, and replacing it with a new and better existence.

Modernism A type of revitalization movement intended to adopt the characteristics of a foreign and "modern" society, in the process abandoning some or all of the "traditional" characteristics of the society undergoing the movement. *See also* **vitalism**.

Modes of religiosity The idea, associated most closely with Harvey Whitehouse, that there are two distinct forms or modes of religion, one based on doctrine and the other based on images and emotion-laden experience.

Monolatry The devotion to one god among the many gods acknowledged to exist.

Monotheism The religious position that one and only one god exists.

Mulid An Islamic celebration, most associated with Sufism, usually related to the birthday of the prophet Muhammad.

Nativism A type of revitalization movement aimed at perpetuating, restoring, or reviving "traditional" cultural practices or characteristics, which are thought to be the source of the group's strength and to be threatened or lost.

Occult economy According to John and Jean Comaroff, the deployment, real or imagined, of magical means for material ends, including ritual murder, the sale of body parts, and the putative production of zombies.

Ontology Ideas about what kinds of things (beings, forces, etc.) exist.

Oracle A religious specialist (or any religious object or process) with the power to forecast the future or answer questions through communication with or manipulation of supernatural forces.

Orientalism Most associated with Edward Said. The claim that Western thinking and research on Islam (and the wider "Eastern" world) has been based on assumptions that render Islam and non-Western societies exotic, incomprehensible, anti-modern, and inferior—the complete "other" of Western society.

Paganism A loose assortment of religious or traditionalist movements or religions that celebrates local or pre-Christian ideas and identities.

Pantheism A form of theism in which it is claimed that "everything" is god, that the universe and all of the material world is the same thing as god, that god is "immanent" in and co-extensive with the physical world.

Participant observation The anthropological field method in which we travel to the society we want to study and spend long periods of time there, not only watching but joining in their culture as much as possible.

Pentecostalism A form of Christianity, usually Protestant, that emphasizes "gifts of the spirit" such as speaking in tongues, ecstatic experiences, and religious healing.

Pilgrimage Movement or travel to religious sites or for religious purposes, involving moving out of everyday space and into and through religious/sacred space.

Pollution Those substances, objects, actions, and perhaps thoughts that cause a person to be "unclean."

Polytheism The religious position that two or more gods exist.

Prayer   A form of linguistic religious behavior in which humans speak and interact with supernatural beings.

Priest   A religious specialist, often full time, who is trained in a religious tradition and acts as a functionary of a religious institution to lead ritual and perpetuate the religious institution.

Primitive mentality   The assumption, associated with Lucien Lévy-Bruhl, that tribal peoples (and certain other humans) think in a distinctive and inferior way.

Prophet   A human who speaks for or receives messages from spirits.

Prosociality   The performance of actions that benefit others at a personal cost.

Reconstructionism   Also known as Dominionism, a Christian movement aimed at "reconstructing" modern society in conformity with Christian (specifically Old Testament) values and institutions.

Revitalization movement   According to Anthony Wallace, the deliberate, organized, and self-conscious effort by members of a society to create a more satisfying culture.

Rite of intensification   A form of ritual in which members of the society are brought into greater communion, in which social bonds are intensified.

Rite of passage   A form of ritual intended to accompany or accomplish a change of status or role of the participants, such as initiation (change from youth to adult) or marriage.

Ritual process   According to Victor Turner, the common structure of ritual actions, which involve separation from everyday life and roles, liminality, and then transformation and re-integration into society.

Sacrifice   A ritual behavior in which something is destroyed or killed, as a form of offering to or communication with supernatural beings, which is usually believed to affect the social or spiritual condition of the sacrificer.

Salafism   From the Arabic *salafiyyah* for "the ancestors" or "the early years." A form of Islam that stresses the piety and practices of the founding generation of Islam and their original (and thereby authoritative) religion.

Salvation ritual   According to Anthony Wallace, the type of ritual that seeks to cause change of personality.

Sannyasin   A Hindu man who renounces home and family and embarks on an itinerant spiritual life.

Sati   The traditional Indian practice in which a widow commits suicide by throwing herself on her dead husband's funeral pyre.

Secular   From the Latin *saeculum* for the present era or generation. That which is distinctive of a particular time period rather than eternal, or that which relates to the present everyday world as opposed to the eternal spiritual world.

Secularization theory   The nineteenth- and twentieth-century position that modern society is incompatible with religion, leading to an inevitable decline in the presence or importance of religion.

Self-mortification   Any of a variety of practices aimed at inflicting discomfort and pain on the self, up to and including death.

Shahadat   The Arabic term for martyrdom (literally "witness").

Shahid   The Arabic term for a martyr.

Shaman   A religious specialist, usually part time, who has personal power, based on unique life experiences or apprenticeship to a senior shaman, to communicate, interact, and sometimes struggle, with supernatural beings or forces, often to heal.

Shari'a   Islamic law.

Sicarii   An ancient Jewish sect of knife-bearers, active during the Roman occupation, who attacked enemies in broad daylight and killed them with a short sword.

Social drama   Public, symbolic scenes (usually ritualized) in which the conflicts or disharmonies of society are played out.

Sorcerer   A religious specialist who uses techniques, including spells and potions, etc., to achieve supernatural effects.

Sorcery   The use of religious techniques to achieve supernatural effects, usually malevolent ones.

Soul   A religious concept of a non-material component or components of a living human. It is widely believed that a soul survives the death of the body, at least temporarily, and continues in another form of existence.

State secularism   The official promotion of secularism (perhaps even anti-religion) by the government.

Structural functionalism   The theory that the function of a cultural trait, particularly an institution, is the creation and preservation of social order and social integration.

Structuralism   The theory, associated most closely with Claude Lévi-Strauss, that the significance of an item (word, role, practice, belief) is not so much in the particular item but in its relationship to others. In other words, the "structure" of multiple items and the location of any one in relation to others is most important.

Symbol   An object, gesture, sound, or image that "stands for" some other idea or concept or object. Something that has "meaning," particularly when the meaning is arbitrary and conventional and thus culturally relative.

Symboling   According to Leslie White, bestowing meaning upon a thing or an act, or grasping and appreciating meanings thus bestowed.

Sympathetic magic   The idea and practice that objects that have something in common with each other (e.g. same shape or texture) have some supernatural connection with each other.

Syncretism   A type of revitalization movement in which elements of two or more cultural sources are blended into a new and more satisfying cultural arrangement.

Taliban   A fundamentalist Islamic movement that seized power in Afghanistan in 1996 and ruled until being ousted by the United States in 2001.

Televangelism   The use of modern mass media (especially television) to practice evangelism or spreading of the Christian message.

Theism   The religious position that at least one god exists.

Theodicy   The practice of explaining the source or cause of suffering or evil in the world, especially in religions that posit a powerful and good god.

Totemism   A term, not widely used today, for the religious conception that human individuals or groups have a symbolic or spiritual connection with particular natural species, objects, or phenomena.

Traditionalization (also traditioning)   The more or less intentional effort to establish ideas, practices, and institutions as "traditions" and to have those things transmitted or handed down, typically by attaching them to "the past" in some way.

Translocal religion   Sometimes labeled "world religion." A religion that coexists in multiple locations around the world; while it may consider itself a single religion, its local forms are often quite divergent.

Vernacular religion   Religion in the "local language," or more broadly, religion that conforms to the ideas, practices, and relations of ordinary people and everyday circumstances, as opposed to official, orthodox, or elite religion.

Vitalism *see* **modernism**

Wahhabism   An Islamic movement founded by Muhammad Ibn 'Abd al-Wahhab, who advocated a purist form of Islam distinguished by opposition to popular superstitions and innovations and the Islamization of society based on scriptural Islam.

Witch   A religious specialist, often conceived as a human with a supernatural ability to harm others, sometimes through possession of an unnatural bodily organ or an unnatural personality; sometimes viewed as an antisocial and even anti-human type who causes misfortune out of excessive greed or anger or jealousy.

Witchcraft   The use of the powers of a witch, usually to cause misfortune or harm.

Bibliography

Abanes, Richard. 1997. "America's Patriot Movement: Infiltrating the Church with the Gospel of Hate." *Christian Research Journal* 19 (3): 10–19, 46.

Ahmad, Irfan. 2009. *Islamism and Democracy in India: the Transformation of Jamaat-e-Islami*. Princeton, NJ: Princeton University Press.

Aitamurto, Kaarina and Alexey Gaidukov. 2013. "Russian Rodnoverie: Six Portraits of a Movement." In Kaarina Aitamurto and Scott Simpson, eds. *Modern Pagan and Native Faith Movements in Central and Eastern Europe*. Durham, UK and Bristol, CT: Acumen, pp. 146–63.

Allerton, Catherine. 2009. "Static Crosses and Working Spirits: Anti-Syncretism and Agricultural Animism in Catholic West Flores." *Anthropological Forum* 19 (3): 271–87.

——2013. *Potent Landscapes: Place and Mobility in Eastern Indonesia*. Honolulu, HI: University of Hawaii Press.

Ammerman, Nancy T. 1987. *Bible Believers: Fundamentalists in the Modern World*. New Brunswick, NJ and London: Rutgers University Press.

——2007. "Introduction: Observing Religious Modern Lives." In Nancy T. Ammerman, ed. *Everyday Religion: Observing Modern Religious Lives*. Oxford and New York: Oxford University Press, pp. 3–20.

Antoun, Richard T. 2001. *Understanding Fundamentalism: Christian, Islamic, and Jewish Movements*. Walnut Creek, CA: AltaMira Press.

Appadurai, Arjun. 1981. *Worship and Conflict under Colonial Rule: A South Indian Case*. Cambridge: Cambridge University Press.

Aran, Gideon. 1991. "Jewish Zionist Fundamentalism: The Bloc of the Faithful in Israel (Gush Emunim)." In Martin Marty and R. Scott Appleby, eds. *Fundamentalisms Observed*. Chicago, IL The University of Chicago Press, pp. 265–344.

Arjomand, Said Amir. 1993. "Shi'ite Jurisprudence and Constitution Making in the Islamic Republic of Iran." In Martin E. Marty and R. Scott Appleby, eds. *Fundamentalisms and the State: Remaking Polities, Economies, and Militance*. Chicago, IL and London: The University of Chicago Press, pp. 88–109.

Armstrong, Karen. 2000. *The Battle for God*. New York: Ballantine Books.

Asad, Talal. 1987. "On Ritual and Discipline in Medieval Christian Monasticism." *Economy and Society* 16 (2): 159–203.

——1993. *Genealogies of Religion: Discipline and Reasons of Power in Christianity and Islam*. Baltimore, MD: Johns Hopkins University Press.

——2003. *Formations of the Secular: Christianity, Islam, Modernity*. Stanford, CA Stanford University Press.

——2009 [1986]. "The Idea of an Anthropology of Islam." *Qui Parle* 17 (2): 1–30.

Asser, Seth M. and Rita Swan. 1998. "Child Fatalities from Religion-Motivated Medical Neglect." *Pediatrics* 101 (4): 625–29.

Atran, Scott. 2002. *In Gods We Trust: The Evolutionary Landscape of Religion*. Oxford: Oxford University Press.

Austin, J. L. 1962. *How To Do Things with Words*. Oxford: Clarendon.

Austin-Broos, Diane. 2003. "The Anthropology of Conversion: An Introduction." In Andrew Buckser and Stephen D. Glazier, eds. *The Anthropology of Religious Conversion*. Lanham, MD: Rowman & Littlefield Publishers, Inc., pp. 1–12.

Bacchiddu, Giovanni. 2011. "Holding the Saint in One's Arms: Miracles in Apiao, Southern Chile." In Anna Fedele and Ruy Llera Blanes, eds. *Encounters of Body and Soul in Contemporary Religious Practices: Anthropological Reflections*. New York and London: Berghahn Books, pp. 23–42.

Bahktin, Mikhail. 1984 [1965]. *Rabelais and His World*, Hélène Iswolsky, trans. Bloomington, IN: Indiana University Press.

Baker, Don. 2002. "The Andrea Yates Case: The Christian God 0 vs. Christianity Meme 3." Online: www.christianitymeme.org/yates.shtml (accessed January 12, 2006).

Barfield, Thomas. 1997. *The Dictionary of Anthropology*. Oxford: Blackwell.

Barker, John. 1993. "'We are *Ekelesia*': Conversion in Uiaku, Papua New Guinea." In Robert Hefner, ed. *Conversion to Christianity: Historical and Anthropological Perspectives on a Great Transformation*. Berkeley, CA: University of California Press, pp. 199–230.

Barkun, Michael. 1997. *Religion and the Racist Right*. Chapel Hill: University of North Carolina Press.

Barnett, Robert. 2012. "Mimetic Re-Enchantment: The Contemporary Chinese State and Tibetan Religious Leadership." In Nils Bubandt and Martijn van Beek, eds. *Varieties of Secularism in Asia: Anthropological Explorations of Religion, Politics, and the Spiritual*. London and New York: Routledge, pp. 29–53.

Barrett, Justin L. 2004. *Why Would Anyone Believe in God?* Lanham, MD: AltaMira Press.

Barth, Fredrik. 1961. *Nomads of South Persia: The Basseri Tribe of the Khamseh Confederacy*. Oslo: Oslo University Press.

Bascom, William R. 1953. "Folklore and Anthropology." *Journal of American Folklore* 66 (262): 283–90.

——1965. "The Forms of Folklore: Prose Narratives." *Journal of American Folklore* 78 (307): 3–20.

Basso, Keith H. 1970. *The Cibecue Apache*. New York: Holt, Rinehart, and Winston.

Bauman, Richard, ed. 1992. *Folklore, Cultural Performances, and Popular Entertainments: A Communications-Centered Handbook*. New York and Oxford: Oxford University Press.

Bauman, Richard. 2001. "Verbal Art as Performance." In Alessandro Duranti, ed. *Linguistic Anthropology: A Reader*. Malden, MA and Oxford: Blackwell Publishing, pp. 165–88.

Beals, Alan R. 1962. *Gopalpur: A South Indian Village*. New York: Holt, Rinehart, and Winston.

Beattie, John. 1960. *Bunyoro: An African Kingdom*. New York: Holt, Rinehart, and Winston.

Beidelman, T. O. 1971. *The Kaguru: A Matrilineal People of East Africa*. New York: Holt, Rinehart, and Winston.

Bell, Catherine. 1992. *Ritual Practice, Ritual Theory*. New York: Oxford University Press.

——1997. *Ritual Perspectives and Dimensions*. New York: Oxford University Press.

Bellah, Robert N. 1957. *Tokugawa Religion: The Values of Pre-Industrial Japan*. New York: The Free Press.

Berger, Peter L. 1999. "The Desecularization of the World: A Global Overview." In Peter L. Berger, ed. *The Desecularization of the World: Resurgent Religion and World Politics*. Grand Rapids, MI: William B. Eerdmans, pp. 1–18.

Berger, Peter and Thomas Luckmann. 1966. *The Social Construction of Reality: A Treatise in the Sociology of Knowledge*. Garden City, NY: Doubleday & Company, Inc.

Berkes, Niyazi. 1998 [1964]. *The Development of Secularism in Turkey*. London: Hurst & Company.

Biale, David. 2011. *Not in the Heavens: The Tradition of Jewish Secular Thought*. Princeton, NJ and Oxford: Princeton University Press.

Bielo, James S. 2011. *Emerging Evangelicals: Faith, Modernity, and the Desire for Authenticity*. New York and London: New York University Press.

Biney, Moses O. 2011. *From Africa to America: Religion and Adaptation among Ghanaian Immigrants in New York*. New York and London: New York University Press.

Bloch, Maurice. 1979. *Ritual, History, and Power: Selected Papers in Anthropology*. London: The Athlone Press.

Boddy, Janice. 1988. "Spirits and Selves in Northern Sudan: The Cultural Therapeutics of Possession and Trance." *American Ethnologist* 15 (1): 4–27.

Boissevain, Jeremy. 1965. *Saints and Fireworks: Religion and Politics in Rural Malta*. London: The Athlone Press.

Bonnefoy, Laurent. 2011. *Salafism in Yemen: Transnationalism and Religious Identity*. New York: Columbia University Press.

Bourdieu, Pierre. 1977. *Outline of a Theory of Practice*. Cambridge: Cambridge University Press.

Bourguignon, Erika. 1976. *Possession*. San Francisco, CA: Chandler & Sharp Publishers, Inc.

Bowen, John R. 2010. *Can Islam be French? Pluralism and Pragmatism in a Secularist State*. Princeton, NJ: Princeton University Press.

——2012. *A New Anthropology of Islam*. Cambridge: Cambridge University Press.

Bowman, Glenn. 2010. "Orthodox-Muslim Interactions at 'Mixed Shrines' in Macedonia." In Chris Hann and Hermann Goltz, eds. *Eastern Christians in Anthropological Perspective*. Berkeley, CA: University of California Press, pp. 195–219.

Bowman, Marion and Ülo Valk. 2012. "Introduction: Vernacular Religion, Generic Expressions and the Dynamics of Belief." In Marion Bowman and Ülo Valk, eds. *Vernacular Religion in Everyday Life: Expressions of Belief*. Sheffield, UK and Bristol, CT: Equinox, pp. 1–19.

Boyer, Pascal. 2001. *Religion Explained: The Evolutionary Origins of Religious Thought*. New York: Basic Books.

Brannigan, Michael. 2005. *Ethics Across Cultures: An Introductory Text with Readings*. Boston: McGraw-Hill.

Bringa, Tone. 1995. *Being Muslims the Bosnian Way: Identity and Community in a Central Bosnian Village*. Princeton, NJ: Princeton University Press.

Bruce, Steve. 2002. *God is Dead: Secularization in the West*. Malden, MA and Oxford: Blackwell Publishing.

Brueggemann, Walter. 2003. *An Introduction to the Old Testament: The Canon and Christian Imagination*. Louisville, KY: Westminster John Knox Press.

Buckser, Andrew. 2005. "Chabad in Copenhagen: Fundamentalism and Modernity in Jewish Denmark." *Ethnology* 44 (2): 125–45.

——2008. "Cultural Change and the Meanings of Belief in Jewish Copenhagen." *Social Analysis* 52 (1): 39–55.

Buechler, Hans C. and Judith-Maria Buechler. 1971. *The Bolivian Aymara*. New York: Holt, Rinehart, and Winston.

Bui, Hum Dac. 1992. *Caodaism: A Novel Religion*. Redlands, CA: Chan Tam Publishers.

Bulbulia, Joseph and Richard Sosis. 2011. "Signalling Theory and the Evolution of Religious Cooperation." *Religion* 41 (3): 363–88.

Burch, Ernest and Werner Forman. 1988. *The Eskimos*. Norman: University of Oklahoma Press.

Burkert, Walter. 1983 [1972]. *Homo Necans: The Anthropology of Ancient Greek Sacrificial Ritual and Myth*. Peter Bing, trans. Berkeley, CA: University of California Press.

Campbell, Colin. 1971. *Toward a Sociology of Irreligion*. New York: Herder and Herder.

Campbell, Joseph. 2001. *Thou Art That: Transforming Religious Metaphor*. Novato, CA: New World Library.

Cannell, Fenella. 2005. "The Christianity of Anthropology." *The Journal of the Royal Anthropological Institute* 11 (2): 335–56.

——2006. "Introduction: The Anthropology of Christianity." In Fenella Cannell, ed. *The Anthropology of Christianity*. Durham, NC and London: Duke University Press, pp. 1–50.

——2010. "The Anthropology of Secularism." *Annual Review of Anthropology* 39: 85–100.

Cao, Nanlai. 2013. "Gender, Modernity, and Pentecostal Christianity in China." In Robert W. Hefner, ed. *Global Pentecostalism in the 21st Century: Gender, Piety, and Politics in the World's Fastest-Growing Faith Tradition*. Bloomington and Indianapolis, IN: Indiana University Press, pp. 149–75.

Carrithers, Michael. 1989. "Naked Ascetics in Southern Digambar Jainism." *Man* (New Series) 24 (2): 219–35.

Carroll, Michael P. 2002. *The Penitente Brotherhood: Patriarchy and Hispano-Catholicism in New Mexico*. Baltimore, MD and London: The Johns Hopkins University Press.

Casanova, José. 1994. *Public Religions in the Modern World*. Chicago, IL: The Chicago University Press.

Cassirer, Ernst. 1954 [1944]. *An Essay on Man: An Introduction to a Philosophy of Human Culture*. Garden City, NY: Doubleday & Company, Inc.

Chagnon, Napoleon. 1992 [1968]. *Yanomamo*, 4th ed. Fort Worth, TX: Harcourt Brace College Publishers.

Chase, Christopher. 2006. "Be Pagan Once Again: Folk Music, Heritage, and Socio-Sacred Networks in Contemporary American Paganism." *The Pomegranate: International Journal of Pagan Studies* 8 (2): 146–60.

Chau, Adam Yuet. 2012. "Efficacy, Not Confessionality: On Ritual Polytropy in China." In Glenn Bowman, ed. *Sharing the Sacra: The Politics and Pragmatics of Intercommunal Relations around Holy Places*. New York and Oxford: Berghahn Books, pp. 79–96.

Chevannes, Barry. 1994. *Rastafari: Roots and Ideology*. Syracuse, NY: Syracuse University Press.

Cigar, Norman. 1995. *Genocide in Bosnia: The Policy of "Ethnic Cleansing."* College Station: Texas A&M University Press.

Clements, Forest E. 1932. "Primitive Concepts of Disease." *University of California Publications in American Archaeology and Ethnology* 32 (2): 185–252.

Coleman, Simon. 2003. "Continuous Conversion? The Rhetoric, Practice, and Rhetorical Practice of Charismatic Protestant Conversion." In Andrew Buckser and Stephen D. Glazier, eds. *The Anthropology of Religious Conversion*. Lanham, MD: Rowman & Littlefield Publishers, Inc., pp. 15–27.

Comaroff, Jean. 1985. *Body of Power, Spirit of Resistance: The Culture and History of a South African People*. Chicago, IL and London: The University of Chicago Press.

——2010. "The Politics of Conviction: Faith on the Neo-Liberal Frontier." In Bruce Kapferer, Kari Telle, and Annelin Eriksen, eds. *Contemporary Religiosities: Emergent Socialities and the Post-Nation State*. New York and Oxford: Berghahn Books, pp. 17–38.

Comaroff, John L. and Jean Comaroff. 1991. *Of Revelation and Revolution: The Dialectics of Modernity on a South African Frontier*, vol. 2. Chicago, IL and London: The University of Chicago Press.

——1999. "Occult Economies and the Violence of Abstraction: Notes from the South African Postcolony." *American Ethnologist* 26 (2): 279–303.

Corr, Rachel. 2008. "Death, Dice, and Divination: Rethinking Religion and Play in South America." *Journal of Latin American and Caribbean Anthropology* 13 (1): 2–21.

Course, Magnus. 2011. *Becoming Mapuche: Person and Ritual in Indigenous Chile*. Urbana, IL: University of Illinois Press.

da Silva Sá, Domingos Bernardo Gialluisi. 2010. "Ayahuasca: The Consciousness of Expansion." In Beatriz Caiuby Labate and Edward MacRae, eds. *Ayahuasca, Ritual, and Religion in Brazil*. London and Oakville, CT: Equinox Publishing, pp. 161–89.

Darwin, Charles. 1882. The Descent of Man and Selection in Relation to Sex, 2nd ed. London: John Murray.

Davidson, Linda Kay and David Gitlitz, eds. 2002. *Pilgrimage: From Ganges to Graceland: An Encyclopedia*. Santa Barbara, CA: ABC-CLIO.

DeHass, Medeia Csoba. 2007. "Daily Negotiation of Traditions in a Russian Orthodox Sugpiaq Village in Alaska." *Ethnology* 46 (3): 205–16.

Deng, Francis Mading. 1972. *The Dinka of the Sudan*. New York: Holt, Rinehart, and Winston.

Denton, Lynn Teskey. 2004. *Female Ascetics in Hinduism*. Albany: State University of New York Press.

de Tocqueville, Alexis. 1955 [1856]. *The Old Regime and the French Revolution*. Stuart Gilbert, trans. New York: Anchor Books.

Dharmadasa, K. N. O. 1992. *Language, Religion, and Ethnic Assertiveness: The Growth of Sinhalese Nationalism in Sri Lanka*. Ann Arbor, MI: The University of Michigan Press.

Dickeman, M. 1975. "Demographic Consequences of Infanticide in Man." *Annual Review of Ecology and Systematics* 6: 107–37.

Dobbin, Jay, with Francis X. Hezel. 2011. *Summoning the Powers Beyond: Traditional Religions in Micronesia*. Honolulu, HI: University of Hawaii Press.

Douglas, Edward Te Kohu and Ian Boxill. 2012. "The Lantern and the Light: Rastafari in Aotearoa (New Zealand)." In Michael Barnett, ed. *Rastafari in the New Millennium*. Syracuse, NY: Syracuse University Press, pp. 35–65.

Douglas, Mary. 1970. *Natural Symbols*. Harmondsworth, UK: Penguin.

——1988 [1966]. *Purity and Danger: An Analysis of the Concepts of Pollution and Taboo*. London and New York: Ark Paperbacks.

Dow, James W. 2001. "Protestantism in Mesoamerica: The Old within the New." In James W. Dow and Alan R. Sandstrom, eds. *Holy Saints and Fiery Preachers: The Anthropology of Protestantism in Mexico and Central America*. Westport, CT: Praeger, pp. 1–23.

Downs, James F. 1972. *The Navajo*. New York: Holt, Rinehart, and Winston.

Dozier, Edward. 1967. *The Kalinga of Northern Luzon, Philippines*. New York: Holt, Rinehart, and Winston.

Driberg, J. H. 1936. "The Secular Aspect of Ancestor-Worship in Africa." *Journal of the Royal African Society* 35 (138): 1–21.

Droge, Arthur J. and James D. Tabor. 1992. *A Noble Death: Suicide and Martyrdom Among Christians and Jews in Antiquity*. New York: HarperSan Francisco.

Droogers, André. 1989. "Syncretism: The Problem of Definition, the Definition of the Problem." In Jerald D. Gort, Hendrick M. Vroom, Rein Frehhout, and Anton Wessels, eds. *Dialogue and Syncretism: An Interdisciplinary Approach*. Grand Rapids, MI: Wm. B. Eerdmans Publishing Co., pp. 7–25.

Dugdale Pointon, T. 2005. "Ikko-Ikki." Online: www.historyofwar.org/articles/weapons_ikko.html (accessed January 18, 2006).

Dumont, Louis. 1980 [1966]. *Homo Hierarchicus: The Caste System and its Implications*. Chicago, IL: The University of Chicago Press.

Dundes, Alan. 1965. "What is Folklore?" In Alan Dundes, ed. *The Study of Folklore*. Englewood Cliffs, NJ: Prentice-Hall, Inc., pp. 1–3.

Durkheim, Émile. 1933 [1893]. *The Division of Labor in Society*. George Simpson, trans. New York: The Free Press.

——1965 [1915]. *The Elementary Forms of the Religious Life*. New York: The Free Press.

Dussart, Françoise. 2000. *The Politics of Ritual in an Aboriginal Settlement: Kinship, Gender, and the Currency of Knowledge*. Washington, DC and London: Smithsonian Institution Press.

Eade, John and Michael J. Sallow, eds. 1991. *Contesting the Sacred: The Anthropology of Pilgrimage*. London and New York: Routledge.

Eagleton, Terry. 1981. *Walter Benjamin: Towards a Revolutionary Criticism*. London: Verso.

Eickelman, Dale F. and James Piscatori, eds. 1990. *Muslim Travellers: Pilgrimage, Migration, and the Religious Imagination*. Berkeley and Los Angeles, CA: University of California Press.

Eliade, Mircea. 1964 [1951]. *Shamanism: Archaic Techniques of Ecstasy*. Princeton, NJ: Princeton University/Bollingen Foundation.

——1970 [1958]. *Patterns in Comparative Religion*. Rosemary Sheed, trans. Cleveland, IN and New York: Meridian Books.

——1998 [1963]. *Myth and Reality*. Willard R. Trask, trans. Prospect Heights, IL: Waveland Press, Inc.

el-Zein, Abdul Hamid. 1977. "Beyond Ideology and Theology: The Search for the Anthropology of Islam." *Annual Review of Anthropology* 6: 227–54.

el-Zein, Amira. 2009. *Islam, Arabs, and the Intelligent World of the Jinn*. Syracuse, NY: Syracuse University Press.

Epstein, Greg M. 2009. *Good Without God: What a Billion Nonreligious People Do Believe*. New York: William Morrow.

Evans-Pritchard, E. E. 1937. *Witchcraft, Oracles, and Magic Among the Azande*. New York: Oxford University Press.

——1949. *The Sanusi of Cyrenaica*. Oxford: Oxford University Press.

——1954. "The Meaning of Sacrifice among the Nuer." *The Journal of the Royal Anthropological Institute of Great Britain and Ireland* 84 (1/2): 21–33.

——1956. *Nuer Religion*. New York and Oxford: Oxford University Press.

——1962. *Social Anthropology and Other Essays*. New York: The Free Press.

Falcone, Jessica Marie. 2012. "Putting the 'Fun' in Fundamentalism: Religious Nationalism and the Split Self at Hindutva Summer Camps in the United States." *Ethos* 40 (2): 164–95.

Falkenberg, Lisa. 2004. "Religiosity Common Among Mothers who Kill Children." *San Antonio Express-News*, December 14.

Feinberg, Richard. 1996. "Spirit Encounters on a Polynesian Outlier: Anuta, Solomon Islands." In Jeannette Marie Mageo and Alan Howard, eds. *Spirits in Culture, History, and Mind*. New York and London: Routledge, pp. 99–120.

Fernando, Mayanthi L. 2010. "Reconfiguring Freedom: Muslim Piety and the Limits of Secular Law and Public Discourse in France." *American Ethnologist* 37 (1): 19–35.

Firth, Raymond. 1940. "The Analysis of Mana." *The Journal of the Polynesian Society* 49: 483-510.

——1973. *Symbols: Public and Private*. Ithaca, NY: Cornell University Press.

——1976. "Conversion from Paganism to Christianity." *RAIN* 14 (May–June): 3–7.

Fisher, Humphrey J. 1973. "Conversion Reconsidered: Some Historical Aspects of Religious Conversion in Black Africa." *Africa* 43 (1): 27–40.

——1985. "The Juggernaut's Apologia: Conversion to Islam in Black Africa." *Africa* 55 (2): 153–73.

Flaskerud, Ingvild. 2010. *Visualizing Belief and Piety in Iranian Shiism*. London and New York: Continuum.

Flower, Scott. 2012. "Christian–Muslim Relations in Papua New Guinea." *Islam and Christian–Muslim Relations* 23 (2): 201–17.

Forbess, Alice. 2010. "The Spirit and the Letter: Monastic Education in a Romanian Orthodox Convent." In Chris Hann and Hermann Goltz, eds. *Eastern Christians in Anthropological Perspective*. Berkeley, CA: University of California Press, pp. 131–54.

Fortes, Meyer. 1959. *Oedipus and Job in West African Religions*. Cambridge: Cambridge University Press.

——1980. "Preface: Anthropologists and Theologians: Common Interests and Divergent Approaches." In M. F. C. Bourdillon and Meyer Fortes, eds. *Sacrifice*. London: Academic Press, pp. v–xix.

——1987. *Religion, Morality, and the Person: Essays on Tallensi Religion*. Jack Goody, ed. Cambridge: Cambridge University Press.

Frazer, James G. 1958 [1922]. *The Golden Bough: A Study in Magic and Religion*. New York: Macmillan.

Freke, Timothy, and Gandy, Peter. 1999. *The Jesus Mysteries: Was the "Original Jesus" a Pagan God?* New York: Harmony Books.

Frey, Nancy Louise. 1998. *Pilgrim Stories: On and Off the Road to Santiago*. Berkeley and Los Angeles, CA and London: University of California Press.

Frykenberg, Robert Eric. 1993. "Hindu Fundamentalism and the Structural Stability of India." In Martin E. Marty and R. Scott Appleby, eds. *Fundamentalisms and the State: Remaking Politics, Economies, and Militance*. Chicago, IL and London: The University of Chicago Press, pp. 233–55.

Galal, Lise Paulsen. 2012. "Coptic Christian Practices: Formations of Sameness and Difference." *Islam and Christian–Muslim Relations* 23 (1): 45–58.

Gateway to Sikhism. 2005. www.allaboutsikhs.com/mansukh/013.htm (accessed February 18, 2007).

Geertz, Clifford. 1968. *Islam Observed: Religious Development in Morocco and Indonesia*. New Haven, CT and London: Yale University Press.

——1973. *The Interpretation of Cultures*. New York: Basic Books.

——1980. *Negara: The Theatre State in Nineteenth-Century Bali*. Princeton, NJ: Princeton University Press.

——1983. *Local Knowledge: Further Essays in Interpretive Anthropology*. New York: Basic Books.

——1984. "Distinguished Lecture: Anti Anti-Relativism." *American Anthropologist* 86 (2): 263–78.

Gell, Alfred. 1998. *Art and Agency: An Anthropological Theory*. Oxford: Clarendon Press.

Gellner, Ernest. 1981. *Muslim Society*. Cambridge: Cambridge University Press.

——1988. *Plough, Sword, and Book: The Structure of Human History*. Chicago, IL: The University of Chicago Press.

——1992. *Postmodernism, Reason, and Religion*. London and New York: Routledge.

Gibbs, Eddie and Ryan Bolger. 2005. *Emerging Churches: Creating Christian Community in Post-modern Cultures*. Grand Rapids, MI: Baker Academic.

Giddens, Anthony. 1994. *Beyond Left and Right: The Future of Radical Politics*. Stanford, CA: Stanford University Press.

Gill, Lesley. 1990. "'Like a Veil to Cover Them': Women and the Pentecostal Movement in La Paz." *American Ethnologist* 17 (4): 708–21.

Gill, Sam D. 1981. *Sacred Words: A Study of Navajo Religion and Prayer*. Westport, CT: Greenwood Press.

Gilsenan, Michael. 2000 [1982]. *Recognizing Islam: Religion and Society in the Modern Middle East*. London and New York: I. B. Tauris Publishers.

Girard, René. 1977. *Violence and the Sacred*. Patrick Gregory, trans. Baltimore, MD: The Johns Hopkins University Press.

Glazier, Stephen D. 1980. "Pentecostal Exorcism and Modernization in Trinidad, West Indies." In Stephen D. Glazier, ed. *Perspectives on Pentecostalism: Case Studies from the Caribbean and Latin America*. Washington, DC: University Press of America, pp.67–80.

Gluckman, Max. 1956. *Custom and Conflict in Africa*. Oxford: Basil Blackwell.

Goffman, Erving. 1959. *The Presentation of Self in Everyday Life*. Garden City, NJ: Doubleday.

Gold, Daniel. 1991. "Organized Hinduisms: From Vedic Truth to Hindu Nation." In Martin Marty and R. Scott Appleby, eds. *Fundamentalisms Observed*. Chicago, IL: The University of Chicago Press, pp. 531–93.

Goldman, Irving. 2004. *Cubeo Hehenewa Religious Thought: Metaphysics of a Northwestern Amazonian People*. New York: Columbia University Press.

Goody, Jack. 1977. "Against 'Ritual': Loosely Structured Thoughts on a Loosely Defined Topic." In Sally F. Moore and Barbara G. Myerhoff, eds. *Secular Ritual*. Amsterdam: Van Gorcum, pp. 25–35.

——1996. "A Kernel of Doubt." *The Journal of the Royal Anthropological Institute* 2 (4): 667–81.

Gough, E. Kathleen. 1971. "Caste in a Tanjore Village." In Edmund R. Leach, ed. *Aspects of Caste in South India, Ceylon, and North-West Pakistan*. Cambridge: Cambridge University Press, pp. 11–60.

Green, Maia. 2003. *Priests, Witches, and Power: Popular Christianity after Mission in Southern Tanzania*. Cambridge: Cambridge University Press.

Greenbaum, Lenora. 1973. "Societal Correlates of Possession Trance in Sub-Saharan Africa." In Erika Bourguignon, ed. *Religion, Altered States of Consciousness, and Social Change*. Columbus, OH: Ohio State University Press, pp. 39–57.

Guthrie, Stewart. 1993. *Faces in the Clouds: A New Theory of Religion*. New York and Oxford: Oxford University Press.

Hadden, Jeffrey. 1993. "The Rise and Fall of American Televangelism." *Annals of the American Academy of Political and Social Science* 527: 113–30.

Hallowell, A. Irving. 1960. "Ojibwa Ontology, Behavior, and World View." In Stanley Diamond, ed. *Culture in History: Essays in Honor of Paul Radin*. New York: Columbia University Press, pp. 19–52.

Hanganu, Gabriel. 2010. "Eastern Christians and Religious Objects: Personal and Material Biographies Entangled." In Chris Hann and Hermann Goltz, eds. *Eastern Christians in Anthropological Perspective*. Berkeley, CA: University of California Press, 33–55.

Hann, Chris. 2007. "The Anthropology of Christianity per se." *European Journal of Sociology* 48 (3): 383–410.

Hann, Chris and Hermann Goltz. 2010. "Introduction: The Other Christianity?" In Chris Hann and Hermann Goltz, eds. *Eastern Christians in Anthropological Perspective*. Berkeley, CA: University of California Press, pp. 1–29.

Harding, Susan Friend. 1991. "Representing Fundamentalism: The Problem of the Repugnant Cultural Other." *Social Research* 58 (2): 373–93.

——2000. *The Book of Jerry Falwell: Fundamentalist Language and Politics*. Princeton, NJ: Princeton University Press.

Harris, Marvin. 1974. *Cows, Pigs, Wars, and Witches: The Riddles of Culture*. New York: Random House.

Hatch, Nathan O. 1989. *The Democratization of American Christianity*. New Haven, CT: Yale University Press.

Haviland, John B. 2009. "Little Rituals." In Gunter Senft and Ellen B. Basso, eds. *Ritual Communication*. Oxford and New York, pp. 21–50.

Heald, Suzette. 1986. "The Ritual Use of Violence: Circumcision among the Gisu of Uganda." In David Riches, ed. *The Anthropology of Violence*. Oxford: Basil Blackwell, pp. 70–85.

Hecht, Jennifer Michael. 2003. *Doubt: A History: The Great Doubters and their Legacy of Innovation from Socrates and Jesus to Thomas Jefferson and Emily Dickinson*. New York: HarperCollins.

Heelas, Paul. 2013. "On Transgressing the Secular: Spiritualities of Life, Idealism, Vitalism." In Steven J. Sutcliffe and Ingvild Saelid Gilhus, eds. *New Age Spirituality: Rethinking Religion*. Durham, UK and Bristol, CT: Acumen, pp. 66–83.

Hefner, Robert W. 1993. "Introduction: World Building and the Rationality of Conversion." In Robert W. Hefner, ed. *Conversion to Christianity: Historical and Anthropological Perspectives on a Great Transformation*. Berkeley, CA: University of California Press, pp. 3–44.

——2013a. "Preface." In Robert W. Hefner, ed. *Global Pentecostalism in the 21st Century: Gender, Piety, and Politics in the World's Fastest-Growing Faith Tradition*. Bloomington and Indianapolis, IN: Indiana University Press, pp. vii–x.

——2013b. "The Unexpected Modern: Gender, Piety, and Politics in the Global Pentecostal Surge." In Robert W. Hefner, ed. *Global Pentecostalism in the 21st Century: Gender, Piety, and Politics in the World's Fastest-Growing Faith Tradition*. Bloomington and Indianapolis, IN: Indiana University Press, pp. 1–36.

Hegland, Mary Elaine. 1998. "Flagellation and Fundamentalism: (Trans)forming Meaning, Identity, and Gender through Pakistani Women's Rituals of Mourning." *American Ethnologist* 25 (2): 240–66.

Heider, Karl. 1979. *Grand Valley Dani: Peaceful Warriors*. New York: Holt, Rinehart, and Winston.

Heo, Angie. 2013. "The Bodily Threat of Miracles: Security, Sacramentality, and the Egyptian Politics of Public Order." *American Ethnologist* 40 (1): 149–64.

Herodotus. 1942. *The Persian Wars*. George Rawlinson, trans. New York: Modern Library.

Herskovits, Melville J. 1938. *Dahomey: An Ancient West African Kingdom*, vol. 2. New York: J. J. Augustin, Publisher.

Hingorani, Alka. 2013. *Making Faces: Self and Image Creation in a Himalayan Valley*. Honolulu, HI: University of Hawaii Press.

Hirschkind, Charles. 2001. "The Ethics of Listening: Cassette Sermon Audition in Contemporary Cairo." *American Ethnologist* 28 (3): 623–49.

Hittman, Michael. 1997. *Wovoka and the Ghost Dance*. Lincoln, NE: University of Nebraska Press.

Hobsbawm, Eric. 1983. "Introduction: Inventing Tradition." In Eric Hobsbawm and Terence Ranger, eds. *The Invention of Tradition*. Cambridge: Cambridge University Press, pp. 1–14.

Hobsbawm, Eric and Terence Ranger, eds. 1983. *The Invention of Tradition*. Cambridge: Cambridge University Press.

Hoebel, E. Adamson. 1960. *The Cheyenne*. New York: Holt, Rinehart, and Winston.

Holtom, Daniel Clarence. 1965 [1938]. *The National Faith of Japan: A Study of Modern Shinto*. New York: Paragon Book Reprint Corp.

Holy, Ladislav. 1991. *Religion and Custom in a Muslim Society: The Berti of Sudan*. Cambridge: Cambridge University Press.

Holyoake, George Jacob. 1871. *The Principles of Secularism Illustrated*, 3rd edn. London: Austin & Co.

Hoover, Stewart M. 2000. "The Cross at Willow Creek: Seeker Religion and the Contemporary Marketplace." In Bruce David Forbes and Jeffrey H. Mahan, eds. *Religion and Popular Culture in America*. Berkeley, CA: University of California Press, pp. 145–59.

Horton, Robin. 1960. "A Definition of Religion, and its Uses." *The Journal of the Royal Anthropological Institute of Great Britain and Ireland* 90 (2): 201–26.

——1972. "African Conversion." *Africa* 41 (2): 85–108.

Howard, Alan. 1996. "Speak of the Devils: Discourse and Belief in Spirits on Rotuma." In Jeannette Marie Mageo and Alan Howard, eds. *Spirits in Culture, History, and Mind*. New York and London: Routledge, pp. 121–45.

Hubert, Henri and Marcel Mauss. 1964 [1898]. *Sacrifice: Its Nature and Function*. Chicago, IL and London: The University of Chicago Press.

Huxley, Thomas. 1902. *Collected Essays*. Volume V: *Science and Christian Tradition*. New York: D. Appleton and Company, pp. 209–62.

Hymes, Dell. 1975. "Folklore's Nature and the Sun's Myth." *The Journal of American Folklore* 88 (350): 345–69.

——2001. "On Communicative Competence." In Alessandro Duranti, ed. *Lingustic Anthropology: A Reader*. Malden, MA and Oxford: Blackwell Publishing, pp. 53–73.

Irons, William. 1996. "Morality as an Evolved Adaptation." In J. P. Hurd, ed. *Investigating the Biological Foundations of Morality*. Lewiston, NY: Edwin Mellon Press, pp. 1–34.

James, E. O. 1971 [1933]. *Origins of Sacrifice: A Study in Comparative Religion*. Port Washington, NY and London: Kennikat Press.

James, William. 1958 [1902]. *The Varieties of Religious Experience: A Study in Human Nature*. New York: Mentor Books.

Jung, Carl G. 1949 [1916]. *Psychology of the Unconscious: A Study of the Transformations and Symbolisms of the Libido*. Beatrice M. Hinkle, trans. New York: Dodd, Mead and Company.

Kan, Sergei. 1999. *Memory Eternal: Tlingit Culture and Russian Orthodox Christianity through Two Centuries*. Seattle, WA: University of Washington Press.

Kang, Yoonhee. 2006. "'Staged' Rituals and 'Veiled' Spells: Multiple Language Ideologies and Transformations in Petalangan Verbal Magic." *Journal of Linguistic Anthropology* 16 (1): 1–22.

Katz, Richard. 1982. *Boiling Energy: Community Healing Among the Kalahari Kung*. Cambridge, MA and London: Harvard University Press.

Keane, Webb. 1997. "Religious Language." *Annual Review of Anthropology* 26: 47–71.

——2007. *Christian Moderns: Freedom and Fetish in the Mission Encounter*. Berkeley, CA: University of California Press.

Kennedy, James. 1997. *Skeptics Answered: Handling Tough Questions About the Christian Faith*. Sisters, OR: Multnomah Publishers, Inc.

Kermani, S. Zohreh. 2013. *Pagan Family Values: Childhood and the Religious Imagination in Contemporary American Paganism*. New York and London: New York University Press.

Keyes, Charles F. 1993a. "Why the Thai Are Not Christians: Buddhist and Christian Conversion in Thailand." In Robert Hefner, ed. *Conversion to Christianity: Historical and Anthropological Perspectives on a Great Transformation*. Berkeley, CA: University of California Press, pp. 259–83.

——1993b. "Buddhist Economics and Buddhist Fundamentalism in Burma and Thailand." In Martin E. Marty and R. Scott Appleby, eds. *Fundamentalisms and the State: Remaking Polities, Economies, and Militance*. Chicago, IL and London: The University of Chicago Press, pp. 367–409.

Kiefer, Thomas M. 1972. *The Tausug: Violence and Law in a Philippine Moslem Society*. New York: Holt, Rinehart, and Winston.

Klima, George J. 1970. *The Barabaig: East African Cattle-Herders*. New York: Holt, Rinehart, and Winston.

Kluckhohn, Clyde. 1965. "Recurrent Themes in Myths and Mythmaking." In Alan Dundes, ed. *The Study of Folklore*. Englewood Cliffs, NJ: Prentice-Hall, Inc., pp. 158–68.

Köllner, Tobias. 2011. "Built with Gold or Tears? Moral Discourses on Church Construction and the Role of Entrepreneurial Donations." In Jarrett Zigon, ed. *Multiple Moralities and Religions in Post-Soviet Russia*. New York and Oxford: Berghahn Books, pp. 191–213.

Kopytoff, Igor. 1971. "Ancestors as Elders in Africa." *Africa: Journal of the International African Institute* 41 (2): 129–42.

Krakauer, Jon. 2003. *Under the Banner of Heaven: A Story of Violent Faith*. New York: Doubleday.

Krings, Matthias. 2008. "Conversion on Screen: A Glimpse at Popular Islâmic Imaginations in Northern Nigeria." *Africa Today* 54 (4): 44–68.

Kuper, Hilda. 1963. *The Swazi: A South African Kingdom*. New York: Holt, Rinehart, and Winston.

La Barre, Weston. 1972 [1970]. *The Ghost Dance: The Origins of Religion*. New York: Dell Publishing Co.

Labate, Beatriz Caiuby, Edward MacRae, and Sandra Lucia Goulart. 2010. "Brazilian Ayahuasca Religions in Perspective." In Beatriz Caiuby Labate and Edward MacRae, eds. *Ayahuasca, Ritual, and Religion in Brazil*. London and Oakville, CT: Equinox Publishing, pp. 1–20.

Lactantius. 1871. *The Works of Lactantius*. W. Fletcher, trans. Edinburgh: T. & T. Clark.

Lambek, Michael. 1981. *Human Spirits: A Cultural Account of Trance in Mayotte*. Cambridge: Cambridge University Press.

Langer, Suzanne K. 1942. *Philosophy in a New Key: A Study in the Symbolism of Reason, Rite, and Art*. New York: Mentor Books.

Larsen, Egon. 1971. *Strange Cults and Sects: A Study of their Origins and Influence*. New York: Hart Publishing Company, Inc.

Laugrand, Frédéric. 2012. "The Transition to Christianity and Modernity among Indigenous Peoples." *Reviews in Anthropology* 41 (1): 1–22.

Lawrence, Bruce B. 1989. *Defenders of God: The Fundamentalist Revolt against the Modern Age*. San Francisco, CA: Harper & Row.

Lawrence, Peter. 1964. *Road Belong Cargo: A Study of the Cargo Movement in the Southern Madang District New Guinea*. Melbourne and Manchester: Melbourne University Press and Manchester University Press.

Leach, Edmund. 1966. "A Discussion of Ritualization of Behavior in Animals and Man." *Philosophical Transactions of the Royal Society of London. Series B, Biological Sciences* 251 (772): 403–8.

Le Bon, Gustave. 1896. *The Crowd: A Study of the Popular Mind*. New York: The Macmillan Company.

Lee, Richard B. 1984. *The Dobe !Kung*. New York: Holt, Rinehart, and Winston.

Lehmann, Arthur C. 2001. "Eyes of the Ngangas: Ethnomedicine and Power in Central African Republic." In Arthur Lehmann and James Myers, eds. *Magic, Witchcraft, and Religion: An Anthropological Study of the Supernatural*, 5th edition. Mountain View, CA: Mayfield Publishing Company, pp. 154–62.

Lessa, William A. 1966. *Ulithi: A Micronesian Design for Living*. New York: Holt, Rinehart, and Winston.

Lester, Tory. 2002. "Oh, Gods!" *The Atlantic Monthly* (February), pp. 37–45.

Lévi-Strauss, Claude. 1963. *Structural Anthropology*. Claire Jacobson and Brook Grundfest Scheepf, trans. New York: Basic Books.

——1966. *The Savage Mind*. George Weidenfeld, trans. Chicago, IL: The University of Chicago Press.

Levy, Leonard W. 1993. *Blasphemy: Verbal Offense against the Sacred, from Moses to Salman Rushdie*. New York: Alfred A. Knopf.

Levy, Robert I., Jeannette Marie Mageo, and Alan Howard. 1996. "Gods, Spirits, and History: A Theoretical Perspective." In Jeannette Marie Mageo and Alan Howard, eds. *Spirits in Culture, History, and Mind*. New York and London: Routledge, pp. 11–27.

Lewis-Williams, J.D. and T.A. Dowson. 1988. "The Signs of All Times: Entoptic Phenomena in Upper Palaeolithic Art." *Current Anthropology* 29 (2): 201–45.

Liebman, Charles S. 1993. "Jewish Fundamentalism and the Israeli Polity." In Martin E. Marty and R. Scott Appleby, eds. *Fundamentalisms and the State: Remaking Polities, Economies, and Militance*. Chicago, IL and London: The University of Chicago Press, pp. 68–87.

Linton, Ralph. 1943. "Nativistic Movements." *American Anthropologist* 45 (2): 230–40.

Londono Sulkin, Carlos David. 2012. *People of Substance: An Ethnography of Morality in the Colombian Amazon*. Toronto: University of Toronto Press.

Louw, Maria. 2012. "Being Muslim the Ironic Way: Secularism, Religion, and Irony in Post-Soviet Kyrgyzstan." In Nils Bubandt and Martijn van Beek, eds. *Varieties of Secularism in Asia: Anthropological Explorations of Religion, Politics, and the Spiritual*. London and New York: Routledge, pp. 143–61.

Luckmann, Thomas. 1970. *The Invisible Religion: The Problem of Religion in Modern Society*. New York: Macmillan.

McCreery, John L. 1995. "Negotiating with Demons: The Uses of Magical Language." *American Ethnologist* 22 (1): 144–64.

McDougall, Debra. 2009. "Becoming Sinless: Converting to Islam in the Christian Solomon Islands." *American Anthropologist* 111 (4): 480–91.

McFarland, H. Neill. 1967. *The Rush Hour of the Gods: A Study of New Religious Movements in Japan*. New York: The Macmillan Company.

McGinty, Anna Mansson. 2006. *Becoming Muslim: Western Women's Conversions to Islam*. New York: Palgrave Macmillan.

McKnight, Scot. 2007. "Five Streams of the Emerging Church." http://www.christianitytoday.com/ct/2007/february/11.35.html (accessed April 15, 2012).

McLoughlin, Seán. 2007. "Islam's in Context: Orientalism and the Anthropology of Muslim Societies and Cultures." *Journal of Beliefs & Values* 28 (3): 273–96.

Malinowski, Bronislaw. 1948. *Magic, Science, and Religion and Other Essays*. Garden City, NY: Doubleday Anchor Books.

——1961 [1945]. *The Dynamics of Culture Change: An Inquiry into Race Relations in Africa*. New Haven, CT: Yale University Press.

Marett, R. R. 1909. *The Threshold of Religion*. London: Methuen & Co.

Marriott, McKim and Ronald B. Inden. 1977. "Toward an Ethnosociology of South Asian Caste Systems." In Kenneth A. David, ed. *The New Wind: Changing Identities in South Asia*. The Hague: Mouton, pp. 277–38.

Marsden, George M. 1990. "Defining American Fundamentalism." In Norman J. Cohen, ed. *The Fundamentalist Phenomenon: A View from Within, A Response from Without*. Grand Rapids, MI: William B. Eerdmans Publishing Company, pp. 22–37.

Marsden, Magnus and Konstantinos Retsikas. 2012. "Introduction." In Magnus Marsden and Konstantinos, eds. *Articulating Islam: Anthropological Approaches to Muslim Worlds*. Dordecht: Springer, pp. 1–31.

Martin, David. 1978. *A General Theory of Secularization*. New York, Evanston, IL, and San Francisco, CA: Harper & Row Publishers.

——1990. *Tongues of Fire: The Explosion of Protestantism in Latin America*. Oxford and Cambridge, MA: Blackwell.

——2013. "Pentecostalism: An Alternative Form of Modernity and Modernization?" In Robert W. Hefner, ed. *Global Pentecostalism in the 21st Century: Gender, Piety, and Politics in the World's Fastest-Growing Faith Tradition*. Bloomington and Indianapolis, IN: Indiana University Press, pp. 37–62.

Martin, Walter. 1976 [1965]. *The Kingdom of the Cults*. Minneapolis, MN: Bethany House.

Marty, Martin E. 1966 [1964]. *Varieties of Unbelief*. New York: Anchor Books.

——1984. *Pilgrims in Their Own Land: 500 Years of Religion in America*. New York: Penguin Books.

Marty, Martin E. and R. Scott Appleby, eds. 1991a. *Fundamentalisms Observed*. Chicago, IL: The University of Chicago Press.

——1991b. "Conclusion: An Interim Report on a Hypothetical Family." In Martin E. Marty and R. Scott Appleby, eds. *Fundamentalisms Observed*. Chicago, IL: The University of Chicago Press, pp. 814–42.

——1993. "Introduction." In Martin E. Marty and R. Scott Appleby, eds. *Fundamentalisms and the State: Remaking Polities, Economies, and Militance*. Chicago, IL and London: The University of Chicago Press, pp. 1–9.

Marx, Karl. 1843. *Critique of Hegel's Philosophy of Right*. Annette Jolin and Joseph O'Malley, trans. Cambridge: Cambridge University Press.

Matos Moctezuma, Eduardo. 1984. "The Templo Mayor of Tenochtitlan: Economics and Ideology." In Elizabeth Boone, ed. *Ritual Human Sacrifice in Mesoamerica*. Washington, DC: Dumbarton Oaks Research Library and Collection, pp. 133–64.

Mayer, Ann Elizabeth. 1993. "The Fundamentalist Impact on Law, Politics, and Constitutions in Iran, Pakistan, and the Sudan." In Martin E. Marty and R. Scott Appleby, eds. *Fundamentalisms and the State: Remaking Polities, Economies, and Militance*. Chicago, IL and London: The University of Chicago Press, pp. 110–51.

Meigs, Anna S. 1984. *Food, Sex, and Pollution: A New Guinea Religion*. New Brunswick, NJ: Rutgers University Press.

Menon, Kalyani Devaki. 2003. "Converted Innocents and their Trickster Heroes: The Politics of Proselytizing In India." In Andrew Buckser and Stephen D. Glazier, eds. *The Anthropology of Religious Conversion*. Lanham, MD: Rowman & Littlefield Publishers, Inc., pp. 43–53.

Meyer, Birgit. 1998. "'Make a Complete Break with the Past': Memory and Post-Colonial Modernity in Ghanaian Pentecostalist Discourse." *Journal of Religion in Africa* 28 (3): 316–49.

——1999. *Translating the Devil: Religion and Modernity Among the Ewe in Ghana*. Edinburgh: Edinburgh University Press.

——2004. "'Praise the Lord': Popular Cinema and Pentecostalite Style in Ghana's New Public Sphere." *American Ethnologist* 31 (1): 92–110.

——2008. "Powerful Pictures: Popular Christian Aesthetics in Southern Ghana." *Journal of the American Academy of Religion* 76 (1): 82–110.

Meyer, Thomas. 2000 [1997]. *Identity Mania: Fundamentalism and the Politicization of Cultural Differences*. London and New York: Zed Books.

Micha, Franz Josef. 1970. "Trade and Change in Australian Aboriginal Cultures: Australian Aboriginal Trade as an Expression of Close Culture Contact and as a Mediator of Culture Change." In Arnold R. Pilling and Richard A. Waterman, eds. *Diprotodon to Detribalization: Studies of Change Among Australian Aboriginals*. East Lansing, MI: Michigan State University Press, pp. 285–313.

Milgram, Stanley. 1963. "Behavioral Study of Obedience." *Journal of Abnormal and Social Psychology* 67 (4): 371–78.

Miller, Donald E. 2009. "Progressive Pentecostalism: An Emergent Trend in Global Christianity." *Journal of Beliefs & Values* 30 (3): 275–87.

Mooney, James. 1896. *The Ghost-Dance Religion and the Sioux Outbreak of 1890*. Washington, DC: Fourteenth Annual Report, Bureau of American Ethnology, part 2.

Morauta, Louise. 1972. "The Politics of Cargo Cults in the Madang Area." *Man* (n.s.) 7 (3): 430–47.

Morgan, David. 1998. *Visual Piety: A History and Theory of Popular Religious Images*. Berkeley, CA: University of California Press.

Morphy, Howard. 1991. *Ancestral Connections: Art and an Aboriginal System of Knowledge*. Chicago, IL: The University of Chicago Press.

Murphree, Marshall. 1969. *Christianity and the Shona*. London: The Athlone Press.

Myerhoff, Barbara C. 1974. *Peyote Hunt: The Sacred Journey of the Huichol Indians*. Ithaca, NY: Cornell University Press.

Nadel, S. F. 1954. *Nupe Religion*. Glencoe, IL: The Free Press.

Nagata, Judith. 2001. "Beyond Theology: Toward an Anthropology of 'Fundamentalism.'" *American Anthropologist* 103 (2): 481–98.

Naiden, F. S. 2013. *Smoke Signals for the Gods: Ancient Greek Sacrifice from the Archaic through Roman Periods*. Oxford and New York: Oxford University Press.

Needham, Rodney. 1972. *Belief, Language, and Experience*. Chicago, IL: The University of Chicago Press.

Newberg, Andrew, Eugene d'Aquili, and Vince Rause. 2002. *Why God Won't Go Away: Brain Science and the Biology of Belief*. New York: Ballantine Books.

Niaah, Jahlani. 2012. "The Rastafari Presence in Ethiopia: A Contemporary Perspective." In Michael Barnett, ed. *Rastafari in the New Millennium*. Syracuse, NY: Syracuse University Press, pp. 66–88.

Nielsen, Kai. 1989. *Why Be Moral?* Buffalo, NY: Prometheus Books.

Nietzsche, Friedrich. 1976. *The Portable Nietzsche*. Walter Kaufmann, ed. Harmondsworth, UK and New York: Penguin Books.

Nock, A. D. 1933. *Conversion: The Old and the New in Religion from Alexander the Great to Augustine of Hippo*. Oxford: Oxford University Press.

Nordstrom, Carolyn and JoAnn Martin. 1992. "The Culture of Conflict: Field Reality and Theory." In Carolyn Nordstrom and JoAnn Martin, eds. *The Paths to Domination, Resistance, and Terror*. Berkeley, CA: University of California Press, pp. 3–17.

Norenzayan, Ara and Azim F. Shariff. 2008. "The Origin and Evolution of Religious Prosociality." *Science* 322 (3 October), 58–62.

North, Gary. 1984. *Backward Christian Soldiers? An Action Manual for Christian Reconstruction*. Tyler, TX: Institute for Christian Economics.

——1986. *The Sinai Strategy: Economics and the Ten Commandments*. Tyler, TX: Institute for Christian Economics.

Obeyesekere, Gananath. 1963. "The Great Tradition and the Little in the Perspective of Sinhalese Buddhism." *The Journal of Asian Studies* 22 (2): 139–53.

——1981. *Medusa's Hair: An Essay on Personal Symbols and Religious Experience*. Chicago, IL: University of Chicago Press.

Ohnuki-Tierney, Emiko. 1974. *The Ainu of the Northwest Coast of Southern Sakhalin*. New York: Holt, Rinehart, and Winston.

Olson, Benjamin Hedge. 2013. "Voice of Our Blood: National Socialist Discourse in Black Metal." In Titus Hjeml, Keith Kahn-Harris, and Mark LeVine, eds. *Heavy Metal: Controversies and Countercultures*. Sheffield, UK and Bristol, CT: Equinox, pp. 136–51.

Ong, Aihwa. 1987. *Spirits of Resistance and Capitalist Discipline: Factory Women in Malaysia*. Albany, NY: State University of New York Press.

——1988. "The Production of Possession: Spirits and the Multinational Corporation in Malaysia." *American Ethnologist* 15 (1): 28–42.

Oring, Elliott. 1986. "Folk Narratives." In Elliott Oring, ed. *Folk Groups and Folklore Genres: An Introduction*. Logan, UT: Utah State University Press, pp. 121–45.

Orta, Andrew. 1998. "Converting Difference: Metaculture, Missionaries, and the Politics of Locality." *Ethnology* 37 (2): 165–85.

Ortiz, Alfonso. 1969. *The Tewa World: Space, Time, Being, and Becoming in a Pueblo Society*. Chicago, IL and London: The University of Chicago Press.

Ortner, Sherry B. 1973. "On Key Symbols." *American Anthropologist* 75 (5): 1338–46.

——1978. *Sherpas Through their Rituals*. Cambridge: Cambridge University Press.

——1989. *High Religion: A Cultural and Political History of Sherpa Buddhism*. Princeton, NJ: Princeton University Press.

Overing, Joanne. 1986. "Images of Cannibalism, Death, and Domination in a 'Non-Violent' Society." In David Riches, ed. *The Anthropology of Violence*. Oxford: Basil Blackwell, pp. 86–102.

Pagels, Elaine. 1995. *The Origin of Satan*. New York: Random House.

Panchenko, Alexander. 2012. "How to Make a Shrine with Your Own Hands: Local Holy Places and Vernacular Religion in Russia." In Marion Bowman and Ülo Valk, eds. *Vernacular Religion in Everyday Life: Expressions of Belief*. Sheffield, UK and Bristol, CT: Equinox, pp. 42–62.

Park, Jungnok. 2012. *How Buddhism Acquired a Soul on the Way to China*. Sheffield, UK and Bristol, CT: Equinox Publishing.

Parks, Douglas. 1996. *Myths and Traditions of the Arikara Indians*. Lincoln, NE and London: University of Nebraska Press.

Paul, Robert A. 1976. "The Sherpa Temple as a Model of the Psyche." *American Ethnologist* 3 (1): 131–46.

Pedersen, Morten Axel. 2011. *Not Quite Shamans: Spirit Worlds and Political Lives in Northern Mongolia*. Ithaca, NY and London: Cornell University Press.

Pelkmans, Mathijs. 2009. "Temporary Conversion: Encounters with Pentecostalism in Muslim Kyrgyzstan." In Mathijs Pelkmans, ed. *Conversion after Socialism: Disruptions, Modernisms and Technologies of Faith in the Former Soviet Union*. Oxford: Berghahn Books, pp. 143–62.

Persinger, Michael. 1987. *Neuropsychological Bases of God Beliefs*. Westport, CT: Praeger Publications.

Pike, Sarah M. 2001. *Earthly Bodies, Magical Selves: Contemporary Pagans and the Search for Community*. Berkeley, CA: University of California Press.

——2004. *New Age and Neopagan Religions in America*. New York: Columbia University Press.

Pinnock, Clark H. 1990. "Defining American Fundamentalism: A Response." In Norman J. Cohen, ed. *The Fundamentalist Phenomenon: A View from Within, A Response from Without*. Grand Rapids, MI: William B. Eerdmans Publishing Company, pp. 38–55.

Poirier, Sylvie. 1993. "'Nomadic' Rituals: Networks of Ritual Exchange between Women of the Australian Western Desert." *Man* (n.s.) 27 (4): 757–76.

Pollock, Donald K. 1993. "Conversion and 'Community' in Amazonia." In Robert Hefner, ed. *Conversion to Christianity: Historical and Anthropological Perspectives on a Great Transformation*. Berkeley, CA: University of California Press, pp. 165–97.

Pospisil, Leopold. 1963. *The Kapauku Papuans of West New Guinea*. New York: Holt, Rinehart, and Winston.

Pouillon, Jean. 1992. "Remarks on the Verb 'To Believe.'" In Michel Izard and Pierre Smith, eds. *Between Belief and Transgression: Structuralist Essays in Religion, History, and Myth*. John Leavitt, trans. Chicago, IL and London: The University of Chicago Press, pp. 1–8.

Primiano, Leonard Norman. 1995. "Vernacular Religion and the Search for Method in Religious Folklife." *Western Folklore* 54 (1): 37–56.

——2012. "Manifestations of the Religious Vernacular: Ambiguity, Power, and Creativity." In Marion Bowman and Ülo Valk, eds. *Vernacular Religion in Everyday Life: Expressions of Belief*. Sheffield, UK and Bristol, CT: Equinox, pp. 382–94.

Pype, Katrien. 2012. *The Making of the Pentecostal Melodrama: Religion, Media, and Gender in Kinshasa*. New York and Oxford: Berghahn Books.

Quack, Johannes. 2012a. *Disenchanting India: Organized Rationalism and Criticism of Religion in India*. Oxford and New York: Oxford University Press.

——2012b. "Organised Atheism in India: An Overview." *Journal of Contemporary Religion* 27 (1): 67–85.

Radcliffe-Brown, A. R. 1965 [1952]. *Structure and Function in Primitive Society*. New York: The Free Press.

Radin, Paul. 1957. *Primitive Religion: Its Nature and Origin*. New York: Dover Publications.

Ramadan, Abdel Azim. 1993. "Fundamentalist Influence in Egypt: The Strategies of the Muslim Brotherhood and the Takfir Groups." In Martin E. Marty and R. Scott Appleby, eds. *Fundamentalisms and the State: Remaking Polities, Economies, and Militance*. Chicago, IL and London: The University of Chicago Press, pp. 152–83.

Ranstorp, Magnus. 2003. "Terrorism in the Name of Religion." In Russell D. Howard and Reid L. Sawyer, eds. *Terrorism and Counterterrorism: Understanding the New Security Environment*. Guilford, CT: Mc-Graw Hill/Dushkin, pp. 121–36.

Rapoport, David C. 1989. "Terrorism and the Messiah: An Ancient Experience and Some Modern Parallels." In David C. Rapoport and Yonah Alexander, eds. *The Morality of Terrorism: Religious and Secular Justifications*. New York: Columbia University Press, pp. 13–42.

Rappaport, Roy. 1992. "Ritual." In Richard Bauman, ed. *Folklore, Cultural Performances, and Popular Entertainment: A Communications-Centered Handbook.* New York: Oxford University Press, pp.249–60.

——1999. *Ritual and Religion in the Making of Humanity.* Cambridge: Cambridge University Press.

Ray, Dorothy Jean. 1967. *Eskimo Masks: Art and Ceremony.* Seattle, WA: University of Washington Press.

Reader, Ian. 1991. *Religion in Contemporary Japan.* Honolulu, HI: University of Hawaii Press.

Redfield, Robert. 1953. *The Primitive World and its Transformations.* Ithaca, NY: Cornell University Press.

Rey, Séverine. 2012. "The Ordinary within the Extraordinary: Sainthood-Making and Everyday Religious Practice in Lesvos, Greece." In Samuli Schielke and Liza Debevec, eds. *Ordinary Lives and Grand Schemes: An Anthropology of Everyday Religion.* New York and Oxford: Berghahn Books, pp. 82–97.

Riches, David. 1986. "The Phenomenon of Violence." In David Riches, ed. *The Anthropology of Violence.* Oxford: Basil Blackwell, pp.1–27.

Roald, Anne Sofie. 2012. "The Conversion Process in Stages: New Muslims in the Twenty-First Century." *Islam and Christian–Muslim Relations* 23 (3): 347–62.

Robbins, Joel. 2003a. "On the Paradoxes of Global Pentecostalism and the Perils of Continuity Thinking." *Religion* 33: 221–31.

——2003b. "What is a Christian? Notes Toward an Anthropology of Christianity." *Religion* 33: 191–99.

——2007. "Continuity Thinking and the Problem of Christian Culture: Belief, Time, and the Anthropology of Christianity." *Current Anthropology* 48 (1): 5–38.

Roes, Frank L. and Michel Raymond. 2003. "Belief in Moralizing Gods." *Evolution and Human Behavior* 24: 126–35.

Rooth, Anna Birgitta. 1957. "The Creation Myths of the North American Indians." *Anthropos* 52: 497–508.

Rudnyckyj, Daromir. 2010. *Spiritual Economies: Islam, Globalization, and the Afterlife of Development.* Ithaca, NY and London: Cornell University Press.

Ruel, Malcolm. 1997. *Belief, Ritual, and the Securing of Life: Reflexive Essays on Bantu Religion.* Leiden: E. J. Brill.

"The Rules and Statutes of the Teutonic Knights." 1969. Indrikis Sterns, trans. Online: www.theorb.net/encyclop/religion/monastic/tk_rule.html (accessed June 30, 2014).

Rushdoony, R. J. 1973. *The Institutes of Biblical Law.* Nutley, NJ: Craig Press.

Sage, Vanessa. 2009. "Encountering the Wilderness, Encountering the Mist: Nature, Romanticism, and Contemporary Paganism." *Anthropology of Consciousness* 20 (1): 27–52.

Sahlins, Marshall. 1976. *The Use and Abuse of Biology: An Anthropological Critique of Sociobiology.* Ann Arbor, MI: University of Michigan Press.

Said, Edward W. 1978. *Orientalism.* New York: Vintage Books.

Schaffer, Matt and Christine Cooper. 1980. *Mandinko: The Ethnography of a West African Holy Land.* New York: Holt, Rinehart, and Winston.

Scheper-Hughes, Nancy and Philippe Bourgois. 2004. "Introduction: Making Sense of Violence." In Nancy Scheper-Hughes and Philippe Bourgois, eds. *Violence in War and Peace: An Anthology.* Malden, MA and Oxford: Blackwell Publishing, pp.1–31.

Schielke, Samuli. 2010. "Second Thoughts about the Anthropology of Islam, or How to Make Sense of Grand Schemes in Everyday Life." Working Papers No. 2, Zentrum Moderner Orient.

——2012. *The Perils of Joy: Contesting Mulid Festivals in Contemporary Egypt.* Syracuse, NY: Syracuse University Press.

Schielke, Samuli and Liza Debevec. 2012. "Introduction." In Samuli Schielke and Liza Debevec, eds. *Ordinary Lives and Grand Schemes: An Anthropology of Everyday Religion.* New York and Oxford: Berghahn Books, pp. 1–16.

Seneviratne, H. L. 1978. *Rituals of the Kandyan State*. Cambridge: Cambridge University Press.

Sethi, Manisha. 2012. *Escaping the World: Women Renouncers among Jains*. London and New York: Routledge.

Shah, Rebecca Samuel and Timothy Samuel Shah. 2013. "Pentecost amid Pujas: Charismatic Christianity and Dalit Women in Twenty-First-Century India." In Robert W. Hefner, ed. *Global Pentecostalism in the 21st Century: Gender, Piety, and Politics in the World's Fastest-Growing Faith Tradition*. Bloomington and Indianapolis, IN: Indiana University Press, pp. 194–222.

Shattuck, Cybelle. 1999. *Hinduism*. London: Routledge.

Shaw, Rosalind and Charles Stewart. 1996. "Introduction: Problematizing Syncretism." In Charles Stewart and Rosalind Shaw, eds. *Syncretism/Anti-syncretism: The Politics of Religious Synthesis*. London and New York: Routledge, pp. 1–26.

Sherzer, Joel. 1983. *Kuna Ways of Speaking*. Austin, TX: University of Texas Press.

Shnirelman, Victor A. 2013. "Russian Neopaganism: From Ethnic Religion to Racial Violence." In Kaarina Aitamurto and Scott Simpson, eds. *Modern Pagan and Native Faith Movements in Central and Eastern Europe*. Durham, UK and Bristol, CT: Acumen, pp. 62–76.

Shorter, Aylward. 1988. *Toward a Theology of Inculturation*. Maryknoll, NY: Orbis Books.

Skorupski, John. 1976. *Symbol and Theory: A Philosophical Study of Theories of Religion in Social Anthropology*. Cambridge: Cambridge University Press.

Smith, Karl. 2012. "From Dividual and Individual Selves to Porous Subjects." *The Australian Journal of Anthropology* 23: 50–64.

Smith, Lacey Baldwin. 1997. *Fools, Martyrs, Traitors: The Story of Martyrdom in the Western World*. New York: Alfred A. Knopf.

Somers, Emily Aoife. 2013. "Transnational Necromancy: W. B. Yeats, Izumi Kyôka and *neo-nô* as Occultic Stagecraft." In Henrik Bogdan and Gordan Djurdjevic, eds. *Occultism in a Global Perspective*. Durham, UK and Bristol, CT: Acumen, pp. 203–30.

Sone, Enongene Mirabeau. 2011. "Religious Poetry as a Vehicle for Social Control in Africa: The Case of the Bakossi Incantatory Poetry." *Folklore* 122 (3): 308–26.

Sosis, Richard and Candace Alcorta. 2003. "Signaling, Solidarity, and the Sacred: The Evolution of Religious Behavior." *Evolutionary Anthropology* 12: 264–74.

Sperber, Dan. 1975. *Rethinking Symbolism*. Alice L. Morton, trans. Cambridge: Cambridge University Press.

Spier, Leslie. 1935. *The Prophet Dance of the Northwest and its Derivatives: The Source of the Ghost Dance*. Menasha, WI: George Banta Publishing Company.

Spindler, George and Louise Spindler. 1971. *Dreamers without Power: The Menomini Indians*. New York: Holt, Rinehart, and Winston.

Spiro, Melford. 1978 [1967]. *Burmese Supernaturalism*, expanded edition. Philadelphia, PA: Institute for the Study of Human Issues.

Sprinzak, Ehud. 1993. "Three Models of Religious Violence: The Case of Jewish Fundamentalism in Israel." In Martin E. Marty and R. Scott Appleby, eds. *Fundamentalisms and the State: Remaking Polities, Economies, and Militance*. Chicago, IL and London: The University of Chicago Press, pp. 462–90.

Srinivas, Tulasi. 2010. *Winged Faith: Rethinking Globalization and Religious Pluralism through the Sathya Sai Movement*. New York: Columbia University Press.

Staal, Frits. 1979. "The Meaningless of Ritual." *Numen* 26 (1): 2–22.

Stallybrass, Peter and Allon White. 1986. *The Politics and Poetics of Transgression*. Ithaca, NY and London: Cornell University Press and Methuen Books.

Stephenson, Peta. 2010. *Islam Dreaming: Indigenous Muslims in Australia*. Sydney: University of New South Wales Press.

Stewart, Charles. 1991. *Demons and the Devil: Moral Imagination in Modern Greek Culture*. Princeton, NJ: Princeton University Press.

Strathern, Marilyn. 1988. *The Gender of the Gift: Problems with Women and Problems with Society in Melanesia*. Berkeley, CA: University of California Press.

Stringer, Martin D. 2008. *Contemporary Western Ethnography and the Definition of Religion.* London and New York: Continuum.

Subedi, Surya P. 2003. "The Concept in Hinduism of 'Just War.'" *Journal of Conflict and Security Law* 8 (2): 339–61.

Susewind, Raphael. 2013. *Being Muslim and Working for Peace: Ambivalence and Ambiguity in Gujarat.* New Delhi and Thousand Oaks, CA: Sage Publications.

Swinburne, Richard. 1977. *The Coherence of Theism.* Oxford: Clarendon Press.

Szilárdi, Réka. 2013. "Neopaganism in Hungary: Under the Spell of Roots." In Kaarina Aitamurto and Scott Simpson, eds. *Modern Pagan and Native Faith Movements in Central and Eastern Europe.* Durham, UK and Bristol, CT: Acumen, pp. 230–48.

Tambar, Kabir. 2009. "Secular Populism and the Semiotics of the Crowd in Turkey." *Public Culture* 21 (3): 517–37.

Tambiah, Stanley J. 1970. *Buddhism and the Spirit Cults in North-East Thailand.* London: Cambridge University Press.

——1979. *A Performative Approach to Ritual.* London: The British Academy and Oxford University Press.

Taussig, Michael. 1977. "The Genesis of Capitalism amongst a South American Peasantry: Devil's Labor and the Baptism of Money." *Comparative Studies in Society and History* 19 (2): 130–55.

Tedlock, Dennis. 1972. *Finding the Center: Narrative Poetry of the Zuni Indians.* New York: The Dial Press.

——1983. *The Spoken Word and the Work of Interpretation.* Philadelphia, PA: University of Pennsylvania Press.

Thompson, J. M. 1962. *Robespierre and the French Revolution.* New York: Collier Books.

Thoms, William. 1846. "Folklore." *The Athenaeum* 982: 862–63.

Tooker, Deborah. 1992. "Identity Systems of Highland Burma: 'Belief,' Akha Zan, and a Critique of Interiorized Notions of Ethno-Religious Identity." *Man* (n.s) 27 (4): 799–819.

Trigger, Bruce G. 1969. *The Huron: Farmers of the North.* New York: Holt, Rinehart, and Winston.

Tucker, Catherine. 2010. "Private Goods and Common Property: Pottery Production in a Honduran Lenca Community." *Human Organization* 69 (1): 43–53.

Turnbull, Colin M. 1961. *The Forest People: A Study of the Pygmies of the Congo.* New York: Touchstone.

Turner, Victor. 1967. *The Forest of Symbols: Aspects of Ndembu Ritual.* Ithaca, NY: Cornell University Press.

——1969. *The Ritual Process: Structure and Anti-Structure.* Chicago, IL: Aldine Publishing.

——1973. "The Center Out There: Pilgrim's Goal." *History of Religion* 12 (3): 191–230.

——1974. *Dramas, Fields, and Metaphors: Symbolic Action in Human Society.* Ithaca, NY and London: Cornell University Press.

——1981 [1968]. *The Drums of Affliction: A Study of Religious Processes among the Ndembu of Zambia.* London: Hutchinson University Library for Africa.

——1984. "Liminality and the Performative Genres." In John J. MacAloon, ed. *Rite, Drama, Festival, Spectacle: Rehearsals toward a Theory of Cultural Performance.* Philadelphia, PA: Institute for the Study of Human Issues, pp.19–41.

Turner, Victor and Edith L. B. Turner. 2011 [1978]. *Image and Pilgrimage in Christian Culture.* New York: Columbia University Press.

Tylor, E. B. 1958 [1871]. *Primitive Culture*, vol. 1. New York: Harper.

Usui, Sachiko. 2007. "The Concept of Pilgrimage in Japan." In Maria Rodriguez del Alisal, Peter Ackermann, and Dolores P. Martinez, eds. *Pilgrimages and Spiritual Quests in Japan.* Abingdon, UK and New York: Routledge, pp. 27–38.

Uzendoski, Michael A. and Edith Felicia Calapucha-Tapuy. 2012. *The Ecology of the Spoken Word: Shamanism among the Napo Runa.* Urbana, Chicago, and Springfield, IL: University of Illinois Press.

Valantasis, Richard. 1995. "A Theory of the Social Function of Asceticism." In Vincent L. Wimbush and Richard Valantasis, eds. *Asceticism.* Oxford and New York: Oxford University Press, pp. 544–52.

Valeri, Valerio. 1985. *Kingship and Sacrifice: Ritual and Society in Ancient Hawaii*. Paula Wissig, trans. Chicago, IL and London: The University of Chicago Press.

van Baalen, Jan Karel. 1956 [1938]. *The Chaos of the Cults*. Grand Rapids, MI: Eerdmans.

Voll, John O. 1991. "Fundamentalism in the Sunni Arab World: Egypt and the Sudan." In Martin Marty and R. Scott Appleby, eds. *Fundamentalisms Observed*. Chicago, IL: The University of Chicago Press, pp. 345–402.

von Fuerer-Haimendorf, Christoph. 1969. *The Konyak Nagas: An Indian Frontier Tribe*. New York: Holt, Rinehart, and Winston.

Wallace, Anthony F. C. 1956. "Revitalization Movements." *American Anthropologist* 58 (2): 264–81.

——1966. *Religion: An Anthropological View*. New York: Random House.

Waterman, Richard A. and Patricia Panyity Waterman. 1970. "Directions of Culture Change in Aboriginal Arnhem Land." In Arnold R. Pilling and Richard A. Waterman, eds. *Diprotodon to Detribalization: Studies of Change Among Australian Aboriginals*. East Lansing, MI: Michigan State University Press, pp. 101–9.

Weinstein, Deena. 2013. "Pagan Metal." In Donna Weston and Andy Bennett, eds. *Pop Pagans: Paganism and Popular Music*. Durham, UK and Bristol, CT: Acumen, pp. 58–75.

Werner, Susan Jayne. 1981. *Peasant Politics and Religious Sectarianism: Peasant and Priest in the Cao Dai in Vietnam*. New Haven, CT: Yale University Southeast Asia Studies.

Westermarck, Edward. 1926. *Ritual and Belief in Morocco*, 2 vols. London: Macmillan & Co.

Westh, Peter. 2011. "Illuminator of the Wide Earth; Unbribable Judge; Strong Weapon of the Gods: Intuitive Ontology and Divine Epithets in Assyro-Babylonian Religious Texts." In Luther H. Martin and Jesper Sorensen, eds. *Past Minds: Studies in Cognitive Historiography*. London and Oakville, CT: Equinox, pp. 48–61.

Wheelwright, Philip, ed. 1966. *The Presocratics*. New York: The Odyssey Press, Inc.

White, Jenny. 2013. *Muslim Nationalism and the New Turks*. Princeton, NJ and Oxford: Princeton University Press.

White, Leslie A. 1959. "The Concept of Culture." *American Anthropologist* 61 (2): 227–51.

Whitehouse, Harvey. 1995. *Inside the Cult: Religious Innovation and Transmission in Papua New Guinea*. Oxford: Clarendon Press.

——2004. *Modes of Religiosity: A Cognitive Theory of Religious Transmission*. Lanham, MD: AltaMira Press.

Wiench, Piotr. 2013. "A Postcolonial Key to Understanding Central and Eastern European Neopaganisms." In Kaarina Aitamurto and Scott Simpson, eds. *Modern Pagan and Native Faith Movements in Central and Eastern Europe*. Durham, UK and Bristol, CT: Acumen, pp. 10–26.

Wilford, Justin G. 2012. *Sacred Subdivisions: The Postsuburban Transformation of American Evangelicalism*. New York and London: New York University Press.

Williams, Thomas Rhys. 1965. *The Dusun: A North Borneo Society*. New York: Holt, Rinehart, and Winston.

Wilmore, Michael J. 2006. "Gatekeepers of Cultural Memory: Televising Religious Rituals in Tansen, Nepal." *Ethnos* 71 (3): 317–42.

Wilson, Bryan. 1982. *Religion in Sociological Perspective*. Oxford: Oxford University Press.

Worsley, Peter. 1968. *The Trumpet Shall Sound: A Study of "Cargo Cults" in Melanesia*. New York: Shocken Books.

Xygalatas, Dimitris. 2012. *The Burning Saints: Cognition and Culture in the Fire-Walking Rituals of the Anastenaria*. Sheffield, UK and Bristol, CT: Equinox.

Yengoyan, Aram A. 1993. "Religion, Morality, and Prophetic Traditions: Conversion among the Pitjantjatjara of Central Australia." In Robert Hefner, ed. *Conversion to Christianity: Historical and Anthropological Perspectives on a Great Transformation*. Berkeley, CA: University of California Press, pp. 231–58.

Yükleyen, Ahmet. 2012. *Localizing Islam in Europe: Turkish Islamic Communities in Germany and the Netherlands*. Syracuse, NY: Syracuse University Press.

Zamorska, Julia. 1998. "Modernity in a Different Way: Cargo Cults in Melanesia as Creative Response to Modernisation." Online: www.geocities.com/southbeach/lagoon/3638/anthro2.html (accessed March 3, 2004).

Zencirci, Gizem. 2012. "Secularism, Islam, and the National Public Sphere: Politics of Commemorative Practices in Turkey." In Alev Cinar, Srirupa Roy, and Mahayudin Haji Yahya, eds. *Visualizing Secularism and Religion: Egypt, Lebanon, Turkey, India.* Ann Arbor, MI: University of Michigan Press, pp. 93–109.

Zimbardo, Philip. 2000. "The Psychology of Evil." *Psi Chi 5* (1): 16–19.

Index